75055

C0-CCJ-097

The Gap between Rich and Poor Nations

OTHER INTERNATIONAL ECONOMIC ASSOCIATION PUBLICATIONS

The Gap between Rich and Poor Nations

Proceedings of a Conference held by the
International Economic Association at
Bled, Yugoslavia

EDITED BY
GUSTAV RANIS

MACMILLAN
ST. MARTIN'S PRESS

First published 1972 by
THE MACMILLAN PRESS LTD
London and Basingstoke
Associated companies in New York Toronto
Dublin Melbourne Johannesburg and Madras

SBN 333 13193 2

Library of Congress catalog card no. 75-185041

Printed in Great Britain by
R. & R. CLARK LTD
Edinburgh

Contents

Acknowledgements

The International Economic Association wishes, as always, to express its gratitude to the two bodies whose financial support made possible the holding of the conference here recorded and the publication of this volume – the Ford Foundation and UNESCO. The interest of both of them in the subject-matter of this conference has been evident in all their policies. For their assistance in making it possible to hold the conference in the very attractive surroundings of Bled in the north of Yugoslavia the Association is deeply indebted to the President and Officers of the Union des Associations d'Économistes de Yougoslavie. May we express our gratitude to the authorities and staff of the Golf Hotel in Bled for all they did for our comfort, and not least for demonstrating to those who came from capitalist countries that the amenities of a socialist holiday-resort hotel are in no sense inferior to those to which they may have been accustomed. Finally this volume will, we believe, provide the best testimony to the Association's debt to Professor Ranis and the programme committee that planned the conference and to the paper-writers who provided the material for its discussion; not least among the latter was Professor Kuznets, whose well-earned Nobel Prize has delighted all who have participated with him in the work of this and other conferences.

List of Participants

Professor Aleksander Bajt, University of Ljubljana, Yugoslavia
Dr. Jack Baranson, Economics Department, World Bank, Washington, U.S.A.
Professor Dr. Mara Bester, University of Ljubljana, Yugoslavia
Professor Jagdish Bhagwati, Massachusetts Institute of Technology, Cambridge, U.S.A.
Professor Ksente Bogoev, University of Skopje, Yugoslavia
Professor Kenneth E. Boulding, Institute of Behavioral Science, University of Colorado, U.S.A.
Professor France Černe, University of Ljubljana, Yugoslavia
Professor Hollis B. Chenery, Harvard University, Cambridge, U.S.A.
Dr. W. M. Corden, Oxford University, Oxford, England
Professor Hector Correa, Tulane University, New Orleans, U.S.A.
Professor H. C. Eastman, University of Toronto, Canada
Mr. Chris Economides, Cyprus Economic Society, Nicosia, Cyprus
Professor Luc Fauvel, Faculté de Droit et des Sciences Économiques, Paris, France
Professor John C. H. Fei, Yale University, New Haven, U.S.A.
Professor R. Findlay, Columbia University, New York, U.S.A.
Dr. Julio Gamba, Buenos Aires University, Argentine
Professor Dharam P. Ghai, Institute of Development Studies, University of Nairobi, Kenya
Professor Bozidar Gluscevich, Institute for Economic Research, Titograd, Yugoslavia
Mr. Roland Granier, Université d'Aix–Marseille, Aix-en-Provence, France
Professor Hassan Hadjiomerovitch, University of Sarajevo, Yugoslavia
Professor D. C. Hague, Manchester Business School, University of Manchester, England
Dr. Mahbub ul Haq, Programming Adviser, International Bank for Reconstruction and Development, Washington, U.S.A.
Professor Sir John Hicks, All Souls College, Oxford, England
Professor Branko Horvat, Institute of Economic Studies, Belgrade, Yugoslavia
Professor Nurul Islam, Pakistan Institute of Development Economics, Karachi, Pakistan
Dr. Nicolas Jéquier, Directorate for Scientific Affairs, O.E.C.D., Paris, France
Professor Harry G. Johnson, The London School of Economics and Political Science, London, England
Professor T. S. Khachaturov, Academy of Sciences of the U.S.S.R., Moscow
Mr. Edo Klansek, Association of Economists of Slovenia, Ljubljana, Yugoslavia
Dr. Bruno Knall, South Asia Institute, University of Heidelberg, Germany
Professor Simon Kuznets, Harvard University, Cambridge, U.S.A.
Professor W. Arthur Lewis, Princeton University, Princeton, U.S.A.
Professor Staffan B. Linder, Stockholm School of Economics, Sweden
Dr. I. M. D. Little, Nuffield College, Oxford, England
Professor E. Lundberg, University of Stockholm, Stockholm, Sweden
Professor Jean Marchal, Faculté de Droit et des Science Économiques, Université de Paris, France
Professor Göran Ohlin, Uppsala University, Uppsala, Sweden
Professor Osman Okyar, Hacettepe University, Ankara, Turkey
Professor Albin Orthaber, University of Ljubljana, Yugoslavia
Professor Josef Pajestka, Komisja Planowania, Warsaw, Poland
Professor Don Patinkin, Hebrew University of Jerusalem, Israel

A 2

Dr. Martin Pfaff, Wayne State University, Detroit, U.S.A.
Dr. Marian Radetzki, Stockholm School of Economics, Sweden
Professor Gustav Ranis, Yale University, New Haven, U.S.A.
Professor P. Nørregaard Rasmussen, University of Copenhagen, Denmark
Professor Austin Robinson, Cambridge University, England
Professor Anthony Scott, University of British Columbia, Canada
Professor Dudley Seers, Institute of Development Studies, Brighton, England
Professor Berislav Sefer, Yugoslav Economists Association, Belgrade, Yugoslavia
Professor T. N. Srinivasan, Indian Statistical Institute, New Delhi, India
Professor Radmila Stoianovitch, University of Belgrade, Yugoslavia
Mr. Paul Streeten, Queen Elizabeth House, Oxford University, England
Professor Luigi M. Tomasini, University of Rome, Italy
Mr. Dusan Tratnik, Association of Economists of Slovenia, Ljubljana, Yugoslavia
Professor Shigeto Tsuru, Hitotsubashi University, Tokyo, Japan
Mr. Baran M. Tuncer, Ankara, Turkey
Professor Raymond Vernon, Harvard University, Cambridge, U.S.A.
Professor Dr. Dragomir Vojnic, University of Zagreb, Yugoslavia
Professor Borivoïe Yelitch, Yugoslav Economists Association, Belgrade, Yugoslavia
Professor Oktay Yenal, Robert College, Istanbul, Turkey

Observers

Miss Anquetil, University of Paris, France
Mr. Edgar Edwards, International Division, The Ford Foundation, New York, U.S.A.
Ursula K. Hicks, Fellow Emeritus, Linacre College, Oxford, England
Dr. Anita B. Pfaff, Wayne State University, Detroit, U.S.A.
Mr. Bevan Stein, O.E.C.D., Paris, France

Introduction

Gustav Ranis

YALE UNIVERSITY
Chairman of Programme Committee

Most of us will agree that, of all the problems on mankind's agenda, three have unmistakably emerged as of overwhelming importance in recent years: the avoidance of nuclear holocaust, the gap between rich and poor and the befouling of spaceship earth – probably, but not necessarily, in that order.

The I.E.A. Conference at Bled (27 August–2 September 1970), which led to the present volume, attempted to deal with the second of these issues, principally, as the title indicates, at the international level. The sessions were organised to permit the Conference to first take up the fundamental question of the meaning of 'the gap', both conceptually and statistically; to then turn to its most important historical causes and contemporary consequences; thirdly, to analyse the various ways in which the co-existence of rich and poor countries helps or hinders in closing the gap, or aiding the process of growth in the poor countries; and finally, to attempt some overall assessment and prognostication on the likely future contours of the problem.

Kuznets' opening paper, dealing mainly with the statistical measurement of the gap over time, in terms of both per capita output and sectoral structure, finds evidence of a growing distance between the rich and poor countries over the long haul, even though convergence in other areas, e.g. literacy and death rates, is also noted. In looking at the historical record and assessing its significance, two main questions seem to arise: one, is 'the gap' really a substantive issue or should we rather be concerned with the problem of growth within the developing world? Second, if we are going to measure gaps between countries, changing over time, should physical gaps, taking into account other measures of welfare (reminiscent of earlier discussions of some of the inadequacies of national income accounting), be viewed as superior? Moreover if the existence of any kind of gap is to be judged mainly a psychological problem – with growth within the L.D.C.s the real criterion of progress – then other amendments to the conventional wisdom currently being put forward, e.g. a new emphasis on intra-country distribution, welfare and employment, must surely also be made consistent with that view. For if man does not live by growth rates alone as he looks horizontally across regions or income groups within a country, why does this argument break down at the national boundaries?

Kuznets keeps reminding us, in his careful, dispassionate fashion, of the fact that, regardless of how we choose to interpret it, disparities in per capita output and in the structure of economies apparently have been increasing over time. Consequently, even though poor country output per head has probably been increasing at a faster rate over the last ten years than ever before – in fact, faster than in rich countries – the continuing widening of the gap in absolute terms can perhaps not be ignored or relegated entirely to the psychological realm. Another Kuznets proposition, that differences in the use of modern technology may serve us as a convenient classificatory or measuring device, is perhaps more open to question. I am not as sure as he is that the use of such technology, certainly if narrowly defined, is as good a criterion as, say, the extent of technological adaptibility or rate of diffusion as a prime cause of differences in performance among rich and poor countries.

The papers on the consequences of the gap, by Ohlin and Yenal, turn out to be as much concerned with its origin as its consequences. While one author places the origins at the time of the Crusades, the other at the time of the Industrial Revolution, both apparently agree that, while the gap has been increasing, it is its perception which has been increasing faster and is causing most of the current tension. Both the analysis of the origins of the gap and of its increased perception must, of course, deal with the nature of the interdependence between rich and poor countries over time. Thus the papers, and the Conference, were forced to inquire into the role of the developed countries in affecting what might have been a 'natural' growth process in the less developed world in the 18th and 19th centuries, during the so-called pre-modern or colonial period. If the spread of knowledge is the main constraint, why did growth not spread evenly throughout the world? Or do we have a case of interrupted 'natural' growth in the overseas countries, an interruption brought about by patterns of political or economic domination of some countries over others? No matter what view, or evidence, we have on the net impact of colonialism, there seems to be general agreement that the historical, as well as the contemporary, importance of the rich to the progress – or lack of it – of the poor far outweighs the importance of the poor to the progress of the rich. Moreover, once divergent paths appear, a variety of demonstration effects, both on the demand and on the supply side, ranging over a wide area of human endeavour, have served to accelerate the process, as well as, incidentally, to give the issue moral force and public attention.

The Conference accordingly next turned to an examination of various dimensions of the acknowledged substantial interdependence of the contemporary rich and poor countries. Boulding and Pfaff, while largely concerned with introducing a new country classificatory scheme, feel that unrequited international capital movements, or grants, have played a relatively small role in creating the gap historically, as well as, to date, in an attempt to help close it. That view is consistent with the position that colonialism was more a psychological than an economic condition and that differential growth patterns since then had more to do with climate, natural resource endowments and domestic policies; but it is equally consistent with the proposition that non-'grants economy' interactions between rich and poor served the two groups unequally.

Other papers, especially those by Horvat and Economides, also deal with the contemporary role of grants flowing from rich to poor – but more in operational terms concerning the nature of the international machinery required – if the Boulding–Pfaff concept of 'community' among all countries is to be realised. Both contributions call for a concerted effort to raise as much as 1 per cent of G.N.P. among the rich countries, such resources to be channelled through some form of world planning agency. But if multilateralism is to constitute the preferred method of channelling resources from rich to poor in the future, it may be necessary to trade off its presumably higher quality and greater poor country acceptability against a lower total volume, since it is difficult – at least today – to imagine a 1 per cent contribution for strictly multilateral-type U.N. programmes.

While the Conference papers do not go into this question in any detail, it is, moreover, by no means clear that the major multilateral agencies, i.e. the World Bank and the various regional banks, will be viewed as satisfactory sole aid instruments by the poor countries. It may be supposed that only a more U.N.-type of internationalism, with both rich and poor subjected to performance reviews, is likely to abate current fears of interventionism and neo-colonialism; and it is this very case in which the quantity the rich are likely to be willing to make available becomes subject to even more severe constraints. If, as most of us would agree, the international grants economy based on a 'community' rather than a 'threats' system, again in Boulding's terms, is likely to remain a rather distant goal, and much of the still substantial current aid flow from rich to poor continues to be politically motivated, there seem to be only two clear options before us: one, a quasi-moratorium on aid, which may well be preferred by many at this time and, while undoubtedly costly, may have a once-and-for-all substantial salutary effect on domestic parameters and then permit everyone to start afresh in a few years' time; or second, while accepting the political motivations of a goodly portion of total foreign assistance, as well as the many unpopular and sometimes self-defeating restrictions which are customarily attached, to continue trying to make the most of it by linking the within-country allocation to necessary structural changes and the improvement of domestic policies.

Given the present state of accumulated frictions between rich and poor, this observer would probably opt for a continuation of aid but under conditions in which the donors take a much less active posture and permit recipients to take much more initiative. This may mean sitting back and letting recipients – if they want to – propose a package of plans, programmes and associated changes, as well as the multi-year aid flows to facilitate them. In such a situation donors would not feel they have to annually chase reluctant recipients with scarce dollars in order to maintain 'country aid levels', while at the same time – and quite unnaturally – insisting on better performance; the recipients would not have to parade around in their underwear on a quarterly basis in response to outsiders' assessments of what was needed at any particular time. There would naturally be room for give and take on any 'package' under discussion, but such a system would put the burden on the poor to approach the rich if and when they were ready to be 'interfered with'.

The same sorts of issues surrounding an increased sensitivity attending the relationships between rich and poor arise with respect to the movement of private capital, especially regarding the multinational corporation, which pits technological flexibility, capital inflow and market access against monopolistic practices and the possible inhibiting tendencies for domestic entrepreneurship, domestic technology and even domestic saving. Both the Vernon and, to some extent, the Jecquier paper, in a later session, deal with this important new phenomenon on the international scene. There apparently is general agreement that the impact of the multinational corporation cannot be measured by its simple balance of payments effects, but rather in terms of its contribution to overall growth and/or other national objectives. However, such agreements break down rather rapidly as between those who argue that any contribution to these objectives is bound to be negative because of the corporation's proclivity to act in its own interests, virtually as a state within a state; and those who contend that it is not any intrinsic anti-social behaviour of such firms which is at fault, but rather misguided protectionist policies of the L.D.C.s themselves which lead to the oft-referred-to pattern of exorbitant profits and inefficient industrial growth. It can readily be agreed that an objective analysis of the whole issue of foreign investment and of the multinational corporation in relation to a much-needed revision of international trade theory represents a major challenge to economic analysis. It clearly makes a good deal of difference whether the type of integration achieved is vertical or horizontal in nature (as our discussion indicated); also whether or not the possibility of renegotiation can be built into the original agreements; whether or not some understanding can be reached among the L.D.C.s both as to their common treatment of the corporation and as to what is meant by an economic analysis of the net benefits and costs of inviting such corporations into a country; and most of all, on whether the corporate drive for economic rationality on a global scale is consistent with the drive for national independence in the L.D.C.s. Certainly this job needs to be tackled before the analysis can proceed much beyond economics.

On the subject of trade, one of the more prominent dimensions of inter-dependence between rich and poor, both the papers and the discussion wonder whether, and why, this particular 'engine of growth' is threatening to sputter. Both the renewed protective threat from the developed countries, who seem to find it easier to liberalise trade with each other than with the poor countries, and the obsession with import substitution by many of the latter, come in for rather conventional chastisement. Bhagwati, while emphasising that excess import substitution in the poor countries has been at the expense of growth, distribution, employment and exports, also makes the important point that once we are in the world of the second best it becomes difficult to determine just how much import substitution is too much, when and how it should be reversed, what is the optimal method of liberalisation and where should it stop. Beyond the general rule of preferring tariffs over quotas, uniform tariffs over discriminatory ones, and tariffs which decrease over time over permanent protection, we really cannot say very much and are desperately in need of a related theory of government. This is even more true because, with liberalisation, equality of access is likely to be accompanied by very unequal market power.

Bhagwati's wise and balanced paper on the sins of omission and of commission on both sides of the trade bargain, does rally to the side of the earlier Prebisch and suggests the regulation of rich country research and development expenditures, away from the displacement of raw materials by synthetics. But, one might ask, just as with export promotion within the poor countries, how much do we really know beyond the fact that competitiveness is 'better' in utilising basic comparative advantage, i.e. are we really in a position to re-allocate research expenditures, even if we accept the objectives indicated. Findlay's contribution, while at a much higher level of abstraction, also demonstrates the importance of overcoming the so-called 'two-gaps' problem', as a disequilibrium situation, through increased allocative efficiency, permitting the generation of exports out of domestic savings.

Little's paper, while focussing a good deal on alternative approaches to project analysis, emphasises the impact of a particular project, public or private, on the total economy and rejects the concentration on only one constraint, e.g. the balance of payments. Whether the cost-benefit calculations are made in foreign or domestic prices, i.e. whether the O.E.C.D. or the UNIDO manual is used, the basic difficulties with partial equilibrium analysis, of course, remain, i.e. the prominence of indirect costs and benefits to justify virtually any project, as well as the interaction among projects – only soluble by constant iteration. But it is undoubtedly true that even better manuals cannot protect us from abuse by policy makers. This observer parenthetically knows precious few cases – either among bilateral or multilateral donors – when a project has ever been rejected because the analysis turned out unfavourable – or accepted because it turned out favourable. Customarily once projects are analysed they have already been 'accepted' in principle; the calculations are then used with or without shadow-price or indirect benefit/cost adjustments until the results justify the initial decision which was usually based largely on 'judgement' and general country expertise; similarly, but less frequently since infant mortality can usually take care of the problem, if there arises a political need to reject a project 'scientifically', the machinery is available, whichever manual is referred to.

The partial resumption of factor mobility between rich and poor which has characterised the recent post-war period of course extends to the movement of labour. The papers by Seers–Jolly and Johnson deal with the international movement of labour and, while carrying on with many of the by now venerable issues surrounding the brain drain debate (see Walter Adams, editor, _The Brain Drain_, which contains the proceedings of a 1967 Conference on this same subject), also manage, in the context of the 'gap' issue, to explore some new ground. For example, the exogenous _v._ endogenous nature of the movement of skilled labour between rich and poor in relation to the widening economic distance between them is explored. Johnson enumerates the costs and benefits of the brain drain to both donor and recipient country in a more complete fashion than previously available, re-emphasises the crucial difference between individual, national and cosmopolitan welfare considerations, but concentrates on the effects on the poor country, in the absence of well-functioning international compensation mechanisms. In summary, he finds that its net impact may turn out to be rather negligible. But even if it did not, he questions the validity of forcing higher talent L.D.C. individuals to subsidise their fellow citizens via a restraint on out-migration unless, of course, the state, or rich country donors, have subsidised his prior education. Seers and Jolly suggest that the brain drain issue be linked to the over-all problem of distorted L.D.C. growth patterns under import substitution and the emerging unemployment-income distribution crisis – within as well as between countries. One can only agree that such a relationship exists – but still wonder whether the absence of a satisfactory blueprint for carrying out the general equilibrium analysis required won't force us into a continued posture of partial equilibrium modesty. One piece of progress reflected in both papers is the distinction drawn between brain and brawn drains, including the totality of L.D.C. environmental conditions affecting the former, and the important 'safety valve' considerations attending the latter. The welfare effects of customary L.D.C. policy mixes with 'over-price' brawn and 'under-price' brain may be quite different at the national and global levels.

The inevitable – and inevitably difficult – subject of the movement of technology between rich and poor is then addressed in papers by Baranson and Fei–Ranis. Baranson's main concern is with the efficiency of the multinational corporation as an agent of technology transfer between rich and poor, as a flexible adaptor of technology to the local scene and as a diffusor of imported and a generator of indigenous technological capacity via local subcontracting and other spill-over effects. In addition to the previously referred to summing up of the political and economic benefits and costs, one specific question that arises in the context of the narrower issue of the technology transfer process proper has to do with the relative flexibility of the multinational corporation in making the 'appropriate' adjustments and adaptations when operating in different endowment situations.

There is episodal evidence on both sides; the validity of the 'how we do it in Kansas' forces must be weighed against the strength of the global division of labour and profit maximisation drive. We certainly need to know a lot more about the relative sensitivity of domestic and foreign firms to international factor price differentials – and beyond this, the relative willingness and ability to adjust factor proportions and output mixes in a fairly substantial fashion. The 'answer', I suspect, will depend in part on the extent to which other global considerations (such as where to show profits for tax or expropriation prevention reasons) or less global considerations (such as the desire to avoid having to deal with too many workers and incipient unions) dwarf technology choice; and in part on the 'distance' at which signals are gathered and decisions made at the nerve centres of alternative types of organisations. The Hymer and Rowthorn[1] view of the foreign firm as part of an impersonal international network run by a few 'distant' men in New York or London is just as plausible as the image of a Schumpeterian extension to the international scene, with less hang-ups about 'prestige technologies' and more single-mindedness in the pursuit of efficiency and profits than its domestic counterpart. The difficulty resides in the absence of very much hard empirical evidence with which to confront our hunches and anecdotes.

The Fei–Ranis paper tries to present a general framework, at a fairly aggregative level, for the examination of the technological transfer mechanism in the context of a transition theory of economic development. A distinction is drawn between the analysis of the act of borrowing from an existing shelf of advanced country technology; the social (or unconscious) L.D.C. innovation process through which transplantation achieves, with time, the same level of efficiency as was initially 'reached for' on the shelf; and, finally – and perhaps most importantly – the private

---

[1] Stephen Hymer and Robert Rowthorn, 'Multinational Corporations and International Oligopoly: The Non-American Challenge', in *The International Corporation*, ed. Charles Kindleberger (M.I.T. Press, Cambridge, 1970).

L.D.C. innovation process through which indigenous capital-stretching innovations are generated and diffused. The theoretical framework is tested against Japanese historical data and is demonstrated to be consistent with it. The key behavioural relations governing both the borrowing and the domestic adaptation process, including the relationship between relative factor endowments in donor and recipient country and entrepreneurial profit maximisation, remain inadequate and need to be further enriched; but the framework does point out at least one way in which the various relevant dimensions of technological change can be brought together and related to output and employment performance in the typical developing country.

While there really exists little professional disagreement on the major weight which must be given to innovation in any explanation of growth, whether in a developed or developing economy context, the papers and the discussion at Bled time and again suggested that the 'ignorance gap' on this subject remains much smaller than any other D.C.-L.D.C. gap we touched on. For example, beyond size of the country, no strong generalisations as to the relative importance of shifts in output mix *v.* shifts in technology for given mixes is likely to be valid – nor do we really begin to understand why 'appropriate' technologies aren't produced in the R. & D. industries of the poor, or marketed with the help of modified and modernised shelf blue-prints of the rich.

Moreover, to many observers it is not at all clear that there exists much, if any, real world flexibility in technology choice. To them the current emphasis on moderating factor price distortions symptomatic of the import substitution syndrome consequently appears exaggerated. If only the co-efficients attaching to the latest vintage machinery produced in the most advanced countries are relevant, all the talk about alternative factor proportions in response to alternative resource endowments does become somewhat irrelevant – or restricted to changes in output mixes via trade.

The evidence on this issue is certainly crucial to the weight one is likely to place on the importance of liberalisation in various L.D.C. markets (foreign exchange, credit, etc.) as a way of ensuring the complementarity of output growth and the fullest use of the economy's relatively abundant supply of unskilled labour. And, happily, the information one is able to gather at the micro level, for Japan historically, and for contemporary Korea and Taiwan, supports the thesis that, except for continuous process industries and industries very close to the crude raw material processing stage, there in fact exists a very substantial potential for factor proportions variability.

For example, Japanese cotton spinning, through the utilisation of triple shifting and higher spindle speeds – as well as the use of coarse counts requiring more labour for repair – was able to absorb from three to seven times the volume of labour per unit of capital as abroad. As late as 1932 weekly man-hours per 1,000 homogeneous spindles of the same quality ranged from 328·8 in Japan to 164·8 in the United Kingdom and 143·1 in the United States.[1] The same general relation obtained in cotton weaving, raw silk, and printed goods. In addition to such modifications in the machine process proper, the Japanese reduced machine-peripheral capital requirements by replacing mechanical with human conveyor belts; and 'stretched' their plant requirements through the use of subcontracting and 'putting out' arrangements with extensions of farm households.

In contemporary Korea examples of capital-stretching adaptations of imported technology abound in textiles, electronics and plywood production. In the manufacture of silk, for example, 1 girl mans 2 looms, as contrasted with 6·8 equivalent looms in contemporary Japan. In reaction to the now rising wages in Japan, Korea is taking over the lower quality yarn spectrum where more girls can be employed to make up for the inferior quality of the raw material. In cotton weaving, one Korean girl mans 3 looms as contrasted with 4 currently in Japan; in spinning, the contrast is between 600 and 900 spindles. Moreover, Korean machinery is run for 3 eight-hour shifts daily, as contrasted with only 2 such shifts in Japan. Peripheral to the machine proper, we may note that the contemporary Japanese use of a conveyor belt system, for example between the carding, gilling and combing operations, is replaced by human hands in Korea.

Even in the production of plywood what at first appears as production processes very similar to those carried on in the U.S., i.e. fixed proportions, in fact, turns out to be quite flexible – interestingly enough mainly because of the greater machine speed combined with much more labour-intensive repair methods used. In Japan, defective pieces of lumber are cut out by hand, the scraps saved and the defect (hole) plugged. Here once again a lower quality raw material can be upgraded to an equivalent quality output through the application of cheap labour. The Korean production line engages 123 workers with equivalent machinery as contrasted with 72 in Japan; moreover, the Korean line is worked a 22-hour day as compared with 20 in Japan; finally, between 10 and 15 per cent more workers are engaged in inspection, repair and maintenance of both materials in process and machinery in place. As a consequence of all this one finds, over all, twice as many workers per unit of capital in this industry than in Japan.

The potential for labour-capital substitution is clearly much greater in fabricating than in continuous flow processes. Electronic assembly and further processing between assembly and final marketing represents perhaps the most dramatic example of this. In transistor assembly operations, for instance, given wage rates 10 per cent higher than the equivalent operators get in the U.S. (in the same firm) the machinery is run at full

[1] *The World Textile Industry: Economic and Social Problems*, vol. 1, International Labour Office (Geneva, 1937), p. 209.

capacity, i.e. six days, three shifts a day, which is 20 per cent above the U.S. equivalent. Moreover certain special operations such as feeding and packaging are usually done by hand on the assembly line, instead of automatically. In spite of the greater use of labour, productivity per worker seems to be higher owing partly to the faster learning process (it was repeatedly stated to take at least two weeks less to train Korean girls in assembly than Americans) but mainly to the greater discipline and attentiveness on the assembly line throughout. For example, in one firm the difference in speed of assembly on identical equipment yields a 30 per cent differential in output (from 68 units per machine hour to 85) and in a die mounting process it rises to more than 100 per cent (from 113 units per hour to 240). These greater speeds of operation, due either to faster machine or operator pacing, are once again accompanied by putting additional girls into more intensive testing, inspection and repair efforts than is encountered in Japan or the U.S. Defective pieces are not thrown away but repaired by hand. Similarly, with machinery itself working at physical full capacity, considerably more manpower is allocated to the maintenance and repair of the in-place capital equipment. In Taiwan, likewise, television set assembly lines utilise twice as many workers as in the U.S. parent plant – with about the same relationship obtaining in plastics fabrication.

What is even more interesting from the point of view of understanding technological change in L.D.C.s is the evidence that a learning process is, in fact, apparently taking place which permits the adaptation process to get better and better with time. For example, the largest electronics firm in Taiwan has increased its capital nine-fold and its employment sixteen-fold between 1965 and 1969. Other related dynamic dimensions may be found in the extensive sub-contracting to local equipment and parts manufacturers going on in both Korea and Taiwan; time and again we are told that after two or three years the smaller domestic parts supplier has become a lower cost producer. The importance of such learning by doing effects for technological diffusion throughout domestic industry as a whole is bound to be substantial.

But the full significance of all this can be seen only when combined with the dramatic changes in output mix which are made possible, especially in the smaller, trade-oriented developing countries. For example, sub-contracting internationally by labour-intensive *v.* technology or capital-intensive stage of production, either between independent firms as in conventional trade theory, or among branches of the increasingly important multinational corporation, is becoming increasingly important. Using bonded export-processing schemes or tariff-free zones into which raw materials are imported and then re-exported, after value in the form of cheap labour has been added, represents a very efficient way of harnessing virtually pure labour services to the development process. Such schemes now yield close to 20 per cent of Korean export value which has itself been rising at almost incredible rates of 30–40 per cent annually over the past half decade.

The powerful combination of interacting technology change and a liberalised trade sector can be demonstrated by the fact that, in 1962, land-based foodstuffs and raw materials made up 75 per cent of total Korean exports, while labour-based light manufacturing industries as a whole, including plywood, raw silk, cotton textile, wigs and footwear, amounted to 15 per cent. By 1968 the situation had been completely reversed, with 77 per cent of the exports in manufacturing and only 14·5 per cent in foodstuffs, livestock and raw materials. It should, moreover, be noted that small scale manufacturing exports, i.e. in units of less than 10 workers, undoubtedly the most labour-intensive part of the spectrum, grew from 18·6 per cent of the total in 1963 to 31·4 per cent in 1968.

For Taiwan, similarly, rice and sugar constituted 78 per cent of export earnings in 1952. By 1969 this had shrunk to 4·8 per cent. During the same period non-traditional agricultural products, including fresh and canned fruits and vegetables, rose from zero to 10 per cent of the total; and, most impressively, manufactured goods, including wood and plywood products, rose from 5 per cent to 69 per cent of the total. The full dimensions of this structural change are recognised when we again note that total export earnings were rising very rapidly, at rates in excess of 20 per cent annually, especially during the 1960s.

All this is intended to demonstrate the point that as L.D.C.s, especially the smaller ones, move out of land-based import substitution into labour-based import promotion capital-stretching innovations may take on major significance. Even in some larger L.D.C.s under partial liberalisation, for example Pakistan, similar conclusions are emerging, e.g. with respect to the diesel and other light machinery industry in the Punjab in the wake of the 'green revolution'. If the still widespread belief of both academicians and policy-makers regarding the assumed tyranny of the technical co-efficients can be overcome – and still entrenched import substitution policies consequently weakened – perhaps this most vital area of contact between rich and poor (the movement of technology) can be made to yield much more substantial fruit than it has in the past.

The present volume concludes, appropriately enough, with an overview and whirlwind tour of the future by Arthur Lewis. In his paper, as well as in the discussion, he takes us by the scruff of our necks and presents us with the uncomfortable question of the possible need for L.D.C.s to choose between economic independence accompanied by a widening gap, on the one hand, and neo-colonial interdependence plus a narrowing gap, on the other. Contemporary L.D.C. voices seem to assert that, given that unhappy choice, they would rather grow in autarky and slowly; others would probably counsel the maintenance of interdependence, even if this wouldn't necessarily guarantee a closing of the gap. The really touchy problem here, of course, is in the realm of private capital movements. And surprisingly, there is not much optimism in evidence on finding ways and means of letting us have the best of both worlds – whether via Hirschman-esque divestment rules, if we are to go the *ad hoc* route, or via multinational control of the multinational corporation, if we are to get ourselves organised. But Lewis concludes a rather pessimistic survey of problems and constraints affecting L.D.C. growth on a surprisingly optimistic note: even if private capital movements are not depended upon unduly, and even if there is no dramatic 'hardening' of these 'soft' states, in terms of fiscal reforms, domestic saving performance, etc., 6 per cent L.D.C. growth rates are feasible in the seventies. He does not exactly tell us why, but it is a good note on which to conclude.

Part 1

The Size and Consequences of the Gap

1 The Gap: Concept, Measurement, Trends

Simon Kuznets

HARVARD UNIVERSITY

I. CONCEPT

(1) Substance (Gap in What?)

By rich nations we presumably mean those that command a volume of economic goods that, relative to population, is significantly larger than some acceptable level. By analogy those nations are poor whose command of economic goods, on a per capita basis, is so much below that acceptable level as to imply major shortcomings and deprivation. This command over goods may be approximated by the stock of material assets, preferably supplemented by some valuation of the human resources at the nation's disposal. But the effective magnitude of such productive assets is best revealed by the annual output which they, in fact, serve to produce. Despite several vexing problems of definition and interpretation, the long-term level of per capita national product is still a reasonable criterion of the wealth and poverty of nations – long-term meaning periods long enough to obviate distortion by transient disturbances and fluctuations.

But some nations, particularly smaller ones, can show a sustained high level of per capita product because they are richly endowed with a natural resource that is desired – and often discovered and operated – by others, and in return for which they receive a large rent. This kind of wealth differs significantly from that of nations whose economy and society are geared to the utilisation of the technological potential of modern economic growth. While some economically developed and modernised countries may also have a natural-resource comparative advantage, we should, in considering the gap between rich and poor countries, exclude those that are rich merely because of bounty of nature, of luck.

We propose to limit the rich nations here to those whose high per capita product is due to an economy and a society that are capable of significant and widespread utilisation of the potentials of modern technology – the economically developed nations. Since no low per capita product nations are economically developed in this sense, the gap between rich and poor is reformulated into a gap between the economically developed nations and the *poor*, less developed nations (less developed by definition).[1] As just

---

[1] This statement implies that the potential of modern economic growth can also be effectively realised and a high per capita product attained in countries without a great natural resource endowment. Japan is the most conspicuous example; but others are the Netherlands, Denmark, Switzerland and even Italy.

indicated, some less developed nations may be windfall rich; other less developed nations, whose levels of modernisation, industrialisation and adoption of modern technology are below that of the developed nations, may have per capita products that place them well above the poor, without windfall riches. Yet the most significant gap for analysis and policy is that between the economically developed and the poor, less developed countries. Of course, it still remains to draw the per capita product line (or band) below which 'poverty' lies; but this can be done best with the help of the statistical data in the next section.

This reformulation of the gap is important because it emphasises the association between the disparity in per capita product and those in economic structures and institutions, in non-economic structures and in social ideology (i.e. views on man and nature prevalent in various societies). The gap is not merely between rich and poor, but between the industrialised, urbanised, mechanised, modernised countries with distinctive economic institutions, demographic processes, political characteristics and ideological patterns, on the one hand; and the largely rural, agricultural, traditional countries, with only small nuclei of modern industry, modern firms, modern government and modern views, on the other. Difficult as it may be to establish the specific connection between economic development, as measured by some index of aggregate product, and economic and social structures, institutions and ideological notions, the evidence on such historical association is too weighty to be denied or neglected. And the association provides a basis for interpreting and analysing the aggregative gap.

(2) Base (*Gap between Whom?*)

The importance of the aggregative and structural gap depends upon the magnitude and number of societies at either end – what might be called the population base. If, despite what we know (confirmed by the statistical appendix), we were to assume that of 3·3 billion of world population, divided among more than 150 states and dependencies (in the mid-1960s), only one country, with some 3 million population, was developed; and only one other, also with a population of 3 million, was poor and less developed (and all others were within a range of say $500 to $600 per capita product and of rather similar structure), the gap – relating to less than 1 per cent of mankind – would hardly deserve much interest. If modern economic growth were not a process affecting a substantial group of nations, and if poverty, caused by the failure to exploit modern economic growth, were not to afflict a large proportion of humanity, the gap would have been viewed as the result of some unusual combination of circumstances – perhaps as an analytical curiosity, but not a significant economic and social problem. It is the nature of modern scholarship to neglect mere intellectual curiosities and concentrate on questions with empirical weight that, at least potentially, seems large.

Given a large population base at each end of the gap, what is the extent of diversity and divisiveness within each base? If, again contrary to reality, we were to assume that there is one large developed country, with a population of say 1 billion, and one large poor less developed country, with a population say of 2 billion (leaving only 300 million for all other nations), the population base of the gap would be large but there would be no diversity or divisiveness at either end (assuming that each country is a fairly unified society). The actual gap, currently observed and illustrated by relevant statistics, is characterised by the many developed, as well as many poor, less developed, countries, and the numerous divergencies among them.

The diversity and divisiveness among nations at both ends are important, particularly with reference to the interrelations or movements *across* the gap, a third aspect of the concept to be noted below. The diversity may relate to size, with major effects on propensity to engage in foreign trade; to level of development (*within* the range indicated by the grouping into developed, and poor, less developed); and to the ideology that governs economic life. The organisation of mankind into nations, and the multiplicity of nations, implies emphasis on the nation's interest as the overriding priority and permits a divisive cumulation of heritage of past history among nations. The gap is thus not merely between the aggregative and structural aspects of economic and social performances of two large groups within the world population, but between the two groups, subdivided into many relatively independent and differing units. There is thus a multiplicity of binary gaps; and the movements across the gap can assume a wide variety of combinations, affected partly by the complementary and partly by the competitive relations among the nations at either end and across the gap.

(3) *Association and Isolation*

Much of the interest in the gap lies in its effect on the flows across the gap – between the rich, developed and poor, less developed, nations – and on the flows within the rich and the poor groups themselves – at least as affected by the gap.

One extreme assumption is that no such flows – either across the gap or within either end – exist; that the two groups are completely isolated from each other and indeed have no knowledge of each other's existence (and that the same is true of the several countries at either end). This is not an entirely unrealistic assumption with respect to much of past history. Until the European explorations of the late 15th century, the societies in middle America lived without knowing of Europeans or being known by them; and did not know of, and were not known to, the societies in Africa. Such cases of complete (or almost complete) isolation were numerous in past history, and their scarcity is a feature of only the recent century. The other extreme assumption – of fully developed and relatively easy economic and other flows across the gap (and within the groups at either end) – is a condition that has only been approached, and is far from fully attained even today.

Isolation or association, the extent and ease of international movements, may apply to economic flows of productive resources, such as man, capital, know-how, etc.; of commodities and services in foreign trade; of monetary and other claims; of consumption patterns via the demonstration effects; and the like. They may relate to flows of intangibles – of knowledge, education, cultural innovations – all fundamental in shaping social and economic life. Finally, the flows may represent exercise of political power – co-operative or aggressive – involving at times substantial flows of economic goods but not as economic activities per se. All these flows and the association or isolation that they spell, condition the co-existence of nations at both ends of the gap. They affect the social and economic stability among the poor countries, the rivalries of developed countries for preferential position with respect to the poor and less developed and the task of optimising the economic flows to enhance the growth prospects of the poor while preserving the pioneering potentials of the developed countries themselves. Indeed much of this conference is devoted to a careful scrutiny of the economic flows across the gap and the specific forms which they assume.

II. MEASUREMENT

Measuring all aspects of the aggregate and structural gap, let alone of the flows across it, is an enormous task and can hardly be attempted here. Furthermore, many of the major quantitative characteristics of the current gap are well known, and it would serve little purpose to demonstrate what is already established. Under the circumstances it seemed best to select for discussion a few statistical findings, and relegate the underlying tables to a statistical appendix.

(1) *Identification and Base*

We identify the developed and poor, less developed countries primarily by their per capita product, using the recent estimates by Hagen and Hawrylyshyn, of G.D.P. in market prices, in U.S. dollars in 1965 (see Table 1.1 which, like all the other tables, contains the specific references). The H-H estimates are based largely on United Nations data, supplemented by a few special sources for the Communist countries.

Developed countries are defined as those with a per capita product in 1965 of $1,000 or more – with two significant exceptions. The first is the exclusion of a few countries with a high per capita product due largely to natural or location advantages (this meant excluding Puerto Rico, Kuwait and Qatar). Second, although Japan's per capita product is given as only $870, we included it among the developed countries because, in view of its scarcity of industrial and natural resources, such a per capita product is a clear indication of a high level of modernisation and development. As thus defined the developed group comprises, among non-Communist countries, Europe, excluding Ireland, Spain, Portugal, Greece, etc.; North America; Australia and New Zealand; Japan and Israel; among the Communist countries, the U.S.S.R., East Germany and Czechoslovakia. It differs from the United Nations definition of non-Communist developed countries by excluding some European countries and South Africa (excluded here because its high per capita income is for its small white population, not its total population). On this definition, the developed countries account for about 861 million people, with a per capita product of some $1,900; or 26 per cent of world population, but 79 per cent of world product.

The 'poor', less developed countries, narrowly defined, comprise all countries with a per capita product in 1965 of $120 or less. This definition segregates many populous countries and accounts for most of the population of Subsaharan Africa and Asia. The population of this group in 1965 was 1,726 million, or 53 per cent of world population. Its per capita product was only $95 – about one-twentieth of that for the developed group – and its share in world product was 7·9 per cent.

These two groups account for about 80 per cent of world population (and for an even higher percentage of world product), leaving somewhat over 20 per cent with a per capita product ranging between $121 and $1,000. Thus the relative magnitude, in terms of population (and product) of the developed countries, on the one hand, and of the 'poor' less developed countries, on the other, would be only slightly affected if we shifted the 'poverty' line upward. A wider definition of the 'poor' L.D.C.s, with the per capita product line set at $300 rather than at $120, would mean a group accounting for 2,089, rather than 1,726 million, or 64 rather than 53 per cent of world population; but its per capita product would still be only $117 (compared with $95 for the narrower definition). This more widely defined, 'poor' group accounts for almost all the population of Asia and Subsaharan Africa, and for a substantial part of the Latin American population.

Two characteristics of the population bases of the gap, familiar though they may be, bear repetition, for their implications are still to be fully explored. The first, given the $120 per capita as a reasonably low line for defining 'poverty' (of which more in the next section), is the relatively large size of the base at the lower end of the gap. That the *'poor'* less developed countries (narrowly defined) account for as much as 53 per cent of world population is to be ascribed largely to the populousness of the countries within the context of the Sinic and Indian civilisations (Mainland China, India, Pakistan and Indonesia, the four alone accounting for 1,295 million in 1965). This, in turn, must be traced to the capacity of these two civilisations to sustain a large and growing population in the past, in ways in which this was not done in Africa, or in the Americas, or even in Europe; and this capacity could hardly have been due to greater natural endowments in Asia. But if the economic and social institutions were responsible, their role in the present economic position of these countries is in question. The second characteristic of the base is that almost all developed countries at the upper end are members of the European civilisation complex, either in Europe or their offshoots overseas or in Asia (Israel). Indeed only Japan can be said to be the one developed country effectively outside the European origin matrix. To be sure, some countries in Europe and offshoots overseas (e.g. Argentina) are not among the developed. Nevertheless a question remains as to the extent to which some elements of 'Europeanness' are a *necessary* if not *sufficient* condition for attaining the status of a developed country, and as to the special conditions in Japan that have provided an adequate substitute or analogue. In short the identification of the bases at both ends of the gap, while indicating their large size in proportion to world population, also raises questions concerning the historically conditioned social and institutional determinants of the difference in development between the two groups of countries.

(2) *Magnitude of the Aggregate Gap*

The estimates shown in Table 1.1 have been converted from domestic currencies to U.S. dollars by conventional exchange rates, modified in case of multiple exchange rates or violent distortions. Such exchange rates differ substantially from approximations to real purchasing power parities of the monetary units, and a wide literature has emerged that deals with the problem and attempts modifications.[1] But the findings of the new usable studies, those by the O.E.E.C. for Western European countries compared with the United States, can easily be summarised.

First, even if exchange rates are assumed to reflect purchasing power parities of goods entering foreign trade, the price structures of the latter do not fully represent the prices of the wider range of goods entering countrywide output and comprising gross domestic product; and more important, the degree of non-representation differs among countries at

---

[1] For a brief review and some attempts at solution, see Wilfred Beckerman, 'International Comparisons of Real Incomes', *O.E.C.D. Development Center Studies* (Paris, 1966). See also the discussion in Simon Kuznets, *Modern Economic Growth: Rate, Structure, and Spread* (Yale University Press, New Haven, 1966), pp. 374–84 (referred to below as *MEG*).

different levels of development and hence of per capita product (as determined by exchange rate conversion). The overstatement (or under-
statement) of the prices in the wider range of G.D.P. is apparently smaller
(or greater) for the country with the lower per capita product (country B)
than for that with the higher per capita product (country A). Hence a shift
from conversion by exchange rates to conversion by purchasing power parities for a wider range of goods *reduces* the disparity among countries in
per capita product. This finding would probably also hold for factor costs
(rather than prices of final products), but I know of no empirical study
containing such a comparison (except incidentally in approximating prices
of final goods, when the latter are services of some one factor).

Second, the use of price levels for a broad range of goods for the two
countries (or sets of countries) yields different relative disparities in their
per capita products (as compared with those attained by conversion by
exchange rates), depending upon which country's price structure is applied
to one and the same set of quantities. If the price structure of the low per
capita product country B is used, the reduction in the disparity measured
by conversion by exchange rates is moderate (the low ratio is raised about
25 per cent for 1950 and less than 20 per cent for 1955, for the sample of
Western European countries relative to the United States – see *MEG*,
Table 7.3, pp. 376–77). If the price structure of the high per capita product
country A is used, the disparity is narrowed appreciably – the more so the
lower country B's per capita product. Thus for Italy, the lowest per capita
product country studied in the O.E.E.C. investigation, the ratio of its per
capita product to that of the United States as 100, on the exchange conversion basis, was 16 in 1950 and 19 in 1955; with the shift to conversion
by the Italian price structure, the ratio increased moderately to 18 in 1950
and 20 in 1955; with the shift to conversion by U.S. prices, it rose to 30
in 1950 and to 35 in 1955.

These findings are due to two underlying associations. The first is the
negative association between quantity and price structures within each
country – more of the relatively cheaper goods (or resources) are used
than of the relatively expensive – with the obvious result of efficiency in
use of resources and of responsiveness of final demand to relative prices.
The second is the negative association in the process of growth (and hence
presumably in disparities among countries that are, at the time of comparison, at different levels of growth) between movements of quantities
and movements of prices – the higher priced goods growing more than the
cheaper goods and their prices declining more (or rising less). Consequently when we value the quantities of country B by the prices of country
A, we assign high prices to relatively abundant goods and resources, and
low prices to relatively scarce goods and resources (e.g. high prices to
labour and agricultural products and low prices to machinery, etc.). And
when we value quantities in country A by prices of country B, we assign

high prices to machinery and capital and low prices to agricultural products and labour. Obviously the upward effects of such valuation by another country's price structure are far greater when this other country is a more developed, higher per capita product nation than when it is less developed. Similar results are found for aggregate growth rates over time: the growth rate is much greater (the disparity is greater) when the weights are *initial* year prices (analogous to prices of country B) than when the weights are *terminal* year prices (analogous to prices of country A).

Third, judging by the sample of the European countries and the United States, the disparity among countries as revealed by exchange rate conversion and that found with direct purchasing power comparisons, is either moderately affected and relatively independent of the country's per capita product when prices of country B are used; or is increasingly reduced the lower country B's per capita product, when prices of country A are used. But even in the latter case, the disparities still remain large despite a possible reduction of a half or six-tenths. Given a gap of over 30 : 1 between the United States and the poor, less developed countries, or one of 20 : 1 between all developed countries and the poor, less developed countries, reduction to 15 or even 10 for the former or to 10 or even 7 for the latter still leaves us with a large gap. And the adjustment has only a slight effect on the relative ranking of countries, taken in substantial groups.

These brief comments on the wide field of international purchasing power parities, which is still to be explored adequately in empirical study, can be supplemented by one, rather speculative, observation. The difference between the aggregative gap when measured by the price structure of country A and the gap when that of country B is used – a problem from the standpoint of formal index number theory – may be analytically revealing. That the relative gap is much narrower when the price weights of country A are used indicates that the gap looks narrower when it is viewed by observers in country A, in the light of that country's judgements as to values of resources and goods; and the same gap looks much wider when it is viewed by observers in country B, using this particular country's judgements as to relative values of goods and resources. Either as a measure of differences in productive capacity or of differences in welfare satisfiable by economic goods, the gap looks wider when judged by the value weights of the 'poorer', less developed country rather than by those of the more developed country.

This comment would be truly significant if the price weights adequately measured productivity assignable to the various factors or reflected the views of the country's population of welfare assignable to various final goods. Needless to say, the prices represent only rough approximations to relative productivity of factors or to welfare weights of final goods. Considering the distortions in factory markets and the effects of income inequalities in all countries, and both perhaps greater in the less developed than in the developed countries, one may doubt that the price structures properly reflect the underlying productivity and welfare ratios. Yet given the conformity of the behaviour of the various price structures to expectations on economically rational grounds, it is hard to deny that the different magnitudes of the gap corresponding to shifts in price structure, i.e. position of the observer, have some significance. The loss in potential productivity and welfare looms more heavily in the less developed countries, that view themselves as sustaining this loss, than in the more developed countries, which appraise the same loss in terms of their own scales of prices and values – granted a question as to the size and social position of the relevant observer classes in the two groups of countries, who may be expected to be aware of the values and quantities involved in the comparison.

(3) *Structural Aspects of the Gap*

Despite the difficult index number problems, we may reasonably conclude that the per capita product gap is wide, indicating a much lower capacity to produce and to consume in the poor, less developed countries than the developed. This conclusion is strongly reinforced by the structural characteristics associated with the level of per capita product – ranging from the purely economic, such as education of the labour force and mechanical energy available per capita; or distribution of labour force and product among major production sectors; or consumption of final goods, ranging from 'necessities' to 'luxuries'; to non-economic processes and characteristics, such as the demographic rates of births, deaths, and migration; or to conditions of life reflected in extent of urbanisation, literacy of population, etc. Wide differences in per capita product are accompanied by wide differences in the characteristics of economic and social structure. If in the developed countries the literacy ratio is close to 100 per cent and in the poor L.D.C.s (narrow definition) it is below 30 per cent; if in the developed countries labour force attached to agriculture is less than 25 per cent of the total and in the poor L.D.C.s it is 75 per cent; if the crude death rates in the poor L.D.C.s are twice as high as in the developed countries, greater reality is imparted to the conclusion that the aggregative gap in economic capacity and performance is wide, and is not a statistical illusion.

A large number of structural characteristics, economic and social, associated with the gap in per capita product, can be measured. However, the documentation for a recent year or period in Table 1.2 – from which the statistics in the preceding paragraph were taken – presents a choice limited to a few characteristics of wide import for which data are easily available. (A more comprehensive survey and discussion are provided in *MEG*, chapter 8, pp. 400–60.) Although it is unnecessary to discuss even

B

the few characteristics given in Table 1.2, let alone others – the major ones are fairly familiar – it may be useful to comment on some problems of interpretation of the gap, which the differences in economic and social structure suggest.

First, the gap, whether in per capita product or in associated structural characteristics, is relative – the levels for the poor L.D.C.s are low (or high, depending upon the characteristics) compared with those for the developed countries. This does not mean that they are low (or high) compared with some other standard. To illustrate: Table 1.2 shows that per capita calorie consumption is a third lower in the poor L.D.C.s than in the developed countries (line 14); and more recent data confirm this disparity.[1] This does not mean that calorie consumption in the L.D.C.s is low relative to requirements set by some nutritional standards. Indeed, in many 'poor' L.D.C.s, according to the table cited in footnote 1 below, the ratio of calorie consumption to requirements is close to 100 per cent (e.g. Pakistan – 98 per cent, Ceylon – 99 per cent, Ethiopia – 95 per cent, Uganda – 97 per cent); and in many L.D.C.s the net protein intake is at or above the required level. Disregarding the problem of unequal distribution of food consumption *within* countries, the averages do not suggest any significant *gap* in the calorie consumption of L.D.C.s with respect to requirements. Not so paradoxically one may interpret the excess of calorie consumption over requirements in the developed countries as a deficiency with respect to desirable standards. Table 1.2 also shows much lower levels of formal education in the L.D.C.s (line 5), and the proportion of people in these countries who have completed higher education is also probably much lower. But it does not follow that there is a shortage with respect to the requirement standards of the actual or proximately higher level of productive capacity. The comment is intended to draw attention to the absolute levels at the low end of the gap, and to the value of relating these levels to such potentially meaningful criteria as mentioned above, than in their relation to the levels at the high end of the gap. The latter comparison implies unrealistically that the developed countries represent an optimum with respect not only to per capita product but also to the various economic and social characteristics that they display.

Second, the associations between per capita product and *some structural* characteristics are close and consistent. Thus as we move from the 'poor' L.D.C.s, narrow definition, to the next group of L.D.C.s, then to the 'non-poor' L.D.C.s, and to the developed countries, the crude death rates drop from 21 to 16 to 11 and to 9 per thousand;[2] the share of labour force in

---

[1] See United Nations, *1967 Report on the World Social Situation* (New York, 1969), Table 2, pp. 36–37.

[2] The sequence and differences for death rates adjusted for age and sex differentials would be even wider, because the higher birth rates in the L.D.C.s result in an age structure dominated by the younger age-classes, with lower age-specific mortality rates.

agriculture declines from 75 to 62 to 46 to 25 per cent, while that in the I-sector rises from 11 to 14 to 27 to 36 per cent; and the share of population in rural areas and small towns declines from 87 to 73 to 66 to 51 per cent (see Table 1.2, lines 22, 27, 33 and 40). Even within the 'poor' L.D.C.s (narrow definition), the lower per capita product for Subsaharan Africa is associated with higher death rates, higher proportions of labour force in agriculture, and greater 'rurality' of population than in the Asian countries with their somewhat higher per capita product (see Table 1.2 lines 23 and 25, and for per capita product line 12, columns 2 and 3, Table 1.1). But even here there is one significant exception: the U.S.S.R., with an appreciably higher per capita product than the top group of L.D.C.s in Latin America, shows as high a proportion of labour force in agriculture and the same extent of rurality (see Table 1.2, lines 21 and 37, col. 4 and 7; and for per capita product, Table 1.1, line 3, col. 6, in parentheses and line 27, col. 5). For other characteristics the association is not consistent. Thus while birth rates are, in general, higher in L.D.C.s than in the developed countries, Latin America, with a larger per capita product than the Asian countries, shows distinctly higher birth rates; and among the developed countries, the overseas offshoots in North America, and Oceania, with much higher per capita product, show significantly higher birth rates than Europe and Japan (see Table 1.2, line 32 compared with line 25, and lines 17–18 compared with lines 16 and 19, col. 1).

Even when the association between per capita product and a structural characteristic or process is close and consistent, per capita product, in itself, should not be interpreted as a direct cause. For example, high death rates for low per capita product countries do not necessarily mean that the low consumption levels due to low per capita product are the major, direct cause of high death rates. The latter may reflect the wide inequality in income distribution in the L.D.C.s, or the general state of economic and social institutions, or the prevailing views which may place no high value on health and life. In short, a complex of factors may result, at one and the same time, in low per capita G.D.P. and in high death rates, with no crucial causal connection between the two. Still a close and consistent association between per capita product and specific characteristics means that the former is a good index of the latter, and can be used to generalise cross-section results from a limited sample and infer levels of these characteristics when they are not directly available.

Third, the association between per capita product and a structural characteristic is often viewed as a basis for extrapolating forward the expected results of a change in per capita product (usually its rise in the process of growth), or estimating backward the change in the characteristic in the past as per capita product grew. But a single cross-section is not a reliable basis for projections *over time* because technological changes and related changes in conditions of life and tastes may shift the cross-section function to a higher or lower level, and such shifts are not reflected in the association within one cross-section. For example, the close inverse correlation between per capita product and death rates in the 1960s does not imply ('predict') the decline between the late 1930s and the mid-1950s in crude death rates in many countries in Asia, Africa, and even Latin America, despite the absence of significant rises in per capita product; and it is highly probable that death rates will also decline in those L.D.C.s in which these rates are comparatively high today, even if per capita product fails to rise. A technological revolution that reduces death rates without large economic inputs or without a radical modification of the social structure means a downward shift of the cross-section, a lowering of death rates without any economic and social changes that would result in a higher per capita product and a more modern social structure. Such gains, with respect to some undesirable corollaries of low per capita product at the lower end of the gap, are not unexpected; but they are necessarily limited and may not reduce the structural gap significantly. The latter may require a significant reduction of the aggregative gap, largely by a higher growth rate of the lower than of the higher per capita product groups.

(4) *Diversity and Divisiveness*

Table 1.3 shows 21 countries in the developed group, and 39 in the 'poor' L.D.C.s group (narrow definition), even though we exclude units with less than 1 million population. Almost all the countries are sovereign states, but include a few territories like Mozambique and Angola, and there are some 120 such units in the world. This multiplicity of sovereign entities, of societies that consider themselves distinct from the rest of the world and their own decision-makers (actually or potentially), affects the interpretation and measurement of the aggregate and structural gaps.

First, when we distinguish individual countries or subgroups within the developed group, or within the 'poor' L.D.C.s, we observe a range of relative magnitudes of the aggregate gap, i.e. a disparity in per capita product. As Table 1.1 shows, per capita G.D.P. for the North American region of the developed countries, at $3,441, is over twice as large as that for developed Europe and about four times as large as that for Japan; whereas within even the 'poor' (narrowly defined) L.D.C. group, the per capita G.D.P. for a sizeable population group in Subsaharan Africa and Asia (of some 260 million) is only about $65. The range in per capita product between North America and this latter group is over 50:1; whereas the range between Japan and the populous less developed countries of Asia is less than 9:1. The range in the gap can obviously vary once we recognise the diversity in per capita product within the developed and less developed groups themselves; and presumably large differences in such relative gaps in per capita product imply similar differences in the gaps in the associated characteristics of economic and social structure. These variations in the 'distance' represented by the aggregate and structural gaps are important and should be kept in mind as a necessary supplement to the overall group averages employed in the discussion.

Second, of more interest, because it introduces characteristics not mentioned so far, is the diversity among the countries in size. Table 1.3 provides a condensed illustration of this diversity, with size measured in terms of population (and, to repeat, excluding units with less than 1 million each, an omission of about 20 million of the world population in 1965 of 3,271 million); but similar diversity would be shown with size measured in terms of area or total economic product.

Within the developed group, 2 of the 21 countries (the United States and the U.S.S.R.) account for about a half, while at the other extreme 6 countries, with less than 6 million each, account for less than 3 per cent of total population in the developed group. The size inequalities are even wider among the less developed countries. Thus of the 39 countries in the 'poor' L.D.C.s group (narrow definition), four (Mainland China, India, Pakistan and Indonesia) account for 1·4 out of 1·72 billion population – whereas 19 countries, with less than 6 million each, account together for 62 million or less than 4 per cent of the total. One should note the many small countries within the less developed group, a result perhaps of the inability to overcome initial divisiveness and to form, through unification, somewhat larger national units.

The importance of size for economic growth attainments and prospects lies in the inevitably greater dependence of small than of large units upon foreign trade, shown by the close inverse correlation between size and proportion of foreign trade to domestic product for countries in which free foreign trade is permitted; and in the problems of organisation and integration that large countries face, particularly if they are less developed and their unifying infrastructures consequently far less advanced than those of an economically developed country. With special reference to the gap one should note that if the small countries must rely on foreign trade and other forms of international division proportionately much more than the large countries, which can count on large internal markets; if the small countries trade mostly with a large country, rather than among themselves (as is usually the case); and if the small less developed countries, like all other less developed countries, trade with one or two large *developed* countries, the inequality represented by the gap – a gap in per capita product magnified by a gap in size – becomes particularly conspicuous. Such inequality in dependence between a small L.D.C., with exports amounting say to a quarter of domestic product and going to a large developed country in which such imports (or exports to pay for them) represent a fraction of 1 per cent of total foreign trade, and even less of domestic product, is clearly potential of great strain – for the smaller trading partner. And it may be observed from Table 1.3 that, if we use 6 million population as a dividing line, as many as 46 non-Communist small countries are presumably trading primarily with six sizeable developed non-Communist countries (with population over 20 million). The strain between the small and large exists also among the Communist countries, even though their foreign trade propensity is generally lower than that of non-Communist countries of similar size and level of development.

Finally, in addition to per capita product and size, other characteristics show great diversity at both ends of the gap. Of these Tables 1.1 and 1.3 illustrate only one, the distinction between Communist and non-Communist countries, which reflects a major type of divisiveness in the current world, a major difference in key aspects of economic and social organisation. There are Communist countries within both the developed group and the 'poor' less developed group (narrowly defined); and some of these are large and some are small. Given the pervasive presence of at least two 'worlds' at both ends of the gap, there is a conspicuous division among countries, and within any gap observed, with respect not only to several major characteristics of economic and social organisation, but also to views as to the optimal pattern of movement toward higher levels of economic and social performance.

(5) *Commodity Trade Flows Across the Gap*

Foreign trade in commodities appears, at least in casual observation, still to be the flow among countries least subject to the type of interventionary restraint that affects even the flow of services, let alone of productive resources, or of such intangibles as elements of the stock of human knowledge and culture. Foreign trade is also an economic flow closely related to economic performance and growth, and is one for which worldwide data are at hand. For these reasons flows across the gap are illustrated only for foreign trade in commodities (Table 1.4).[1]

Two factors affecting the proportion of commodity trade to total output have already been noted. Communist countries, with their governmental control over foreign trade, are characterised by lower trade proportions than non-Communist countries. In Table 1.4 the ratio for the former of the total of exports and imports to G.N.P. is 10·7 per cent, contrasted with one for the non-Communist countries of 20·5 per cent (in both cases

---

[1] For a more detailed discussion see Simon Kuznets, 'Quantitative Aspects of the Economic Growth of Nations: IX. Level and Structure of Foreign Trade – Comparisons for Recent Years', *Economic Development and Cultural Change*, vol. XIII, no. 1, Part II (October 1964). In recent years exports of services were about a quarter of the exports of commodities and imports of services about a sixth of the imports of commodities. Total trade in services tends to be a somewhat higher proportion of total trade in commodities in the more developed than in the less developed countries (see e.g. Table 1.1, pp. 4–5).

the ratio of the sums of exports and imports to the sums of G.D.P.); and the difference would probably be even more marked if the foreign trade in services could be included, given the lesser importance of finance and transport as well as of tourist services in the international flows to and from the Communist countries. Part of the difference can be attributed to a lower proportion of small countries and a lower per capita product within the Communist bloc – both of which would make for a lower foreign trade ratio. But the magnitude of the difference, the sharp decline in trade proportions in the countries into which the Communist organisation was introduced, and the obvious effects of control over foreign trade, all suggest that the major source of lower propensity to trade probably lies in the Communist organisation of economic activity.

The second, and most dominant, factor is size. The paper cited in footnote 1 on the previous page shows for a large sample of non-Communist countries proportions of commodity trade to G.N.P. for countries classified by size of either population or G.N.P. For some twelve groups of countries the foreign trade proportion ranges from a low of 12 to a high of 109 per cent; for groups classified by size of population it ranges from 17 to 81 per cent, or about two-thirds of the full range; for groups by size of G.N.P. it ranges from 19 to 73 per cent, over half of the full range (see Table 1.2, Panel B, p. 35). Further analysis shows that the narrower range of effect for countries grouped by size of G.N.P. is due to the reduction of the inverse correlation with total G.N.P. by the positive correlation of foreign trade proportions with G.N.P. per capita. It is, therefore, the size factor that explains the somewhat lower trade proportion for the total of developed countries than that for the 'poor' L.D.C.s (wide definition, but not the narrow) or than that for all the L.D.C.s – 19, 24 and 28 per cent respectively (Table 1.4, col. 5, lines 4, 12 and 18). For the one developed group that contains a fair number of small countries, Western Europe, the foreign trade proportion, 33·4 per cent, is among the highest, surpassed only by Subsaharan Africa and the Middle East with their many very small countries (col. 5, lines 1, 10 and 13).

But the most relevant finding, bearing directly upon flows *across* the gap, is in Panel B of Table 1.4 – which shows exports by provenance and destination for economic classes of countries, of which Class I is quite close to the non-Communist developed countries as we define them, and Class II is close to the non-Communist L.D.C.s (taken as a whole). If we exclude the Communist countries, whose share in total world foreign trade (and in the trade of the large sub-divisions of the non-Communist countries) is small, we find that of the total exports of L.D.C.s to non-Communist countries (93·5 per cent of their total exports) about eight-tenths were sent to developed countries, and less than two-tenths to other L.D.C.s. Likewise, of the total imports (exports received) by L.D.C.s from non-Communist countries (92 per cent of their total imports), about eight-tenths were received from the developed countries and only about two-tenths from the other L.D.C.s. To put it crudely, the L.D.C.s depend on the developed countries for eight-tenths of their foreign trade, which means overall about a fifth of their output. By contrast, the developed countries send about eight-tenths of their exports to non-Communist countries (about 96 per cent of their total exports), to other developed countries; and receive about eight-tenths of their imports from non-Communist countries (96 per cent of the total), from other developed countries. The developed countries are thus dependent on the non-Communist L.D.C.s only for about two-tenths of their trade (other than that with the Communist bloc), or roughly speaking, to less than 4 per cent of their total domestic output. As already mentioned, this contrast is even wider for individual large developed and small less developed countries.

Finally Panel B indicates that among the Communist countries (Economic Class III) the developed and less developed countries within Europe are fairly closely tied in: most of the exports received by Eastern Europe and the U.S.S.R. originate within the Communist bloc (71 per cent of all exports received by Eastern Europe and 65 per cent of all exports received by the U.S.S.R., line 31, col. 5 and 6). But the Asian Communist countries (dominated by Mainland China) receive only a third of their imports (exports received) from the Communist bloc, and close to a half from the non-Communist developed countries (col. 7, lines 29–31). Presumably, the allocation of exports originating in the U.S.S.R. and Eastern Europe also differs from that for Communist Asia.

III. LONG-TERM TRENDS

We deal here with the gap between the developed and the 'poor' L.D.C.s (largely narrow definition) and view the movement over the past century to century and a quarter, the period of modern economic growth for most presently developed countries. The following major trends can be suggested: (1) widening of the absolute, and even relative gap, in per capita product; (2) widening of the gap in some aspects of economic and social structure, but not in others; (3) increasing interdependencies among nations combined with increasing diversity and divisiveness – the former associated with continuing major improvements in transport and communication and advancing technology; the latter with the growing number of sovereign units, and of large developed nations, and increasing diversity in political and ideological orientation.

(1) *Widening Gap in Per Capita Product*

The evidence, while limited in reliable detail, is compelling. Most of the presently developed countries entered into modern economic growth about a century ago, or more. The typical growth rates in per capita product for these countries meant multiplication over a century by a factor of 5, implying an annual growth rate of about 1.6 per cent (see *MEG*, Table 2.5, pp. 64–65). In none of the 'poor' L.C.D.s (narrow definition) did per capita product rise at such a rate over a century; and, indeed, if we work back from the mid-1950s when the per capita product of this group was between \$80 and \$90 (in 1965 \$), a *doubling* over a century would have brought per capita product down to between \$40 and \$45. But even doubling is too large a factor, at least for the 'narrowly poor' countries of today. Of these we have an approximation only for India, for which the suggested rise from the 1860s to mid-1955 is about two-thirds, or a multiplication factor of 1·8 per century.[1] For Egypt (within the range of the 'poor', wider definition), the records suggest practically no growth in per capita product (but considerable growth in population) between 1895–99 and the mid-or late 1950s; and only for Ghana, another country within the widely defined 'poor' L.D.C.s, do some estimates suggest a substantial growth in product (amounting to almost a tripling between 1890 and the 1950s).[2]

A reasonable conjecture is that, in comparison with the quintupling of the per capita product of developed countries over the last century, the per capita product of the 'poor' L.D.C.s rose two-thirds at most; and that this relation would hold roughly, even if we were to measure the century back from 1965 (rather than from the mid-1950s). This suggests that the gap that existed at the beginning of the century tripled in 100 years. Since the present relative gap is either 20 : 1 or 16 : 1, depending upon the definition of 'poor' at the lower end (see Table 1.1), a century ago the average per capita product of developed countries (taken together) was already from 5 to 7 times as high as the per capita product of the current 'poor' L.D.C.s. However, this widening of the gap was not due to a decline or stagnation of the per capita product of the L.D.C.s as a whole; even if it had quadrupled over the century, the absolute and relative gap would have widened. In fact, if the records can be trusted, the per capita product of many L.D.C.s rose substantially and for no such country can a significant long-term decline be found.

As Tables 1.5 and 1.6 (limited to non-Communist countries) indicate,

[1] See M. Mukherjee, *National Income of India: Trends and Structure* (Calcutta, 1969) Table 2.5, p. 61. An even lower estimate is suggested in Krishan G. Saini, 'The Growth of the Indian Economy: 1860–1960', *The Review of Income and Wealth* (September 1969), pp. 247–63.

[2] The estimates for Egypt are extrapolations back from 1945–49 on the basis of indexes of agricultural output, their relation to labour force engaged in agriculture and the ratio of product per worker in the A and non-A sectors. Those for Ghana are taken largely from R. Szereszewski, *Structural Changes in the Economy of Ghana, 1891–1911* (London, 1965). For details see Simon Kuznets, *Economic Growth of Nations: Total Output and Production Structure*, Chapter I, Table 3 (Harvard University Press, in press).

B 2

even in the post-World War II period, when there was a marked acceleration in the growth of per capita product of the L.D.C.s – with some growth
rates more than 2 per cent per year, i.e. higher than the 1·6 per cent for the
developed countries over the past century – the gap continued to spread.
The reason for this is that the growth rate of per capita product for the
developed countries, more than 3 per cent per year in this period, rose
even more. It should be noted that the rate of growth of *total* product was
higher for the L.D.C.s than for the developed countries – at least for the
longer periods of 15 and 10 years (Table 1.5, lines 1 and 2, col. 5 and 6); it
is the higher growth rate of population in the L.D.C.s that yields a lower
rate of growth of per capita product – although no necessary causal association is involved.

The gap in per capita product between the developed countries and the
L.D.C.s appears to have widened also in the Communist bloc, at least as
suggested by the comparison between the U.S.S.R. and China over the
period since the early 1950s. According to rough estimates by western
scholars, net domestic product per capita for Mainland China rose only 20
per cent between 1952 and 1965 or 1·4 per cent per year (although it rose
32 per cent from 1952 to 1958); by contrast, in the U.S.S.R. per capita
product rose 5·2 per cent per year from 1950 to 1958 and 3·5 per cent from
1958 to 1964.[1]

The continuous widening of the gap between the developed and the
'poor', less developed countries may seem puzzling, given some obvious
economic implications of a wide gap, of a great lag. A wide gap implies a
large potential of material technology, and of social and institutional
inventions, as yet unexploited by the L.D.C.s, and correspondingly the
possibility of a much higher growth rate for the L.D.C.s, once whatever
barriers prevented it in the past are removed. But growth potentials at
different levels of material technology (and associated social and institutional structures) may differ, and those at higher levels of technology
are not necessarily more limited than at the lower levels – assuming that
additions at the former may be of limited relevance to additions at the
latter. To use the recent decades as an illustration: the emergence of atomic
energy, electronic industries, space exploration and some new chemicals,
may mean little to the proximate growth potentials of the 'poor' L.D.C.s;
and the growth rates that these new industries generate in the developed
countries need not be lower than the potential growth rates of the 'poor'
L.D.C.s, even with relatively successful exploitation of the modern technology relevant to their condition and needs. Similar reasoning applies to

[1] The estimates for China are from Nai-Ruenn Chen and Walter Galenson, *The
Chinese Economy under Communism* (Chicago, 1969), Table VII–2, p. 169. Those for the
U.S.S.R. are from the 89th Congress, 2nd Session, Joint Economic Committee Print,
New Directions in the Soviet Economy, Part II–A (Washington, 1966), Table 2, p. 105
(in a paper by Stanley H. Cohn).

possible differences in growth potentials between the 'advanced' levels of material technology and those relevant to the L.D.C.s, as they might have been in the 19th and earlier 20 century.[1]

Three further comments on the post-World War II widening of the gap are relevant. First, the greater growth of population in the 'poor' L.D.C.s than in the developed countries is largely the result of a recent sharp decline in the death rates, accompanied by continued high birth rates. This more rapid population growth than in developed regions is a recent phenomenon, which has emerged only since the early 1940s. Before then and back to the late 18th century, population in developed countries had grown more rapidly than in the less developed (both groups taken as a whole).

Second, the trends in per capita product in Table 1.5 for developed and less developed countries, taken as groups, are affected by shifts of population weights, as well as by the difference in absolute per capita product, both *within* the groups. Thus, the percentage growth rate for per capita product of the United States has a large weight within the developed group because the U.S. per capita is so high; and a shift in population in favour of the United States will raise per capita product for the developed group as a whole, even if per capita product for each subregion taken separately remains constant. Likewise Latin America, with the highest per capita product among the L.D.C.s, will have a similar effect on the per capita product for the group as a whole. There is much to be said for weighting per capita growth rates for each subregion by a constant share of population – so that a 20 per cent rise in per capita product will be weighted the same for members of different nations or subregions. (Indeed one might argue that these percentage rises, or declines, should be weighted more heavily, the lower the per capita product.) Lines 18–20 of Table 1.5 show that if we use fixed population weights, the growth rate of per capita product for the developed group as a whole is greater than shown in the calculation based directly on the comprehensive indices (3·57 instead of 3·03 per cent for the longest period of coverage, line 18, col. 1 and 2); whereas the same adjustment reduces the growth rate for the L.D.C.s (1·94 instead of 2·13 per cent). The per capita product growth rate of the L.D.C.s in this population-weighted calculation is still lower than that for the developed countries, even if we exclude Japan from the latter (it is then 1·94 compared with 2·86 per cent).

Finally, the details in Table 1.6 on the sectoral shares reveal that the larger weight of the A, and smaller weights of the I and S sectors in the L.D.C.s, combined with the generally higher growth rates of the I sector

[1] For a discussion of this point in application to the case of Japan see Simon Kuznets, 'Notes on Japan's Economic Growth', in Lawrence Klein and Kazushi Ohkawa, eds., *Economic Growth: The Japanese Experience since the Meiji Era*, Richard R. Irwin for the Economic Growth Center of Yale University (Homewood, 1968), pp. 388–95.

(as well as of the S), would produce a lower growth rate of *total* per capita product in the L.D.C.s – even if the rate of growth of per capita output of each sector taken separately were the *same* in the two groups of countries. If technological or other constraints restrict the growth rates of the A sector to lower levels than those of the I sector (the S sector may be left out because fully adequate bases for measurement of its 'real' output are still to be established), the L.D.C.s, in order to match or exceed the growth rates of per capita product of the developed countries, would have to attain much higher rates of growth in either the A or the I sector, and most likely in both. With substantial growth rate of product per capita in the developed countries, achievement of such high rates in both the A and the I sectors of the L.D.C.s, particularly in the former, is a difficult task.[1]

(2) *Trends in Structural Gap*

The long-term widening of the gap in per capita product was obviously accompanied by a widening of the gap in some aspects of economic structure. Thus if the rise in per capita product in the course of modern economic growth was associated with a marked decline in the share of the A sector in product and in labour force, the slower rise of per capita product in the L.D.C.s than in the developed countries was likely to be accompanied by a lesser decline in the share of the A sector in labour force and in product, widening the gap in the production structure (between the A and non-A sectors). This trend can be readily documented in terms of shares in labour force. The share of the A sector in the total labour force in the non-Communist developed countries (Europe, North America, Australia and New Zealand, Japan and Union of South Africa) declined from 56 per cent in 1880 to 48 in 1900 and to 23 in 1960; whereas the share in the non-Communist L.D.C.s (all other countries) was 78 per cent in 1900, 77 in 1930 and 71 in 1960.[2] In 1880 the spread between 56

---

[1] The effects of this difference in weights of the A and I sectors can be shown in a simple calculation based on Table 1.6. The relative gap between the developed countries and the Asian subregion in per capita product of the A sector barely changed between 1950–52 and 1965–67 (from 2.36 to 2.49, line 10); that for per capita product of the I sector dropped appreciably (from 34.3 to 29.7, line 21). But if we combine the A and I sectors, the relative gap in the combined per capita product rises from 11.1 to 13.4, by about a fifth. Likewise, the gap in per capita product of the A sector between the developed countries and Latin America remained unchanged (1.45 and 1.44, line 11); and that in per capita product of the I sector barely changed (5.6 and 5.8, line 22). But when the two are combined, the gap rises from 3.9 to 4.3, about a tenth.

Moreover these effects of the small weights of the I and the large weights of the A sector would be accentuated if we were to allow for the higher prices of I sector products relative to A sector products in the L.D.C.s (i.e. apply the world market price structure, or that characterising more developed countries).

[2] See P. Bairoch and J. M. Limbor, 'Changes in the Industrial Distribution of the World Labour Force by Region, 1880–1960', *International Labour Review*, vol. 98, no. 4 (October 1968), Table IV, pp. 320–21 and Table V, p. 324.

per cent in the A sector in the developed countries and probably about 80 per cent in the L.D.C.s was 24 percentage points; in 1960, the two percentages were 23 and 71, a spread of 48 percentage points. And presumably the disparity in the share of the A sector in total product also widened (for the movement of this share in developed countries see *MEG*, Table 3.1, pp. 88–93). The decline in the share of the A sector in labour force must have been accompanied by a drop in the share of rural and small town population, a rise in urbanisation and increasing divergence in this respect also between developed countries and L.D.C.s. Evidence on this point is available, limited however to the period 1920–60. In 1920, 70·7 per cent of the population of the developed regions (all of Europe, North America, the U.S.S.R., Japan, and Australia and New Zealand) were in rural areas and small towns (less than 20,000); and 13·7 per cent were in large cities (over 500,000); while in the same year 93·9 per cent of the population in the L.D.C.s (rest of the world) were in rural-small town areas and 1·4 per cent in large cities. The spread in percentage points was 23·2 for shares of rural-small town areas and 12·3 for shares of large cities. By 1960, the share of rural-small town population dropped to 54·2 per cent for developed regions, but was still 84·0 per cent for the L.D.C.s, and the spread widened to 29·8 percentage points; while the share of large cities population rose to 22·3 per cent in developed countries but to only 6·9 per cent in the L.D.C.s, and the spread widened to 15·4 percentage points.[1]

There should have been, at least among the non-Communist countries, a widening disparity in other aspects of the production structure, e.g. in the distribution of factors and output among various types of organisation, and of productive establishment (by status of workers, scale of enterprise, type of ownership, etc.). The growth of per capita product in the developed countries must have been accompanied by changes in the character of organisation of the economic unit and the scale of the production unit, which accentuated the existing differences in this respect from the less developed regions of the world.

Although the statistical measures indicate widening divergence in such structural aspects as shares of non-A sectors, of urban population, of large scale economic units, etc., important elements of convergence do exist. The rises, limited as they are, in the shares of the I sector within the L.D.C.s may be associated with the emergence of modern technology, of the modern infrastructure and of some modern industry; and this emergence, although it brings only a modicum of modern technology and economy within the boundaries of a less developed country, represents a significant movement *toward* developed status – even if the share in the

[1] See United Nations, *Growth of the World's Urban and Rural Population, 1920–2000* (New York, 1969), Tables 47, 48 and 51, pp. 115–16 and 119. Temperate South America was shifted to the less developed regions.

developed countries of such modern elements has measurably increased more, absolutely or proportionately to aggregate product. And the A sector, the rural population, and the small scale economic units may be affected by these nuclei of modern economy and technology in ways that are not reflected in the types of shares cited above.

Yet in some aspects of economic and social structure this penetration of elements of modern economic growth brings about a *measurable* convergence between the L.D.C.s and developed countries, even though the disparity in per capita product widens. Thus the increasing involvement of less developed regions in the network of international trade must have raised their foreign trade proportions and brought them closer in this respect to the developed countries which had had, in earlier times, higher foreign trade proportions – a point to which we will return in the next section – and in some, in many ways more important, non-economic aspects of social structure convergence also took place. Thus as already observed in the discussion of Tables 1.5 and 1.6 in connection with the post-World War II growth of developed and less developed regions, the death rates in many of the latter regions declined markedly, and more than in the developed countries. Comparison of death rates, and perhaps even morbidity rates, between the 1920s and the 1960s – a period over which the gap in per capita product must have widened – would show marked convergence (except for some L.D.C.s in Africa). Literacy, with its rapid rise in the less developed countries, and its approach to practically the 100 per cent ceiling in developed countries, would also show convergence; and so would proportions of population receiving primary education.

Finally, there is much evidence of convergence in political and ideological aspects, uncertain as an economist's judgement of such aspects must be. We can particularly interpret the shift from colonial status to political independence and national sovereignty, which began after World War I and spread rapidly and widely after World War II, as an instance of convergence between the L.D.C.s and the developed countries with respect to the formal character of political structure. Before World War II and even more before World War I most of the low income, less developed countries, were colonial in status; and although some developed units (such as Canada, Australia and New Zealand) were also colonies, the character of their relationship to the mother country was quite different. The shift to national sovereignty that occurred is clearly a major case of convergence in political form that accompanied divergence in economic performance and some aspects of economic structure.

Analogous to the shift in political form was the movement toward what might be called modern ideology. The often-referred-to 'revolution of rising expectations' that is assumed to characterise the less developed regions of the world, means that their populations (or groups within them) have begun to emphasise material (economic) achievement, and are accepting the belief in the capacity of modern technology and society to reach high levels of material output per capita, and expect that these material attainments can and should be secured. All these are typical views on the modern economy and society that have evolved in the developed countries (largely from experience with the impressive achievements of modern technology), and are quite different from the views held by pre-modern societies and by traditional societies even in recent times. This represents a significant convergence which, in combination with the widening gap in economic per capita performance, may have some explosive possibilities. But I know of no measures of such expectations among the populations of the less developed countries, or of the dissatisfaction produced by the widening gap, when combined with a significant rise in the absolute per capita product and consumption.

(3) *Trends in Interdependence and Divisiveness*

The rapid advance in technology, characteristic of modern economic growth, both facilitated and induced larger flows among nations and also across the gap between the developed and the less developed countries. And these larger flows made for greater mutual dependence of nations than in earlier times, when groups of nations could live isolated from each other. The continuing technological revolution in transport and communication, from the application of steam to land and water transport, to the internal combustion engine on land and in the air, to the recent emergence of jet and rocket propulsion in space; the spread of electric and short wave power in communication – let alone a host of subsidiary inventions in preservation and storage and reproduction – had an obvious and profound effect on the ease with which goods, people and ideas could be moved across long distances and among widely separated nations. Growing materials-technology and the readiness of population in developed countries to accept new goods made for a continuing economic (in addition to political) stimulus for the developed countries to reach out to the less developed – in the search of the resources that the new technology made accessible and valuable (e.g. petroleum and uranium ores, previously of little value) and for which potential markets within the developed countries could be large. This dependence of developed countries on the resources of the less developed, although mitigated by the capacity of modern technology to produce substitutes, obviously has grown in comparison with the state of relative isolation a century to a century and a quarter ago. Concomitantly, although the less developed countries were often unwilling parties to the establishment of trade and political ties that sometimes limited their freedom of decision, the growing exploitation of their natural resources and their closer acquaintance with modern goods, technology and society, in turn increased the dependence of these L.D.C.s on the rest of the world, largely the developed countries.

Such growing interdependence was reflected not only in economic and material flows but also in the spread of consumer tastes and social inventions and philosophy. For foreign trade in commodities this process can, however, be readily measured, with the help of long-term estimates of the total volume of foreign commodity trade since the early 19th century, and subdivided between the developed and less developed for more recent periods. Between 1820 and 1850 volume of world foreign trade per capita grew over 42 per cent per decade; between 1850 and 1880, 38 per cent; between 1870 and 1900 about 30 per cent; between 1881 and 1913, 34 per cent.[1] Since the growth of per capita product in the developed countries was less than 20 per cent per decade, and for the world as a whole, including the less developed countries, must have been much lower, the proportion of foreign trade to total output rose markedly between the early 19th century and 1913, demonstrating greater involvement and interdependence among nations. The proportion of world commodity trade to output (i.e. of combined exports and imports to world product) must have risen from a few percentage points in 1800 to about a third in 1913 (see Paper X, p. 7).

Even in the period from 1913 to 1963, which was affected by two world wars and a major world depression, the volume of world trade per capita grew 14·4 per cent per decade (Paper X, Table 1), and this rate would probably be raised one or two percentage points if we were to add the four years to 1967. Even at this much reduced level, the growth rate of world trade per capita was probably not far short, if at all, of the growth rate of world output per capita – which means that although the trade proportion for the world did not rise, by the late 1960s for the world as a whole (if not for some distinct regions) it was not significantly below the peak before World War I.

The *shares* of the less developed part of the world (all except Western Europe and North America from 1800 to the 1870s, excluding also Oceania, South Africa and Japan for later years, and excluding the Communist countries after 1913) in this rapidly growing volume of world foreign trade remained constant in the 19th century – at either 20 or 30 per cent, depending upon the estimate – and tended to rise slowly from the beginning of the 20th century to just before World War II (Paper X, Table 2, pp. 11–12). This meant that the volume of foreign trade of the less developed part of the world grew at equally high or higher rates than that of the developed countries, through most of the long period back to the early 19th century if not in the recent decade. Indeed direct calculations for 1876–80 to 1913, and even for 1913 to 1963, show decadal rates of

[1] See Simon Kuznets, 'Quantitative Aspects of the Economic Growth of Nations: X. Level and Structure of Foreign Trade: Long-Term Trends', *Economic Development and Cultural Change*, vol. 15, no. 2, Part II (January 1967), Table 1, p. 4; referred to in the text as Paper X.

growth in the per capita volume of foreign trade of 28·6 and 11·0 per cent respectively for the L.D.C.s, and 25·6 and 10·4 per cent respectively for the developed countries (Paper X, Table 3, p. 16, based on a somewhat different set from that cited above). The foreign trade *proportions* therefore rose much more in the L.D.C.s than in the developed countries – which was only natural for those less developed countries that entered the network of foreign trade for the first time during this long period: but since it was widespread, it is a good index of increasing engagement. Moreover, if in the earlier periods foreign trade proportions were lower in the less developed regions than in the developed countries, these trade proportions in the L.D.C.s moved closer to those in the developed regions – convergence in another aspect of economic structure despite widening per capita product differentials (as already noted in the preceding section). However, in the post-World War II decade the foreign trade proportion for the L.D.C.s rose less than that for the developed countries, and for Latin America it even declined over a longer period.[1]

Two final brief comments on this trend toward increasing interdependence may be added. First, technological and related breakthroughs

[1] Paper X, Table 3, p. 16, shows that between 1913 and 1963 per capita volume of foreign trade for all non-Communist L.D.C.s grew 11·0 per cent per decade, but that for Latin America *declined*, whereas that for Asia and Africa (excluding Japan and the Union of South Africa) grew 14·8 per cent per decade. For the post-World War II decade from 1955–57 to 1965–67, we derived the growth rates for the country groupings in Table 1.5 from quantum indices of exports and imports given in United Nations, *Yearbook of International Trade Statistics 1967* (New York, 1969), Table C, pp. 32–33, and extrapolated back to 1965 the indexes in the *Yearbook of International Trade Statistics 1959* (New York, 1960), Table C, pp. 28–29. Classes I and II in the 1967 *Yearbook* and developed and less developed categories in the 1959 *Yearbook* were taken to represent developed and less developed regions (non-Communist). The regional groupings in the two *Yearbooks* are similar.

GROWTH RATES PER YEAR, G.D.P. AND FOREIGN TRADE
FOR 1955–57 TO 1965–67, NON-COMMUNIST COUNTRIES

	G.D.P. (from Table 5)	Exports	Imports
	(1)	(2)	(3)
1. Developed countries	4·44	6·80	7·79
2. L.D.C.s	4·65	5·12	4·18
3. Asia (E. and S.E.)	4·26	4·01	5·03
4. Latin America	4·90	3·53	2·21

The marked decline in the foreign trade proportion for Latin America, particularly in the import proportion, is clear; yet for Asia, the proportion of exports declines slightly but the import proportion rises, and the trade proportions for the developed countries rise noticeably. However, such movements over the post-World War II decade should be interpreted in the perspective of much longer trends, back to the 1920s, to 1913, or even further. In this longer perspective, the foreign trade proportion rose more in the L.D.C.s than in the developed countries, before 1913; and for Asia-Africa, but not Latin America, even for the long stretch from 1913 to date.

in transport, communication and the stock of general knowledge have enormously facilitated and affected not only the peaceful types of flows, but also the exercise of political pressure or military power – particularly of the developed countries *vis-à-vis* each other or in relation to the less developed regions. The consequences, combined with increasing divisiveness, are obvious and need not be discussed here; but clearly the enormous economic magnitudes involved in major wars and explicable largely in terms of the complex technology of producing, transporting and delivering weapons, played a major role in the disruption and retardation of the growth of the international trade network. Second, and much less obvious, are the possible worldwide effects of increasing power of modern technology, even when exercised within the boundaries of the developed countries proper. The pollution of air streams by jets and atomic weapon tests and the heat pollution of the atmosphere by power plants, while largely originating in the developed regions, spread across the globe and affect even distant less developed regions. These unforeseen, and certainly unintended, effects of the application of modern technology, combined with the rapid consumption, chiefly by developed regions, of the apparently non-reproducible and non-replaceable natural resources of the world, suggest a dependence of the rest of the world on the technology of the developed regions – not only on its bounty, but also on its adverse effects on ecology of the world, which means a dependence also on its capacity to provide substitutes and to offset such adverse effects.

These trends towards increasing interdependence assume particular weight when viewed together with the trends toward increasing divisiveness, which have emerged, if not concurrently, since World War I. This divisiveness, particularly with respect to political structure and ideological positions, is a difficult subject for an economist. Yet it is too important to be passed by without comment. Let me then conclude with a few brief remarks, which are offered as notes on trends that seem of direct bearing upon the economic gap between rich and poor nations, although no claim is made that these trends have been closely scrutinised.

First, although the rapid dissolution of colonial empires and attainment of national sovereignty by the former colonies promise many potential benefits, they also mean a multiplication of foci of decision, a large addition to the number of nations (many small), and thus, at least in the short run, a great increase in points of friction and division. Our earlier comment on the many small countries in the world, and particularly in the less developed regions, illustrated in Table 1.3, should be repeated here. The colonial liberation movement has added, since World War II alone, at least 26 new nations in Subsaharan Africa (not counting Southern Rhodesia); at least 5 in North Africa and the Middle East; 11 in Asia – counting only countries with over a million population, and outside the Communist bloc (see the source used for Table 1). Thus over 40 of some

120 units counted in Table 1.3 have attained political sovereignty at most only two decades ago. The number, particularly in the Middle East, would be even larger if we extended the period to the World War I decade.

To be sure, we cannot say that the conflicts among, or within, these new nations (e.g. between India and Pakistan; or North and South Vietnam; or the internal revolts in the Sudan, the Congo and Nigeria) are a more divisive element than the tensions, incidents and squabbles in the past among colonial powers in their struggles for protection or extension of their spheres of interest. But regardless of how one compares the two situations, the significance of the gap between poor and rich nations must be considered in the light of the recent large increase in the number of these poor nations of most diverse historical origin; the continuing struggles to establish a viable political framework within many of them, as well as the unresolved conflicts that emerged when many of these new nations attained independence; and the prospect that many will continue to be relatively small and a few extremely large, with all the problems of independent economic growth that such size characteristics suggest.

Second, the number of *large developed* countries implies increased divisiveness so long as the organisation of national states persists and newly developed large national states claim their 'rightful' share in the world. Pax Britannica lasted well as long as Great Britain was the only truly developed large country, but it eroded rapidly in the last quarter of the 19th century, by which time Germany, France and the United States joined the ranks of large, developed nations. If one may speak of a trend when so few units are involved, there has been an increase in divisiveness associated with the rise in the number of large economically developed societies organised politically into sovereign nations with competing claims as to their position in an already divided world. That a large country can, in a short time and without substantial industrialisation, move toward greater economic (and hence political) power, and thus have unsettling and divisive effects, is illustrated by the recent history of the relations between Mainland China and the rest of the world.

Third, the emergence after World War I of the U.S.S.R. and its rapid attainment of substantial industrialisation, if not of complete economic and social development, meant, as already indicated, the beginning of a major fissure in the world. For a century and a quarter before 1917, although modern economic growth, as it was spreading, was accompanied by tensions and wars among economically advanced nations or between them and some less developed units, no ideological cleavage emerged in the major organisational form of society in which economic development was taking place. Even the Marxian doctrine adhered to by some social groups within developed countries envisioned socialism as a final phase of development after the breakdown of capitalism, but did not consider the possibility of by-passing the long evolution of capitalist, free market, democratic society. Against this background, the U.S.S.R., a large nation that, having industrialised, operated under an ideology hostile to that of all other developed countries and thus served as an exponent of an alternative road from pre-modern to modern economic organisation, was something new, and inevitably increased the divisiveness in the world. The significance of its effect on less developed countries through competing claims and policies needs no expounding. We do not intend here to pass judgement on the validity of ideological claims, or to indicate whether such divisiveness, particularly among the developed countries, is beneficial for the economic growth of less developed regions. The reference is simply to obvious facts of political and ideological life on the international canvas of the world, which must be considered in analysing various aspects of the economic gap.

STATISTICAL APPENDIX

List of Tables

TABLE 1.1

DISTRIBUTION OF WORLD POPULATION BY PER CAPITA
GROSS DOMESTIC PRODUCT (AT MARKET PRICES) AND BY
MAJOR REGIONS, 1965

(Population in millions; per capita G.D.P. in U.S. dollars)

	World	Sub-saharan Africa	Asia	Middle East	Latin America	Europe	Oceania	North America
	(1)	(2)	(3)	(4)	(5)	(6)	(7)	(8)
1. Total population	3,271	223	1,789	110	243	675	17·4	214
Developed Countries								
2. Population	861 (262)	0	98·0	2·6	0	532 (262)	14·0	214
3. Per capita G.D.P.	1,892 (1,166)	0	870	1,407	0	1,455 (1,166)	2,033	3,441
4. Percentage of population of region	26·3 (8·0)	0	5·5	2·4	0	78·9 (38·8)	80·3	100
Less Developed Countries (grouped by per capita G.D.P.)								
$80 or less								
5. Population	267 (19·0)	80·1	178 (19·0)	7·2	0	0	2·2	0
6. Per capita G.D.P.	65·6 (70)	58·4	69·5 (70)	54·0	0	0	50·0	0
7. Percentage of population of region	8·2 (0·6)	35·9	9·9 (1·1)	6·6	0	0	12·3	0

TABLE 1.1 (*continued*)

	World	Sub-saharan Africa	Asia	Middle East	Latin America	Europe	Oceania	North America
	(1)	(2)	(3)	(4)	(5)	(6)	(7)	(8)

$81–$120

	World	Sub-saharan Africa	Asia	Middle East	Latin America	Europe	Oceania	North America
8. Population	1,459 (713)	93·5	1,347 (713)	13·5	4·7	0	0	0
9. Per capita G.D.P.	100 (100)	92·3	101 (100)	103	85·1	0	0	0
10. Percentage of population of region	44·6 (21·8)	41·9	75·3 (39·9)	12·3	1·9	0	0	0

'*Poor*' *L.D.C., narrow definition* (*per capita G.D.P.* $120 *or less*)

	World	Sub-saharan Africa	Asia	Middle East	Latin America	Europe	Oceania	North America
11. Population	1,726 (732)	174	1,525 (732)	20·8	4·7	0	2·2	0
12. Per capita G.D.P.	95 (99)	77	97 (99)	86	85	0	50	0
13. Percentage of population of region	52·8 (22·4)	77·8	85·2 (41·0)	18·9	1·9	0	12·3	0

$121–$180

	World	Sub-saharan Africa	Asia	Middle East	Latin America	Europe	Oceania	North America
14. Population	121	5·4	82·2	29·6	3·8	0	0	0
15. Per capita G.D.P.	147	147	142	159	166	0	0	0
16. Percentage of population of region	3·7	2·4	4·6	26·9	1·6	0	0	0

$181–$300

	World	Sub-saharan Africa	Asia	Middle East	Latin America	Europe	Oceania	North America
17. Population	241 (1·9)	25·3	67·4	52·4	93·6	(1·9)	0·8	0
18. Per capita G.D.P.	259 (185)	258	266	237	268	(185)	300	0
19. Percentage of population of region	7·4 (0·1)	11·3	3·8	47·7	38·5	(0·3)	4·8	0

'*Poor*' *L.D.C., wide definition* (*per capita G.D.P. of* $300 *or less*)

	World	Sub-saharan Africa	Asia	Middle East	Latin America	Europe	Oceania	North America
20. Population	2,089 (734)	204	1,675 (732)	103	102	(1·9)	3·0	0
21. Per capita G.D.P.	117 (99)	101	106 (99)	184	255	(185)	50	0
22. Percentage of population of region	63·9 (22·4)	91·5	93·7 (41·0)	93·5	42·0	(0·3)	17·1	0

$301–$450

	World	Sub-saharan Africa	Asia	Middle East	Latin America	Europe	Oceania	North America
23. Population	88·5 (19·5)	0·5	13·2	2·4	42·9	29·1 (19·5)	0·5	0
24. Per capita G.D.P.	349 (371)	448	324	323	334	380 (370)	435	0
25. Percentage of population of region	2·7 (0·6)	0·2	0·7	2·2	17·6	4·3 (2·9)	2·6	0

Table 1.1 (continued)

	World	Regions						
		Sub-saharan Africa	Asia	Middle East	Latin America	Europe	Oceania	North America
	(1)	(2)	(3)	(4)	(5)	(6)	(7)	(8)
$451 or more								
26. Population	233 (76·4)	18·4	2·6	2·1	98·1 (7·6)	112 (68·8)	0	0
27. Per capita G.D.P.	675 (735)	589	542	1,619	608 (530)	734 (757)	0	0
28. Percentage of population of region	7·1 (2·3)	8·3	0·1	1·9	40·4 (3·1)	16·5 (10·2)	0	0
All Less Developed Countries								
29. Population	2,410 (830)	223	1,691 (732)	107	243 (7·6)	143 (90·2)	3·4	0
30. Per capita G.D.P.	179 (164)	142	108 (99)	216	411 (530)	655 (662)	162	0
31. Percentage of population of region	73·7 (25·3)	100	94·5 (41·0)	97·6	100 (3·1)	21·1 (13·4)	19·7	0

Notes: Entries in parentheses refer to Communist countries (included in relevant totals). We classified Yugoslavia and Cuba with the usual list of Communist countries in Asia and Eastern Europe.

The underlying estimates are from Everett E. Hagen and Oli Hawrylyshyn, 'Analysis of World Income and Growth, 1955–1965', *Economic Development and Cultural Change*, vol. 18, no. 1, Part II (October 1969). These are based largely on United Nations estimates, supplemented by auxiliary sources (particularly for the Communist countries), and use conventional conversion rates to U.S. dollars in 1965. The estimates for the individual countries are given in Tables 3B, pp. 16–19; 4B, pp. 23–25; 5B, pp. 31–33; 6B, pp. 36–37; 7B, p. 39; and 8B, p. 41. The estimates for Communist countries have been adjusted to conform to the international G.D.P. concept.

The regions distinguished here conform to the continental divisions, with the following exceptions. Subsaharan Africa includes all of Africa except Sudan, Egypt, Libya, Tunisia, Algeria and Morocco. The latter, together with Aden, Gaza Strip, Muscat and Oman, Yemen, Bahrain, Jordan, Syria, Lebanon, Iraq, Saudi Arabia, Kuwait, Qatar and Israel constitute the Middle East. Europe includes Asiatic U.S.S.R., but excludes Turkey, which is covered under Asia. Latin America is the Western Hemisphere, except Canada and the United States (the latter two constituting North America), and therefore includes minor population groups (e.g. in Greenland) not usually included under Latin America.

The developed countries include most countries with per capita gross domestic product of $1,000 or more and Japan, for which per capita G.D.P. was given as $870. However, we excluded those countries with per capita G.D.P. above $1,000 in which this high level is due to some exceptional natural resource endowment or some advantageous strategic location. These countries – the Netherlands, Antilles, Puerto Rico, Kuwait and Qatar – were placed among the less developed. The developed countries include most of Europe (except some in Eastern and Southern Europe and Ireland); Australia and New Zealand; North America; Japan; and Israel (whose per capita product is set at over $1,400, and would be well over $1,000 even allowing for unrequited imports). The definition differs from that used by the United Nations in excluding South Africa, where the high income of the white population is offset by the low income of the much larger non-white (the per capita G.D.P. is set at less than $600); and in excluding parts of Europe (Greece, Portugal, Spain, Ireland).

TABLE 1.2

STRUCTURAL ASPECTS ASSOCIATED WITH PER CAPITA INCOME OR PRODUCT, LATE 1950s AND EARLY 1960s

A. *Large Sample of Non-Communist Countries, Late 1950s*
(Classes by Per Capita National Income, 1956–58)

N.I. 1956–58 / G.D.P. 1965	Developed			Less Developed		
	$575–1,000 (811–1,410)	$1,000 and over (1,410 and over)	Total	Under $100 (under 133)	$100–200 (133–266)	Total
	(1)	(2)	(3)	(4)	(5)	(6)
1. Average per capita income (1956–58 $)	760	1,366	1,063	72	161	102
2. Equivalent, G.D.P. in 1965 $	1,072	1,926	1,500	96	214	135
3. Per capita energy consumption, kilos of coal equivalent, 1956–58	2,710	3,900	3,305	114	265	164
4. Percentage of population literate, 15 years of age and over (about 1950)	94	98	96	29	51	36
5. School enrolment (ex. pre-primary and higher education) as % of four-fifths of 5–19 age group (one year, 1956–58)	84	91	87	37	48	41
6. Percentage of male labour force in agriculture (about 1956)	21	17	19	74	64	71
7. Percentage of national income originating in agriculture (latest year)	10·9	11·4	11·15	40·8	33·4	38·3
8. Relative product per worker, agriculture (line 7: line 6)	0·52	0·67	0·59	0·55	0·52	0·54
9. Relative product per worker in non-agriculture (100 minus line 7): (100 minus line 6)	1·13	1·07	1·10	2·28	1·85	2·13
10. Intersectoral ratio, line 9: line 8	2·17	1·60	1·86	4·15	3·56	3·94
11. Level of urbanisation (% of population in metrop. communities of over 100,000), 1955	39	43	41	9	14	11
12. Expectation of life (yrs) at birth, 1955–58	67·7	70·6	69·1	41·7	50·0	44·5
13. Infant mortality (per 1,000), 1955–58	41·9	24·9	33·4	180	131	164
14. Per capita calorie consumption, latest year	2,944	3,153	3,048	2,070	2,240	2,127
15. Starchy staples as % of calories consumed, latest year	53	45	49	77	70	75

(Vital Crude Rates per 1,000)

	1960–64			Percentage Shares in Labour Force			Percentage Shares in Population		
	Birth Rates	Death Rates	R.N.I.	A	I–	S+	Rural & small towns	20,000–500,000	over 500,000
	(1)	(2)	(3)	(4)	(5)	(6)	(7)	(8)	(9)
Developed Regions									
16. Europe (Western and Northern, plus Italy)	18·2	10·8	7·4	15·4	44·1	40·5	48·2	27·7	24·1
17. North America	23	9	14	8	39	53	42·0	21·5	36·5
18. Australia and New Zealand	23	9	14	12	40	48	35·4	23·7	40·9
19. Japan	17	7	10	33	28	39	54·0	19·7	26·3
20. All non-Communist (lines 16–19)	19·8	9·5	10·3	16·2	39·4	44·4	46·7	24·1	29·2
21. U.S.S.R.	23	7	16	45	28	27	63·6	23·9	12·5
22. All developed (lines 20 and 21)	20·7	8·8	11·9	25·3	35·8	38·9	51·3	24·1	24·6
'Poor' L.D.C.s, Narrow Definition									
23. Subsaharan Africa ex. South Africa	48·5	25·1	23·4	81·6	7·3	11·1	92·7	6·7	0·6
24. Mainland China	35	21	14	75	10	15	86·2	6·5	7·3
25. Middle, South and South-East Asia	41·5	20·2	21·3	72·1	12·4	15·5	87·0	8·1	4·9
26. Total, non-Communist incl. Melanesia	42·9	21·1	21·8	74·1	11·3	14·6	88·1	7·9	4·0
27. Total, incl. Melanesia	39·8	21·1	18·7	74·5	10·7	14·8	87·3	7·4	5·3
Next Group of L.D.C.s (add for 'Poor', Wide Definition)									
28. North Africa	43	19	24	71	10	19	74·4	14·8	10·8
29. South-West Asia	42	18	24	69	14	17	77·2	17·0	5·8
30. Middle East (28–29)	42·5	18·5	24·0	70·0	11·9	18·1	75·7	15·9	8·4
31. Other East Asia	39	15	24	62	12	26	70·5	17·3	12·2
32. Tropical Latin America	43	15	28	61·7	13·9	24·4	72·7	15·8	11·5
33. Total above (lines 30–32)	42·1	16·5	25·6						
'Poor' L.D.C.s, Wide Definition									
34. Non-Communist	42·7	20·1	22·6	71·8	11·8	16·4	84·7	9·6	5·7
35. All	40·2	20·4	19·8	73·0	11·1	15·9	85·2	8·6	6·2
All Other L.D.C.s									
36. South Africa	42	19	23	37	29	34	67·6	17·6	14·8
37. Latin America (Middle, Temperate, Caribbean)	38·6	13·2	25·4	44·7	23·1	32·2	63·6	17·7	18·7
38. Eastern Europe	18	9	9	45	31	24	68·1	21·3	10·6
39. South Europe (excl. Italy)	22·5	8·3	14·2	50	26	24	66·4	20·8	12·8
40. Total incl. Melanesia (36–39)	28·2	11·0	17·2	45·6	27·4	27·0	66·1	19·7	14·2

TABLE 1.2 (*continued*)

Notes: *Lines 1, 3–7, 11–15, columns 1–2 and 4–5:* Underlying data are from United Nations, *Report on the World Social Situation* (New York, 1961), Chapter III, Table 1, p. 41 (and following discussion and tables).

Line 2: National income in 1956–58 prices was converted to gross domestic product at market prices, in 1965 prices (both in U.S. dollars) in three steps. First, we calculated the ratio, for the late 1950s, of gross domestic product at market prices to national income (the difference being indirect taxes minus subsidies, capital consumption charges and net factor income from abroad). This ratio was calculated separately for the low and high income countries (both limited to those in which the net income from abroad was relatively negligible) on the basis of United Nations, *Yearbook of National Accounts Statistics 1968*, vol. II, *International Tables* (New York, 1969), Table 1. The average ratio of G.D.P. at market prices to N.I. was about 1·165 for the low per capita product countries and 1·24 for the high per capita product countries. Next we calculated the change in the general price level (implicit in gross national product) from 1956–58 to 1965 for the United States, based on the *Economic Report of the President* (Washington, D.C., February 1968), Table B–3, p. 212; was 14·1 per cent. Finally the adjustment factor for the high per capita countries, derived as (1·24 × 1·141), was 1·41; for the low per capita product countries it was (1·165 × 1·141), or 1·33.

Panel A
Columns 3 and 6: For the developed countries, we weighted the entries in columns 1 and 2 equally, judging by the rough population magnitudes in the two income class groups (non-Communist countries). For the 'poor', less developed countries (wide definition) the weights for columns 4 and 5 were 2 and 1 respectively, as suggested by the population for the non-Communist countries in Table 1.1.

Panel B
The regional groupings in the three sources from which the demographic and labour force data were taken are identical. We tried to fit these groups roughly into the categories distinguished in our Table 1.1, shifting Italy out of Southern Europe (with the remainder classified under less developed countries).
The rough consilience is indicated by comparison of the population totals underlying Panel B with those shown in Table 1.1 (for 1965). For the developed countries, the total underlying Panel B is 831 million, compared with 861 in Table 1.1; for the 'poor' L.D.C.s, narrow definition, it is 1,823 million in Panel B compared with 1,726 in Table 1.1; for the 'poor' L.D.C.s, wide definition, it is 2,149 million in Panel B and 2,089 million in Table 1.1; and for 'other' L.D.C.s, it is 305 million in Panel B and 322 in Table 1.1.
Columns 1–3: The vital rates in columns 1 and 2 and underlying population totals are from United Nations, *Demographic Yearbook 1965* (New York, 1967), Table 1, p. 103 (and relevant tables for Italy in the same volume). Rates for larger groups were calculated by weighting the rates for the subcomponents by the arithmetic mean of the population for 1960 and 1965.
Columns 4–6: Underlying data are from Samuel Baum, 'The World's Labour Force and Its Industrial Distribution', *International Labour Review*, vol. 95, nos. 1–2 (January–February 1967), pp. 96–112. I– includes mining, manufacturing, construction, electric power, gas and water. Transport and communications are included with services in S + . Agriculture includes related industries, such as fishing, forestry and hunting. Weighting is by total labour force.
Columns 7–9: Underlying data are from United Nations, Population Studies no. 44, *Growth of the World's Urban and Rural Population, 1920–2000* (New York, 1969), Tables 47, 48, 49 and 51, pp. 115–17 and 119; and for Italy, Tables 41 and 43, pp. 98–100 and 102–3. Weighting is by total population in 1960.

TABLE 1.3

DISTRIBUTION OF COUNTRIES, WITH POPULATION OF
1 MILLION AND OVER, BY SIZE OF POPULATION,
DEVELOPED AND LESS DEVELOPED, NON-COMMUNIST AND
COMMUNIST COUNTRIES, 1965

(Size of Population Groups (in Millions))

	1·0–2·99	3·0–5·99	6·0–9·99	10·0–19·99	20·0–49·99	50·0–99·99	100 and over	Total
	(1)	(2)	(3)	(4)	(5)	(6)	(7)	(8)
Developed Countries								
1. Number	2	4	3	5	1	4	2	21
				(2)			(1)	(3)
2. Population	5·2	19·0	24·5	74·4	48·9	263·2	425	860·0
				(31·2)			(231)	(262·0)
'Poor' L.D.C.s, Narrow Definition								
3. Number	7	12	4	8	4	0	4	39
	(1)			(2)			(1)	(4)
4. Population	12·3	50·1	30·3	112·0	119·7	0	1,395	1,719·0
	(1·1)			(31·0)			(700	(732·0)
'Poor' L.D.C.s, Wide Definition								
5. Number	15	20	8	12	9	1	4	69
	(2)			(2)			(1)	(5)
6. Population	28·1	84·1	59·2	160·8	268	81·3	1,395	2,077·0
	(3·0)			(31·0)			(700	(734·0)
Other L.D.C.s								
7. Number	10	3	7	6	4	0	0	30
				(2)	(3)	(1)		(6)
8. Population	20·2	11·9	60·3	96·0	126·1	0	0	314·0
				(15·8)	(48·7)	(31·4)		(95·9)
All L.D.C.s								
9. Number	25	23	15	18	13	1	4	99
	(2)			(2)	(5)	(1)	(1)	(11)
10. Population	48·3	96·0	119·5	256·8	394	81·3	1,395	2,391·0
	(3·0)			(15·8)	(79·7)	(31·4)	(700	(830·0)
World (excluding countries with population less than 1·0)								
All								
11. Number	27	27	18	23	14	5	6	120
12. Population	53·5	115	144	331	443	345	1,820	3,251
Non-Communist Countries								
13. Number	25	27	16	16	13	5	4	106
14. Population	50·5	115	128	220	412	345	889	2,159
Communist Countries								
15. Number	2	0	2	7	1	0	2	14
16. Population	3·0	0	15·8	111	31·4	0	931	1,092

TABLE 1.3 (*continued*)

Notes: Entries in parentheses in lines 1–10 relate to the number and population of the Communist countries (included in the relevant totals). Cuba was classified among the Communist countries.

For underlying population totals see the Hagen-Hawrylyshyn paper cited in the notes to Table 1.1.

TABLE 1.4

COMMODITY FOREIGN TRADE, 1965, PROPORTION TO GROSS DOMESTIC PRODUCT AND STRUCTURE OF EXPORTS BY ECONOMIC CLASSES OF PROVENANCE AND DESTINATION (G.D.P. AND I.E. IN BILLIONS OF $)

A. *Proportion to G.D.P., Market Prices*

	Total G.D.P. in Group	G.D.P. covered by I.E.	Proportions to G.D.P., %			Proportion to World Trade, %
			I	E	I and E	
	(1)	(2)	(3)	(4)	(5)	(6)
NON-COMMUNIST COUNTRIES						
Developed						
1. Europe (Western, Northern, Italy)	469·5	469·5	17·4	16·0	33·4	41·4
2. North America	737·1	737·1	4·3	4·8	9·1	17·8
3. Japan	85·2	85·2	9·6	9·9	19·5	4·4
4. Total (incl. Australia, New Zealand, Israel)	1,323·9	1,323·9	9·6	9·3	18·9	66·2
'Poor' L.D.C.s, Narrow Definition						
5. Subsaharan Africa	13·3	12·8	22·2	19·7	41·9	1·4
6. Asia (M.S. and S.E.)	75·4	72·7	7·6	4·7	12·3	2·4
7. Total (incl. Melanesia)	91·0	87·6	10·4	7·3	17·7	4·1
'Poor' L.D.C.s, Wide Definition						
8. Subsaharan Africa	20·6	20·1	24·0	23·1	47·1	2·5
9. Asia	105·0	102·3	9·6	7·5	17·1	4·6
10. Middle East	18·9	18·7	21·8	25·5	47·3	2·3
11. Latin America	26·1	26·1	7·0	8·9	15·9	1·1
12. Total (incl. Melanesia)	171·0	167·3	12·4	11·6	24·0	10·6
All L.D.C.s						
13. Subsaharan Africa	31·7	31·1	23·5	20·0	43·5	3·6
14. Asia	110·7	107·9	13·0	10·3	23·3	6·6
15. Middle East	23·1	20·6	23·6	27·4	51·0	2·8
16. Latin America	96·0	92·6	11·3	12·9	24·2	5·9
17. Europe	33·7	33·7	18·4	7·5	25·9	2·3

TABLE 1.4 (*continued*)

	Total G.D.P. in Group (1)	G.D.P. covered by I.E. (2)	Proportions to G.D.P., %			Proportion to World Trade, %
			I (3)	E (4)	I and E (5)	(6)
18. All L.D.C.s (non-Communist), incl. Oceania	295·7	286·3	15·0	13·1	28·1	21·3
COMMUNIST COUNTRIES						
19. Developed (U.S.S.R., Czechoslovakia and East Germany)	305·3	305·3	4·3	4·5	8·8	7·1
20. 'Poor' L.D.C.s (wide definition, Europe and Asia)	73·0	70·1	3·1	2·9	6·0	1·1
21. Other L.D.C.s (Cuba and rest of Eastern Europe)	63·4	63·4	13·0	12·3	25·3	4·2

B. Structure of Exports by Economic Class of Region of Provenance and Destination

Regions of Destination

Regions of Provenance	Economic Class I (1)	Economic Class II (2)	Economic Class III (3)	Total (4)	U.S.S.R. (5)	E. Europe (6)	Asia III (7)
			Values of Exports (Billion $)				
22. Ec. Cl. I	95·74	26·99	4·99	127·72	1·63	2·45	0·91
23. Ec. Cl. II	26·11	7·65	2·39	36·15	1·08	0·80	0·51
24. Ec. Cl. III	4·68	2·94	13·77	21·39	5·10	7·97	0·70
25. Total	126·53	37·58	21·15	185·26	7·81	11·22	2·12
			Shares in Total Exports Sent Out (%)				
26. Ec. Cl. I	75·0	21·1	3·9	100·0	1·28	1·92	0·71
27. Ec. Cl. II	72·2	21·2	6·6	100·0	2·99	2·21	1·41
28. Ec. Cl. III	21·9	13·7	64·4	100·0	23·84	37·26	3·27
			Shares in Total Exports Received (%)				
29. From Class I	75·7	71·8	23·6		20·9	21·8	42·9
30. From Class II	20·6	20·4	11·3		13·8	7·1	24·1
31. From Class III	3·7	7·8	65·1		65·3	71·1	33·0
32. Total	100·0	100·0	100·0		100·0	100·0	100·0

Notes:
Panel A

The underlying data for imports (c.i.f.) and exports (f.o.b.), in U.S. dollars, for individual countries are from United Nations, *Yearbook of International Trade Statistics, 1967* (New York, 1969). Summary Table A, pp. 12–19, and from Table 1.1 of the country tables for Iran, Afghanistan, Iraq and Saudi Arabia. The data for individual countries were combined into the groups set up in Table 1.1.

The gross domestic product estimates are from the source cited for Table 1.1.

Panel B

The underlying data are from the *Yearbook of International Trade Statistics, 1967*, Summary Table B, pp. 20–33. Economic Class I includes the United States, Canada, Western Europe, Australia, New Zealand, South Africa, Japan. However Western Europe, as defined in the source, includes, in addition to the non-Communist developed countries, the less developed (such as Portugal, Spain and Greece), as well as Turkey (classified by us under Asia) and Yugoslavia (classified by us as Communist). Nevertheless the proportional difference between the trade of what we define as non-Communist developed countries and Economic Class I is minor, one or two percentage points at most. Economic Class III covers the Communist countries – U.S.S.R. and other Eastern Europe, and the four in Asia. Economic Class II, the rest of the world, is roughly coterminous with what we define as non-Communist, less developed countries, but it includes Cuba, classified by us as Communist.

TABLE 1.5

GROWTH OF GROSS DOMESTIC PRODUCT, TOTAL AND PER CAPITA, NON-COMMUNIST COUNTRIES, 1950–67

	1950–52	1955–57	1960–62	1965–67	\multicolumn{3}{c}{Growth Per Year (%)}		
					Col. 1–3	2–4	3–4
	(1)	(2)	(3)	(4)	(5)	(6)	(7)
Gross Domestic Product (1963, $ factor costs, in billions)							
1. Developed countries	654	798	959	1,232	3·90	4·44	4·31
2. Less developed countries	116·3	147·2	185·5	231·9	4·78	4·65	4·71
3. East and S.E. Asia (excl. Japan)	53·5	65·5	80·4	99·4	4·16	4·26	4·22
4. Latin America	42·5	54·5	69·4	87·9	5·03	4·90	4·96
Population (in millions)							
5. Developed countries	589	626	669	711	1·28	1·28	1·26
6. Less developed countries	1,082	1,200	1,356	1,542	2·28	2·54	2·39
7. E. and S.E. Asia (excl. Japan)	685	759	853	961	2·22	2·39	2·28
8. Latin America	162	185	211	244	2·68	2·82	2·77
G.D.P. per capita (1963, $ FC)							
9. Developed countries	1,111	1,274	1,433	1,733	2·59	3·12	3·01
10. Les developed countries	107·5	122·6	136·8	150·4	2·44	2·07	2·27
11. Asia	78·1	86·3	94·2	103·4	1·90	1·83	1·89
12. Latin America	262	295	329	361	2·29	2·03	2·13
Relative Gap							
13. Line 9: Line 10	10·3	10·4	10·5	11·5			
14. Line 9: Line 11	14·2	14·8	15·2	16·8			
15. Line 9: Line 12	4·2	4·3	4·4	4·8			

TABLE 1.5 (*continued*)

COMPARISON OF GROWTH RATES OF G.D.P. PER CAPITA, MOVING G.D.P. (G) WEIGHTS AND FIXED POPULATION (P) WEIGHTS

	Developed Countries			Less Developed Countries	
	G	P	P, excl. Japan	G	P
	(1)	(2)	(3)	(4)	(5)
16. 1955–57 to 1965–67	3·13	3·69	2·88	2·03	1·86
17. 1950–52 to 1965–67	3·03	3·57	2·86	2·13	1·94

Notes: Total and per capita gross domestic product are from United Nations, *Yearbook of National Accounts Statistics, 1968*, Vol. II, *International Tables* (New York, 1969), Table 7B, pp. 119–25 (for annual indices from 1950 to 1957); and Table 2B, pp. 54–59, for estimates of 1963 total gross domestic product, at factor costs, in U.S. dollars for the non-Communist countries. Population indices were derived by dividing the indices for total G.D.P. by those for per capita G.D.P. The absolute totals for population in 1963 are from United Nations, *Demographic Yearbook 1967* (New York, 1968), Table 1 and Table 4 for individual countries excluded or shifted for comparability with product.

The entries in columns 1–4 were derived by applying arithmetic means of the indices for the years indicated in the stub to the absolute totals of G.D.P. and population in 1963. The per capita G.D.P. was derived by division.

Developed countries in the source include all of non-Communist Europe (plus Cyprus and Turkey), North America, Oceania, Japan, Israel and South Africa. The less developed countries include East and Southeast Asia (excluding Japan); the Middle East (Southwest Asia excluding Cyprus, Turkey and Israel); Africa (except South Africa); and Latin America (including the Caribbean).

Lines 16–17: When changing per capita G.D.P. is derived by dividing total G.D.P. by total population (as is done in lines 9–12), and a region comprises subregions with different levels of G.D.P. per capita, the per capita average can change because of a shift in weights of population among subgroups with different per capita G.D.P. levels. The per capita levels are thus derived by the use of different and moving G.D.P. and population weights. One can remove the effect of shifts in relative population weights, as well as the effect of a percentage change in the higher per capita G.D.P. levels, by weighting the growth rates in per capita for each subregion separately by fixed population weights. This was done for the population weight calculation, using the 1963 population totals.

Entries in columns 1 and 4, lines 16–17, are comparable with those in lines 9 and 10, col. 5–7, except that here developed countries had to be limited to the sum of E.E.C. and EFTA countries in Europe, North America, Oceania and Japan; and the less developed countries to the sum of E. and S.E. Asia (excluding Japan) and Latin America. For countries included under E.E.C. and EFTA in Europe see the notes to *The Yearbook of National Accounts Statistics*, Table 7B, referred to above.

TABLE 1.6

GROWTH OF GROSS DOMESTIC PRODUCT, BY THREE
MAJOR PRODUCTION SECTORS, NON-COMMUNIST
COUNTRIES, 1950–67

	1950–52	1955–57	1960–62	1965–67	Growth per Year (%) Cols. 1–3	2–4	3–4
	(1)	(2)	(3)	(4)	(5)	(6)	(7)
Agriculture and Related Industries (A Sector)							
G.D.P. Originating (bill. $, 1963 FC)							
1. Developed countries	54·7	59·8	67·3	74·8	2·10	2·26	2·11
2. L.D.C.s	45·5	54·2	63·8	71·8	3·44	2·85	3·09
3. E. and S.E. Asia (excl. Japan)	26·9	31·6	37·0	40·5	3·21	2·51	2·76
4. Latin America	10·4	12·5	14·9	17·8	3·66	3·60	3·65
G.D.P. Originating in A, per capita of total population ($, 1963 FC)							
5. Developed countries	92·8	95·5	100·6	105·2	0·80	0·97	0·83
6. L.D.C.s	42·1	45·2	47·1	46·6	1·13	0·30	0·68
7. E. and S.E. Asia (excl. Japan)	39·3	41·7	43·3	42·2	1·00	0·12	0·47
8. Latin America	64·1	67·6	70·7	73·1	0·96	0·76	0·86
Relative Gap							
9. Line 5: Line 6	2·20	2·11	2·14	2·26			
10. Line 5: Line 7	2·36	2·29	2·32	2·49			
11. Line 5: Line 8	1·45	1·41	1·42	1·44			
Industry Sector (I Sector)							
G.D.P. Originating (bill. $, 1963 FC)							
12. Developed countries	298	373	447	592	4·14	4·73	4·68
13. L.D.C.s	29·9	41·6	57·2	77·4	6·70	6·41	6·55
14. E. and S.E. Asia (excl. Japan)	10·1	14·0	19·1	26·9	6·58	6·75	6·73
15. Latin America	14·5	19·7	26·6	34·7	6·26	5·82	5·99
G.D.P. Originating in I, per capita of total population ($, 1963)							
16. Developed countries	507	596	668	832	2·82	3·40	3·38
17. L.D.C.s	27·7	34·7	42·2	50·2	4·32	3·77	4·06
18. E. and S.E. Asia (excl. Japan)	14·8	18·4	22·4	28·0	4·34	4·33	4·36
19. Latin America	89·7	106·5	126·3	142·4	3·48	2·94	3·13
Relative Gap							
20. Line 16: Line 17	18·3	17·2	15·8	16·6			
21. Line 16: Line 18	34·3	32·3	29·8	29·7			
22. Line 16: Line 19	5·6	5·6	5·3	5·8			

TABLE 1.6 (*continued*)

	1950–52	1955–57	1960–62	1965–67	Growth per Year (%)		
					Cols. 1–3	2–4	3–4
	(1)	(2)	(3)	(4)	(5)	(6)	(7)

Service Sector (S Sector)

G.D.P. Originating (*bill. of $, 1963 FC*)

	(1)	(2)	(3)	(4)	(5)	(6)	(7)
23. Developed countries	302	365	445	566	3·95	4·48	4·28
24. L.D.C.s	40·8	51·4	64·5	82·6	4·69	4·86	4·81
25. E. and S.E. Asia (excl. Japan)	16·5	19·9	24·3	32·0	3·95	4·86	4·51
26. Latin America	17·5	22·3	27·8	35·4	4·74	4·73	4·72

G.D.P. Originating in S, per capita of total population (*$, 1963*)

	(1)	(2)	(3)	(4)	(5)	(6)	(7)
27. Developed countries	512	583	665	796	2·64	3·16	2·98
28. L.D.C.s	37·7	42·8	47·6	53·6	2·35	2·26	2·36
29. E. and S.E. Asia (excl. Japan)	24·1	26·2	28·5	33·3	1·69	2·42	2·18
30. Latin America	108	120	132	145	2·01	1·87	1·90

Relative Gap

	(1)	(2)	(3)	(4)
31. Line 27: Line 28	13·6	13·6	14·0	14·9
32. Line 27: Line 29	21·3	22·3	23·3	23·9
33. Line 27: Line 30	4·7	4·8	5·0	5·5

Notes: The underlying data are from the sources cited in the notes to Table 1.5.

The I sector includes mining, manufacturing, electric power, gas and water, construction, and transport and communications. The S sector includes trade, professional and government services, and all other services. The A sector includes besides agriculture such related industries as fishing, hunting and forestry.

For the methods of calculation see the notes to Table 1.5.

C

Discussion of the Paper by
Simon Kuznets

Professor Tomasini, opening the discussion, commented on the paper by Professor Kuznets. He said that Professor Kuznets had often before provided the economics profession with valuable statistical information and had now given them an immensely valuable analysis of the gap between rich and poor countries. This kind of conference could not be held without his participation, and it was right that he should present the first paper. The problem of investigating the 'gap' was strictly tied to the idea of measurement. We could hardly speak of a gap if we had no index by which to measure it. Did we have such a measure; was it valid; did it reflect the differences we observed between nations, as distinct from the gap which referred in some obscure sense to an economic distance? If it did, must we continue to talk of the gap as a magic word to cover our inability to analyse the problem of differences between countries?

The use of per capita income or G.N.P. as good indicators of economic development had been attacked in the literature for at least twenty years. Economists had contended that the data were poor for many reasons, and that these ways of measuring ignored important aspects of development. While he agreed with much of this criticism, he thought that many of the issues raised missed the essential point. We should concentrate more on understanding differences between countries, and less on identifying the 'gap'.

One should avoid considering as developed those countries which had a high per capita G.N.P. based on the ownership of natural resources which gave rise to rents. One could then emphasise, as some economists had, the role that technology played in the development process in different countries. If technology were to be the main element differentiating countries, he was inclined to accept such a hypothesis in part. It was essential, however, to explain how one could use a measure to rank countries according to level of development.

Technology was hardly quantifiable and, even if it were, one could not speak of an 'optimum' amount of technology outside a given economic setting. In other words, even if it were possible to establish a useful measure of technology, the quantity or quality of 'technology' employed in different countries must still depend on the socio-economic variables which differed between countries. If we could not talk of quantity of technology *per se* without relating it to socio-economic structure, we were in fact suggesting that it was not possible to measure the 'distance' between countries by such an indicator. He thought that the problem extended to all measurements used by economists: the cardinal, lexicographic, etc. He did not exclude the possibility of comparing different countries according to their use of given technologies; comparisons did not require ranking. However this not only left us without a measure of the gap, but also forced us to question the validity of the concept.

A way out could be to rank countries according to rates of per capita growth. Growth rates had no normative content so that we should be restricted to an ordinal ranking. Even this type of ranking was misleading, because in most cases measures of G.N.P. excluded social costs. He would therefore argue that if we persisted in wanting to measure the distance between countries we should at least consider social costs (pollution, discrimination, etc.) as well as the benefits of various growth rates. In addition, of course, per capita growth rates, and also per capita income measures, ignored the distribution of the social product. The actual distribution of the benefits and costs of development was the most important issue in economic change.

Where we were concerned with promoting either higher growth rates or more equal distribution of per capita income between countries, or a more equitable distribution of the benefits and costs of development, we must concentrate our attention on the socio-economic structure. Professor Kuznets showed his concern for this aspect of development but Professor Tomasini regretted that he did not pursue it in more detail.

Professor Tomasini went on to consider specific issues raised by Professor Kuznets' paper. This distinguished between economies which were capable of 'significant and widespread' use of modern technology (economically-developed countries) and others, which were not. While he was uncertain about the meaning of 'significant and widespread' one could say that the U.S.A. was not economically-developed since the potential of modern technology was not spread among all the firms, even within one of its industries. Only a few U.S. firms, in some sectors, adopted modern technology on a significant scale.

Although the paper emphasised technology and economic structure, Professor Kuznets' analysis of the gap used per capita product as the main indicator. He eliminated countries which ranked high in per capita product, but low by other characteristics. It might be useful for this sort of analysis to establish a number of socio-economic indicators, ranging from per capita income to air pollution. If weights were attached to these indicators, countries could be ranked in a way which would at least provide a more comprehensive description of the economic distance between nations. However he would prefer that we abandoned searching for a measure of the gap, and *a fortiori* even the recognition that a gap existed.

The association between per capita product and some structural characteristics must not be used, as Kuznets wanted, to extrapolate changes in per capita product. Professor Tomasini said he would even make this position more general. What we should be interested in was the structure of the economy of each country and how changes in that structure could raise per capita income or produce a more egalitarian income distribution. Economic comparisons among countries remained valuable in this sort of analysis, but it removed the need to rank them.

He agreed with Professor Kuznets that the size of a country was important for economic growth, just as economies of scale were important in production. The problem of size was particularly interesting and complex because it related not only to economic but to socio-political considerations too.

Professor Kuznets held that once some barriers were eliminated, less developed countries would have higher growth rates because they could call upon the large potential of modern technological knowledge. That proposition was based on the assumption that technology which was considered obsolete in developed countries could contribute to growth in underdeveloped countries. This idea was generally accepted in economic literature but Professor Tomasini had three reservations about it. First, in many cases, new technology was associated with the introduction of new goods or with changes in old ones. This might reduce the total demand for traditional goods, and would certainly hold back their rate of expansion. This phenomenon held in both developed and developing countries, so that old technology might be a liability to developing countries. Second, even where new technology was not associated with the introduction of new goods, what might be termed 'an emulation effect' made developing countries unwilling to adopt the old technology. Third, while it was often said that developing countries could choose from a wide range of technologies, this was not quite true. Patent restrictions, lack of skilled labour, lack of raw materials and socio-economic factors all meant that the set of feasible technologies was very restricted. The size of the set of feasible technologies was closely associated with the level of development.

Professor Kuznets had noted a widening disparity in production structure and labour share in certain sectors, counterbalanced by a convergence in some socio-cultural characteristics. For example, there was a reduction in death rates, a rise in literacy rates and the solution of certain chronic health problems.

In Professor Tomasini's opinion these contradictory trends supported the contention that we should concentrate our attention on socio-economic indicators which measured welfare in different countries, and not on the size of the gap. As we knew, only welfare status could be compared.

Professor Tomasini wanted to draw one conclusion from these comments; both the actual development process and theories of economic development would benefit from more concern with project analysis and less with macroeconomic theories of measurement.

Professor Kuznets said that, in response to Professor Tomasini, he would like to make some general comments. In recent years there had been a great deal of criticism of aggregate measures of economic performance, and much emphasis on the need to study structure. While he agreed with this emphasis, he thought that perhaps the criticism was overdone. The solution to the difficulties raised by aggregate measures was not to scrap them but to improve them. While accepting the value of comparing structural characteristics, he pointed to the need to use aggregate measures when different structural elements had to be assigned proper weights. The process of historical change was one of an inter-relation between various dynamic elements, with some of these elements more dynamic than others. The story was not only one of identifying significant elements in a given period, but of identifying the response of the main, perhaps more slowly moving, factors in the system, and weighting all of them properly. Assigning weights to structural elements, changing at different rates, could not be done without introducing aggregates of which these elements were commensurable parts.

Professor Kuznets wondered whether it was not the task of national income accounting to improve the system of measurement and definition of input and output components. Particular emphasis might, perhaps, be put on the neglected diseconomies which Professor Tomasini mentioned. As to measures of the gap which were alternatives to those in total product per capita, Professor Tomasini knew well enough that all the direct measures of technological and economic performance – horse-power of mechanical energy, the extent of the introduction of new industries, the consumption of major commodities and services per head – were all closely correlated with product per head, especially if one left out a few small countries whose high product per head was due largely to unusually rich natural resources. Thus, the close association between product per head and socio-economic structures and factors suggested that the former was a measure that could be used as a substitute for a variety of associated technical, economic and social-structural characteristics.

Professor Kuznets admitted that the size-distribution of income had been understressed in his paper, but it could be clearly shown that there was also a difference between developed and less developed countries in the inequality of the internal distribution of income. Inequality of income distribution was greater in the less developed countries, and there too the position might be getting worse rather than better as time passed by. Professor Kuznets had been working on the problem recently, but there was a great deal of technical detail to be covered, and he had therefore left it out of this paper.

He had also left out another major point, because he had not been asked to cover it. But he would raise it now. Historical evidence showed that the widening gap was accompanied by *increasing* output per head in the less developed countries. There had been no *absolute* fall in output per head in these countries. Indeed, the recent rise in output per head in many less developed countries had been at a higher rate than that in developed countries before 1939. There had been a big rise in output per head in all countries, largely associated with the acceleration of growth rates in developed countries – particularly in Europe and Japan. What was less clear was how far the increase in output per man in less developed countries *depended* on the increase in output per man in the developed countries. How much was due to technological progress – some relevant to less developed countries, some not?

If he could be devil's advocate for a moment, he would argue that inequalities in development provided an opportunity for technological (and social) advance in less developed countries that would not have been possible had there been no inequality. Perhaps there was a conflict between growth and equality. This tended to be ignored because discussions concentrated on the 'gap' rather than on growth. But he wondered what was the significance of a high level of output per man in developed countries for the general advance of technology in the world at large. If such technology were turned toward helping less developed countries, it could do a great deal. If there were no reserves for doing so in developed countries, perhaps one could not get such benefits. Professor Kuznets therefore wondered whether we overlooked the positive role played by inequality, once given, whether in the past or in its potential for the future.

Professor Lundberg said we had similar discussions about inequality within countries. We seemed to worry if the rich in a particular country got richer relatively to the poorer. But he always suspected the argument. Indeed, he wondered why we used it all. Perhaps it was a question of conscience. Perhaps we asked at what cost the rich got richer. Drawing this analogy with the whole world might be dangerous, but we had to discuss the problem on a world scale.

Professor Bhagwati said that the problem of pollution and its effect on the gap was somewhat more complex than Professor Tomasini seemed to suggest. It raised issues similar to those raised, by Professor Kuznets himself among others, many years ago, about the evaluation of defence expenditures in national income accounts. Of course, an important aspect of pollution was the externality issue: how could we get decentralised firms to do something about pollution when the market did not require that they counted it in as a cost in their operations? On the other hand, the gap problem raised in turn the question of how pollution should be entered in the national income accounts. Here we had to reckon with the fact that, under present practices, anti-pollution activity was already included as part of national income. Thus garbage disposal was an economic activity in the market-place and resources devoted to it were counted as adding to national income. The suggestion now was that pollution should be evaluated and subtracted from national income to arrive at 'true' national income (and that this would reduce the gap as the affluent countries had more pollution than the L.D.C.s). If we combined this idea with the current accounting conventions, it would mean that a society which merely 'threw out' garbage would find its national income reduced by the imputed value/cost of this garbage, whereas if the society had a garbage-disposal activity, this would be treated as part of national income. National income measurement would change arbitrarily according to whether garbage-disposal was within the market system or outside it. One therefore needed a consistent system of accounting conventions to deal with the question of pollution, which was only 'generalised garbage'. And one had to recognise that the conceptual problems here were identical to those discussed some decades ago in relation to defence, intermediate inputs, justice, police, etc.

Professor Bhagwati also thought that a proper understanding of the structural gap required that one should look not merely at proportions but also at absolute magnitudes. The change in the occupational structure in India, after a hundred years of development, might not seem important if one simply looked at percentages. However, the absolute scale of modern activity was very big and this had changed the character of the society. This was obvious also if one made a cross-section study of Nepal and India: one would find the same income per head and a similar occupational structure. Yet the countries were very different because the scale of modern industrial activity was so much greater in India. In order to look at the 'distance' between countries, one clearly needed to look at scale as well.

In his paper, Professor Ohlin had suggested that however good the rate of growth was in underdeveloped countries there would be no fall in the relative (or even absolute) gap by the year 2000. This raised the question whether there was not some other way in which a country could obtain national satisfaction. For example, China appeared to have done so by developing the H-bomb. While he did not approve of this particular way of solving the problem, Professor Bhagwati wondered whether the really challenging and fruitful question was how a country could 'join the big league' even though there was still an economic gap between it and other developed countries.

Dr. Mahbul ul Haq said that, as a planner from an underdeveloped country, he did not find the constant preoccupation with the measurement of the gap either a fruitful exercise or very helpful in policy making.

The gap was a fairly meaningless measure for policy makers for at least three reasons. First, the traditional measurement of the gap considerably exaggerated differences in real income. For example, a per capita monthly income of about £3 in India still made living at least possible at the subsistence level because of the way Indian society was presently organised. A similar income in America did not provide a subsistence existence.

Second, the measurement of the gap often assumed that the sense of values and the structure of economy prevalent in the most developed country, i.e. the U.S.A., was the only correct basis for measurement. This was false since many artificial demands were created in an affluent society such as advertising, the space programme, etc. which the developing countries could do well without. It was perfectly possible for an economy to survive without having a number of industries which were found in the U.S.A., including the flourishing cosmetics and lingerie industries.

Third, measurement of the gap did not lead to any useful policy conclusions but only heightened a sense of frustration in underdeveloped countries. While it was true that a single year's aggregate increase in real G.N.P. in the U.S.A. could not be achieved in India over the course of a century at the present rates of growth, such a comparison was frustrating and, in fact, irrelevant. One did no service to the developing countries to convince them that life began at £1,000 per capita income, when the prospects for attaining such a level were fairly remote for most of them over the course of the next century. Many developing countries would be quite content to aim at a per capita income of about £200 (which would still give them a reasonable standard of living) and not pursue elusive goals.

Dr. Haq wondered whether it would be more appropriate to measure the gap in physical rather than financial terms – in terms of food, clothing, housing, education and health? This would make the gap more manageable as well as more relevant for policy-makers. For instance, if per capita food consumption was about 2,000 calories in India while it was about 3,000 calories in the developed world, this gap could be reduced and even eliminated in the next few decades through sensible planning. Similarly, it was quite possible to reduce the gap in education and health facilities fairly quickly with the application of modern knowledge and techniques. In many fields it would be found that the gap was less alarming in physical terms than it was made out to be in financial terms because the question here was not simply a quantitative measurement of G.N.P. Qualitative factors were also relevant. He concluded that while the existing concept of the gap as expressed in financial terms might be useful in pressurising developed countries into higher levels of foreign assistance, at least for planning purposes the gap concept should be expressed more in physical terms. They both gave a more accurate idea of the gap and directed planning effort to right priorities.

Professor Johnson said that several points which had been raised during the discussion were worth thinking about. First, there was the question of how to measure national income, if one allowed for pollution, etc. If one looked round Bled one saw plenty of private pollution but this was part of the existing way of life. It was only when a country became rich that this kind of problem became really serious. It was true that a lot of national income in developed countries was part of the cost of living rather than part of national satisfaction. Garbage disposal was an example. However, if one took away from the national income of an underdeveloped country that part of the national income which was incurred in meeting costs of pollution which were part of the way of life, one would probably find a similar gap to the one we had now.

The problem was that the cost of living rose with the standard of living. Urbanisation increased the costs of moving foodstuffs and other products, so that one needed to allow for more than differences in national income between countries. This would make the problem easier, but he wondered whether those in underdeveloped countries wanted to narrow the gap completely. Did they really want to be living the life of the current citizen of America in fifty years' time? It was not just a question of studying the present gap and trying to eliminate it.

However, Professor Johnson thought that participants had been less than fair to Professor Kuznets. The latter had written the paper he had been asked to write. This gave us the material required for a good deal of broad thinking about the nature of the whole development process.

Dr. Nurul Islam returned to the specific question of defence expenditure raised by Professor Bhagwati. This was important for many developing countries. There were two issues. There was the problem of social evaluation. How did one evaluate added-value in the fields of defence or public administration? With other services, prices were supposed to reflect margin utilities. Unfortunately they did not do so in the public sector. While this was well known he thought it needed emphasising.

There was also the problem of competitive defence spending. If an underdeveloped country spent a good deal on defence, this was likely to be because it regarded two or three other countries as potential threats. Yet if country A increased its defence expenditure, the likelihood was that countries B, C and D would then raise their expenditures still farther. If so, one could argue that the security that country A was purchasing would go down. Indeed, if the other countries really did increase their defence expenditure by more than country A, one could argue that there had been a decline in A's real G.N.P.

Professor Lewis said he wanted to do battle with the devil. Professor Kuznets had argued that the high relative rate of growth in developed countries was good because growth in underdeveloped countries depended on it. Historically this was true. Prebisch was right that in the late 19th century underdeveloped countries did well out of European development. Then, in 1920–40, income per head in countries like India and Egypt fell because of the bad economic performance of developed countries. However this particular link was no longer necessary. It was not the case that the progress of India or Brazil now depended on trade with developed countries.

As the advocate of the angels, he would suggest that underdeveloped countries had all they needed for fast growth. They had surpluses of raw materials and fuel; could produce food; could acquire manufacturing skills; and could save if they needed to. Therefore one could say that it need make no difference to them in the long run whether or not all the developed countries sank under the sea. There would be immediate losses. For example, terms of trade would change. However underdeveloped countries would then discover that they could use their own resources, save for themselves and educate themselves. They would find that they could grow just as fast as they had done *with* the developed countries. So what had been historically true need be true no longer.

Dr. Radetzki pointed out that Professor Kuznets had argued that the existence of a wide gap implied that developed countries could help underdeveloped countries – provided there were no barriers. The question was what were these barriers? Dir. Radetzki suggested that they might partly be caused *by* the gap itself. For example, a big gap was said to increase political or economic subordination and so hinder growth. Professor Kuznets had also argued that the gap might be decreased by social legislation, with poor countries copying social legislation in richer countries. Yet copying a rich country's social legislation could actually *decrease* the ability of a poor country to grow.

On trade relations, Dr. Radetzki said that problems of social change in underdeveloped countries and rapidly changing demand patterns in rich ones made it difficult to adapt exports. Poor countries found it difficult to change their supply patterns to match changes in demand in rich countries. Professor Kuznets had claimed that the gap helped because it allowed the rich to get richer. Looking at the statistics one could argue that the growth in underdeveloped countries had been concentrated on the richer underdeveloped countries. The growth of the poorer ones was not necessarily equally impressive.

Professor Chenery argued that we were talking about the less interesting aspects of the gap and not the important fact that in a country with a low per capita income it was hard to achieve what was needed. The question was what could we *do*. Perhaps we should look at the problem as a dynamic one. One then had to look at population growth relatively to the level of income, and so at the total effect over a period. He was hopeful that the time taken to move from a state of underdevelopment to one of development was shortening. He would define the point at which a country became developed as one where per capita income was $800 per annum. He would similarly define a country which was still underdeveloped as one with a per capita income of less than $200 per annum. Countries in between he would class as transitional. Japan had moved from underdevelopment to development in about seventy years – between about 1910 and 1965. He would like to look at some of the relevant relationships by plotting the proportion of an economy which was devoted to a particular industry against income per head.

During the transitional period one would find an industry growing faster than in either underdeveloped or developed countries. This was true in total, the population was growing because of the widening gap between birth and death rates. The important question was how far we could go through the transitional stage more rapidly. Europe had taken about a hundred years; Japan seventy years; he thought that Yugoslavia, Israel and Korea would do it in forty to fifty years. He therefore thought that we should introduce a time dimension into the discussion.

Professor Correa thought we should emphasise the importance of the gap in terms of welfare and not only in quantitative economic terms. We all knew the problems of measuring welfare and he would like to suggest a new measure. One might treat the uses of income in different countries as revealing preferences. Using factor analysis, one might then be able to work out an index of revealed preferences, weighting particular elements in consumption. This would give an index of welfare which would enable one to compare levels of welfare between different countries.

On Professor Lewis's point, he thought that developed countries were a definite obstacle to the development of underdeveloped countries. Indeed, it

c 2

was probably a pre-condition for the development of backward countries that
the advanced countries should sink under the sea.

Professor Patinkin thought that part of the discussion had sounded like those
on how to compare standards of living in different countries which had gone on
since 1950. Many of the points made today had already been made. For example, earlier studies had considered the costs of modern life, of transportation,
of time taken in travelling, of pollution and of maintaining the legal and administrative framework for economic activity. We had already looked at the
question; what is net productivity in a net sense? We were now dealing with a
much broader question, which had already been recognised in parts. Professor
Patinkin thought that all these factors worked against developed countries and
narrowed the gap. However there was one factor which widened it. Leisure was
not included in national income, and there was more leisure in developed
countries. When leisure was included, it was no longer clear that correcting the
gap would narrow it.

As for the 'other' measures which Professor Tomasini had mentioned, put in
technical language what Professor Tomasini was saying was that we were interested in the first or second derivatives of the function of productivity per man. If
one found that technology was not reflected in per capita output, it could hardly
be said to be making a useful contribution.

The relevant question was what had happened to the rate of change of the
gap. Was it increasing more quickly or more slowly? If Professor Tomasini's
factors were important, then the gap might be increasing but its rate of increase
should be falling. It was not clear from the data presented in Professor Kuznets'
paper that this was true.

Professor Patinkin made several comments on Professor Juznets' assumptions.
First, he wondered how valid it was to eliminate countries with a high level of
income because they happened to be situated in the right part of the world –
with large oil resources, for example. Was this merely a question of luck? Was
it not a very puritan attitude to say that one was lucky to be born into a society
with a large stock of capital equipment? It was possible today to be a Hippy
simply because one was in a society with a high standard of living and a large
stock of capital. Both were inheritances from the past, and a gift of nature was
rather similar.

Professor Patinkin thought that the view of population which regarded it as a
drag on growth was putting too much emphasis on conditions in South East
Asia. African countries did not worry similarly about population growth. It
seemed that the revealed preferences of some developed countries suggested
that they wanted to raise population. Perhaps this was linked to what Professor
Bhagwati had said about scale. One had to look at particular increases in population and ask whether they were desired.

Professor Findlay said he was now confused over which was the angel and
which was the devil. Professor Lewis claimed that if the developed countries
would sink, the underdeveloped countries could still maintain their rates of
growth, citing India and Brazil. But Professor Lewis had lost sight of some
smaller countries like Thailand, Taiwan and South Korea, which had been
much more successful. When one spoke of internationalising the engine of
growth among dozens of underdeveloped countries, it was important only to

remember that India, Brazil and Pakistan were big countries. For the remainder, international trade must remain the engine of growth. Professor Lewis was using a closed large-country model. The U.S.S.R. and China had shown what such large countries could do – at a very high cost. They could make more capital goods, but at a big opportunity cost in terms of consumer goods sacrificed. The sacrifice might possibly be feasible only if one had a very big country. For the others, there was the problem of scale – through international integration alone could they do what they wanted. This was particularly true of countries in South East Asia and Latin America. Indeed, Professor Findlay wondered how useful it was to look at the underdeveloped countries 'as a whole'. Unless there was world integration he did not think this was a reasonable method. Each underdeveloped country was alone, or in a narrow grouping. He thought the idea that the developed world could 'sink' was the advocacy of the devil. It diverted attention from the need to keep the drive to liberalisation of trade going. Unfortunately, this had now lost its thrust.

Professor Johnson wanted to defend Professor Lewis. In his contribution, Professor Lewis had simply summarised a large part of his Wicksell Lectures, in which he had wondered whether, if the developed countries disappeared, the development of underdeveloped countries would turn out to depend so categorically as had been thought on trade with developed countries. Professor Lewis had shown in the Wicksell Lectures that a good deal of development in backward countries depended on internal factors and he was *not* arguing that each underdeveloped country could go it alone. What he held was that the whole tropical region could develop institutions that would allow development to go ahead. How far colonial relations and the existing pattern of international trade kept trade from changing to new patterns was another question.

Professor Lewis expanded his earlier remarks. What he had been trying to say was that much of the 'energy' of underdeveloped countries ran to waste because these countries believed, erroneously, that they could not make real economic progress if they were unable to increase trade with developed countries. He was trying hard to dispute this view, and anyone who advocated it – like Professors Kuznets and Findlay – was speaking for the devil.

Dr. Pfaff said that in contemporary measurement of the gap non-market factors were neglected. The gap was overstated because the present system of national accounts neglected household production and other types of non-market output. The latter was presumably larger in less developed countries than in industrialised countries. However, according to a recent study of *Non-market Components of National Accounts*, published by the University of Michigan's Survey Research Centre, the average value of a family's unpaid output was about 50 per cent of disposable income, even in the United States. To discuss the problem meaningfully we needed a broader framework.

On the other hand, the present system of national accounts focussed attention on important indicators. By implication it perhaps had more effect on improving economic welfare than other more esoteric concepts.

To attempt to arrive at a broader concept of national income or welfare, a system would have to be found that reflected performance at four levels: the cultural, social, political and economic. One could measure the gap at any of these levels. If a society were viewed as a dynamic system, however, account would have to be taken of the lagged effects of one system-level on the rest of the system. Furthermore, such a way of measuring welfare required agreement on a suitable social discount rate, as well as on a time horizon for the allocation of resources. Furthermore, a measurement system based on such a socio-economic model would have to take account of questions of equity and other systemic considerations. In the absence of agreement about the structure of such a model and of the social preference function for alternative goals, the large numbers of statistics that had to be studied could not be interrelated meaningfully.

Mr. Streeten wondered whether, if Professor Lewis wanted to show that underdeveloped countries were wasting their effort in preaching at the rich countries, preaching at the L.D.C.s in turn to improve the movement of goods and men between them was going to be any easier.

What Professor Lewis had said was not really a reply to Professor Kuznets. Professor Kuznets had been talking about knowledge, science and technology; Professor Lewis's argument was about the demand for exports and the terms of trade. Mr. Streeten wondered whether it would help if we focussed on the various ways in which the interdependence of developed and underdeveloped countries helped or hindered the development of the underdeveloped.

So far not much had been said about the way in which the gap affected the supply of savings, skills or some other important factors. Perhaps we could be more specific than we had so far been on how intervention by policy could help to reduce the detrimental and encourage the beneficial effects.

At the end of his paper, Professor Kuznets suggested how interdependence and divisiveness posed problems. But what was Professor Tomasini's conclusion about underdeveloped countries not wanting second-hand or obsolete equipment, because an improvement in technology brought with it an improvement in the product? Perhaps we should shift attention from changes in processes and technology to changes in the type of product. Frances Stewart had recently drawn attention to the possibility that underdeveloped countries needed 'intermediate' i.e. more appropriate, goods. Many products sold in rich countries satisfied a wide range of needs simultaneously, and one might be able to eliminate the satisfaction of 'excess' needs when adapting them to poor countries. A problem was that there was a gap in the range of goods to meet particular needs. Many modern goods 'overkilled' in the sense that they provided for a wider range of satisfactions than underdeveloped countries required or could afford. Professor Tomasini had mentioned drip-dry nylon shirts. There was no need to have a shirt that saved labour in ironing in underdeveloped countries. It might be better for such countries to have less-sophisticated products whose production was more appropriate to their factor endowments. He thought this was true of houses, fruit drinks and other consumer goods. The question was whether these could be produced at lower costs than mass-produced sophisticated products, and whether they would be wanted by consumers. He thought one needed to widen choice by providing 'appropriate' products, as well as providing appropriate technologies.

Professor Srinivasan said that two suggestions for measuring the gap had emerged. Dr. Haq thought that it should be measured in physical terms – for example, in calorie intake per head. Professor Chenery suggested that the gap should be measured in terms of the time needed to close it. Professor Srinivasan thought that by shifting the measurement of the gap to physical terms, one might reach misleading conclusions. In terms of calorie intake, the gap was 2 : 1 as compared with 30 : 1 in terms of per capita income. This did not necessarily mean that the calorie gap could be closed more easily or quickly. But, by adding a time dimension, one obtained very different estimates of the time needed to close the gap, depending on the institutional assumptions one made. For example, if the calorie intake per person of the poorest 10 per cent in India was to be brought to the average level for the U.S.A., the length of time taken would depend on whether one assumed that efforts to close the gap were to be made in the context of consumer sovereignty and the existing income distribution. With such an assumption, to raise the calorie intake of the poorest 10 per cent one would have to increase aggregate income far more than if one were to do it by some non-market arrangement, where food was allocated to the needy, regardless of their ability to pay. Further, so long as one kept the assumption of consumer sovereignty, the production pattern necessarily had to be related to the pattern of consumer demand, regardless of whether this would lead to a quicker closing of the gap, however measured.

Professor Robinson had been interested in the arguments on the inadequacy of the data Professor Kuznets had provided in his paper. However he thought there was still interest in the figures. For example, on p. 40 Professor Kuznets gave figures for the rate of growth of G.N.P. and population in various areas. He showed, for example, that the G.N.P.s of underdeveloped countries had grown slightly faster – at 4·65 per cent – than the G.N.P.s of developed countries – at 4·44 per cent. But at the same time, the populations of underdeveloped countries had grown at 2·45 per cent per annum – twice that of the 1·27 per cent rate for developed countries. This was why one had big differences in the rate of increase of income per head.

Professor Robinson said he had recently been working in Bangkok on ECAFE statistics. These were all revalued at constant 1960 prices. This implied that the terms of trade were the same as in 1960 which was, for ECAFE countries, very far from a good assumption. He wondered whether national income statistics, in some contexts at least, should be adjusted for changes in the terms of trade. If one had a country with an import ratio and an export ratio of 25 per cent, then a 4 per cent change in the terms of trade by itself represented a loss to the country equal to 1 per cent of G.N.P. We were looking at very small differences compared with this. He wondered whether Professor Kuznets' figures allowed for changes in terms of trade. He noted that this problem was equally important for the U.K. The national income statistics failed in certain periods to allow for *favourable* changes in the U.K.'s terms of trade.

On population we had to remember the extraordinary effects of what was happening. If a country had a 3 per cent population growth, as in South East Asia, it would have to allow for a 33 per cent increase in population in a decade. In India, during each decade, the addition to the population was equal to the total populations of the U.K., France and Germany. All this needed investment, and so much of current investment in underdeveloped countries was devoted to enabling them to stand still. It was not just a question of looking at G.N.P. per head in underdeveloped countries. We had to see what would be left over after one had provided for the existing rate of growth of population. Professor

Kuznets said that there were few underdeveloped countries where income per head was falling. But it would be easier to find countries where the amount of private consumption per capita was falling. In India, as the result of a higher level of investment and saving, private consumption expenditure had been rising at a little less than the rate of growth of population; there was a slight fall in private consumption per head. If we began to think in terms of equalising the rate of growth of personal consumption expenditure in different countries, we had a long way to go before we would start closing the gap.

Professor Vernon said that consideration of the gap required the introduction of psychological evidence, where the economist had limited qualifications. The gap implied that levels of satisfaction were a function not only of one's own growth, but also of the growth of others. Did we, as economists, really know? It might even be that levels of satisfaction were reduced, not increased, as the size of the gap declined. An example was the increased unhappiness of blacks in the United States as the gap between blacks and whites grew smaller.

The implication of what Professor Kuznets had said was that a large gap generated a free good, namely, technology, that the underdeveloped countries were in a position to use without further cost. Technology was then better thought of as a necessary, rather than a sufficient, prerequisite for increased productivity. Countries applying technology needed to know how to apply it, which required investment in the learning process and in organisational structures. This was probably a much bigger need than was generally recognised. On the other hand, this kind of investment was probably going on at a greater rate than was generally recognised, especially in countries at the upper end of the less developed scale. The cost of such effort was reflected in the high price of import substitutes, rather than being recorded as investment in human capital, where, perhaps, it more properly belonged.

Professor Ohlin referred to the direct impact of the income gap on income distribution. Professor Kuznets had said that perhaps income distribution was becoming more unequal in underdeveloped countries. In these circumstances, one could not overlook the link between the incomes and expenditures of the elite in these countries and the international demonstration effect. One began to feel the wisdom of isolation.

This led to the question of dualism in developing countries. We were back to an old question. Are national units very meaningful? When we talked about gaps, we felt that there was not just a quantitative but also a qualitative, perhaps political, difference between developed and underdeveloped countries. Professor Chenery had argued that the real issue was to raise income per head from $200 to $800 perhaps. If a country had a modern sector, like that in nearby industrial countries, and a lot of undevelopment pulling down the average income, what did one say? Did one take the low average? Or did one treat this country as two countries, one with a highly industrialised economy and the other with a primitive economy? While Professor Vernon believed that we ought to ignore the gap, it was what we had come here to discuss and we could not avoid this kind of question.

Professor Kuznets said that in this discussion during the first session, we had returned to a number of perennial problems in national income definition and accounting. He wanted to mention three broad groups of such problems.

First, there was the question of intermediate products – some of which should perhaps not be regarded as part of the final product (as they now are) – for example, defence, government administration and the like. Could we treat these as necessary inputs in the production function? Or were they historical accidents in the sense of *not* constituting requirements for total output and its growth? Second, there was the question of the valuation of different commodities and services, which has been only slightly touched upon during the discussion. Third, there was the dependence of the definition of the scope of economic product on basic properties of the economic and social system.

All these were problems that could be 'solved' only by approximation, but such continuously changing approximations were important and indispensable if measures were to provide a proper basis for the analysis of changing reality. We should note that from the 1940s U.S. national income statistics had not changed in response to such problems, because the changing approximations might impair a valuable guide which the U.S. government had for measuring and regulating short-term economic performance. National income accounting was closely linked to the short-run theory of Keynesian economics; rendered great service; and its very success led to rigidity. The national accounting framework would have to be changed significantly, if it were to be fully useful for the study of growth and long-run problems.

The second group of questions was concerned with the significance of the measures of the gap. Dr. Haq, particularly, had spoken about the need for different criteria. Since Professor Kuznets had suggested in his own paper that comparison of product per capita was not necessarily the right criterion, he would say no more. But it led to the question of what was the goal of economic activity, a question suggested by two possible meanings of the gap. One was the gap in the sense of a shortfall from some desirable standards. The other began with the measurement of differences in levels of economic performance, as conventionally measured. But the range of 30 : 1 revealed was important not so much as a significant value, but as showing that styles of life must differ – since people survived despite these apparently impossible differentials. He would oppose Professor Vernon's view of the gap as a purely psychological problem. He thought it was much more a testimony of real and wide differences in economic performance. He was not saying whether the gap was deplorable or not; simply that, in the second meaning, as conventionally measured, it existed. We should accept the gap as a fact of co-existence in a world of societies with different economic and social systems, different levels of performance, perhaps different ideas of life. Co-existence was basic, and a key to the flows between countries and inter-relations among them.

On angels versus devils, Professor Kuznets said that the existence of the higher-level technology of developed countries *was* a resource for the world at large, and also for the less developed countries. It did not only operate via the demand side, where it had been important even in recent years: the technology of the developed countries had worked to generate the natural and other resources of the less developed. He was speaking here not only of material technology. Even more important was the character of the technology – which was problem-solving. The social inventions of developed countries also helped the poorer countries. Whether the less developed countries had to produce their own technology, in time, was another question. His own impression was that an important channel of accelerated growth in less developed countries would be an attempt to mobilise some of their resources to work on technological innovations there. A few well-trained groups could do a great deal.

He felt that the implication of these comments was that viability of developed countries was important for the world at large. It was necessary for the former to survive as viable units. If internal pressures caused the developed countries to turn more of their attention to their internal problems, it was a real question whether they would be able to spare even 1 per cent of their product for the less developed regions; and if the resources could be spared, whether the long-run returns, even for the world at large, would look sufficiently great relative to those from internal use. The difficulty was that this was a period where we had too little foreknowledge of what the future might be like, and where we were dealing with complex and untested inter-relations.

2 The Contemporary Consequences of the Gap

Göran Ohlin
UPPSALA UNIVERSITY

I. THE MAGNITUDE AND SIGNIFICANCE OF THE GAP

Nobody disputes the existence of a gap between rich countries and poor, and it probably does not matter to this conception whether, measured in terms of G.N.P. per head, the differential is of the order of 20 : 1 or 10 : 1. For one thing, the gap is perceived as the qualitative difference between industrialised and 'modernised' nations on the one hand, and archaic and agricultural communities on the other. For another, income comparisons seem arbitary on many grounds. Quite apart from their reliability and meaningfulness, they depend heavily on the grouping.

Among the industrialised countries themselves there is an income gap of the magnitude of 4 : 1. Below them are a number of relatively well-to-do countries in the 'developing' world, covering another range of a factor of 4. Then comes the bulk of the poor countries which again differ by roughly a factor of 4. Thus a comparison between, say, Argentina and Italy will be a very different matter from a comparison between India and the U.S.A.

What income comparisons do is to range countries in a way which is fairly well correlated with other rankings on the basis of any conceivable measures of social advancement which we have been able to think up. This in turn lends some credence to the belief that economic and social development proceeds along a path where the overridingly important factor is that command over the niggardliness of nature which is expressed in productivity.

Paradoxically, therefore, income measurements which demonstrate the magnitude of the gap also tend to soften its edges and to draw attention to the unity of human experience. Many other differences, which at first sight loom very large – differences of culture, race, religion, etc. – do not seem to preclude an essentially similar economic development.

This is important because it makes the gap rather less awe-inspiring. Looking back one is amazed at how, until quite recently, the gap was seen as part of a natural order. Today it is not, and the basically economic conception of the gap tends to create the opposite conviction that it could and should be eliminated forthwith.

Only a fool could presume to know the consequences of the gap as it exists and as is perceived today. It is cited, in innumerable ringing declarations, as a great and ominous threat to the world community, but when the gap is discussed in advocacy of foreign aid it is usually in an exhortatory mode which lacks precision, consistency and at times even conviction. It strikes a note of urgency, but the gap is going to yield only slowly, if at all, to whatever measures are taken.

The dilemma is exemplified by the Pearson report, which starts from the awesome challenge of the gap and ends up suggesting that aid might be phased out by the year 2000 when the gap would be no smaller than today, even on the report's assumption that the majority of developing countries will then be launched on self-sufficient growth at the significant rate of 6 per cent.

There is thus reason to examine more dispassionately some of the issues which do not fit easily into the more officious language of the development gospel. I propose to raise a few of them, without providing more than tentative answers.

II. THE ORIGIN OF THE GAP

Many arguments about the gap, and not least their normal tenor, stem directly from a specific notion about its 'causes'.

Most of what has been termed the 'economic distance' between the industrialised and the less developed countries has arisen within the course of the last one hundred years. But even at the time of the Industrial Revolution, some Western countries seem to have had higher levels of G.N.P. per head than very poor L.D.C.s today. One might well speculate that, broadly speaking, the economic superiority of the West evolved *pari passu* with the European offensive against the rest of the world which began with the Crusades and ended with the colonial empires of the late 19th century.

It is precisely this rough correlation between Western power and Western prosperity which gives rise to two different ways of looking at the matter:

(1) The emergence of Western capitalism and industrialism may be seen as a consequence primarily of internal social change unique to the West. The West grew away from the rest of the world, slowly at first and then rapidly. The assertion of Western power was a more or less incidental consequence of economic disparity, with the flag following trade.

(2) Alternatively, the exercise of power in colonial trade and 'exploitation' were indispensable elements in Western growth, the pillars on which Western prosperity rested. Conversely, economic conditions in the colonial world deteriorated through actual immiserisation or

were held back by the halting of social change which would have brought development.

The overwhelming weight of evidence and argument seems to favour the first of these views. This is not to exonerate the rapacity of colonialism but merely to say that its contributions to Western economic growth seem secondary rather than primary. Similarly, although the West was responsible for violent disruption of social and political structures elsewhere, there is little to suggest that this interrupted a process of economic development which would have resulted in something similar to Western growth. It might even be argued that in many cases colonial rule, by removing ancient institutions, laid the groundwork for more rapid social and political modernisation. At the end of colonial rule few have wished to return to a *status quo ante*.

On the other hand, living conditions certainly deteriorated in Latin America, where complex civilisations were destroyed and the bulk of the native population perished. Even where there is no evidence of a clear drop in levels of living, as in Asia and Africa, such a change is quite possible. After all, a serious deterioration in levels of living seems to have occurred in Europe itself between the beginning of the 16th and the middle of the 18th century, in spite of simultaneous improvements in commerce and technology.

In L.D.C.s themselves and among many Western radicals it is certainly an often asserted view that the abuse of Western power was the chief factor in the historical evolution of the gap, and that even today the practices of Western countries in commercial policy, the promotion of foreign investment, and perhaps even their foreign aid constitute major obstacles to L.D.C. development. It may be said that these are rhetorical figures of speech which are not to be taken too seriously, and that in any case there is more than a grain of truth to charges of this kind. But do they not deflect attention from more valuable lessons about the dynamics of internal social change which marked the modernising nations?

III. THE POLITICAL MORALITY OF INTERNATIONAL EGALITARIANISM

The misdeeds of colonialism provide sufficient nourishment for those who wish to postulate the 'guilt' of the West. But on the reading of history which I have suggested above it makes little sense to hold the West responsible for the poverty of the non-industrialised countries.

Even so it is perfectly possible to find the gross inequalities in the world offensive or unhealthy. Indeed a principal function of estimates of the gap is to be used in pleas for more foreign aid and other support of developing countries. Advocates of foreign aid sometimes seem to believe that the

mere existence of a large gap should be enough to persuade governments
and tax payers in rich countries of the need for action to reduce it.

Actually there are of course two strands, to some extent contradictory,
in the philosophy of foreign aid as so far practised. One represents an
international egalitarianism which is an extension of principles which have
come increasingly to illuminate the domestic policies of industrialised
countries. The second strand sees foreign aid as 'an instrument of foreign
policy', to use the phrase which must have found its way into internal
policy memoranda in all donor countries. It emphasises the hazards to
world peace of stark inequalities and/or unsettled conditions in the Third
World. It also usually claims that specific political, strategic and economic
advantages may be legitimately pursued by individual donors by the use of
foreign aid as a tool of economic diplomacy.

As to the first of these views, one may oneself subscribe to a vague
notion of international solidarity without, however, holding high hopes of
its significance as an effective force in the world of today. Gross disparities among individual members of the community are contrary to the
principle of 'natural equality', which has figured in Western thought since
the Schoolmen although its application to the international scene is
startlingly recent. What matters is not the existence of the gap but the
perception of community.

As Tawney noted,

> what a community requires, as the word itself suggests, is common
> culture. . . . But a common culture cannot be created merely by desiring
> it. It rests upon economic foundations. It is incompatible with the ex-
> istence of too violent a contrast between classes, for such a contrast
> has as its result, not a common culture, but servility or resentment, on
> the one hand, and patronage or arrogance, on the other. It involves, in
> short, a large measure of economic equality.[1]

Tawney was, in the early thirties, speaking of equality inside the nation,
as indeed all commentators on equality in the past. A hasty perusal of the
literature does not uncover any references, before the post-war years, to
international inequality as a moral or political problem, except in the
muted form of references to missionary activity or colonial trusteeship.
Even today, although internationalism is a factor to be counted with and
has found institutional expression in a host of international organisations,
it is only too apparent how limited its political significance remains. For
one thing, the developing countries are too preoccupied with nation
building and the creation of a sense of community within their own
borders to be particularly receptive to the appeal of internationalism. For
another, their own internal inequalities of income and wealth frustrate
attempts to apply Western egalitarianism on an international scale without

[1] R. H. Tawney, *Equality* (London, 1931), p. 41.

the objection that the poor in rich countries aid the rich in poor countries. Thirdly, governments in rich countries remain above all guardians of the national interest.

Attempts to construe the precepts of international solidarity as being in a deeper sense consistent with national interest are usually too far-sighted and visionary to be compelling. It is not cynical but realistic to recognise that in spite of the lipservice paid to international co-operation in the interest of decorum, conflicts between domestic and foreign interests will usually find governments acting on behalf of their nationals or their own presumed interests of state, except in cases where they feel bound by international law.

The argument that the gap is a threat to international security is sometimes taken to suggest that rich countries, as small islands of prosperity, will find themselves besieged and attacked by the populous underprivileged nations surrounding them. This appeal to the fears of the prosperous, reminiscent of the argument for levelling inside the industrial countries, does not have much warrant in history. Rich countries have been more likely to make war on poor countries than vice versa.

Technology may of course change that and many other things. The 'shrinking-world' argument hints at forces which willy-nilly link all nations more closely: instantaneous communication, rapid transport, growing trade, world-wide problems of health-control, over-population, pollution and the control of multinational corporations. Extrapolations of current trends do indeed suggest that such global issues will exert a growing pressure for international co-operation in specific technical fields, which is where it has proved remarkably successful in the past. But whether this will create a community of interests within which the gap is recognised as a joint concern of the first order seems doubtful.

A more down-to-earth argument is that many developing countries represent international danger spots where political instability threatens to involve the great powers in escalating conflicts. But the critical element in this view is political turmoil. How clear is it that the gap or even the absolute poverty of developing countries is the cause of the weaknesses and the instability of their political systems? Their economic development will, if history is any guide, be yet another unsettling force, although it may ultimately provide a new base for national community and stability.

Even if it is accepted that the gulf between the two worlds is a source of international tension, each of the industrialised countries finds itself in a 'prisoner's dilemma'. The individual country can do little to affect the situation, and for that matter even collective action to provide development assistance will only make a marginal contribution to development and might well be unable to do more than keep the gap from widening.

It is thus not surprising that the bulk of foreign aid remains bilateral, to all appearances directed less towards the gap as such than towards the pursuit of particular relationships or specific advantages. Within the framework of a long colonial association links have often formed which make it natural 'to help our friends', as a white paper with disarming simplicity described the purpose of British aid. But there is also a convergence of other objectives: the mystique of *rayonnement*, the protection and promotion of investments and trade, collaboration in the U.N., etc. Similarly, in the important case of the United States, genuine idealism has combined with hard-headed notions of military and political strategy. These motives and objectives pull in different directions in the allocation of aid: the disinterested ones steer it towards the needy while relatively well-to-do L.D.C.s may have more interesting *quid pro quos* to offer and may use their bargaining power in the international 'grants economy' more effectively.

Only in the international organisations is there so far an institutionalised concern with the welfare of the world community as a whole. They wrestle with great difficulties of internal efficiency and with the intrinsic challenge of growing into more than the sum of their member governments. Yet it is by the slow accretion of power on behalf of the international community as such that the gap and all it represents stand the greatest chance of becoming the factor in world politics which it is so far only in form but not in substance.

IV. GAP OR POVERTY?

The 'gap' is often no more than a shorthand expression for a blurred notion of the plight of developing countries. When the focus is sharpened there are at least three, and probably many more, notions of what is the central problem:

(1) *Absolute Poverty*

The plight of the street-dwellers of Calcutta may perhaps stand for the whole complex of deprivation implied in a subsistence or sub-subsistence level. Starvation and disease will, at least in prosperous communities, arouse far greater compassion than mere poverty. The uncomfortable truth that there is a fairly close correlation between incomes on the one hand and nutrition and health on the other is a persuasive leveller, and the notion of a sharply defined subsistence income was modified already by Ricardo. It has, however, acquired a new relevance today.

(2) *Stagnation*

Development economics is generally concerned with the attainment of growth and social improvement, without any precise notion of the speed. A rate of growth of income per capita of, say, 3·5 per cent is historically impressive and quadruples incomes in 50 years which cannot fail to change a society profoundly. Supposing that requirements of social justice are met, and that significant improvement is recorded, is it meaningful to call this inadequate?

(3) *Gap Poverty*

In terms of relative performance it may well appear inadequate, if richer countries continue to grow at the same or higher rates. Absolute and relative international income comparisons will be a reminder of the large and possibly widening disparities. Is this relatively abstract measure really more important than the quality of life and the quality of the community in question, judged on its own terms? If this is not so, it might be preferable not to interpret the 'gap' too literally, but to put more stress on the elimination of destitution and the launching of steady growth.

V. THE POSSIBILITY OF ELIMINATING THE GAP

It is easy enough to make mechanical extrapolations of growth trends to show that, if industrialised countries continue to grow at recent rates, it will take a very long time for L.D.C.s to catch up unless they achieve Japanese growth rates. Even if they managed to raise incomes per head 2 per cent faster than rich countries, a gap of 20 : 1 would only be closed in 150 years.

At present average rates the gap will hardly ever be closed, and the time required for the bulk of L.D.C.s to reach even today's European income levels would be of the order of a century – not much for a historian, but impossibly remote as a time horizon for impatient politicians. The conclusion that development aspirations must be tempered by patience might seem almost inescapable. But a number of points are worth recalling.

In the first place, the development record is enormously mixed. Some countries will succeed better than others, although there is no way of telling which will be most successful over the long haul.

Secondly, a general acceleration may be expected with increasing industrialisation. There is not even a guarantee that new Japans will not emerge.

Thirdly, it cannot be blithely assumed that the growth of the rich countries will remain as buoyant as it has been over the last exceptional decades. A dwindling industrial sector will reduce the opportunities of genuine productivity improvements through applied science, pollution problems which increase the cost of air, water, and space may raise conventional G.N.P. but not welfare.

Demographic projections have in the past been rather consistently wrong whenever the horizon was pushed beyond a decade or two. To forecast economic development even a generation ahead is probably impossible. Projections of the probable course of the gap are likely to lead to defeatist conclusions even when they represent little more than idle doodles.

It might also be asked what 'closing the gap' should really mean. European countries have not closed the gap with the U.S.A., but they are clearly in the same league. The definition of an 'industrialised' or 'developed' country is not immutable, and it is certainly not expressed in terms of a fixed real income level. A reasonable and realistic objective for world policy might well be to move the poorer countries across the qualitative gulf which now divides them from industrial nations. To make them members of the same league seems, in fact, to be what the whole thing is really about. There is no way of telling, off-hand, at what levels of income this might be brought about, as it will all depend.

If the richest countries move into a new 'post-industrial' condition which is clearly recognised as setting them apart from younger industrial nations, international egalitarianism might suffer but the present dichotomy of rich and poor countries would be mitigated. Much of the organisation of international development tends, however, to perpetuate polarisation. UNCTAD tends to confront the O.E.C.D., and inside the international organisations similar battle lines are drawn which may in the future be difficult to cross, no matter what the record of development of individual countries.

VI. DOES THE GAP ITSELF IMPEDE DEVELOPMENT?

Apart from its political and moral implications, does the gap itself have purely economic consequences? If the economic disparity affects the growth chances of the developing countries unfavourably and perhaps also enhances those of the already rich, then poor and rich will tend to grow further apart.

It is clear for anyone to see that economic growth has an uneven impact on regions in one and the same country. It is easy to enumerate a number of positive and negative effects that growth in one region is likely to have on another. Among the positive ones are the stimulation of exports, the appearance of cheaper imports, the outflow of surplus labour. Among the negative ones – Myrdal's 'backwash' – may be the displacement of traditional exports and even of production for local use, depopulation and selective emigration. Whether positive or negative effects will predominate will depend on too many 'structural' factors for even a general presumption.

In the case of the developing countries, a number of unfavourable consequences of the disparity are often cited as making development more difficult for them than it would be in the absence of the much richer countries. But most such suggestions are ambiguous, and the disadvantages, while real enough, are only the back side of equally real advantages.

Technology is a case in point. The labour-saving technology of the West, with its large economies of scale, is held responsible for its part in the employment problem of L.D.C.s. There is much to blame in the inappropriate choice of technology in L.D.C.s but it is difficult to accept the view that a widening of the spectrum of technological possibilities could in itself be detrimental. It would in fact seem clear that the large reservoir of technological knowledge available today is basically an enormous asset from which L.D.C.s have also drawn considerable benefits.

Public health has undoubtedly played a major part in precipitating the population explosion, but it is rash to condemn it on that account. The direct gains in well-being which are reflected in longer life-expectancy well bear comparison, as contributions to welfare, with sizeable economic gains. It is difficult to establish a trade-off between the two. In fact, health-improvements *per se* undoubtedly contribute to productivity, and the detrimental effects of rapid population growth are not as self-evident as many schematic calculations suggest.

The brain drain from developing countries is another backwash effect, but closer scrutiny suggests that behind the emigration of professionals usually lies a lack of employment opportunities for the relevant categories of manpower rather than a mere pull of higher wage levels. In a more open world than ours, should not the proper remedy for many of the problems of L.D.C.s be greater possibilities of outmigration rather than fewer?

The 'demonstration effect' of Western consumption patterns, emanating from much higher income levels, is sometimes denounced for its tendency to displace traditional needs which might be more easily satisfied. This criticism would often seem to be more properly directed against excessively unequal patterns of income distribution. In the matter of consumer goods for mass consumption, the process of growth has always involved changes of the items which enter the consumer's basket, and to complain of products which find wide acceptance among consumers in L.D.C.s requires a vision of a pattern of development in which consumer wants are not taken very seriously.

It is probably in the fields of trade that disadvantages of the weaker and poorer partners have most often been claimed – naturally so, as this is where direct transactions are involved. It would lead too far afield to summarise all the suggested drawbacks of the situation of the L.D.C.s as trading partners. One implication of the gap is cheap labour cost, unless the efficiency of labour is so low as to offset the wage differential. Protectionist practice in industrialised countries tends to obstruct this and other advantages when domestic industries are seriously embarrassed by L.D.C. competition. But this is hardly a consequence of the gap. Protectionist countries tend to resort to protectionism against all comers. And even though protectionism in some cases renders access to the markets of rich countries more difficult, it does not eliminate it, and the large and dynamic markets of industrial countries have been indispensable to the impressive record of world trade which has benefited L.D.C.s although their share has fallen as a result of the predominance of traditional products.

In sum, there can be no clear verdict against the gap. The presence of the industrialised countries is a challenge to the leadership of the developing world which may seem frustratingly great, far greater than that which in the past was confronted by reformist governments in Prussia, Japan and elsewhere. The magnetic pull exerted by the example of the richer countries seems indisputable, even though it may be deplored by social critics inside these countries themselves. The difficulties involved in telescoping vast social and economic change are obvious – but that the gap itself should on balance add to these difficulties seems an extravagant idea.

VII. THE POWER GAP

The great divide among nations is one of the facts which basically affects the modern view of the world. The awakening to this fact has been as sudden as the great wave of colonial emancipation which more than any other factor gave rise to the new awareness of world poverty. The attainment of *égalité de droit* has always preceded *égalité de fait*. In the suddenness of the transformation there has been an understandable tendency to invest the economic gap with a profound significance in virtually all respects. I have tried to suggest why some of these arguments seem dubious, inconsistent or fanciful.

Indisputably, however, the gap is directly pertinent to the distribution of power in the world. I would submit that this, rather than the distribution of amenities, is at the heart of the problem. Power is a nebulous term and economists widely seek to eschew it. But when the investments, trade, and even aid of the industrialised countries are branded as neo-colonialist this is not to be waived aside. In dealings between rich and poor countries, economic power is an omnipresent reality. Even if it is not abused by design or thoughtlessness, it colours the relationship in innumerable ways. It stems from inequalities among nations rather than among individuals. In negotiations the representative of an Asian country may well be a richer man than the official from an industrialised country in West or East. But the arrogance of power, and the resentment, will be dictated by G.N.P. or even G.N.P. per head.

I am not capable of judging whether this source of tension and irritation is a genuine threat to the viability of the international system of states, or whether it is a more serious problem than the conflicts between nations with superior power. But at any rate it does not make for a healthy international community, and the collaborative effort to reduce the economic distance between nations imposes itself as an inescapable attempt to make the world less imperfect.

3 The Contemporary Consequences of the Gap

Oktay Yenal

ROBERT COLLEGE, ISTANBUL, TURKEY

I. THE EMERGENCE OF THE GAP

Throughout the settled history of mankind, riches and poverty have existed as the twin fates not only of individuals, but also of societies whether defined as tribes or organised as states. But whilst the differences of well-being among the individuals or the families in a country have, for centuries, posed problems for analysis and public policy, the differences of living standards among the various regions of the world have not been taken up as a major issue either of international policy or of economic thought until recent times. It is only in the last two decades that the difference of prosperity between the rich and the poor countries, now called the gap, has attracted increasing attention of both the policy makers and the thinkers. Indeed it is no exaggeration to say that the gap which is the concern of international economics and politics *par excellence* nowadays was hardly noticed during the century before the Second World War although it was there for anybody who had an eye for it. This paper, after referring to the change of world political and intellectual attitude towards the difference in living standards between the rich and the poor regions, will attempt to review the main consequences that the large or increasing gap, or the awareness of it, has on international relations – political and economic – and on the development problems and prospects of the poor countries.

History abounds with accounts of settlements coinciding in time and proximate in space which varied in degrees of prosperity; but never before had the differences in amenities of life approached the scale of the present gap, the origin of which may be traced back to the aftermath of the Industrial Revolution. Indeed in terms of the per capita income levels, the experience of Western Europe and North America during the last century and more is unique. Although the beginnings of the innovations and organisational changes referred to as the industrial revolution were already in the making during the 18th century, it was only during the first half of the 19th that the full impact of the new technology became evident on the productive capacity and the living standards of what are now industrialised countries. By 1850 the differential between the rich and the poor lands had already reached a significant level [1]. Setting a beginning date as such is not to ignore the part played by the evolution of the institutions and the formation of attitudes through the previous ages which had prepared the climate for the big leap forward. What is stressed is the fact not always fully appreciated that the gap we are discussing has a history of little more than a century.

To our generation, with its limited historical perspective, the fact that the gap between the rich and the poor countries, as we know it, has a short past may come as a surprise. But to a generation with pretensions of high moral and ethical norms, it may come as a shock to see how little awareness of this gap as a problem existed until recently. The lack of seeing the gap as a problem was the result of not being concerned with the economic development of what were called the 'backward' regions, which in turn was the natural consequence of the colonial set-up in the 19th century – a world divided into a small developed block of independent states and a large backward block of dependent regions. This is, of course, an oversimplification. There were big states which were independent and yet poor compared with the Western countries. In Europe and Asia, Russia was lagging behind, and the Ottoman Empire had already lagged behind. In the Far East, Japan and China had closed themselves to the impact of the Western industrial system. But the relative poverty of these states as well as those of the colonies was viewed, both within and without, more as an issue of political development than as a case in economic progress. The focus of attention was on faulty political systems, inefficient administrations and peoples which were still in their pre-civilised state. The dichotomy centred on civilised *v.* barbaric. In other words, the gap was perceived more as a political gap or a civilisation gap than as an economic gap. This is reflected in the writings of John Stuart Mill where he speaks of 'those backward states of society in which the race itself may be considered as in its nonage' [2].

II. AWARENESS OF THE GAP

We now live in an age when the gap between the rich and the poor regions of the world has reached unprecedented proportions. Furthermore, the awareness of the size and the trend of the gap is very much in the consciousness of not only the politicians and the social scientists, but also of the masses both better and worse off. This awareness is mostly the result of backward regions becoming independent, although the improved techniques in measuring economic well-being and the spread of information through better communications have also contributed to it. As Professor Robbins points out, the concern with economic development has always been closely related with the emergence of national states:

It was the rise of the nation state which gave the impulse to the conception of economic development as a desirable objective of policy.

Under the Roman Empire the area of administration was so vast, under feudalism the concentration of power so feeble, that the idea of policies deliberately adopted to bring about or facilitate economic change cannot readily have suggested itself to the speculative intelligence. But the emergence of the national unit, with all that that has implied for the consolidation of the Curse of Babel and the perpetuation of international anarchy, did mean that there had emerged a definite forum for the consideration of policy [3].

Extending the same observation it can be argued that there was not much international concern for the development of the 'backward' regions until the backward regions started becoming politically independent entities and were promoted, as it were, to the status of 'underdeveloped' countries – a term which implied a hope as well as the gap.

The gap and the awareness of it is no doubt at the root of the present international tensions as well as being the source of frustrations internal to the poor states. However, particularly in accounting for the latter difficulties, it is important at the outset to draw a distinction between the consequences of the large or the growing gap and the problems arising from the efforts of the poor countries to develop. The process of development and the repercussions of the prosperity differentials among nations are related in many ways as will be discussed at length below. The urge to move to higher living standards is itself usually the outcome of nations becoming gap-conscious. And the gap is likely to have significant effects, positive or negative, upon the processes that are vehicles to development. But given the will of a country, or the decision of its rulers, to achieve faster rates of progress, stresses and strains appear in the society irrespective of whether there exist rich neighbours around, or whether the income differential between the more and the less prosperous neighbours is growing. Development is a painful process involving change and sacrifice, and development policy issues can easily lead to controversy and strife even if not coupled with the added complication of rich neighbours never tiring of getting richer. However not only are some of these problems magnified by the growing gap, but new factors also enter the scene.

III. DOES THE GAP PUT POOR COUNTRIES AT A COMPETITIVE DISADVANTAGE?

One major characteristic of the international relations between the rich and the poor countries in recent decades has been the extensive use of economic means for political ends. This has not been limited to what is sometimes referred to as 'aid-diplomacy' alone but to almost all the spheres of economic or social activity. Disputes that were in the past resolved in the military field or through the mechanism of alliances are now finding their expression in the economic threats and promises concerning mainly international economic flows of trade, aid and capital. The same development in world politics that led to the collapse of the colonial empires and to the birth of the new nations – a move towards rule by consent and away from rule by force – has led to the present emphasis on economic factors and de-emphasis on military strength. On the other hand it is the existence of the large gap which enables the rich countries to influence poor nations through economic relations. At the risk of over-simplification, it can be argued that the sequence of causation in the classical definition of 'imperialism' has been reversed. Instead of the economic motives determining the politics of the big powers as was suggested in the past, we now have a situation where the political considerations are shaping the style of economic relations between the rich and poor countries. It is this process which comes nearest to the current definitions of neo-colonialism or neo-imperialism.

The appearance or the awareness of the gap between the rich and the poor nations has coincided with the growing pessimism in theory regarding the efficacy of natural market forces between the nations – i.e. economic transactions and flows – in narrowing the gap. In a dynamic setting not much faith is bestowed on the comparative advantage mechanism to perform this function no matter what the theoretical implications of the factor equalisation theorem and the Heckscher-Ohlin model are. Even in a dynamic setting, the earlier hopes of the economists based on right or wrong interpretations of the 19th century experience of foreign trade acting as an 'engine of growth' have, it seems, faded away [4]. However, there is some confusion as to whether this is an analytical or an empirical inference – and this makes an important difference. The inability of the market forces to spread prosperity is usually presented as an empirical evidence, in which case a legitimate question is to what extent the obstacles put in the way of the natural market forces have been responsible for this inertia. In other words, the issue of how the natural market flows affect the relative growth rates and the issue of the extent to which these market forces are allowed to function are two separate questions [5].

Whether in actual fact the existence of a wide gap in income levels between countries will put the poorer at the mercy of the richer or not, the fear of this happening was probably one of the factors which have led to extensive advocacy and practice of protectionism and central planning in the underdeveloped world. Nor have the rich countries refrained from putting barriers on the channels of international flows at their end. Whatever dynamic forces trade and other flows might have, these forces were in a sense paralysed in degrees by these administrative interferences. Therefore if the consciousness of the gap has brought any new pattern into the international trade flows, it has been in the direction of obstructing or interfering with these flows. It is conceivable that some of the interferences in the international transactions by the poor countries had a favourable effect on their industrialisation process or on the share of their gains from trade. But taking an overall view, it seems likely that the barriers to the movements of goods, capital and labour force have reduced the effectiveness of the international flows as a mechanism of transmitting growth without, however, actually reducing the dependence of the poor countries on foreign goods and services. The growing trade gap as manifested in the growing *ex ante* deficit of most developing countries is evidence of this.

IV. INTERNATIONAL FLOWS AND THE GAP

One novelty, perhaps the only one in the area of international flows, has been the unilateral transfers to the poor countries in the form of government assistance or credits through the international organisations during the last two decades. For the first time in history large sums of money were given by the rich countries as grants or credits at concessionary terms to the independent underdeveloped countries. However, although the magnitude of this kind of transfer was unprecedented in history, it was not large in terms of the prosperity of the donors, nor was it sufficient with respect to the needs of the recipients to have a significant overall impact. Unfortunately the total of such transfers is now on a declining trend. What is perhaps more important is that the attempts from various circles to formulate and organise a worldwide co-ordinated programme of soft capital transfers to the underdeveloped world has not met with success. The responsibility for this lies at the threshold of the governments of the big powers who, jealous of their contributions and caught in their short-sightedness, are keen to continue to use aid flows as a lever for their political objectives. It remains a sad fact that no matter how much humanitarian sympathy might lie at the root of the donations by the taxpayers of the rich nations, their governments would not live up to the challenge of participating in multilateral aid programmes whose main objective would be to reduce the gap. And the result has been a growing disillusionment on the part of all concerned.

Whereas the market-oriented flows or the policy-determined transfers have been declining or at least stagnating, a vague category which can be called the knowledge flow, including technology, know-how, information or even culture has been jumping over the gap at high speeds towards the poor countries as a result of the communications revolution. It is this flow which seems to have made the most profound impact on the economic processes, certainly much more than the other more tangible flows mentioned above. But the flow of information, whether embodied in the imported commodities or disseminated through the news media, is also influencing the values, ethics and æsthetics in the poor countries. Here lies the chief impact of the gap.

As mentioned above, the objective of development is related to the gap in the sense that the urge to develop is the result of knowing about the more prosperous countries. The poor people living a life of deprivation and misery do not have to know about the luxuries of life in the rich countries to feel frustrated. Pockets of riches that exist in all societies are enough to create dissatisfaction in the have-nots. But the size of the gap between the two groups of nations dramatises the situation mainly for the intelligentsia and the governments of the poor states who are eager to move their countries as rapidly as possible out of poverty. And the continuous technical progress with the seemingly limitless growth of prosperity in the rich nations adds another dimension to the frustrations of the poor countries. This is the urge for *relative* development, that is, catching up with the developed countries. In other words the question centres on what the race is for. Is the race for arriving at a decent minimum standard of living, or achieving a level at which the economy gains momentum, or is this a race just for the sake of racing?

Flow of information to the poor regions on the ways man controls his environment has certainly facilitated economic development in the under-developed countries. The impact of modern technology on easing the toil and trouble of the poor may be even larger than is usually reflected in the quantitative measurements. Furthermore, the positive contributions of some advanced research and technology may actually be greater in the deprived regions. Methods of providing cheap proteins or new varieties of seeds which have only a marginal effect in the rich countries make a difference between starvation and adequate nutrition for the poor. In this sense the progress of the developed nations would be expected to enhance the prosperity of the poor countries to the extent that this progress leads to the advancement of science and technology which can be used to alleviate poverty. But these are the products of progress in technology *per se* and not the result of a widening gap.

V. MEDICAL KNOWLEDGE, POPULATION GROWTH AND THE GAP

Almost all these favourable developments are in danger of being wiped out by another impact of the knowledge flow. I am referring to the precedence in time of the discoveries in medicine and improvements in sanitation within easy access of the poor countries, leading to the reduction of death rates before the fertility rates in these countries started to decline in their natural course, or before the easy and cheap methods of birth control were available and could be widely applied in the underdeveloped regions. Thus the progress in medicine and sanitation which was surely

D

a blessing when we are concerned with the individuals, has led to the greatest social problem of our day, namely the population explosion. As Toynbee says, 'It threatens to divide mankind into two camps: a majority camp of increasingly resentful have-nots and a minority camp of increasingly uneasy haves' [6].

Although in recent years significant advances have been accomplished in birth control methods, the application of these technologies in the poor regions has not approached by any means the spectacular success that was achieved with preventive medicine and improved sanitation methods during the last two or three decades. This is understandable. The dilemma lies in the fact that, contrary to the case of preserving life, birth control is an activity with a social benefit significantly above the private benefit, which may even be negative. In other words the value attached by the individuals to reducing the number of their offspring may be lower than the value of birth control to the society. But the extent of the social benefit is not always fully appreciated by the authorities whose business it is to be concerned about social benefits. Even when the social benefit is appreciated, the application of birth control methods involves heavy subsidies to compensate for the difference between social and individual benefits, and to the extent the private benefits are negative, the subsidy has to be on an individual basis – which makes the implementation of these policies very difficult.

VI. DEMONSTRATION EFFECTS

The most direct link between the gap and the development opportunities of the poor countries can be found in the international version of the demonstration effect argument which, at one stage, was one of the main tenets of the vicious circle theorems. Nurkse summarised the argument as follows:

> A high income and consumption level in an advanced country can do harm in that it tends to reduce the domestic means of capital formation in the underdeveloped countries; it puts extra pressure on countries with a relatively low income to spend a high proportion of it [7].

Presented in this way, an important negative link is suggested between the gap and the development opportunities of the poor, the gap causing the widening of the gap. On *a priori* grounds it is not clear that the knowledge about higher standards will lead to a higher consumption level because there is no reason why individuals will want to maximise their present consumption at the cost of forgoing investment – that is higher income flows in future. They may rather maximise their income streams over a period of time unless they have very short time horizons. As pointed out by Nathan Rosenberg, the low level of savings ratios in the underdeveloped countries may be due more to lack of investment opportunities [8]. Indeed poor countries with their underdeveloped financial systems offer very limited opportunities to small savers who are not entrepreneurs at the same time. An interesting case of how incentives can make a difference is provided by the behaviour of the Turkish workers in Germany who continue to live probably even below what would have been their standards in Turkey just for the sake of saving as much as they can, being well aware of the advantages that their savings in foreign exchange will entitle them to.

It is not possible to make a strong case for the demonstration effect hypothesis in the case of public current expenditures either. Again in Nurkse's words, the effect is suggested as follows:

> The international disparities can inhibit not only voluntary private saving but also the use of public finance as an instrument of capital formation [9].

Whether the level of public consumption in the poor countries is high or low is difficult to say in the absence of a norm. It can perhaps be argued that the average or the marginal propensity to consume in the public sector of some underdeveloped countries is high. However, on closer examination, this may turn out to be due to excessive or increasing number of government employees than be the result of high or increasing salaries. On the contrary, in most of these countries the earnings in the public sector lag behind the pays in the private sector. Since overemployment or disguised unemployment in the public sector cannot be considered a consequence of the demonstration effect, the existence of rich neighbours is not enough to explain this phenomenon directly. One can, of course, cite examples of large expenditures on luxury buildings and public works. But these should more appropriately be viewed as investments rather than as consumption.

In fact the waste incurred by imitating the *investment* pattern of the rich witnessed in many poor nations, in both the private and the public sector, is possibly far in excess of the loss incurred by the imitation of rich men's *consumption* habits. It is interesting to observe the case of public buildings where huge fortunes are spent for the capital outlay but very little is provided for maintenance. The desires of the governments of the underdeveloped countries to be like their rich neighbours lead them to imitate the production methods of the richer economies. This desire is translated into action either through the direct economic activities of the public sector or through the policies which shape the allocation of resources in the private sector and is reflected in the interferences of the governments in investment decisions and in the relative prices (including the exchange rate, the interest rate and the wage rate). It can be argued that the planning strategies have more often than not been based upon imitation of developed economies. Thus development planning becomes an exercise in technocratic imitation, usually carried out by the engineers or bureaucrats with little respect for the economic analysis of the situations. To what extent this has been a wise strategy cannot be resolved in any simple manner. However it remains a fact that many burning issues of development such as emphasis on industrialisation at the cost of neglecting agriculture, import substitutions and growing unemployment have part of their origins in the policy makers imitating the structures, products and technologies of the richer countries.

VII. THE LONG-TERM OUTLOOK

It seems that the gap has not set in motion any significant equilibriating mechanism in terms of economic forces; on the contrary, it may have affected the growth opportunities of some regions adversely. Thus the gap has, in a sense, squeezed the poor nations between rising expectations and limited or, in some cases, narrowing means. In the words of the porter in *Macbeth*, 'It provokes the desire, but takes away the performance'. Although most underdeveloped countries are showing signs of modest economic growth in terms of per capita incomes, one margin that is getting narrower, particularly under the pressure of the population explosion, is the time for orderly change. Caught in this dilemma, most nations of the world inhabited by two-thirds of its population, are forced to imitate – the stimulus for imitation itself being a consequence of the knowledge flows. But international imitation is a painful process, not just limited to a narrow definition of technology but penetrating into every cell of human life. As a result of this imitative change the poor societies are being shaken to their roots, producing tensions of a social and political nature.

This turbulence has both short- and long-term implications. In the short run even the nationhood of some poor countries is threatened. In the vocabulary of political scientists, differentiation in the underdeveloped countries meaning 'the establishment of more specialised and more autonomous social units' has probably become a rapid process under the impact of the institutions and ideas from the developed countries, before the economic capacity is ready to work out integrative solutions. The problems are aggravated and an orderly change is difficult when a cushion of prosperity is missing. As the Turks say, one grain of prosperity conceals a thousand vices. Again we see the dilemma of poor societies over-anxious for centralist action just when the integrated authority for this type of action is getting weaker, thus preparing the ground for political crises and social upheaval.

The frustration created by the gap also has implications, in a longer perspective, on the development of cultures and civilisations. Three-quarters of the world population in their rush for survival are driven to choose between the two 'model' societies. There seems to be no time to embark upon new experiments. The delight and the excitement of trying new horizons is gone; the dull atmosphere of imitating technologies, and through this, imitating cultures is here with us to stay. Whether the poor nations will eventually become 'successful' replicas of the Western countries or the Socialist countries remains to be seen. But not much hope is in store for the development of their own civilisation and cultures.

Forty years ago Keynes could be optimistic even in the midst of depression in describing the prospects for the grandchildren of his generation in the following terms:

> The course of affairs will simply be that there will be ever larger and larger classes and groups of people from whom problems of economic necessity have been practically removed. The critical difference will be realised when this condition has become so general that the nature of men's duty to one's neighbour is changed. For it will remain reasonable to be economically purposive for others after it has ceased to be purposive for oneself' [10].

In the time that has elapsed since Keynes wrote, the world has probably moved further away from the target of economic bliss he had in mind. This is so not only because there has been a tremendous increase in the size of the economically deprived people, but also because no change of attitude is discernible in the behaviour of prospering classes to justify Keynes' hope in human nature. If his hopes were to come true there would not be a problem of the gap, but merely an issue of development aiming at providing a decent living standard for the poor of the world. In the words of John Stuart Mill, ideal state of economic development would be 'that which while no one is poor, no one desires to be richer, nor has any reason to fear being thrust back, by the efforts of others to push themselves forward' [11]. But in the present political atmosphere and given the ethics of our day, the fear of being thrust back is very much with everybody. Thus the gap is an issue in relative development, and the race goes on with increasing blindness just because others are racing too.

REFERENCES

[1] J. Patel, 'World Economy in Transition (1850–2060)' in *Socialism, Capitalism and Economic Growth* (Cambridge, England, 1967).
[2] J. S. Mill, *On Liberty*, p. 13.
[3] Lord Robbins, *The Theory of Economic Development* (New York, 1968), p. 158.
[4] Ragnar Nurkse, *Equilibrium and Growth in the World Economy* (Cambridge, Mass.), 1961.
    Gunnar Myrdal, *Rich Lands and Poor* (New York, 1957).

John Hicks, 'National Economic Development in the International Setting', in *Essays in World Economics* (London, 1959).

[5] H. G. Johnson, *Economic Policies Towards Less Developed Countries* (New York, 1967), pp. 49–50.

[6] Arnold Toynbee, 'The Menace of Population', in *Our Crowded Planet*, edited by F. Osborn (New York, 1962), p. 136.

[7] Ragnar Nurkse, *Problems of Capital Formation in Underdeveloped Countries* (Oxford, 1953), p. 68.

[8] Nathan Rosenberg, 'Capital Formation in Underdeveloped Countries', *American Economic Review*, vol. 1, no. 4 (Sept. 1960).

[9] Ragnar Nurkse, *Problems of Capital Formation in Underdeveloped Countries*, *op. cit.*, p. 70.

[10] J. M. Keynes, 'Economic Possibilities for our Grandchildren', in *Essays in Persuasion* (London, 1931).

[11] J. S. Mill, *Principles of Political Economy*, pp. 753–4.

Discussion of Papers by
Goran Ohlin and Oktay Yenal

Professor Hicks introduced both papers. He said that it was difficult to summarise these two (to him very congenial) papers. For they covered (as they were
bound to do) an enormous field; they could not possibly cover it in any but a
very summary fashion. When one tried to summarise one found oneself left with
nothing but headlines to newspaper articles. He did not blame the authors for
this. 'Only a fool could presume to know the consequences of the gap as it
exists and is perceived today', said Professor Ohlin. Professor Hicks quite
agreed.

He therefore proposed to do no more than mention a few particular points
which we might usefully discuss, though they might not be closely connected
with one another.

One point which we could hardly avoid, though we might not be very fitted to
discuss it, was the historical origin of the gap we were discussing. Professor
Ohlin talked about an economic superiority of the 'West' going back to the time
of the Crusades; Professor Yenal seemed to think it went back only to the Industrial Revolution (say 1800). His own impression was that there were great
inequalities between nations well before the latter date. He would hazard the
guess that the real income of a considerable fraction of the population (perhaps
the upper quarter) would even in 1750 have been higher in England, Holland
and Switzerland than in France or Italy; and far higher in Japan than in India.
But of course it was true that these differences were not changing, as they had now
come to change; and that they were not brought to people's attention, so that
little was known about them. What was known was very often wrong. When the
Europeans first went to India they thought that it was a rich country, a dazzlingly
rich country. Only when they took over responsibility for ruling it did they find
out how wrong they were.

Second, he would further maintain that these initial inequalities were very
important in explaining what had happened since. For (as had been observed in
several of the papers) the initial stages of industrialisation, when they could not
be financed by foreign borrowing, were a terrible strain. It was much easier for a
country which was initially wealthy to take that strain. This is what Sir Arthur
Lewis seemed to him to have overlooked in his picture of the developed countries
sinking under the sea!

Third, he would turn to the distinction, which seemed to emerge in both of
the papers, between the effects of the actual differences in growth rates and the
effects of the knowledge that they existed. There was a tendency to think of the
effects of this knowledge as being wholly bad – 'demonstration effects' and so on.
Of course, the existence of *bad* demonstration effects must be admitted; he liked
Professor Yenal's insistence that they were to be found in the public as well as in
the private sector. Also, they were important in investment as well as in consumption; which linked on to the wise remark of Professor Kuznets about the
inadequacy of our Keynesian concepts to deal with these things. But were we
really to say that the effect of the knowledge of what was going on elsewhere was
wholly bad? He would have thought that there were many 'less-developed

countries' which would have had no development at all had it not been for such emulation.

In conclusion, he liked Professor Yenal's method of treating the population problem in Pigouvian terms – as a difference between marginal social and marginal private product. He would like to suggest one practical conclusion which seemed to follow from it. An effective way to control the population explosion would be to provide all children with expensive school meals – to be paid for by their parents.

Professor Ghai also commented on the paper by Professor Yenal. The main points of the paper could be summarised quite simply; the gap between rich and poor countries was a relatively modern phenomenon – going back about a hundred years. But consciousness of the gap was an even more recent phenomenon, dating back no more than a couple of decades. The existence of an awareness of the gap had had profound and manifold consequences, both at the national and at the international level.

The perception of the gap was at the root of the present international tensions. At the national level it had influenced the economic organisation and policy of developing countries towards central planning and protectionism. Through imitation of rich countries the gap was partly responsible in L.D.C.s for wasteful policies of industrialisation, import substitution and the neglect of agriculture. Although as modern technology had developed in advanced countries it had brought many benefits to less developed ones, it had not been without major drawbacks, principally in contributing to the population explosion. While the adverse consequences of the international demonstration effect as it operated on savings and expenditure in the developing countries had perhaps been exaggerated in the literature, its effects on the pattern of investment might be more serious but had been largely neglected. Professor Yenal did not draw up a balance sheet of the implications of the gap for the development of poor countries, but it seemed that he regarded it as having a net adverse effect.

One difficulty in writing on this kind of subject lay in deciding which developments in the poor countries one should attribute to the existence of the gap. If one were not careful it was easy to end up by attributing everything in underdeveloped countries to it. His basic reaction to the paper was that Professor Yenal attributed some consequences to the gap which he himself would not regard as in any sense specially dependent on it; yet there were other consequences which seemed much more important but which were not brought out sufficiently in the paper.

For example, Professor Yenal wrote that 'the gap and the awareness of it is no doubt at the root of international tensions'. Neither he nor Professor Yenal was an expert on international politics, but it was clear that inernational tensions and wars were the outcome of conflicts of national interest and ambition; that they had existed from time immemorial and would no doubt continue indefinitely. While the gap might have had some impact on the nature and frequency of such tensions, it seemed more likely that they were, in the main, independent of it. Similarly Professor Yenal attributed much internal tension in developing countries to awareness of the gap. While it might have contributed to this, it seemed more likely that the causes of unrest and turbulence in developing countries were very complex, and were to be sought much more in ethnic, tribal, linguistic and other factors. They might also depend on lack of national unity, on corruption, on wasteful and extravagant expenditure by governments, etc., rather than on the existence and perception of the gap.

Finally, he felt that Professor Yenal exaggerated the importance of the gap between rich and poor countries, when he linked the gap with the growth of central planning, protectionism and industrialisation in poor countries. The consequences of the gap between rich and poor nations that impressed him most were quite different. Although they were touched upon in Professor Yenal's paper, they were nowhere brought out sufficiently. They arose from the fact that, because of the dominance of rich countries in the world, there was a continuous and accelerating transfer of product, technology, institutions and attitudes – indeed a whole way of life – from rich to poor countries. The changes that took place in rich countries – whether in the form of new technology, new products, improvement of old products or indeed different kinds of social organisation – reflected a response to the special needs and problems of these countries. Many forces in the modern world resulted in the rapid transmission of such innovations to developing countries.

It did not require much imagination to see that when the innovations were transplanted to developing countries, with quite different economic structures and lines of development, it would be pure accident if they proved beneficial. Economists had, in the past, concentrated their attention on only a few such transfers – those of technology, patterns of consumption and income distribution. But the impact of developments in rich countries on poor countries was much deeper and wider. Indeed the extent of dependence was frightening to contemplate. With the exception of basic foodstuffs, the quality and type of product consumed in poor countries was largely determined by rich countries. The schools, colleges and universities their citizens went to were imported from advanced countries; the films and television programmes they watched were all imported too. It was hardly surprising therefore that in most cases the products produced in developing countries, the technologies used and the education they gave, were largely irrelevant to their needs. Caught in a situation where ways of life appropriate to a completely different and alien socio-economic structure were being imposed on them by powerful forces, the developing countries had two options – apart, of course, from doing nothing. They could either seal themselves off from the rest of the world: or they could learn to innovate; to adapt transplanted products, technologies and institutions in the light of their own needs; to select and reject. The former option had been taken by China, and a few small countries like Burma had attempted to do the same. For the overwhelming majority of L.D.C.s this was not a genuine option at all. They could not shut themselves off from the rest of the world without inflicting incalculable injury on themselves. Their only escape from a world dominated by rich countries, where they were passive recipients of alien and largely irrelevant institutions, products, technologies, etc., was to develop a capacity to innovate, to adapt, to select and to reject. But the absence of this very capability was the hallmark of underdevelopment.

Professor Robinson said that the discussion of when the gap emerged went back to the kind of issues raised in the I.E.A. conference at Konstanz in 1960, when there was a good deal of discussion of Professor Rostow's ideas about why

D 2

particular countries 'took off' at particular times. Why did not some underdeveloped countries 'take off' earlier? Why did the Indian railway age, when
ports and other infrastructure were also developed, not lead to a take-off? Why
had Brazil taken off so late?

This was a separate question from that raised in Professor Yenal's paper on
the relations of the developed to the underdeveloped world, and how relationships
between the two inhibited or favoured growth in underdeveloped countries.

Professor Kuznets said that, on the historical issue, he thought that the
historical perspective should be explored for the emergence of consciousness of
the gap as well. The importance of such consciousness was noted in both papers.
On the historical origins, quantitative records suggested that most developed
countries (Western Europe and its overseas offshoots such as U.S.A., Canada,
Australia and New Zealand, but excluding South Africa) had a product per
head in the late 18th and early 19th century appreciably higher than at present in
the less developed parts of the world. Currently we said that if a country had a
G.D.P. per capita of less than $120 it should be classified as less developed.
Product per head in the developed countries of Europe had been $200 to $300
per head even before modern economic growth began (in the late 18th century
in Great Britain; the first quarter of the 19th century in France and somewhat
later in other Western European countries). In the overseas offshoots it was
even higher (particularly in Australia, which in the 1890s had the highest income per head in the world). The difficulty in going further back was the lack of
statistics. One would like to know a good deal about China and India in the
later 18th century, but one did not. His guess was that Europe had a higher
per capita product by the 18th and perhaps by mid-17th centuries.

There was an interesting discussion in Europe in the second half of the 18th
century about all this – discussions of the Ancients versus the Moderns, and of
the role of Chinese emperors as benign monarchs whose intelligence should be
emulated. The intellectual leaders of Europe at that time could seriously debate
whether standards of economic performance in advanced Europe of the time
(England, Holland and France) was any higher than in the golden age of an-
tiquity. Much of the discussion was politically motivated and biased by the in-
tention to criticise the existing European regimes for their wastefulness. It was
therefore natural that the discussion would minimise current achievements.
However, the fact that serious discussion of the question did take place showed
how limited economic attainment must have looked in those early days. Only
the critical Hume could say that the discussion was based on unsound data and
led to highly dubious conclusions.

We had to remember that, except for Japan, the initial level from which the
presently-developed countries began their modern economic growth and industrialisation was two to three times as high as the *present* level in the populous
less developed countries of Asia (and probably of most of Africa). At the same
time, agriculture in these countries was much more effective than in the less
developed countries of Asia and Africa today. But we now have new technologies and should not draw the wrong conclusions from this very low starting
point in many of the less developed countries today.

As to why the gap became the focus of attention, perhaps this was because of
a change in view of the basic sources of modern economic growth. A clear

example of this change was the Point Four Declaration of President Truman twenty years ago. It reflected a theory that economic growth depended on knowledge more than on material resources; and it suggested that by transferring knowledge and technology, sharing it, and with only marginal transfers of material capital, one could overcome the existing economic backwardness in a large part of the world. This was an over-simplified view, because the transfer and application of knowledge and know-how were not that simple; indeed, the results were disappointing. Nevertheless if one accepted the view that the main source of economic growth was the rapid accumulation and application of useful knowledge, the gap led to a problem. If the only thing a country needed to do was to draw on the world's stock of knowledge, why did three-quarters of the world fail to do so? If there had been more emphasis on natural resources or capital accumulation, there would have been less of a puzzle.

The significance of the gap now was that it represented a huge loss of potential output and welfare, because less developed countries, for one reason or another, could not use effectively their resources, particularly human resources. In the old days the developed countries were much more interested in the natural resources of the less developed countries. Now with more interest in the human resources, the loss of welfare and output was felt more keenly.

With national independence the gap among national units had become of concern both as an intellectual puzzle and as a practical problem in loss of welfare and in political weakness.

Professor Findlay wondered whether the growth of the West had become parasitic on the East at some stage. Professor Ohlin argued that the development of the West was basically autonomous, and he agreed. However, since the conference was in a historical mood, he would go deeper. Perhaps the Marxists could expand on this idea, because Marx had the theory of primitive socialist accumulation. During the period in the West between the Middle Ages and the Industrial Revolution, this had played a significant role and had led to later developments. Most Western economists would dismiss this idea, but the Industrial Revolution was based very much on cotton, and so on slavery. Yet most people would say that the main determinant was technological. It was hard to see how primitive accumulation itself lead to increased knowledge and to technological change. Perhaps the Western countries had needed the resources implied by primitive accumulation in order to develop technology and knowledge.

Professor Ranis recalled that Professor Kuznets had asked what had gone wrong with the Point Four philosophy; he deserved an answer. Professor Ohlin had said that perhaps the existence of the underdeveloped countries was not important to the development of the richer countries, which would have gone on independently. Less had been said about the more important question of the relationship between developed and underdeveloped countries today. It might help to examine the relationships in the colonial period.

Was the growth of the advanced countries something which could have taken place in any case, developing from local changes, but which was interrupted by the colonial pattern? The effect of the demand for raw materials had been mentioned. More important, perhaps, was the net effect of colonial intervention on the gradual development of a pattern of trade and investment. With colonialism there were far more bilateral arrangements. Had a process of regional, inter-regional and international trade been developing, which was interrupted by colonialism? For example, had the advent of colonial countries inhibited the development of domestic industry in underdeveloped countries?

This suggested the pessimistic conclusion that what had happened in the 19th century was not necessarily true any longer. Perhaps we should think in terms of two phases. First there was the colonial phase. Second, there was national development, mainly since 1945, where attempts were made to alter the colonial pattern to allow national development. Largely autarchic methods were used, and there had been no attempt to bring about national development by using 19th-century tools, not for colonial but for national development. In so far as attempts had been made, which was not very much, the results suggested that growth could be quite rapid and the transfer of knowledge quite successful. However, this required a number of changes. All countries would have to participate in the world economy but without colonial methods and consequences.

Professor Horvat spoke of the historical origins of the gap. He said that as economists we tended to generalise because this was the only way the science progressed. However, history was not orderly. There were many fortuitous and haphazard events. If the conference were being held 1,500 kilometres farther south, on Lake Ohrid, we should be in a poor part of Yugoslavia which had one-fifth of the income per head in Bled. Yet around the 10th century this had been a highly developed region, with high standards of craftsmanship, the first university and modern painting. The old culture had been destroyed by invasion from the south.

A comparison was often made between Yugoslavia and England, both of which had approximately the same territory. In medieval times they had had the same population and had been about equally developed in economic terms. Now England had $2\frac{1}{2}$ times the population and 3 times the income of Yugoslavia. The reason often suggested was that England was an island, while Yugoslavia had been frequently invaded – from all four sides.

When one tried to explain why development occurred, one had to look beyond technical categories like capital, technology and skill. Ordinary historical events like invasion and the location of the country often played the decisive role.

Replying to Professor Findlay on exploitation, Professor Horvat said it was well known that many people tried to show that colonies were a burden on colonial powers, and that on the whole the colonial power experienced a deficit in flows of goods and services. He did not question the validity of these statistical studies, but there was one simple point. If colonies really were a burden, then why did countries insist on continuing to be colonial powers? The answer was that development was not influenced only by economic variables. A colonial power could exert political force. Being more powerful helped the country economically, even though one could not show a clear economic gain. If there were weak and powerful countries, then one had a relationship of exploitation between the two, whatever the calculations showed. A lack of equality in power – and states were power organisations – meant that there must be exploitation.

Professor Patinkin said that we had been talking about *the* gap. In fact the gap being discussed was one in modern European history. If we went back to medieval times we should have to revise what we said, with China probably ahead of the rest. *The* gap related only to our present situation.

In a similar way, he would object to what Professor Ranis had said about *the* colonial exploitation. Again we were thinking particularly in terms of South East Asia and Africa. Yet both North and South America had been colonies, but what had happened there had been different. For example, why had North America and Latin America, both of which had experienced considerable immigration, followed different patterns? Again there was a variety of colonial experiences. Only by looking at this variety could we throw light on the different patterns of exploitation today.

Dr. Pfaff said that an explanation in terms of growth of G.N.P. would not only have to take account of movements along the production function brought about by increases in factor supply, but of the more important shifts in the production functions due to technical change. These, in turn, were caused by a variety of long-run socio-economic forces, and by a variety of historical accidents.

As a start one could take some simple evolutionary theories to explain long-run changes in factor inputs and in the level of technology. In the Marxian theory, technology expressed by the forces of production – which influenced the relations and superstructure of production – was the major explanator of long-run development. As an alternative to this simple model we might use several explanatory variables. Taking only additional *economic* variables into the scheme and going back in time only a few centuries, we might arrive at a *negative* developmental gap for the period preceding the 18th century; by adding *attitudinal*, *social* and *political* variables as well, and by making a heroic leap backward as far as the emergence of secularism in the 12th century as followed by the rise of Renaissance culture in the 14th and 15th centuries, we might conclude that these were the 'ultimate' explanators of secular changes leading to the present gap. Alternatively, one could point to the 'Protestant ethic' and the accompanying change in attitudes towards interest and capital accumulation as most important factors.

Even if these broad explanatory schemes were valid as guides to historic changes, they might not be very significant for present-day less developed countries. Through education and other means of acculturation, major changes could and did occur within one or two generations. While it was interesting to explain the forces leading to the present gap, it was more important to help to narrow it by the techniques of 'social engineering' – education and planned socio-economic change.

Dr. Radetski thought it was interesting that colonial exploitation took place simultaneously with the Industrial Revolution. Transfers of profit and capital did occur between the colonies and Western Europe. This was shown by the experience of European companies, like the British East India Company and the activities of Rhodes, and of the Belgians in the Congo.

An interesting part of the explanation of development in Western Europe was perhaps a spin-off from colonialism – rather like the spin-off from the space programme. This could explain part of European development through the growth of the exploratory spirit, the development of cotton or new impressions gained from trade with foreign countries. Not least, there was the need to control the colonial empire which itself taught Western countries a good deal.

Dr. Anita Pfaff suggested that there was an important cultural reason for the development of the gap. Christian civilisations had not considered pagan civilisations as their equals. Technological innovation was therefore not transmitted to present-day less developed countries, at the time of its development, because it seemed logical and reasonable to colonial powers that colonies should provide raw materials and not share in advancement. On the other hand, other developed countries had been able quite easily to obtain technological innovations from the country where they were developed originally. It involved only transmitting technical methods. More recently, when developed countries became interested in transmitting technology to less developed countries, the barrier had become quite forbidding, involving the sudden transfer of a new way of life rather than just a method of production.

Professor Tsuru had been perturbed by Professor Ohlin's remarks that 'the reading of history shows clearly'. He would just remind the conference that Schumpeter had said that a feudal society could be a stationary society; a socialist society could be stationary; but stationary capitalism was a contradiction in terms. This told us a great deal about events in countries like Japan – and reasons why they did or did not develop.

Mr. Economides said he was reminded of what Keynes said in the *Treatise on Money* about the origins of the U.K.'s investment overseas. The original gold brought back by Drake from piratical exploits in the 16th century had allowed Queen Elizabeth to give £42,000 to the formation of the Levant, and later the East India Company. These were the main foundation of England's foreign investments. That amount, compounded from 1580 to 1930 at the estimated reinvested net yield of $3\frac{1}{4}$ per cent per annum, grew to £4,200 million, which coincided with the total of all British foreign investments in 1930.

Professor Robinson said that he would like to mention, in a light-hearted vein, that he had first made this calculation. In his earliest research work on foreign investment in the 1920s under Keynes, he had tried to see how the value of a bar of gold would accumulate over time. He had shown his calculations to Keynes, who had much improved on the idea in the *Treatise*.

Professor Chenery said that he wanted to take up the question of economic distance. All economic advance was bound to be uneven because development was, as Professor Kuznets said, adjustment to technological change. Therefore, if one had to have uneven advance, one had to accept some gaps. The question was what one should do about it. Estimates of economic distance were that it was not getting any greater. In 1900 many countries had been a hundred years behind the leaders. Professor Ohlin suggested that the estimate was still the same. He would himself say that fifty countries were now within fifty years of the leaders. Perhaps twenty of them would catch up within fifty years. We knew, for example, from South East Asia, how rapidly countries with good educational systems in a minimum of social structure could catch up. He thought it might well take India a hundred years, but the problem there was not so much organisational but political. As for the relationships between the leaders and the laggarts, not all wanted to follow the same path. Professor Kuznets showed that so far this had been a similar path, but it might well be that more countries would want to advance differently in future. They did not have to follow the present path followed by countries which had already developed, but it was possible to learn how one wished to advance from studying what had happened to countries that had developed.

Professor Vernon said that the critical question was how far policies were; working. Professor Ohlin suggested that they were working after a fashion; Professor Yenal said no, not really, things were going from bad to worse. Yet he thought that some policies *were* 'working'.

Market forces were contributing to the growth of countries with oil. Tourism was contributing to the growth of Mediterranean countries. Labour-intensive exports were contributing to the growth of Hong Kong, Taiwan, Korea, Mexico and so on. Foreign aid had also demonstrably contributed to growth in Pakistan, Korea and a number of other countries. In the aggregate, the exceptions to Professor Yenal's generalisations bulked large and might be the rule.

Professor Yenal had posed a dilemma. If the advanced countries did not provide support to less developed countries, they would be unable to narrow the gap; if they did provide support, they would inevitably influence the less developed countries by affecting their tastes and technologies. If Professor Yenal wanted support that excluded this sort of influence, he was ejecting all possibilities.

In any case, could the elites of less developed countries purport to speak for their lowest-income groups? This was a moral issue as well as a question of fact. The gap between those who spoke for the L.D.C.s and their ordinary citizens was huge. It was hard to accept that such spokesmen could speak authoritatively for their own people in matters of preference and taste. We should note that peasants in these countries preferred cities and radios, whatever their spokesmen might prefer.

Professor Tsuru referred to the distinction between the effects of the gap and the effects of knowledge of the gap. He thought institutional constraints were quite important. Knowledge about tested – and often desirable – institutions in developed countries was compelling. During the time when Japan had been developing there had been no demonstration effect. Social security, public health measures, etc., were unknown. The knowledge of such tested and working institutions tended to induce L.D.C.s to collapse the historical process. He wondered whether the capitalistic way of development could be consistent with this type of development. Could one collapse the process and remain consistent with capitalistic development?

Professor Horvat was not happy with Professor Chenery's time measures. He would prefer to look at the 'catching-up' time. For example, one might have two countries which, a hundred years ago, had been in the relation of 1 : 5 and were still the same. Suppose the rate of growth of the less developed country was now 4 per cent instead of 2 per cent. The time distance in Professor Chenery's terminology was half. However, if the developed country now increased its growth rate to 5 per cent, the distance was even lengthened. One now had a dilemma over which was the more appropriate measure. It was not just a question of metaphysics, but of describing what the situation was today. One could not predict the future, but one did need to take into account rates of growth as well as existing levels.

Dr. Corden suggested that one could reformulate the problem of the gap as follows: is there a positive or negative relationship between income per head in developed and undeveloped countries? The answer was that there was a positive relationship. This was not a question of ideology. It was perfectly possible that the rate of growth in developed countries might fall; it was also possible to have the mutual destruction of the U.S.A. and the U.S.S.R.

Dr. Corden suggested five reasons why less developed countries benefited from growth in developed countries. First, they provided markets. Despite the development of synthetics which replaced the raw materials of less developed countries, on the whole economic growth in developed countries improved the terms of trade of less developed countries. Secondly, there was a fall in real import prices; the development of new products benefited the less developed countries. Third, there was technical spillover. Fourth, there was the challenge that a high level of technological development in advanced countries presented. Fifth, there was the potentiality of aid.

One needed also to bear in mind the effect on death rates. Here the gap was narrowing – although this had the opposite effect on real income per head. Perhaps we ought to allow for the effect of greater life expectancy on human welfare in our calculations of changes in real income per head.

Mr. Streeten said that in an earlier session we had taken the existence of developed countries as good or neutral. Now we saw it as detrimental. Rather than discuss the total net effects of the gap we should disaggregate them. We should ask which specific events or policies were detrimental in order to alter or mitigate them.

He thought one could draw some general distinctions. First, there were the differential effects of higher *levels* of production and all that went with them in richer countries; second, there were higher *rates of growth* of income or again of income per head in developed countries, with their effects on the supply of capital, the demand for skills, the rate of innovation and the terms of trade. One should therefore distinguish, first, between differential *levels* and differential *rates of growth*; next between, on the one hand, economic and technical causes and, on the other, the effects of government policies such as protection. For example, the amount, direction and nature of research and development expenditure was partly the result of policy decisions. The percentage of research and development carried out in underdeveloped countries or on the problems of underdeveloped countries was very small indeed.

We might also ask how far differences in either levels or rates of growth affected policies and vice versa. These would be useful questions to look at as a preparation for sorting out the gross contributions from various sources to the net effects of the gap.

Professor Srinivasan said that Professor Yenal seemed to suggest that the gap and the awareness of it was the major cause of international tension. But was this correct? He agreed with Professor Ghai that the awareness of patterns of consumption and production in developed countries had harmful effects on the investment allocations of L.D.C.s It seemed to him, first, that some tensions in some developing countries were not the result of the gap between nations, but of the gap between regions and individuals within the country. Second, there were harmful consequences flowing from the international demonstration effect. These arose more from the unequal distribution of income, particularly personal income, within the developing countries.

The rèsult was that, given the existing distribution of income and political power, only the elite of these countries were aware of the patterns of investment and consumption in developing countries. They were able to shift the allocation of investment resources to the production of such goods and services as they desired. Even such desirable technical breakthroughs as the emergence of new types of grain mainly benefited the upper income groups, who held substantial amounts of irrigated land, had access to credit and so on. In other words, the consequences of the gap for patterns of consumption, technology, etc., would be quite different if the income and power distribution in the developing countries were itself different.

Dr. Nurul Islam wanted to reverse the question asked by Professor Lewis in the previous session. What would happen to developed countries if the developing countries were to sink beneath the sea? We all knew that more than 80 per cent of the trade between developing countries took place between themselves. Technological progress in rich countries tended to reduce their dependence on underdeveloped countries because of the use of synthetic raw materials, the discovery of ways of economising on raw materials, the protection of agriculture in developed countries, etc.

There was also a problem of the market. The advantage of having access to the markets of poor countries could be replaced by increased trade among developed countries. In fact, one often felt that the policies of rich countries were directed towards reducing their dependence on the poor countries, if one analysed their restrictive trade and immigration policies. He therefore thought that the developed countries would lose only marginally if all the developing countries were to 'sink'.

Since the developing countries were there to stay, what was the appropriate relationship for rich countries to seek with them? Part of the answer could be increased trade and private investment in poor countries. In the light of this, the case, or rationale for foreign aid – concessional aid or grants – from the point of view of the rich countries was a weak one, at least in purely economic terms. The subject had been analysed quite exhaustively in recent discussions on foreign trade, including Professor Ohlin's paper. He thought there were two main reasons for aid: moral and political. The first moral reason seemed to be that it was right for the rich to help the poor. The second was that the ethical values of the rich led them to help the poor in their own countries so that they felt it was right to help the poor in other countries as well. On the political side there was the short-term political advantage of winning friends and influencing other countries. This was the possibility of gaining a strategic advantage over other rich countries in the context of international rivalry for influence. In the long run there was the political advantage of ensuring a peaceful and prosperous world – although this was a very nebulous idea.

These factors all influenced the allocation of aid. For example, American grants were highly correlated with military assistance. American loans were highly correlated with income per head as well. United Nations loans were not related to population per head but the World Bank loans were. American government loans were highly correlated with the voting pattern of countries in the United Nations. All of these criteria were obviously haphazard and unevenly distributed.

Professor Kuznets thought Nural Islam was right about the forces behind the aid programme, but as economists and social scientists we had to stress a major selfish reason why developed countries should help less developed countries to develop as rapidly as possible. If economic and social progress depended on the production of knowledge, and if millions of people in the less developed countries could produce knowledge too, given the opportunity, then the potential loss we were currently sustaining was substantial. This might not be the kind of argument that impressed governments and legislators, but it should impress general opinion in the world through an appeal to the enlightened self-interest of aid-givers.

Professor Horvat commented that Professor Kuznets might be right in a socialist world. But since the world was not a socialist one the reverse was true. There was no consciousness in the U.S.A. of the advantage of increasing knowledge in China.

Professor Scott recalled that Professor Ohlin had noted that the literature showed no 'references, before the post-war years, to international inequality as a moral or political problem, except in the muted form of references to missionary activity or colonial trusteeship'.

Simiarly, Professor Yenal suggested that there had been no interest in international equality between the 19th century and the 1950s. Everyone seemed to have been very punctilious over economic history during the session, but there had been very cavalier treatment of ideas and policy. He was reminded of a hearing on the pollution of the Great Lakes. The members of the inquiry were mostly old people; the witnesses were mostly students who emphasised the carelessness of the older generation for the environment. One said, 'My generation is the first which ever considered the human environment. At least, I think that's true because it's the only generation I have ever known.'

Similarly our discussions of the gap today were based on what we remembered and it reminded him of one concern, based on the idea of an optimum population. This was much discussed during the inter-war years, and was applied not so much to birth control as to mass migration. He remembered a series of lectures in 1939–40 in which it had been suggested that developed countries should subsidise emigration from the West Indies, China, Japan, etc., to Europe and Australia. There was no question that while the main factor lying behind all this was political, economists, and especially those in the Institute of Pacific Relations, were looking at this problem very seriously. We should remember that there had been many other thoughts on this subject in addition to the ones we had now.

Pro'essor Ranis said that he did not quarrel with Professor Islam about the motives governing the quantity and allocation of aid, though he did not think that U.N. votes were very relevant. He certainly did not want to defend the way in which the size and allocation of aid was currently determined.

He would emphasise that enlightened self-interest in both underdeveloped and developed countries should lead us to tackle the problem of the gap. While there were some baser motives governing allocation *between* countries, these did not often apply to the way in which aid was allocated *within* countries. A country could take advantage of aid, however basely motivated the initial grant might be.

Professor Ohlin said that some questions in social science were more interesting in their pursuit than in their solution. The historical origin of the gap was probably one. Perhaps if we went back into the whole historical process, the views expressed today might seem to have made too light of the problem of colonialism. In a varied spectrum there were obviously examples of what must, at the very best, be called 'exploitation'. Racial conflict and dominance were important too, although they had not been mentioned today. It was hard to believe that the problem of exploitation could be solved by a reference to weak and powerful partners, to the belief that such imbalance *must* always lead to exploitation, and that it must do this whatever were the facts. The notion of power was diffuse and many market relations were not much affected by it. But he would grant that the complexities of imperialism had had a great affect on free trade – although this was not our subject. The same was true of many accidents of history, wars, etc.

A much closer problem was that of population. One of the more surprising things was that the population explosion had not been expected as little as twenty years ago. It was thought that the population of the underdeveloped countries would continue to grow quite slowly. As social scientists we did not have much insight into these problems, or indeed of the strength of public health measures. Yet without the population increase our problem would not seem so difficult.

Professor Ohlin said he would concede that his treatment of many issues had been cavalier, and he agreed with Professor Scott that there was a growing concern with the problem of the 'gap' in the inter-war period, expressed in the whole trusteeship notion. However, it was probably true that only since 1945 had there been one world. In this situation, the gap had attracted more attention.

As to whether the gap was a product of colonialism, this was not clear. Colonialism took shape in centuries of growth of the network of trade and economic contacts. Technology was more important than economics, and with it the development of communications and the altered view of the world. Probably Professor Islam's analysis took things as far as one could go but, among the considerations Professor Islam mentioned, the awareness of the world as one was more important (though more nebulous) than many other factors.

Professor Ohlin admitted that some short-term forces behind aid were fading while new links were replacing colonialism.

There had been references to global problems but, as Professor Kuznets said, more important was the convergence of new societies, cutting across ideological boundaries. There was nowadays a common way of viewing the human position.

Professor Yenal summed up, saying that the discussion had concentrated more on the origin than on the consequences of the gap, and he must perhaps take part of the blame for this since he had touched upon the topic by way of introduction to his paper. The question of how far back the gap went was related to the definition of the gap which had been discussed in earlier sessions. It could be shown that income differentials between Western Europe and other parts of the world had appeared much earlier than the 19th century. But the important question was when this difference became a significant one, in the sense of a difference in the league that the nations belong to.

The importance of trying to trace the origins of the gap might be to gain insight into the sources of development. Speculation on the original sources of development could be stretched in all directions, including explanations in terms of the impact of religions – such as the role of the Protestant ethic. As historical explanations these ideas were complex; but for one coming from a totally Moslem country he hoped that the whole of the explanation did not lie in Calvinism. This was why theories emphasising the economic determinants of development had produced a new hope in our age. Nor did he see that much light could be shed on present-day problems by going back to the origins of the gap in order to distribute blame. It would be more fruitful to emphasise the consequences of the gap rather than its origins.

On consciousness of the gap, he would like to point out that although there were examples in the inter-war period of countries which had become conscious of it – one example was Turkey – this did not change the fact that general world consciousness of the gap did not exist before the Second World War.

On the consequences of the gap, he was sorry that so much ideology dominated the debate that even the papers of an international conference were read with coloured glasses. Whereas Professor Ghai had found that his paper put too little emphasis on the consequences of the negative attitude of the richer countries, Professor Vernon had interpreted it as yet another assault on capitalism and imperialism, and lacking in its understanding of market forces. Professor Yenal thought this was ironic, since he was known in his own country as an exaggerator of market forces. A careful study of the paper might show more awareness of market influence than Professor Vernon thought.

However, one had to examine critically the relation of market forces to the gap. First, there was the question of whether, in our day, they provided an engine of growth for the poor countries. Would the expansion of international trade be on a sufficient scale to produce the necessary stimulus for the developing world? Some examples of success stories could be quoted – for example, Taiwan and South Korea. But if all, or most, underdeveloped countries tried to sell shoes to the U.S.A., would *all* succeed as well as South Korea had? Then there was the question of whether the market forces which might help the poor countries appeared as a result of the gap or were exaggerated by it.

On the impact of aid one could not be categorical, but it was hard to argue that aid had made a big impact on underdeveloped countries. It was still harder to argue that a particular type, or scale, of aid had made much contribution to shrinking the 'distance'.

If we wanted to see the *consequences* of the gap, we would have to specify our point of view much more precisely. We would have to specify the characteristics of a gapless world in order to provide a model for comparison with the actual world. What would happen to the poor countries if the developed countries sank into the sea? Did we want this to happen immediately or in ten or twenty years? What would be the consequences if the developing countries adopted an isolationist policy? The assumptions about the alternative we envisaged would make a difference to the conclusions we reached about the consequences of the gap.

Professor Robinson commented light-heartedly that fifty years ago he had been taught by Professor Dennis Robertson that only the educated economist could appreciate that trade could benefit both parties. The layman thought that a gain to A was necessarily a loss to B. Now we found sophisticated economists arguing that there would be a loss to one party and a gain to another through exploitation and that evidence of a gain to one party from trade must mean that the other had lost. He did not think that the world was either so different or so simple. Perhaps there was still room to go on to try and improve our explanations.

He would also like to ask what really would have happened in India if the British administrators had not been honest believers in John Stuart Mill. What would they have done differently if they had been educated in modern development economics, Keynesian economics, growth economics and the rest? Or what would have been different if the British had left India in 1860? Would India have been further along the road now? Was the colonial period (bad as it had undoubtedly been politically and psychologically) as bad economically as was sometimes believed? Although this was not an answer, we should remember that the protection of Indian industries was introduced in the 1920s, long before the end of the colonial period.

4 The Gap between Rich and Poor Nations from the Socialist Viewpoint

Branko Horvat

INSTITUTE OF ECONOMIC STUDIES, BELGRADE

I. THE SOCIALIST VIEWPOINT

Socialism is not about nations; it is about individuals. That is why the original title of the paper I was invited to present – 'The Gap from the Socialist Countries' Perspective' – was somewhat misleading. Even the present modified title is not altogether satisfying: it stops at the international level and neglects the intra-national analysis. We are all citizens of one single world. If some of us happen to be born into rich nations while others belong to poor nations that simply means that some of us are privileged while others are underprivileged citizens of that same single world. The privilege of the man in a rich country is not earned; it is as arbitrary as the privilege connected with inherited property or the one that was associated with inherited feudal titles. The history books tell us about class polarisation within particular countries. The contemporary world has produced a similar, yet new, form of social polarisation: the one between rich and poor nations. In our world human beings are clearly not born equal.

But socialism is exactly about equality – equality of opportunity, to be more precise. An individual performs three fundamental roles in his active life. He is a producer, a consumer and a citizen. In a socialist system he would enjoy equal opportunity in performing any of his roles. As a producer he would have equal access to productive capital as anybody else. This implies not only full employment but also the choice of occupation. As a consumer he would share in the available supply of goods proportionally to his own productive contribution. This implies that inherited wealth – either nationwise or familywise – plays no role in income distribution. As a citizen he would enjoy the same self-governing rights as any other citizen. This implies political participation on equal terms not only nationally but internationally.

If the wealth is distributed among individuals very unequally, all those conditions are violated. Privileged and underprivileged social classes arise. We get an exploitative society. Similarly, if wealth is distributed among nations very unequally, the ensuing social polarisation generates exploitation. The rich nations are strong and they exploit poor nations which are weak. This exploitation proceeds in innumerable ways. The most obvious form is political domination. Economic pressures, military threats, preventive wars and occupations, various subtle and less subtle interferences in domestic affairs, are familiar ways of running the world on behalf of a higher civilisation. Next, even in a utopian world of political non-interference, completely free trade would act strongly against the poor and in favour of the rich. By now it is well known that in a situation of sufficiently different levels of development, free market generates economic polarisation and not a compensatory movement of resoruces. And even if a multinational corporation moves to an underdeveloped country in search of profit, profit is maximised from the point of view of the corporation not of the host country.[1] It is also well known that in practice these two interests widely and consistently differ. Finally, the labour and brain drain is a relatively new form of counterproductive movement of resources, namely of such movement that leads to relative, sometime even absolute, impoverishment of the already poor.

It is therefore in the nature of things that rich nations exploit poor nations. But no one likes exploitation. Tensions mount. Social explosions are inevitable. They occur from time to time. Since we live in one single small world, we cannot afford to ignore them. Thus the socialist viewpoint is likely to become the point of view of our epoch, if the human race is to survive.

II. A SHORT SURVEY OF FACTS

About two-thirds of the world population live in less developed countries. They earn only one-eighth of the world income. This income inequality has been and continues to be increasing over time. In the past century, from 1860 to 1960, the richest quarter of the world population increased their share in the world income from 58 to 72 per cent, and the share of the poorest quarter dropped from 12·5 to 3 per cent.[2] In the last decade gross national product of the two poorest regions in the world – of Africa and South Asia – was increasing at a rate of about 4 per cent per year, while industrialised countries experienced annual growth of 4·8 per cent.[3] The output of some 37 countries with about one-half of the total population of the underdeveloped world was expanding at a rate less than 4 per cent per year.[4] In view of the rapid population growth, per capita income was expanding around 1 per cent per annum. Slow output

---

[1] In the words of R. Prebisch: '. . . executive arms are multinational, but the decision making centre is national'. (*Transformacion y desarollo. La gran tarea de America Latina* (Santiago de Chile, April 1970), p. 113. To be called the *Prebisch Report*.)

[2] B. Higgins, *Economic Development* (Norton, New York, 1968), p. 5.

[3] *Partners in Development: Report of the Commission on International Development* (Praeger, New York, 1969), pp. 27–29. It will be called the *Pearson Report*.

[4] Council of Europe, Committee on Economic Affairs and Development *Draft Report On the Role of Council of Europe Member States in the Second United Nations Development Decade* (Strasbourg, 1969), p. 18. It will be called the *Vedovato Report*.

growth implies a low rate of employment increase.[1] If the present trends continue, we may expect unemployment to grow at a fantastic rate. The most developed countries enjoy per capita income some twenty times higher than most of the underdeveloped countries. This means that in order to match an annual increase in per capita income in the first group, the population of the second group has to work as long as one generation or so. In more extreme cases, differences become really frightening. In the period 1960–67, per capita gross national product of the United States was increasing at the rate of $144, that of India at the rate of $1.20 per annum.[2] In other words, India needs more than a century to match the annual American per capita increase of output!

Development implies industrialisation, industrialisation means filling up the empty cells of an input-output table. Only a few of the very large countries with rich and varied resources can establish simultaneously an integrated set of industries and thus advance in a balanced way. Most countries can adopt only an unbalanced growth pattern. An incomplete industrial structure will have to be supplemented by increased imports. Thus in order to support industrialisation, imports will have to grow faster than total social product. Imports are bought by exports. Consequently a rapid expansion of exports is a precondition for fast growth.[3]

Table 1 gives output and export performance of various regions in the last decade.

TABLE 1

ANNUAL RATES OF GROWTH OF G.N.P.
AND EXPORTS 1960–67
(percentages)

	G.N.P.	Exports
Southern Europe	7·1	13·7
Middle East	7·2	8·7
East Asia	5·6	5·4
Latin America	4·5	4·8
Africa	4·0	5·4
South Asia	4·1	1·5
Developing countries	5·0	6·1
Industrialised countries	4·8	8·8

Source: *Pearson Report*, p. 27, para. 47.

Only Southern Europe achieved satisfactory export results. This is also the most developed part of the underdeveloped world. Middle East exports are based on oil and so cannot be repeated in other countries.

[1] In Latin America even manufacturing employment has been increasing at a rate lower than the rate of growth of the labour force (*Pearson Report*, p. 243).
[2] *Vedovato Report*, p. 19.
[3] 'The growth rates of individual developing countries since 1950 correlate better with their export performance than with any other single economic indicator' (*Pearson Report*, p. 45).

Exports in the rest of the underdeveloped world have been disappointing. The explanation of the failure is not difficult to find. Developing countries (1) export tropical food products (tea, coffee, cocoa, bananas) for which the aggregate world demand expands only very slowly; (2) they also export products competing with agricultural products from the temperate zone (sugar, rice, vegetable oils). In this case demand is expanding even more slowly because industrialised countries artificially stimulate their own home production. In the period 1954–67, the share of developing countries in the world commodity trade dropped from 54 per cent to 42 per cent, mainly as a result of the great increase in agricultural production in the industrialised countries;[1] (3) they export raw materials competing with man-made products (rubber, jute, hard fibres, cotton) whose demands also expand at a slow rate; (4) only a few fortunate countries export non-substitutable industrial raw materials – oil and minerals – whose demand is rapidly increasing. In general, developing countries derive almost 90 per cent of export earnings from primary products[2] for most of which the world demand is increasing at a substantially lower rate than for manufactured goods.

Nor is this the whole story. The exports mentioned are vulnerable because they are not diversified and prices oscillate. In almost one-half of developing countries more than 50 per cent of export earnings are derived from one commodity; three commodities contribute more than 60 per cent of export earnings in three-quarters of developing countries. Under such conditions the supply often exceeds demand and the terms of trade turn against developing countries. In Africa, for instance, the loss in terms of trade in 1966 relative to 1957 amounted to $1–3 billion, which was sufficient to wipe out all contributions of aid.[3]

The alarming state of affairs was recognised a long time ago. Aid programmes were initiated by various industrialised countries. In 1961 the General Assembly of the United Nations launched the Development Decade 1961–70. But the results so far have been rather disappointing – the gap between rich and poor countries is rapidly widening. The effective transfer of resources has been insignificant. Higgins quotes the UNCTAD estimates according to which in the period 1951–60 the net flow of private and public capital – after interest and profit remittances and the loss due to terms of trade were deducted – amounted to $13 billion annually for all 75 underdeveloped countries or $16 million per country. 'Such figures', Higgins comments, 'hardly sound relevant to national economies at all; they sound more like report of individual corporations.'[4] About 90 per cent of official assistance is bilateral. Three-quarters of that aid is tied,

---

[1] *Vedovato Report*, p. 41.　　　　　　　　　[2] *Pearson Report*, p. 81.
[3] P. Ady, 'Trade and Liquidity in Africa', paper presented to the Columbia University Conference on International Economic Development, 1970, p. 6.
[4] Higgins, *op. cit.*, p. 295.

which reduces the value of aid by some 15–20 per cent. The assistance appropriations are often made on an annual basis which renders efficient programming impossible. The assistance is distributed in a haphazard way. In 1964–66 net official assistance per head (multilateral and the D.A.C. countries) varied between $2·5 for India and $36·6 for Jordan.[1] And, of course, the assistance policies of the rich are influenced by all sorts of extra-economic considerations. No wonder results have been less than meagre.

III. THE NEED FOR CO-ORDINATED INTERNATIONAL ACTION

Official international development assistance has been stagnating (around $6·4 billion per year) or even falling in recent years. There are no signs that development performance of most developing countries will substantially improve. Thus the process of relative impoverishment will continue. Owing to the educational efforts of the last decade or so, in many of the developing countries native intelligentsia is in process of being created. These educated men and women are fully aware of the growing disparities in opportunities in the modern world. There is little doubt that they will waken up the consciousness of their peoples on that issue. Thus there will be an increasing desire to share in the advantages – both material and non-material – of the modern civilisation, and there will be an increasing frustration for not being able to do so. The rapidly increasing army of unemployed – unskilled, skilled and highly educated – can only intensify frustration and discontent. Unless concerted international action is taken in time, we may expect major social and political upheavals and military conflagrations. We may also note that all advanced countries but one (Japan) are populated by white people, while all poor countries of Asia and Africa, without exception, are populated by coloured people. When extreme income disparities are coupled with racial differences, the consequences are known only too well.

Development is clearly the primary responsibility of the less developed countries themselves. They can secure permanent development results only by their own efforts. But their own developmental efforts have so far been frustrated by at least three groups of causes:

  (1) the lack of access to the markets of industrialised countries;
  (2) the insufficient transfer of resources;
  (3) the organisational inefficiencies.

(1) *Access to the Markets*

For obvious reasons developing countries find it extremely difficult to compete with industrialised countries in markets for manufactured goods.

[1] *Pearson Report*, p. 298.

But even when they are well equipped for competition – or for instance in the production of textiles or semi-finished products based on metals – they encounter special barriers.

In many instances the imports in question – observes A. G. Hart – compete with industries in the advanced countries that are regarded there as 'sick'. Having been reduced essentially to routine and having been carried on in industrial countries so long that there are whole regions burdened with obsolescent skills, the very industries the under-developed countries can most rapidly bring to a competitive cost level are industries whose competition is threatening to the 'retarded regions' of the advanced countries.[1]

In all advanced countries agriculture represents serious political problems. When it comes to agriculture, these countries do not hesitate to violate the GATT rules in the most disgraceful way. The Common Market prohibitive variable levies are perhaps the best example of that conduct.

In order to equalise the trade conditions on the world market, the advanced countries will have to undertake a unilateral reduction, preferably elimination, of tariffs in favour of developing countries. However, even if they were willing to do so, in the two most important cases discussed under (1) and (2) they cannot act immediately and in isolation. Structural adjustments can be effected only gradually.[2] A co-ordinated international action and long-term programming appear indispensable.

(2) *Transfer of Resources*

This transfer may be private or public (official). Both are necessary and both are in an utterly unsatisfactory state. An international corporation like General Motors produces an annual output larger than the gross national product of a country like Bulgaria; and Bulgaria is not exactly the least developed or the smallest country. The United States Steel Corporation produces more steel than do most nations in Western Europe.[3] When large international corporations enter the market or invest in a developing country, they do not compete on equal terms with domestic firms. Some sort of international control appears necessary. Its task will be to make sure that the import of private foreign capital contributes most to the development of the host country and to guarantee fair treatment for the foreign investor.

[1] A. G. Hart, 'The Latin American Potential for Expanding Industrial Exports', paper presented to the Columbia University Conference on International Economic Development (Williamsburg, 1970), p. 30.

[2] In the meantime the loss of export earnings to the L.D.C.s owing to the imposition of quotas can be compensated for by the rich nations that impose the quotas making appropriate payments under GATT auspices (J. N. Bhagwati, *Trade Policies for Development*).

[3] D. R. Frisfeld, 'Fascist Democracy in the United States', *The Conference Papers of the Union for Radical Political Economy* (Philadelphia, 1968), p. 4.

In order to meet the needs at least partly, public transfers of resources should be substantially expanded. In order to increase efficiency of development assistance, it should be untied and it should be appropriated over several years. Both these changes require a concerted action. Industrialised countries are not likely to transfer a larger amount of their resources unless an international agreement is reached. Next, if some lenders soften their terms while others do not, the soft lenders will soon finance the payment of interest to hard lenders. Similarly, countries with untied loans may find their money being used to finance exports from countries with tied loans. And in the atmosphere of annual budgets parliaments will not be ready to commit future budgetary resources for longer term assistance programmes, unless this has become an international obligation.

(3) *Organisational Efficiency*

If the development assistance is to be efficiently used, it has to be distributed according to some performance criteria and according to some rules that are binding for donors. Neither can be achieved in bilateral arrangements. A recipient country clearly cannot impose conditions upon the conduct of a donor. A donor country cannot hope to undertake performance assessment – however justified – without provoking strong resentment on the part of a recipient.

It is well-known that external economies play an important role in economic development. Thus a co-ordinated multilateral programme will be more efficient than the sum of separate bilateral programmes. Further, there are economies of scale: documentation, advice, guidance and auditing can be organised more efficiently. Finally, the regional distribution of development assistance may be rendered more rational and inter-regional integration facilitated under a multilateral arrangement.

On a basis of the foregoing analysis we can derive a fairly obvious conclusion: if there is to be a substantial change, if the underdeveloped countries are to begin to catch up with their more fortunate industrial neighbours, a concerted international action ought to be undertaken. Little wonder that all five recent reports on international economic development – Jackson, Pearson, Vedovato, Peterson and Prebisch – recommend multilaterisation of development assistance.[1]

---

[1] The internationalisation of development assistance may have important favourable social and political effects. Thus no country can ask for international assistance in order to reduce international income differences if its own distribution of income among various social groups is so unequal as to deviate strongly from the accepted contemporary standards. Similarly, no country will be able to receive assistance if it wages a war against its neighbours. Consequently the peace may be strengthened and social reforms encouraged as a result of an intelligently organised international economic co-operation.

The same position has now been taken by many other writers in this field.[1]
Co-ordinated international economic development means planning on
the world level.

IV. WORLD ECONOMIC PLANNING

In the last two centuries sometime fragmented feudal economies were
integrated into national economies and also into the world economy
through the operation of the (free) market. Since about the time of the
First World War it was becoming clear that the market alone had not
been a satisfactory co-ordinating device. The Soviet Union introduced
central planning and Western countries, after the economic disaster in the
early 1930s, introduced various sorts of short-term planning by means of
various policy instruments. After the Second World War, with Marshall
Plan and activities of various international agencies, the first steps in the
direction of world economic planning have been made. By planning, I
mean an agreed upon *ex ante* co-ordination of economic activities. Now,
and for some time to come, the extremely uneven economic development of
various parts of the world calls most urgently for world planning. But
regulating the relations between rich and poor countries does not exhaust
the need for economic planning. Similarly as national economic planning
means more than bringing about an orderly regional development, planning on an international scale will gradually replace more primitive and
barbaric methods of running world economic affairs in general. However,
within the confines of my theme, I shall concentrate exclusively on the

---

[1] E. K. Hamilton warns the government of his country – the largest donor – that
'after a decade of great effort and accomplishment, U.S. policy should take into account
that the world has reached a point where the politics of predominantly bilateral aid are
untenable over the long term and where the multilateral community appears capable, if
assiduously enlarged and improved, of taking on a much larger share of the task. . . .
The problem is to develop a programme which inspires the confidence necessary to
begin a cycle of longer-term mandates. . . .' ('Towards Public Confidence in Foreign
Aid', *World Affairs*, 4, 1970, pp. 300 and 303). On the other hand, R. Robinson shows
that not only multilateralism is preferable and necessary, but also that bilateralism – if
used for political purposes – is self-defeating: 'Historically the necessity for great
powers to intervene imperialistically as rivals in the internal affairs of underdeveloped
states has arisen more often from the latter's internal weakness and collapse than from
the nature of the former's interests in them. Today similarly advanced countries'
interests are at risk from foreign intervention and great powers' rivalry so long as
underdeveloped states remain economically and politically weak. In the light of history
therefore the best method for advanced states to secure their interests is not to use aid
to play politics against each other. This merely weakens the recipient more and so
raises the risk to foreign interests. The best method is to use aid to strengthen his economy and government. The highest risk to foreign interests arises from economic
failure and consequent political instability on the part of the recipient.' (R. Robinson,
ed., *International Co-operation in Aid*, Cambridge University Overseas Studies Committee, Cambridge, 1966, p. 17.)

'regional' aspects of planning, those aspects that may lead to faster economic betterment of the underprivileged poor majority of the world. I shall first tackle organisational problems. In the next section I shall consider the necessary policy measures.

The existing international institutions, though engaging in numerous partial planning activities, are not designed in such a way as to perform an overall co-ordination. The World Bank group handles more than one half of total official aid, has accumulated great developmental experience and could perhaps be built up into a World Planning Agency. But the developing countries have 'misgivings about its weighted voting and limited membership'.[1] Thus the Bank, although doing a good job, is often criticised and distrusted and is opposed by an entire group of countries. It is also true that investment and planning are not exactly the same activities. We are left with the United Nations machinery or a possible alternative. There, however, the bureaucratic red tape and political pressures may be so strong as to prevent the functioning of a viable, useful and efficient W.P.A. These considerations lead one to suggest that the World Planning Agency be set up as an independent institution with the strong participation of the World Bank and under the political (not administrative) control of the United Nations. Both organisations can only gain under this arrangement: the World Bank would be relieved of an extremely time-consuming work of replenishing the IDA funds; UNO would get a co-ordinative agency without expanding – possibly reducing – its administrative apparatus. Without going into unnecessary details, the formal organisational structure may be envisioned as follows:

The W.P.A. could be headed by a director who is responsible for day-to-day operations. Development programmes and major policy recommendations are reviewed by the World Economic Development Council, whose (rotating) president would be the president of the U.N. Economic and Social Council, the (permanent) vice president would be the director of the W.P.A. and members would be the U.N. under-secretary for economic affairs and secretaries of the U.N. regional commissions, presidents of the World Bank, International Monetary Fund, U.N.D.P. and regional banks and the director of the Institute of Social and Technological Research. The W.P.A. would have specialised committees composed of internationally known experts that serve in their personal capacities. The W.P.A. staff, in co-operation with committees and specialised international agencies, prepares development and investment allocation programmes. These programmes are reviewed by the Council and become operative when approved by ECOSOC which acts as a specialised international parliament.

For necessary research work the W.P.A. could rely first of all on its

[1] United Nations, *A Study of the Capacity of the United Nations Development System*, Vol. I (Geneva, 1969), p. vii. To be called the *Jackson Report*.

Institute which is a combination of a research institution and a university, both designed so as to cover all social and technical disciplines essential for development. The Institute will educate university teachers, research workers and other experts for less developed countries. It will engage in technological and medical research essential for less developed countries and not undertaken elsewhere. The Institute may be expected to conduct extensive research in economic, social and political aspects of development with an aim to achieve an operational knowledge about appropriate institutions' design – knowledge that is so conspicuously lacking today. The last mentioned field of research is obviously not restricted to the less developed parts of the world; it is of equal importance for industrialised countries and for a civilised survival of the world as a whole.

The W.P.A. is supposed to improve upon the present practices in international economic development in all four major fields: financing development; stabilising commodities flows; promoting trade; advising and assisting in the implementation of programmes. In order to do that, it would have to engage in the following activities:

(a) Co-ordination of the activities of the existing international agencies (F.A.O., WHO, UNICEF, UNESCO, U.N.D.P., UNIDO, World Bank, I.M.F., I.L.O., GATT, UNCTAD, O.E.C.D., etc.). There is a recognised urgent need for such a co-ordination.[1] By co-ordination is meant a commonly agreed plan of action. The W.P.A. is expected to use, not to replace, the existing facilities. It will provide an informational and data clearing function.

(b) Working out development forecasts and development programmes for the United Nations and associated institutions. For this purpose it may incorporate the present United Nations Centre for Development Planning, Projections and Policies. The W.P.A. may also suggest policy measures on its own initiative. The national planning bureaus may become affiliated to the W.P.A., and so world planning may be conducted in a truly democratic way with full information accessible to anybody concerned. Nor should one under-estimate the political educational value of such co-operation.

(c) Giving advice and rendering other services in the field of development either when ordered to do so or on its own initiative. The W.P.A. should become a place where any government can confidently turn any time for advice and help. Most of the work will be probably done in other agencies outside the W.P.A., but the W.P.A. must provide for an efficient channelling of requests.

(d) Proposing the distribution of available resources among regions and countries. The distribution programme becomes operative when approved by ECOSOC.

[1] The *Jackson Report* is entirely dedicated to a careful examination of this need.

(e) Assessing the performance of assistance recipients and controlling the conduct of assistance donors.

In order to win confidence and function efficiently, the W.P.A. must be administratively independent, display a high degree of professional competence and intellectual excellence and have sufficient financial resources. The first condition is a matter of organisation, the second hinges very much upon the success of the Institute, the third can be fulfilled by a world income tax.

An orderly development of the world in which we live is a formidable task. The W.P.A. and its institute must be able to assemble the best brains if we are to improve upon the present sad state of affairs.

V. SUGGESTED POLICY MEASURES

The underdeveloped part of the world is not at all homogeneous. We would commit serious mistakes if we continued to speak in such undifferentiated terms – as is usually done. There are great differences among developing countries. There are at least five different regions that can be conveniently classified into two groups:

(1) Countries in the Initial Stage of Development

(i) *Black Africa.* Least developed region of the world with per capita incomes less than $100 in most countries. Many small states sparsely populated. Native intelligentsia almost non-existent, educational systems in an early stage of development. In the period 1960–67 in 19 countries with 37 per cent of total population G.N.P. per capita grew at a rate less than 1 per cent or even declined.

(ii) *Asia* (except Middle East). Almost equally poor but mostly overpopulated region with relatively high educational standards. The social infra-structure necessary for fast growth (educated groups, competent civil service, political institutions) is available. North and South Korea, Taiwan and (probably, but reliable statistics are not available) China have shown how fast growth is possible.

The average per capita income of the two regions is around $100. Gabon, Malaysia, Philippines, Ghana, Ivory Coast, Senegal and Zambia represent exceptions with per capita income above $150.

(2) Semi-developed Countries

(i) *Arab countries and Iran.* Relatively fast growing region whose economy is mostly based on oil exploitation.

(ii) *Latin America.* Sparsely populated region with relatively high educational standards and with often antiquated social structures.[1]

(iii) *Southern Europe.* The most dynamic and most uniformly developed of all less developed regions comprising some of the fastest growing economies in the world.

Group (2), and each of its subgroups, diplay much wider differences in development than the first group. For most countries per capita income falls in the range $200–$1,000. Haiti, Yemen, U.A.E., Bolivia and Syria represent exceptions with per capita incomes less than $200.

Before proceeding, we must make two more distinctions. Development investment can be classified into two categories: investment in social overhead capital (schools, hospitals and possibly the transportation network which only slowly pays off) and directly productive investment. The development assistance consists of unilateral transfers (grants), loans on concessional terms and commercial loans. The first category is essentially a budgetary subsidy; the other two represent development loans.

As far as the transfer of resources is concerned, we may postulate the following criteria. If a man, regardless of where he was born, is to be treated as a human being, he must enjoy an adequate diet,[2] and must have access to medical and educational facilities. These three requirements will in principle be met by budgetary subsidies (unilateral transfers) administered perhaps by UNICEF, WHO and UNESCO. There is also another reason for this approach. If we succeed in educating the people and keep them healthy, they will soon find ways and means of generating fast growth. In the very poor countries investment in the transportation network (roads, ports, railway lines) qualifies also for budgetary subsidies. Otherwise such countries soon become saddled with heavy debt service requirements which have depressing effects on growth.

A U.N. study indicates that as a country reaches per capita income of about $400 on the average, it comes very close to the health and educational standards (as measured by the life expectation, infant mortality, caloric value of food consumption, quality of the diet, enrolment ratio and literacy rate) characteristic for the contemporary civilisation.[3] In other words, at a certain not very high level of development an average country manages to finance its social services out of its own income and so there is no need for further subsidisation.

In general, group (1) of regions will rely heavily on subsidies and very soft loans, group (2) may perhaps replace subsidies by very soft loans, or

---

[1] Prebisch estimates that the inequality of income distribution is increasing and that now low income groups – comprising 60 per cent of Latin American population – share in total consumption with only 22·5 per cent (*Prebisch Report*, p. 194).

[2] For instance, it is now known that protein deficiencies in the early years of life have an adverse effect on future physical and mental development.

[3] United Nations, *Report of the World Social Situation* (New York, 1961), p. 41.

E

(in its upper income levels, say in region iii) eliminate this category of projects altogether and use only near-commercial and commercial loans for development investment.

The money for subsidies and for soft loans is to come from 1 per cent income tax imposed upon all industrialised and group (1) countries. Whether 1 per cent is sufficient or not is not worth while discussing.[1] As every planner knows from his own experience, such percentages are determined by considerations of political feasibility. The 1 per cent target (although total, not only public transfers) has been popularised for years and by now sounds familiar to political bodies. All countries are, of course, free to use additional resources for bilateral arrangements. This 1 per cent income tax represents resources to be allocated by the World Planning Agency. In this way the official assistance is, of course, completely untied. If it turns out that some donors suffer temporary economic disadvantages, a simple procedure can be worked out so as to ensure that the value of purchases by the recipients in the donor countries be equal to the portion of income taxed away in these same countries. The tying of tax-aid can perhaps be practised in the case of the aid given by the group (2) of the L.D.C.s. The required finance corresponding to the one per cent income tax can be rendered acceptable to the public in the donor countries by using taxes on, for instance, tobacco and liquor for this purpose.

Loans, even if they are soft, have to be repaid. For that exports must continuously expand. Thus we come to consider our second development condition, an access to the market of industrialised countries. It seems reasonable to suggest that industrialised countries eliminate tariffs (and other trade barriers) on all imports from group (1) countries and reduce tariffs (and other barriers) by, say, 50 per cent for imports from group (2) countries. In exchange for this concession the group (2) will reduce tariffs by 50 per cent on imports from group (1) countries. Obviously such an elimination of trade barriers cannot be accomplished overnight. We have already discussed the problem of sick industries and agriculture. The W.P.A. will be asked to work out longer term programmes of gradual elimination of trade barriers in co-operation with the GATT and UNCTAD.

With assured finance for the social infrastructure, with large amounts of foreign exchange at their disposal, with expanding foreign markets providing sufficient proceeds for the repayment of debts and with an access to

---

[1] In fact it means a lot since it represents net transfers which will be only partly used for grants. Thus the other part will be accumulated at a certain interest rate and so available resources in proportion to income of developed countries will gradually increase. Next, 1 per cent of advanced countries' income represents 7 per cent of less developed countries' income. If the assistance multiplier is about $1\frac{1}{2}$, the less developed countries will more than double their present rate of growth.

development finance depending on the performance standards, most less developed countries should be able to accelerate their growth appreciably and begin to close the degrading gap between the rich and the poor.

The conclusion just derived is probably not controversial. What is controversial, however, is the willingness of industrialised countries to act as required.

VI. POLITICAL FEASIBILITY OF THE SUGGESTED APPROACH

If all governments were socialist, opinions might differ regarding the technicalities, but the suggested approach would seem perfectly natural and so acceptable. Since most governments are not socialist, a socialist approach will surely not be enthusiastically applauded. Particularly one cannot expect the big powers to be ready to surrender their arbitrary power to an internationally controlled agency. Thus it is more likely that the initiative will be first accepted by smaller industrialised countries. Such an acceptance cannot, of course, have important quantitative consequences. But it may help to educate the world public opinion and to exert pressure on superpowers until a complete acceptance is achieved. Let me briefly review some of the pros and cons of the proposed scheme.

Few people are likely to oppose openly an international development effort, but many will argue that it is impractical since money is simply not available. There are at least three possible answers to this objection. The required transfer of resources is just a fraction of the existing military expenditures.[1] If an agreement could be reached whereby military expenditures would be reduced and resources used for international economic development, everybody in the world stands to gain. Next, if the 19th century capital export is taken as a standard, the United States would have to reproduce Marshall Plan twice per annum in order to match British lending abroad in the 19th century as measured in proportion to national income.[2] Thirdly, five European countries exceeded 1 per cent target in terms of total flow of financial resources (Switzerland 1·4 per cent, France 1·2 per cent, Federal Republic German 1·2 per cent, Belgium 1·2 per cent, the Netherlands 1·1 per cent, all in 1968). The official assistance of France has exceeded 0·7 per cent.[3]

[1] Addressing the Columbia University Conference on International Economic Development, Mr. MacNamara – formerly a defence minister and now the president of the World Bank – found it necessary to point out: 'It is tragic and senseless that the world today is spending $175 billion a year on armaments, a sum so huge that it is 25 times larger than the total spent in all foreign assistance programmes'. Professor Frisfeld estimates that military expenditures in the U.S.S.R. are about as large as the total G.N.P. of India; the U.S. military expenditures are possibly 50 per cent larger (*op. cit.*, pp. 10–12).

[2] B. Higgins, *Economic Development* (Norton, New York, 1968), p. 197.

[3] *Vedovato Report*, p. 22.

Suppose we have the money – our conservative opponents may continue to argue – why should we send it abroad instead of using it to deal with the pressing needs at home? Charity is certainly not a meaningful answer; it is not convincing for the donors, it is offending for the recipients and it is simply not true. The moralist explanation – the obligation of the rich to help the poor, or to remedy the injustices of colonialism – may appeal to some noble souls, but is not likely to be very effective. The *Pearson Report* sees the motive for international action in an enlightened long-run self-interest:

> It is a recognition that concern with improvement of the human condition is no longer divisible. If the rich countries . . . concentrate on the elimination of poverty and backwardness at home and ignore them abroad, what would happen to the principles by which they seek to live? Could the moral and social foundations of their own societies remain living and steady if they shed their hands of the plight of others?[1]

Similar reasoning, with a somewhat more pragmatic touch, one finds in the report that the American banker R. A. Peterson prepared for his government:

> . . . the developing countries contain two-thirds of the world population. Their future success or failure will influence profoundly the kind of world we live in. The nations of the world are growing more interdependent – in trade, in finance, in technology and in the critical area of political change. U.S. decision-making in such important areas or military expenditures will be influenced by the amounts of turbulence in the developing countries of the world, and U.S. prosperity will be influenced by their economic progress.[2]

Summarising the proceedings of a conference on international co-operation in aid held in Cambridge, England, in 1966, R. Robinson points out that

> economic aid is a sensible insurance against neo-colonialist rivalry, the revival of imperialism and its risks to international peace . . . if in the past the internal crises in developing countries arising from flagrant mismanagement of their relations with the outside world have frequently invited juggernauts to clash and intervene, it is cheaper and better to prevent these occasions arising again by helping economic and social construction.[3]

An approach motivated by some immediate and very tangible economic gains, Vedovato calls the realist approach. Donor countries have benefited from the tied aid, they have established footholds in overseas markets. 'Others have financed, through exports of private capital, the

---

[1] *Pearson Report*, p. 8.   [2] *Peterson Report*, p. 8.   [3] *Op. cit.*, p. 15.

prospecting and exploitation of oil, mineral ores and other raw materials needed by their national industry.'[1]

In connection with the access to the market, one can invoke the classical free trade argument. Why should Japan impose a 200 per cent tariff on the import of rice from her Asian neighbours and the Common Market countries a combined levy of 50–80 per cent on the import of meat from Yugoslavia, and why should developed countries grow sugar beet when it is so much cheaper to import cane sugar from tropical countries? Why should industrialised countries spend $1 billion annually on research intended to develop substitutes for tropical agricultural products,[2] when these products are already available? Clearly, costs could be substantially reduced, trade substantially increased and everybody concerned could substantially gain if trade barriers were eliminated. Next, since most of the developed countries surely do not operate at the absorptive capacity limits, the world income tax means an expansion of foreign markets by the same amount due to the purchases effected by the less developed countries. In fact foreign trade will expand by more than that amount because the increase in the domestic output of developing countries will generate some additional imports and exports. A scheme may be devised so as to ensure a fair participation in gains of trade by all donors. The budgetary subsidy, when used to finance the adequate diet, may help to relieve the United States, Canada and other agricultural producers of their surpluses. In short, an international co-operation will lead to a better utilisation of the world's human and physical resources.

Finally, the international community has also some means to exert pressure when necessary. The membership in the United Nations Organisation may be made conditional upon the fulfilment of the economic development co-operation obligations.

We have reached the point of conclusion. The contemporary world seems to be structured in such a way as to make the socialist – some may prefer to call it the humanist – solution not only desirable, but also necessary. The moralist and the realist approach work in the same direction. There seems to be no other viable and rational long-run alternative.

[1] *Vedovato Report*, p. 13.
[2] IMF-IBRD, *The Problem of Stabilization of Prices of Primary Products* (A Staff Study, Part I, 1969), p. 26.

Discussion of the Paper by Branko Horvat

Professor Knall, opening the discussion, pointed out that the original title of the paper, 'The Gap between the rich and the poor Nations from the Socialist Countries' Perspective', had been changed by the author to 'The Gap from the Socialist Viewpoint'. The reason was, as Professor Horvat said, that 'Socialism is not about nations; it is about individuals'. If wealth were distributed among individuals very unequally, the conditions for equality of opportunity were violated. Professor Horvat felt that, 'Socialism is exactly about equality'; while, on the contrary, 'in a situation of sufficiently different levels of development, a free market economy generates economic polarisation and not a compensatory movement of resources'.

Given this, Professor Horvat believed that it was in the nature of things that rich nations should exploit poor nations. From this increasing frustration would arise and, unless concerted international action was taken in time, one might expect social and political upheavals. The way of avoiding a social explosion – according to Professor Horvat – was the socialist viewpoint. He said that this was likely to become the point of view of our epoch. Professor Knall could not see what was specifically socialist about this, unless by 'socialist' Professor Horvat meant the awareness of the gap between rich and poor nations *and* a willingness to undertake concerted international action to give assistance. If this was the socialist viewpoint, then Professor Knall thought we were all 'socialists'.

The author went on to survey briefly the data about the inequality of income in the world and of the unfavourable situation in developing countries. This alarming state of affairs had been recognised and aid programmes initiated by all inustrialised countries, as well as by the U.N. family. Professor Horvat rightly underlined that 'development is clearly the primary responsibility of the less developed countries themselves. . . . But their own developmental efforts have so far been frustrated by at least three groups of causes: (1) the lack of access to the markets of industrialised countries; (2) the insufficient transfer of private and public resources; (3) the organisational inefficiencies of developmental assistance.'

On the basis of his analysis, Professor Horvat derived a 'fairly obvious conclusion: If there is to be a substantial change, if the underdeveloped countries are to begin to catch up with their more fortunate industrial neighbours, a concerted international action ought to be undertaken'. This led him to a proposal for a world planning agency – the *pièce de résistance* of Professor Horvat's paper. The world planning agency (W.P.A.) should be an independent institution under the political (but not administrative) control of the U.N. The organisational structure that Professor Horvat favoured was given on pages 104–5 of his paper.

As far as the necessary policy measures were concerned, Professor Horvat classified the developing world into two groups: (1) countries in the initial stages of development; (2) semi-developed countries. To the first group belonged the countries of black Africa and Asia (except the Middle East). In the second group he included the Arab countries and Iran, Latin America and Southern Europe.

This group, and each of its subgroups, displayed much wider differences in development than the first group. As a general rule for development policy, the countries in group 1 would rely heavily on subsidies (unilateral transfers) and very soft loans. Group 2 might perhaps replace subsidies by very soft loans or (in its upper income levels, say, in Southern Europe) use only near-commercial and commercial loans for development investment.

The money required for W.P.A. would come from a 1 per cent income tax imposed on all industrial and group 2 countries. Official assistance by the W.P.A. would be completely *untied*. However, a simple procedure could be worked out to ensure that the value of purchases by the recipients of the donor countries were equal to the portion of income taxed away in these countries.

At the end of his paper Professor Horvat dealt with the political feasibility of his approach. He started with a statement which would certainly arouse discussion: 'If all governments were socialist, opinions might differ regarding the technicalities, but the suggested approach would seem perfectly natural and so acceptable. Since most governments are not socialist, a socialist approach will surely not be enthusiastically applauded.'

The author ended his paper by reviewing briefly the pros and cons of the proposed scheme. First, many people would say that it was impractical since money was simply not available. Second, even if we had the money, why should we give it to developing countries instead of using it for pressing needs at home? In conclusion, the author stressed the pressing necessity for effective international co-operation, which seemed to be the only way for a better use of the world's human and physical resources.

Professor Knall pointed out that the paper did, of course, give much more detail about various matters – especially the organisation and procedures of the proposed W.P.A. This was not a completely new proposal because the need for such an agency had been expressed from time to time. For example, in the papers presented to the conference, Mr. Economides mentioned a 'world development planning authority' which would also act as a clearing house for all development grants. The Pearson Report, in chapter 11, on 'An International Framework for Development' also contained some interesting thoughts on how multilateral machinery could be enlarged and improved; however, this presupposed a thorough review of the present system of international organisations.

Professor Horvat's proposal was more coherent and more comprehensive than previous schemes. The main difficulty was one very important question: were the industrialised countries willing to act as required? In this respect he felt that Professor Horvat's statement that 'if all governments were socialist, the suggested approach would seem acceptable', sounded somewhat optimistic. The bigger nations of the socialist, and also of the capitalist, world would not surrender their power easily to an international control agency. There were many reasons for continuing to use bilateral channels, some of them listed in the Pearson Report (p. 209). However he did agree with Professor Horvat when he presumed that it was more likely that the suggested agency would first be accepted by the smaller industrialised countries.

What Professor Horvat said about the W.P.A. covered most of the items which could be dealt with in a paper of this kind. Despite its shortness it was an excellent starting point for further consideration, research and action. It seemed that the time had come when the internationalisation of development effort should enter a more operational phase. International surveys like the Jackson and Pearson reports had already prepared the ground by emphasising the crucial need for concerted international action. What future research could and should do to work out more concisely the aims, the organisational structure and the procedures of the W.P.A. Within this research work, an important aspect was the elaboration of criteria which would be applied to the transfer of resources. Another was the financing of the W.P.A. The suggested 1 per cent income tax could eventually be combined with a scheme like that proposed by Hirschman and Bird in their essay 'Foreign Aid – the Critique and Proposal' (*Essays in International Finance*, no. 169, Princeton University, July 1968, pp. 15–16). Through this individual taxpayers could claim a full tax credit for the foreign-aid contribution up to 5 per cent of their income tax, or $10,000, whichever was smaller.

If the participants in the conference believed that the proposal for a W.P.A. was sound, then our discussion might perhaps concentrate on points which needed elaborating. Whatever the soundness and rationality of the project, however, the most difficult thing would be the political willingness of donor countries. Would they accept the idea both of internationalisation and institutionalisation of their development efforts? This, of course, goes far beyond the province of economists.

Professor Horvat said that Professor Knall had agreed with most of the points he had made, so that he was able only to agree in return. He would, however, like to elaborate two points. First, what was a socialist? If a readiness to improve the world was socialism, then indeed we all were socialists. However in the real world decision-makers were not socialists. Not every 'socialist' was a socialist. What mattered was what nations did. Professor Knall said that big countries, both socialist and capitalist, would keep to bilateral relationships. If they did, then they were not socialists. On how new the idea of the W.P.A. was, he agreed that Jackson had said much the same thing at a Cambridge conference in 1960. Today there was general agreement that we needed to move to multilateral arrangements. However, people associated planning with administrative order-giving. He used the word to mean prediction, anticipation and co-ordination. Administrative order-giving had no place. It was also said that we needed a world government if we were to plan. He did not agree with this.

Professor Vernon wanted to deal with the paper delicately, because its use of the words 'planning' and 'socialism' did not give them the normal meanings. In the paper, socialism excluded state socialism; planning excluded a large administrative apparatus; planning objectives were limited to the things that were socially good. In sum, Professor Horvat was basically talking about benign, open activities by benign open participants. Such activities were obviously for the good. Should the world move to world planning? All, no doubt, would agree that we needed more multilateral activity. But would the L.D.C.s themselves be willing to plan? The last ten years suggested a decline in the disposition to do so. Would they be willing to accept guidance from a world planning agency? This, too, seemed to be a declining propensity among L.D.C.s. Still, more multilateral activity was probably desirable. It might entail the risk of less aid, but the shift might be accompanied by less tension.

Dr. Little suggested that Professor Horvat was wrong to claim that aid would not increase because the leaders of developed countries were not socialist. The fact was that in developed countries public opinion mattered very much – and aid was not popular. As a result, the analogy between equality within countries and between countries broke down. There was little feeling of community with other countries. While he would agree with Professor Vernon that we needed more multilateral aid, few would want a monolithic administrative structure of the kind Professor Horvat suggested. Multilateral co-ordination was not always better *in practice* than a good deal of bilateralism. And even if *all* aid were multilateral, there would be a lot to be said for different aid organisations, because this would mean differences in style. It would probably be very wrong to go for one style.

Professor Černe said that when one spoke about the gap, one had to ask between whom. In the papers, one found the words 'country' and 'nation'. Both were categories to be used cautiously. Within a country one had rich and poor – not just in G.N.P. but in wealth too. Professor Černe thought that the contrast between developed and underdeveloped countries and between Communist and non-Communist countries was wrong. As we knew, if we ranked countries in terms of income per head, some countries were less developed than others. His own finding was that the less-developed Communist countries did twice as well as the non-Communist ones. Why was this? Were there tendencies to eliminate the economic gap the same in Communist and non-Communist L.D.C.s? Or was the effect of changes in L.D.C.s a result of the Marxian laws of tendency to capital accumulation? Did not the widening gap between non-Communist L.D.C.s and developed countries require a solution in theory and in practice? It was a question not just of aid but of future generations. To allow the rich to get richer was not helping co-existence. It was rather advocating the Schumpeterian idea of a 'destructive destruction'. The idea of a world planning agency was not necessarily a socialist institution; indeed, it might at present be even against the socialist idea of what was needed.

Professor Robinson strongly agreed with Dr. Little. Everyone would prefer multilateral to bilateral arrangements; if one could guarantee the same total amount of aid either way, then multilateral arrangements were better. Yet if some countries were prepared to give more in bilateral aid than if forced to give aid multilaterally, was it really clear that we *must* rule out the bilateral solution?

However if one had a world planning organisation, how would it allocate funds? Would not all the old political pressures arise? Should we not end up by giving so much per head in all countries? How could one get a rational allocation of funds? Without going all the way with Professor Rosenstein-Rodan, he would suggest that one might feel that different countries at different moments of time could use aid more effectively and were poised to carry out a 'big push'. Might not the best ways of helping L.D.C.s be to help some a great deal at a particular time? If so, would this be better done by a monolithic organisation? Might it not be best to persuade a number of countries to go and help one L.D.C. at a particular moment. He thought that there was great virtue in *distributing* the process of decision-making over aid.

Professor Johnson argued that this was all right provided one did not go too deeply. The distinction between multilateral and bilateral aid was becoming an unreal dispute, a play on words. We did seem to have an aid-givers' view of these things now. It followed that a variety of decision takers would not be likely to reach different conclusions.

There was then the question of whether a multilateral view would be more monolithic. At the moment one could argue that the whole process was much too unco-ordinated. Perhaps we paid too much attention to governments. Since we did not like national policies, we tried to move toward international arrangements in the hope that we would do better. The problem at that level, as Dr. Little had said, was that the general public was not interested in aid. There was, therefore much to be said for bilateral arrangements. The U.K., for example, could help India and Pakistan more easily than Taiwan. There could be much more aid on a country-to-country basis than on the basis of common humanity.

Professor Knall had suggested that there would be a lot of public support for the notion of contributing to development assistance on a humanitarian basis. Perhaps the solution would be to mobilise aid nationally, coercing those who did not want to give. This brought us back to bilateral rather than multilateral solutions. It was easier to resist a world tax rather than a national one. Perhaps we should clear the way to allow individuals and groups to give to development and then obtain tax remissions. Individuals might feel that they had much more control over the way tax resources were used.

Professor Correa wanted to challenge Professor Vernon on the remark that underdeveloped countries should take guidance. In his view those who needed guidance were developed countries. Underdeveloped countries did not use economic power to get benefit for themselves; developed countries did. This had been seen, for example, in the Geneva World Trade Conference. The underdeveloped countries had suggested ways in which the more favoured countries could help them. None had been accepted.

Dr. Mahbub ul Haq expressed some sympathy with Professor Horvat in his contention that the socialist viewpoint would inevitably triumph in underdeveloped countries. He felt that many of these countries had experimented with mixed economies, often with a blend of capitalist institutions and socialist objectives, but there was an increasing disenchantment with such experiments and a growing tendency to turn socialist, at least at the intellectual if not at the institutional level.

He cited the experience of Pakistan. Pakistan had openly accepted the capitalist road to development in the 1960s. It had introduced all the usual incentives for saving and investment, experimented with dismantling of economic controls and allocation through price mechanism, and aided and abetted the process of rapid capital formation, irrespective of income inequality so long as the end result was an acceleration in the growth rate. This worked fairly well until about the middle of the 1960s, since foreign aid kept increasing and protected domestic consumption, especially through the provision of PL480 foodgrains. However, the system broke down in the late 1960s when there was a decline in foreign assistance and the squeeze resulting from a wish to protect the growth rate fell on the urban areas. Real wages of industrial workers declined by about one-third.

Dr. Haq reflected that the capitalist way of development could be protected only if the Western world was prepared to give massive doses of foreign assist-ance so that pressure on domestic consumption could be cushioned in a period of rapid development. Otherwise, the income inequalities inherent in the process of capitalist growth would become an explosive issue and the developing countries would settle for a lower growth rate rather than a distorted pattern of income distribution. He also speculated that, after about two decades of aimless development, the underdeveloped countries were more likely to turn inwards and to debate policy questions like domestic income distribution, the justice of rewards from the development process, the basic structure of society, etc. If socialism was about equality of opportunity (and that was how Professor Horvat had defined it), then this would be a triumph of the socialist point of view.

As for the world planning organisation, he was not sure whether Professor Horvat would like to impose the tyranny of centralised world planning on under-developed countries or whether his proposal amounted only to better co-ordination of aid. He argued that unless proposals for better co-ordination of aid and for the monitoring of economic performance were accompanied by a major increase in aid, the underdeveloped countries were likely to reject them, as the discipline implied in these proposals would not be compensated by the promise of any carrot.

Dr. Haq concluded that if a world planning agency was to be established, it would be irksome, impractical and unacceptable. The underdeveloped countries should be allowed to develop in their own fashion, according to their own stages of development, without being subjected to pre-fabricated models of develop-ment from a central agency. Economists would do better by helping to improve the aid climate than by sitting in judgement on how the diminishing volume of aid should be co-ordinated.

Professor Khachaturov said that the problem of the gap was dynamic – a result of the factors of economic growth. He thought that it was essential to examine the influence of these factors. Countries developed unequally; their rates of growth at different times were different. Some countries went ahead while others lagged behind. Their relative positions were changing all the time.

He thought there were two groups of factors. First, there were natural factors like location, climate and natural resources. Second, there were social factors like the economic system, international relations, technology and science, and education. He thought that social factors were the most important. It was likely that such advantages as the presence of important natural resources or the proximity of seaways could lead in certain social situations to the acceleration of growth, but in other situations to the country becoming a colony. This was why he thought it useful to study historical, economic and social conditions for the development of different countries in order to find the causes of the gap. When one saw what these causes were, it was possible to work out how to remove them.

It might well be that to raise the rate of growth of underdeveloped countries one could learn by looking at the U.S.S.R., which had made the transition from an underdeveloped to a developed country. There were also some republics, parts of the Soviet Union especially in Central Asia and the Trans-Caucasus, which before the revolution were underdeveloped borderlands of the Russian

Empire. These regions had now become developed Soviet republics and provided a greater share of the G.N.P. of the U.S.S.R. and of its investment.

If one looked at other socialist countries, one found that, as a whole, these were growing faster than the rest of the world. The co-ordination of their development was very important for the economic growth of socialist countries. They did not have to be identical. They had different resources and different traditions. Between 1950 and 1968 considerable differences in the rates of growth had been allowed in order to equalise the levels of economic achievement in these countries, with the highest rates of growth in the least developed socialist countries. With the development of the socialist system, discrepancies in such overall measures as output per man should be reduced.

There was a need for social control over the economy. Mutual assistance became more essential. The interests of underdeveloped socialist countries were taken into account in planning and co-ordination within the socialist world. The exchange of scientific knowledge was also important. Prices and the amount of foreign aid were fixed so as to benefit underdeveloped countries. Underdeveloped countries in the socialist world obtained funds from industrialised countries or from the investment bank.

As for the underdeveloped countries outside of the socialist system, one could mention that central planning would help them to redistribute resources and increase short-run economic growth. There were many ways to remove the obstacles to their development and to give more opportunities for their productive forces. But this appeared to be a matter for separate discussion.

Professor Patinkin said that there seemed to be an implicit contradiction between the development assistance that underdeveloped countries felt they should get and that provided by the market mechanism. Funds did not go to underdeveloped countries for the purposes they wanted. Yet if a country had oil, the oil companies would compete to exploit it. This implied that developed countries gave aid only for political purposes.

If underdeveloped countries wanted to keep out politically-motivated assistance, how should they behave? They might support multilateral arrangements because these implied less political influence. For example, they might use the World Bank – though this was conservative. What they wanted was an institution that was risk-taking. The dilemma seemed to remain.

On exemption from income tax, Professor Patinkin suggested that all finance ministers in countries which did not yet have these arrangements would say that the government wanted to decide how to use its own tax revenue and not leave this to taxpayers. It was not realistic to think that such schemes would spread much more widely. In any case, he doubted whether they would raise much money.

Professor Ohlin still could not find what was specifically socialist about Professor Horvat's paper. Equality was not the same as socialism. He agreed that social ideology would affect what happened to a country, but with variation and diversity. As for the gap, did socialist thought have any more to say about it than that in the rest of the world?

Passing to the suggestion for a world planning organisation, he was surprised that this came from a Yugoslav. He thought that Yugoslavs had seen that central planning had its problems and were not sure that a world planning agency would make things *less* barbaric. A monolithic agency scared him. There was much difficulty today because there was too much co-ordination. What we wanted was workable competition to break up the task of the international organisations.

Professor Eastman said that Canadian income tax regulations permitted the deduction from taxable income of certain contributions for charitable purposes in developing countries. Modest sums were given this way, of which the government in effect paid about half. He expected that, if regulations allowed taxpayers to designate how their tax payments should be spent, large sums would initially be allotted to foreign aid because each taxpayer would imagine his contribution to be costless to himself. However it would soon become evident that the increased foreign aid expenditures were not at the expense of other governmental expenditure but largely additional to them, and taxes would rise. Professor Eastman believed that total foreign aid contributions would then probably fall below present levels as individual taxpayers came to realise that their own action influenced the total tax paid. In any event he did not think that governments would tolerate a system causing substantial loss of control over budgetary decisions and probably great budgetary instability. He noted that Canada had very recently increased its foreign aid expenditure, partly because of falling defence spending. Perhaps the main hope for foreign aid lay in a falling defence expenditure, because governments preferred to spend money rather than reduce taxation.

Professor Yenal thought that if one could talk of the 'socialist view' of the gap, the relevant issues would be the impact of the gap on economic systems, especially in poor countries, or the effect of these systems in widening the gap. These issues were different from the general topic of capitalism *versus* socialism, since countries might choose a particular way of life for quite other reasons than the effect of economic systems on the gap. As far as the impact of the gap on the economic systems of the poor countries was concerned, he wondered how far increasing aid could push or pull countries out of the orbit of one economic system into another. On the other hand it was not clear to him how the choice of economic systems might remedy the trend of the widening gap.

Multilateral aid had been discussed at great length. Apart from the expression of a general desire for international equality, he did not see how a socialist (or, for that matter, a capitalist) view related to international flow of funds. When we spoke of *multilateral* arrangements we really meant *multinational* arrangements. The fundamental problem faced was strong nationalism and the pursuit of national interests – whether socialist or capitalist. And the answer was to be sought in moderating nationalism and fostering internationalism, rather than in a movement towards one system rather than another.

Dr. Anita Pfaff said that Professor Horvat had used the term socialism in a very broad sense. She would rather call this a systematic view than a socialist view. In an aid process both donors and recipients could be distinguished. However, both were members of a system. A system could be defined by a set of members, a set of joint goals and a pattern of interdependence between members. The process of aid was an expression and function of the underlying interdependence between donor and recipient. In a systematic view two general types of motivation for giving could be identified: (1) the integrative system resulted in giving because there was a sense of community between grantor and grantee (love, compassion, pity); (2) giving under the threat system was aimed at diverting a direct or potential threat from the grantee to the grantor – the grantee considered withdrawing from the system or destroying it. Blackmail and bribery were cases in point. In economic terms, one-way flows resulted in an imbalance in the system. In psychological terms, what appeared as unilateral economic relationships were very often bilateral. The act of giving resulted in increased prestige for the grantor; or satisfaction due to a realisation of his self-image. It often put him 'above' the grantee. Alternatively, the grant or gift was given as a pay-off for a past wrong. In narrow economic terms these aspects appeared irrational and irrelevant. In a behavioural sense they provided the cause and motivation for economic action.

Current international aid had historical roots. Either there were guilt feelings towards the former colonial countries or a sense of community with them was developed by former colonial powers, resulting in a flow of aid to the former colony.

An optimal system required a sense of community, efficiency and equity. Multilateral aid might or might not prove more efficient than bilateral aid. Multilateral aid arrangements might result in a more equitable distribution of grants; the main problem, however, lay in the formulation of operational equity criteria. Yet some recipient countries would lose relative to bilateral arrangements based on historic or other ties.

Turning to private giving, Dr. Pfaff said that private gifts (charitable contributions) had totalled about $12 billion in 1968 in the U.S.A. A price incentive effect was clearly present in giving, a person with an annual income of over $500,000 had to bear a real cost of only 36c per dollar of a charitable contribution because income tax could be deducted. Increased charitable giving by rich people had been observed. Of course, this was partly a consequence of the higher income, but most probably it was also due to the lower 'price of giving' for the rich. International private giving might, therefore, be fostered by tax incentives. However, most countries would grant such tax incentives very discriminatingly, if at all, since this would provide governments with a tool for directing their citizens' grants to particular recipients.

Professor Horvat replied to the debate. As Professor Vernon had indicated he had not used the word 'planning' in a normal sense. He had not used it in the sense in which it was used in the U.S.A. or Europe. But he had used it in the way it was used in Yugoslavia, and he felt free to do so in Bled. Professor Vernon saw socialism as open, benign and co-operative. He did not agree. It was not just a matter of good wishes.

To Dr. Little, Professor Horvat said that the claim that rich countries had to bother with public opinion was in contrast with what Professor Eastman had said. He would draw attention to the 'tax effect'. If left to themselves, taxpayers would not provide foreign aid; they did so because there was a tax advantage. If there was an international law for all to pay 1 per cent of income tax to poor countries, this would achieve the desired result.

Since he had written his paper, an article in *World Affairs* (No. 4, 1970) by Hamilton, suggested that policies of bilateral aid were untenable; multilateral aid must come. Neither public pressure nor attention to Congress would help enough. We needed a longer-term mandate. He had recently met an international group of decision-makers and found them much more receptive to these ideas than a few years ago. Perhaps future policy making would start from different premises.

He would recall that in 1960 when there was discussion as to whether a new United Nations Committee – later UNIDO – could be set up, everyone had said that this would be difficult because the U.S.A. and the U.S.S.R. would not agree; yet an agreement had been signed within three weeks.

When Professor Robinson asked what the agency would do, he agreed that there were difficulties. However his own paper had been selected by the programme committee and he could not go into details. He felt that one should distinguish subsidies and development loans. The criterion used for subsidies should be need – with more going to poor countries. This was a result of socialist (humanist) views. Neither loans nor subsidies should affect things like medical and educational facilities, which must depend on the criterion of performance.

He would say to Professor Robinson that no planning agency could avoid political pressure whatever was done. He did not want to prevent foreign aid being more than 1 per cent of international income tax. He just wanted an obligatory base. Professor Johnson had referred to tax deduction and so had others. There had been some support for a tax on tobacco and liquor used to benefit underdeveloped countries. There were many suggestions about how one might raise the money. Whatever method was used, it would not be too hard to raise 1 per cent of tax revenue. Professor Eastman's problems would then be solved because deductions would take place only within the 1 per cent limit.

Professor Ohlin had wondered whether the socialist tradition had more to say than other writers about equality in economic development. It did, though he did not argue the point in his paper.

To Dr. Anita Pfaff, Professor Horvat said that socialism via systems analysis was interesting. One could go on to look at problems of threat and integration. The threat system was still with us, but it did not belong to the socialist system. Only integration belonged to the socialist approach. Everyone was part of the same system – citizens of the same world. In medieval and feudal times humanism had been concerned with family or village solidarity. In modern capitalism it dealt with the whole nation. We were now entering an era where the community covered the whole world – a socialist community, he hoped, and therefore an integrative system.

5 Reduction of a Gap between Rich and Poor Regions within a Planned Economy: The Case of Yugoslavia

Albin Orthaber

UNIVERSITY OF LJUBLJANA, YUGOSLAVIA

I. INTRODUCTORY

This paper aims to show the problems that have arisen in reducing the gap between the developed and the less developed regions of Yugoslavia and the ways in which these have been tackled. For this purpose it has been divided into two parts. The paper itself deals analytically with some of the general and specific issues that have presented themselves.

An appendix contains some of the factual information relevant to the problems of reducing the gap. A reader who is not familiar with present conditions in Yugoslavia may find the paper itself easier to understand if he begins by reading the appendix.

This paper is deliberately confined to examination of the limited field of economic development, without dealing with the numerous objectives and measures in the fields of cultural and social life and human relations, though the author is well aware of their immense importance.

II

Within the framework of the national plan, the current objectives and measures designed to reduce the gap are set out. They depend principally on the material conditions prevailing in the country as a whole, on the progress made, on the rate of growth and on the structure of economy in the developed and the less developed regions, and in particular, on the extent of the gap. In addition, they are closely dependent also on the institutional conditions and on general economic conditions.

There have been considerable changes and inconsistencies in the policies and in the public attitudes regarding the size, motives, methods and timing of the removal of the gap.

So far as concerns the period and the dimensions of the problem of removing the gap, in the first stages of building up the planned economy there was a belief that an adequate equalisation of the two regions, the less developed (L.D.R.s) and the developed (D.R.s) could be achieved within a relatively short period. At the same time there was also a belief that national resources could be effectively redistributed through centralised decisions, taking into account the accepted criteria of solidarity and equality of rights.

Faced with the dilemma of growth or equalisation, the new economic system, aiming at as rapid a growth of the whole national economy as possible, decided in favour of the first alternative, implying a primary dependence of equalisation on growth. In particular, after the Reform in 1965 it explored the possibility that inter-regional allocation can be achieved on the principles of economic profitability, invoking in addition the criteria of solidarity when necessary.

In this way a considerable volume of resources is, it is true, made available without being specifically devoted to the purpose of closing the gap. But at the same time an attempt is made to follow the principle of increasing social utility. A further, considerably smaller proportion of the total resources is transferred to the L.D.R.s in accordance with the criteria of business interest (in the case of raw materials or products), or else calls for a certain profitability (as in the case of participation of enterprises in the D.R.s in the financing and profits of those of the L.D.R.s). There is a current tendency to increase the volume of such transfers. A considerable proportion of the available funds, however, is today still allocated on the basis of political bargaining.

In framing the strategy to reduce the gap and provide the necessary resources to do so, the conflicting aspirations of individual groups of interests are often apparent. In most cases they represent the divergent interests of individual regions. Although the realities of existing circumstances and the limited practical possibilities of reducing the gap prevent the achievement of maximum objectives – for instance, a very short-term elimination of the gap – the estimates of realistic targets and of possible sources and volumes of resources for their achievement, as well as views on ways of using them, differ considerably. This is a phenomenon that cannot be escaped in any type of society, whatever its institutions.

Furthermore, tendencies have been emerging to introduce in one and the same country, in addition to already differentiated development, policies towards various types of regions and economic policies that should to some extent discriminate between different developed regions and discriminate again between different less developed regions. Such tendencies have led to many controversies although, in the ultimate analysis, there is no denying the view that a duality in the system does not follow from a substantive duality within a modern state.

In view of the strains and conflicts between the developed and less developed parts of the country and the harm done by these, there is a steadily growing conviction that the social benefits that would result from the elimination of this effective duality would be greater than the direct and indirect social costs of elimination.

In consequence the central problem of raising the standard of the developed has been moved into a new focus. There are a number of factors dictating a further reconsideration of the principles of solidarity and of equality of rights. It is in the interest of the economy as a whole, when one is dealing with the reduction of the gap, that the costs of achieving it shall be as low as possible and the benefits as great as possible. As this depends partly on the time factor, it is necessary to discover the optimal time horizon in which a determined reduction of the gap can be achieved.

There are a number of alternative ways of achieving any objective of this kind, both in terms of locations and of sectors; it is necessary to select from among them, on the basis of appropriate political and economic criteria. These criteria, however, can be formulated and established satisfactorily only within the framework of a development plan. Such methods are being introduced rather slowly and partially. At present those responsible use in practice the remnants of the old and new systems. But in addition there are being evolved more vigorous concepts deriving from the logic of the Reform. Apart from the former centralised inter-regional allocations, made on the basis of subjective and red-tape criteria, there remain allocations that are exposed to market anomalies and individual profiteering. It is against a background of these that there are increasing tendencies to introduce into the inter-regional allocations, decisions based on the consideration of common social benefits, recognised and measured by scientific methods.

To make it possible to discuss the methodological problems of such programming we must first formulate afresh the general objective. The fundamental problem is to achieve, as soon as possible and as completely as possible, the reduction of the gap; but to do this in a way that will least affect the efficiency and growth of the national economy as a whole, and avoid harmful repercussions on the dynamic growth path of the economy.

Any comparison of the theoretical differences between the D.R.s and the L.D.R.s on a world scale with the actual differences between the developed and the less developed regions of Yugoslavia shows us that the latter possess some specific features. Most of these differences derive from the basic fact that the less developed regions of Yugoslavia still have the 'classical' characteristics of never having been developed, while the developed areas of Yugoslavia do not possess the complete attributes of a state of full development. The characteristics of the L.D.R. are everywhere, and equally in Yugoslavia: a lack of capital; a low saving capacity; a rapid increase of population and surplus of manpower, combined with shortage of higher skills; low efficiency and a low level of production associated with slow growth, particularly if the region is wholly dependent on its own potentialities for development. The familiar characteristics of all less developed regions include an inadequate infrastructure, low and undiversified demands in the local market, and similar features.

While all these typical characteristics of a less developed region are apparent in the L.D.R.s of Yugoslavia, one cannot discover in its developed regions all the attributes of a state of development. Capital is still a scarce factor. In spite of a slower increase in population, shortage of unskilled labour is not a characteristic of all the developed areas of Yugoslavia. There is surplus labour leaving Croatia, Slovenia and Serbia to go abroad, particularly since the Reform eliminated disguised unemployment. The fundamental structural characteristic of a state of development, with a high proportion of industrial production and a relatively small proportion of employment in agriculture, is not yet fully evident. Neither the productive nor the non-productive infrastructures are yet completed in the D.R.s. The qualifications of highly skilled manpower are not appreciably greater than are required by the level of the technology currently in use. These specific features of the current economic state of the regions exercise decisive influence on the possible methods of reducing the gap between the L.D.R.s and the D.R.s of Yugoslavia.

A second group of factors influencing strongly the choice of policies and measures to reduce the gap, are the institutional features, including those of the economic system of the country. Among other things it is relevant, in regard to the policy of removing the gap, to establish who makes decisions about future development, in whose interest, and by what criteria. On these questions there are preconceptions with regard to socialist countries, formed in the early post-war era, which only in part correspond to the realities of today. According to these preconceptions the main decision-makers are the central state organs, which supposedly make their decisions on the basis of proposals submitted by the central state planning agencies on behalf of individual regions. They supposedly take principally into account the often conflicting criteria of the so-called public interest in which political and ideological concepts are strongly represented. These stereotyped ideas about the institutional pattern of planning can be applied to Yugoslavia scarcely at all.

The fact that in Yugoslavia the main decision-makers are economic organisations, managed by the producers themselves, is of considerable importance for the policy of removing the gap, and particularly for the measures to transfer resources from the D.R.s to the L.D.R.s. The producers make the decisions about the continually increasing proportion of the national income they create, and this reduces the possibilities of a centralised budgetary reallocation of resources to the less developed regions. As the organs of self-management in the various enterprises make autonomous decisions over wide fields of economic operations, any inter-regional arrangements must considerably depend on agreements reached by the enterprises themselves. The introduction of the criterion of profitability as the principal criterion of business decision-making has moreover led the economic organisations to base their decisions concerning non-obligatory inter-regional transfers on expected profitability. This implies that inter-regional transfers of resources have to be stimulated increasingly by indirect policy measures designed to create more favourable conditions for transfers and investments in the L.D.R.s, in the form of tax concessions, credit terms, and the like. At the same time these relative attractions are also directly affected by the random conditions of the market, by the greediness of enterprises for profits, to the disregard of their wider common interests, or by lack of interest if the projects concerned do not satisfy their short-term commercial interests.

III

Following normal lines, the Yugoslav planning strategy to reduce the inter-regional differences is designed generally along the following lines:

The transition from an economy with a low level of production and efficiency is to be achieved mainly by reallocating resources and through creating, by appropriate intervention, a more suitable environment for the development of the L.D.R.s. For closing the gap the most important transfers, apart from inter-regional movements (D.R.s to L.D.R.s), are transfers between sectors of production (agriculture to industry) and the intra-sectoral transfers between institutions. Here the point is primarily to strengthen these sectors in the economy which have development potential (the public sector, the co-operative sector, the social sector).[1]

It is well-known that regional planning, and thus also the programming to reduce the gap, takes the form in the planned economies of a combination of overall planning, sectorial planning, selection of individual projects and the detailed plans of enterprises.

The process of overall planning includes programming or forecasting changes in the basic relationships between the L.D.R.s and the D.R.s and in the various rates of growth, taking account of the growth of population and manpower increases. The volumes of productivity and similar factors are estimated. On this basis the volumes of inter-regional transfers and possible foreign borrowings are calculated, as well as the total effects of the various changes on productivity and the maintenance of any necessary balances. The programme at this stage contains not only quanti-

---

[1] For the purpose of structural change in an economy production sectors must be divided into those producing (a) for the local market, which are inherently immobile sectors, (b) those able to produce for the national economy as a whole and for areas wider than regions; and finally (c) those that can be located in any region (mobile sectors), in particular in whichever region, as a result of location, will ensure the greatest efficiency. There is sometimes also a division into national and international sectors, on the one hand, and regional and local sectors on the other hand.

tatively defined targets but possibly also the measures proposed for their implementation. In this work the use of dual models is normal, and ordinarily the regional and the sectorial approaches are reconciled at this stage.

There is a further scope for reducing the gap in planning the structural changes of the national economy, particularly in the plans for production. This is done chiefly in two or three fields and sometimes as separate operations. In the first phases of the transition of a L.D.R. the most important structural change is in the planned expansion of the industrial sectors for the benefit of the agrarian section. This is achieved through a preferential allocation of the resources of the whole economy to industry and through movement of manpower from the agrarian sector to the industrial sectors.

At this stage some countries have given preference first in their plans to creating a productive infrastructure and setting up basic industries, while in a number of other countries development was started successfully through a more rapid and cumulative development of manufacturing industries. Each of these two basic solutions has different effects on the rate and extent of reduction of the gap.

Once basic industries and the necessary infrastructure have been created, preference can be given to those 'national' and 'international' sectors that show the most favourable opportunity costs and are competitive in the foreign market. The speed and results of this process in developing the less developed regions depend to a considerable extent on the strategy adopted in planning, in the country concerned. Aspirations towards creating a predominantly consumers' society or an heroic or humanitarian society can fundamentally alter the basis of allocating resources to sectors and thus also the structure of the economy in the less developed regions.

One of the conditions which can make it possible for this process to escape major trouble and disequilibrium is a more rapid growth of productivity in agriculture. The latter has to succeed in producing more raw materials for manufacturing and more food for the workers employed in manufacture while itself employing less manpower. If as a result the disposable income earned by the farmers has been increased up to the extent of enabling them to purchase a part of the increased industrial production, and at the same time to modernise technologically their own production, a number of important potential dangers of economic imbalance will thus have been removed.

An important part in the structural change of the economy, the absorption of the surplus of manpower, the creation of opportunities for employment, the raising of the standard of life and thus the closing of the gap, is played by the tertiary sector. Its problems cannot however be discussed here.

The strategy for reducing the gap which I have outlined is too over-simplified to satisfy anyone either in practice or in theory, although it is adopted in the majority of countries with less developed regions. Its value in the present context is that it provides a clearer illustration of the specific problems that are arising, in relation to the programmes for reducing the gap here in Yugoslavia.

IV. SOME PRACTICAL PROBLEMS OF REDUCING THE GAP

Certain specific characteristics and differences between the developed and the less developed regions in Yugoslavia, together with the institutional peculiarities of the country, have created a number of special problems affecting the strategy of closing the gap.

Some specific characteristics and differences between the developed and the less developed regions in Yugoslavia, along with her institutional specific features, are the reason why the strategy for reducing the gap in Yugoslavia raises a series of special problems.

Experience has shown that in Yugoslavia as elsewhere it is difficult in a rapidly developing country to achieve a faster growth of the L.D.R.s than the average national growth. The fundamental and purely economic causes of this are not only the lack of availability of factors required for development and the magnitudes of the necessary transfers, but largely also the existing structure of the L.D.R., and the retarding force exercised on such a region by lack of a more modernised and economically developed environment.

While the developed regions have already passed the threshold between undevelopment and development, the less developed regions are still in the phase of transition to modern growth. At this stage of development the rate of growth depends on a number of inevitable preconditions, necessary for future development but for the moment lowering the rate of growth in the L.D.R.

The less developed structure of the economy compels the L.D.R. to invest its own and any external resources in infrastructure and in basic industry. These are branches of slow growth which because of the price-level of recent years do not show a high profitability and a cumulative increase. Apart from these a considerable proportion of the available resources has to be devoted to non-productive infrastructure; while it is true that this is in part a necessary condition of the growth of production, by itself it does not directly contribute to it.

Most of the developed countries of today built up their infrastructure in a period of slower growth, low wages and thus a greater surplus value of labour, when the capital intensity of production was smaller. A modern economy must operate under different economies of scale and, therefore, must invest larger quantities of capital to achieve the same result.

The volumes of capital flowing into the L.D.R.s depend on the transfers from the developed regions, where capital is still a scarce factor with a wide range of opportunities for employment at home. This has a retarding effect, especially in cases where capital, owing to the special circumstances in a L.D.R., is likely to be employed under less favourable conditions and at greater risk than in its own region of origin, or when it has greater opportunity of establishing comparative advantage at home.

The development of the regions takes place today, moreover, in an era of rapid technological progress. This aggravates the antithesis between the objective of achieving more rapid technological progress in production and the objective of solving the problem of full employment that is familiar in any dual economy. Considerable differences exist in Yugoslavia between the level of employment in a L.D.R. and a D.R., and the difference would be even greater if disguised unemployment could be taken into account. As a consequence some of these less developed regions show an exceedingly high inter-regional and only slightly lower international mobility of manpower.

It is of additional importance that those less developed regions which have comparative advantages in agricultural production too, encounter difficulties in achieving agricultural expansion in these later years of the 20th century. For many of the products agricultural output is rapidly reaching the point of saturation within the present pattern of consumption. As a production sector with a small elasticity of income demand in Europe [1], its upper limits of expansion are severely limited. The expansion of agriculture in the L.D.R.s is also limited by the fact that the income earned in the local market is not yet sufficient to make it possible to replace the existing farm equipment with more equipment at a higher technical level. This is, moreover, one of the reasons why traditional forms of land ownership have survived with the accompaniment of atomised holdings, of technologically backward methods of production and of little surplus for the market.

The surplus of manpower and the need to create a modern infrastructure and modern basic industries using up-to-date technologies has led to a controversy, relevant to the development of all less developed regions under modern conditions. In the less developed regions possessing a surplus of manpower, it is argued, the restructuring of production should proceed by giving priority to labour-intensive productive sectors [2]. This, however, very frequently conflicts with the objective of increased productivity.

Propensity to consume has been intensified in Yugoslavia because the demonstration effect of consumption in neighbouring countries affects Yugoslavia more than it does other socialist countries. Yugoslavia has practically open frontiers, and the psychological impact she receives from the north and west influence propensity to consume in the south. One of the results of the demonstration effect is a reduced propensity to save. This is faced by a high propensity to invest, which is apt to be in excess of the propensity to save. For the high propensity to invest there are several causes. One of them is that income earned depends on producers' success in raising production and thus on the adoption in production of technological, organisational, managerial and other innovations, all of which require investment.

V

From what has been said thus far, it might be easy to conclude that the closing of the gap cannot be achieved successfully, either through centralised planning or by dependence on transfers of national resources motivated by market forces or by current regional interests.

The structure of the economy in the less developed regions, their lack of infrastructure and of basic industries, their scarcity of certain essential factors such as capital and highly skilled labour, their labour surpluses and other circumstances, all require that the process of closing the gap shall be planned and programmed. In addition to a medium-term plan, a long-term strategy also needs to be drawn up. Instead of depending exclusively on political solutions, scientific decision-making methods must be employed.

The analysis of the methodological problems of operating dual economies has no long theoretical tradition. Practical experience is slight when compared with the importance of the problem. With the exception of a few outstanding works, such as those by H. Chenery, J. Tinbergen, Vera Cao Pina in respect of the Mezzogiorno, R. Carrillo Arronte in respect of Mexico, purely methodological studies capable of practical application seem to be rare. Those responsible for the gap between theory and practice that exists in this field are likely to be on both sides of the fence.

The reason for this inadequacy in the scientific studies seems predominantly to be the difficulty of calculating and forecasting the various processes in the succeeding phases of application. This has led hitherto to inadequate certainty in decision-making. This interpretation is indicated by the almost impossible tasks assigned to the methodology of programming a gap reduction.

In planning the strategy for long-term development in Yugoslavia, certain principles for programming the reduction of disparities in development were formulated under the reformed economic system. Some of the problems and conclusions can be briefly summarised as follows:

(a) As is well known, any plan must solve the problem of how to allocate optimally scarce resources in order to achieve certain given targets within the limitations imposed by certain given constraints. Since we have to deal with a dual economy, each of these elements of the programme – the resources, the targets and the constraints – must be handled in respect of both the L.D.R.s and the D.R.s, whether it is proposed to treat the problem by a system of unconnected equations or by a completely formalised dual mode.

(b) For this purpose the programming can be presented either as a maximisation of targets or as a minimisation programme in respect of the use of scarce goods or resources.

(c) The programme can be handled as a one-factor programme or as a multifactor programme. For the purpose in hand we have already restricted ourselves in our verbal exposition to handling at most three factors – capital, manpower and possibly technological progress.

(d) If a regionally homogeneous economy was under consideration, the planning problem would be how to distribute optimally the scarce resources so as to reach a maximal growth in using minimal resources or development factors. In a dual economy the problem has to be formulated differently. In principle all target variables of objectives and data, parameters or structural constants must be established for each region, L.D.R. or D.R. At the same time the fundamental objective of the programming must be reformulated to correspond. The objective is now to find a solution of the problem of how to allocate the national resources between the D.R.s and the L.D.R.s in such proportions that the rate of national growth will be least affected by the volume of resources transferred.

(e) From the point of view of efficiency the question for a programmer is formulated in a different way: how a certain volume of resources can be regionally allocated so that, consistent with maximum possible growth of efficiency in the L.D.R.s, the efficiency in the D.R.s (or in L.D.R.s plus D.R.s) is decreased least. This solution is more manageable in a sectoral approach. Because of the existence, for example, of four subregions in Yugoslavia with different efficiencies, some regional overall solution is required. In the sectoral approach the objective described is modified to that of how to allocate, by sectors and regionally, the resources used in the D.R.s and in the L.D.R.s respectively so that a maximal growth of efficiency is achieved in the L.D.R.s, consistent with a minimal decrease in the rate of growth of efficiency in the D.R.s (or in the L.D.R.s plus D.R.s). The relationships of maximisation and minimisation cannot be formulated in any other way, since it must be expected that in any case smaller values will result in the trends of productivity and national growth.

(f) Such inter-regional project selection cannot be implemented in practice through automatic elimination by individual profitability in the market or through 'planning' by verbal argument. It raises a number of very sophisticated problems. In seeking optimal solutions ordinary market prices cannot be used; the prices used reflect the true scarcity of all the components of cost. Thus the use of shadow prices is associated with the cost-benefit analysis. Their computation and use in Yugoslav regional planning raise no less problems than they do in market economies. Since such a procedure is more manageable in the project phase and less so in the sector phase of the choice of an optimal production pattern as between the individual regions, its use has proved to be difficult and expensive in consequence of the long time horizon of the strategy (extending to 1985) and the huge number of projects involved.

(g) In any dual economy the optimisation must proceed simultaneously along two lines – that of the geographical area and that of the sector. But it is impossible to apply identical procedures and criteria of choice to all groups of sectors. Immobile activities, or activities that must exist where they can directly meet on the spot the demand for goods, and particularly for services, do not depend for their existence on inclusion in the programme. They are included in the structure of the economy and reserve social resources automatically, for example in the cases of transport, power, building materials, and the like. The principle of efficiency or cost minimisation must be respected, and thus there is need to introduce technological innovations where necessary. There is a completely different situation in the case of mobile activities and of those with a national or international market. Their whole existence depends on whether they do or do not achieve a comparative advantage. If they are not capable of production at relatively more favourable opportunity costs, there is no point in allocating resources to them.

(h) The formulation attempted above represents only a half-truth. With international division of labour any economy is more or less open; this applies equally and with greater force to any regional economy in its relation to the national economy. And for this reason opportunity costs in the classical sense must be applied to it. If, for instance, a D.R. produced A and B groups of products at lower costs than a L.D.R. and the L.D.R. produced in its region only the B group more favourably, the division of labour between the regions would have to take account of this and assign to the L.D.R. only those products in the B group in which it had a comparative advantage.

REFERENCES

[1] Simon Kuznets, *Modern Economic Growth* (Yale University Press, New Haven, 1966), Chapter III.
[2] J. Fei and G. Ranis, *Innovation, Capital Accumulation, and Economic Development* (Yale University, New Haven, 1963).

APPENDIX
BACKGROUND INFORMATION RELATING TO YUGOSLAVIA

In Yugoslavia 30 per cent of the population, living in an area representing 40 per cent of the total of the country, produce only 20 to 22 per cent of the total social product. Three of the total of six republics that compose Yugoslavia – Bosnia and Herzegovina, Montenegro and Macedonia with the addition of the autonomous region of Kosovo, form according to the official definition the less developed regions of Yugoslavia. Within these less developed regions there are considerable differences again. While the inhabitants of Bosnia and Herzegovina have a per capita income two-thirds of the average of Yugoslavia, the inhabitants of the Kosovo region have an average income only one-third to a half of the average of Yugoslavia. Similar ratios apply inter-regionally to wealth per head and to most of the elements of the material, social and cultural standard of living.

Compared with the gap between the developed and the less developed countries of the world, the gap within Yugoslavia does not represent one of the most dramatic examples in the world of today. Yet its consequences powerfully affect the people who have to suffer from it; they have to live under circumstances of grave inequality within the same country. The gap exists under a socialist system which was historically brought into existence because it promised to eradicate these and similar differences.

For these reasons a progressive removal of the gap is a continually urgent task for the economic, social and cultural policies of Yugoslavia. The practical objectives within the specific period of time and the more detailed measures to carry them into effect form a regular element in the medium-term plans of the country; the objectives that only can be achieved in a longer period form a part of the long-term development policies.

The creation of conditions favourable to the removal of differences between regions, together with a partial decentralisation, remains one of the important responsibilities entrusted to the federal organs by the Constitution.

The original and underlying causes of the inadequate development of the regions that lie chiefly to the south of the river Sava are not a matter of deficiency of resources or manpower. They are primarily of historical, geographical and political character. The areas occupied by these regions were for centuries border-areas of the long-dying Ottoman Empire, or represented buffer zones for the defence of Europe against inroads from the Ottoman territories. At the time when capitalist production and international trade began to expand they were inaccessible and distant from the continental routes along which the main flows of the market economy were developing. Their natural resources failed to be exploited fully because of their low population density and inaccessibility to transport. Nor was there any considerable development, of a colonial character, of infrastructure for exploiting raw materials with industrial manufacturing industries based on them. Since these regions remained only partially independent until well into this century and were partially under the rule of various foreign empires, they were in no position to establish for themselves any considerable mutual economic interdependence. The differences of per capita income that emerged in this way could not be eradicated during the twenty-three years, from 1918 to 1941, of the existence of the Old Yugoslavia, formed from the remnants of Austria-Hungary and Serbia. Thus the differences have remained to be dealt with after the Second World War, and present one of the major problems of the new State.

In its task of closing the gap between the less developed and developed regions since the Second World War Yugoslavia has had notable success. The national income of the less developed regions rose from 1948 to the Reform in 1965 by an average of 7 per cent annually, at constant prices until 1960; the increase was as high as 8·5 per cent for the period from 1961 to 1965. In the developed regions of Yugoslavia it rose in the same two periods by 7 per cent and 7·2 per cent respectively. In the period 1966 to 1970 the annual average increase in all the less developed regions of the world amounted to 5 per cent. The high population growth, however, reduced the rate of increase of income per head to about 2·5 per cent in the 1960s which is none the less regarded as a remarkable acceleration.[1]

After the Yugoslav economic Reform of 1965, the rate of growth of the less developed regions at first fell behind that of the country as a whole, but it has been accelerating again recently, and in the period from 1966 to 1970 it will be equal to the national growth rate. At the same time a fixed capital investment and welfare expenditures for schools, hospitals and houses have been increasing. Personal consumption has been increased. The less developed regions have started to export, and non-productive consumption has been considerably increased.

Distinction has to be made between two or more phases in considering the ways in which it is proposed to reduce the gap in Yugoslavia. In the first phase an equalisation, to be achieved as soon as possible, was set as a target in respect of the development of the less developed regions, as compared with the developed ones. The funds devoted to this purpose were allocated directly from the central budget and were in the main not repayable. The use of the funds was dependent upon the approval of the central planning agency; the criteria for their use, natural in view of the general shortage of all goods and services immediately after the war, allowed the employment of simple national balance sheet accounts, showing funds on one side and objectives on the other. The choice between alternatives, judged by the criteria of economic efficiency and profitability, played at that time a smaller role in planning in general; thus they were not employed even in this field of inter-regional transfer of resources. In measures affecting the system as a whole, and in particular in those concerned with fiscal and credit policies, there was no favouring of the less developed, and the system was fairly neutral in relation to regional policy.

Within the then existing system of administrative centralism, the main considerations in allocating national funds to less developed regions were solidarity and equality of rights between the developed and the less developed regions. This simple unelaborated administrative system of centralised allocation of

[1] L. R. Pearson, *Partners in Development*, Report of the Commission on International Development (Praeger, New York, 1969), p. 12.

funds favoured, it is true, the less developed. But in the end it showed through-out the economy, and not only in respect of the less developed regions, the same deficiencies – an insufficiently rational and economic allocation and use of the available funds, and thereby, in spite of immense work and effort, often in-adequate results.

The far-reaching institutional and organisational changes that were intro-duced in 1951–52 extended to changes in the measures used to remove the gap. These changes were characterised by the decentralisation of decision-making and by the democratisation of public life; by the introduction of self-manage-ment of these occupied in enterprises; by a greater role played by market forces and competition; by a new way of distributing income, taking into account the contribution of the individual or enterprise to the volume, quality and economic rationality of the organisation's production or activity. The economic organisa-tions or enterprises have become the decision-makers, retaining, in order to make them as independent as possible, more and more of the funds flowing from their operations. The state organs play a constantly declining role, their interventions being reduced to those involved in creating general conditions as favourable as possible for economic management, but in no way interfering with the operations and planning of the enterprises. As a result the role of the central state budget, which in the earlier phase used to transfer most of the national funds available to the less developed regions, has been reduced in importance, and has been limited mainly to the expenditures for state admini-stration and for defence. In consequence of these general changes in the system of financing the less developed regions, alternative new sources of funds have had to be found; new organisations and instruments for their distribution have had to be established; new criteria of allocation, suitable to the new system, have had to be created.

The changes in the economic and social systems, and in particular those embodied in the Reform of 1965, included among the principal economic targets an acceleration of economic growth in general, and to this end an emphasis on efficiency of economic management, making this the principal criterion for making all decisions relating to production, investment, export and import, and similar issues. For the moment we are not concerned with the broader aims involved in raising material, social and cultural standards of life and human relations.

It will be appreciated that, with such changes in the economic system, the principles of solidarity and of equality of rights that are an undeniable element of the socialist society, could not remain as the principal and only criteria for inter-regional allocation of national funds. In addition to them a start was made to follow also in this field the principles of the reformed economy with its emphasis on a constantly increasing efficiency in all the sectors of economic management and in all branches of activity. In the relationships between the less developed and the developed regions this must mean that, as a principle, the development of those particular projects and of those particular regions should be favoured in which the greatest possible comparative increase in the efficiency of management can be ensured.

This, however, introduces an important new element into the relationship between the developed and the less developed regions – the difference between the efficiency of resources allocated where they will maximise the economic growth of the economy as a whole, and the efficiency of the same resources and of allocations of national funds when used in the less developed regions.

The attempts made to deal with these problems have been reinforced by the following measures taken by the community:

(a) a special fund for the development of the less developed regions;
(b) additional funds for the development of social services;
(c) a supply of funds transferred from the developed regions, on strictly business principles;
(d) foreign funds;
(e) various measures affecting the whole economic system, in particular through incentives to investors in developed regions to make investments in the less developed regions.

Each of the above-mentioned measures has its own specific purpose: some of them follow, in part, the criterion of strictly economic operation and of efficient economic management; some of them follow, in part, the principles of solidarity.

The trends shown with regard to the use of funds and the adoption of these measures fairly illustrate the fundamental and sometimes opposing aspirations that underlie the policy of reducing the gap.

The results of this development, with all the accompanying changes, are differently assessed by different observers with different interests and pre-conceptions. No one can deny that the growth of the less developed regions, which amounts to an annual average of 7 per cent, is unusually rapid. Yet considering the high level of growth of the economy as a whole and considering that the gap can be reduced only through a more rapid growth of the less developed regions, there are some who have expressed concern at the relatively slow progress of the less developed regions as compared with the developed ones.

A number of fascinating theoretical and practical problems are posed by this fundamental question. Some of them are examined in the general body of this paper.

Discussion of the Paper by Albin Orthaber

Professor Rasmussen stressed that the gap considered by Professor Orthaber was different from the one to be the main topic for the Conference. Professor Orthaber's gap was a regional one, and in this sense it existed everywhere, in every developed as well as in every developing country. As far as could be judged from Professor Orthaber's paper, it seemed to be even smaller in Yugoslavia than in most countries. This was very surprising and Professor Rasmussen felt that much more information on this subject must be available. We learned from the paper (which was made available only a few hours before the session) that 30 per cent of the Yugoslav population produced 20 per cent to 22 per cent of the total social product. But this did not point to a really grave problem. Similar figures for other European countries, for the U.S.A. and for many, if not most, developing countries, would show much greater regional inequalities.

Considering regional differences from a policy point of view, one was always facing a dilemma which, surprisingly enough, Professor Orthaber did not explicitly mention. Regional gaps might be reduced either by attempts to increase the rate of growth in the weaker regions relatively to the overall rate or by moving the population to the more prosperous regions. For the sake of argument he would assume these two possibilities to be alternatives. (In the real world, of course, this was not the case.)

If we assumed the optimisation of the allocation of resources to be a target it was easy in principle, though difficult in practice, to resolve the dilemma. If the reason for the gap was a lack of infrastructure in a wide sense in the less developed regions, the logic would be to see to it that this infrastructure was constructed. If, however, the gap was due to unfortunate natural circumstances, including the location of resources and industry, the remedy should rather be an active labour market policy, involving the gradual transfer of part of the population to the developed regions.

Such transfers might be beneficial to those remaining in the less developed regions. The benefits here depended on the shape of the production functions. Secondly, the transfers might be beneficial to the developed regions, again depending on the production functions. If there were to be a positive gain in both regions, the production functions must be different. However, experiences seemed to indicate that this was very often the case. It had been shown that over the last two decades overall growth had been higher in those countries where the urban sector had been able to draw on a reservoir of manpower in the rural sector. One could compare the case of Japan with that of the U.K. Such facts pointed to significant regional differences in production functions.

In passing, Professor Rasmussen stressed a line of thought in Professor Horvat's paper, namely that the developing, as well as the developed, countries were suffering probably substantial losses in welfare because of the subsidies paid to agriculture in the developed countries. This was undoubtedly hampering the beneficial transfer of manpower in the developed countries to urban activities.

This way of looking at regional gaps met two major difficulties. The first was a political one, as there would always be in such cases heavy pressure to maintain the *status quo*. Second, there was the intricate problem of judging whether or not the less developed regions would have a chance to catch up in the longer run. There was no reason to be afraid of *temporary* subsidies; there was every reason to be afraid of *permanent* subsidies, because these involved a continuing non-optimal allocation of resources.

The calculus, of course, should be modified, with due account being taken of the true social costs and benefits of a transfer, including the external economies and diseconomies involved. Also, there might be non-economic reasons for accepting losses due to misallocation. In each case, however, it was important for the politicians to know what the costs actually were – and it might be hard to judge the gains from a transfer of resources. But we knew they existed and could easily point to the facts.

An active manpower policy was, it must be admitted, confronted with many difficulties. Local conditions, languages and traditions might be so different that a transfer in the short run – though perhaps not in the long run – became virtually impossible. In this case a regional subsidy might be justified by reference to national solidarity. How far one should go must in turn be a purely political problem, as p. 123 of the paper showed. Professor Orthaber returned to this question again and again. However he did not think that, as economists, we could contribute very much to its solution. It remained a truly political problem. Experience seemed to show that the politicians were willing to sacrifice a great deal in order to bring about more regional equality. However, experience also seemed to show that politicians – for good reasons – compromised. Regional gaps were narrowed, but Professor Rasmussen knew of no case where regional policy had gone so far as to equalise incomes completely. One of the main functions of an active labour market policy must be to inform all concerned about the possible gains from a transfer. Basically – but this was a purely personal judgement – he was inclined to argue that if people wanted to remain where they were in spite of well-known gains, perhaps for good human reasons they should be allowed to do so. But it was doubtful whether this attitude could justify a subsidy at the cost of the nation.

Finally, Professor Rasmussen wanted to present a concrete, though really extreme, case of regional problems and policy – the desperate case of Greenland. Up to 1950 the economy of Greenland was, on the whole, self-sustained. The Greenlanders had merely survived, the individual usually not for very long as the average expectation of life was less than thirty years. Those responsible had become aware of the issue two decades ago, and a huge and accelerating programme had started. Today the average expectation of life was seventy years. Infrastructure had been constructed – the investment in Greenland had in some periods been almost equal to the region's total income – and income per head had doubled several times. At the same time there had been a population explosion – the rate of increase of the population had for a period been 4 per cent per year. Today the annual transfer from Denmark amounted to $90 million to a native population of 40,000, i.e. more than $2,000 per head, and of the order of $10,000 per family. At the same time climatic conditions seemed to deteriorate and fish, the only natural resource, was disappearing.

For years it had been impossible to mention the possibility of emigration to Denmark without being considered a traitor. Now this issue had become an open question which could be mentioned. The case of Greenland proved that the situation could become so desperate that it was acceptable to supplement a regional policy of subsidies by other measures. Nobody dreamed of equalising income per head in Greenland with that of Denmark by way of capital transfers, in spite of the fact that overall growth in Denmark would hardly be affected. He was sincerely convinced that a population became demoralised if it had to live on subsidies throughout. If so, this was a point in favour of using subsidies as the short-run, but active manpower policy as the long-run, regional policy.

Professor Rasmussen would have liked to see this point discussed in Professor Orthaber's paper. The reason why it was not discussed might be that Yugoslavia did not have regional disparities of a very serious order of magnitude. This was what appeared from the paper, but on this point he was sceptical. He would have thought that regional differences were much greater, and also that more data than had been made available in this paper could prove this point.

Professor Horvat wondered whether Professor Rasmussen had looked at the idea that the Greenlanders might sooner go to Iceland, financed by the Danish government.

Professor Orthaber said he had two kinds of comment to make. First he wanted to talk about Yugoslavia's policy to close the gap Professor Rasmussen. had said the gap was not really big enough to cause much concern. However the gap probably looked smaller than it really was. Indices of income were not the only ones; other factors hampered the equalisation of income.

There was also the movement of people. This was the problem of the poor nephew of the rich uncle who always reacted negatively. There were big differences between the less developed regions themselves, so that any illustrations perhaps were misleading, like all aggregate indices.

On how to narrow the gap, could one really move six million people? The size of the problem affected its difficulty. The causes of the gap were explained in the paper and the main one was historical. Location played a different role at different times and perhaps today was not so important as a hundred years ago. Better transport, for example, had helped. But regions outside the main economic flows were not in a position to develop modern industrial production.

There were conflicts, in countries like Yugoslavia, between the aim of increasing production for the whole economy and that of finding the optimal relationship with the less developed part of it. Achieving optimal results was more difficult because of a number of factors: the growth of the country; the growth of the region; the efficiency of the region, etc. In the paper he had given his views on this problem.

Professor Scott welcomed the paper because regional disparities were an important example of economic inequality. Also some regions were almost rich (or poor) nations. They could well be considered as L.D.C.s in their own right.

Professor Scott agreed with Professor Rasmussen that the paper had at least one deficiency in that it did not look at internal migration. Professor Orthaber *might* say that migration in Yugoslavia was either impracticable or impolitic. However, Yugoslav labour *was* internationally mobile. Surely there could be some migration within the country.

What Professor Orthaber did say was that poor regions were poor because of historical accident rather than because of the absence of labour and capital. The

F

implication was that it would be better to make capital mobile rather than people. While Professor Scott could see the force of this argument, he thought there were some points in favour of migration beyond those made by Professor Rasmussen.

Migration did have a catalytic effect in forcing the losing region to restructure agriculture in order to develop rural industry. It might also be that, when some people left, marginal productivity in the region rose. Emigration could well raise income per head. It could do this both in the losing and in the gaining region. In what he had said about Greenland, Professor Rasmussen had argued that it might be even cheaper to move everybody out. Possibly one could do this by force, but it turned out that assistance and migration were not policy alternatives; they were complements. One implied the other. First, assistance implied or required migration, which might mean emigration or immigration. But if one decided on emigration, then social policy in many countries showed that it was difficult to get people to move if they were in grinding poverty. One needed to raise their standard of living to a minimum level before migration could be contemplated. While migration helped the poor this should go in both directions, with some migration and some capital movement.

Professor Robinson recalled that the I.E.A. had held a conference in 1967 on backward areas in advanced countries and had discussed Yugoslavia in this context. It had been found there that almost all countries, of all kinds – capitalist, socialist and mixed – had underdeveloped regions. In many cases it had become clear that what was now regarded as a nation was in reality a confederation of previously separate nations, and that what led people to want to stay in backward areas was their cultural and linguistic groupings more than economic considerations. In this earlier conference, the need to move work to the workers had been emphasised. In other words the Conference had looked at the social versus the private benefits of concentration. It had been agreed that it was arguable that in such instances there was a case for subsidising the movement of work to the workers rather than encouraging migration out of the cultural and linguistic group.

Professor Rasmussen said that of course if the Greenlanders wanted they should be allowed to go to Iceland. It was perfectly possible for the Danish government to finance this. In early spring plans had been set up for a labour exchange in Greenland, and a public statement had been made that this exchange would advise anyone who wanted to leave Greenland. They would be encouraged to go to Iceland, Denmark or anywhere else where they understood the language. To Professor Scott, Professor Rasmussen said that one had to consider all alternatives. Given the world we lived in he would certainly not argue that policy over Greenland had been senseless. It was very hard to move primitive people to civilised areas. Children had to be educated first.

Professor Orthaber said that on migration he appeared to have given the impression in his paper that Yugoslavia had neglected its possibilities. This was not true. Ten per cent of the labour force in Slovenia, for example, came from elsewhere. In addition, 7 per cent of Yugoslav labour worked abroad.

Part 2

International Flows and their
Effects on the Gap

6 The Grants Economy and the Development Gap

Kenneth E. Boulding
UNIVERSITY OF COLORADO

and

Martin Pfaff
WAYNE STATE UNIVERSITY

I. THE NATURE OF THE PROBLEM

The problem of the gap between rich and poor countries is a familiar one, and we need not spend much time in repeating what everybody knows about it. Nevertheless Figure 6.1 may throw some additional light on the nature of the problem. Here we plot, for as many countries as data could be obtained, the rate of growth of per capita G.N.P. against the per capita G.N.P. itself on a logarithmic scale.[1] It is clear that the nations of the world divide out into two fairly distinct groups, which we may call the 'A' nations and the 'B' nations. The A nations are clearly participating in a long-term growth process of some kind. They lie approximately on a straight line, suggesting that the growth process itself is logistic, with the rate of growth diminishing as growth proceeds. For the A nations it is clear that 'the poorer the faster, the richer the slower'. The implication of this is that for these nations growth will proceed until all are about equally rich and are proceeding towards an asymptotic rate of growth which is zero, which seems to be somewhere between $5,000 and $10,000 of the per capita G.N.P. Two interesting facts emerge about the A nations – they are nearly all within the Temperate Zone, or just outside it, and it does not seem to make any difference, at least from this point of view, whether they are socialist or capitalist.

The B nations on the other hand do not exhibit any clear relationship between the rate of growth and the per capita G.N.P. Most of them are in the tropics, with three notable exceptions from the Temperate Zone of South America. Their rates of growth are all below what their existing per capita G.N.P. would lead us to expect if they were in the A group. Most of them are poorer than the countries of the A group and none of them are growing as fast as the poor countries of the A group. The statistical impression that is created is that these are countries in which the rate of

[1] A similar diagram for 1950–60 (obtainable on request from K. E. Boulding) shows a very similar pattern.

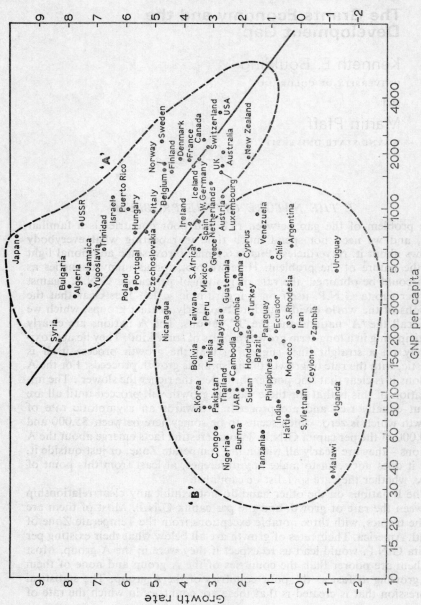

FIG. 6.1. Per cent per annum rate of growth in 1960–1965.[1]

1 The time space was a little different in a few cases. Data from the *United Nations Yearbook*

growth is somewhat sporadic and due to random factors of good luck or bad luck in any particular period, but none of them are really on a sustained growth path.

Gross statistics as used in Figure 6.1 of course must be used with the greatest of caution, especially where the original data on which they are based are often very unsatisfactory. The Gross National Product itself, even if based on accurate data, is a very inadequate measure of human welfare. It neglects non-market elements in the economy, especially those of the household. It does not account adequately for the exhaustion of exhaustible resources or for pollution, that is, the production of negative commodities. The rate of growth can be very misleading. It sometimes represents merely a transfer from non-market into market activities or it represents the increase of public goods of dubious value, like national defence. The average figure, furthermore, may easily hide wide disparities in the internal distribution of income. The distribution of income between rich and poor people is not the same as the distribution between rich and poor countries, so that two countries with the same rate of growth, the same per capita G.N.P. and the same official statistics may easily be in a very different situation in regard to human welfare and economic potential.

In spite of these deficiencies of the average G.N.P. figures, the picture which emerges is so clear and striking that the problem to which it points cannot be neglected. It is a world picture, furthermore, which can occasion no satisfaction to anyone who has the welfare of the human race at heart. It is a picture of a world separating out roughly into a rich temperate zone and a poor tropical zone, with the rich countries on the whole following a line of development which will end up with their all being quite rich, and with many poor countries barely managing to prevent themselves falling down into even deeper poverty. A planet in which about one-third of the people live in countries which are clearly advancing towards greater riches, while two-thirds of the population live in countries which are not so advancing, is one which no one can contemplate with satisfaction. Abraham Lincoln's famous remark of more than a hundred years ago, that 'I believe this government cannot endure permanently half slave and half free', can be adapted pertinently to the modern world, and the question has to be faced as to whether a planet can survive in which less than half is rich and getting richer, and more than half is poor and in danger of getting poorer.

II. REASONS FOR THE GAP

When we ask ourselves the reasons for this division of the planet Earth into A countries and B countries no single simple answer emerges, though we can make some general suggestions. In the first place no simple theory of climatological or genetic determinism is acceptable. The shared *genetic heritage* of the human race is so enormous by comparison with regional or racial differences, and the genetic variation of individuals within the regional and racial groups of mankind is so large, that genetic explanations of these differences could explain only a minute fraction of the variability.

Climatic explanations perhaps carry a little more weight, particularly when as in the past these have been associated with the incidence of debilitating diseases, like malaria. If we look over the whole course of human history, however, it is clear that many tropical societies have achieved complex social structures, great architecture and art, and that human organisation and learning capacity have been able to overcome in many instances the unfavourable aspects of climate. Thus in the 16th century the civilisation of northern India was certainly as advanced technologically and artistically as that of Europe. The Mayans and the Khmers produced tropical civilisations as architecturally elaborate as those of the ancient Mediterranean. Tropical Africa has had a great continuous artistic tradition, and the more we know of even what used to be thought of as primitive societies, the more complex and remarkable their achievements become. This rather sharp differentiation indeed between the developing temperate zone and the stagnant tropics is a relatively modern phenomenon, and we must look for its explanation in the events of the last two or three centuries.

Just as any simple climatological or genetic explanations of the developmental gap are quite inadequate, so any simple explanation in terms of *exploitation* is inadequate. The difference between the rich and the poor countries is not a result of exploitation in the simple sense, that the poor countries produce a great deal and the rich countries take it away from them without giving anything in return. The immediate difference between the rich and the poor countries is a result of the fact that the rich countries produce a great deal per capita and the poor countries produce very little. It is the *difference in productivity* that makes the largest explanatory factor, not any differences in exploitation. This is not to say, of course, that exploitation does not exist or even that it is unimportant. It has certainly existed more in the past than it has in the present. Furthermore colonial and dependent relationships have created a psychological exploitation, as Everett Hagen has suggested, which may have had very serious long-run consequences. Simple exploitation, which is a one-way transfer of economic values from the exploited to the exploiter as a result of some relationship of coercive inequality, is a case of a larger class of economic relationships, that of one-way transfers in general which has come to be called the 'grants economy'. It is the main purpose of this paper then to examine the role of the whole grants economy in the explanation of the developmental gap.

III. THE CONCEPT OF THE GRANTS ECONOMY

A 'grant' we define simply as a one-way transfer of exchangeables, which in an accounting sense increases the net worth of the recipient and diminishes the net worth of the grantor. Thus suppose in Figure 6.2 we have a square matrix; along both OX and OY we arrange the three billion people of the world, with each point representing a person, each in the same arbitrary order. Suppose that N and M are two persons in the world population at the positions shown on OX and OY. We will adopt the convention that the points on the upper side of the diagonal OS, such as P, can be assigned a number which measures the total economic value (in 'dollars' worth') of goods and services, which flows from the person on the vertical scale to the person on the horizontal scale. Thus if we think of the point P as a little square of the matrix, we could write in this square the total value flow from M to N. Similarly the point Q represents the total value flow from N to M. The squares on the diagonals, such as at R and at S, could be used to represent some kind of internal flows, such as self-produced and self-consumed output.

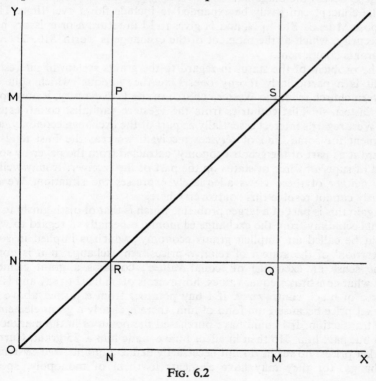

Fɪɢ. 6.2

If now the relationship between M and N is a pure exchange relationship, we would expect the figures at P and at Q to be the same. If M, for instance, buys $10 worth of potatoes from N, the figure in the square P would be $10, representing $10 outflow of money. The figure in the sqaure Q would also be $10, representing $10 outflow of potatoes. If, however, there is a grants component in the economy between some pairs of transactors, the figures at P and Q will not be the same. Thus suppose M gives $10 to N and obtains nothing in return. The figure at P is $10, the figure at Q is zero. Or suppose that M gives N $10 and N only gives M $3 worth of potatoes. The figure at P is 10 and at Q is 3. There is then a net grant at P of 7, and at Q of −7, indicating that M has given N $7 more than he has received, and N has received from M $7 more than he has given. From the total economic flows matrix, therefore, we can easily construct the *grants matrix* by subtracting the flow at each point P from the flow at the mirror image point Q. The grants matrix has the property that it is symmetrical about the diagonal OS with the signs changed, that is, the figure at any point P will have an equal negative figure at its mirror image Q across the diagonal.

The concept can easily be expanded to include flows over time. Thus suppose M lends $10 to N, and N gives to M in return a promissory note or security, which at the moment of the exchange is worth $10. There is no grants component.

The problem of the status in regard to the grants system of interest or profit is a particularly thorny one. Like the 'filioque' which split the Eastern church from the Western church in the 11th century, it now splits the Eastern socialist countries from the Western capitalist countries; for the West regards interest essentially as part of the exchange economy, as a payment for some kind of services received, whereas the East tends to regard it as part of the grants economy, extracted from the payer by some kind of superior force or status on the part of the receiver. It may well be that neither of these views adequately expresses the situation. We obviously cannot resolve this controversy here.

Again this is part of a larger problem, which is that of distinguishing the grants economy from the exchange economy, especially in regard to what might be called an 'implicit grants economy', which is implied in some 'distortion' of the system of relative prices. An exchange, if it is not in some sense an exchange of 'equal values', contains a grant element. Just what constitutes equal values, however, is often hard to say and is the source of much controversy. If I buy potatoes from a farmer above the market price because I am fond of him, there is clearly a grant element in this transaction. If I could have purchased the potatoes in the market for $10 but paid him $15 then in effect I have made him a $5 grant. Current market prices, however, do not necessarily define a 'grants-free' system of exchange, for they may have elements in them of monopoly, special privilege due to quotas or import restrictions, and hence the existing structure of market prices may well hide an implicit grants element. Western economists have generally regarded that system of relative prices which corresponded to alternative costs as an essentially 'grant-free' price structure. While this assumption provides a very useful base, there may be good arguments for modifying it. These however are subtle and difficult problems which we do not have time to discuss here and which will be more fully discussed in some forthcoming volumes [1].

IV. SOURCES OF GRANTS

One of the paradoxes of the grants economy is that it arises out of three quite different sources, which we might describe very briefly as love, fear and ignorance. If N gives something to M and receives nothing in return, this may be either because N feels benevolent towards M, identifies with him, regards an increase in his welfare as equivalent to an increase in his own, and hence is willing to sacrifice something himself in order to ensure that M's position is improved. The relation of a parent to a child is frequently, though not always, of this character. A parent makes sacrifices for the child because the parent's own identity is realised in the welfare of the child. At the other end of the scale a grant may be a form of tribute, that is, a response to a credible threat. The bandit who says, 'Your money or your life' is setting up a threat system. If I give him my money I am making him a grant, that is, the unilateral transfer of an exchangeable. There is something here which is a kind of parody of exchange. I give him my money, he gives me my life, but the exchange of goods for what might be called a 'negative bad', that is, the abstention from doing something bad, is very different from the exchange of goods for goods. The third source of grants, ignorance, is apt to arise, as we have noticed, when exchanges take place between partners of unequal status. The poor in all societies tend to be made poorer because of their ignorance, even of the opportunities which exist for them, and the clever and the knowledgeable have always been able to manipulate social structures in their own favour.

Grants which are made out of threat or out of ignorance both deserve the title 'exploitative'. Grants which are made out of genuine benevolence are not exploitative, with the exception of the case in which the benevolence is 'undeserved'. It is not unknown, for instance, for a person to exploit the affection which a friend feels for him and demand grants either of time, attention or even of goods and services, which are essentially exploitative. Because of a phenomenon which we may call the 'sacrifice trap', these grants of exploitative benevolence are by no means rare. A nation exploits the love of its citizens; a husband the love of his wife. Children may exploit their parents and parents their children. A church may exploit its members or the parishioners may exploit the clergy. Wherever sacrifice, i.e. grants, is demanded and given, the identity of the sacrificer becomes bound up with that of the object or organisation for which the sacrifice was made. Hence this organisation can frequently go on demanding sacrifice and become exploitative. Likewise a sense of guilt can be exploited. Those who have been done injury may sometimes exploit the guilt of the injurer, even beyond the injury which has been done. It is clear that what we have here is an immensely complicated social phenomenon of which not even the description, much less the explanation, can be accomplished in a short paper.

V. *INTERNATIONAL GRANTS AND THE DEVELOPMENT GAP*

Let us now turn to the problem with which we started, that of the gap between the A countries and the B countries, and ask ourselves in the first place how far the structure of the grants economy on a world scale has produced this gap and in the second place what might be the role of the world's grants economy in reducing it. Neither of these questions is capable of definitive answers in the present state of knowledge. Nevertheless even in our present degree of ignorance certain propositions suggest themselves as probable and the theory of the grants economy suggests important directions in which knowledge may be improved by further research.

The tentative answer to the first question would seem to be that quantitatively the grants economy in any of its forms has played a relatively minor role in the processes of development which led to the development gap. Grants made out of benevolence and a sense of community, which we might call 'gifts', have always been rather small relative to the exchange economy. Private gifts, such as charitable contributions, immigrants' remittances, missionary grants and so on, have been a noticeable part, at least in the relations between the A countries and the B countries, but quantitatively as a proportion of the income of either set of countries, the amounts are very small indeed, and it is extremely doubtful whether they ever exceeded more than a fraction of 1 per cent of the total income, either of the donor or of the recipient, except for short periods and particular places, such as disaster relief.

Furthermore foundation grants for international activities play a similarly minor role in the context of overall monetary flows between nations, though they may have a qualitative impact beyond this minute quantitative importance, due to their role in international education and training for development. Table 6.1, for example, shows the grants (of $10,000 or more) given for international activities by all U.S. foundations (these were about 12 per cent of all U.S. foundations giving) in 1968. Of the $92·73 million granted, a combined total of 65 per cent went for such

TABLE 6.1

TOTAL GRANTS OF $10,000 OR MORE GIVEN
FOR INTERNATIONAL ACTIVITIES BY U.S.
FOUNDATIONS, 1968

	Grant (U.S. $000's)	%
General	525	1
Cultural Relations	4,675	5
Education	24,215	26
Exchange of Persons	2,162	2
Health and Medicine	17,238	19
International Studies	21,771	23
Peace and International Co-operation	3,806	4
Relief and Refugees	3,442	4
Technical Assistance	14,896	16
Total	92,730	100

Source: Foundation Library Center, *Foundation News Bulletin*, January 1969, p. 4.

developmental activities (26 per cent were allotted for education, 23 per cent for international studies and 16 per cent for technical assistance). The effect of highly skilled scientific, engineering and managerial manpower in leading to increased productivity – and thus, to keeping the gap between A and B continuing to present levels, as compared to a still wider discrepancy – can only be surmised in very vague terms.

Non-governmental transfers have decreased in relative importance since World War II. This is illustrated, for example, in Table 6.2, which depicts 'personal transfers' to foreigners (made by individuals, nonprofit institutions, the business sector, etc.) as compared with government transfers, for the United States, for the period 1929–68. While personal transfers were about ten times as large as government transfers in 1929, they were about a third of government transfers in 1969. While the U.S. case cannot be generalised for all countries, particularly for the period prior to 1946, it none the less established a strong presumption for the shift from private to public means of international aid.

Public international grants consist of three categories: (1) grant-like flows, being the sum of loans payable in the recipients' currencies and transfer of resources through sales for recipients currencies; (2) net official grants, reparations and indemnification payments, being gifts in money or in kind for which no payment is required; and (3) grant elements of net official loans, being grant elements of loans extended by government and official agencies in currencies other than that of the recipient country, with maturities of over one year, for which repayment is required in convertible currencies or in kind.

TABLE 6.2

U.S. INTERNATIONAL TRANSFERS 1929–68[1]
(millions of dollars)

Year	Personal Remittances in kind (1)	Total Personal (2)	Govt. (3)	Total 2+3 (4)	G.N.P. (5)	Personal Remittances as a % of G.N.P. (1) (6)	Total Personal as a % of G.N.P. (2) (7)	Govt. as a % of G.N.P. (3) (8)	Total (2+3) as a % of G.N.P. (9)
1929		343	34	377	103,095		0·333	0·033	0·366
1930		306	36	342	90.367		0·339	0·040	0·378
1931		279	40	319	75,820		0·368	0·053	0·421
1932		217	21	238	58,049		0·374	0·036	0·410
1933		191	17	208	55,601		0·344	0·031	0·374
1934		162	10	172	65,054		0·249	0·015	0·264
1935		162	20	182	72,247		0·224	0·028	0·252
1936		176	32	208	82,481		0·213	0·039	0·252
1937	1	175	60	235	90,446	0·001	0·194	0·066	0·260
1938	1	153	29	182	84,670	0·001	0·181	0·034	0·215
1939		151	27	178	90,494		0·167	0·030	0·197
1940		178	32	210	99,678		0·179	0·032	0·211
1941		179	14	165	124,540		0·144		0·132
1942		123	90	213	157,910		0·078	0·057	0·135
1943		249	53	196	191,592		0·130		0·102
1944		357	88	269	210,104		0·170		0·128
1945	30	473	352	825	211,945	0·014	0·223	0·166	0·389
1946	272	673	2,249	2,922	208,509	0·130	0·323	0·079	0·014
1947	339	682	1,943	2,625	231,323	0·147	0·295	0·840	1·135
1948	264	697	3,828	4,525	257,562	0·102	0·270	1·486	1·757
1949	155	532	5,106	5,638	256,484	0·060	0·207	1·991	2·200
1950	130	454	3,563	4,017	284,769	0·046	0·159	1·251	1·410
1951	106	409	3,106	3,515	328,404	0·032	0·125	0·946	1·070
1952	107	443	2,088	2,531	345,498	0·031	0·128	0·604	0·732
1953	122	503	1,978	2,481	364,593	0·033	0·138	0·543	0·681
1954	98	504	1,776	2,280	364,841	0·027	0·138	0·487	0·625
1955	80	456	2,042	2,498	397,960	0·020	0·115	0·513	0·628
1956	107	555	1,868	2,423	419,238	0·026	0·132	0·446	0·578
1957	123	570	1,775	2,345	441,134	0·028	0·129	0·402	0·532
1958	107	563	1,798	2,361	447,334	0·024	0·126	0·402	0·528
1959	110	599	1,849	2,448	483,663	0·023	0·124	0·382	0·506
1960	136	484	1,878	2,362	503,734	0·027	0·096	0·373	0·469
1961	130	497	2,089	2,586	520,097	0·025	0·096	0·402	0·497
1962	118	512	2,164	2,676	560,325	0·021	0·091	0·091	0·478
1963	132	605	2,179	2,784	590,503	0·022	0·103	0·369	0·471
1964	133	600	2,165	2,765	631,712	0·021	0·095	0·343	0·437
1965	145	658	2,177	2,835	684,884	0·021	0·096	0·318	0·414
1966	144	556	2,277	2,833	749,857	0·020	0·074	0·304	0·378
1967	180	755	2,243	2,998	793,544	0·023	0·095	0·283	0·378
1968	187	753	2,112	2,865	865,701	0·022	0·087	0·244	0·331

[1] Source: (1) For the years 1929–64:
U.S. Department of Commerce, Office of Business Economics, *The National Income and Product Accounts of the United States, 1929–1965*, Statistical Tables, A Supplement to the Survey of Current Business, U.S. Government Printing Office, Washington, D.C. (Personal remittances in kind: Table 2.5, line 102; Personal and Government Transfers: Table 4.1, lines 6 and 7).

(2) For the years 1965–68:
U.S. Department of Commerce, Office of Business Economics, *Survey of Current Business*, July 1969, Vol. 49, No. 7 (National Income Issue), U.S. Government Printing Office, Washington, D.C.

It is indeed questionable as to whether grant-like flows can be fully included as non-market flows: they do involve a *quid pro quo* whose exchange-equivalent is much smaller than their face value, owing to problems of inconvertibility, etc. There is little doubt about the nature of net official grants, reparations and indemnification payments as being true grants. In the case of grant-elements, the magnitude included depends on the selection of an appropriate discount rate for the estimation of the present value of future repayment streams to donors and recipients. The real cost to donors will differ from the real benefits of recipients, since different interest rates prevail in the donor and lender countries [2].

A grants matrix of the non-Communist world is presented in Appendix Table 1. It depicts the sum of grants under all three categories, made by Development Assistance Committee (DAC) countries to developing countries on the major regions of the world, during 1965.[1] A similar computation for grants made by the Communist regions – U.S.S.R., Eastern Europe and Mainland China – is formulated on the basis of some plausible assumptions about the terms of loans or grants made during the period 1954–67. (See Appendix Table 2.)

These matrices reflect, in the objective light of economic inquiry, a gamut of cultural, social, political and economic forces of great complexity. Only a few of the dominant patterns on the grantor and grantee side may be mentioned:

(1) *A spectrum of economic aid relations* characterises the interaction between grantors and grantees. This is reflected in a shifting mix of grant-loan arrangements. This mix ranges from countries which give only pure grants and no low-interest loans (e.g. Australia), to those who give low-interest loans (e.g. Austria and Mainland China) and to others whose loans are not very liberal in the year studied (e.g. Japan, whose grant element is only 11 per cent of the face value of loans).

(2) The *degree of concentration* or dispersion differs; while countries like Austria, Germany and Canada give small amounts to almost all countries, others focus their grants on more clearly defined regions of interest. Australia and Japan, for example, provide assistance mainly to S.E. Asia, France mainly to French-speaking Africa where 90 per cent of its grants go), and the U.S.S.R. gave 50 per cent of its aid to three countries – India, U.A.R., and Afghanistan.

(3) The *political background* and relationship between grantor and grantee is a major explanator of grants. In fact a perusal of relative grant shares by region (in both Appendix Tables 1 and 2) may serve as a striking summary of relative power relations of major donor countries in that particular part of the world. This shows up in the

[1] A matrix which excludes grant-like flows is available from the authors.

major interest sphere of the U.S.A., U.S.S.R., Mainland China, U.K., France and of other formerly colonial powers. (The status of 'former colonial ruler' conveys a very expensive distinction indeed!)

(4) The whole system is dominated by the aid granted by the superpowers, primarily the United States. However, in particular regions, the relative influence of more concentrated aid-giving of smaller nations may be inferred from the grants network. (For example France follows an independent policy of supporting 'neutrals'.)

(5) The main conclusion from the pattern of grantor behaviour may be summarised as follows: While the network of international trade may reflect patterns of economic self-interest and current trading opportunities, the pattern of grants reflects the presence of past community and present ties; or else, the attempts of a major power to promote a sense of community and political domination. (For example, the concentration of Soviet foreign aid to the Middle East presages eventual influence even before the Six-Day War made such an influence transparent in political terms.)

Turning now to a view of grantee patterns, we may conclude the following:

(1) 'Need' in itself is not a guarantor of aid. The relatively wealthier of the less developed countries were apparently more successful in attracting foreign aid than the relatively poor. (This is true particularly for European and Latin American grantee countries.)

(2) A 'special political relationship' with one or more major powers – either through colonial dependence or through a current political liaison – is likely to lead to enhanced grants.

(3) Relatively less populated countries have a better chance to obtain a relatively higher per capita aid than the relatively more populated and larger countries.

When both grantor and grantee patterns are integrated we conclude that international grants may serve to (1) maintain a system of special relations between major and minor powers, (2) promote special patterns of community based on regional or political interest, (3) increase the dominance of some major powers in the international system; *but they do not appear as a generally effective instrument in narrowing the gap between the A and B countries, even though it may be of importance in some special cases. The magnitudes of grants are relatively small, and the patterns of allocation do not necessarily support the notion that economic growth is truly the major aim of international grants policy.* The capacity of particular countries for internal reorganisation far exceeds in importance any particular advantages which a country may have had from its position in the international grants economy.

The case of Japan in the 19th century is a good example. Japan received virtually no grants from anybody. Yet because of its internal reorganisation it was able to enter the 'A' group of nations, certainly by about 1880, and it has made spectacular, indeed record breaking advances in per capita G.N.P. in the last twenty years, with a relatively small amount of outside assistance. Even if we look at the most undesirable aspect of grants, i.e. grants from poor countries to rich ones, these also turn out to have been very small. Thus in the case of India and Great Britain the 'home charges' which India paid to Great Britain during most of the 19th century hardly ever amounted to more than 0·5 per cent of the Indian G.N.P. and were more than counterbalanced by the advantages which India received from the ability to borrow at low rates of interest in the London money market [3]. There is a great deal of evidence accumulating indeed that even under the relationship of political imperialism, such as prevailed before the Second World War, the grants economy was more on the side of the colonies exploiting the mother country, at least in terms of flows of exchangeables, than on the side of the imperial power exploiting its colonies. Often indeed as we have suggested earlier the indirect effects may have been serious. Colonialism indeed was a system which was twice cursed. It injured both the colonies and the imperial power, as Adam Smith indeed pointed out in 1776.

The tribute element in the international grants economy therefore has always been quite small quantitatively, except perhaps in certain times and places in classical civilisation and it has become increasingly insignificant with the rate of science-based technology.

If we describe grants which are made out of ignorance as 'fraud', it is clear that this element in the grants economy likewise is quantitatively of relatively little importance today, except in so far as a dominant class may deliberately keep a subordinate class in ignorance. Slave societies certainly have an exploitative grants economy of this kind, although even here the tribute element is of great importance, that is, the slave gives to the slave owner more than he receives from him because the slave owner has the power to kill him and the slave has no legal rights. Here again, however, as we move into the modern world it becomes harder and harder to keep people in ignorance, simply because ignorance pays off less and less well for the exploiter. In modern societies, though there are certainly pockets of ignorance and fraud, especially, say, in the poorest 20 per cent of the population, this is not a phenomenon which can explain the development gap, either within or between societies, except in certain marginal cases.

Finally we may mention the 'Prebisch Thesis' concerning the effect of grants in alleviating the monopolistic exploitation of less developed countries and in improving the worsening terms of trade between the industrialised exporting (= grantor) and the agricultural importing (= grantee) countries. No doubt grants may act as vehicles of system maintenance: by improving the relative position of an 'injured' party, the stronger party attempts to prevent the withdrawal of the weaker party. Threat-capability through mere switching of economic or political allegiance may serve to attract a larger share of international grants. Unfortunately the empirical evidence on the terms of trade prevailing between industrialised and less developed countries does not necessarily support such a contention: system maintenance it may be, but more of the political than of the economic system.

Furthermore one would expect that an industry will suffer a deterioration in terms of trade if, first, it has been marked by technological progress, and second, if it produces products for which substitutes are developed. Worsening in terms of trade is, therefore, a reflection of the dynamic price system which should act as a signal for a country to 'get out of' these exporting activities. In fact one might argue that the grants economy would be misapplied if it were used solely to stop dynamic processes inherent in the exchange economy. One might even go further and argue that the grants economy ought to be applied to speed up such processes. In other words if there are worsening terms of trade, the grants economy – that is, the tax-transfer system – ought to be used to further worsen these terms of trade. However such an argument is unlikely to be popular with the raw-material producing countries which may have but a few alternatives for earning exchange income.

There is, however, not enough evidence to suggest that the terms of trade on the whole had worsened for all developing countries. Moreover as the raw material resources and the resources of the environment get more and more exhausted in the industrialised countries, there is likely to be an improvement in the secular terms of trade of the less developed over the next forty to sixty years.

II. THE INTERNAL NATIONAL GRANTS ECONOMY

One of the factors that might explain the presence and magnitude of the developmental gap may be found in the internal processes of the developing country itself, namely, the intra-nation grants processes and their role in promoting overall growth. Grants arise within the nation from a variety of private and public sources, such as individual and corporate contributions, foundation grants, the activities of non-profit institutions, the transferring role in-kind of the government, the transfer payments from the public to individuals, subsidies made to industries and implicit grants present in a variety of public actions.

What then is the internal function of the grants economy in national development? The first and major function is its role in helping bring about a speedier reallocation of resources than what would be inherent in the logic of the market mechanism itself. This reorganisation function might be termed the *anti-entropic function* of grants. Its main purpose is to concentrate resources in a way that the market itself may not be able to do. In traditional societies resources tend to be highly diffused. It is very hard to bring them together in a concentrated form. This is not to deny that development processes *do* occur in the market economy. After all, the principle of division of labour and the development of organisation are a consequence of market opportunity. This is particularly true through the development of capital markets which fulfil the same kind of function. It is indeed an important question to ask as to whether the exchange of the grants economy would be more successful in such marshalling of resources. If the political institutions of a country are better developed than its economic institutions, then presumably a case could be made for the use of the grants economy in bringing about such a concentration of resources for development. This may very well be the key to the decision as to whether a country would want to go the private or the public road in development. In Japan, for example, a nearly optimum mix of the two was presumably obtained. After the Meiji restoration Japan relied extensively on the use of the public grants economy. However as soon as the industries which were developed under the impetus of the public grants economy were viable, they tended to be 'shunted off' into the private sector. This is an excellent example of how the grants economy may be used as an agent for the development of the exchange economy. On the other hand this use of the grants economy may have some perverse consequences. As the case of Japan has indicated, the military may 'capture' the grants economy for its own ends. It may be one of the problems of socialist development that in the absence of a well-organised capital market the grants economy is essential for the marshalling of resources. Whenever a capital market itself is not considered legitimate, other and often less efficient means for the concentration of resources for development are used. On the positive side, one of the advantages of socialism may precisely consist in its ability to divert a larger share of the surplus of development, using whatever 'means of collective persuasion' that are available. However this is attained at the cost of losing an efficient capital market. Some kind of 'shadow price' for capital can only be presumed by the directors of the central planning authority. It is, therefore, important to recognise that there are implicit trade-offs involved whatever instruments are used for the marshalling of resources.

Another major source of pathology of the grants economy results from the distributive effects of those measures that are instituted to promote growth. Very often rapid economic development entails redistributions that are highly inequitable. These then, if considered illegitimate, may lead to a collapse of the total system and to a withdrawal of legitimacy from the grants and exchange apparatus set up to promote growth. It is ironic that the exchange economy is usually criticised for bringing about in-equitable results, while the grants economy – whose function presumably is the amelioration of such inequities – may lead to *further* inequities in the system. When we think of a symbol of development, such as the high dams erected for water control, we have in fact a very vivid example of these effects of the grants economy. If we look at the costs and benefits of the dams, such as the Aswan or the Volta Dam, we must ask our-selves the question as to who gets the benefits and who pays the costs of development. The Volta Dam, for example, displaced about 80,000 people in Ghana who are not likely to recover in the near future from this trau-matic change. These social casualties of development are likely to impose a very heavy cost on society for decades to come. Unfortunately the logic of the benefit-cost analysis provokes far less conviction when the benefits accrue to the wealthy and the costs to the poor! This pattern of distributive effects accruing from development may find its parallel in developed countries in those measures that are designed to alleviate environmental deficiencies at the cost of the poor.

Another way of judging the success of the grants economy in develop-ment is generally found in its integrative or disintegrative results. In the case of those who have been displaced by development, a significant dis-integrative effect is all too likely. Similarly, the questions of the integrative or disintegrative effects of the taxes that are raised to finance these public development projects must not be lost sight of. Particularly if the legiti-macy of the existing tax system is questioned by the poor, the sense of community or integration is not likely to be fostered.

Distributive consequences result also from those inflationary spirals that are generated by heavy development spending which does not show up in the short-term in an increase of tangible products. While we do not know very much about distributive effects of inflation and its various ramifications, no doubt certain segments of the population – particularly the fixed-income earning middle class – are likely to be affected negatively.

The 'failure' of the grants economy of a developing country to marshal resources for development, together with failures of markets, may thus be blamed in part for the existence of a development gap. However the nature and magnitude of grants themselves are a reflection of a sense of community which gives rise to the willingness to make transfers.

VII. SCIENTIFIC KNOWLEDGE AND TECHNOLOGY IN DEVELOPMENT

If it is not the international grants economy and not entirely the internal national grants economy which explain the development gap in either its exploitative or its non-exploitative form, what does explain it? The answer must lie in the process out of which this extraordinary development of the last two or three hundred years has arisen. The development – which has carried us from per capita incomes of about $100 per head, characteristic in all classical civilisations and indeed in all civilisations up to about the 17th or 18th century, to the $1,000-$4,000 per head characteristic of the rich countries today – is a phenomenon intimately associated with the remarkable explosion of knowledge arising out of the subculture of science. We can trace indeed a substantial improvement in productivity beginning with the neolithic revolution and the invention of agriculture and the domestication of crops and livestock, which proceeds irregularly throughout the whole age of civilisation and which might almost be said to culminate in the so-called Industrial Revolution of the 18th century in England. By the 16th and 17th centuries, however, this long, slow process of improvement of folk knowledge and folk technology had reached the point where the *breakthrough in science* could take place, partly because of instrumentation, such as the telescope and the microscope, partly because of social inventions, such as the Puritan ethic, and partly perhaps because of sheer luck. Whatever the reasons, and they are by no means clear, the breakthrough into science occurred in Western Europe and not in China, where it might have been expected, as China was in the forefront in the development of folk knowledge and technology for almost 2,000 years. The remoteness and the inclement climate of the European peninsula of the largest world island may also have helped to create a situation in which the mutation into science could occur, as Europe escaped to a considerable extent the depredations of the Mongols who devastated Islam as well as China. Another factor was the peculiar geographic situation of the time which enabled Europe, as it were, to explode in population and influence, both eastward into northern Asia and westward into the Americas, both of which can be regarded as geographic extensions of the European cultural phyla.

Another consequence of this expansion was that most of the tropical countries came under European colonial domination by the end of the 19th century. Even though this may not have represented much in the way of direct exploitation in the shape of tribute, it created a cultural trauma which made it hard for the non-European populations to absorb the new knowledge into their own cultural development. A further factor in the situation is that science-based technology originated primarily as a Temperate Zone subculture and was often ill-adapted to tropical conditions. Consequently even well-meaning attempts to expand Western technology into the tropics have often created ecological disasters, simply because Western-trained scientists and engineers have tried to apply methods which are suitable to Temperate Zone ecosystems to tropical ecosystems where they are not suitable at all.

The demographic factor also has considerable importance, at least in explaining some of the difficulties of the last generation. The spread of scientific medicine, and especially public health and the elimination of malaria about 1950, have created a serious demographic crisis in the tropics. In many tropical countries the rate of population increase is now so high that the population doubles almost every generation, which is an enormous burden on the developmental process. In addition the change in the age composition of the population has resulted in a situation with relatively small proportions of the population of working age and a large proportion of children and young people to feed and educate. This again might almost be regarded as the result of the impact of a Temperate Zone medicine on tropical culture, which has not yet had time to make the adjustments in fertility which the spectacular diminution in mortality required.

VIII. SOCIAL AND PSYCHOLOGICAL PROCESSES IN DEVELOPMENT

The most difficult questions, and yet perhaps the most important, revolve around the qualitative impact of the various elements of society on the developmental process. The rough aggregates and averages with which we have been dealing obscure an immensely complex qualitative structure, which is very hard to reduce to simple terms. There is, for instance, the problem of the structure of substitutability. Obviously any commodity or element in a process which has no substitutes is in a highly strategic position, and its absence may inhibit or destroy a whole process which depends on it. Some crucial and non-substitutable raw material, for instance, might well be an example, which may be quite insignificant in the overall aggregate statistics, but may nevertheless have a crucial importance. The real difficulty is that we know very little about the structure of substitutability. One has a suspicion that the whole impact of modern technology is enormously to increase the range of possible substitutes and hence to diminish the importance of these strategic elements. But in the absence of any real information system about this, it is impossible to be certain.

It may well be indeed that the most strategic elements in the whole process are in the human nervous system and in the total learning process which goes on in society, and which goes on in each individual right from the moment of birth. It may be also that some of the most strategic factors in the development process are certain moral attitudes towards the world and towards one's self which are learned very early in life. Perhaps the greatest obstacle to development either in the person or in the society is an attitude of self-pity, which is strongly related to a kind of pathological dependency. The converse of this, which is an attitude which looks in a pragmatic way to the opportunities of the future rather than to burdens in the past, is the most favourable psychological climate for almost any developmental process. What produces these subtle cultural and personal traits, however, is a profound mystery. We do not really know what are the inputs that produce these particular outputs.

IX. CONCLUSION

When we look at the qualitative aspects of the development process the grants element in the social system may take on much more importance than its quantitative significance would suggest, simply because the grants economy tends to be affected with a higher moral intensity than the exchange economy and hence tends to seek out strategic points at which it can operate. Both foundations and governments as granting agencies are not much interested in the commonplace, bread-and-butter kind of operations. They always want to find a situation in which they can exercise leverage, that is, in which each dollar granted produces a large ultimate effect. Though this search for leverage may not always be successful, the fact that it goes on much more intensely in the grants sector suggests that qualitatively this may have a substantial impact. We see this particularly in the tendency for grants sectors to go towards education, research and the infrastructure in general, which may be highly strategic points with large 'multipliers' in the system as a whole.

We have to admit, however, that we know very little about the effect of grants. One of the great difficulties in the whole grants sector of the economy is that it has very poor feedback. The great virtue of exchange as an organiser is that the feedback from mistakes is very rapid. If a firm produces a commodity for the market which nobody wants, it will very soon find this out. If a strong demand develops for something, it will not be long before suppliers will learn about this. The price system, in other words, is a great teacher, which is why it has a crucial role in the development process, fundamentally a learning process after all. This is why preventing the price system from operating without providing any substitutes is one of the surest recipes for developmental failure. In the grants sector, on the other hand, feedback is erratic and slow. If a foundation makes a grant it may never find out whether the grant is effective, simply because the success of the grant does not affect very much the future functioning of the foundation. Practically the same is true of government grants. Governments, after all, are public foundations, and foundations are private governments. There is, furthermore, a strong reluctance in any bureaucracy to find out about its mistakes, and even greater reluctance to publicise them. Consequently the learning process is extremely slow and there are good reasons therefore for supposing that the grants economy in general is much less efficient as a learning process than the exchange economy. This does not mean, of course, that the grants economy is not essential. It is indeed indispensable in the provision of public goods and eradication of public 'bads', like pollution, and in the identification of strategic 'fulcrums of change' which the exchange economy because of its very success, is likely to overlook.

The final conclusion, therefore, is that the success of the developmental process depends in the first place on keeping a proper balance between the exchange sector and the grants sector, and in the second place improving the efficiency of the grants sector so that it does not fail in its essential functions. It can be argued strongly, for instance, that the developmental success of the United States was a result perhaps as much of good luck as of good management, but was partly the result also of a willingness to use the grants sector, both private and public, very extensively as a supplement to the exchange economy. The same could certainly be said of Japan. On the other hand, the failures of development in other capitalist societies, especially Latin America for instance, may be laid partly at the door of the failure of the grants economy, in particular the public grants economy, to provide the kind of infrastructure or strategic overhead which is necessary for the proper functioning of the exchange economy.

On the other hand, in the socialist camp the greater success of Yugoslavia, which seems to be the most rapidly developing country of this block, may well be the result of a recognition of the essential role of the exchange economy in a socialist country. It is not absurd indeed to hope that the whole socialist-capitalist controversy may be resolved as we learn more about the relative role of the exchange sector and the grants sector in development and in increasing the quality of human life. If we think of a capitalist society as an exchange economy modified by grants, and a socialist society as a grants economy modified by exchange, it is clear that the difference between them becomes much more quantitative than it is qualitative. We can then perceive all the various systems as part of a spectrum, and out of the experience of the various types of societies we may develop a learning process which will enable each society to find the mixture which is most appropriate for its own culture and its own state of development.

REFERENCES

[1] (a) Martin Pfaff and Anita B. Pfaff, with an Introduction by Kenneth E. Boulding, *The Grants Economy*, Wadsworth Publishing Company, Belmont, California (forthcoming in 1971).
  (b) K. E. Boulding and Martin Pfaff (eds.), *Redistribution to the Rich and the Poor: The Role of the Grants Economy in Income Distribution*, Wadsworth Publishing Company, Belmont, California (forthcoming in 1971).
  (c) Kenneth E. Boulding, Martin Pfaff, and Anita B. Pfaff (eds.), *Transfers in an Urbanized Economy: Theories and Effects of the Grants Economy*, Wadsworth Publishing Company, Belmont, California (forthcoming in 1971).

(d) Kenneth E. Boulding, Janos Horvath, and Martin Pfaff (eds.), *The Grants Economy in International Perspective*, Wadsworth Publishing Company, Belmont, California (forthcoming in 1971).

[2] John Pincus, 'Costs and Benefits of Aid', United Nations Conference on Trade and Development, TD/7/Supp. 10 (26 October 1967).

[3] K. E. Boulding and T. Mukerjee, *Unprofitable Empire: Britain and India 1880–1947. A Critique of the Hobson–Lewin Thesis on Imperialism*, to be published in the Proceedings of the Seventh European Conference, Peace Research Society (International) (Rome, Italy, 30–31 August 1970).

STATISTICAL APPENDIX

TABLE 1

TOTAL GRANTS, GRANT ELEMENTS AND GRANT-LIKE FLOWS
(U.S. $. millions)

Recipients—	Australia (1)	Austria (2)	Belgium (3)	Canada (4)	Denmark (5)	France (6)	Germany (7)	Japan (8)	Netherlands (9)	Norway (10)	Portugal (11)	Sweden (12)	Switzerland (13)	Italy (14)	United Kingdom (15)	United States (16)	Total (17)
Europe:																	
Cyprus	—	—	—	0·02	—	—	0·27	—	—	—	—	—	—	*	5·07	0·29	5·65
Gibraltar	—	—	0·03	*	—	—	—	—	—	—	—	—	—	—	0·81	—	0·81
Greece	—	0·01	—	0·01	—	—	0·69	—	—	—	—	—0·01	0·15	0·88	0·01	0·41	11·17
Malta	—	—	—	—	—	—	0·01	—	—	—	—	—	—	0·04	13·62	0·39	14·07
Spain	—	—0·01	0·84	—	0·08	—	6·21	—	—	—	—	—	—	0·40	—	7·07	13·67
Turkey	—	0·16	—	—	—	—	7·13	0·10	0·54	0·13	—	0·12	0·24	0·29	7·42	42·22	58·33
Yugoslavia	—	—0·03	—	—	—	—	—0·44	*	—	—	—	0·07	0·01	3·72	—2·77	15·90	16·40
Unallocated	—	—	—0·01	—	—	4·70	—0·01	—	—	—	—	—	—	—	*	0·20	4·88
Total	—	0·13	0·86	0·03	0·08	4·70	13·83	0·10	0·54	0·13	—	0·18	0·40	4·74	29·72	75·48	130·92
North Africa:																	
Algeria	—	—	—	*	—	127·46	0·91	—	—	*	—	0·30	0·20	0·13	0·01	7·36	136·37
Libya	—	—	—	—	—	—	0·66	*	—	—	—	0·02	—	1·25	2·28	2·66	6·87
Morocco	—	—	0·05	0·09	—	22·21	3·51	—	—	—	—	0·04	0·03	0·47	*	51·50	77·91
Tunisia	—	0·25	0·07	0·17	0·04	16·73	3·19	—	0·01	—	—	0·81	0·15	0·09	0·08	40·34	61·95
U.A.R. (Egypt)	—	0·01	—	—	0·04	—	4·31	0·05	—	0·02	—	—	—	1·54	0·17	76·28	82·40
Unallocated	—	—	—	—	—	—	—0·01	—	0·01	0·01	—	0·04	—	—	—	—	0·04
Total	—	0·26	0·12	0·26	0·08	166·40	12·57	0·05	0·01	0·03	—	1·21	0·38	3·49	2·54	78·13	365·55
South Africa:																	
Botswana (Bechuanaland)	*	—	—	0·04	—	—	—	—	—	—	—	—	—	—	5·58	—	9·62
Burundi	—	—	2·73	—	—	—	0·05	—	—	—	—	—	0·07	—	0·03	0·12	3·00
Congo (Kinshasa)	—	0·01	87·90	0·55	—	—	0·34	—	—	—	—	—	0·34	0·91	0·65	40·82	132·26
Ethiopia	*	0·01	—	—	0·67	—	1·24	0·02	—	0·10	—	1·40	0·01	0·32	0·55	11·19	15·84
French Franc Area:																	
African and Malagasy States:																	
Cameroon	—	—	—	0·30	—	13·38	1·16	*	—	—	—	—	0·28	0·11	0·28	3·93	19·44
Central African Republic	—	0·01	—	0·01	—	9·46	0·09	—	—	—	—	—	—	—	—	1·12	10·69
Chad	—	—	—	0·11	—	11·43	0·06	—	—	—	—	—	0·03	—	*	1·12	12·75

																	Total
Gabon						6·50	0·30									1·24	8·04
Ivory Coast						20·59	0·25					0·10				0·70	21·67
Madagascar						30·21	1·77		0·21							1·45	33·71
Mali						6·37	0·32									2·22	9·10
Mauritania						7·17	0·04	0·04								0·13	7·34
Niger						12·76	0·26	0·01				0·02				1·08	14·15
Senegal						30·40	1·16	*				0·14				0·71	32·44
Togo						4·85	1·94					0·11				1·31	8·26
Upper Volta						9·75	0·27									0·70	10·82
Total						254·83	7·98	0·21								17·87	283·09
Fr. Overseas Terr. and Depts.						50·48										0·08	50·56
Total						305·31	7·98	0·21								17·95	333·89
Gambia				0·02			0·11	0·05							0·12		4·05
Ghana	0·07			1·55			1·68	0·11	0·07						9·12	3·79	14·53
Guinea				0·08		-0·29	0·98	0·16							20·94		21·83
Kenya	0·08		0·37	0·70			1·03	0·16	0·14						7·14	36·67	46·82
Lesotho (Basutoland)	0·01		0·10	0·10			0·14									8·85	9·24
Liberia			0·22	0·08			2·44								13·61	0·15	16·55
Malawi	0·04			0·20			-0·47							*	3·37	27·88	31·98
Mauritius	0·01			0·11											0·07	1·52	1·71
Nigeria	0·18			1·93	0·01		1·68	0·05	0·19	0·02				0·54	22·76	2·62	40·12
Portuguese Overseas Prov.:																	
Angola											0·62						0·64
Cape Verde											1·08						1·08
Maeso							*								0·43		0·43
Mozambique											0·28						0·28
Portuguese Guinea											0·05						0·05
Sao Tome and Principe											0·05						0·05
Timor											0·11						0·11
Total	0·02							*			9·17					0·43	9·62
Rhodesia	0·02		0·49	0·16			0·07			0·08					4·87		5·20
Ruanda		4·00		0·73			0·28							0·01	0·63		6·14
Seychelles			*	*											0·04		1·54
Sierra Leone	0·03		0·16	0·16			0·39	0·01					0·01		5·76	1·50	7·63
Somalia							2·73					0·02	13·14		7·50	1·25	23·40
St. Helena															0·01	0·01	0·65
Sudan	0·02						3·41	0·03		0·01		0·01			4·48	0·64	9·59
Swaziland	0·01			0·01			3·47	0·02	0·08	1·24		0·03			6·62	1·66	10·24
Tanzania	0·10	0·04		0·90			0·27	0·02		0·01		*		0·01	3·15	10·18	26·25
Uganda	0·02			0·58			0·13	0·02		0·03		0·05		0·01	0·74	13·00	14·40
Zambia	0·03			0·11			0·87	*		-0·01		-0·02			0·01	11·32	12·41
Unallocated		0·19							0·02						1·89		2·99
Total	0·65	0·44	94·63	9·00	1·42	305·02	29·76	0·47	0·41	1·11	9·17	3·46	1·55	17·29	160·20	18·47	815·84

(continued)

TABLE 1 (continued)

Recipients— \ Donors—	Australia (1)	Austria (2)	Belgium (3)	Canada (4)	Denmark (5)	France (6)	Germany (7)	Japan (8)	Netherlands (9)	Norway (10)	Portugal (11)	Sweden (12)	Switzerland (13)	Italy (14)	United Kingdom (15)	United States (16)	Total (17)
North and Central America:																	
Bahamas	—	—	—	—	—	—	—	—	—	—	—	—	—	—	0·06	—	0·06
Bermuda	—	0·07	—	*	—	—	—	—	—	—	—	—	—	—	0·05	—	0·05
Costa Rica	—	—	—	—	—	—	0·23	*	—	—	—	—	*	0·01	0·01	7·03	7·35
Cuba	—	—	—	—	—	—	*	*	—	—	—	—	*	—	—	—	*
Dominican Republic	—	0·09	—	—	—	—	0·15	—	—	—	—	—	—	0·01	—	67·85	68·01
El Salvador	—	—	—	—	—	—	0·20	—	—	—	—	—	—	—	0·07	7·23	7·53
Guatemala	—	—	—	—	—	—	0·72	0·03	—	—	—	—	—	*	—	8·86	9·68
Haiti	—	—	—	0·10	—	—	0·30	—	—	—	—	—	0·01	*	—	2·55	2·88
Honduras (Br.)	—	—	—	—	—	—	—	—	—	—	—	—	0·02	—	1·51	0·36	1·97
Honduras	—	—	—	—	—	—	0·12	—	—	—	—	—	—	0·01	0·01	5·17	5·31
Jamaica	—	—	—	0·28	—	—	0·01	*	—	—	—	—	*	*	2·78	3·07	6·14
Mexico	—	0·11	—	1·17	—	0·05	0·26	0·06	—	—	—	—	*	*	0·06	13·28	15·86
Netherlands Antilles	—	—	—	—	—	—	0·01	—	3·60	—	—	—	—	0·37	—	—	3·61
Nicaragua	—	—	—	—	—	—	0·13	—	—	*	—	—	—	—	—	7·56	9·70
Panama	—	—	—	—	—	—	0·08	*	—	—	—	—	—	0·01	*	12·37	13·25
Trinidad and Tobago	—	—	—	0·43	—	—	*	—	—	—	—	—	*	0·80	0·01	15·45	15·89
West Indies (Br.)	—	—	—	1·08	—	—	—	—	—	—	—	*	—	—	9·74	0·39	11·21
Unallocated	—	—	—	—	—	12·60	0·12	0·01	—	—	—	—	0·01	—	-0·02	0·85	13·57
Total	—	0·27	—	3·06	—	12·65	2·33	0·10	3·60	—	—	—	0·04	1·22	14·28	152·02	189·57
South America:																	
Argentina	—	0·05	—	-0·60	—	-0·53	-3·84	-1·02	0·16	—	—	—	0·14	-0·89	-3·43	4·86	-6·67
Bolivia	—	0·01	—	—	—	—	0·04	-0·02	—	—	—	—	0·01	0·03	0·23	24·86	26·24
Brazil	—	0·03	—	0·27	—	2·54	15·60	3·37	0·27	*	—	—	0·24	0·10	0·72	69·74	92·82
Chile	—	0·01	0·96	0·38	0·14	0·35	0·52	0·14	0·13	0·01	—	—	0·02	-0·07	1·22	44·07	47·87
Colombia	—	—	—	—	0·04	—	1·22	0·02	0·04	—	—	—	*	—	0·07	22·50	23·90
Ecuador	—	0·02	—	—	—	—	0·42	0·02	0·04	—	—	—	*	—	*	14·40	14·86
Falkland Islands	—	—	—	—	—	—	—	—	—	—	—	—	—	—	0·05	—	0·05
Guyana	—	—	—	0·21	—	—	*	—	—	—	—	—	—	—	2·00	3·22	5·43
Paraguay	—	—	—	—	—	—	0·59	-0·03	—	—	—	—	—	0·02	*	5·29	5·87
Peru	—	0·03	0·27	—	0·08	—	5·44	-0·06	—	—	—	—	0·15	0·04	0·36	19·96	30·63
Surinam	—	—	—	—	—	—	—	—	5·65	—	—	—	—	—	—	0·31	5·96
Uruguay	—	0·15	—	—	—	—	0·65	*	—	—	—	—	—	0·08	*	2·25	2·98
Venezuela	—	—	—	—	—	—	0·63	0·02	—	—	—	—	-0·01	-1·63	0·08	16·74	15·99
Unallocated	—	—	—	—	—	—	0·12	0·01	—	—	—	—	—	—	0·01	—	0·13
Total																	

Israel	—	—	—	—	-0·03	—	-0·08	75·64	0·01	*	—	0·10	37·68	113·32
Jordan	—	0·10	—	—	—	—	0·01	1·34	0·01	*	—	0·08	37·02	45·10
Kuwait	—	—	—	—	—	—	*	—	—	0·01	—	0·10	0·10	1·06
Lebanon	—	0·02	—	—	—	—	*	0·63	—	—	0·01	0·01	—	0·10
Muscat and Oman	—	—	—	—	—	—	—	—	—	—	—	—	—	—
Qatar	—	—	—	—	—	—	0·01	0·02	—	—	—	—	0·03	0·07
Saudi Arabia	—	—	—	—	—	—	—	—	—	—	0·02	25·99	0·03	26·01
South Arabia Federation	—	0·02	—	0·04	—	—	0·02	0·15	—	—	0·02	0·18	-1·66	-1·22
Syria	—	—	—	—	—	—	—	—	—	—	0·02	1·49	—	1·49
Trucial Oman	—	—	—	—	3·60	—	—	0·64	—	—	0·14	0·02	4·50	5·30
Yemen	—	—	0·01	0·01	3·52	—	0·07	*	0·01	—	-0·01	—	-0·03	3·57
Unallocated	—	—	0·08	0·08	—	—	0·21	0·21	0·07	0·55	0·10	0·10	84·65	207·03
Total	—	0·48	0·03	0·08	—	—	0·07	81·33	0·21	0·07	0·23	—	35·84	207·03
Asia: South														
Afghanistan	0·03	0·02	0·01	—	—	—	0·10	6·35	—	0·01	0·15	0·01	0·06	33·37	40·67
Bhutan	0·15	—	—	—	—	—	0·01	0·01	—	—	—	—	—	—	0·16
Burma	1·06	—	0·22	—	—	—	11·79	-0·02	—	—	0·32	*	0·05	2·96	16·69
Ceylon	1·53	—	3·02	—	—	—	0·13	0·99	0·01	—	0·28	*	0·12	3·89	10·02
India	9·56	0·09	20·16	0·20	—	—	6·68	17·21	1·37	3·35	3·41	0·66	0·02	26·67	582·21	671·59
Maldive Islands	—	—	0·01	—	—	—	0·09	0·30	—	—	—	0·40	*	0·08	0·09
Nepal	0·05	—	0·01	—	—	—	0·09	0·30	—	—	2·39	0·18	0·08	15·62	16·52
Pakistan	1·71	—	12·05	0·08	—	—	4·08	13·48	0·33	—	-0·01	14·58	214·12	263·99
Unallocated	2·76	—	-0·01	—	—	—	-0·01	*	-0·01	—	0·18	-0·02	-0·02	2·71
Total	16·85	0·11	36·38	0·28	—	—	22·88	38·30	3·68	6·54	1·25	0·21	42·45	852·15	1022·44
Asia: Far East														
Brunei	*	—	0·01	—	—	—	*	—	—	—	—	—	0·02	—	0·03
Cambodia	0·32	—	0·10	—	4·29	—	0·45	0·64	—	—	—	—	0·04	1·62	7·96
China (Taiwan)	—	—	—	—	—	—	0·25	0·47	—	—	—	—	—	29·97	30·73
Hong Kong	0·02	—	0·05	—	—	—	0·04	2·33	—	—	—	0·02	0·12	1·91	4·49
Indonesia	1·54	0·01	0·08	—	—	—	21·52	4·88	—	—	—	—	0·03	6·87	35·36
Korea (South)	0·27	—	0·05	0·57	—	—	9·37	1·70	0·54	0·49	0·01	0·43	0·14	162·70	175·91
Laos	0·75	—	0·12	—	3·06	—	0·56	0·29	—	—	—	—	0·07	3·98	58·40	67·16
Malaysia:														
Malaya	0·92	—	—	—	—	—	—	—	*	—	—	—	0·34	—	1·26
Sabah	0·31	—	—	—	—	—	—	—	—	—	—	—	1·74	—	2·05
Sarawak	1·42	—	1·82	—	—	—	—	—	—	—	—	—	2·09	—	3·51
Unallocated	—	—	—	—	—	—	0·24	0·45	—	—	—	*	7·08	3·61	13·20
Total	2·65	—	1·82	—	—	—	0·24	0·45	*	—	—	*	11·25	3·61	20·02
Philippines	0·18	—	3·04	—	—	—	35·30	1·17	0·01	—	0·01	0·01	0·19	34·65	74·57
Rhu-kyu (U.S.)	—	—	—	—	—	—	—	—	—	—	—	—	—	15·12	15·03
Singapore	0·60	—	0·50	—	—	—	0·07	0·06	—	—	—	—	1·25	0·01	2·49
Thailand	2·07	0·19	0·28	0·15	—	—	3·86	2·90	0·01	—	0·05	0·03	0·63	22·73	32·90
Vietnam (South)	0·84	—	0·58	—	4·87	—	0·21	1·99	*	—	0·02	0·14	0·23	300·10	308·98
Unallocated	*	—	—	—	—	—	-0·01	0·04	0·01	0·02	0·01	0·01	—	-0·01	0·06
Total	9·24	0·20	6·63	0·72	12·22	—	71·85	16·92	0·57	0·51	0·11	0·74	17·88	637·48	775·27

(continued)

TABLE 1 (*continued*)

TOTAL GRANTS, GRANT ELEMENTS AND GRANT-LIKE FLOWS
(U.S. $ millions)

Donors— Recipients—	Australia	Austria	Canada	France	United Kingdom	United States	OECD
Oceania:							
Fiji Islands	*	—	*	—	4·37	0·01	4·38
French Overseas Territories	*	—	—	23·62	—	—	23·62
Gilbert and Ellice Islands	*	—	—	—	0·42	—	0·42
New Guinea and Papua (Austr.)	82·51	—	—	—	—	*	82·51
New Hebrides (Br. and Fr.)	*	—	—	—	0·58	—	0·58
Solomon Islands (Br.)	*	—	—	—	3·82	0·11	3·93
Tonga	*	—	—	—	0·17	0·17	0·34
Trust Territory of the Pacific Islands (U.S.)	—	—	—	—	—	18·16	18·16
Western Samoa	*	—	0·01	—	—	—	0·01
Unallocated	0·02	—	0·01	—	0·01	−0·01	0·03
Total	82·53	—	0·02	23·62	9·37	18·44	133·98

Source:
(1) Grant-like flows, net official grants, reparations and indemnification payments: Organisation for Economic Co-operation and Development, *Geographical Distribution of Financial Flows to Less Developed Countries* – (Disbursements) 1960–65, Paris, 1966–67.

(2) Grant-Equivalents of Development Assistance Committee Countries loans: John Pincus, *Costs and Benefits of Aid*, United Nations Conference on Trade and Development, TD/7/Supplement 10, 26 October 1967.

TABLE 2

GRANT ELEMENT OF LOANS GIVEN BY CENTRALLY
CONTROLLED ECONOMIES TO LESS DEVELOPED
COUNTRIES, 1954–67
(U.S. $ millions)

	U.S.S.R.[1]	*Eastern Europe*[2]	*Mainland China*[3]	*Total*
Grant element	36%[a]	24%[b]	60%[c]	
TOTAL	2156	504	536	3196
Africa	309	71	178	558
Algeria	84	5	30	119
Cameroon	3			3
Central African Republic			2	2
Congo Brazzaville	3		15	18
Ethiopia	37	4		41
Ghana	32	24	24	80
Guinea	26	6	15	47
Kenya	16		11	27
Mali	20	6	14	40
Mauritania	1		2	3
Morocco	16	8		24
Nigeria		3		3
Senegal	2			2
Sierra Leone	10			10
Somalia	24	1	13	28
Sudan	8	6		14
Tanzania	8	1	32	41
Tunisia	12	5		17
Uganda	6		9	15
Zambia	2		10	12
Far East	148	71	143	362
Burma	5	6	50	61
Cambodia	9	1	30	40
Indonesia	134	63	63	260
Latin America	67	59		126
Argentina	16	1		17
Brazil	31	54		85
Chile	20			20
Ecuador		1		1
Uruguay		2		2
Near East and South Asia	1633	303	215	2151
Afghanistan	205	3	17	225
Ceylon	11	12	25	48
Greece	30			30
India	573	85		658
Iran	119	13		132
Iraq	66			66

(*continued*)

TABLE 2 (*continued*)

Near East and South Asia (contd.)	U.S.S.R.	Eastern Europe[2]	Mainland China[3]	Total
Nepal	7		36	43
Pakistan	64	13	40	117
Syria	84	34	10	128
Turkey	76	2		78
UAR	364	135	64	563
Yemen	33	4	24	61

Sources:
   [1] I.N.R. Research Memorandum; U.S. Department of State (14 August 1968) Communist Government and Delevoping Nations: Aid and Trade in 1967, pp. 2–3.
   [2] U.S. Congress-Joint Economic Committee: Soviet Economic Performance 1966–67, p. 127.
   [3] 'The Foreign Aid Programs of the Soviet Bloc and Communist China': An Analysis by Kurt Muller, pp. 218–39.

Notes on calculation of grant elements.
   [a] Grant element based on repayment terms of 2·5 per cent per annum for 12 years compared with I.B.R.D. lending rate of 5·5 per cent per annum in 1960 (3% × 12 = 36%).
   [b] Grant element based on repayment terms of 2·5 per cent per annum for 8 years compated to I.B.R.D. lending rate of 5·5 per cent per annum 1960 (3% × 8 = 24%).
   [c] Grant element based on repayment terms with a weighted average of 0·5 per cent per annum for 12 years compared with I.B.R.D. lending rate of 5·5 per cent per annum in 1960 (5% × 12 = 60%).

7 Should the Rich Countries Help the Poor? How could they do so?

Chris Economides
CYPRUS ECONOMIC SOCIETY

I. HOW DID THE 'GAP' EMERGE? IS IT WIDENING?

Although the gap in income per head in the rich countries and the poor countries may be an economic problem, its causation and solution extends beyond the narrow borders of economics into the domain of other social and human sciences, such as politics, ethics, demography and humanism.

It may be said in general terms that the 'gap' has emerged and has been widening as a result of the continuing advance of the industrialised countries' economies on the one hand, and the stagnation or low pace of the primary producing countries' economies, on the other. By applying science and technology to their production, the advanced industrial countries have raised their labour productivity considerably. At the same time, through imperfect and oligopolistic competition, and with the assistance of a high elasticity of demand of their products, they have managed to appropriate to themselves almost all the fruits of higher productivity, instead of sharing them with their trade-partners, the primary producing countries, through lower prices and free movement of capital and labour.

On the other hand, the primary producing countries' economies have remained mostly backward and poor because:

(a) their products have been marketed under conditions of almost perfect competition and inelastic demand, and their increases of labour productivity (where they have occurred) have mostly been passed on to the buyers of their products in the form of lower prices.

(b) the industrialised countries have, on the one hand, been competing with the backward primary producing countries, both with agricultural products of their own and with synthetic materials manufactured by them; they have, on the other hand, discriminated against the backward primary producing countries by introducing subsidies and high tariffs in favour of their own agricultural products;

(c) in most cases and for long periods, the backward primary producing countries were colonies of industrialised countries, who

G

treated and 'developed' them mainly as suppliers of cheap food and raw materials and as consumers of their industrial products.

II. CONTEMPORARY EMPIRICAL EVIDENCE

The thesis that I have outlined above is, I think, supported by the trends of the past two decades and by the events taking place before our eyes today, which provide much more convincing evidence than the uncertain statistics of earlier epochs.

(1) *Post-War Productivity and Prices in Manufacturing*

According to U.N. statistics, between 1948 and 1967 labour productivity in the manufacturing industries of all the developed market economies rose by nearly 100 per cent.[1] During the same period, the unit value index of the world exports of manufactured goods, instead of falling by at least 33 per cent[2] as it might have been expected to have done under conditions of perfect competition, actually rose by 13 per cent.[3] During the period 1948 to 1967, the wholesale price index of finished goods in the U.S.A. rose by 26 per cent.[4]

(2) *Post-War Prices of Agricultural Products*

During the same period the price indices of exports of food and agricultural non-food products from all developing countries fell by 14 per cent and 21 per cent respectively[5] and the wholesale price index of farm products in U.S.A. fell by 15 per cent.[6]

(3) *The Typical Case of British Agriculture*

British agriculture is one of the most efficient in the world. During the past ten years its labour productivity has risen annually by 6 per cent and,

---

[1] *U.N. Statistical Yearbook 1968* (pp. 42, 50). Indices of World Manufacturing Production 1948 = 45; 1967 = 127. World manufacturing employment rose from 72 to 106. Thus the index of manufacturing productivity rose from 62 to 120; i.e. from 100 to 194.

[2] On the assumption that unit labour-costs (which fell by 50 per cent) constitute two-thirds of the price and that the other components of the price remain stable per unit.

[3] U.N. Yearbook 1968 (p. 66). Unit value index of World Exports of Manufactured Goods: 1948 = 95; 1967 = 107.

[4] U.N. Yearbooks 1957 (p. 464) and 1968 (p. 539). Indices of Wholesale Prices of finished goods in U.S.A. 1948/1953, 94/100; 1953/1967, 91/107. Therefore Indices 1948/1967, 94/118 = 100/126.

[5] Food Exports price indices: U.N. Yearbooks 1957 (p. 435), 1959 (p. 404), 1968 (p. 406); 1948/1953, 100/100; 1953/1958, 100/94; 1958/1967, 111/101. Therefore 1948/1967, 100/86.

[6] U.N. Yearbooks 1957 (p. 464), 1968 (p. 539). Wholesale Price Indices of Farm Products in U.S.A. 1948/1953, 111/100; 1953/1967, 111/104. Therefore 1948/1967, 111/94 = 100/85.

although it now employs only 3 per cent of the total labour force in U.K., it supplies about 50 per cent of the country's needs.[1] Yet, in spite of such increased productivity, the British agricultural sector needs state support equal to 100 per cent of its net income, in order to reach the average per capita income of the whole country,[2] whilst the annual earnings of its hired farm workers are only 68 per cent of those in other industries.[3]

(4) *Price-making by Manufacturers*

If one follows the business columns of the press, one can see how manufacturers all over the world, by a concerted action, and under the price-leadership of the large corporations, raise their prices, passing on to consumers any increase in their unit labour and other costs. Here are some typical examples:

> Ford Increases Tractor Prices. Ford, the second largest tractor manufacturer in the United Kingdom, yesterday became the last of the companies in the industry to announce an increase in prices. The move – averaging 10 per cent over the whole Ford range – follows Massey Ferguson's unannounced increases; averaging 8 per cent, early last month. . . . The £33m. industry's latest rises, the second round in just over a year, will add some £3 m. to farmers' bills. Ford, which has 30 per cent of the British market compared with Massey Ferguson's 39 per cent, blamed the need for the increases on rising materials and manufacturing costs.[4]

> ICI and Monsanto Raise Prices. More chemical prices are going up. Imperial Chemical Industries and Monsanto are raising prices of polyethylene products, such as polymers, powders and compounds, by about 7 per cent. Other major producers of the material, Shell and British Petroleum, are thought to be reviewing their prices. I.C.I. and Monsanto are among those who recently increased the cost of polystyrene. Together they probably account for 230,000 tons of polyethylene production in this country. I.C.I.'s material is marketed under the brand name Alkathene.[5]

[1] See U.K. Agriculture's Import Saving Role, E.D.C. for Agriculture, H.M.S.O. (1968), pp. 4, 24, 26.

[2] See *Annual Review and Determination of Guarantees, 1970*, H.M.S.O., Cmnd 4321 (1970), pp. 11, 38, 43. The average annual net farming income in the U.K. from 1964/5 to 1968/9 was £484 million, of which £241m. came from state support grants, such as deficiency payments (the implementation of guaranteed prices), subsidies and other production grants (excluding administrative expenses).

[3] *U.K. Annual Abstract of Statistics, 1969*, pp. 142, 198. Men's average weekly earnings in manufacturing industries in October 1968 were £23.12.4d.; those of agricultural workers 1968/69 were £16.2.1d.

[4] *The Times* (London, 7 May 1970), p. 30.

[5] *Ibid.* (3 July 1970), p. 24.

W. Germany. Daimler-Benz Price Rise Likely. Substantial increases in material and wage costs this year will most probably force Daimler-Benz to increase prices on all products. The outlook for the year suggests that profits will not be able to grow at the same rate as in 1969. Dr. Joachim Zahn, company chairman, said that Deutsche mark revaluation and the West German inflation had led to vast cost rises. For the year so far these rises had been about 10 per cent.

But, in the autumn, the company would have to conclude a new wage agreement, which without doubt would very substantially add to the mounting overhead costs.[1]

(5) *Price-acceptance by Farmers*

On the other hand the plight of farmers all over the world, caught between the Scylla of rising costs and the Charybdis of the falling prices of their own products, is seen in such press reports as the following:

Australia. Cost-Prices Crisis Upsets Farmers. The farmers are caught in a vicious cost-price circle and are conspicuously tightening their belts. Had not Australia a minerals boom, the country would not be facing its biggest crisis. . . . Australia is not continuing to ride on the sheep's back, even though wool (21·3 per cent) and wheat (7·7 per cent) still lead exports. Because of the sharp decline in wool prices growers are facing bankruptcy, and only massive subsidies are holding together the wheat, dairy and other industries. The statistics for wheat are particularly alarming; last year growers produced 515 m. bushels, of which only 299 m. were sold; even after next year's harvest, only 275 m. bushels are expected to be marketed. This year, because of poor overseas returns, the Government could pay up to £18 m. in subsidies under the wheat stabilisation scheme. It also has had to find £76 m. from loan funds to allow the Wheat Board to repay its Reserve Bank overdraft for 1968. . . . Other rural sectors are also badly hit. The price of cropping produce (cereals, vegetables, fruit, sugar) is now only 6 per cent higher than in 1961. Beef cattle prices have gone up 15 per cent, dairy produce 2–3 per cent, and wool down by 5 per cent. Against this costs of equipment and supplies have risen by 12 per cent, services and overheads by 30 per cent, and marketing by 16 per cent. . . . Despite subsidies, various estimates put the number of Australia's 200,000 farmers earning less than £470 a year as 30,000, and a third of all farmers are supposedly economically redundant. Even to maintain this situation, subsidies and other means of support are costing the taxpayer, according to the Institute of Public Affairs, about £930 a farm each year. The actual subsidy is now more than £93 m.[2]

[1] *The Times* (2 July 1970), p. 19.
[2] *Ibid.* (2 April 1970).

IV. THE RICH INDUSTRIALISED COUNTRIES' MORAL DEBT TO THE POOR PRIMARY PRODUCING COUNTRIES

If the thesis argued above is correct – that is, if the gap has been created mostly by the usurpation by the industrialised countries of the lion's share of the joint product of the international division of labour and the international collaboration through world trade with the primary producing countries – the moral inference is that the former countries owe a moral debt to the latter which they should repay by giving them sufficient unrequited financial and technical aid to enable them to narrow the gap and to become really equal partners in human society. But is a moral debt enforceable in a world in which might is still right? I think it may be, if such a moral debt is backed by the concensus of world opinion and by the debtors' feeling that such repayment is in their own long-term self-interest.

V. THE RICH COUNTRIES' LONG-TERM SELF-INTEREST

The rich industrialised countries have reached a point where their main concern is not the scarcity of resources in relation to their needs, but a real or imaginary threat from external enemies. This is the reason why the largest share of their budgets goes to military expenditure, including research directly or indirectly connected with 'defence'. For example, the NATO countries are now spending over \$100 billion for their 'defence' which represents about 10 per cent of their collective G.D.P. and the whole world is spending probably \$200 billion for the same purpose. At present underdeveloped countries, as such, do not appear to be a threat to the developed countries, since the economic gap also involves a military strength gap, the more so because of the development of modern sophisticated weapons.

The case of Communist China should, however, be seen not simply as that of a country ruled by a government ideologically hostile to both Soviet and Western countries, but rather as a case of a densely populated poor underdeveloped country which may, one day, when it feels strong enough, try to solve its demographic and economic problems by aggression. The past history of mankind shows that pressure of population (in relation to the available resources), backed by sufficient strength, often leads to desperate aggression, such as the invasions and devastation of Europe by the Huns under Attila in the 5th century and by the Mongols under Genghis Khan in the 13th century. China has also proved that even an underdeveloped country can make nuclear weapons and rockets. In actual fact scientists in many countries now appear to be on the threshold of inventing cheap methods of enrichment of uranium 235 and making nuclear bombs at low cost, in which case nuclear arms will be sooner or later at the disposal of poor countries as well as rich.

In these circumstances, poor underdeveloped countries should be viewed by the rich developed ones not simply as poor needing help for development – whether in the form of charity or repayment of a moral debt – but as a three-fourths majority of mankind, whom they have the choice either to collaborate with in creating a better world in which all nations, big and small, will have equal rights and opportunities in raising their living standards, or to abandon to their fate at the risk of turning them into potential enemies possessing nuclear weapons through which human life may possibly be annihilated from the face of earth. It is poor consolation for the rich countries to think that the people of the poor countries may also perish, for, by definition, the haves have more to lose than the have-nots. This is well illustrated by some of the recent successful aircraft hijackings by desperados and even by bluffers.

VI. HOW CAN THE GAP BE NARROWED AND BRIDGED?

One must first ask what do the poor countries need? In general terms, in order to narrow and bridge the gap, the poor countries need mainly:

(i) *More food* to abolish hunger and malnutrition and to raise the standard of living of their people. Food may be made available, in the short run, by imports from abroad, either as free gifts or at low subsidised prices, and in the long run, by raising either the productivity of domestic agriculture or the productivity of other industries for export at remunerative prices to pay for imported food.

(ii) *Birth control* to solve the problem of population growth which is as urgent a problem as the related one of abolishing hunger and malnutrition. This involves disseminating information, providing medical advice and facilities and offering birth-avoidance incentive payments. The rich countries could help the governments of poor countries in this respect by intensifying research in contraception and early termination of pregnancy and by making available to them medical practitioners, teachers, nurses and free birth control devices and pills.

(iii) *Education and technical training* is needed to enable the poor countries to adopt new scientific and technological methods in production, management and marketing.

(iv) *Price-compensatory grants to farmers* are needed since, as we have seen, international market forces are adverse to agricultural producers and since any prospective rise in agricultural productivity, however desirable it may be, is followed, as is now happening with the 'green revolution', by the unprofitable fall in their export prices and even in their total export earnings. To offset this producers should be paid compensatory grants, similar to the deficiency payments given by the U.K. government to its own farmers. As a result there would be, on the one hand, an incentive for farmers to increase their productivity and, on the other hand, food prices would be kept low for the benefit of the masses of consumers.

(v) *Industrialisation* is ultimately the only way to narrow and bridge the gap. It is desirable to help the poor countries to industrialise so that, on the one hand, that part of their labour force which is now unemployed or underemployed may be given productive employment, and on the other hand, they may produce the goods that they need to raise living standards, to make possible higher investments and provide goods to be exported to acquire the imports needed for these purposes.

To achieve these objectives, what the poor countries need are, first, capital equipment and know-how for the establishment and operation of plants and factories and, secondly, markets for their products. The former can initially be supplied only by the rich industrialised countries. In order, however, that these infant industries be able to grow, they need to be given not only protection in their domestic markets but also preferential treatment in the rich countries' markets. At the same time, in view of the considerable external economies, economies of scale and other advantages enjoyed by their competitor industries in rich countries, the newly established industries in poor countries need to be given investment grants and other incentives, similar to those given by industrialised countries to industries newly established in their own 'development' areas.

With sufficient financial resources and with sufficient will and determination, men can perform the seemingly impossible. To achieve all the above prerequisites for narrowing and bridging the gap between the rich and the poor nations, all we need is sufficient financial resources, accompanied by the will and determination of governments to solve this vital problem for the future of mankind. The world has now enough scientists, technologists and other qualified personnel ready to be mobilised for the solution of any problem, however difficult it may at first sight appear, provided reasonable salaries and employment terms are offered to them.

Take, for example, the two incredible achievements of the last thirty years: the fission of the atom and the landing of man on the moon. By mobilising brains from all over the world and by placing at their disposal adequate financial resources, America achieved the seemingly impossible. In the light of these miraculous achievements, can anyone doubt that the rich industrialised countries can, if they have the will, solve this gap problem, however difficult it may now appear?

Let us first consider the present trends. If world affairs are left to continue their present course, and the rich countries' aid to the poor ones is no larger than at present, the gap must be expected to continue to widen both proportionately and, *a fortiori*, in absolute terms. According to World

Bank's 1969 Report,[1] during the period 1950 to 1967, the G.D.P.s of the developing countries rose annually by 4·8 per cent, their population rose by 2·4 per cent and their per capita G.D.P. by 2·4 per cent. On the other hand the G.D.P.s of the industrialised countries rose by 4·3 per cent, their population by 1·2 per cent and their per capita G.D.P. by 3·1 per cent. According to U.N. statistics[2] the average per capita G.D.P. of the industrialised countries in 1967 was about $U.S. 2,200 and that of developing countries only about $180. If the 1950–67 trend continues, by the year 2000 the annual average per capita G.D.P. of the industrialised countries will be increased by $3,800 to reach $6,000 and that of developing countries by only $220 to $400 (at 1967 prices).[3] Thus the present average gap which is about 12 : 1 will rise to over 15 : 1. It should also be borne in mind that if the present trends continue, the population of the developing countries which, in 1967, was about 73 per cent of the world (excluding China, U.S.S.R. and the other socialist countries) may be expected to rise by the year 2000 to 80 per cent of the world.[4]

VII. A TARGET OF $1,000 PER HEAD FOR L.D.C.s BY THE YEAR 2000

If the gap is to be narrowed, a target should be set to increase by the year 2000 the average annual per capita G.D.P. of the L.D.C.s to at least $1,000 (at 1967 prices), and thus reduce the gap to 6 : 1, on the assumption that the average per capita G.D.P. of the present industrialised countries will grow as mentioned above by 3·1 per cent per annum to $6,000. To achieve this target, the birth rates in the L.D.C.s will have to be substantially reduced. If, for instance, the population growth of the L.D.C.s can be restricted to an annual average of 1·7 per cent, then the annual growth of G.D.P. needed to achieve the target of $1,000 per

---

[1] See *World Bank Annual Report 1969*, p. 46. According to the Bank's definition, the industrialised countries are the following 22 countries: the U.S.A., Canada, the E.E.C. (6), EFTA (except Portugal) (6), Finland, Ireland, Iceland, Japan, Puerto Rico, South Africa, Australia and New Zealand. All the other countries of the world, except the U.S.S.R., China and the other Centrally Planned Economies, are included in the definition of 'Developing Countries' or 'L.D.C.s'. These definitions are adopted in this paper.

[2] *United Nations Yearbook 1968*, pp. 78–86 and 585–9. The population of the 'industrialised countries' in 1967 was about 640 million, and that of the 'L.D.C.s' about 1,700 million. The G.D.P.s of the former totalled $1,400 billion; those of the latter about $300 billion. (In 1963 they were estimated by U.N. to be about $230 billion.)

[3] $100 in 33 years at 3·1 per cent p.a. compound, grow to 274; $2,200 × 2·74 = $6,028. $100 in 33 years at 2·4 per cent p.a. grow to 219; $180 × 2·19 = $394.

[4] Present population, per footnote 2, above, L.D.C. 1,700 m. (73 per cent) out of total 2,340 million. By year 2000 if L.D.C. population grows by 2·4 per cent p.a., × 219 = 3,700 million, whereas the present industrialised countries' population, 640 million, growing at 1·2 per cent × 148 will be 950 million.

capita by the year 2000 is 7 per cent.[1] Such a growth, though difficult to realise, is not impossible, if one remembers that probably some 20 per cent of human resources in L.D.C.s are now idle.

If we are to increase the annual growth rate to 7 per cent, the resources transferred from the industrialised countries to L.D.C.s will need to be increased substantially. In 1968 some $13 billion were transferred to the L.D.C.s, of which only one-third were government grants or grant-like contributions.[2] The annual servicing of debts, however, by L.D.C.s amounted to $4 billion[3] and the total annual outflow of resources from L.D.C.s has been estimated by UNCTAD to amount (in 1967) to about $8 billion, including profits, dividends, interest and amortisation, but excluding any funds, of which the total is unknown, involved in the flight of indigenous capital.[4]

Thus not only will more resources need to be transferred to the L.D.C.s, but also most of them will need to be unrequited transfers.

Thus new sources of aid will need to be tapped. Besides the usual sources of development aid – official disbursements (multilateral and bilateral), technical aid and private investments and loans – it is suggested that the following potential sources should be tapped:

(a) *The Counterpart of Special Drawing Rights.* As is known, the I.M.F. has, as from 1 January 1970, inaugurated a new and radical scheme for the increase of international liquidity – the Special Drawing Rights. Unlike other drawings from the I.M.F., the beneficiaries of the S.D.R. do not have to give in exchange an equivalent amount of their own currency. At the same time, the recipients are not obliged to reconstitute their holdings of S.D.R. by more than 30 per cent on the average.[5] Thus, in practice, 70 per cent of the S.D.R. allocated to each country is a gift of international purchasing power.

One might have expected that such gifts would have been allocated in proportion to each country's needs of international purchasing power. Yet the allocation was made in proportion to each country's quota in the I.M.F. which practically means, in proportion to each country's economic strength. For example, America's share in the first year's allocation will be $867 million and the other industrial countries' share is $1,587 million out of a world total of $3,414 million. On the other hand, all the L.D.C.s shares together amount to no more than $960 million.[6]

[1] $100 in 33 years at 5·3 per cent p.a. grow to 550; $180 × 5·50 = $990.

[2] Pearson's 'Partners in Development' Report, p. 137, Table 7.1: total new flow of resources to L.D.C. in 1968 $12·8 billion, of which only $4·1 billion were 'grants and grant-like contributions'.

[3] Pearson's 'Partners in Development' Report, p. 372, Table 10: debt servicing 1968 estimated at $4 billion.

[4] See UNCTAD Secretariat study TD/B/C.3/73 quoted in *UNCTAD Monthly Bulletin* No. 45 (May 1970).   [5] See *I.M.F. Articles*, Schedule G.

[6] See I.M.F. quarterly *Finance and Development* (June 1970), p. 62.

G 2

In these circumstances, if it were to be agreed that the rich industrialised countries have a moral duty and/or a self-interest in making substantial unrequited transfers of resources to the L.D.C.s, a most convenient and equitable method would be for them to place, for this purpose, at the disposal of either one of the existing world development bodies, such as the I.D.A., or one to be established for co-ordinating the international division of labour, as is suggested below, amounts of each country's own currency equivalent to its S.D.R. allocations.

(b) *Part of Disarmament Savings.* As stated above, the rich countries are wasting 10 per cent of their G.D.P.s on real or imaginary security measures. If the world is to come to its sense it should, sooner or later – the sooner the better – reach a disarmament agreement which will both create a more relaxed international climate and release large resources for constructive purposes. In such a case, part of those resources should be utilised for world development designed to improve still further international relations.

(c) *Income Tax Credits for Foreign Aid Contributions by Citizens of Rich Countries.* An ingenious scheme for both increasing foreign aid contributions and getting the people of the donor countries to become actively interested in world development has been proposed by Harvard Professors Albert O. Hirschman and Richard M. Bird in their study *Foreign Aid – a Critique and a Proposal* published by the International Finance Section of Princeton University. The essence of their plan is

> to involve the individual tax payer of the donor countries in the foreign-aid program. Instead of paying taxes for a package of government expenditures that includes foreign aid together with all domestic programs, taxpayers could elect to use a limited portion of their income-tax obligation for contribution to one or several World Development Funds. . . . For their 'contributions to foreign aid' the taxpayers would receive a full tax credit from the Internal Revenue Service.

In more detail, they suggest that

> the tax-credit mechanism might work somewhat as follows: individual taxpayers could claim a full tax credit for their foreign aid contributions, up to 5 per cent of their income tax or $10,000, whichever is smaller. A hypothetical average taxpayer with an adjusted gross income of $16,000 and a tax liability of $2,030 could, for example, obtain a tax credit of $102 under this scheme. The claim for credit would have to be substantiated by a receipt from the depository bank or other satisfactory document. The limits of 5 per cent and $10,000, while arbitrary, are designed to eliminate the possibility of undue influence by wealthy individuals on the operations of the Development Funds and to hold

the potential cost of the scheme to the Treasury to reasonable dimensions.[1]

The above described imaginative scheme which has the important advantage of arousing the interest of the rich countries' people in world development aid, could perhaps be given a trial by one or more governments of the industrialised countries.

VIII. CONSCIOUS AND RATIONAL PLANNING OF INTERNATIONAL DIVISION OF LABOUR AND DEVELOPMENT

As I have argued above, the present international division of labour resulting from market forces is, from the point of view of humanity, utterly disappointing; it has left, on the one hand, vast human resources idle, and on the other hand, three-fourths of mankind in poverty and misery. Though we live in the age of science, by means of which man has solved most physical problems, in our attempt to solve social problems such as the one under discussion, we still depend almost wholly on random forces rather than on conscious and rational planning and on implementation by scientific methods. To organise world economic affairs more rationally and to bridge the 'gap', a world body needs to be established, preferably under the auspices of the U.N. ECOSOC, which will coordinate all aid programmes and direct them towards an international division of labour which will take into account both *social* and also wider *ecological costs*.

This body, which might be called, let us say, the W.D.P.A. (the World Development Planning Authority), could also act as a clearing house for all development grants. On the one hand, each rich country, in order to avoid balance of payments difficulties, would place at the disposal of the W.D.P.A. its contribution to world development, in the form of its own currency to be used for the purchase from it of any material and human resources that it could make available for export. On the other hand, each poor country would submit to the W.D.P.A. a priority list of its needs. The task of the W.D.P.A. would then be, in collaboration with the World Bank, the I.D.A. and other U.N. bodies dealing with development, to prepare a world plan and allocate to each poor country its priority share out of the pool of the rich countries' contributions in material and human resources. The W.D.P.A. would also help the governments of L.D.C.s to prepare their own domestic economic and social structures, such as land reform, which can expedite development. I believe that in the age of the modern electronic computer, and granted the necessary will and determination, it is possible to make and implement such a world plan, however difficult it may appear at first sight.

[1] *Essays in International Finance*, No. 69 (July 1968), pp. 15–16.

IX. THE ROLE OF THE ECONOMIST

Since the problem of the 'gap' is basically an economic problem, economists can and must play a major role in its solution, by helping to create a world climate of opinion and consensus that this is a problem vital to the future of mankind and by devising practical ways and means for its solution. May I end by expressing my hope that this Conference will make its own very considerable contribution to these ends.

Discussion of Papers by
Kenneth Boulding, Martin Pfaff and Chris Economides

Dr. Mahbub ul Haq introduced the paper by Professor Boulding and Dr. Pfaff. He said he faced a particular dilemma in summarising this paper since he understood so little of it and disagreed with the little he understood. Consequently he was not quite sure if he could be relied upon to present an entirely fair summary. He would ask the authors to correct the record if they felt that their views had not been properly presented.

To summarise, the authors attempted to analyse (i) how far the structure of the grants economy on a world scale had produced the development gap between rich and poor nations, and (ii) what role the world grants economy could play in reducing this gap. In order to throw more light on the nature of the gap, the authors divided the world into A and B nations – A nations participating in some sort of long-term growth, while B nations merely drifted along. The authors found no simple explanation of the gap between A and B nations; neither climate, nor genetic heritage nor exploitation of the poor by the rich was wholly satisfactory. Instead, they turned to explore the role of international grants in initially creating, and eventually bridging, this gap. Their conclusions were negative on both scores. They found that international grants had played a rather minor role in the past in the process of development that had led to the emergence of the gap. They also concluded, after an exhaustive quantitative study of the grants element in the assistance currently provided by the Western and Communist worlds, that international grants were unlikely to be of great consequence in reducing the gap.

Indeed they found no economic factors which were dominant in deciding the pattern of allocation of international grants. In their view, this mostly served to maintain a system of special relations between major and minor powers and to protect the political interests of donors. Having discarded grants as a significant factor in explaining the development gap, the authors turned to certain forms of intra-national grants, which again did not provide a very adequate explanation of the gap. The authors then briefly searched for an explanation in the failure of scientific and technological knowledge to spread to the underdeveloped world – and in the social and psychological processes of development. However, these social processes proved elusive and mysterious and the authors appeared to give up the chase. Their final conclusion was that 'the success of the development process depends in the first place on keeping a proper balance between the exchange sector and the grants sector, and in the second place improving the efficiency of the grants sector so that it does not fail in its essential function'.

It was refreshing to learn from the authors that our world was divided not so much between developed and underdeveloped countries as between A nations and B nations. The A nations comprised both developed and underdeveloped countries, while the B nations were all underdeveloped. This gave the authors a new way of dividing up the world, and they fondly drew new boundaries round their zones A and B and plotted them neatly on a graph. It did not bother them much that their A zone contained only six developing countries – Israel, Jamaica,

Trinidad, Puerto Rico, Syria and Algeria – which together constituted about 1 per cent of the total population of the L.D.C.s. They were equally unconcerned about the special factors which might explain the rapid growth of the six developing countries they had chosen to join group A. These were, of course, minor inconveniences, and the authors were not going to be denied their exciting discovery that the world could be divided in more ways than one.

However, they were a little uncertain what to do with the discovery. They were intrigued by the fact that the A nations were all in the temperate zone, and the B nations mostly in the tropical one. However, they did not quite wish to opt for a climatic explanation of the gap. Yet they did not quite give it up. This left a considerable confusion. Climate kept coming in again and again. If scientific knowledge had not spread to the underdeveloped world, it was because 'science-based technology originated primarily as a temperate zone sub-culture that was often ill-adapted to tropical conditions'. Even the demographic crisis was confined to the tropics. The authors frequently talked about 'the developing temperature zone and the stagnant tropic zone'. Thus, despite their protests to the contrary, the authors left a strong impression that the underdeveloped world had been cursed not so much by the stars as by the sun.

The main questions that this part of the paper raised were to what extent was such a division between A and B nations really valid? And how useful was it in shedding any further light on the gap? He hoped we could debate this.

Another question we might well debate was the concept of the grants economy itself and its usefulness in explaining or reducing the gap. He had to confess that though he did know what a grant was (or thought he knew before he read the paper) he found it very difficult to understand what a grants economy really was and what relationship, legitimate or illegitimate, it had with the development gap. Perhaps all the authors were wanting to discuss was whether a sizeable net transfer of resources had taken place from the currently underdeveloped to the currently developed world in the last two centuries, so as to create the present gap; and whether there was now the possibility of a major net transfer of resources from the developed to the underdeveloped world to help reduce it. If this *was* the real issue, it could have been stated a little more simply.

He had to confess that he found the authors' conclusions about earlier transfers of resources between the colonial powers and their colonies extremely fascinating. The authors concluded that it was 'the colonies which exploited the mother country, at least in terms of flows of exchangeables'. He was quoting, not exaggerating! They estimated that the 'home charges' which India paid to Great Britain during most of the 19th century hardly ever amounted to more than 0·5 per cent of the Indian G.N.P., and were more than counter-balanced by the advantages which India received from her ability to borrow at low rates of interest in the London money market. So, the tail wagged the dog and the colony happily exploited the mother country – but somehow got impoverished in the process. This fact did seem to bother the authors, so they looked for the explanation in the mystical Indian pysche, and in India's traditional values and its reluctance to accept modern science and ideas – and of course, lest we forgot, the fact that India happened to be in the tropical zone.

It was commendable that the authors had estimated the Indian G.N.P. for the 19th century, while India was having considerable difficulty in estimating its

G.N.P. today at all accurately. Nor could he find any reasonable excuse to explain why India was contributing only 0·5 per cent of its G.N.P. in home charges, not even conforming to the 1 per cent rule. However, he did find some difficulty with the one advantage that the authors quoted – the ability to borrow in the London money market at low rates. Borrowing for what? To finance an industrial revolution and an agricultural breakthrough, or to pay for a large army to maintain the British raj? What was this reverse transfer of resources? Home charges were real and imperial preferences were real, and the scale of agricultural production on deteriorating terms of trade was real. What were the counterbalancing factors the authors had in mind to prove that there was a net transfer of resources from the colonial power to the colony? One looked in vain for evidence, but found only one, lone phrase saying 'there is a great deal of evidence accumulating that . . .' Unless more evidence was presented than mere assertion, speculation like this and calculations like these merely added a calculated insult to a historical injury.

What was more, did we really have to go over all this again? There had been a good deal of discussion already about the origins of the gap. Perhaps there was a feeling that if we could once find out its real causes we should have a sure-fire formula for reducing or eliminating it. But was that true? What if the gap were the result of complex historical forces, subject to widely different interpretations? What was gained by an obsession with the causes of the gap if the past was an imperfect guide to the future? And how much did it really help to know whether colonies were a good or a bad thing for economic development?

We could no longer count on the sense of guilt of the developed world or on its moral obligations. This theme had lost its novelty for the West and its utility for the underdeveloped world. And we were not claiming the repayment of an old debt even though we could have done. He had made a lighthearted calculation, that even if India had transferred only $100 million to Great Britain in the early 19th century, it would have multiplied to over $400 billion by now, at 6 per cent interest. Yet, India was in no position to collect the debt, nor did it want to keep reminding the U.K. of it. But did Professor Boulding and Dr. Pfaff have to add the charge of exploitation to the fact of India's backwardness? Was it really necessary to rewrite history to soothe a troubled conscience? It was true that India's structural transformation had been delayed, and quick changes had had to be brought about. Did one have to peep into the Indian social psyche every time and reassure oneself whether the Indians were really sane and whether they could manage structural changes?

Why could we not accept the simple fact that most developing countries were colonies only two decades ago, and that economic development was no one's priority; only political freedom was. The Governor-General of India had a simple directive: to maintain law and order, and to club the natives whenever they got a little restive. The Governor-General was usually a serious fellow who took his duties seriously. He did maintain law and order and, from time to time, clubbed the natives – some of them fairly hard. It was not very strange that the natives devoted most of their energy to regaining political freedom rather than attaining an agricultural breakthrough. The British did many good things, of course, and the colonies did produce some infrastructure and growth.

But this missed the basic point, which was that most of the creative energies of the system were devoted to regaining political freedom. It was an objective transcending all else.

As an aside he might add that it would be interesting to speculate what would have happened to the creative energy of America if it had not ceased to be a colony in 1776. Or, what would have happened had the Indian mutiny succeeded in 1857 and India gained its independence then rather than now. It was, after all, on historical facts like this that history turned, rather than the production functions.

Anyway, the structural transformation of many developing countries was delayed and development became a priority only in the last two decades. Since then, despite all the breast-beating and disenchantment, two-thirds of humanity had managed to increase its production and effect structural change at a rate never before witnessed in history for so much of mankind. If the rate of change was still found disappointing by the masses, it was because the task was so huge and because so much time had been lost – not because the pace was slow. The pace could have been quicker probably and the change faster – but that was not the point. He simply wanted to ask the authors in what respect they found underdeveloped societies resisting change so that they had to explore the hidden depths of the psyche and reach the conclusion that 'the most strategic elements of the whole process are in the human nervous system'.

In fact the rate at which the so-called traditional society accepted modern ideas and technology was truly amazing. The illiterate village housewife in India or Pakistan accepted family planning devices with a calm that would have shocked an American housewife even in the early 20th century. Illiterate farmers had been literally flocking to use modern fertiliser when its use was made economic and profitable. The change in urban and social patterns had been more swift and shattering than the West had ever known. And let no one forget the reluctance of those who were supposed to transfer technology. He recalled that when Pakistan had built its biggest project, the $900 million Mangla Dam, the Pakistani chief engineer of the project had been relegated to looking after the maintenance of houses and cars. He and his colleagues were not even allowed in the project area. Was this really an example of the transfer of scientific knowledge and technology that the underdeveloped work was strongly resisting?

Finally he wished to say a word about the role of foreign assistance in reducing the development gap which, for some mistaken reason, he thought was to be the main theme of the session. The authors had devoted very little space to it in their paper. Their conclusion, on the basis of a fairly limited quantitative analysis, was that international grants were not motivated by any economic factors but were based on special political relations. The brutal message underlying most of the paper was that international grants were not going to be important in the future development of the underdeveloped world, that they carried no moral or economic obligation on the part of the developed world and that they would be given mostly on political considerations with little attention to economic performance.

If this were true and accepted, then the L.D.C.s would have to draw up their future plans and programmes more realistically and stop chasing elusive standards. They would have to turn inwards and plan on the basis of self-reliance.

Indeed, if this were true, Western intellectuals should advocate a complete termination of aid programmes. The shock waves from this would strengthen national will in that part of the unfortunate world which kept waiting aimlessly for foreign doles, and did not get psychologically geared up to make an assault on the problem of poverty through its own resources and its own will. A little aid, like a little knowledge, could be a dangerous thing. If the authors were right (and he stressed the word 'if'), then we should take their findings to their logical conclusion and advocate that all aid must end.

Professor Eastman introduced the paper by Mr. Economides. He said this paper followed very well on earlier discussions, because it gave evidence for the gap, speculated on the reasons for it and established a goal of an L.D.C. per capita income of $1,000 in the year 2000. The paper also indicated why developed countries should aid L.D.C.s, listed the needs that developed countries should meet, suggested some means of financing aid and proposed the establishment of a world development planning authority.

Evidence for the gap had already been fully discussed and Professor Eastman did not think we need take more time now with Mr. Economides' statistics. But why was there a gap? Mr. Economides identified the principal causes. Firstly, there was price maintenance by developed countries which exported manufactured goods and did not pass on gains in productivity to purchasers in L.D.C.s Secondly, there was discrimination by advanced countries against imports of agricultural products. Thirdly, the colonial policies of earlier periods had designated L.D.C.s as suppliers of food and raw materials. It was, of course, difficult to deal with all L.D.C.s at once, but it seemed to Professor Eastman that other, perhaps more fundamental, reasons existed for their low incomes. However, we could look at the factors identified by Mr. Economides as some especially subject to what went on in developed countries, though there might be less agreement with the first and third reasons listed as causes of underdevelopment than with the agricultural policies of advanced countries.

Restrictive practices in industrial production were better in explaining cyclical movements in the terms of trade between exports of industrial goods and agricultural goods and raw materials, than in providing a cause for secular industrial underdevelopment. On the contrary, if prices of manufactured goods were kept up in the long run, this made production in the L.D.C.s more feasible.

Whatever the contribution of colonialism to the present economic structure of the world, an economy specialising in the production of food and raw materials was not necessarily treated unfavourably. Comparative advantage might lie that way and be consistent with maximising its income.

As for agriculture, one should recognise that tropical foodstuffs were not generally discriminated against so long as they were not substitutes for domestic production in developed countries. Also some L.D.C.s, exporting other things, benefited from low world agricultural prices. Even so, the seriousness of the protectionist policies of developed countries in agriculture could hardly be over-emphasised, especially if account was also taken of widespread quantitative restrictions of various sorts on imports of textiles, shoes, etc., by developed countries. The former encouraged over-production in agriculture in developed countries and turned the terms of trade against the agriculture of the L.D.C.s, which otherwise would have a greater comparative advantage in agriculture.

This induced them to expand into labour-intensive manufacturing, where their production, if competitive, tended to meet quantitative restrictions abroad. Or they developed into high-cost import substitution, including the production of capital goods, which was wasteful.

The agricultural policies of developed countries directly damaged some L.D.C.s, but they also damaged some important developed countries, with consequent dangers for the L.D.C.s as well. It seemed that no further progress in trade liberalisation was possible without agreement on agriculture in the developed countries. Worse, difficulties in agriculture in these countries threatened to promote a general retreat from trade liberalisation through the gradual extension of non-tariff barriers, if not from increased duties. Yet the domestic political cost of measures to rationalise agriculture in developed countries was obviously often high and any progress would be slow. If there was progress in reducing agricultural protection, it would come only from negotiations between developed countries, because only they had sufficient bargaining power to affect the problem.

Mr. Economides had written that developed countries should aid L.D.C.s because they had in the past obtained the greater portion of gains from trade with them, and because he detected dissatisfaction and impatience in the L.D.C.s that might lead to violence which would harm advanced countries. He indicated that advanced countries could act in several fields, of which Professor Eastman mentioned two. First was the provision of food by a combination of gifts (at least in the short run) and the payment of subsidies to L.D.C. farmers to offset the consequences of low prices or farm incomes. Second, developed countries could aid industrialisation in L.D.C.s by providing capital and know-how and by opening their own markets. Professor Eastman would personally reverse this order because granting tariff preference for manufactured goods from L.D.C.s, and especially removing quantitative restrictions and so-called voluntary restraints on exports, would immediately greatly improve the trade prospects of some L.D.C.s. It also struck him that there was plenty of capital and know-how available from private and official sources. What was in short supply was profitable investment opportunities in L.D.C.s.

He thought that the provision of the most useful know-how first required its development. Reference had been made earlier to the development of final products more suitable to consumers in L.D.C.s. Similarly, the international subsidisation of the development and design of suitable techniques of production for the relative factor prices existing in L.D.C.s might bring big returns. At present, processors and manufacturers outside the developed countries, where designing took place, had a choice. They might adapt old techniques now obsolete in developed countries, but more suitable to their own relative factor prices; or they could design best-practice techniques for economies with low labour costs. Businessmen in L.D.C.s typically chose the latter, which showed that the gains that had occurred from developing technology more than offset inefficiencies caused by applying it to inappropriate factor prices. The gains from altering the latter largely remained, and the public financing of design costs for techniques suited to the factor prices of L.D.C.s was the kind of subsidy that might bring good results.

Mr. Economides had suggested some new means of financing aid. First, if

Professor Eastman understood correctly, developed countries should buy their S.D.R. allocations from an international development agency. Professor Eastman could not himself see the connection between the international need for liquidity and foreign aid. Second, foreign aid contributions could be made deductible from income tax to a specified maximum in developed countries. He had already explained that he thought such a scheme would lead to maximum contributions, in the first instance, when individual taxpayers thought their contributions were free, that was to say at the expense of others. As they came to appreciate that their collective decisions resulted in an equal change in the tax bill because other government expenditures had to be financed anyway, the total allocation would probably fall below present aid levels.

Professor Eastman said that he agreed with Mr. Economides when the latter foresaw that a substantial part of any prospective reduction in armament expenditure would go to foreign aid. Finally, Mr. Economides had proposed the creation of a world development planning organisation to co-ordinate all aid programmes. This was a subject which had been discussed in a previous session.

Mr. Economides wanted to clarify what had been said by Professor Eastman about S.D.R.s. These were a gift of international purchasing power. They should therefore have been given according to needs not wealth – which was what happened when they were allocated on the basis of the quotas in the I.M.F. That being so, Mr. Economides suggested that the rich recipients of S.D.R.s should, in their turn, give to the poor countries for development purposes amounts equal to such S.D.R.s, in accordance with the dictum: freely ye have received, freely give.

Professor Boulding thought there had been some misunderstanding. His A and B countries were at least classified in terms of two variables rather than one. He did not believe in much of the diagram, but there was a pattern in it. The gap was not simply between rich and poor countries. It also seemed to be between those that had not begun to grow through a dynamic process over time, which came from the development of science and science-based technology. It was an accident that this happened in Europe rather than in China where it should have done. Part of the problem lay in the speed at which it could happen.

However, there was something more fundamental. The rest of the world was not in on the process; the question was how to get in. In fact, many Latin American countries had 'fallen off' the main line.

The idea of the 'grants' economy was unfamiliar, but he had found it very useful. The difficulty was that economists were obsessed with the idea of exchange. If one expanded the idea to exchangeables, one found that there were a lot of one-way transactions. The grants economy was simply a set of such one-way transactions. It was an economy because there was scarcity. If I got a grant, you did not. One could certainly develop a system on these lines.

On imperialism, what he had said was largely a product of other work. The point was simply that economic relationships between colonies and colonial countries were small; they could hardly explain differences either way. The paper was certainly not a defence of imperialism. He thought that Dr. Haq had given a false impression. The criticism of imperialism was that its major impact was psychological. Economic aspects of imperialism were both dull and irrelevant. The difficulty was that economics had no answers to important problems.

His interest in the grants economy had grown because he had lost interest in economics. The grants economy was a first, approximate measure of an integrated system. One had to treat these issues positively; it was no good just preaching. He wanted to know how a positive system could be changed. It was no good saying that something was what we should do without having a programme for achieving it. We did not know what were the main factors underlying the grants economy. With our obsession over the traditional framework of exchange, we often lost sight of all these factors.

Dr. Pfaff thought that Dr. Haq was guilty of some misrepresentation and distortion, although he had made some perceptive comments on some of the weaknesses of the paper. He simply wished Dr. Haq had used economic reasoning rather than political propaganda to make his points. He added that Dr. Haq had thus set up several strawmen to be knocked down during the discussion.

First of all, he wished to disassociate himself emphatically from the impression created by Dr. Haq's presentation. He neither condoned imperialism in general nor British exploitation of India in particular. On the contrary, he thought that exploitation took many forms and had many effects on both exploiter and exploited. Against this background he interpreted the comments cited by Dr. Haq to mean that, in terms of *net* real resource transfers between a colonial power and its colony, exploitation might not even have been as 'successful' as generally believed. This was meant as an indictment of the 'inefficiency of colonialism' rather than as an apology for the past.

The description of the role of the grants economy *vis-à-vis* the development gap, as expressed by the paper, was intended not as a normative statement of what grants *should* do to narrow the gap, but as a 'positive' or descriptive account of its *de facto failure* to help close the gap. If further empirical evidence came up to contravene these conclusions, the authors would be happy to revise them. Nevertheless he still thought that the main explanator for the rise of the international grants economy was a sense of community arising between some nations, just as failures of the grants economy could be attributed to a lack of sense of community felt by others.

The concept of the grants economy was a complement to the concept of the exchange economy. It was useful because it provided a macroeconomic framework within which one could relate international aid to international trade. In a more formal vein one could show that both exchange and grant behaviour were special examples of general economic behaviour. Neoclassical formulations of the theory of international trade thus became a 'special case' of a more general theory of international behaviour.

Professor Ranis commented that economists were, by and large, a traditionally-oriented group and found it very hard to accept new paradigms. He wondered how the grants economy idea helped our understanding. The idea of unrequited transfers was not new. The question was how different they were if one had a mixed economic package for L.D.C.s to go with them.

Professor Ranis agreed with Dr. Haq that we should not spend much time discussing 'who beat whom' in the 19th century, though he wished that Dr. Haq had kept to his own injunction. The interesting thing was to discover what had caused the gap, because then we might be able to understand the present problem of attitudinal change and the future. We might be able to do this better if we could see what had interrupted development in the 19th century. Rather than ending aid we should perhaps look at this problem.

The 19th-century economy was a world economy for better or worse. Free trade must have had some effect on the market. The question now, when countries were trying to use their resources for national development or structural change, was which set of policy packages would be best. If an open economy meant a market economy and that meant colonialism, then most countries would want none of it. However if the conclusion was that one needed to draw back and think, they would welcome this.

It was fairly clear that most of the countries Dr. Haq spoke for were not ready for East-European Socialism. Were they ready for what Professor Tsuru had suggested in an earlier discussion? What choice was to be made? How was one to galvanise peasants into action? Were these societies to be autarchic or outward-looking, though with government controls? (Professor Ranis did not worry about any country's psyche any more than Dr. Haq did.) But how did one mobilise them? The enlightened self-interest of underdeveloped countries would surely lead to a package that was very different from present ones. He would simply re-emphasise what he had said earlier; aid gave a country additional opportunity to use its own resources once it had decided what was the best thing to do.

Professor Kuznets referred to the chart in the paper by Professor Boulding and Dr. Pfaff. If this new classification were to be taken seriously, more effort should have been given to documenting it. First, Professor Kuznets wondered what 'the early sixties' were. A growth process was a time process, over a specified and hopefully long enough period to reveal trends. Whatever one thought about the brevity of the implied period, the findings were still surprising. How had Bolivia done better than Mexico? And how had Cambodia done so well? Any structural, cross-section diagram needed critical examination of the components. Second, if one took the A countries, the line showed a negative correlation between growth rates and G.N.P. per head. But in the top corner group one had six Communist countries listed by Dr. Haq, and five others with Japan on top. Eliminating the Communist countries, and taking out Israel (which was not underdeveloped), Puerto Rico and Algeria (because of the civil war), one would find that the line had a positive, not a negative, slope. The comparison then became one essentially between developed and less developed countries, with the per capita product of the former growing more rapidly than that of the latter.

The general rule in any such cross-section diagram was that one had to specify the period, the sample, the methods and the basis of classification – on objective grounds that could then be checked by other observers. He was sorry that this statistically oversimplified finding had entered into the discussion.

Dr. Baranson recalled that Dr. Haq had asked if we should end aid. Dr. Baranson thought the 'devils versus angels' argument had been misinterpreted. The real question was whether the underdeveloped countries would have to fend for themselves. He thought that in the end self-reliance was the only answer. He would like to say, after Shakespeare, that the fault, dear Brutus, lay in ourselves. As far as underdeveloped countries were concerned, in reference to an ability to adapt technology, the ultimate model was perhaps in Japan. In the past century Japan had developed the inner discipline required to do this. Similarly, in the United States, craftsmen during the Colonial days spent much time learning from the United Kingdom and in developing indigenous skills. From this lineage came the modern world of licensing and investment. Dr. Baranson also alluded to his experience in Yugoslavia. In the motor car industry, a Yugoslav firm (Crvena Zastava) negotiated for updated technology from FIAT. On the other hand, the truck manufacturers were much less effective in structuring their industry. Ultimately firms in the L.D.C.s have to rely on their own capabilities to deal with the world.

Mr. Granier said that we could agree to play the authors' 'game' and accept the 'A countries' as effectively homogeneous and objectively selected. The temptation was then very great, in looking at the A countries, to conclude that there had been a reduction of variation between them. Pushing the authors' reasoning further, one quickly ended by thinking that, for these countries, growth followed a logistic process, growth rates becoming inversely proportional to levels of output per man. This question merited discussion.

Could one show that growth rates fell in line with increasing income per head? If so, how did we deal with Belgium, France, Germany and the U.S.A., all of which were in Group A, and in the last twenty years had achieved higher growth rates than before? All he wanted to do was to raise this question. Even if the authors' regression line was obtained by technically impeccable method, had they the right to give a time scale to a purely statistical study? This simply brought together, at one moment, growth rates that were very diverse. The experience of rich countries seemed to counsel prudence. In particular, one could hardly have believed in the 1930s that the developed world would emerge from stagnation so successfully after 1945. It was perhaps too risky to suggest that the contemporary world presented a picture of logistic growth. Was this not equally true for part of the world?

Mr. Granier also wanted to make a point about the behaviour of total output (not per capita output) in the world at present. The statistics published in the past few years by the U.N. showed that over a long period, at least for fifteen years, the less rich countries had achieved annual average growth rates higher than those of rich countries. More important, their performance was even better if one looked at sectoral growth rates, especially in agriculture and industry. This being so, did we concentrate too much attention on output per man?

Professor Horvat also commented on the chart. He agreed with Professor Kuznets that more care had been needed. Though less harsh than Professor Kuznets, he would suggest that, if one took the figures for the last decade, countries like Greece, Spain, Taiwan and South Korea would go into the A group, and one or two A countries into the B group. This would change the pattern and one could probably draw different conclusions.

He agreed with Mr. Granier that the use of total G.N.P. was more relevant than G.N.P. per head. He thought that the table would be less meaningless then; indeed, it would be consistent with the Chenery distinction between underdeveloped countries, transitional countries and developed countries. It would also be consistent with his own classification of countries with incomes of less than $150; those with incomes of between $150 and $1,000; and the advanced countries above this. One could identify these groups with territorial distinctions and find the underdeveloped countries in black Africa and Asia. The transitional countries were in the Mediterranean and Latin America.

One could also classify countries by their internal systems. Then the centrally-planned, underdeveloped and transitional countries would have higher growth rates than the rest. In the A countries this would not be true. This approach seemed potentially fruitful and it might be possible to develop a quantitatively-based theory of growth.

Professor Horvat said that he would conclude that there was no tendency for the rate of growth to converge to zero. It must be remembered that this was a static graph. The regression line would shift and so, in the reasonably foreseeable future, there was no reason to think that it would cross at 0.

On page 162 of the paper the authors said that the 'success of Yugoslavia may well be the result of a recognition of the essential role of the exchange economy even in a Socialist country'. This sentence did not seem to make sense; especially the word 'even'. There was no contradiction between an exchange economy and socialism. What socialists objected to was the concentration of economic power in a market economy. This fostered one group at the expense of another. If one could have an exchange economy without the concentration of power, then one should use it.

Mr. Baranson thought that the use of the term 'grants economy' was unfortunate. Economists already distinguished between social and private costs and benefits. The market-place did impose one kind of discipline. The developing countries were interested in improving their economic performance. Long-term investment in education, infrastructure etc., were not the immediate concern of private economic activity. If one thought in terms of social and private costs and benefits, then the bridgehead Professor Boulding and Dr. Pfaff had created could be used to reduce real differences of interest by conflict rather than by resolution.

Dr. Radetski wondered if Mr. Economides was right in suggesting that developed countries consciously operated quite so much to the detriment of poor primary producers. First, he was not certain about the price theories. For example, there had been significant changes in the quality of manufactured goods, not least car manufacturing. This might explain a good deal of price increase. In Sweden turbines for power generation had increased in price only at the same rate as their productivity.

There were other grounds for doubt too. In 1948–52, Sweden, for instance, had exported mainly iron ore, wood, steel, etc. Since then ore had been found in other places and Swedish ore prices had been severely reduced. Recent technological development in wood pulp manufacture also meant that almost any kind of wood could now be used. This again had reduced pulp prices. Despite it, the value of Swedish exports had risen rapidly. This was because the exports had moved away from primary products to manufactured goods of various kinds.

In pulp and ore, conditions in the market were far removed from perfect competition. Both markets were, in fact, highly cartelised. Pulp and ore prices had fallen nevertheless, simply because supply had increased more rapidly than demand. Generalising from Swedish experience it was hard to say that there was a moral debt on the part of the purchasers of primary products to sellers because prices had fallen.

Professor Fei noted that Professors Chenery and Boulding had each produced a classification of countries. On the whole, they confirmed each other's findings. One had eight industrial countries where there was an inverse relationship between the rate of growth and real income per head. There was a second group of countries in transition where on the whole there was a positive relation between income per head and growth.

As for the time dimension, if one accepted the major hypothesis that it was possible to do this correlation, then the time dimension became less important. However, Professor Kuznets' remarks did question the usefulness of the diagrams. Professor Fei thought that, at the least, it began to suggest a growth theory. One would expect individual A countries to slide in a south-easterly direction rapidly over time. Similarly one would expect the countries in transition to slide rapidly in a north-easterly direction. This diagram appeared to relate to the early 1960s. In the late 1960s and the early 1970s, one should be able to see if these predictions were being borne out. If so, then the approach was helpful.

The important group of countries was that where national income was rising but the rate of growth was near zero. The question was whether these could get into the transitional crowd. Professor Chenery's answer was that they failed to do so because of population growth etc. He did not think that Professor Chenery had thought the theory fully through, and the real one would be very complex. For example, industrial advance clearly needed the routinisation of innovation. Perhaps the general equilibrium framework could explain what was happening. As for transitional countries that were moving to the north-east, one needed a different explanation. One had to explain why income distribution and savings capacity increased.

Professor Fei thought the diagram hid too much. For example, with primary producing countries he thought that if the main activity was linked to the land, the country would not grow rapidly. Development seemed to require moving away from the land to a better use of labour. This was what was happening in Taiwan. He thought this was a promising approach if underlying factors could thereby be more carefully investigated.

Dr. Nurul Islam said that there had been several attempts to measure the relationship of growth to the influx of foreign aid. Few of them had been conclusive. However they confirmed the general impression that there were a host of other factors. Contribution from aid was probably marginal.

Over the last two decades, he would argue that 85 per cent of development had been financed internally. Therefore variations in internal policy were the crucial element. Cross-section studies relating export earnings and the percentage of aid to G.N.P. showed that aid was more important. The oil countries apart, countries whose exports increased fast were also countries where there was a policy for using internal resources more effectively. So we should look for changes in domestic policy that would help growth. Aid was then a marginal addition to total resources; a necessary, but not a sufficient, condition for growth. Indeed, aid might postpone changes that were conducive to growth; it might postpone institutional changes which were necessary in both developed and underdeveloped countries. The radical left certainly held this view and argued for a moratorium on aid.

The aid-givers were in a dilemma. How could one make the aid-receivers change their systems? Aid always strengthened the hand of the government in power, however bad. It was hard for aid-givers to attack the way in which domestic resources were being mobilised or aid used. Yet the use of aid was governed by a complex of institutions, with many non-economic problems arising.

Professor Johnson said the discussion had drifted away from the papers. He found the paper on the grants economy unhelpful. It developed a new concept; it was rather like putting old wine into new bottles and claiming that something had been added. He thought that it was a pity that Professor Boulding had lost his interest in economics. Economics had recognised these problems and advances had been made in discovering what the problems were.

First, governments and foundations both faced problems of optimisation subject to constraints. They were not the usual constraints; and the maximand was different too. One problem was that the staff of both foundations and governments turned over rather rapidly. If one looked at organisation theory, one was hardly surprised to find that new appointees always wanted to innovate. They went for new activities rather than repeating old ones.

Similarly there was now an economic theory of government which saw governments exchanging services with the public in return for increased tax capacity. One had a theory of government which thought that government had to operate so as to maximise their chances of being re-elected. At the same time they had to motivate the electorate to generate some kinds of development in order to increase tax tevenue.

We had a behavioural theory in the sense that it was able to make predictions. As for the foundations, no American economist could have failed to notice their extreme reluctance to make grants to researchers in other countries. He must have asked himself, if only mildly, why some people got grants for research and others did not.

Professor Johnson suggested that we might get further with the concept of public goods. We accepted that there were some things the market could not do; there were traces of this theory in the paper. For example, the effective cost of collecting revenue for particular services was so high that collective provision of these services was financed by taxes. Or the nature of the goods might make it hard for the market to cope with supplying them. This was especially true of the kind of thing that foundations were concerned with, for example, basic research. In this way perhaps we needed the grants economy to take care of these activities, where there were externalities. The problem was one of allocating resources among these activities; much had been said of the problem of technology, know-how, etc., where the time dimension and the problem of capturing a return made it hard for the market to work.

Another problem, touched on in the paper, was that the market had failures and biases, but that the process of decision-taking itself was biased too, by the political dynamics of government and committees. Bureaucracy multiplied; government proliferated. This was a major problem in underdeveloped countries. There were two points. The market was good in its own context, but it could not handle many modern goods. Second, government processes were often inadequate to deal with these problems because they were so difficult. It was hardly surprising that Professor Boulding found it so hard to marshal the uncertain concept of the grants economy. He was an amateur working in a field where others had already been operating – Professor Johnson thought very much better.

Professor Chenery thought that Professor Boulding and Dr. Pfaff might have written a better paper had they used normal econometric techniques. This had been done, for example, by Alan Stroud. He had used simple hypotheses about how donors behaved to explain in a regression sense on the basis of income per head, population and political affiliations. He came up with a 'shadow price' for having been, for example, a French possession. Professor Chenery said that one should not lump all underdeveloped countries together, add up all aid and say that it led to only 15 per cent investment. If one looked at the facts, one say that 30 countries had a growth rate above 5 per cent. To achieve this, the rules seemed to be: be Communist; have a high capital income; have a lot of aid. Of these 30 countries, 10 appeared to have grown rapidly because of aid. Aid concentrated in these countries probably make a big difference. He did not think that 15 per cent was quite the same thing as 10 out of 30. The important thing was to concentrate on the transition, discovering what circumstances foreign aid helped in. He did not like averaging processes.

Dr. Little felt that there was a muted challenge in the meeting to the whole aid concept. It might have come from Professor Boulding's paper which de-emphasised grants. Professor Boulding said one should not pity oneself. Professor Tsuru said that Japan had developed with no aid, little trade and no emulation. Dr. Haq suggested that we should abandon the whole aid process. And Dr. Baranson seemed to be making the same choice. Then came Professor Islam, who argued that aid supported the government in power. There were some in the U.K. who opposed aid on these grounds, arguing that it went to wicked governments which ought to be overthrown.

The suggestion had also been made that aid undermined self-reliance. If true, this was serious; but why should it? He would like to be reassured on this, though he had never seen much evidence of it himself. Maybe the argument was that it sapped the government's willingness to tax: or that public law 480 had reduced domestic efforts to raise agricultural production.

We should go to the heart of the problem and face it more explicitly. He was for aid, and did not see why we should not keep both it *and* the domestic drive to develop. Why did one have to say that aid sapped these things? He hoped someone would reassure him in thinking that aid was desirable.

Dr. Baranson argued that there seemed to be something in what Professor Boulding said about the special motives governments had in changing ideology. This Round Table needed some answers to the question: what are the motives that prompt governments and private foundations to provide aid and assistance to L.D.C.s? In his Wicksell lectures, Professor Johnson had said that 'product cycle' theory had helped to explain private firms' investment in research and development. Was there any analogous theory to explain the flow of funds from public sources and private foundations?

Professor Johnson found it hard to answer this question because then one would have to ask what was the product of government. Maybe there was a product cycle in what governments were about. American governments had certainly changed their views of their role. For example, it had been said about 1930 that the market did not work then, when in fact it was the government that did not work. This led to the idea that the government knew better than the market. Perhaps the economist could bring the understanding that this was an ideological response (not necessarily valid) to changing circumstances.

Dr. Baranson replied that there must be something in what Professor Boulding said about the motives governments had in changing ideology. What would grip this kind of conference was an answer to the question: What gets government to act?

Professor Johnson said that the start of the theory of government was that its role was to provide alternatives to the market system. This was why, for example, we did not have major land reforms. However he was not sure that Professor Boulding would say this was the government's role. Professor Johnson wanted to say two things. First, development was a process of transformation, and one had to find people to carry it out. Society restricted their freedom to do this. Entrepreneurs typically came from groups of immigrants – debarred from political success. If political success became easier, then one had the restriction of social change in the name of promoting it. The political process controlled property. It was a social process; one could talk about development without anything happening. At the same time one could have development without anyone consciously promoting it.

Second, there was the problem of how to establish government agencies to bring about change. One criticism of U.S. aid policy was that the 'green revolution' was a product of a private foundation. The American government did little or nothing except talk and produce propaganda. Talk did not imply that anything that was relevant was being done.

Professor Patinkin thought that one basic element affecting all aid programmes was corruption. It occurred in both recipient and donor countries. It might well be a very important element explaining the different degrees of success of aid in different countries. One should perhaps talk about the 'corruption economy' as well as the grants economy. He would like to argue that a most significant external economy was lack of corruption; honesty was a great economic asset.

Dr. Little had spoken of the possible adverse effects of aid. Israel had greatly benefited from aid but, apart from the general effects, there had been two specific unfavourable results. First, in the early 1950s there had been little discrimination about what to finance. Shadow prices had been ignored, and there had been instances of poor allocations of resources. Although Israel was learning, there was still a tendency to continue some projects in the hope that they would turn out well after all. Without aid one might be harsher in the criteria one used.

One also found that the degree of business savings used to finance development was very small in Israel, especially as compared with the U.S.A. Aid as an alternative source of funds was reducing the incentive to corporate saving. If one asked why this mattered, the answer was that it mattered if the country wanted to be independent.

Professor Ranis said that, in order to reassure Dr. Little, he would argue that the important thing was not the spread of aid. The most important thing was the ability to influence domestic policies – to convince officials that they could take measures which they would not be prepared to take without extra aid inflows. He would not argue that there was an effect across the board. Aid-givers often did put new wine into old bottles. However where some of the bureaucracy in the receiving country saw the need for change, aid could help. This ought to give us a lesson in what aid could not do, if it was not across the board. For example, household savings were probably more important than public savings, and these could be released with the help of aid.

Dr. Anita Pfaff said that she had tried to stay out of the discussion for obvious reasons, but felt that Professor Johnson misunderstood the concept of the grants economy. The paper used the term 'grants' as a generic one to signify *one-way* flows. In fact, a research grant from a foundation would most likely not be a 'grant' at all in that sense; at least it was not a 'primary grant'. It involved the obligation on the part of the recipient to provide something in return – a piece of research. In view of the great variance in the possible return output, she would term this relationship a 'probabilistic exchange'. They might be using old wine but were adding some new ingredients as well.

Professor Johnson responded by asking what had been gained by rechristening a unilateral transfer. All social relations, including slavery, could be called exchanges. Did changing the name of the concept really help us to understand the process any better?

Professor Boulding thought that the paper had fulfilled its function. It was extraordinarily difficult for anyone to accept a new idea, but he and Dr. Pfaff had had to use new bottles, because the wine would not go into the old ones. If some participants had not so far found the concept of the grants economy useful, he hoped that they would not close their minds to it, but go on trying to understand. All he was saying was that his concept made a grant a one-way transfer of an exchangeable. The accounting test of this was whether the net worth of the recipient increased and that of the donor decreased. These elements had something in common. One could have one-way transfers in all kinds of conditions. The bias of the economist in seeing everything as exchange distorted his view because he saw this as an integrated relationship. There were other grants which could be extorted under threat.

Professor Boulding pointed out that one could not talk about international grants without talking about community. The important questions were: What is the public? What are grants? We needed a theory of community, benevolence and malevolence. It would not be found in the economist's literature, even though that might be important. The idea of the 'grants economy' was simply a 'hatstand'. However, he and his co-authors had found it very useful because they had been able to hang on it a lot of hats they had found lying around.

Professor Boudling was sorry about the diagram, which had turned out to be something of a red herring. He had put it in because he was preparing the paper for an intelligent audience, and thought that such an audience might be prepared to agree that such a diagram could be suggestive if not definitive. The question was whether there was a main line of development. He did not know but felt that the growth process must be logistic. Exponential growth in any field could not go on for very long. The question was that kind of logistic process it was. All processes of this kind were interrupted, perhaps by invasion, by revolution or by the great depression of the 1930s. Dynamic processes were often interrupted by the evolutionary potential they created. A mechanical process was perfectly all right, provided one did not believe in it. Professor Boulding was inclined to think after the afternoon's discussion that perhaps the invention of statistics had been an international disaster. Statistical significance, it should be remembered, was not the same as epistomological significance. All he asked was that members of the Round Table should not prejudge a new idea. Some might find it useful.

Perhaps a crucial point was that the public goods problem and the redistribution problem overlapped a good deal; however, they were different. The problem of the grants economy was the problem of the nature of community. This was unsatisfactory because there was no world community. We all had loyalties to units smaller than the whole human race. None of us saw ourselves as human beings; otherwise we should be in jail. But this was not final; he saw a growth in the idea of community. He did not know why, but it was certainly a basic problem.

Dr. Pfaff said that the paper had touched only briefly on the concepts and theory of the grants economy, focussing mainly on a general assessment of the role of the international grants economy in helping to narrow the developmental gap. He would identify therefore some of the major underpinnings of grants economics:

First, the concept of the grants economy was a macro-economic concept. It included all private and public bilateral or exchange processes. It thus differed from the traditional theory of public finance which distinguished only between the private or market economy and the public or government economy. The traditional approach therefore neglected the nature and increased economic significance of non-profit institutions in the private sector, which give rise to transfers or grants, and also of 'government business' in the public sector which reflected exchange or market processes.

Second, many economic processes could only be understood if the exchange element were separated from the grants element. An example of the power of this concept was found in the usefulness of the 'grant-equivalent of foreign aid' which measures not the monetary, but the real-resource cost of aid, thus providing a more objective definition of the aid-component of international flows.

Third, the rationale for a theory of the grants economy might be derived from the theory of market failures. Because of externalities in production and consumption, increasing returns to scale, indivisibilities and the presence of monopoly or oligopoly relations, markets failed to function efficiently, thus achieving less than maximum *economic* welfare. Positive or negative transfers – grants or taxes – were generally called for to help remedy this economic deficiency. Furthermore, due to the distributive results and the cyclical instabilities introduced into employment and prices, markets also failed to achieve maximum *social* welfare. The grants economy could thus be explained by the need to provide an extraneous mechanism for co-ordination and regulation whenever the signal-system of market prices could not be relied upon to achieve the desired results.

Fourth, the polar distinction between purely private and purely public goods maintained in the neo-classical approach to the theory of the public economy neglected the fact that most goods conformed to neither of these extreme points. If, for the purely private good, *no* externalities were present; and for the pure public good *all* benefits were externalised, very few goods could be explained by such a model. On the other land, grants economics distinguished between market goods (characterised by relatively small externalities) and social goods (characterised by relatively large externalities). The former tended to be financed through the exchange economy and the latter through the grants economy. The distinction between 'private' and 'public' was thus misleading, particularly since social goods were accompanied by bilateral flows in both the private and public sectors. Even as a purely technical taxonomy, private and public goods would be viewed as two special cases of the market-social-goods continuum.

Fifth, grants economics was formally based on three pillars. At the micro-level, it rested on the assumption of *interdependence* of consumers' utility functions resulting from various degrees of identification of one individual with others in his community or peer group. The assumption of independence of utility functions which constituted the platform of neo-classical welfare economics, thus became a special case of the more general assumption on the nature of socio-economic man. It assumed the presence of atomistic individuals. Empirical evidence on granting behaviour, whether private or public, i.e. through the tax-transfer mechanism, further suggested that this was an unrealistic assumption.

At the macro-level, it was based on the assumption of the systemic interdependence of the components of the system within a cybernetic entity. This was distinguished from the mechanistic or Newtonian view of reality, embodied in neo-classical welfare economics.

It rested on the view that multiple and often conflicting goals guided the activities of individuals and the community. Markets, if left to themselves, were instruments for the attainment of 'market efficiency' or 'efficiency in the narrow sense', but not of 'general efficiency' or 'efficiency in the broad sense'. The latter reflected also the norms of stability, growth, equity, economic freedom and social security, integration, system maintenance and so forth. The allocation of resources via the grants economy was designed to produce market-offsets. It reflected a concern with *general* efficiency norms.

Dr. Pfaff hoped that participants would not take the paper as a comprehensive statement of the relations between the grants economy and the development gap, nor as a complete statement as to what grants economics was all about. He hoped they would not prejudge the entire area of the study of the grants economy on the basis of this narrow preliminary paper, that they would keep an open mind till the more comprehensive set of publications came out.

Mr. Economides also replied to the discussion. He doubted if improvement in quality played any significant role in the rise of industrial-good prices. Industrial workers, through their strong trade-unions managed to get increases in wages and salaries over and above increases in productivity, and industrial businesses, thanks to imperfect competition and high-income elasticity of demand, passed on such increases to world consumers. Market forces were biased in favour of manufactured goods. Since international production depended on the international division of labour, he thought it was only fair that this bias should be corrected by unrequited transfers.

8 On Measuring the Value of Private Direct Overseas Investment

I. M. D. Little

NUFFIELD COLLEGE, OXFORD

I. INTRODUCTION

There are few subjects more charged with emotion than the value of private investment to developing countries: and the Pearson Commission (later referred to as 'Pearson') as well as the D.A.C. have been accused of presenting it in too favourable a light. There were a number of papers, presented to the recent Columbia Conference on Internal Economic Development, which reacted strongly.

One of the issues, raised at that Conference by Mr. Streeten, was that of measuring the balance of payments effect of such investment [1]. This appears, prima facie, to be closely related to the issue of whether it is reasonable to present net private (or public) capital movements as a 'transfer of resources' without subtracting interest and dividends – whether in fact the standard D.A.C. practice is misleading. If it were reasonable to measure, as Pearson denies and Streeten maintains, the balance of payments effect of a particular investment by the net capital inflows while subtracting repatriated profits, it would also be true that subtracting repatriated profits and interest from D.A.C. figures would give the balance of payments effect of aid plus private foreign investment in developing countries. I shall be arguing that this hypothesis is wrong, but this does not imply that those who prefer to subtract dividends and interest when considering the 'transfer of resources' have not got a good case.

The above is the first issue I want to consider. But the second one – not raised directly by Pearson or, so far as I know, at the Columbia Conference – is the relationship between net benefit and the balance of payments effect. This is of some importance because UNCTAD and others are studying the balance of payments effect of private overseas investment (P.O.I.): while the O.E.C.D. Development Centre and UNIDO have produced, respectively, a Manual [2] and a Guidelines [3] which purport to measure the net profits of particular investments – which can certainly include P.O.I. This work seems to be unrelated at present.

These are the two main issues which I want to raise. They are certainly relevant to the question of how far private investment deserves promotion – a vast subject to which, of course, a great deal else besides is relevant. I shall, in a final section, permit myself merely a few reflections on this grand and infinitely debatable topic – reflections arising out of recent work on protection and project analysis.

II. WHAT WOULD OR SHOULD HAVE HAPPENED IF THE PRIVATE OVERSEAS INVESTMENT HAD NOT TAKEN PLACE

This is obviously crucial to any cost-benefit analysis, or to any analysis of balance of payments effects. No evaluation of any operation is possible without establishing or postulating the state of affairs both 'with' and 'without' that operation.

It has become abundantly clear, especially in recent discussions concerning the difference (if any) between the Manual and the Guidelines referred to above, that the economist must be very clear about the difference between 'would' and 'should'. Does he make the comparison between the optimal state of affairs with and without, or between what he thinks is the most likely state of affairs with and without?

There is, presumably, no such dilemma for the economic historian who is not interested in optimisation. But the dilemma is real for those who are concerned (whether they like it or not) with making rather than explaining change.

The value (and the balance of payments effect) of a project often depends very much on whether or not the government will or will not promote other investments, or make other policy changes. Will it or will it not alter the quota on an important input or output? Will it or will it not alter price policies so that the output substitutes for A, which saves a lot of foreign exchange, rather than B which does not? The more actively interventionist the government, and the more often it shifts policy, the more frequent and serious is this dilemma.

Where the value of the input or output is very important in the evaluation, then it is not too difficult for the evaluator who is (however indirectly or humbly) influencing events to get off the horns of his dilemma. He can say, for example, 'if the government will do A the estimated present value of this investment is X; if not it is only Y'. But he cannot do this for very many things without getting the sack. So the dilemma remains. It is arguable how far he should assume, and he has to assume something for twenty years or so, that the government will be apparently rational (i.e. pursue means most conducive to its apparent goals), or will continue with policies which he believes he can show to be irrational in this sense. On the one hand it can be argued that the government may sometimes consider as an end what the economist usually takes to be a means: and, on the other hand, that governments often do things without realising their side-effects, and that when such side-effects become very apparent, policy is likely to change – an example may be the institution of excessive protection as a side-effect of meeting a balance of payments crisis by the use of quantitative restrictions. The O.E.C.D. Manual took the line that where an evaluator was in doubt about what future policy would be, then he should assume (when the issue could not be presented to the government) that it would be rational in the above sense. The UNIDO Guidelines seems to take the line that he should assume, when in doubt, that no detail of policy would change – e.g. a fixed quota would remain fixed, etc.[1]

III. CRITICISM OF THE PEARSON COMMISSION VIEWS

The reader may well be wondering how exactly the above relates to the issues raised at the beginning of this paper, in particular to the balance of payments effect of P.O.I. Pearson stressed that 'what *would* have happened without', is the only correct method of assessing the balance of payments effect and that all indirect effects must be included. Streeten says 'what matters is not what historically preceded the foreign investment, but what the next best alternative would have been'. He goes on to outline a number of possibilities as to the next best alternative, which I shall consider later.

But I do not think Pearson was thinking of the past. The 'would have been' is counterfactual. I imagine that they had in mind a future P.O.I., and are telling the analyst to ask what would have happened if the government had not agreed to it. The difference is between Pearson's 'would' and Streeten's 'should': the latter seeming, on this issue, to be *plus Manual que le Manual*, insisting that it is the next best alternative which is relevant.

There is no doubt that, if one is advising a recipient country, one should at least investigate what is the next best alternative to a P.O.I., and see whether the government should not be advised to adopt this – bearing in mind also that some much less good alternative may be the realistic one. But this is not the point of view of Pearson, which was advocating P.O.I. in general. To try to decide whether such advocacy is right from a global point of view one must, I think, take the most typical alternative likely in fact to occur if there were less P.O.I.

Streeten goes on to envisage the following alternatives to overseas investment, e.g., in a cement plant:

(1) to raise the capital and other resources domestically and set up an indigenous cement plant;

[1] This, I believe, is the only significant difference between the two approaches. It is a pity that this difference of emphasis remains. A small increase in the consultation which did occur between authors could probably have resulted in an agreed statement of the pros and cons – with consequently less confusion.

H

(2) to borrow money abroad, hire engineers and managers and buy the know-how through a licensing arrangement;
(3) any partial combination between (1) and (2), including joint ventures with foreign firms, management contracts, etc.;
(4) to import the finished product;
(5) not to carry out the investment now nor to import the product, but to do without it for the time being.

It is normal, and I think justifiable, to assume that we need not, or should not, consider Keynesian unemployment – that is, a situation in which a general increase in demand would be plainly beneficial. In which case either (a) the domestically financed but otherwise equivalent investment results in a fall in investment elsewhere, or in consumption, or both; or (b) it is financed from reserves.

Take case (a) first, and suppose the fall is in investment only (the normal assumption, justifiable if the government is already doing the best it can to restrain consumption). We usually have no way of telling what will be the composition of the fall in investment, and can thus generally proceed only by supposing that the (average) marginal investment has a certain foreign exchange yield. This yield can be estimated only by carefully tracing all the direct and indirect consequences, and then valuing them in terms of their impact on the balance of payments. This 'foreign exchange yield' is then the rate of discount to use for the foreign finance and subsequent outflows associated with the P.O.I. (discounting is essential because the timing of the gains and losses will not be the same for the two sides of the comparison).

If the sacrifice were consumption, then the balance of payments saving of the P.O.I. is the present discounted value of the foreign financing *less* the foreign exchange equivalent of the consumption forgone. Obviously this bears no relation to the benefit of the P.O.I.

It would be tedious to spell out the intermediate positions, when the sacrifice is partly investment and partly consumption. But it is important to note that, despite appearances, alternatives (1), (2) and (3)[1] involve one in estimating in detail the balance of payments effect of producing or consuming particular goods and services, i.e. those of the investment or consumption forgone elsewhere in the economy.

There is, however, one conceivable case in which the alternative to P.O.I. is the identical project with identical out-turn financed by reserves which yield nothing, either in interest or by affecting internal policies

---

[1] Streeten's second option differs little from the first. The project again goes ahead, with no significant difference in input or output, except for some expenditure on licences and expatriates which would have to be allowed for. Apart from this, we merely compare the terms of the loan with the probable P.O.I. financing. And option (3) is an amalgam of (1) and (2).

favourably – reserves which are purely a store of value and nothing else. Then the balance of payments effect is simply the undiscounted sum of the foreign exchange inflows and outflows associated with the project, because all general equilibrium effects have been removed by assumption. This appears to be the assumed alternative which Streeten asks one to accept as the basis for measuring the balance of payments effect. For after criticising Pearson (and some unidentified D.A.C. papers) for their 'would have been' approach, and for assuming unemployment and unemployability of the domestic resources used by the P.O.I. (the only evidence that they make this mistake is the mention of the use of local labour services as a contribution – which it usually is, in part), Streeten goes on to say

the analysis which runs in terms of capital inflow (including retained profits) and profit outflow, crude though it is, has therefore stronger logical validity and operational use than the analysis based on 'indirect' effects. . . .

These first three options all involve the possibility of the project going ahead without the P.O.I. It is undoubtedly right that these options be examined. But from the point of view of what would have happened in the case of any P.O.I. which actually occurs, they cannot often be relevant. I think that *usually* a government which permits a P.O.I. will have considered these options and will have rejected them as not being feasible.

It seems to me that some combination of options (4) and (5) is relevant in the great majority of cases (if we add in the possibility of changing exports). More generally, it seems most realistic to assume that the alternative is not to have the project, which involves tracing all the differences this makes to the economy, and estimating the impact on the balance of payments. This is generally the alternative either because the government cannot increase its own investment, for macroeconomic reasons, or because the domestic alternative is not feasible for managerial or technical reasons (if one is considering what *should* be the alternative, then this is true *a fortiori*). It is also rather easier than estimating the consequences of not doing some other unidentified marginal investment, or of reducing consumption.

IV. THE O.E.C.D. MANUAL'S APPROACH

Let us now turn to the Manual's approach, which assumes that the alternative versions of the project would already have been examined and the best selected. These alternatives could cover Streeten's options (1), (2) and (3). It is simply that the story is taken up when alternative versions have been rejected and it is now a matter of acceptance or rejection.

The aim is to estimate the net benefit of investments, not the balance of payments effect. But, because the Manual chose to value everything in terms of the yardstick of freely disposable foreign exchange, the transition from benefit to balance of payments effect is quite easy.

First consider the impersonal inputs and outputs of a project. These are all valued, whether they are of domestic or foreign provenance, in terms of their estimated impact on the balance of payments (we revert later to a description of how this is done). Consequently the net value added (5), so expressed, is an estimate of the balance of payments effect of production, excluding any effect on the balance of payments of employment.

Next consider employment. This has a production effect, calculated by estimating marginal products in alternative occupations in terms of foreign exchange. But employment may also have an effect on consumption. The question then arises as to whether any allowance should be made for the effect of increased consumption on the balance of payments. In a developed economy the normal procedure would be to make no allowance, on the grounds that employment on a new project has no overall consumption effect. But in a developing country which has difficulty in increasing taxation, increased employment will generally result in increased consumption as a direct effect of the new investment, and this will worsen the balance of payments. However, one can have it both ways, with and without the consumption effect. For instance, in the latter case, one would value unskilled labour at the foreign exchange value of the marginal product in its alternative occupation (m). Thus the balance of payments effect of the project is $V - lm$, where l stands for employment.

In the former case, one subtracts an estimate of the foreign exchange value of the increase in overall consumption which is attributable to the project. In the Manual this was assumed to be ($c - m$), where c is the foreign exchange equivalent of the consumption level of the newly-employed worker. Then the balance of payments effect becomes ($V - lm$) − $l(c - m) = V - lc$.

The previous paragraph shows that an estimation of the *total* balance of payments effect requires setting the shadow wage equal to c. This implies that if all investments were chosen with this value for the shadow wage, the maximum positive balance of payments would be achieved. It is indeed a commonplace in the literature on shadow wages and the 'choice of techniques', that this is also the maximum growth solution. It should be no surprise that the same set of project choices would serve both ends, maximising the balance of payments, and maximising savings expressed in terms of foreign exchange: for free foreign exchange can either be retained or be used for any investment.

No country can ever give absolute priority to either of the above ends – anyway, not for long. It follows that no investment, P.O.I. or any other, should be assessed just by reference to its total balance of payments effect. We surely want to know the benefit of it, which implies placing *some* positive value on the increased present consumption which it may cause – but which is detrimental to the balance of payments.

If we put as much positive value on the extra consumption as we do on saving foreign exchange, then the correct expression for benefit is $V - lm$, which is the same as the foreign exchange effect *without* allowance for the deterioration caused by increased consumption. The shadow wage becomes m, and this is appropriate if the aim is maximum output. But maximum output, without regard to savings and the balance of payments, is often not the appropriate aim either. Consequently the Manual suggested a compromise shadow wage rate to be used for assessing the social profitability (benefit) of a project which was $c - \dfrac{1}{s}(c - m)$, the value of this expression lying between c and m, depending on s which is defined to be the number of rupees' worth of consumption which is socially equivalent to a rupee's worth of money in the hands of the government, and is presumed to lie between 1 and infinity. With this value for the shadow wage, the shadow profit measures the benefit, but not the balance of payments effect.

Now let us describe how the balance of payment effect of the changed demands and supplies for particular goods is estimated. Inputs and outputs are divided into those assumed to affect mainly trade (called traded goods – Ts) and those assumed to affect mainly domestic production (called non-traded goods – NTs). Thus, for instance, an increased demand is assumed not, in general, to result in a reduction of use as a result of price rises or rationing, although in reality this may occur to some extent. Increased supply is assumed to affect trade, or to satisfy an increasing domestic demand.[1]

The impact of changes in trade on the balance of payments needs no discussion. But how does one assess the impact of, say, an increased demand for electricity, construction, services, etc.? The Manual assumed, in general, that supplies would increase, and that there would be an import content to this increase: the remainder in turn would consist of NTs (labour also is an NT), which could again be broken down into Ts and NTs. Eventually the whole cost is thus assessed in terms of foreign exchange. The Manual also assumed, in general, constant returns to scale for NTs (no other assumption is manageable, except for some very important individual item).

In dealing with NTs, which affect domestic demands and supplies,

---

[1] The UNIDO Guidelines provides a more theoretically correct treatment, in which every purchase or sale is divided into its effect on trade, production and use: on production the same ramification would occur at the second stage; on use, the further effects of this on production, trade and use would need to be assessed; and all such effects would need to be dated. But this is plainly impractical.

some macroeconomic assumptions become relevant. The need for such assumptions, if any effect on the balance of payments is to be estimated, has been well put by Professor Reddaway in a related context [4]. He rightly stresses that such assumptions are always debatable, and can never be better than approximately true. Nevertheless applied economics must proceed, so don't shoot the pianist!

Now the Manual assesses each project against the yardstick of some (unknown) marginal investment, the social yield of which is reflected in the rate of discount. Although each project has to be considered as an extra investment in order to determine its consequences, this does not imply that its acceptance increases total investment. Nevertheless macroeconomic assumptions are required, mainly because one project may use NTs more than another (and also, but less important, a different mix of NTs); and these demands for NTs may affect the domestic economy.

Now the Manual methods imply that the entire consequences of an increase in the demand for NTs, valued at shadow prices, fall on the balance of payments. This sounds peculiar. Suppose that (1) there is a fixed exchange rate, (2) there is full capacity working in NTs, and (3) the government does nothing to counteract the increased demand for NTs, then, with constant returns to scale, the full shadow cost of the increased demand will fall on the balance of payments as more NTs are supplied. But, it may be very reasonably objected, there cannot be an instantaneous increase in capacity. In that event there might be some increase in production, by stretching capacity, which would cost the balance of payments less than predicted; but there might also be some reduction in use elsewhere in the economy (perhaps resulting from price rises), which would in turn have some balance of payments effect. So far as I can see the error could go either way. Later capacity will adjust, and the error would then be eliminated. Moreover, the objection that capacity cannot instantaneously expand is not quite as strong as it sounds. For many decisions are being taken in the economy which affect the demand for, say, electricity, and investment is a continuing business. Correct feedback from project analysis, which anticipates the overall demands that will be made, has the same effect as instantaneous adjustment. Of course, such optimal planning is too much to hope for. But where any large maladjustment in the supply and demand for an NT, which is important to the project under analysis, is known to exist, the Manual would in any case try to make a better estimate than would be given by its normal method.

The effectiveness of this kind of adjustment discussed in the above paragraph, which occurs without price changes, in theory depends heavily on constant costs – which will be a lot for some to stomach, although in fact a great deal of applied economics (including e.g. Reddaway's estimates[1]) proceeds, willy-nilly, on this assumption.

[1] Op. cit., and Final Report, ibid.

The above paragraphs assumed an *increase* in demand for NTs. But if our project makes, rupee for rupee, a lower demand on NTs as compared with (average) marginal investment, then some excess capacity might emerge unless the trade-intensive nature of this and other investments had been properly anticipated. This possibility brings one conveniently to the second macroeconomic assumption which validates the Manual procedure.

We can assume that the government keeps a constant pressure of demand for NTs, rather than allowing it to fluctuate a little in response to different investment decisions at the margin. But it should not do this by changing the discount rate (for it would not be total expenditure which had gone wrong, but the division between domestic and foreign). Nor should it, we hope, change taxes – for these have been set for other purposes and our methods of valuation assume no change. What it should change is the exchange rate. We then have a model in which the pressure of demand for 'domestic' resources is kept stable by changes in the exchange rate. Such changes in the exchange rate would affect the relative shadow prices only in so far as they changed the real value of the consumption of labour, and therefore, in theory, the shadow wage. But one would probably want, in practice, to estimate the shadow wage from a long-run point of view, and forget the fluctuations due to the real wage's reacting to out-of-phase charges in money wages and the exchange rate.

Sooner or later countries do change their rates to keep their non-traded domestic resources competitive. But, with too many countries, it is later rather than sooner. We then have to rely, in the short or medium term, on the hope that small variations in the demand for domestic resources do not make very much difference to our valuations – this taken together with the rider that, if it is clear that there will be excess or deficient demand for certain NTs, we can write up or down their shadow prices (which, as always, measure the effect on the balance of payments) by what we would hope to be appropriate amounts. The upshot is a claim that the Manual provides a good and workable method of estimating either balance of payments effects or net benefits. The difference between the two lies only in the choice of the shadow wage rate to apply. But, in the present context, where we are concerned with the desirability of P.O.I., I think we have to be a little more firmly on the side of asking 'what would have happened', than seemed appropriate for the purposes of the Manual where rather more stress was put on what the *best* alternative would have been. This could, e.g., make a difference to whether a particular good is deemed to affect mainly trade or mainly production.

Having estimated, in the above manner, the benefits (and, less important, the balance of payments effects) of a project as if it were domestically financed, it is very easy to subtract or add the foreign financing flows to give the flows of net benefits after allowing for the foreign financing.

V. THE FORMS IN WHICH BENEFIT OR LOSS STEMS FROM A P.O.I.

I ignore, as throughout this paper, the various external economies and diseconomies, whether economic, social or political, which are often suggested and stressed by protagonists and opponents of P.O.I.

Any promotion of economies of scale external to the project is either included in the above disclaimer or may be included in the shadow pricing of inputs or outputs.

Apart from these effects, direct taxation is the obvious source of benefit which is most stressed. Thus G. D. A. MacDougall,

> The most important direct gains to Australia from more rather than less private investment from abroad seem likely to come through higher tax revenue from foreign profits (at least if the higher investment is not ended by lower tax rates), through economies of scale and through external economies generally [5].

The divergences which arise between the prices paid or received by the P.O.I. from the real marginal costs of supply have received much less stress. Monopolistic profit has been occasionally mentioned, but little else before the Pearson Commission which says (p. 102):

> Foreign investment generally produces a net benefit for the host country, but there are instances where this is not the case. For example, the level of tariffs, especially for manufactured goods, is often inappropriate. A protective tariff (or quantitative export control) involves the payment of a subsidy by the economy as a whole to producers in the industry protested.

Pearson then devotes two paragraphs to the point that tariff-jumping or quota-avoiding small-scale import-substitution investments by foreign companies may well cause a loss to the host country as a result of these subsidies to foreigners. If the social profit is negative, then there is also, *a fortiori*, a foreign exchange loss.

In the now quite large number of project studies done in connection with the Manual, and using its procedures, there is ample confirmation of the point.[1]

I shall deal first with domestic projects, which often however involved foreign exchange payments for royalties or managerial fees. I later consider what differences foreign financing makes.

---

[1] Some of these studies are summarised in *Industrialization in Seven Developing Countries*, I. M. D. Little, T. Scitovsky and M. FG. Scott (O.U.P. 1970). The individual studies are, regrettably, mostly confidential as disclosing information from firms.

The extreme case is that of negative domestic value added at border prices. In other words, the imported components, plus fees, etc., together with the foreign exchange cost involved in the purchase of domestic supplies, add up to more than the final product would have cost to import. This may not be very common, but I believe that it is more than a freak case. It results, of course, from excessive protection.[1]

Less bad, but still resulting in a loss to the host economy, is the case when, although valued added at border prices is positive, the 'social profit', which differs from value added by the subtraction of the real cost implied by the use of indigenous people, is negative. I believe that negative social profit is common in manufacturing.

Now, if the project is a P.O.I., the situation is worse. Even when there is negative value added at border prices, the enterprise may be profitable at domestic prices – in which case there is the extra loss in the shape of profits accruing to the foreigner. Thus a time stream of social profits may be turned into a stream of social losses when the profits of the foreigners are subtracted. Where domestic prices are seriously distorted the local profitability of a P.O.I. ceases to be any guide at all as to whether the host country benefits.

But, of course, the price distortion may work the other way. Probably most manufacturing units, but especially foreign ones, pay wages which are higher than the social opportunity cost of labour. The benefits of P.O.I. are likely to be greatest where the investment is labour-intensive, and the product is either unprotected or is exported without subsidy – provided of course, that the country does not have *both* the capital *and* the expertise to go it alone. Yet, in many countries, it is this kind of plantation or extractive enterprise which attracts the greatest xenophobia. Private foreign capital is more acceptable in manufacturing. But where it flows into capital-intensive industries which are very highly protected, there is considerable risk that the host country actually loses thereby.

The Author, together with Mr. D. Tipping, has done a study of the British Commonwealth Development Corporation's Oil Palm Estate at Kulai in West Malaysia. This was a post-mortem for nineteen years, followed by projections to establish the terminal value. The commercial return at market prices worked out at 8·2 per cent. We then worked out a social return, in

[1] Mr. Kidron believes it is common with joint ventures in India, 'If India is at all typical, materials, components and know-how supplied by the foreign investor frequently cost the local associates more than the landed price of the final goods they were meant to displace'. ('Pearson on Private Foreign Investment', Columbia University Conference on International Economic Development, mimeo.) But, oddly enough, Kidron seems to blame this on the foreign investor, perhaps abetted by the local capitalists. But it is really a product of the host government's economic policies: sometimes it is probably an unintentional by-product but it certainly also occurs with ventures which are misguidedly but actively promoted by the government. It also occurs in the public sector and in private firms acting without foreign collaboration.

the sense of what the return would have been if Malaysia had put in all the capital but everything else remained the same. A palm oil estate combines imported machinery with local labour and land, and exports the output. There is plenty of jungle, and very little besides labour is bought from or sold to the rest of the economy – so the correct relative price of labour and foreign exchange is what really matters for a social cost benefit analysis. When labour was valued at the market rate (adjusted for comparability with foreign exchange – see below), the social return was 13·2 per cent. This would also have been our estimate of the foreign exchange rate of return. The difference between the 8·2 per cent and the 13·2 per cent was largely taxation, but part of it was due to the fact that we valued the few purchases of goods and services and labour from the domestic economy at 90 per cent of their face value for the sake of comparability with the large inputs and outputs of foreign exchange. But we also made a guess at the marginal product of labour in alternative peasant occupations (rice-growing, coconuts, pineapples). Using this figure which was about one-third of the actual wages paid, the estimate of the social rate of return was lifted to 19·4 per cent. This would be our estimate of the real social return which exceeds the foreign exchange rate of return in that the latter takes no credit for the increased consumption flowing from the project.

VI. THE CONSEQUENCES OF REDUCED PROTECTION IN DEVELOPING COUNTRIES

Now if developing countries reformed their industrialisation policies, to make internal prices correspond closely to national scarcities and priorities, there should be no question of loss arising from P.O.I. If the foreign company will come in without protection, then the host country must gain the tax and any difference between the wages paid to locals and their real opportunity cost – although this difference would have to be reduced by subsidies, as an alternative to protection. Now, under these conditions, the developing country would certainly cease to attract most of the capital-intensive, import-substitution, assembly-type investments which have come in the past. Some such industries might be run down as well. Since Western industry is capital-intensive, and often rather unlikely to design techniques specifically for use in developing countries, there would be less P.O.I. on this score – but our contention is that this would probably be no bad thing. As against this, there would be much greater incentive for Western firms to manufacture components, to be exported back to themselves, perhaps under some 'co-production agreement', [6] or to use developing countries as manufacturing bases for export. The fact that many Western firms restrict exports from developing countries is regrettable, but not surprising when the investment in the developing country was of the tariff-jumping kind intended for import substitution in the local market, and when their main base for exporting is elsewhere. At the same time there is evidence that many companies are willing to use developing countries as export bases when the local system does not inhibit exports by heavy protection.

Whether or not a large reduction in protection combined with other incentives to industry, such as labour subsidies, would result in more or less P.O.I. in manufacturing one cannot say. But it would certainly raise its value and ensure that it did not actually do harm.

VII. CONCLUDING REMARKS

It seems to me that some of the grounds of objection to P.O.I. are misplaced – but others are not!

Quite a lot of confusion is caused by looking only at transfers of resources. It is quite legitimate to define 'transfer of resources' as net of dividends and interest, unlike the D.A.C. But, in that case, it should be made very clear that benefit does not depend on a positive transfer of resources. It is in the nature of P.O.I., and indeed of public loans (unless aid goes on for ever), that eventually there must be transfers back to the investor or lender. But this does not mean that the country is not then better off, nor does it mean that it is not then importing more than it would have done if it had never accepted the P.O.I.[1] Nor, of course, does it mean that the country is not currently benefiting from the operations of the foreigners. It just means that there is a transfer of resources to them – that they are getting more than nothing out of it! The inevitability of this is no great cause for excitement. If the country is still below the international poverty line, it can be aided to pay interest on its private debts – which also removes the temptation of nationalisation of the assets without proper compensation. I see nothing conspirational or sinister in 'bribing' a country not to throw out its foreign capitalists.

But the extent to which P.O.I. benefits the host country (and it should be a truism that it is the benefit, not the balance of payments effect, that matters) is a subject of much, often very emotional, debate. Wide disagreement is possible, because so little is known about the economic benefits of particular P.O.I.s. So long as the profitability of manufacturing (and it is manufacturing that is important, because this is the sector where public aid is of little help) is a poor guide to its social benefit, the best way of getting further enlightenment is by project studies. This would still leave

---

[1] Admittedly it can then profit still more, and be perhaps still better off, if it nationalises the foreign investment and pays inadequate or no compensation – which can and does happen. But if P.O.I. has a role to play for a great many years in benefiting developing countries, such behaviour, while it may benefit that country, will harm other developing countries.

room for significant disagreement concerning possible social and political
side effects (as well as the immeasurable economic externalities), but it
would take one quite a long way.

In the meantime, should rich country governments take special measures
to encourage P.O.I.? I find this very hard to answer. Given their own
inability or unwillingness to manage their foreign trade and payments
through the price mechanism, it is quite likely that increased P.O.I. would
be at the expense of public aid, even international public aid. Public aid
is cheaper for developing countries, and the donors can exercise some
surveillance which may help to prevent the worst investments – but it is
difficult for it to do the same job as P.O.I. in the manufacturing sector.
The trouble is that some P.O.I. is probably very good, and some very bad:
and we really do not know the shape of the distribution between these
extremes. The fact that I have doubts is because I take the reservations of
Pearson, quoted above on page 210, more seriously than the Commission
itself did. If I had more confidence in the way many developing countries
are, and have been, going about industrialisation, I think there would be
no doubt. Perhaps the best thing is to persuade the rich to encourage it
and the poor to look at it with considerable suspicion – recognising that
it is mostly their own policies which make suspicion necessary. Certainly
quite simple cost-benefit analysis of projects would eliminate acceptance
of P.O.I.s with the features described by Kidron and referred to earlier.

REFERENCES

[1] 'The Contribution of Private Overseas Investment to Development', Conference
    on International Development (Columbia, 1970): and *Venture*, The Fabian Society
    (January 1970).
[2] *Manual of Industrial Project Analysis*, Volume II, I. M. D. Little, and J. A. Mirrlees
    (O.E.C.D. 1969).
[3] *Guidelines for Project Evaluation* (UNIDO, mimeo, May 1970).
[4] *Effects of U.K. Direct Investment Overseas: An Interim Report*, Appendix C (C.U.P.
    1967).
[5] G. D. A. MacDougall, 'The Benefits and Costs of Private Investment from Abroad:
    A Theoretical Approach', *The Economic Record* (1960).
[6] See R. Vernon, 'Conflict and Resolution between Foreign Direct Investors and
    Less Developed Countries', *Public Policy*, Vol. XVII (1968).

9 United States Enterprise in the Less Developed Countries: Evaluation of Cost and Benefit[1]

Raymond Vernon
HARVARD UNIVERSITY

I. THE SCALE OF INVESTMENT IN FOREIGN SUBSIDIARIES BY UNITED STATES PARENT COMPANIES

A striking phenomenon of the last decade has been the growth in the less developed countries of the subsidiaries of U.S. parent companies. Despite constant political excursions and alarums, despite repeated incidents of inflation and devaluation, the commitments proliferate and grow.

In 1967, a group of 187 U.S. parent companies – a group responsible for about three-quarters of all foreign direct investment from the United States – reported about 2,600 subsidiaries operating in the less developed countries; 1,900 in Latin America and 700 in the underdeveloped parts of Africa and Asia. The investment stake of all U.S. parents in branches and subsidiaries in those areas was on the order of $16 billion. The number of employees in these subsidiaries totalled about 3,500,000, including 29,000 Americans. The activities conducted within the subsidiaries consisted mostly of manufacturing and raw material extraction, but sales and services also were well represented. The manufacturing industries represented by the subsidiaries covered the range from simple food processing to complex instrument manufacture.

The growth and spread of U.S. subsidiaries in less developed areas has matched their proliferation in the advanced countries. From 1957 to 1966, for instance, the number of subsidiaries in less developed areas of the 187 U.S. parent enterprises mentioned earlier exactly doubled, while the recorded investment itself came close to tripling. Meanwhile the spread by country and by industry was striking.

For all that, only the most halting progress has been made toward measuring the economic consequences of the growth. To be sure, public policy in a field as difficult and as sensitive as foreign investment cannot be

[1] The preparation of this article was financed by grants from the Ford Foundation to the Harvard Business School and the Harvard Center for International Affairs. Some of the main ideas will be contained, in amended and elaborated form, in a book under my authorship, *Troubled Horizons: The Multinational spread of U.S. Enterprise* (New York, Basic Books, 1971).

determined by economic consequences alone; the political and social aspects are bound to be overwhelming in the final assessment of policy. Nevertheless economic costs and benefits, as the economist weighs them, still manage to have a bearing.

II. THE NATURE OF SUBSIDIARY ACTIVITY

To assess economic effects one has to adopt some conceptual framework. Until very recently the simplifying paradigm that served economists as a basis for the observation of foreign private direct investment was that of a portfolio investment; a subsidiary was seen and measured as a movement of capital from the 'lending' to the 'borrowing' country [1]. Of late, however, the obvious inadequacies of that approach have begun to chafe [2].

When a subsidiary has been established in a less developed country, it generally has taken its place as a part of an ongoing international organisation. In effect the subsidiary has been expected to contribute certain strengths to the organisation and to receive certain resources from it.

As a rule finance capital has been only one of the various kinds of resources with which the parent has endowed the subsidiary. Contrary to Hobsonian hypothesis, excess U.S. saving seems to have had little to do with the establishment of overseas subsidiaries in the less developed areas. Where capital was involved, parents have shown a distinct preference for raising the needed funds locally rather than for transferring them from the United States. For every dollar transferred across the exchanges, another has been ploughed back from local earnings and two more have been raised from local capital sources.[1]

More critical than the seed capital that accompanied the establishment of the subsidiary has been the subsidiary's attachment to the multinational system of which it was a part. The subsidiary has been assigned a set of tasks on behalf of the system: producing oil, or digging ore, or assembling automobiles, or selling radios. It has been given access to certain facilities of the system: a cadre of managers and specialists; an international search capability to locate other resources; downstream market outlets for the products generated by the subsidiary; upstream sources of supply for the products required by the subsidiary.

These things have generally been made available to the subsidiary at a price. The subsidiaries have paid in dividends, in royalties, in administrative charges or in invoiced prices in transactions with affiliates and parents. At times the charges and prices have patently been below the going market value of the goods or services involved; at other times they have been determined by the market; at still other times they have been

---

[1] Based on Survey of Current Business data. Estimates of this sort require some heroic assumptions; but the figure is reliable as an order of magnitude.

demonstrably in excess of market prices. But there have also been numerous cases when the goods and services being transferred were sufficiently unique that market prices could not serve as a guide. Access to common trademarks, to guarantees, to emergency services provided by the parent cannot easily be priced or costed. In cases of this sort the intra-firm pricing could only be arbitrary.

In any case, the object of any multinational enterprise in the allocation and pricing of rights and resources among its subsidiaries is to follow a course that best serves the interests of the enterprise as a whole. Sometimes the pricing is designed principally to ensure that the more efficient subsidiary managers see their efforts reflected in larger subsidiary profits. But there are other objectives as well, such as reducing the aggregate tax burden of the multinational enterprise, reducing its foreign exchange risk exposure, exploiting the legitimate channels for moving funds through a foreign exchange licensing system or placating an irate government ministry.

Accordingly, to weigh the costs and benefits attaching to a subsidiary of a multinational enterprise by looking on the activity as a portfolio investment invites acute distortion. The capital that is nominally assigned to the subsidiary is unlikely to reflect the resources available to it. The profit that is nominally generated by the subsidiary is unlikely to represent its private yield to the multinational enterprise or its social yield to the host country. The businessman who directs the strategy of a multinational enterprise, if he behaves like an economic man, gauges the performance by its marginal contribution to the multinational system, wherever that benefit may nominally appear in the system.[1] The economist measuring social yield, if he is faithful to his discipline, will look for the marginal impact of the whole multinational system upon the country in which the subsidiary is located.

III. EVALUATING COSTS AND BENEFITS: THE FORM OF THE QUESTION

Before the 'effects' of U.S.-controlled subsidiaries in less developed countries can be weighed, one other kind of issue has to be confronted. 'Effects', as has so often been noted, can only be measured by comparing a state of being with some explicit alternative. In this case, to measure the effects of the U.S. investment, one has to assume what would have happened in the countries concerned if the U.S.-controlled subsidiaries had not been created. Should it be assumed, for instance, that the local economy would have acquired equivalent foreign resources – principally

[1] As an illustration, see *Continental Oil Company*, PP 170 R, Harvard Business School case, 1969.

capital, human skills and access to markets – on some other basis. If so, on what basis? And what assumptions should be made about the alternative uses of the local resources mobilised by the U.S.-controlled subsidiary?

Lest queries of this sort be regarded as diversionary and captious, the reader is warned that past efforts to measure the 'effects' of foreign direct investment have demonstrated – if they have demonstrated nothing else – that the results are quite sensitive to assumptions of this sort. It matters very much, for instance, whether other countries would have found the means for creating the enterprises concerned if U.S. parent companies had not done so. It matters also whether the internal demand patterns of such countries can be taken as invariant, or whether they are affected by the existence of a U.S.-controlled subsidiary in the country. Finally, there is the question whether the productivity of the countries involved would be much different when actual history and the likely alternative versions of history are compared.

The space occupied by the words of the last paragraph is less than their significance warrants. Each of the queries, each of the alternatives, opens up major avenues of speculation and raises the possibility of widely different estimates of the 'effect' of U.S. foreign direct investment.

In the execution of the studies done so far, it has not been possible to deal squarely with many of these issues. Some have been bypassed and some suppressed, as analysts have tried to make the best net judgements that their facts and techniques permitted. In general they have tried to measure social cost and benefit by focussing on three kinds of questions: the resources transferred and the payment for those resources; the balance of payment effects generated; and the degree of national independence lost.

IV. THE RESOURCE TRANSFER

If the appropriate measure of resource transfer consisted of finance capital alone, the annual amount being moved from outside sources into less developed areas by way of multinational enterprises would have to be counted as trivial. If the capital moving across the exchanges and the internally generated funds ploughed back into such subsidiaries are all totted up, the annual totals come to only a little over $1 billion. From the viewpoint of the host government, however, the 'resource transfer' includes such benefits as may be associated with being attached to the multinational enterprise as a whole. Where such added benefits exist, they generally are thought of under such rubrics as access to technology and management, and access to markets.

The value of such access varies, of course, according to circumstances. In industries that are organised on tight, vertically integrated lines, such as the aluminium industry, the material-producing countries place a very

high value on access to markets; in industries where the vertical structure
is less pervasive, as in copper and oil, countries producing the raw materials usually sense that market access may have a little less value; in cocoa
or palm oil, where a free international market exists, guaranteed market
access may have little value for the less developed country.

To complicate matters a bit further, the value to host countries of
access to markets or technology can change over the life of a foreign-
owned subsidiary. In the first import-substituting stage, as foreign-
owned manufacturing subsidiaries set up their facilities to serve the local
market, the host country places no value at all on 'market access'; its
access to organisation and technology, however, may be very valuable
indeed. As the problems of manufacturing automobiles and refrigera-
tors lose their occult quality, however, the access to organisation and
technology may decline in value. On the other hand the loss is not inevitable. If the foreign-owned subsidiary eventually moves into more
complex manufacturing processes, then the economy of the less-developed
country can be seen as on the receiving end of a new resource. And if the
foreign-owned subsidiary goes a step further and begins to export its
product abroad, then the value of market access must be brought into the
calculation.[1]

The manageability of this concept, however, is impaired somewhat
by another consideration. The operations of a foreign-owned subsidiary
can stimulate local entrepreneurship and train up local skills, thus creating
a social dividend for the host country; this has been a widely observed by-
product of the operations of foreign-owned automobile assembly plants,
especially those required to use components made locally. In other instances, however, those operations can conceivably stifle the emergence of
local skills or local entrepreneurship; local producers of toilet soap, for
instance, could be choked off by the competion of foreign-owned subsidiaries, especially subsidiaries selling their product on the strength of a
well-known international brand name. Some way of reflecting these gains
and losses has to be bought into the calculus of net benefit.

In putting a price on the elusive and evanescent benefits that have been
discussed so far, the use of going market prices can help a little. After all,
management can sometimes be hired under contract; technology can be
transferred under licence; marketing can be arranged at a price; and the
training of entrepreneurs and technicians can be conceived of as a pur-
chaseable service. But the efficiency of approaching the valuation question
in this way depends on its realism. It may be quite realistic to evaluate a

---

[1] A more extended treatment of these questions will appear in the book mentioned
earlier, based on the work of the Harvard Multinational Enterprise Project. See also my
'Conflict and Resolution Between Foreign Direct Investors and Less Developed
Countries', J. D. Montgomery and A. O. Hirschman (eds.), *Public Policy* (Cambridge:
Harvard University Press, 1968), Vol. XVII, pp. 333–51.

foreign-owned subsidiary engaged in manufacture or steel production in
terms of the market price of alternatives, while it may not be very useful
to evaluate bauxite mining on this basis.

The problem of putting a value on the foreign-owned subsidiary's
operations is complicated by one more major question: how to appraise
the value of the avoidance of risk. Risk rears its complex head in two
contexts. First there is the well-known Arrow dilemma – the fact that in
some cases the value of knowledge cannot be priced by the buyer until
he already has that very knowledge in his possession [3]; buying knowledge, therefore, involves a special gamble. The second risk-related problem
has to do with comparing the value of guaranteed access to foreign markets
with the value of freedom to choose when and where to sell. That problem
is illustrated by the dilemma of the copper producing countries. They see
virtue in the stability that goes with selling through the vertically integrated copper companies but they also see virtue in the freedom that goes
with selling in a free market at more variable prices and quantities.

There are no simple answers to valuation problems of this sort, when
they are approached in general terms. It is almost comically irrelevant
to introduce untreated 'yield on investment' figures as bearing on the
valuation issue. The 'investment' is not what the host countries received
when appropriately valued by the country. Besides, the 'yield' is probably
not what the host country paid, when a proper value is placed upon it.
Those payments, as noted earlier, eventually are reflected through many
different channels: the sums that the economy is charged for imports or
receives on exports as a result of the presence of the foreign-owned subsidiary; the amounts that are paid as interest, royalties and administrative charges, as a result of the subsidiary's presence; and so on.

The complexity of that calculation is disconcerting. If the oil exporting
economies get a higher price for their oil by selling through multinational
enterprises than by selling in the open market, as seemed to be the case
in 1970, then this fact must be weighed in the calculation; on the other
hand, if oil-importing economies pay a higher price for their oil by buying
through multinational enterprises, as they well may, then this fact increases their payments to such enterprises [4]. If less developed countries
pay more for the imported materials of their pharmaceutical and electronics plants because their plants are tied to producers located abroad,
then this is a part of the economy's payments to the multinational enterprise.[1]

There is nothing inevitable about the relation of benefits to costs, and
little that offers easy comfort to ideologues either on the right or on the
left. Yet the empirical evidence begins to suggest a few general propositions.

[1] Recent unpublished studies of Colombian imports, undertaken by Constantine V.
Vaitsos, suggest that this factor may be of considerable importance in some industries.

If finance capital is the main resource being transferred by way of the foreign-owned subsidiary, then the net positive impact of the investment can be expected to be at a peak early in the life of the subsidiary and to decline thereafter. If access to organisation and to technology are the resources being transferred, then the same tendency probably holds. But the point of decline can be postponed if the subsidiary enlarges its character and function.

The value of 'access to markets' follows a pattern that is a bit more complex. For the raw material exporting countries, access to overseas markets may be most valuable early in the project's life and may decline over time. For foreign-owned import-substituting facilities, however, market access may be quite irrelevant from the viewpoint of the host country from the very first; yet it may grow valuable again if the import-substituting operation eventually becomes the basis for a flow of exports to overseas markets.

VI. BALANCE-OF-PAYMENT EFFECTS

In the less developed countries themselves, the popular contention with regard to the balance-of-payment impact of foreign-owned subsidiaries is that the operations of such subsidiaries eventually 'decapitalise' the host country. The demonstration is simple: From 1960 to 1968, for example, while $1 billion or so of fresh capital was being transferred annually to U.S.-controlled subsidiaries in the less developed areas, something like $2·5 billion were being withdrawn annually in the form of 'income' alone.[1] If withdrawals in the form of royalties and overpricing of intermediate goods were added, the figure might be larger still.

To substitute more adequate estimates for this statistical *tour de force* is not easy. Obviously, the presence of the foreign-owned subsidiary affects not only the capital and remissions figures in the balance-of-payments but the trade accounts as well. The challenge is to estimate the effect on all these accounts, comparing reality with some specified alternative.

At least one comprehensive effort of this sort has been so far attempted; this effort, limited to the manufacturing subsidiaries of U.S. enterprises, was designed to reflect the condition and relationships of the early and middle 1960s [5]. The principal lesson to be learned from the effort is how difficult a defensible calculation can be.

Table 9.1 indicates some of the main results of the analysis. The figures in the table are derived from two different estimating models. Model A, the 'free choice' model, assumes that the U.S. enterprise was not obliged to make the investment in its manufacturing subsidiary in the less developed area; that if the investment had not been made, the enterprise could still

[1] *Survey of Current Business*, October 1969, p. 30.

TABLE 9.1

TWO MODELS OF BALANCE-OF-PAYMENT IMPACT ON
LESS DEVELOPED COUNTRIES FROM TRANSACTIONS WITH
UNITED STATES ASSOCIATED WITH $1.00 OF DIRECT
INVESTMENT IN U.S.-CONTROLLED MANUFACTURING
SUBSIDIARIES
(in U.S. cents)

	Impact on Latin America		Impact on Areas Outside Canada, Europe and Latin America	
	First Year After	Tenth Year After	First Year After	Tenth Year After
Model A – The 'Free Choice' Investment[a]				
Income, royalties, fees to U.S.	− 5·4	− 9·0	− 10·2	− 23·0
Net replacement of imports from U.S.	+ 37·4	+ 62·5	+ 84·1	+ 190·5
Other trade effects with U.S.	− 19·3	− 32·3	− 18·9	− 43·0
Total effects with U.S.	+ 12·7	+ 21·2	+ 55·0	+ 124·5
Model B – The 'Defensive' Investment[a]				
Income, royalties, fees to U.S.	− 5·4	− 9·0	− 10·2	− 23·0
Net replacement of imports from U.S.	− 7·5	− 12·6	+ 22·5	+ 51·0
Other trade effects with U.S.	+ 2·9	+ 4·9	− 3·0	− 6·7
Total effects with U.S.	− 10·0	− 16·7	+ 9·3	+ 21·3
Total Sales	92·0	154·0	111·0	251·3

Source: G. C. Hufbauer and M. H. Adler, *Overseas Manufacturing Investment and the Balance of Payments* (Washington: U.S. Treasury Department, 1968).

[a] See the text for the differences in the assumptions embodied in the models.

have supplied its market in the less developed area from its U.S. facilities. Model B, however, is based on the assumption that the investment is 'defensive', that is to say, that the investment displaces an equal amount of investment which would have been made by local businessmen in the less developed area for the production of the same product.[1]

The two balance-of-payment estimates in Table 9.1. are quite similar to one another, yet strikingly different from the generalisations that tend to dominate the literature on the subject. They offer only slight encouragement to the school that sees investment in import-substituting manufacturing facilities as the answer to the foreign exchange shortages of the less developed countries. And they offer almost no comfort at all to the

[1] Another assumption that distinguishes the two models concerns aggregate investment. In Model A, U.S. aggregate investment at home is reduced by $1.00, while aggregate investment in the less developed countries is increased by $1.00; in Model B, aggregate investment is unchanged in the U.S. and in the less developed countries.

school that sees foreign direct investment as a drain on the payments of those countries.

The main point of interest to be extracted from the two models is the critical importance of the import-substituting effects. Other possible balance-of-payment influences arising out of the investment, such as profits, royalties and fees paid to the U.S. parent, turn out to be less important in determining the net balance of payment influence of the U.S. investment.[1]

This formulation of the results, of course, begs the central question: To what extent do U.S.-controlled subsidiaries in the less developed countries actually contribute to import substitution? The truth about import substitution in individual cases probably lies somewhere between the assumption of Model A and that of Model B, in that frustrating middle ground which imperils categorical generalisations.[2] Moreover, the formulation bypasses some of the most interesting balance-of-payment questions of all: whether, through increased efficiency, the balance-of-payment position of the country is improved;[3] whether, through increased income and heightened import demand, that position is burdened; and so on.

The problems of estimating the balance-of-payments impact of U.S.-controlled enterprises in the less developed areas, difficult enough in the manufacturing industries, have grown even more complex with respect to investment in raw materials. The challenge in such cases is to estimate what would have happened to the balance-of-payment aspect of the economy if the foreigner had not been invited to exploit the country's raw materials. Would the materials have been located, developed and exploited? If so, under what conditions? And how would the output have been marketed and at what prices?

In the case of raw materials produced in tightly integrated industries, the presumption is strong that U.S.-controlled investment contributes

---

[1] There is a question whether the profits and royalties figures are fully reflected in the table. The Vaitsos study, mentioned earlier, indicates that profits are often transmitted to the parent by way of elevated transfer prices on imports from the parents or affiliates. In that case, the balance-of-payment impact of the profits so transmitted would not escape the statistical net, but would be caught in the 'other trade effects' figure.

[2] The reader who hopes to make serious use of estimates of the Hufbauer-Adler type is warned that space restraints here prevent an adequate elaboration of the many points of critical vulnerability that such estimates entail. For a more adequate discussion, see my *U.S. Controls on Foreign Direct Investment—A Reevaluation* (New York: Financial Executives Research Foundation, 1969), pp. 39–64. Also R. N Cooper's review of the Hufbauer-Adler study in *Journal of Economic Literature*, VII, 4 December 1969, pp. 1208–9.

[3] J. M. Katz, *Production Functions, Foreign Investment and Growth* (Amsterdam: North Holland Publishing Company, 1969) shows a high positive correlation in Argentina between (1) the proportion of foreign direct investment in an industry in Argentina, and (2) its rate of productivity increase over time.

favourably to the balance-of-payments position of the host country. It would be hard to doubt, for instance, that countries like Saudi Arabia, Libya and Venezuela have been helped in balance-of-payments terms by the U.S.-controlled oil-producing subsidiaries, as compared with any plausible alternative. But the kind of meticulous estimating approach that is implicit in models of the type described earlier obviously has no bearing here. Clearly the assumption that such investments are a matter of 'free choice' as in Model A, or the alternative assumption that the investments are 'defensive' as in Model B, implies a restructuring of the big raw materials producing industries on lines that are radically different from those in existence. Price patterns would change; tax effects would be shifted; efficiency levels would be altered; demand would be modified. In the case of raw materials even more than in manufactures, the inability to handle these issues explicitly deprives the model's results of any predictive value.

Still, even in raw material industries, one cannot say that the effect of U.S. foreign direct investment is forever favourable to the balance-of-payments of less developed areas. The existence of large raw material industries in some countries tends to create an equilibrium rate of exchange over the long run that blights the possibility of developing competitive manufactured goods exports and that handicaps the possibility of competitive import substituting industries. At some stage, therefore, the balance-of-payment effect of such investment becomes indeterminate; the case of Venezuela is a classic case in point. Even here one is reduced to equivocal statements about the long-run balance-of-payment effects of foreign direct investment.

VII. DISTORTION AND DEPENDENCE

Concern over the impact of U.S.-controlled subsidiaries in the less developed areas takes still another turn. Because these enterprises have their origins in the advanced countries, it can be assumed that they are most at home with a certain technology; they think in terms of large scale, of relatively expensive labour [6]. This kind of orientation is thought to produce various harmful effects on the economies of the less developed countries. One of these is the misuse of local resources – misuse in the sense that too much capital and too little labour are used, given the relative price and supply of these local factors.

The facts themselves, as usual, are obscure. There are no comprehensive data on the degree to which multinational enterprises adapt their production processes to the conditions of the less developed countries, and scarcely any data at all on the comparative response of local competitors. The prolonged debate among economists over factor reversals and factor proportions has left behind a litter of conflicting and half-documented views.

To the extent that data do exist at the individual enterprise level, they suggest that in some cases a considerable amount of adaptation actually does take place, as multinational enterprises move their products and processes across international boundaries into less developed areas [7].

This is not to say that many enterprises approach the question of an appropriate technology with a totally clean slate. Few ask: If we were beginning from ground zero, how best would we produce in less developed areas, given the differences in scale, in factor costs, and in the reliability of supplies? Still, adaptation occurs.

Some enterprises, following the easiest path toward adaptation, fall back on the use of a product or process that they may already have outgrown in their more advanced markets. Adjustments of this sort generally move the enterprise towards processes that are appropriate to a smaller scale of output and to more labour-intensive methods. (Of course, when multinational enterprises take this step, desirable though it may be, they court the risk of being charged with dumping second-hand machinery or obsolete products on the less developed host economy.)

The degree of adaptation in which different enterprises engage may well be accidental in part, depending on the experience and sensitivity of the production men involved. But there is some evidence that the propensity to adapt is not wholly idiosyncratic. According to one small study [8], those U.S.-controlled multinational enterprises that think of their market position as being based on product quality are loathe to experiment with changes in their production processes, much more loathe than enterprises that think of their market position as being dependent mainly on cost and price consideration. The same study suggests that adaptation is less likely to occur if production costs are a small part of the total sale price (as in pharmaceuticals) than if production costs are a large part of price (as in sewing machines). In this case one sees a reflection of the fact that management is a rationed resource; when management is scarce and overburdened, as it commonly is, first things come first.

Here and there, in the spotty anecdotal materials on the subject, there are indications that the unwillingness of foreign-owned subsidiaries to shift from capital-intensive to labour-intensive projects, when unwillingness exists, may be due to a quite rational evaluation of the consequences of shifting, rather than to ignorance and indifference regarding the advantages of a shift. In some cases engineers have deliberately designed plants and products for use in less developed areas in such a way as to avoid having to rely on scarce types of local labour, such as maintenance specialists, supervisors and inspectors [9]. It may be, too, that production specialists have always been aware of what economists are just beginning to realise, namely, that labour in underdeveloped areas tends to be more efficient, relative to labour in the advanced areas, in activities that are machine paced [10]. Even where labour's efficiency has not been adversely affected by labour-intensive methods, rational decision-makers have had to consider whether such methods added to the length of the production cycle and hence to the capital costs of the process. Finally, there have been even a few situations in which capital intensive technology have been preferred because the local labour force could not be counted on to report regularly for work.

It is not clear whether foreign-owned subsidiaries are more responsive to the forces making for capital-intensive processes than are their local competitors. Where cases do seem to permit comparison, the result is often corrupted by differences in the scale of the enterprises being compared. With higher volumes of production, there is a strong case for the substitution of capital for labour [11].

There is another kind of 'distortion' associated with the investments of U.S.-controlled enterprises, however, whose character is more obvious. If capital-intensive processes tend to be overstressed and if monopoly profits tend to abound, then income-distributing consequences follow. As nations grow, these consequences increase in importance. The concern of the political and intellectual elite shifts from 'How should we develop?' to 'How should we share the rewards of development?' In many countries, including India, Pakistan, Colombia, Mexico and Chile, there has been a growing emphasis on this question and a mounting resistance to the increased wealth and increased status of a new industrial and commercial class.

As part of that syndrome of protest, the question of ties between the local business elite and foreign investors has begun to gain a certain prominence. That tie has been made particularly explicit among intellectuals in Latin America, and has been supported by scholars in the United States itself. The foreign-owned enterprise in the less developed countries, especially the U.S.-controlled subsidiary, is seen as the instrument of an aggressive foreign culture. In the process the U.S. enterprises have found local partners in the countries of the less developed world, men who are prepared to contribute their local influence and their local resources to establishing and maintaining an oligopoly in partnership with the foreign-owned enterprises. Two consequences ensue: the local interests share in the monopoly profits of the foreigners; and the local economy is delivered over to the foreigner's control. This is the *dependencia* syndrome.[1]

The usual question elicits the usual uncertain answer: Dependence and distortion, as compared with what?

The reliance of less developed economies on foreign trade is to some extent unavoidable, irrespective of the internal role of foreign-owned

---

[1] An important subsidiary theme is that foreign-owned enterprise, by sharing a part of its monopoly profits with local workers through the payment of an elevated wage, subverts the worker and blunts his will for social protest.

enterprise. If the economy is small, the reliance on outside markets is likely to be great; if the economy is committed to rapid growth, the reliance may be greater still. Iran, now undisputed owner of its natural oil reserves, is no less dependent on access to outside markets than it was in the days of Mossadegh two decades earlier. Cuba as a socialist state relies no less on her outside markets than it did as a capitalist economy. The issue of dependence, therefore, is much less one of reliance on outside markets and resources than it is one of the distribution of income, status and power inside the less developed countries.

If the issue of dependence and distortion were posed in these terms, the reaction in the less developed countries would be clear and unequivocal.[1] Better a situation in which the foreigner's role was remote and indirect than one in which the foreigner's hand was more visible and the benefits to him more direct. And if it is unavoidable that foreigners should exert influence and derive benefits, then better a situation in which the foreigner came from relatively small or remote countries than from the United States. These basic preferences, it may be, are what lie behind much of the objection in the less developed world to U.S.-controlled direct investment.

[1] These points are elaborately developed by S. H. Hymer in a number of recent publications. See, for instance, his 'The Multinational Corporation and the Law of Uneven Development', in J. N. Bhagwati (ed.), *Economics and World Order* (New York: World Law Fund, 1970). For a critical appraisal of less developed area reactions, see H. G. Johnson, 'The Multi-National Corporation as an Agency of Economic Development: Some Exploratory Observations', presented at the Columbia University Conference on International Economic Development, February 1970 (mimeo).

REFERENCES

[1] J. A. Hobson, *Imperialism, A Study* (London, Archibald Constable & Co., 1905); H. W. Singer, 'The Distribution of Gains between Investing and Borrowing Countries', *American Economic Review*, Vol. II, No. 1 (May 1950). More recently, P. B. Musgrave, *United States Taxation of Foreign Investment Income* (Cambridge: Harvard Law School, 1969), pp. 9–25; R. Z. Aliber, 'A Theory of Direct Investment', C. P. Kindleberger (ed.), *The International Corporation* (Cambridge: MIT Press, 1970), pp. 17–34.

[2] H. G. Johnson, 'The Efficiency and Welfare Implications of the International Corporation', in the Kindleberger symposium just cited; R. E. Caves, 'Foreign Investment, Trade and Industrial Growth', Royer Lectures (University of California (Berkeley), mimeo, 1969) pp. 4–5; C. P. Kindleberger, *American Business Abroad* (New Haven: Yale University Press, 1969), pp. 1–36.

[3] K. J. Arrow, 'Economic Welfare and the Allocation of Resources for Invention', in R. R. Nelson (ed.), *The Rate and Direction of Inventive Activity* (Princeton: Princeton University Press, 1962), pp. 614–19.

[4] Michael Tanzer, *The Political Economy of International Oil and the Underdeveloped Countries* (Boston: Beacon Press, 1969), pp. 194–257.

[5] G. C. Hufbauer and F. M. Adler, *Overseas Manufacturing Investment and the Balance of Payments* (Washington: U.S. Treasury Department, 1968).

[6] Meir Merhav, *Technological Dependence, Monopoly and Growth* (New York: Pergamon Press, 1969).

[7] Jack Baranson, *Manufacturing Problems in India* (Syracuse: Syracuse University Press, 1967), pp. 18–81; G. S. Edelberg, *The Procurement Practices of the Mexican Affiliates of Selected United States Automobile Firms*, unpublished D.B.A. thesis, Harvard Business School, 1963, pp. 30–135; W. A. Yeoman, *Selection of Production Processes for the Manufacturing Subsidiaries of U.S.-Based Multinational Companies*, unpublished D.B.A. thesis, Harvard Business School, 1968, pp. 78–97

[8] See the Yeoman thesis, *op. cit*, pp. 98–126.

[9] W. P. Strassmann, *Technological Change and Economic Development* (Ithaca: Cornell University Press, 1968), p. 200.

[10] Christopher Clague, 'The Determinants of Efficiency in Manufacturing Industries in an Underdeveloped Country', *Economic Development and Cultural Change*, Vol. 18, No. 2, January 1970, pp. 188–205.

[11] W.P . Strassmann, *Technological Change*, pp. 157–84.

Discussion of Papers by
Raymond Vernon and Dr. Ian Little

Dr. Little was invited to explain in more detail the O.E.C.D. Manual. He said that his paper did not depend closely on the manual, but only on the insistence that project evaluation in most underdeveloped countries required shadow prices. One almost had to reconstruct the country's whole price mechanism. He was convinced that the industrial sector of underdeveloped countries had a price mechanism that was so distorted that actual prices were almost useless in decision taking. The O.E.C.D. Manual tried to recreate the price system. It was not unique; there was also a draft UNIDO Manual. He did refer to differences between them in his paper, but they were not important. The O.E.C.D. authors (himself and Professor Mirrlees) assumed that the alternatives being considered were optimal. This assumption was too crude, but when in doubt one had to assume that governments used rational policies of programming, choice and international trade. The U.N. Manual was slightly different, saying that, if in doubt, one should assume that, for example, any quota would continue indefinitely.

The approaches might look different because of the numeraire which the O.E.C.D. used. The O.E.C.D.'s numeraire was savings measured in free foreign exchange. Everything was thus valued in terms of its impact on the balance of payments. The United Nations was more conventional in using domestic prices. The O.E.C.D. Manual revalued domestic resources: the U.N. Manual revalued foreign resources. However, as was to be expected, where they made the same assumptions they reached the same conclusions. The paper really only depended on the use that these manuals made of shadow prices.

The way that Little and Mirrlees had used foreign exchange made it possible to get easily and quickly from the net benefit of a project or programme to the balance of payments. However he did not accept the balance of payments effect as a measure of the benefit of a programme. We had to assume that in underdeveloped countries each project had an effect on the consumption, especially in the industrial sector. This was because wages were greater than the opportunity cost of labour. Governments did not have complete control over the level of consumption. The O.E.C.D. Manual associated an increase in consumption with the undertaking of projects, and therefore saw an effect on the balance of payments as a result of this increased consumption. He thought that this must be included in any estimates of the effect of projects on the balance of payments. However one could estimate the balance of payments simply by adding the consumption effect.

Professor Chenery, introducing Dr. Little's paper, said that there were two lines that might be followed in the discussion. One could focus on project evaluation; or one could look mainly at the foreign capital flow and methods of evaluating this. On the evaluation of projects, however financed, this was the difficult technique to master. Perhaps if one had learned it one way it was harder to shift to doing it a different way. He would therefore like to concentrate on the domestic resource cost problem and its relation to the effect of protection. The domestic resource cost came from translating overall development programmes into specific criteria for specific projects. An example was the work by Dr. Bruno in Israel. It was similar to using shadow prices, but applying an equilibrium constraint over all individual projects. If the effect on the balance of payments was to be big, then he thought two things followed. First, one had to think of all projects in this way; second, if one thought of foreign exchange and capital, one had to do a linear programme with two constraints. One was the balance of payments; the other was domestic savings plus the inflow of capital. Obviously activities used capital. The crucial result from this linear programming calculation was the tradeoff which came from its solution. One started from the constraints. Some projects had a big effect on the balance of payments – for example, production of oil, because this broke the foreign exchange constraint and enabled other activities to take place. He therefore thought that the idea of two constraints was good. Perhaps it was better than the ideas in the Little-Mirrlees manual. If one used equilibrium prices then one could get these from the linear programme and this made project evaluation reasonably easy. One started from the domestic value as numeraire and found domestic cost. Activities whose main result was to increase consumption or activities with not much effect on the balance of payments mainly had a domestic cost.

Professor Chenery said that the second main question was perhaps better understood if one read the fourth section of Dr. Little's paper before the second and third. Dr. Little's dispute with Mr. Streeten was as to how differently one should treat foreign as distinct from domestic investment projects. Dr. Little said that there were two steps. First, one asked whether there was an opportunity for investment where not less than three choices were concerned and where one could make the product domestically or import it. One would evaluate this first with shadow prices. Then, having narrowed the choice to either spending foreign exchange or doing nothing, one could go on as in the paper. One could think of cases where one would need to calculate the choices simultaneously. Dr. Little would do the three options first and then take up the analysis from there. The analysis used should be similar for foreign and domestic investment decisions. However, Professor Chenery knew from previous discussion that members of conferences like the present one did not always think that this was correct.

Dr. Corden, introducing Professor Vernon's paper, said that it fell into four parts. First, there was a discussion of the nature of the activities of the subsidiaries of multinational corporations. Second, the paper discussed the question of the transfer of the resources which this caused. There were problems of measurement and evaluation. For example, it was difficult to find market prices for the services provided to less developed countries by links with multinational corporations. Third, Professor Vernon looked at the balance of payments effects of foreign investment and stressed correctly that it was not enough to consider financial capital inflow and profit reimbursement. The main conclusion was the critical importance of the import substitution effect. The final part of the paper dealt with a number of other topics, like the argument that multinational corporations distorted factor proportions. The conclusion was that their activities were unlikely to be too capital intensive. The paper was the tip of an iceberg of economic research, which was apparently to hit the world fairly soon. There were few formal models in the paper, but Dr. Corden would assume that they existed. The whole subject of foreign investment and multi-national corporations was a challenge to economists to provide clear and simple methods of analysis. All these ideas were quite recent, but were now being extended, not least by Professor Johnson. Dr. Corden wanted to contribute some suggestions about methods of analysis and classification.

He would give his views under the four headings in which he had analysed Professor Vernon's paper. On the nature of the relationship between the subsidiary and the parent, he thought this could be decomposed into three main elements. First, there was a movement of financial capital. This problem had been formulated analytically by Sir Donald MacDougall and others. It was emphasised that there might be little actual inflow, since the multinational corporation might finance investment by ploughing back what it earned in the underdeveloped country or might borrow locally.

Second, there was a horizontal relationship – ordinary horizontal integration from industrial economics. However, this was now international. Where a multinational corporation set up a new car assembly plant, there was horizontal integration. Even so, if a Japanese firm producing motor cars set out to produce iron ore in Australia this would not be horizontal organisation, unless the Japanese firm was also producing iron ore elsewhere. Horizontal integration, in turn, led to two kinds of issue. On the one side, there would be a transfer of knowledge. The horizontal relationship itself caused this. Professor Johnson had emphasised the horizontal relationship, and perhaps understressed others. On the other hand, there was also a monopolistic aspect. The firm would supply imports and also domestic products. If it supplied a large proportion of them, this could lead to difficulties. Alternatively, the multinational corporation might be exporting and competing with the exports of its own subsidiaries from this country. But if exports were being made at given world prices, and the country itself was small, then the price level would be little affected. In Australia there had been a good deal of talk of the subsidiaries of multinational corporations holding down exports in order to avoid competition with the parent firm and with other subsidiaries.

Third, there was the likelihood that there would be vertical integration by the multinational corporation. Professor Vernon emphasised this aspect. This integration could be both backward and forward. Dr. Corden felt that it was on this aspect that he had learned most from Professor Vernon's paper.

On how to analyse the gains and losses of the subsidiaries – this was much more than a question of capital movements. Professor Vernon had tried to look both at inflows and at payments back. Perhaps this was too difficult. Dr. Corden suggested that one might conceive of an imaginary island. It had economic relations with the rest of the world. Its economy was initially in balance. Then a ship moored alongside. It took workers from the island, paid them and sent them back home to sleep. The king of the island might tax the ship or, indeed, subsidise it to come or to moor alongside. Products might be sent aboard instead of to the island. However, the activities on the ship might be mysterious. One might not be able to know what happened on it or how it was related to the fleet. For example, some of its outputs and inputs might leave and arrive in small boats under cover of darkness.

If we were interested in the welfare of the island, we need not measure the transactions on the ship. What we needed to know were the links between the ship and the island. The rest of its activities were irrelevant for this purpose. The ship was like an enclave, and represented the multinational corporation. We might trace the monetary links with the island – taxes, subsidies, wages paid – as well as any external effects. So the focus was on the linkages of the ship (the foreign corporations) with the island. One really had a three-country model: the rest of the world, the ship and the national economy. For purposes of analysis one should not merge the ship and the national economy.

There were also similar ways of analysing the balance of payments effects of foreign investment, and these could easily be linked to orthodox balance of payments theory and to the gains and losses from foreign investment.

Professor Srinivasan said he was not quite clear about the distinction that Dr. Little was drawing between the views of the Pearson Commission and those of Mr. Streeten. It seemed to him that the problem could be posed as follows. We could assume for the moment that the planner knew the social valuation of all inputs and outputs relating to a project or set of projects from now until eternity. He also knew the social rate of time preference at each point. The question then simply boiled down to checking whether the present value of the stream of values of outputs from the project exceed that of inputs. There was no separate balance of payments effect or employment effect, direct or indirect, that needed to be considered. These were already taken care of in the calculation, because of the assumption that the planner knew the social value of each input and output.

This computation was the first stage of project evaluation. Suppose the decision was to undertake the project. The next question one needed to consider was whether such a decision would alter any of the social values of the inputs and outputs that were used in the first place. If it did not, the problem of choice was solved. If it did, and if one could obtain a new set of social values, one then had to recalculate the present values of all the previously-included projects to see whether, at the new valuation, any of them remained included or became excluded. If some new ones were included, then the social values had again to be recomputed and the projects re-evaluated. This iterative procedure would have to continue (hoping that it did converge) until a set of equilibrium social values was realised, at which the present value of each included project at least covered its cost and those of the excluded projects did not.

It was doubtful if this iterative scheme was feasible in practice. It was often suggested that if one could not do such an elaborate exercise, one could at least improve decision-making by correcting such distortions as arose from over-valued exchange rates, over-pricing of labour, under-pricing of capital, etc. in relation to their presumed social valuations.

He was not at all clear that correcting or adjusting such a set of prices and leaving others alone would necessarily improve decision-making in the sense of giving a choice of projects that led to higher social welfare.

Professor Tuncer wanted to take a wider view. The impact of foreign private investment on underdeveloped countries was full of important political and social implications, which were so far-reaching that they could not be overlooked. However, he would stick to economics. Private foreign investment had long been treated in the textbooks as a capital transfer from developed to underdeveloped countries. This was no longer claimed. As Professor Vernon said, in 1960–68 $1 billion of new capital had left the U.S.A. for underdeveloped countries. Yet their repayments had been $2½ billion per annum. The flow of international private capital was a source neither of capital nor of foreign exchange. One had to look elsewhere for benefits.

Professor Tuncer agreed with Dr. Little that the benefit of foreign private investment was not on the balance of payments only, but on other factors too. He would, however, like to emphasise the balance of payments effect, mainly because balance of payments difficulties became increasingly important for underdeveloped countries as foreign investment in them increased. Turkey was a good example. Private foreign investment in Turkish manufacturing had been not more than $7 to 8 million per annum in 1960–66. However, profit transfers had risen from about 1 per cent of export earnings in 1965 to about 8 per cent in 1966. Each year multinational corporations in Turkey could transfer abroad over 20 per cent of the capital they brought in. With current trends, in fifteen years, profit transfers would equal 25 per cent of export earnings. Turkey was also repaying foreign debt at the rate of 20 per cent of its export earnings. So, in fifteen years' time, Turkey might well be paying out almost 50 per cent of its export earnings in profit reimbursement and the servicing and repayment of the national debt.

One also had to consider export earnings. Investment by foreign countries in Turkey was not earning Turkey foreign exchange. The investments were designed not to export but to capture local markets. So there was little, if any, benefit to Turkish exports. Nor was there much import replacement; the investment was basically of the assembly type. Many imported semi-manufactured components were used.

Professor Tuncer said he would not draw far-reaching conclusions from this, but thought that this experience was quite common. Relying heavily on private foreign investment could have big disadvantages for underdeveloped countries, though he did not deny that there were other benefits.

Professor Horvat wanted to make a small point about footnote 3 on page 223 of Professor Vernon's paper. The correlation noted there might be spurious. Research by himself and others suggested that foreign investment usually went into expanding industries – industries expanding faster than average. These industries were also increasing productivity faster than average. The correlation between growth and productivity was close for two reasons. First, there were economies of scale; second, if these industries expanded rapidly they were able to invest in new plants and therefore new technologies. His conclusion was therefore that foreign investment went into rapidly expanding industries, increased productivity rapidly and so raised profitability in these industries.

Professor Tsuru wanted to look at some other aspect of Professor Vernon's remarks about distortion and dependence. The paper summarised very well the points about static and dynamic efficiency problems. However, for the gap, the more important question was the effects on the consumption function and the saving ratio. For example, in Thailand in the early 1950s the country had brought in Pepsi Cola and Coca Cola. There were even Pepsi Cola and Coca Cola political parties. The reason was that important people had given concessions and the political parties benefited from the consumption of these drinks.

The cost of consuming one bottle per person per week of Coca Cola was something like one-tenth of total consumer expenditure. This might have been all right now, but in the 1950s there had been drawbacks. Professor Tsuru thought there were many examples of producers' sovereignty like this.

Dr. Baranson pointed out that there were cases where the Little method ran into difficulties. First, there was a difficulty in calculating the indirect effect of a particular project. For example, New Zealand had been interested in building a steel billet mill. The extra cost of steel billets was nominal, but in eventually rolling the full range of steel products there would be secondary and tertiary effects of rising costs in a market of New Zealand's limited size.

Second, there was the problem of determining the international (c.i.f.) prices, which stemmed from differential pricing in world markets. In the New Zealand example, if one took the U.K. home price as a base, it was £51 per ton (£44 plus £7 delivery charge to New Zealand); if one took the Japanese export price delivered to New Zealand it was £35 per ton. This was obviously a critical difference. Underdeveloped countries generally argue that they could not compete with 'dumping' prices.

Third, there was the problem of computing indirect supplier costs. For example, with automobiles, something between 30 and 70 per cent of components were purchased outside. For these costs, taxes and foreign exchange had to be used. Of course, this defeated the basic approach of direct calculation.

Fourth, when one was evaluating a project one needed a bench mark of acceptable levels of inefficiency – say, for example the cost premium over c.i.f. prices. Without some bench mark, one still did not know what the results in a particular project analysis meant. At present the World Bank used its intuition in taking the view that somewhere between 25 per cent and 50 per cent above the world price was all right, but the Little method did not itself show the way out.

Fifth, and not least important, the method was essentially an *a posteriori* technique. For project appraisal, all the comparisons would have to be made on projected figures and postulated levels of efficiency.

Professor Johnson wanted to make a general comment on the papers. Economists in this area tended to be confused over what were and were not real problems. For example, they bothered about balance of payments effects. This was a purely monetary phenomenon and talking always in these terms was nonsense. Yet the papers paid lip service to the idea, assuming that an estimate of real effects would give the balance of payments effect. He was not sure that he agreed with what Dr. Little had said. One should concentrate on real effects, and he thought that balance of payments effects were a false problem, arising because one had a fixed exchange rate and no internationally-imposed disciplines. The fact was that the policy-makers at the international level had created a problem for themselves; but we did not need to treat this as a problem for ourselves as well.

Professor Johnson felt that what Professor Tuncer had said was orthodox but, in his view, nonsense. It assumed that the concept of capital was not relevant and that money flows were the only thing. The point was not that capital gained returns – this was the essence of the notion of the rate of interest, and some of us knew that it had existed for hundreds of years. One obviously had to pay interest. Development theorists had suddenly discovered that if one did not include interest in one's calculation, one could make a fortune! The question was whether using the capital gave the country any benefit; the real issue was not whether the country could service the debt, but what effect importing the capital would have on the country's net productive capacity.

This led to the policies of government. There was evidence in Turkey that high-cost industries had been attracted because they had been given so much protection. The fact that foreigners then gained was perhaps important – but it was the government's own fault. Professor Johnson repeated that in a recent conference he had attended it had been decided that governments gave far too much incentive to foreign investment – so this was a political and economic problem.

On the narrow question of the gap, Dr. Corden's analogy of the ship was useful. It might be elementary, but elementary things were what economists tended to forget. One had to remember that a country did not necessarily gain if it acquired improved technology; it could pay too much. One had to look at a variety of things. For example, there were tax receipts and subsidies. There was a lower price for consumers and a higher price for domestic factors. There was the effect in training local labour and management. There was the hope, for example, that the advent of the multinational corporation would lead the domestic economy to perform better. One hoped that it might persuade local labour to be more punctual in arriving at work and to save time while it was working.

If we looked at the contribution of the multinational corporation, to narrow the gap, it was not an easy route. Underdeveloped countries would have to rely more on their own entrepreneurs. First, however, one should not pay too much for what the multinational corporation gave. Second, one should hope for long-run effects in developing workers, managers and a modern industrial attitude.

Professor Bhagwati agreed with Professor Johnson that the balance of payments was a monetary phenomenon and that the focus on the foreign-exchange-bottleneck idea, while correct in itself, had led to a widespread confusion among policy-makers. However, he wished to defend Dr. Little against the charge of confusion on this point. Clearly Dr. Little was merely applying the principle of international prices as representing correct opportunity costs, and hence everything was being evaluated at its 'international price equivalent' so that, in this very specific sense, he was perfectly right in calling it a 'balance-of-payments impact' analysis. Of course, what actually happened to the balance of payments in the conventional sense would depend also on other things, such as the effect of the foreign investment on domestic expenditure *vis-à-vis* domestic income.

Professor Bhagwati also wished to argue that the separation of economic and political issues, as suggested by some discussants, was somewhat artificial. All economic issues had some political element about them; and, leaving aside questions relating to satellite status, private foreign investment could affect things like foreign aid. And the relationship could go either way. Thus most political economists had noted that private foreign-investor lobbies were generally against foreign aid flows and wished their replacement by an opportunity to penetrate foreign markets through their investment instead, a trend which seemed to be increasing in the United States today. Yet Indian experience suggested some beneficial connections as well. In India, foreign investors, who

I

saw their profits linked positively with the availability of foreign aid for importing raw materials, had been a useful lobby for getting more aid allocated in the form of 'maintenance imports' and less in the form of 'projects', thereby increasing the productivity of the aid flow.

On the question of restrictions on private foreign investment, he wished to note that sometimes specific areas which were considered 'low priority' were ruled out from the scope of private foreign investment. This was a case of misplaced concreteness. So long as, for example, the foreign investor brought in foreign exchange to buy an interest in a 'low-priority' area (e.g. buying up a restaurant), that foreign exchange could always be utilised to invest in a 'high-priority' area (e.g. to buy machinery for a tractor plant). One reason for such specific restrictions could be that, if other governmental restrictions, say on entry, made for large monopoly profits for investment in this industry, these monopoly profits could accrue to the foreigner and thus raise the cost of investment to the economy.

Professor Patinkin said that the basically objectionable thing was that the government created monopoly profits and gave them to individuals. Surely this was just as important whether the monopoly profits went to foreigners or to citizens.

Professor Bhagwati replied that it was clear that monopoly profits going to the foreigners added to the foreign country's welfare whereas if they accrued to the domestic entrepreneur, they were a transfer within the system, no matter how undesirable.

Professor Chenery said he wanted to reply to Professor Johnson. It was not true that development economists were failed general equilibrium theorists. The relationship between general equilibrium models and development had never been tackled. Yet there were plenty of examples of countries growing with disequilibrium. So, in the real world, one had to accept that governments could not manage the balance of payments in an ideal way. This was particularly true because the demand for imports grew 50 per cent faster than the G.N.P. If one used general weapons to intervene in the economy, enormous interference was needed. So, to talk about general equilibrium analysis simply avoided the problem. If one looked at the facts rather than the theory, then balance effects were important, particularly because growth was a disequilibrium process.

Professor Johnson said he preferred general economic theories rather than simple arithmetic calculations that ignored monetary effects. To do one's calculations on the basis of ignoring the theory was not helpful; though, of course, it did later provide jobs for experts to put things right.

To Professor Bhagwati he said that what he had been saying about Dr. Little was that the latter looked at real calculations. His only criticism was the suggestion that these calculations could give one a balance of payments effect. In fact one needed to include something about aggregate demand and/or exchange rate policies.

Professor Ranis agreed Dr. Little's main point had not been that we had to accept the protectionist's structure, but that the existence of the protectionist structure need not be accepted.

As far as Professor Vernon's paper was concerned, we should ask whether private foreign investment led to different degrees of flexibility in using domestic resources and a different product mix. Vertical integration was relevant. He had recently been studying electronic firms in South Korea. This led him to the question of the blanket statement that the multinational firm got more flexibility in using cheap labour than a domestic firm or a foreign non-subsidiary. There was a series of stages in making this product, and most firms used labour-intensive methods on assembly. But the subsidiary of a U.S. corporation could not go beyond the assembly stage because of the policy of the parent firm, and movement between processes was inhibited. This was not true in the non-subsidiary. There, differences in factor proportions were very big. He would accept the notion of Dr. Corden's ship, but it *was* important for these benefits whether it was a single ship or whether it was part of a fleet.

Professor Kuznets wanted to ask a question of Dr. Corden. He wondered how one could measure the effects of the ship without knowing what it was doing or how the ship was connected with the rest of the fleet. Professor Vernon's paper ignored the question as to how to do the calculation. If Dr. Corden had an answer, he would like to have it given more explicitly.

Professor Fei returned to the role of the multinational corporation in transferring technology. What he said was based on recent studies in Korea and Taiwan. The aim of the American multinational corporation was to use available labour supplies there. Production was aimed mainly at the U.S. market so that firms were really conforming to the development process in Taiwan in producing labour-intensive exports. There was a direct export effect and foreign earnings were increased.

He had been looking at the amount of labour and capital used in Taiwan in order to see what assimilation of technology there had been to make production more appropriate to the factor proportions in Taiwan. The result was not clear. Some firms were strongly interested in taking advantage of different factor endowments; some were not. In the end he had looked at a good deal of engineering information. If the product used a good deal of labour, it was usually possible to use more. But the closer one got to the raw material stage, the smaller the alteration in labour-intensiveness. On the quality of the product, more control required more labour. He thought the history of the firm was important. A long-established firm had more technical knowledge and could use older technology which had been used in the parent firm in earlier years. On the whole, the quantity of labour used was likely to be small, but also there was likely to be a good deal of sub-contracting of making parts in the future, which would presumably be more labour-using.

Professor Findlay said that on page 220 of Professor Vernon's paper, there seemed to be a confusion of real and monetary factors. Where there was specialisation in raw materials exports were desirable, whether financed by foreigners or domestically. It was hard to blame foreign investment for over-specialisation in raw materials. A country could, after all, decide how far to go in. If it went too far, then there was a reduction of flexibility in future, but the desired result could be obtained if care was taken.

To Dr. Corden, Professor Findlay said that we should restrict ourselves if we ignored what went on in the ship and in the fleet. For many matters, like the transfer of technology, the multinational corporation would have a rule-of-thumb so that one would be unable to predict the effects of the multinational corporation on development economics if one did not look at the rule-of-thumb used by the whole fleet. What was important was what happened in the country, but in order to see that one had to study both the multinational corporation and the country itself.

The Little–Mirrlees manual implied that calculating in dollars got round the problem of having a shadow price for foreign exchange. Few could calculate this. One would have to look at non-traded goods and rate of transformation between them and traded goods. *Dr. Little* said that the dollar was a numeraire, but was he saying this in the same sense as in general equilibrium theory? Did he mean that it did not matter which commodity one used as the numeraire, or was there more involved?

Dr. Corden said he had tried to provide an approach that would lead to a better answer. He was interested in both the ship and the fleet. However, to calculate the effect on the national economy, one need only focus on the links between the ship and the island (the national economy).

His approach was that there was no need to measure the profitability of the ship – which was probably impossible anyhow. One simply looked at tax revenues. As for technical transfers, much went from the fleet to the ship (the subsidiary); his approach ignored this too. Only non-market spillovers to the country were considered. For example, the Australian subsidiary of General Motors yielded some spillover, but this often meant that suppliers were supplied at lower prices than the General Motors subsidiary. He knew the problem was still complex, but thought that his approach avoided some difficult problems. If labour was overpriced in the economy, one could get a figure for the difference between the social and private costs of labour. One did not need to value the whole output of the subsidiary.

Mr. Streeten said that what was emerging was that the multinational corporation could be, and often was, efficient. However, it had an uneven impact on the host country. There were conflicts between efficiency and social and political objectives. It was not just that there were uneven effects on income distribution; there was also unevenness between regions, sectors (extractive and modern manufacturing rather than agricultural and small-scale) and between large and small firms. It was ironic that countries, in harmony with the multinational corporations, often prided themselves on the splendid performance of the corporation when its impact, through raising wage rates or introducing excessive social services, or resisting multi-shift working, was bad for development.

What could one do about this? He thought a country had in principle two sources of compensation, though in practice one was often relinquished. First, there was tax; second, official aid. On tax, countries often gave concessions and then, by imposing conditions, went on to interfere with the efficiency of the firm to which the concession had been given. He thought it was much better to allow firms to get on with doing an efficient job. To get the right tax policy, then, the island/ship metaphor did not help. He thought underdeveloped countries should get together to work out joint tax policies, as the oil producing countries had through OPEC. The islands must co-ordinate and co-operate; they must also know what the right amount of tax was and must therefore know what goes on inside the ship. Tax negotiations took the form of bilateral monopoly or bilateral oligopoly. There was a gap between the maximum tax payment that the multinational corporation was prepared to make and still invest the same amount, and the minimum the country was prepared to accept and still permit the investment. The host should try to know what this range was. To do this it needed to know transfer prices, fees, royalties, etc. – all the secrets that lay hidden inside the ship. One country was too weak to discover this and co-ordination was required.

There was also a case for an international agency to collect information and to co-ordinate and strengthen the bargaining powers of underdeveloped countries. There might be international incorporation of some companies for the collection of taxes.

On aid, he thought that official aid was complementary to foreign private investment because it made it possible to service debt incurred on foreign borrowings and profit remittances. It also allowed joint ventures with local participation, which were desirable on political and social grounds, as well as allowing countries to use aid for buying-out options.

Professor Lewis returned to the issue of Dr. Corden's ship. This was not a new idea; it was what Phyllis Deane did originally in calculating the national income of Northern Rhodesia some thirty years ago. It involved unconsciously taking a side in a political argument. The copper industry in Northern Rhodesia was behaving like a ship, and the Africans intended to stop this once they got political power. They wanted to tame it, control its employment policies, force it to buy local intermediate products, etc. They were agreed that all income produced in Northern Rhodesia was Rhodesian. So what one needed to know depended on what one intended to do with the information. Dr. Corden's ship was all right for the days of extra-territorial rights – not for the world of today.

As for what approach was required to find the impact of private foreign capital on the economy, we had been looking at the impact on the balance of payments and on incomes. What about the effect on long-run productive ability? This required savings and savings came from profits. If an economy was dominated by foreigners, it would never have enough savings capacity of its own. It might well adopt unnecessarily capital-intensive processes because capital imports were available. Inefficient domestic producers might develop a bigger savings potential for the economy than foreigners who took more savings out. It did matter for productive ability in the long run whether income was produced by nationals or by foreigners.

What effect would a multinational corporation have on domestic entrepreneurial ability? It could destroy it; it often prevented its increase. For example, this might be the effect of Indians in East Africa, or of the United Africa Company on Africans in West Africa.

The multinational corporation affected domestic technology, domestic management ability and domestic saving potential. It could affect all three positively; equally, it could affect any of the three adversely.

Dr. Haq emphasised that multinational corporations were a fact of life and that underdeveloped countries had to learn to live with them. The essential thing was to evolve a framework of rational policy to deal with these corporations if underdeveloped countries wished to benefit by a large inflow of foreign capital and technology.

Illustrating from the experience of Pakistan, he summarised some of the rules of the game. First, the corporations were generally prohibited to go into the manufacture of simple consumer's goods and confined to such fields as required large capital and new technology. Second, they were confined more to the export sector than to import substitution industries since means of remittance could be easily earned. Third, a certain proportion of local staff had to be employed in all technical and administrative jobs. (This was about 50 per cent in Pakistan, though it had merely resulted in a brain drain of highly educated personnel who were drawn away to jobs not commensurate with their abilities.) Fourth, equal pay was generally prescribed for local staff and foreign personnel. Fifth, market domination was avoided by limiting the corporations to a certain share of the domestic market (such as less than one-third in the case of Pakistan).

Dr. Haq observed that despite such 'enlightened' rules of the game, the inflow of private foreign investment into Pakistan had declined and was now around 0·1 per cent of the G.N.P. The outflow of remittances was about twice this amount. He was not quite sure what the moral of the story was. Did it mean that if the developing countries really wanted foreign capital they had to forgo many of their current rules and regulations and give a freer hand to these corporations to exploit the domestic market? Or did it mean that present rules of the game in most developing countries were not quite rational and needed to be re-examined in the light of economic and political conditions in each country? He expressed some doubt about the future role of multinational corporations in underdeveloped countries as political conditions were increasingly turning against their free and uninhibited operations.

Professor Ohlin said that the basic way of looking at how far multinational corporations could reduce the gap had changed drastically as the gap had come into notice. Twenty years ago it had been assumed that the natural way was to transfer resources and technology through private markets and activities. In the specific political conditions of the last twenty years public aid had come to be regarded, not as an exception but as natural, and one now asked whether private capital movements were acceptable at all.

Differences had been revealed in the discussion of problems of valuation and comparison. What did one compare private foreign investment with? Dr. Corden's ship arrived, and we thought that it essentially created an accounting problem. But then Professor Lewis said that this was not true at all because one could always buy or lease a new ship. We had used many bases of comparison in the discussion. If one compared foreign and domestic investment, one saw that there were many untoward consequences of foreign investment, but this was less evident if the alternative was no investment.

Mr. Streeten's international agency would help underdeveloped countries to cope with multinational corporations, and this was one of the more valuable proposals made during the morning. The economic problem of foreign investment hardly existed in strict static terms, but the dynamic aspects, which included the whole complex of social change, were hard to handle. All we had were hunches based on historical experience and instincts based on our political proclivities.

Professor Horvat had been trying hard to find consistent advice from the papers and discussions. It was clear that one needed a single theory of investment that covered both foreign and domestic investment. It was also clear that

there was not much hope of a general theory. So one had to specify carefully
the conditions of the economy one was studying. In Yugoslavia the problem had
two main aspects. First, there was a surplus of labour. Second, foreign exchange
was the main bottleneck. Yugoslavia knew that investment could expand at 12
to 15 per cent per annum. To expand by more than that meant a negative
marginal efficiency of investment. So the necessary accumulation to finance expansion came from ordinary economic policies. One could forget money flows,
savings, taxation, etc., though these were important in textbook general equilibrium theory. If the capital/output ratio in Yugoslavia was 3 (2 in manufacturing) the social rate of return was between 30 and 50 per cent.

Within this Yugoslavia could accommodate all its investment projects until
the 12 to 15 per cent increase was achieved. They were selected according to
priority and profitability was looked at in terms of foreign exchange. This was
general equilibrium analysis only in the sense that input/output calculations
gave the overall effect of the foreign exchange constraint. He did not see why
there had been the argument over the foreign exchange rate. One had to maximise foreign exchange gains; one could then devise a way of calculating the
effects on investment.

On multinational corporations, Professor Horvat saw a paradox in their role
in development. When one needed foreign capital most it was most dangerous
because it could stifle development. There were many examples from Yugoslavia in the archives of multinational corporations which were preserved after
nationalisation. There were examples in other countries as well. When the
countries were strong enough to have an equal partnership with multinational
corporations, the latter did not matter much. Indeed countries began to set up
their own. Fresh thinking was needed. One possibility was international control,
through an organisation like GATT, and perhaps international corporations
should be created, with international top management, with something like
Hirschmann's divestment corporations and with supervision by international
agencies.

Professor Chenery said he had hoped for some clarification on whether the
investment and the balance of payments was similar or not. Perhaps we understated the effects of private investment. In five years this had been responsible for
half of the increase in foreign capital for underdeveloped countries. So it was
growing, and the question was how to make the best use of it. He thought that
all countries needed both; yet no one seemed to be looking for the right mix.
Though Turkey had problems, Korea, for example, had fast growing exports
financed by foreign investment. and so could afford repayment. It was true that
repayment in the near future was more arduous with private capital than with
foreign aid.

Dr. Corden said that Professor Lewis had given his ship an ideological interpretation which was not there. His was simply a theory of positive economics, a
variety of the enclave notion. To Professor Ohlin, Dr. Corden said he had been
concerned with the accounting problem of measuring *ex post* gains or losses
from foreign investment to the national economy, because this was what Professor Vernon's paper was concerned with. It was not the only problem, of
course, but estimates of such gains and losses were useful for political decision-
taking.

When he thought of the future of the multinational version of the vast modern corporation he was disturbed. He believed in capitalism, but with controls and constraints. Governments needed to intervene to correct the price system for external economies and diseconomies, or to substitute for it where appropriate. If they used tariffs or subsidies, they should not do so because of pressure from private enterprise. He had cases in mind, and not just in the international field. Firms did put pressure on governments for tariffs, tax remission, quotas, etc., or to prevent necessary controls or interventions. It would need very strong governments indeed to deal with, and stay independent of, the large multinational corporations of the future.

Dr. Little said that the main point of his paper had been to emphasise the importance of project studies. Countries engaged in too much programming and macro-planning and not enough micro-analysis. Dr. Srinivasan had said that micro-prices would be altered as additional projects were accepted, and that much iterative programming was needed to arrive at shadow prices. In theory this was true. In practice, one could get near enough to optimal shadow prices without much programming to do a great deal of good with project analysis. He had himself looked at thirty projects, which gave returns ranging from minus infinity to plus 50 per cent. He was certain that the top ten would be in any optimal plan, and the bottom ten not. His doubts were about the middle ten. So simple project analysis could do a great deal of good.

On private foreign investment, he thought that one should try to estimate social returns on projects. If the shadow prices showed a social return greater than the private return, then the project was beneficial. But if the return went to foreigners the project might still not be acceptable. Going it alone might be even better. One project he had looked at gave a private rate of return of 200 per cent; the estimate of the social return was 40 per cent. It was a good project but the fact that it was carried out by foreigners may have made it a bad one. The private return was absurdly high because of very high effective protection. He did not say that one ought to drive private foreign capital into extractive industries, simply that one had to get the prices right – or evaluate on the basis of shadow prices.

The important thing was not the balance of payments but the national benefit. To close the 'gap' we needed maximum benefit from projects, not a solution to the balance of payments problem. One could get reasonable estimates of balance of payments effects from his method, but this was not a very important point.

Dr. Baranson had pointed out that there were many world prices. However, this was not a matter of the numeraire. Whatever the numeraire one got the the same problem. Project analysis was different but it was a part of life. One was often wrong, but he had enough faith in reason to believe that it was better than random choice. His paper had not been concerned with the World Bank rules. However, he would observe that one might have a good project if an input was important, whereas it would be bad if that input was made by a local industry that should not have been there. There was no blanket rule; he simply asked for proper project analysis. If there were a benefit, even if the product was domestically made, and one could not get the government to alter its ways, then one should go ahead. But one could not do this by generalised 15 per cent or 25 per cent rules.

Professors Bhagwati and Johnson knew that he agreed with all, or almost all, they had said. He had answered the main point made by Professor Bhagwati by his reference to the fantastic rate of return on some projects in India.

To Professor Ranis he said that he felt that private foreign capital often was harmful, but this was the recipient's failure. Recipients should use the capital well.

Professor Findlay had asked if there was a deeper meaning to the use of dollars or gold as numeraire. The broad answer was that there was not. He certainly did not imply that foreign exchange was the only bottleneck. He had chosen this numeraire because it seemed more in line with World Bank procedures; also (very naughtily) he had done so because he realised that some people might accept the Manual because they thought that foreign exchange *was* a bottleneck.

To Dr. Corden he would say only that one might sometimes have to reject a good project because of its foreignness. He was then saying that on some occasions one might have to sink the ship.

He did not agree with Professor Horvat that foreign exchange was the main bottleneck. Measuring the desirability of private foreign investment by flows over the exchanges was doubly misleading. To see balance of payments effects we must look at all repercussions, quite apart from externalities which he de-emphasised anyway and which he had ignored in his paper. The obvious and real inputs and outputs were, in his opinion, the most important, and he thought that the project studies he had made supported this.

Professor Vernon thought that in a suitable environment a multinational corporation could add to global welfare. The big problem was the national distribution of this welfare. There were two kinds of situation. First, most countries were too lazy or too fearful to cope with the multinational corporation. There were some examples of countries where multinational corporations did not fit in with the national structure so that changes in institutions were needed. A good deal of study was required, including the study of suggestions like those made by Professor Horvat and Mr. Streeten.

To Dr. Corden, Professor Vernon said that the problem of evaluation was that in political terms one had to make the decision at the outset, before the figures were available. This was why we had to know whether the ship was part of the fleet. One could measure capital fairly easily, but one needed other measures too.

He was not sure whether Dr. Little's or Dr. Corden's measures would help. He thought that both overstated the value of their measures. Measurement was certainly difficult. Resources entered and left; all transactions did not take place at arm's length as in Dr. Corden's model. The complication was that resources often had no prices at all. We did not know how to estimate the value of achieving stability in markets. For example, how could one make the comparison for Chile of selling copper to Anaconda at fixed prices, rather than selling it on the open market?

On Dr. Little's example of a project bringing a profit of 200 per cent, he thought that for the particular project, he could probably reduce this to 3 per cent or raise it to 600 per cent, by suitable adjustments of the value of capital and of cash flow. One did not necessarily get a good answer if one merely looked at the data in a simple way.

I 2

We were dealing with an extremely dynamic problem. So, if the observations on Turkey were correct, here was an exceptional case. The multinational corporation had long shed the concept of being an assembly and packaging plant and it was now very often deeply embedded in the receiving country. It was also responsible for much of a country's exports. For example, 40 per cent of Latin America's manufactured exports came from multinational corporations.

To Professor Tsuru, Professor Vernon said he hoped he would agree that the example of Coca-Cola had too many emotional overtones. Where Coca-Cola was not available, the local population often drank something else. The question was whether the resources used in producing the alternative had welfare implications. One would be arrogant to say that there were no welfare benefits in drinking Coca-Cola. He usually found that the man making this kind of judgement had a glass of Heineken in his hand! We ought to try to think of general welfare in terms other than those of an élite group with its own set of values.

10 Trade Policies for Development[1]

Jagdish N. Bhagwati
MASSACHUSETTS INSTITUTE OF TECHNOLOGY

I. INTRODUCTORY

The division of the world into rich and poor nations is a disturbing phenomenon, which is frequently traced back to the Industrial Revolution. The Industrial Revolution undoubtedly initiated a period of rapid income growth, based largely on the continual accretion of technological innovation (which has now come to be regarded as the primary component of substained economic growth) in a number of countries, spreading out from England in the late 18th century but bypassing a number of countries on the 'periphery'. But it is an historical fact that such disparities in economic standards of living obtained, between different regions of the world, at a number of different periods of modern history stemming from what Cipolla describes as the Agricultural Revolution of 10,000 years ago when the Mesolithic Age passed away.[2]

The unique characteristic of the post-Industrial-Revolution era, therefore, consists rather in the emergence of an acute *consciousness* of the disparities in incomes across the world and of consequential concern at the ethical offensiveness of this inequality and also at the alarming possibility of the gap widening further rather than narrowing. Furthermore, the emergence of this consciousness at a socially and politically significant level seems to be a phenomenon of the present century.

That the gap, whether measured in income or consumption levels per capita (or in terms of other indices such as literacy, infant mortality, etc., which also are generally well-correlated with income and consumption levels), will necessarily widen by (say) A.D. 2000 in *relative* terms, if present-day trends continue into the future, is difficult to assert. It is just conceivable that the rich nations, for example, experience a deceleration in their G.N.P. growth. The United States, for example, is likely to have to spend significantly more on domestic problems such as race and the ghetto,[3] while the Soviet Union will most likely be diverting substantial

[1] The research support of the National Science Foundation and the facilities of the Indian Statistical Institute in the preparation of this paper are gratefully acknowledged.

[2] For speculation as to the uneven spread of the Agricultural Revolution among different regions of the world, see C. Cipolla, *The Economic History of World Population* (Penguin Books, 1967).

[3] This should reduce the resources available for direct investment and hence the growth of incomes. On the other hand, it is arguable that the resources used will be

resources away from investment and growth to consumption. There could also be a growing trend towards substituting leisure for income at the margin (thus reducing income growth, as conventionally measured). And finally the increasing shift to services in the consumption pattern (and hence in production as well, owing to the fractional nature of trade in G.N.P. as also the generally non-tradeable nature of services) may hinder the rapid growth of incomes since the accrual of technical change and productivity in services has historically been less dramatic than in material production.[1] At the same time, the L.D.C.s may well accelerate their economic performance, as the investment which has been undertaken in infrastructure, agricultural extension and research since the Second World War begins to pay dividends.

In absolute terms, however, the logic of compound interest and the harsh facts of our post-war experience with the difficulties attending upon attempts at accelerating the growth of the L.D.C.s make it virtually certain that the gap will widen if current trends, resulting from the present mix of policies and actions, continue into the future.[2] The urgency of adapting the international order in the direction of accelerating the economic development of the L.D.C.s is thus manifest.

On the other hand, in the fields of *both* trade and aid policies of the rich nations, there are signs of serious retrogress in recent years. In the United States, in particular, the revival of protectionist sentiment is likely to end up having its principal impact on labour-intensive 'cheap-labour' imports from the L.D.C.s. At the same time, aid flows on the basis of U.S. legislative commitments already made, are certain to record a drastic fall during 1971 and 1972 while they are already below even the

---

diverted from uses such as defence expenditures and that the expenditures on slum clearance and race problems may in turn improve the economic efficiency of the system by improving the productivity of the poor.

[1] Indeed, what appears to be a dramatic difference between services and material production has prompted Nicholas Kaldor into recommending the Selective Employment Tax in the U.K. to tax labour out of services into manufacturing. To consider, however, that it is an inevitable law of life that services should lag behind in technical progress seems dubious and naive. It is quite likely that most services have traditionally been in *either* the *public sector* (e.g. bureaucracy and the Post Office) where the incentives to undertake R. & D. expenditures and/or implement new technology from external sources have been generally absent or weak, *or* the *small-scale* sector (e.g. retail shops in English villages, the favourite example of English economists) which is typically ill-suited to undertake Schumpeterian innovation or even imitation. It is just possible therefore that the growth of larger-scale service establishments, and the increasing diversity of services as affluence grows, will lead to rapid increases in the technological knowhow in the area of services as well, in the long run.

[2] For projections of the gap into the year A.D. 2000, admittedly of a 'surprise-fee' variety, see H. Kahn and A. Weiner, *The Year 2000* (Macmillan, New York, 1965). Variations on these projections can be found in Paul Rosenstein-Rodan's paper in J. Bhagwati (ed.), *Economics and World Order: 1990–2000*, World Law Fund (Macmillan, New York, 1971).

nominal level of seven years ago. And, on current evidence of Republican thinking, it seems likely that *private* foreign investment will eventually be preferred to official aid flows.[1]

The following discussion of trade policies for development, both by the rich nations (Section II) and the poor nations (Section III), is therefore to be viewed against this backdrop of a growing sense of urgency about the state of international economic order and the consequent need to reverse certain disturbing trends, at minimum.

II. TRADE POLICIES OF THE RICH NATIONS

The trade policies of the rich nations are directly relevant to the development of the poor nations in two different ways.

The availability of trade opportunities can trigger off 'export-led' growth: trade then being the 'engine of growth' in Robertson's famous phrase.[2] Alternatively this may make more rapid growth possible if export opportunities are opened up and thus the incidence of a 'structural' bottleneck (i.e. a 'foreign exchange gap') is reduced: trade is then 'permissive' and makes growth possible instead of initiating it.

The focus on planned development (or at least on targeted rates of growth of incomes) since the Second World War has in fact led many L.D.C.s into viewing the problem of trade primarily as a bottleneck to growth. Admittedly, as we shall note in the next section, the trade and exchange rate policies of the L.D.C.s have themselves contributed to this phenomenon. Furthermore, the 'two-gap' exercises of Hollis Chenery and his associates typically tend to exaggerate the structural problems of growth because of the rigidities which are built into these macro-models. None the less the proposition that, at the margin, the productivity of additional domestic savings is intolerably low because transforming it into productive investment through trade would yield extremely poor returns in view of the available trade opportunities, seems to be empirically tenable for the L.D.C.-block as a whole and for some important,

---

[1] Thus, for example, the *Peterson Task Force Report*, 1970, has failed to endorse any quantitative goals for increased aid flows; and its recommendation that the U.S.A.I.D. be replaced by a Bank which would, in turn, have 50 per cent representation by U.S. business on its Board represents an ideological shift in the general direction of private enterprise at a time when many important L.D.C.s are shifting in the contrary, 'left' direction (e.g. India, Chile, Peru, Bolivia, Ceylon and possibly Pakistan).

[2] Of course, as Ronald Findlay elegantly points out in his companion paper in this session, it does not take much ingenuity to construct a paradoxical model where more exports mean a smaller growth rate. For example, if exports can exceed imports, a faster rate of growth of exports than imports could well imply a sufficiently large loss of resources to the outside world to outweigh the impact of such export growth on domestic incomes. However, the empirical relevance of such 'perverse' linkages between the growth of exports and of income seems dubious.

individual L.D.C.s as well. And it leads directly to the question as to what
can be done to improve these trade opportunities.[1]

At the outset we must note however that trade generally differs from
aid in the important respect that trade can be a non-zero game, benefiting
both parties to the transaction, whereas aid is a one-way transfer and
what the donor loses the recipient gains.[2] In principle, therefore, we
should expect trade policy changes in the rich nations, which are frequently being suggested, to go through with far less difficulty than the
aid programmes have run into.

But there are two major qualifications to this argument:

(1) Some of the demands for changes in trade policy of the rich
nations are, in fact, demands for unilateral transfers. This is the case,
for example, with the traditional Prebisch-type thesis that the terms of
trade of the L.D.C.s show a secular decline and therefore schemes for
paying a 'just' or a 'fair' price must be devised and implemented. These
demands are nothing but the international equivalent of the domestic
demands (which are different only in being successful) within the Western
countries for parity payments and related support for agriculture; and
the Prebisch-thesis, whose factual basis has frequently been shown to
be weak, is to be politically construed as an (unsuccessful) attempt at
inducing 'compensatory' resource flows from the rich nations by
generating a guilt feeling.

(2) On the other hand, even when tariff cuts and expansion of quotas
(which should normally increase both the access of the L.D.C.s to the
rich nations' markets as also the real incomes of these nations) are
proposed, these run into exceptionally great difficulties. And here the
problem is mainly that in the case of the labour-intensive manufactures
(which include cotton textiles, shoes, manmade fibres, woollens, etc.),
the rich nations have still not been able to accept the consequences of
the fact that the L.D.C.s naturally have comparative advantage in these
items. The real problem has been that these industries are frequently
located in the poor areas of the rich nations, the 'L.D.C.-enclaves',
where the mobility of labour is low, alternative job opportunities in the
same location are scarce and the labour force is frequently attached to
its traditional occupations, as with shoes in Massachusetts and textiles
in the Southern United States. This is also the central problem of the
agricultural protectionism to be found in the Western rich nations.

---

[1] The economists who do not wish to accept the 'trade-as-a-bottleneck' idea could
none the less manage to come to similar policy prescriptions by reworking the problem
in terms of the familiar 'gains-from-trade' theory.

[2] Of course, the political economy of aid flows requires that the public in the donor
countries be appealed to in terms of their own 'self-enlightened interest', so that even
the unilateral transfer of economic resources may be conceived of as producing some
political *quid pro quo* in exchange.

The effects of the trade and non-trade barriers (as also domestic excises on tropical imports) on the export performance of the L.D.C.s have been well-documented now in the literature. Their effects have been approximated by Harry Johnson for primary products as follows:[1]

Item	Loss in Annual L.D.C. Export Earnings (in millions)
1. Agricultural protectionism in developed countries	$2,000
2. Sugar protection by existing methods as contrasted with protection by deficiency payments	$357–525
3. European duties or excises on coffee, cocoa and bananas	$110–125
4. U.S. lead and zinc quotas (not applied now)	less than $45
5. U.S. petroleum quotas	$1,109
6. U.S. surplus disposal	$685

The figures are approximate and not fully additive; but they suggest important orders of magnitude. At the same time they relate only to barriers on primary products. When it comes to manufactures, Bela Balassa's important empirical work on the tariff structure of the industrial countries has shown (Table 10.1) that the effective protective tariffs (E.P.R.s) show escalation by stage of manufacture (a complaint of long standing at the GATT by L.D.C.s) and that are they generally higher, by big margins, than the nominal tariffs.

Of equal importance are the *potential* tariffs and Q.R.s which threaten successful labour-intensive exports of manufactures to the rich nations. The 1962 Cotton Textiles Agreement, undertaken within the framework of GATT and imposing 'voluntary' quotas on the exporting countries, is only a systematised version of the fate which can afflict any successful entry into the markets of the rich nations. The recent history of what is increasingly likely to be a U.S. reversal of its liberal position on world trading arrangements, with President Nixon supporting restrictive quotas imposed by law on manmade fibres and woollen textiles, may well be marking a turning point in U.S. trade policy which is as alarming as the recent emasculation of the U.S. aid programme. The surrender to the demand for textile quotas has been the thin end of the wedge, leading to demands for similar treatment from a number of U.S. industries under pressure from imports: shoes, steel and electronics among them; and, with the Cotton Textile Agreement due to expire, there is likelihood of the cotton textiles also coming under the Administration's new support for legislated textile quotas.[2]

[1] Cf. his *Economic Policies Towards Less Developed Countries*, Brookings Institution (Washington, D.C., 1967), p. 94.

[2] On the question of the importance of non-tariff barriers, particularly now that the Kennedy Round has made serious dents in the tariff barriers, an excellent source is Robert Baldwin, *Non-Tariff Distortions of International Trade*, Brookings Institution (1970), especially Chapter 2.

TABLE 10.1

NOMINAL AND EFFECTIVE TARIFF RATES ON MANUFACTURES OF EXPORT INTEREST TO LESS DEVELOPED COUNTRIES[a]

(percentages)

Industry	United States		United Kingdom		Common Market		Sweden		Japan	
	Nominal	Effective	Nominal	Effective	Nominal	Effective	Nominal	Effective	Nominal	Effective
(1)	(2)	(3)	(4)	(5)	(6)	(7)	(8)	(9)	(10)	(11)
Intermediate Products I[b]										
Thread and yarn	11.7	31.8	10.5	27.9	2.9	3.6	2.2	4.3	2.7	1.4
Wood products including furniture	12.8	26.4	14.8	25.5	15.1	28.6	6.8	14.5	19.5	33.9
Leather	9.6	25.7	14.9	34.3	7.3	18.3	7.0	21.7	19.9	59.0
Synthetic materials	18.6	33.5	12.7	17.1	12.0	17.6	7.2	12.9	19.1	32.1
Other chemical materials	12.3	26.6	19.4	39.2	11.3	20.5	4.5	9.7	12.2	22.6
Average of nine manufactures that make up intermediate Products I	8.8	17.6	11.1	23.1	7.6	12.0	3.0	5.3	11.4	23.8
Intermediate Products II[c]										
Textile fabrics	24.1	50.6	20.7	42.2	17.6	44.4	12.7	33.4	19.7	48.8
Rubber goods	9.3	16.1	20.2	42.9	15.1	33.6	10.8	26.1	12.9	23.6
Plastic articles	21.0	27.0	17.9	30.1	20.6	30.0	15.0	25.5	24.9	35.5
Miscellaneous chemical products	12.6	15.6	15.4	16.7	11.6	13.1	2.5	0.0	16.8	22.9
Ingots and other primary steel forms	10.6	106.7	11.1	98.9	6.4	28.9	3.8	40.0	13.0	58.9
Metal manufactures	14.4	28.5	19.0	35.9	14.0	25.6	8.4	16.2	18.1	27.7

Clothing	25·1	35·9	25·5	40·5	18·5	25·1	14·0	21·1	25·2	42·4
Other textile articles	19·0	22·7	24·5	42·4	22·0	38·8	13·0	21·2	14·8	13·0
Shoes	16·6	25·3	24·0	36·2	19·0	33·0	14·0	22·8	29·5	45·1
Leather goods other than shoes	15·5	24·5	18·7	26·4	14·7	24·3	12·2	20·7	23·6	33·6
Bicycles and motorcycles	14·4	26·1	22·4	39·2	20·9	39·7	17·1	35·8	25·0	45·0
Precision instruments	21·4	32·2	25·7	44·2	13·5	24·2	6·6	9·1	23·2	38·5
Sport goods, toys, jewellery, etc.	25·0	41·8	22·3	35·6	17·9	26·6	10·6	10·6	21·6	31·2
Average of ten manufactures that make up Consumer Goods	17·5	25·9	23·8	40·4	17·8	30·9	12·4	23·9	27·5	50·5
Investment Goods										
Non-electrical machinery	11·0	16·1	16·1	21·2	10·3	12·2	8·8	11·6	16·8	21·4
Electrical machinery	12·2	18·1	19·7	30·0	14·5	21·5	10·7	17·7	18·1	25·3
Average of five manufactures that make up Investment Goods	10·3	13·9	17·0	23·0	11·7	15·0	8·5	12·1	17·1	22·0
Average of 34 manufactured goods included in categories above	11·6	20·0	15·5	27·8	11·9	18·6	6·8	12·5	16·2	29·5

Source: Harry Johnson, *Economic Policies Towards Less Developed Countries* (Brookings Institution, 1967). Originally from Bela A. Balassa, 'Tariff Protection in Industrial Countries: An Evaluation', *Journal of Political Economy*, Vol. 73 (December 1965).

[a] Tariff averages are weighted by the combined imports of the countries.
[b] Manufactures whose main inputs are natural raw materials.
[c] Intermediate goods at higher levels of fabrication.

TABLE 10.2

RELATIONSHIP BETWEEN NOMINAL AND EFFECTIVE TARIFFS IN RECENT STUDIES

| Country and year | Number of Industries | Spearman Rank Correlation | $U = a+bN$ | | R^2 | F |
			a (T ratio)	b (T ratio)		
(0)	(1)	(2)	(3)	(4)	(5)	(6)
Argentina, 1953	29	0·89	− 15·02 (− 1·44)	1·15 (9·72)	0·78	94·4
Belgium, 1959	29	0·83	− 6·98 (− 2·42)	1·50 (7·75)	0·69	60·1
Brazil, 1966	21	0·96	21·0 (5·68)	0·32 (11)	0·86	120·4
Brazil, 1967	21	0·95	2·78 (0·56)	0·72 (8·89)	0·81	79·0
E.E.C., 1959	29	0·94	− 9·75 (− 6·85)	1·50 (17·2)	0·92	296·1
E.E.C., 1962	36	0·85	− 4·60 (− 1·81)	1·61 (8·68)	0·69	75·3
France, 1959	29	0·92	− 13·88 (4·37)	1·22 (12·80)	0·86	163·9
Israel, 1961	30	0·80	− 3·38 (− 0·37)	0·70 (5·09)	0·48	25·9
Italy, 1959	29	0·96	− 12·95 (− 7·20)	1·56 (17·4)	0·92	303·3
Japan, 1962	36	0·71	3·09 (0·97)	1·11 (6·65)	0·57	44·2
Korea, 1963–65	218	0·92	6·48 (2·47)	0·61 (17·2)	0·58	297·3
Malaysia, 1963	45	0·73	3·00 (0·50)	0·48 (1·44)	0·05[1]	2·1
Malaysia, 1965	45	0·86	2·19 (0·43)	0·76 (3·07)	0·18	9·5
Netherlands, 1959	29	0·87	− 11·75 (− 5·95)	2·29 (8·76)	0·74	76·7
Pakistan prices, 1963–64	32	0·49	53·1 (2·01)	0·36 (1·92)	0·11[1]	3·7
Pakistan, 1963–64	32	0·72	− 0·88 (− 0·08)	0·64 (4·06)	0·45	24·6
Philippines, 1961–65	89	0·92	13·93 (1·63)	0·84 (9·08)	0·49	82·4
Sweden, 1962	36	0·81	1·20 (0·67)	1·49 (8·08)	0·66	65·3
Taiwan, 1965	37	0·80	26·8 (6·05)	0·53 (5·68)	0·48	32·3
Turkey, 1960s	7	0·06	68·3 (3·01)	− 0·05 (0·17)	0·01[1]	0·03
U.K., 1962	36	0·76	3·03	1·13	0·48	31·0
U.S.A., 1962	236	0·84	2·89 (0·33)	1·24 (6·54)	0·56	342·7
U.S.A., 1958–60	281	0·37	2·00 (1·98)	1·14 (17·88)	0·53	319·6
West Germany, 1959	29	0·93	− 10·70 (− 12·0)	1·60 (15·1)	0·89	228·7

[1] Not significant at 1 per cent level.
U = effective tariff (with *domestic* value added in the denominator)
N = nominal tariff
Source: Benjamin Cohen, 'The Use of Effective Tariffs', *Economic Growth Center Discussion Paper No. 62* (Yale University, 24 February 1969).

These developments only underline the major policy failure of the rich nations: their inability to deal with the problem of social and economic mobility effectively. While the capitalist system is supposed to work efficiently on the Darwinian principle, in practice this is not possible because the groups which lose from Pareto-better policies require to be compensated and, when they are not, they resist the change even more fiercely. Cheaper labour-intensive imports are good for the rich nations; but the costs of adjustment are localised on those who lose employment in their trades and must therefore often retrain themselves and even geographically migrate. The London *Economist* describes the situation well for the New England shoe industry:

> The haranguing in Washington about the undesirability of restrictions on foreign trade does not interest many people in Massachusetts. They see only that the local factory is shut and that there are few jobs for those turned off. The shoeworkers are a relatively old labour force – their average age is 45 – and their skills are not easily adaptable to any other industry. They are reluctant to move away from the small towns and ethnic concentrations formed by their immigrant fathers who were drawn to the shoe factories 50 or 60 years ago. And in general the New England Shoe Manufacturers' Association reports that 'the majority are not getting new jobs. They have gone on relief.'[1]

Far more effective compensatory policies to improve the domestic mobility of labour are clearly necessary than have been legislated for in the rich nations, if trade policy is to be suitably amended in the interest of international division of labour and of the L.D.C.s in particular. At the same time it is clearly necessary to build into the world trading system a compensation mechanism so that any (estimated) loss of export earnings to the L.D.C.s by the imposition of quotas is compensated for by the rich nations imposing these quotas, through an appropriate payment under GATT auspices. This would both act as a tax on such practices as also meet the difficulty which L.D.C.s face in building up their foreign exchange resources.

This selective review of the trade barriers, quantitative and non-quantitative, actual and potential, agricultural and on manufactures, may be supplemented by some remarks concerning the role of aid and technological progress in the rich nations in influencing the trade performance of the L.D.C.s.

(1) The aid flows since early 1960s have become increasingly tied by source. The deficit of the U.S. has led to all U.S. aid being tied by now, with a number of safeguards also being developed to ensure that switching is minimised and the aid flow does not effectively get untied. The surplus countries, such as West Germany, have also followed suit, mainly in

[1] *The Economist* (27 June–3 July 1970), p. 50.

capitulation to their exporting interests: it has been difficult to tell German exporters that U.S. exporters should be allowed to tender for German-aid-financed projects when German exporters are excluded from the U.S.-aid-financed markets. Thus aid has come to be almost comprehensively tied by source.[1]

In addition, however, to the direct losses inflicted upon the recipient countries, the source-tying has also hurt the possibilities of developing L.D.C. exports to other L.D.C.s. Along with the developed countries, the L.D.C.s have been excluded from a market of up to $7·00 billion per annum.[2]

The only exceptions to this have been the Policy Determination 31 of U.S.A.I.D. under which eight L.D.C.s have been allowed for some time to tender for U.S. aid-financed contracts (subject to restricted accounts arrangements and certain constraints on what can be tendered for) and the recent U.S. extension of this practice to Latin American countries for U.S. aid to Latin America.

Thus the aid policies have hurt the exports of the L.D.C.s not merely through the effects of surplus-disposal programmes (which represent automatic aid-tying) on the sales of 'third' L.D.C.s (e.g. the effect of surplus cotton disposal on Egyptian exports of cotton), but also through aid-tying practices of a more general nature.

(2) Further, the role of technological research in the rich nations needs to be re-examined. The development of synthetics and substitutes for traditional raw materials from the L.D.C.s has tended to influence adversely the export markets of the L.D.C.s. Admittedly we must qualify this argument by noting that the production of synthetics in turn creates at times demands for new imports from L.D.C.s; and, as we know from the 'dollar-shortage' analysis, even technical progress in import-competing industries *can* lead to secondary benefits for the outside world. But the empirical significance of these qualifications has hardly ever been studied systematically and seems to be limited.

If therefore the technical innovativeness of the rich nations is indeed directed at replacing materials imported from the L.D.C.s, is this desirable? This important question has been sidetracked in the familiar Nurkse-Cairncross debate about the respective role of demand and supply factors in explaining the phenomenon of technical progress and the partial or total displacement of certain primary materials from export markets in consequence. That technical progress will follow largely from R. & D. expenditures undertaken in search of profits is clear enough; and, in this case, it is natural that industries using (imported) materials will develop

---

[1] Cf. J. Bhagwati, *The Tying of Aid*, UNCTAD Document at the Second UNCTAD Conference in New Delhi; reprinted in Bhagwati and Eckaus, *Foreign Aid*, Readings in Modern Economics (Penguin Ltd., 1970).

[2] This figure would have to be adjusted downwards if one wishes to exclude food aid.

knowhow aimed at economising the use of such materials, especially if the supply situation is not considered satisfactory.

But this leaves open the question whether such technical progress as is so induced and organised in the rich capitalist nations represents an optimal way of spending R. & D. resources, either from the point of view of world welfare or, more pertinently, from the viewpoint of L.D.C. welfare. The inadequacy of the present market system in utilising available technology and the potentialities of technological innovation to prevent pollution in the affluent nations has dramatically brought home to us the fact that we have here an important question for economic analysis.

And the same question (as with pollution) carries over to the problem of technological research, as currently organised in the rich nations, when it comes to the problem of R. & D. expenditures which infringe directly on the exports of the L.D.C.s. The scorn which economists are therefore fond of directing at the occasional demand for 'stopping research on synthetics', dismissing it as a neanderthal sentiment, is uncalled for: there is a basic problem of social choice here as to the optimal allocation of R. & D. resources among alternative uses and there is little reason to believe that the market system of organising such allocations at the moment is optimal from the viewpoint of developed-country, L.D.C. or world welfare.

III. TRADE POLICIES OF THE POOR NATIONS

While therefore the trade policies of the rich nations have certainly hindered the growth of the L.D.C.s, and they can be improved in a number of ways, the trade policies of the L.D.C.s have also played a contributory role.

Although it is difficult (and also rash) to generalise about the complex set of countries that constitute the L.D.C.-bloc, the post-war experience in a number of important L.D.C.s suggests certain common patterns of behaviour.

(1) Unlike the (European) rich nations, which reached near-convertibility generally within a decade of the end of War, many L.D.C.s (with the notable exception of Thailand and many African countries) have experienced the reverse trend: in the shape of intensified Q.R. and exchange-control regimes.

(2) At the same time, a number of L.D.C.s in Latin America, as also Asian countries such as India and Pakistan, have undertaken what is generally described now as an 'import substitution' strategy of development. The Q.R. and exchange-control regimes, plus occasional high tariffs, have either prompted import-substituting industrialisation (as in

much of Latin America) or have been used *deliberately* as policy instruments for prompting import substitution (as in India and Pakistan).

The resulting pattern of resource allocation has been now studied in depth by numerous economists and its principal defects are now better understood.

(A) *The degree of import substitution* which has been observed in several L.D.C.s appears at times to have gone too far.

The question of 'how much' import substitution a country should have is related to what its trade opportunities are. The optimum tariff argument, which applies as soon as a 'foreign exchange gap' situation obtains,[1] implies that import substitution (in the sense of *departure* from the free-trade allocation of resources *via* imposition of suitable trade tariffs) *is* optimal. The real question here therefore is whether the L.D.C.s, for whom export markets are certainly not characterised by infinitely elastic demands, have carried the process too far because of 'elasticity pessimism'.

That this happened in countries such as India is clear from the evidence now available.[2] In fact, it is evident now that import-substituting strategies might even be self-reinforcing because elasticity pessimism leads to emphasis on import-substitution implying poor export performance which, in turn, is taken as evidence in support of the original pessimism about possible export performance!

A considerable volume of evidence has now accumulated (a) on how overvalued exchange rates and the accompanying emphasis on import substitution have discriminated against superior export performance (in Latin America, in Pakistan and in India); (b) showing that the price elasticities for L.D.C. exports of manufactures are 'high enough' to be taken seriously into consideration;[3] and (c) showing that a number of individual L.D.C.s could have improved their export performance even in primary exports by following suitable pricing policies.[4]

[1] The foreign exchange gap obtains if ex-ante savings are frustrated by declining terms of trade; but if terms of trade will decline as more exports are attempted, then the country has 'monopoly power in trade' and there necessarily follows an optimal tariff.

[2] See, for instance, Manmohan Singh, *India's Export Trends* (Oxford, England, Clarendon Press, 1964), for a convincing analysis of how India's export performance during the Second and (first half of the) Third Plans was adversely affected by *domestic* policies and that the degree of justifiable 'elasticity pessimism' was therefore exaggerated in Indian policy thinking. Also see J. Bhagwati and Padma Desai, *India: Planning for Industrialization*, Oxford University Press, 1970, Chapters 18–20.

[3] This is, for example, the conclusion reached for Argentina, Brazil, Colombia and Mexico by Henry Bruton, *Latin American Exports and Import Substitution Policies*, Research Memorandum No. 32 (Centre for Development Economics, Williams College, November 1969).

[4] Thus, for example, India lost ground in tea and jute textiles to other countries during the late fifties and early sixties, and it is arguable that this share could have been

But the effect of the Q.R. and/or high-tariff regimes in several L.D.C.s on their export performance cannot be captured merely through the price discrimination implied against exports. Q.R.s in particular, even when originally imposed on balance-of-payments grounds, have often resulted in sheltered markets. Where the degree of this sheltering is pronounced, as in India where imports are automatically ruled out if 'indigenous availability' exists, quality-consciousness and technological innovativeness are at a discount. The development of exports, in highly-aggressive and quality-conscious markets, then becomes extremely difficult. At the same time, the rigidities built into the direct-allocational Q.R.-regimes necessarily prevent exporters from being able to increase production and/or capacity quickly to execute export orders: the situation being compounded in India by the legal impossibility in general of buying imports (in addition to the direct allocations to each firm) in a general market.

(B) *The pattern (as distinct from the degree) of import substitution* which has been observed in many L.D.C.s has also been chaotically inefficient.

(1) The growth of several small-scale plants in a number of industrial activities, with consequent loss of economies of scale, has been noted in both Latin America and Asia. In Latin America the growth of such inefficient enterprises has been both induced and maintained by high tariff walls which make profitable production at almost any scale possible. Besides, this phenomenon appears to have occurred in Latin America (in the automobile industry, for example) despite free entry, suggesting that most firms got into the act simultaneously and are consequently in an inefficient but stable equilibrium where none wishes to expand at the expense of the other since each can play at the same game. It is puzzling however that although many of the plants/firms in these industries are *foreign*-owned, the governments have not decided to lower the tariff rate sufficiently to maintain output at the *same* level but in fewer plants and hence at lower cost in view of the economies of scale. The absence of the *domestic* industrial pressure groups seems to have been compensated for

---

maintained by more aggressive pricing policies. However, two remarks are warranted here. (i) An oligopolistic situation where a country is a major supplier makes it difficult for the country to retain its share if new suppliers are keen to move in and have the resources to wage a price war whose costs to the larger supplier are very much greater. (ii) The success of some countries in their export performance *vis-à-vis* other countries, in certain markets, often leads to the unduly optimistic conclusion that if only the latter group of countries would change their trade policies and improve their price-competitiveness, they would do equally well too. But this does not follow for the obvious reason that, if the export price-elasticity for the *product* itself is low, as is indeed the case for many primary exports, the net result could be a deterioration in the export earnings of all the exporting countries. In a real sense therefore the *success* of Pakistan, for example, in building up her jute exports, with the assistance of the Bonus Voucher Scheme which constitutes an export subsidy, is to be attributed to the *failure* of India in countering aggressively the price cutting practised by Pakistan.

TABLE 10.3

EFFECTIVE AND NOMINAL TARIFF RATES IN SELECTED INDIAN INDUSTRIES: 1961 AND 1962

Industry	Effective Tariff (%)			Nominal Tariff (percentage)
1961	Due to Q.R.s	Due to Tariffs	Total	
A. Consumer Goods				
1. Soap and Glycerine	99·06	226·03	325·09	100
2. Matches	− 173·30	246·46	73·16	143
3. Electric fans	364·30	105·20	469·50	54·6
4. Glass and glassware	− 73·51	69·44	− 4·07	56·25
5. Leather and leather mfs.	− 348·13	− 2,089·55	− 2,437·68	100
6. Bicycles	− 207·83	30·22	− 177·61	75 (65%)
7. Sewing Machines	− 2,274·73	32·96	− 2,241·71	45 (35%)
8. Electric lamps	1,870·10	468·00	2,338·10	85
9. Rubber and rubber mfs.	0·59	68·16	68·75	50
B. Intermediates and Raw Materials				
10. Paper and paper board	161·27	325·77	487·04	74·7
11. Non-ferrous metal	− 539·81	− 7·15	− 546·96	44·9
12. Iron and steel	354·20	9·98	364·18	21·25 (15·75)
13. Turpentine and rosin	80·57	33·08	113·65	29·50
14. Plastics	68·71	− 1·52	67·19	20
C. Capital Goods				
15. Textile machinery	580·88	− 11·67	569·21	15
16. Automobiles	− 1,999·28	− 122·04	− 2,121·32	50·9 (46·1)
17. Ship building	1,342·60	− 7·81	1,334·79	20
1962				
A. Consumer Goods				
1. Soap and Glycerine	—	—	—	—
2. Matches	− 37·93	− 449·04	− 486·97	143
3. Electric fans	212·54	77·50	290·04	54·6
4. Glass and glassware	− 72·26	71·74	− 0·52	56·25
5. Leather and leather mfs.	− 59·50	906·60	847·10	100
6. Bicycles	− 374·94	8·52	− 366·42	75 (65%)
7. Sewing machines	210·20	33·90	244·10	45 (35%)
8. Electric lamps	256·95	250·68	507·63	85
9. Rubber and rubber mfs.	23·23	89·05	112·28	50
B. Intermediates and Raw Materials				
10. Paper and paper board	27·72	204·75	232·47	74·7
11. Non-ferrous metal	− 284·64	26·17	− 258·47	44·9
12. Iron and steel	− 348·18	33·27	− 314·91	15·75
13. Turpentine and rosin	40·99	33·31	74·30	29·50
14. Plastics	326·96	39·52	366·48	20
C. Capital Goods				
15. Textile machinery	532·64	− 87·07	445·57	15
16. Automobiles	1,235·42	280·49	1,515·91	46
17. Ship building	224·71	12·32	237·03	20

Note: The bracketed figures relate to preferential tariffs.
Source: J. Bhagwati and Padma Desai, *India: Planning for Industrialization* (Oxford University Press, 1970); calculated from Tables 17.1 and 17.2 as averages of four alternative estimates.

by either trade union interests at the plant level or by the foreign entre-preneurial pressure groups which may be operating effectively *via* the aid mechanism or more covert means of the kind which the theory of neo-colonialism seeks to identify. In any case, the Latin American tariff and Q.R. policies have made this inefficient industrial structure *feasible*.

In Asia, on the Indian sub-continent in particular, the Q.R. policies have also made inefficient production in uneconomic-scale plants profit-able: but the primary, proximate cause has been industrial licensing policy, combined with (a) political pressures to give different parts of the country a share of the targeted investments in each activity, and (b) a fallacious economic theory that meaningful domestic competition can be introduced, despite controls on entry *via* industrial and import licensing, by merely increasing the number of firms/plants.[1]

(2) But, quite aside from the proliferation of uneconomic-scale plants, which tariffs and/or Q.R.s have stimulated or made possible, even the *total* output levels of different industries have been so low in many cases that significant economies of scale could not possibly have been achieved. This has been the result of substantially autarkic, 'inward-looking' policies in these L.D.C.s. The swing towards significant import-substituting in-dustrialisation was generally accompanied by geographically non-discrimi-natory protection against imports of manufactured goods from every-where. Thus each L.D.C. tried to industrialise in most products, losing greatly in consequence both economies of scale and the advantages of international division of labour.

It has now been realised, and Raul Prebisch was among the early converts to this view, that it is possible to industrialise at *lower* cost, con-sistent with attaining a given degree of industrialisation, by suitably adapting the tariff structure in a way which would permit greater ex-ploitation of both comparative advantage and economies of scale.[2]

It is against this theoretical view that one can make sense of the in-creasing attempts at liberalising trade *among* L.D.C.s: they are intended to protect the nascent industrialisation of participating L.D.C.s against the industrialised rich nations, while permitting fruitful specialisation in industries among one another. Of course, it cannot be shown that all such liberalisation among L.D.C.s will necessarily improve welfare over the

---

[1] Cf. Bhagwati and Desai, *op. cit.*, Chapters 14–17.

[2] The theoretical writings of Cooper and Massell, Johnson and Bhagwati have ex-plored these questions at some length as well. Cf. C. A. Cooper and B. Massell, 'To-wards a General Theory of Customs Unions for Developing Countries', *Journal of Political Economy*, 1965; H. G. Johnson, 'An Economic Theory of Protectionism, Tariff Bargaining and the Formation of Customs Unions', *Journal of Political Economy*, 1965; and J. Bhagwati, 'Trade Liberalization Among L.D.C.s, Trade Theory and GATT Rules', in J. N. Wolfe (ed.), *Value, Capital and Growth* (Edinburgh University Press, 1968).

otherwise-autarkic policies which have characterised many L.D.C.s in the last two decades: but so can one not argue that a 100 per cent preferential tariff reduction, which GATT sanctions, is necessarily better than (say) a 50 per cent preferential tariff reduction, which GATT does not sanction. On balance it seems quite probable that modification of the GATT rules to permit preferential tariff concessions among L.D.C.s will improve L.D.C. incomes and will also promote a more rapid, eventual move towards non-discriminatory world trading arrangements.

(3) An inefficient allocation of resources among alternative import-competing activities has also been noted for the import-substitution-strategy L.D.C.s.

In analysing this phenomenon, two different but related approaches have been used: the effective protection (E.P.R.) method and the domestic resource cost (D.R.C.) method. The latter, when adopted correctly, is nothing but an application of ideal cost-benefit analysis: it enables one to rank alternative projects and industries by the domestic resource cost of earning foreign exchange and thus one can pin down the inefficiency losses arising from misallocation of resources.[1] It has been used by Anne Krueger, in a classic article on Turkey, to argue that very large losses have been imposed on the Turkish economy by the Q.R.-regime.[2]

The E.P.R. theory, on the other hand, utilises similar data to arrive at measures of the proportional increment in value-added over the free trade value-added. Industries are then ranked by this measure of effective protective rates. This is then taken as a relative ranking of industries by their truly effective protection. rather than by their nominal tariffs which relate only to the output of these industries, indicating how resource allocation has shifted.[3]

There are a number of difficulties, both conceptual and statistical, with these E.P.R. indices. Chief among them are the following:

[1] Where tariffs or Q.R.s are used, there would also be additional *consumption* losses (which are ignored in several estimates actually made for a number of countries).

[2] Cf. Anne Krueger, 'Some Economic Costs of Exchange Control: The Turkish Case', *Journal of Political Economy* (October 1966). However, her large estimates of losses relate only to the few industries which she studied; and even if they were representative, we could not readily infer equally large losses for the economy *as a whole* because of less-than-infinitely-elastic demands for many exports, in particular. Nonetheless, her estimates are an extremely useful step in the right direction.

[3] The E.P.R. theory has been developed by a number of economists, including Corden, Barber, Travis, Ruffin, Tan, Johnson, Balassa, Ramaswami and Srinivasan, and Jones. See, in particular, W. M. Corden, 'The Structure of a Tariff System and the Effective Protective Rate', *Journal of Political Economy* (June 1966); Augustine Tan, 'Differential Tariffs, Negative Value-added and the Theory of Effective Protection in General Equilibrium', *American Economic Review* (March 1970); and V. K. Ramaswami and T. N. Srinivasan, 'Tariff Structure and Resource Allocation in the Presence of Factor Substitution', in J. Bhagwati, R. Jones, R. Mundell and J. Vanek (eds.), *Trade, Payments and Growth: Essays in International Economics in Honor of C. P. Kindleberger* (M.I.T. Press, 1971).

(1) Ramaswami and Srinivasan have shown that, in the presence of generalised substitution between domestic and imported factors, E.P.R. indices cannot be constructed so as to yield necessarily accurate resource-allocational effects.[1] This is a criticism of empirical relevance as well: not merely are intermediates often substitutable for capital goods and labour, but it is also wrong to identify imports with intermediate goods since many L.D.C.s import a large quantum of capital goods which are admitted to be generally substitutable for (domestic) labour.

(2) The problem of whether non-traded goods should be treated as part of value-added or as inputs is still theoretically unresolved; and the studies on India, Pakistan and other countries show that the estimates of E.P.R.s can be quite sensitive to which method is adopted.[2]

(3) The evaluation of value-added at international prices also poses two difficult questions. (a) Since, with transport costs, there are both c.i.f. and f.o.b. prices, we have to decide which of these two prices we wish to use for any output or input in our calculations. As is well known, any equilibrium rate of exchange will have an associated classification of commodities and services into exportables, importables, and non-traded goods. Since we observe only the protected-situation exchange rate and *its* division of goods and services into these three categories, we are generally left to guess about which items should be evaluated as exportables (f.o.b. price), importables (c.i.f. price) and non-traded goods (somewhere between c.i.f. and f.o.b. prices) in the hypothesised free-trade situation. In practice, this issue is fudged in all the estimates of E.P.R.s and the observed classification of commodities and services into these three categories seems to be adopted for both the free-trade and the protection-inclusive calculations of value-added. Clearly a sensitivity analysis at minimum would seem to be in order. (b) Another difficulty arises from the fact that contrary to the assumption of present-day E.P.R. theory and calculations, the exports and imports of any country are rarely characterised by *infinite* elasticities of world demand and supply. This is particularly the case for exports – and especially so for the primary exports of a number of L.D.C.s. And this *does* affect the exercise because primary exportables enter into many of the import-competing industries for which E.P.R. calculations are

---

[1] Corden has ingeniously shown later that, for a restricted class of production functions, $X = X[V(K, L), M]$, where X is output, K and L are domestic factors in given supply and M is the imported factor, and generalised substitution holds between V and M, an E.P.R. index can be constructed. However, this seems to have little *practical* significance.

[2] Cf. Bhagwati and Desai, *op. cit.*, Chapter 17; and Lewis and Guisinger, 'Measuring Protection in a Developing Country: The Case of Pakistan', *Journal of Political Economy* (1969).

made and therefore they have to be evaluated at international prices as well.[1]

(4) A number of statistical difficulties also attend upon these calculations: specific tariffs have to be turned into *ad valorem* rates; preferential tariffs frequently intrude for specific sources (e.g. Commonwealth preferences); the correct tariffs have to be identified and related to data in input-output tables on input inefficients which are necessarily highly aggregative; where Q.R.s obtain, the premia on imports must be taken into account and are nearly always difficult to obtain with any accuracy in Q.R.-regime L.D.C.s; and so on.[2]

None the less, the E.P.R. calculations are of interest and broadly underline the fact that tariffs and Q.R.-regimes have permitted or prompted extremely high-cost industries to emerge and flourish. Thus effective rates of protection have been observed, in a number of studies, which range at times up to several thousand per cent: a result which is particularly evident in Q.R.-regimes as is clear from the Indian E.P.R. calculations presented in Table 10.3. There the effective protection is broken down into the part available, thanks to Q.R.s and the part attributable to tariffs. It is evident that Q.R.s add significantly large protection to different activities and that the (total) effective tariffs are significantly larger than the nominal tariffs.[3]

These data, as also similar calculations for Pakistan by Lewis and Guisinger, underline the chaotic, variable and generally unforeseeable nature of the protection which the Q.R.-regime manages to offer.[4] The losses which these bizarre tariffs entail are also brought home dramatically

[1] These conceptual difficulties have made a number of economists sceptical of the utility of the E.P.R. concept while recognising that nominal tariffs are not useful from the point of view of predicting resource-allocational effects either. This scepticism has been reinforced also by the facts that (1) *at most*, the ranking of E.P.R.s could tell one that the highest-E.P.R. industry has attracted resources and the lowest-E.P.R. industry has lost them, whereas for all the others in between, *nothing* can be inferred at all, as with nominal tariffs; and (2) the ranking of industries by their nominal and effective tariffs, in practice, seems to be highly correlated anyway (see Table 10.2): hence we might as well save ourselves all the bother!

[2] For a detailed analysis of such difficulties in the context of the Indian Q.R.-regime, which is particularly complex, see Bhagwati and Desai, *op. cit.*, Chapter 17.

[3] Since the rates are calculated with *international* value added in the denominator, negative rates in excess of 100 per cent are also 'high' rates from the point of view of the degree of protection afforded. To avoid confusion on this score, the rates are sometimes presented with *domestic* value added in the denominator, as in Table 2.

[4] In fact, countries such as India (where the principle of 'indigenous availability' is used to exclude imports whenever domestic production is available, regardless of costs) and Brazil (where the Law of Similars is used often with equivalent results), one must contend with the fact of *automatic* protection as soon as an industry is started; hence the structure of relative incentives among alternative activities is not conveyed fully by the measures of *actual*, observed tariff rates.

by several instances of 'value subtracting' activities which have come to light in the studies on Pakistan, India, Philippines and Brazil, among other countries.[1]

(3) *The pattern of raw material import allocations* under certain Q.R. regimes also seems to have been instrumental in reducing the efficiency of resource utilisation. Thus, in both Pakistan and India, the Q.R. system has operated so as to give import licences *pro rata* to installed capacity. Thus in a situation of excess capacity due to shortages of imported materials, the system has set up incentives for creating yet more excess capacity. This follows because, with the import premium in an overvalued exchange rate system, entrepreneurs would be able to get hold of additional imports at premium-*exclusive* prices if they installed more capacity and produced more, whereas additional production *via* further utilisation of existing capacity would require purchase of these imported materials from the market at higher premium-*inclusive* prices.

Furthermore, there are the standard and well-known inefficiencies of such regimes, in the shape of delays and bottle-necks which create disproportionately large losses throughout the system because of the slowness and limited flexibility of the direct-allocational systems in practice.

(4) *The inefficiency of the industrialisation and trade pattern has also been reinforced in other 'dynamic' ways.* The growth of industry and entrepreneurship in a sheltered market appears to involve nurturing of these in a harmful environment: cost-minimisation and innovativeness are not fostered in such a climate. Bruton, for example, has found that labour and factor productivity growth rates are inversely correlated with the degree of protection furnished, in Latin American experience. In India there is no evidence of R. & D. expenditures by industry since planning in a sheltered market began; and quality complaints in several industries have persisted long and, at times, have even increased. The small-scale plants and firms which have been encouraged are also ill-adapted to technological innovativeness of any kind: such progressiveness is usually associated with larger firms. Also, the tariff-jumping and Q.R.-jumping foreign investments which usually accompany the import-substitution strategy are also often characterised by small scale; and typically, as the Canadians have long noted, the parent company nearly always have their R. & D. establishments 'at home', thus confining the host L.D.C.s to 'trickle-down' benefits but not the advantages of having more appropriate technology develop in an indigenous setting.

(5) *These 'dynamic' inefficiencies are probably accompanied also by a failure of the Q.R.-regimes to improve the domestic rate of saving.* Bruton

---

[1] For an extended discussion of the analytical significance of this phenomenon, see Bhagwati and Desai, *op. cit.*, Appendix to Ch. 17, and the brilliant papers of Tan, *op. cit.*, and S. Guisinger, 'Negative Value-added and the Theory of Effective Protection', *Quarterly Journal of Economics* (August 1969).

has argued, for example, that the typical tendency of import-substituting industrialisation to reduce imports to ('essential') intermediates, raw materials and capital goods is likely to impair the ability of the government to raise taxes through import duties and hence savings, because domestic taxes are more difficult to raise. Similarly, following Power, he has argued that the growth of indigenous, import-substituted consumer goods may well have reduced the marginal savings rate in Pakistan because with more consumer goods reduced, it would be difficult to resist pressures for additional consumption, especially if an overvalued exchange rate prevents their exportation.[1]

The evidence on these 'dynamic' linkages between the trade and exchange rate regimes and the efficiency of the economic system, operating *via* technological innovation and capital accumulation, is however too tenuous at this stage for us to reach firm conclusions. None the less, what *is* available, and the *a priori* arguments, suggest that the 'static' inefficiencies (discussed under (A)–(C) above) are certainly not outweighed by dynamic benefits and, if anything, both point in the direction of a change to a superior trade and exchange-rate mechanism.

IV. A SHIFT TO MORE 'LIBERAL' TRADE REGIMES

A move away from the overvalued-currency and Q.R. regimes, with protection being furnished *via* identifiable methods such as tariffs rather than Q.R.s and for limited periods and in limited degree, is clearly called for if the arguments and the evidence presented so far are to be accepted.

Now it is indeed true that the L.D.C.s have had a number of devaluations in the post-war period, with a frequency and of a magnitude which compare favourably with the rich nations (Tables 10.4 and 10.5). As Margaret de Vries has correctly pointed out, if the exchange rate changes are adjusted for relative purchasing power changes, then the L.D.C.s have generally devalued *more* than the developed countries (Table 10.6 where a figure less than 100 means that the parity devaluation exceeds the rise in the price level of the country *relative* to that abroad).

But these devaluations have largely been in response to developing payments situations. While representing axiomatically liberalisation attempts in the sense that a successful devaluation would reduce the pressure on the direct-allocational Q.R.-regime, the more interesting attempts at liberalisation have been where a 'policy package' has been presented to the L.D.C., usually embracing devaluation, import liberalisation, external credits and (in some cases) internal stabilisation measures. Such packages have been

---

[1] This argument is the inverse of the Mahalanobis-type argument once used in India: if you produce steel, you will necessarily raise the rate of saving because you cannot eat steel. Actually steel does get exported, is used for domestic furniture and you can also have excess capacity for lack of demand!

TABLE 10.4

MAGNITUDES OF EXCHANGE DEPRECIATION, 1948–67: DISTRIBUTION OF 21 MORE DEVELOPED AND 88 LESS DEVELOPED COUNTRIES BY DEGREE OF DEPRECIATION
(Magnitudes in per cent)

Magnitude of Depreciation	Number of More Developed Countries	Country Identification[1]	Number of Less Developed Countries	Country Identification[1]
Zero, virtually zero, or appreciation	3	A	10	F
0–29	6	B	6	G
30–39	5	C	17	H
40–75	6	D	33	I
More than 75	1	E	22	J

[1] The letter symbols stand for the following countries, listed in order of increasing depreciation.

A. Japan, Switzerland, United States
B. Canada, Italy, Belgium, Luxembourg, Germany, Netherlands
C. Australia, Norway, South Africa, Sweden, Denmark
D. Ireland, United Kingdom, New Zealand, France, Austria, Finland
E. Iceland
F. Lebanon, Cuba, Dominican Republic, El Salvador, Guatemala, Haiti, Honduras, Liberia, Panama, Ethiopia
G. Costa Rica, Syrian Arab Republic, Saudi Arabia, Portugal, Venezuela, Nicaragua
H. Burma, Iraq, Jordan, Kenya, Kuwait, Libya, Malaysia, Nigeria, Pakistan, Sierra Leone, Singapore, Somalia, Sudan, Tanzania, Uganda, Zambia, Ecuador
I. Cyprus, The Gambia, Jamaica, Malawi, Trinidad and Tobago, Guyana, Burundi, United Arab Republic, Ceylon, Philippines, Thailand, India, Rwanda, Peru, Iran, Mexico, Nepal, Turkey, China, Cameroon, Central African Republic, Chad, Dahomey, Gabon, Guinea, Ivory Coast, Malagasy Republic, Mali, Mauritania, Niger, Senegal, Togo, Upper Volta
J. Ghana, Algeria, Tunisia, Morocco, Congo (Brazzaville), Colombia, Greece, Spain, Laos, Viet-Nam, Israel, Yugoslavia, Paraguay, Argentina, Chile, Congo (Democratic Republic of), Uruguay, Bolivia, Afghanistan, Brazil, Indonesia, Korea

Source: Margaret G. de Vries, 'Exchange Depreciation in Developing Countries', *IMF Staff Papers* (November 1968), p. 562.

attempted recently in India, South Korea, Colombia and elsewhere under I.B.R.D. and U.S.A.I.D. auspices.

Unfortunately, however, as of now enough analytical examination of these cases has not become available. None the less a few pertinent points can be made which seem critical to the question of devising an optimal and feasible transition to a freer trade regime:

(1) In so far as devaluation is part of the package, cross-sectional analysis as also detailed examination of individual devaluations in L.D.C.s suggest that a devaluation is best undertaken after a good

TABLE 10.5

EXTENT OF EXCHANGE DEPRECIATION, 1948–67,
SHOWN IN ARITHMETIC MEANS[1]
(in per cent)

Country Grouping	Unweighted Means	Weighted Means[2]
All countries	47·8	22·8
More developed countries	30·1	15·0
Less developed countries:		
Africa	55·6	49·4
Asia	59·4	46·2
Europe	70·6	77·0
Latin America	43·0	60·9
Middle East	40·6	37·1

[1] Means were calculated from individual country data rather
than from grouped data.
[2] Weighted by share in aggregate exports in 1966.
Source: Margaret G. de Vries, *op. cit.*, p. 565.

TABLE 10.6

RATIOS BETWEEN PURCHASING POWER PARITY RATES
AND ACTUAL EXCHANGE RATES: 1967 ON BASE 1948,
AVERAGED BY REGIONS; AND 1967 ON BASE 1955,
AVERAGED BY REGIONS

Country Grouping	Number of Countries in Group	Country Identifica-tion[1]	Average Ratio (× 100) (1948 Base)	Average Ratio (× 100) (1955 Base)
More developed countries	20	A	96·9	106·8
Less developed countries:				
Africa	5	B	80·9	97·5
Asia	9	C	67·9	93·2
Europe	5	D	69·0	95·9
Latin America	20	E	88·3	83·3
Middle East	5	F	45·1	95·8

[1] The letter symbols stand for the following countries:
A. Australia, Austria, Belgium, Canada, Denmark, Finland, France, Germany,
   Iceland, Ireland, Italy, Japan, Luxembourg, Netherlands, New Zealand, Norway,
   South Africa, Sweden, Switzerland, United Kingdom
B. Ghana, Morocco, Nigeria, Sudan, Tunisia
C. Ceylon, China, India, Korea, Malaysia, Pakistan, Philippines, Thailand, Viet-
   Nam
D. Greece, Portugal, Spain, Turkey, Yugoslavia
E. Argentina, Bolivia, Brazil, Chile, Colombia, Costa Rica, Dominican Republic,
   Ecuador, El Salvador, Guatemala, Haiti, Honduras, Jamaica, Mexico, Nicaragua,
   Panama, Paraguay, Peru, Uruguay, Venezuela
F. Iran, Iraq, Israel, Syrian Arab Republic, United Arab Republic

Source: Margaret G. de Vries, *op. cit.*, pp. 568, 570.

harvest. This is because a bad harvest will mean *both* a general price increase and, since most L.D.C. exports still tend to be agricultural and agriculture-based manufactures, that the export performance is likely to decelerate – both of these phenomena being exogenous to the devaluation. But *post hoc ergo propter hoc* is quite common, and devaluations are condemned for what follows rather than for what they have led to.

(2) Furthermore, formal devaluations frequently *replace* inefficient, *de facto* devaluations which have already taken place *via* the imposition of import duties and the grant of export subsidies. In Table 10.7, we

TABLE 10.7

NOMINAL AND EFFECTIVE CURRENCY DEVALUATION

Country	Time of Devaluation	Nominal Devaluation[a]	Effective Devaluation	
			Exports	Imports
			(per cent change in dollars per unit of local currency)	
Argentina	Jan. 1959	66	63	61
Brazil	Sept. 1964	66[b]	65[b]	61[b]
Canada	June 1961–May 1962	5	5	10[c]
Colombia	Nov. 1962	26	13	23
Colombia	Sept. 1965	33	6	25
Costa Rica	Sept. 1961	15	14	6
Ecuador	July 1961	17	10	16
Greece	April 1953	50	31	41
Iceland	Feb. 1960	57	54	41
Iceland	June 1961	12	12[d]	11[d]
India	June 1966	37	n.a.	27[c]
Israel	Feb. 1962	40	12[c]	26[c]
Korea	Feb. 1960	25	29	34
Korea	Feb. 1961	50	35	36
Korea	May 1964	49	44	50
Mexico	April 1954	31	28	31
Morocco	Oct. 1959	17	17	12[c]
Pakistan	July 1955	30	28	28
Peru	Jan. 1959–Apr. 1959	31	31	31
Philippines	Jan. 1962	40	14	16
Philippines	Nov. 1965	10	10	10
Spain	July 1959	30	24[d]	26[d]
Tunisia	Sept. 1964	20	20	17
Turkey	Aug. 1958	56	39[d]	

[a] Parity or principal import rate.
[b] During calendar year 1964.
[c] Includes known changes in import duties and export subsidies.
[d] Effective devaluation calculated for goods and services; the remainder for merchandise only.

Source: Richard N. Cooper, 'Currency Devaluation in Developing Countries: A Cross-Sectional Assessment', *Economic Growth Center Discussion Paper No. 72*, (Yale University, July 1969).

K

have data on several recent L.D.C. devaluations, put together by Richard Cooper, which underline this fact. The result is that, as export incentives and import duties are *reduced* with the change in the parity, the net or effective devaluation is *smaller* than the gross or nominal devaluation. In the 1966 Indian case, for example, the formal devaluation implied that a unit dollar worth of exports would earn 57·5 per cent more Indian rupees; but when allowance is made for the simultaneous removal of several export subsidies and the imposition of countervailing export duties on primary exports, the figure changes to 17·5 per cent. And yet the devaluation was judged primarily in terms of the 57·5 per cent change: the lack of dramatic improvement in export performance being contrasted with the 'largeness' of the (formal) devaluation! Public opinion needs therefore to be educated on the difference between gross and net devaluations (as was singularly not done in the Indian case).

(3) The Indian case also highlights the tricky nature of aid diplomacy in introducing such policy packages. In a very real sense, the donor countries, under I.B.R.D. consortium auspices, forced the package deal upon a hesitant Indian government. The result was a practically unanimous political reaction of resentment in the country: the Right, the centrists and the Left were united in their condemnation of the devaluation on this ground! The moral seems to be that, if a politically difficult decision has to be made, it is best not forced on the L.D.C. government, as such arm-twisting tactics will only compound the political difficulties.

(4) The role of external credits in a liberalisation package is also somewhat more complex than has often been supposed. These credits are often thought of as methods of achieving a simultaneous relaxation of import controls instead of awaiting the impact of the devaluation on export earnings; and, in case of excess capacity in industry, it is believed that an increased availability of raw materials will also accelerate export performance.

On the other hand, it is possible that they may be disruptive in the sense of bringing about a recession: a phenomenon which has been observed in some countries to follow after a devaluation. This could happen quite naturally for example if more imports lead to greater competitiveness in the import-competing industries and hence to a deceleration in their investment plans whereas export industries, asymmetrically expecting that the devaluation might soon be neutralised by price increases, may not be accelerating *their* investment plans. The role of expectations and time lags is clearly critical in evaluating this type of problem; again, however, we know little that is systematic on it yet.

In general, therefore, the problem of a transition to a more flexible and liberalised trade and payments regime is a complex one.[1] But it is critical, as the success of L.D.C.s in getting out of their current framework of trade and exchange rate policies will greatly influence the success, in turn, of their developmental efforts.

[1] Several other complexities have been discussed elsewhere by Anne Krueger and myself in an N.B.E.R. document (1970) which provides the analytical framework for guiding twelve L.D.C. studies, to be directed by them, of the cost of exchange control regimes and of their attempts at liberalisation: Brazil, Ceylon, Chile, Colombia, Egypt, Ghana, India, Israel, Pakistan, Philippines, South Korea and Turkey.

11   Some Theoretical Notes on the Trade-Growth Nexus

Ronald Findlay
COLUMBIA UNIVERSITY

I. INTRODUCTORY

The mutual inter-relationships of trade and growth have been perceived by economists from the earliest days of the development of the subject. Adam Smith's 'productivity' and 'vent for surplus' theories of the interaction between trade and growth have been revived recently by Hla Myint, and perhaps the current interest in Cambridge growth theory will draw attention away from the static trade model of Ricardo's *Principles* and towards the fascinating link between trade, income distribution and growth that he explores in his earlier *Essay on the Influence of a Low Price of Corn on the Profits of Stock*. Marshall's view that the causes of economic development are to be sought in the theory of international trade, and D. H. Robertson's famous phrase about trade being an 'engine of growth', show the awareness of the relation by neo-classical writers, although it must be said that the experience of the 20th century points more in the direction of growth being an 'engine of trade' rather than the reverse.

Since the Second World War the emergence of the newly independent developing countries has created an enormously wide range of interest in problems of trade and development. Export instability, external debt burdens, commodity agreements, direct foreign investment and trade preferences are only some of the issues that have come under extensive discussion in this field, and the literature on each of these topics itself is already large and growing exponentially. Obviously, it would be quite fruitless to attempt to say something about all of these issues. Instead I shall attempt to consider just some of what I consider to be the more basic theoretical problems of the trade-growth nexus.

In the next section the focus is on the relationships between the rate of growth of exports and the rate of growth of income. This leads to a discussion of the so-called 'two-gap' theory in the next section. The final section considers some of the influential and controversial views of Dr. Raul Prebisch on the problems of trade and development.

II. THE RELATIONSHIPS BETWEEN THE RATE OF GROWTH OF EXPORTS AND THE RATE GROWTH OF INCOME

It is perhaps most convenient to begin our discussion of the relations between growth and trade by considering the simplest possible growth model, the celebrated construction of Harrod and Domar, as extended to the open economy [1]. Starting with the familiar Keynesian equation connecting investment, exports, savings and imports we have

$$I + X = S + M$$

If it is assumed that savings and imports are proportional to income, that exports grow exogenously at the rate x and that income is proportional to the stock of capital, the Keynesian relation becomes a differential equation in K, as shown below:

$$\frac{dK}{dt} = (s + m) bK - X_0 \exp(xt)$$

where s, m and b are the marginal propensities to save and import and the output-capital ratio respectively. The solution of this equation gives us the stock of capital and hence the flow of income, at any time t in the future.

$$K(t) = \left(K_0 - \frac{X_0}{(s+m)b - x}\right) \exp[(s+m)bt] + \frac{X_0}{(s+m)b - x}\exp(xt)$$

where K_0 is the intitial stock of capital and X_0 the initial export level.

This equation requires some interpretation. What it shows is that the capital stock can be divided into two parts, each of which grows at a different rate. One of these parts, which we shall call K_x, is that part of the capital stock which produces the output directly and indirectly used for the supply of exports. The total output produced by K_x will be bK_x but not all of this will be available for export. An amount cbK_x has to be deducted as consumption of domestic goods corresponding to the level of income bK_x. Then an amount xK_x has to be set aside as investment to provide for the growth of exports at the rate x. We therefore have the relation

$$X_0 = bK_x - cbK_x - xK_x = [(1-c)b - x] K_x$$

Since $\quad (1 - c) = (s + m)$

we have $\quad K_x = \dfrac{X_0}{(s+m)b - x}$

which is the co-efficient of the second exponential term in the solution of the differential equation. The co-efficient of the first term is the residual capital stock, which provides investment and the associated induced domestic consumption. The rate of growth of this residual is $(s + m) b$ or $(1 - c) b$, that is to say the product of the 're-investment ratio' and the output-capital ratio. The overall growth rate thus lies in between this rate and x, the rate of growth of exports. The model, as we have interpreted it, requires that $(s + m) b$ be greater than x. If this inequality is reversed the model gives the absurd result that output will eventually become negative.

Subject to this restriction, it is easily seen that an increase in the growth rate of exports will reduce the growth rate of the system as a whole. A rise in x will raise K_x, and therefore lower $K_0 - K_x$, at any point of time, and since the latter grows faster at any future time the total capital stock will be less. This result can also be checked by differentiating the expression for the capital stock with respect to x, for any fixed value of t. Similarly, a rise in the propensity to import will *raise* the growth rate of the system, for any fixed value of s, since this is equivalent to a reduction in c, the propensity to consume domestic output, which means that K_x will be reduced and $K_0 - K_x$ increased as well as the growth rate of the latter component of the capital stock raised permanently since the 're-investment ratio' is increased. An increase in s, with m constant, will also obviously have the same effect of raising the rate of growth of the economy and the level of capital and income at any time in the future.

The effect of changes in x and m on the growth rate, however, is somewhat paradoxical in view of the widespread belief that the growth of developing countries has been restricted by too low a growth rate of exports and too high a propensity to import. Kindleberger, for example, in considering alternative simple models for the explanation of trade growth interactions in Britain and France from 1850 to 1913, says of one of his cases that 'trade is tied in with a Harrod-Domar growth model, and more trade means more growth' [1]. As we have seen, only half of this statement is formally correct and it would appear not to be the half that Kindleberger really meant, namely that more exports means more growth.

The paradox disappears, however, as soon as some of the crucial assumptions of the model considered above are brought out. These are that investment has no imported component and that there is a perfectly elastic supply of international credit, with balance of payments deficits or surpluses capable of being accumulated indefinitely. Since in actual fact a high proportion of investment costs in developing countries is for imported capital equipment and foreign exchanges credits are scarce, the Harrod-Domar model, when extended to the open economy in the fashion described above, does not capture what seems to be to many the essence of the problem of trade and development.

An alternative but related simple model, however, can readily be constructed to accommodate this feature. We start with the relation

$$I = \alpha(X - M)$$

where α is the ratio of the total value of investment to its imported component, X is total exports and M is imports of consumer goods only. If we assume that the latter is proportional to income, and as before that income is proportional to the stock of capital, and that exports grow at a fixed rate, x, we have

$$\frac{dK}{dt} = \alpha(X_0 \exp(xt) - mbK)$$

The solution of this differential equation is easily obtained as:

$$K(t) = \frac{\alpha}{x + \alpha mb} X_0 \exp(xt) + \left(K_0 - \frac{\alpha X_0}{x + \alpha mb}\right) \exp(-\alpha mbt)$$

Since the second term diminishes with time we have the result that the capital stock and hence income grows eventually at the same rate as the exogenously determined growth rate of exports. This, in the simplest and crudest way, displays foreign trade as the 'engine of growth'.

Examination of this formula shows that the rate of saving does not explicitly appear anywhere. Since investment has a domestic component as well it is clear that the saving rate must accommodate itself to the growth rate determined by the formula, if the complementary domestic resources for investment are to be provided.[1] Since we are assuming balanced trade we must have

$$\frac{dK}{dt} = sbK(t)$$

from which it follows that

$$s = \frac{\alpha}{b} \left(\frac{X_0 \exp(xt)}{K(t)} - mb\right)$$

This shows that the rate of saving will change over time, as a function of the changing ratio of exports to capital stock, and hence of exports to national income. As time tends to infinity, however, we have from the solution of the differential equation that

$$\frac{X_0 \exp(xt)}{K(t)} = \frac{x + \alpha mb}{\alpha}$$

which means that in the limit

$$s = \frac{x}{b}$$

Recalling that the growth rate of national income is equal to the growth rate of exports in the limit, this corresponds to the familiar Harrod-Domar

[1] The author is greatly indebted to Sir John Hicks and Professor T. N. Srinivasan for drawing his attention to conceptual and algebraic errors in the treatment of this question in the original manuscript. The rest of this section of the paper has been completely rewritten as a result. They are not of course responsible in any way for whatever errors remain in the amended version, which they have not seen.

formula for the relation between the saving rate and growth rate of national income in a closed economy.

What we have now arrived at is essentially the 'two-gap' theory of Professor Hollis Chenery and his various associates [3]. For suppose that the *s* which we calculate in the manner described turns out to be too large for the economy to sustain. It is then prevented from taking advantage of the growth possibilities inherent in its foreign trade situation, and we have 'savings-limited' growth. On the other hand, if it can attain a larger *s* than the one required then we have 'foreign exchange-limited' growth, the answer to which is a higher *x* or a lower *m* or both. The next section attempts to examine the logical basis of the 'two-gap' theory a little further.

III. THE TWO-GAP THEORY

In its most rigid form the 'two-gap' theory assumes that there is a fixed ceiling on foreign exchange earnings, that imported and domestic goods are required in fixed proportions for investment and that there are either no imports of consumer goods or that these are held down to some irreducible minimum. These assumptions result in an increase in the rate of saving having no effect on the rate of growth beyond a certain point, determined by the domestic output requirements of an investment level set by the ceiling on the net foreign exchange available for imported investment inputs. Alteration of any of these assumptions makes it impossible to assert that it is the shortage of foreign exchange alone that constrains the rate of growth. For example, suppose that we retain all the assumptions mentioned above except that we allow for substitution in consumption between imported and domestic goods, in response to changes in the relative prices of these two classes of consumer goods. If, as seems reasonable, the import content of investment is higher than that of consumption at any relative price-ratio of domestic and imported goods, an increase in the rate of saving will raise the demand for imported goods. The total available is fixed but the rise in the relative price of imported goods will cause consumers to substitute away from imports, releasing more foreign exchange for investment and hence raise the rate of growth. Since the terms of trade shift adversely the capital-output ratio rises and the rise in the rate of growth will be less than proportional to the increase in the rate of saving, so that although increases in the rate of saving always have some effect on growth, the relation is subject to diminishing returns [4].

At a recent conference of the International Economic Association, Hla Myint strongly criticised what he called the 'UNCTAD approach' to the problems of trade and development, especially the 'foreign exchange gap' analysis which appears to be the logical basis of this approach [5]. One of his criticisms is the familiar one that countries such as Puerto Rico and

Hong Kong, as well as the more recent examples of Taiwan, South Korea and Thailand, have all been able to achieve remarkable rates of export growth. While these examples show that individual small countries can escape from the foreign exchange scarcity trap, it still may be true that for the developing world as a whole there are serious obstacles to export expansion on a large scale to finance capital goods imports. Myint also points out that historically the bulk of the total value of investment consists of domestic goods for such things as construction, agricultural capital, roads, and so on. Why cannot these useful activities be expanded, even if foreign exchange is scarce? The crux of the matter, however, is not the relative magnitudes of the two components of investment but their substitutability for each other. In its usual formulation the two-gap theory assumes either that substitution is not possible or that the productivity of domestic goods for investment is zero at the margin.

Once substitutability between domestic and imported components of investment is permitted it follows that there is a need to balance the allocation of domestic output between exports and investment. More exports means the possibility of more imported inputs for investment but also less domestic inputs for the same purpose. We have a typical optimising problem in marginal analysis that does not appear in either of the macro models considered in the first section, since each of them concentrates on an extreme case, no imported investment inputs in the Harrod–Domar case and no scarcity of domestic investment inputs in the 'foreign exchange gap' case.

The nature of the problem and the solution in the case of substitutability can be clearly brought out by the following simple model. Suppose that domestic output can be used for investment, consumption or export. The level of domestic output is a function of labour and the stocks of two types of capital, domestic and imported. For simplicity it is assumed that there are no imports of consumer goods. If the input of labour is held constant we can draw a family of isoquants each showing alternative combinations of imported and domestic capital that can produce the same level of domestic output.

In Fig. 11.1 the axes measure the stocks of domestic and imported capital equipment, OA being the existing amount of the former and OB of the latter. These inputs of the two types of capital and the fixed labour input determine the current level of domestic output. Deducting the fixed amount that goes for consumption the surplus is available for use either as exports in exchange for imported capital or directly for domestic capital. If all of the surplus domestic output is added to the domestic capital stock this will increase by the amount $O'A'$. If all of it is exported in exchange for imported capital equipment the stock of this will increase by the amount $O'B'$. The line $A'B'$ shows the alternative combinations of the two types of investment that are open to the economy, on the assumption that the marginal cost of imported capital equipment is increasing. With fixed terms of trade $A'B'$ would be linear instead of concave to the origin.

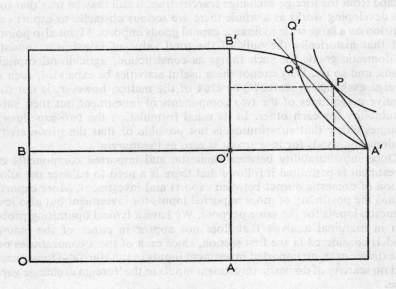

FIG. 11.1 Domestic capital

The optimal 'mix' of investment between imported and domestic components is determined by the point P, where the curve $A'B'$ is tangential to the highest attainable domestic output isoquant. P will obviously be superior to either one of the extreme points A' and B', which correspond to maximisation of domestic investment and exports (for import of foreign capital equipment) respectively. It is of course possible that for particular shapes of the $A'B'$ curve and the isoquants a 'corner solution' at either extreme may occur. In general export optimisation and export maximisation will not coincide. How significant a growth of domestic output can be achieved as a result of following the optimal allocation policy depends upon the terms on which foreign capital equipment can be obtained in exchange for exports, which determines the position of $A'B'$, and on the efficiency with which both types of capital equipment and labour are used, which determines the output levels on the isoquants for inputs. The 'UNCTAD approach' to development can be conceived of as trying to push out $A'B'$ while the neo-classical 'efficiency approach' tends to take $A'B'$ as given and to concentrate on selecting the best point on it, and also on trying to get the most output out of the optimally selected inputs.

Import substitution for capital goods has been advocated in proposals for schemas of Latin American economic integration. Although serving regional instead of national markets and hence taking advantage of economies of scale such schemas of protection will, at least initially, have unfavourable effects on growth. In terms of the diagram A' B' will be shifted inwards, since the transformation into capital goods of the previously imported type will be less efficient.

If capital goods are imported under conditions of increasing costs it is readily seen, however, that free trade will not give the optimum solution. The curve A' Q Q' in Fig. 11.1 shows the combination of imported and domestic capital formation that will be selected at any given price-ratio of the two types of goods, which is equal to the terms of trade. Free trade equilibrium will take place at Q which is inferior to the optimum point P. For P to be attained a suitable 'optimum tariff' will have to be imposed [6].

IV. THE ARGUMENTS OF DR. PREBISCH

No discussion of the inter-relations of trade and development problems, however selective, can avoid consideration at some point of ideas associated with the name of Dr. Raul Prebisch. In spite of the voluminous literature on the 'Prebisch thesis' or, more correctly, the 'Prebisch theses', there has not yet emerged any consensus as to the correctness or otherwise of his views, or indeed even of what his views precisely are. One assertion in his early pamphlet on the economic development of Latin America, that there is a secular tendency for the terms of trade to turn against the developing countries, has apparently been refuted. His statement was based on early studies of U.K. experience which apparently showed the terms of trade improving. The inference that they must therefore have turned against the developing countries that traded with her has been questioned, since the fall in transport costs has made it possible for f.o.b. export prices to rise in the developing countries at the same time as c.i.f. import prices fell in the U.K. Later research by Kindleberger on Europe and Robert Lipsey on the United States has disclosed no evidence of a secular change in the terms of trade in either direction. These points have often been made by critics of Prebisch, but what is more interesting for our present purpose are the various theoretical arguments that he has advanced, not always very clearly or rigorously, on the links between technological progress, industrial protection in developing countries and the terms of trade.

Prebisch repeatedly asserts that the effects of technological progress are not symmetrical for the 'centre' and the 'periphery'. Improvements at the 'periphery' are transferred to the 'centre' in the form of lower prices for primary products, whereas the same is not true, or less true, for improvements occurring in the 'centre' itself. Two quite different reasons are advanced by Prebisch for this striking proposition. The first and much better known, in his famous ECLA pamphlet, was in terms of price and wage rigidity due to monopolistic market structure in the 'centre' as contrasted with flexibility of prices and wages in the primary producing sectors at the 'periphery'. No empirical evidence was offered and the logic of the argument is also not developed at all convincingly. In his *American Economic Review* article [7], however, Prebisch develops the proposition in terms of the single-factor, many-good Ricardian model expounded by Edgeworth, Graham and other writers in the mainstream of theoretical doctrine in the field of international trade.

In terms of relative labour productivities at the 'centre' and the 'periphery', primary products are at one end of the 'chain of comparative advantage' and manufactures at the other. Let there now be a reduction in labour input required per unit of some primary commodity exported by the 'periphery'. Its cost, and hence, under competitive conditions, its price must fall. Assume, however, that the price-elasticity of demand for any primary product is less than unity. The increase in demand is, therefore, insufficient to maintain the previous level of employment in the sector experiencing the increase in productivity. The resulting unemployment will reduce the wage-rate and hence prices all round, stimulating expansion of demand sufficient to absorb all the labour released. The greater the average degree of price-inelasticity of demand, however, the greater the drop in wages and prices, and hence the greater the deterioration in the terms of trade.

But there is another route to adjustment that needs to be explored. A fall in the wage-rate at the 'periphery' will normally shift the margin of comparative advantage in some industrial goods to the other side of the line and hence there is the possibility that prices on existing exports need not have to fall appreciably in order to absorb the labour released, which is taken up by production of the formerly imported industrial goods. Prebisch asserts, however, that labour productivity at the 'periphery' in these goods is relatively so low that it takes sharp reduction in the wage-rate for the shift to occur, so that there is no escape from the adverse movement of the terms of trade. In the case of technical progress at the 'centre' price-elasticity of demand for its export commodities is high so that wages need not fall, or at least not appreciably, so that there is no significant adverse effect on the terms of trade. Furthermore, if labour productivity relative to wages is quite high, even for primary products that are normally imported, a slight decline in the wage-rate can shift some primary commodities over the line so that the terms of trade are protected by this mechanism also.

The same model can also be applied to the case of continuous increase in labour force and productivity in the two regions. Growth at the same rate will result in balance of payments deficit for the 'periphery' since the income-elasticity of demand for imports is assumed to be higher for industrial than for primary imports. This induces a fall in money wages that does not lead to switching of imports to exports because of the 'wide technological disparities', i.e. very low relative labour productivity of the 'periphery' in industrial goods. The kind of adjustment that can take place for balance of payments disequilibrium between two industrial areas, such as Europe and America, by reversal in the direction of trade for marginal commodities, is, therefore, not possible and decline in the terms of trade brought about by wage reduction or exchange depreciation is the only solution.

The policy conclusion drawn by Prebisch from his analysis of the asymmetrical effects of technical progress at the 'centre' and the 'periphery' is not that technical progress should be held back in the export sector of the latter region but that there should be a deliberate policy of industrialisation to complement this process. Industrialisation for him does not mean merely the establishment of high-cost factories, as many of his critics seem to assume, but a policy of raising industrial productivity which, in addition to bringing direct gains, will counteract the unfavourable effect on the terms of trade of technical progress in primary products. Since at the outset industrial costs will be high the 'infant industry' argument may also be involved, but it is important to realise that Prebisch sees this problem in a wider dynamic context than the traditional Mill-Bastable case.

As we have seen, Prebisch formulates his model of technical progress and the terms of trade in terms of the Ricardian model with many commodities. The same broad conclusions could be derived, perhaps more elegantly, from the analysis of factor accumulation and technical change in the context of the neo-classical two-sector, two-factor model undertaken in recent years by Rybczynski, Johnson, Corden, Bhagwati, Findlay and Grubert and other authors.

Prebisch also has a further argument for protection, to which he even devotes a diagram, which turns out on closer examination to be a special case of the familiar 'optimum tariff' argument, but applied to the use of incremental rather than total resources. This argument for tariffs is of course accepted by all writers on the subject as a valid exception to the general case for free trade.

REFERENCES

[1] H. G. Johnson, *International Trade and Economic Growth* (1957), Chapter V.
[2] C. P. Kindleberger, 'Foreign Trade and Economic Growth: Lessons from Britain and France, 1850 to 1913', *Economic History Review*, Vol. XIV, No. 2 (1961).

[3] H. B. Chenery and A. Strout, 'Foreign Assistance and Economic Development', *American Economic Review* (September 1966) and R. McKinnon, 'Foreign Exchange Constraints in Economic Development and Efficient Aid Allocation', *Economic Journal* (June 1964).

[4] R. Findlay, 'The "Foreign Exchange Gap" and Growth in Developing Economies' forthcoming in *Essays in Honor of C. P. Kindleberger* (1970).

[5] Hla Myint, 'International Trade and the Developing Countries' in P. A. Samuelson (ed.) *International Economic Relations* (1969).

[6] For a more detailed analysis see R. Findlay, 'Efficient Accumulation, International Trade and the Optimum Tariff', *Oxford Economic Papers* (July 1968).

[7] R. Prebisch, 'Commercial Policy in the Underdeveloped Countries', *American Economic Review* (May 1959).

Discussion of Papers by
Jagdish Bhagwati and Ronald Findlay

Professor Linder introduced the discussion, saying that he hoped he might be able to do justice to what was an interesting and fine paper. The introduction to the paper covered old ground, but Professor Bhagwati went on to deal with the danger of potential obstacles, including the risk of increasing protectionism against the exports of underdeveloped countries. It would be interesting to see whether any American participants would be prepared to comment on the position over protectionism from the United States at the moment. Trade restrictions were interesting because they represented a non-zero-sum game. But some, like commodity agreements, represented aid rather than trade.

Underdeveloped countries competed with industries in 'poor areas' of developed countries, said Bhagwati. But was this just an unhappy accident? We needed an explanation of whether it would continue. There might be a good deal to say about this, and one could argue that developed countries would always be competing with the industries of underdeveloped countries whose products had low income elasticity. Underdeveloped countries were likely to break into industries with low technology and with units that found it difficult to move out into other activities. Perhaps the underdeveloped countries should concentrate on a narrow production spectrum though this might lead to problems in the trade policies of developed countries.

On policy measures, Professor Bhagwati suggested that we should be interested in labour-market policies in developed countries. These were good not only for developed countries but in bringing about more liberal trade policies. Professor Bhagwati further suggested that there might be systems of fines for countries which broke the GATT rules, but Professor Linder wondered whether any international association of this kind could function so smoothly as to be able to impose fines.

Professor Bhagwati discussed the role of aid. He said that there was increased tying and, through this, a reduced grant element. But the willingness to give aid was a function of tying, and tying stopped a good deal of intra-trade. This might be an important disadvantage, but aid represented a transfer of resources, which must be allowed to leave developed countries. So he wondered whether the tying of aid really could stop net intra-trade. The discussion of research into synthetics was dubious because one could make the same point about all research. Why should one concentrate particularly on synthetics? Could one, anyway, divert this research into more constructive fields?

On underdeveloped countries, Professor Bhagwati said that the degree of import substitution had now gone too far, merely making economic performance worse. The pattern of import substitution had led to plants and industries that were both too small. On customs unions, perhaps Professor Bhagwati could have said more – at the expense of his argument on domestic resource costs.

There was an interesting point on licences for raw material imports. If these were given to instal capacity, this gave an incentive to firms to increase capacity, whether or not it was needed. At the same time Professor Bhagwati gave a short discussion of technical inefficiency and the possible negative effects on savings.

On protection, Professor Bhagwati wanted visible protection (by tariffs rather than quotas) of limited degree and for a limited time. One could argue that this was an easy recommendation. But how could one decide on the optimum degree of trade interference? In the early part of the paper there seemed to be uncertainty over how to handle the two-gap theory. Professor Bhagwati took what was perhaps the eclectic position, that a foreign exchange bottleneck might provide a specific case for trade policy. Professor Linder did not agree. A foreign exchange gap meant that one could not have both external and internal equilibrium simultaneously. On the other hand, if Professor Bhagwati simply accepted ordinary tariff theory, there was none the less no discussion of how to determine whether actual trade restrictions were too severe or not. He gave evidence that there might be negative value added in these circumstances but did not say what was acceptable and what was unacceptable interference.

Perhaps we needed a political theory on why one could have too much import substitution? How could one get away from it? There was good reason why it might be attractive to politicians to intervene too much, because it showed their community that they were active. If one accepted this kind of risk, one ought to think more about what kinds of rules politicians should be given when deciding whether to intervene. If one accepted that there were strong arguments for protection, one had to tell the politicians to interfere. However, if there was a weak case for protection, economists were to be blamed for providing a list of protectionist arguments which proved difficult for politicians to handle.

Professor Vernon said that the paper opened the relevant issues in a constructive way and he hoped he would not be misunderstood. However, he would like to suggest that developed countries had made enormous efforts to reduce their import barriers. Professor Bhagwati gave a description of these efforts which was historically distorted. It was certainly useful to belabour developed countries to go further, but one ought to look at the facts first. In particular one should remember that it was a normal part of the political struggle in the United States, most of the time, to be fighting to stop an increase in protection. There were times when import restrictions were being reduced, but these were very brief. Most of the time there was a great deal of opposition to such efforts. One therefore had short bursts of trade liberalisation, followed by long periods of pressure for protection. Even so, tariffs now were only one-third to one-half of what they had been in 1948, and the fall in effective tariff rates was not much different. Contrary to what Professor Bhagwati's paper said, the internal adjustment process in the United States was exceedingly effective, and the shoe and textile industries had changed their locations drastically in the last two decades. The American capacity to adjust was therefore much bigger than the paper indicated. Moreover, Professor Bhagwati used historical trade data to estimate the effect of the incremental trade to be hoped for in L.D.C.s. Where one did get expansion in these countries, the advantages were considerable.

Professor Bhagwati accepted Harry Johnson's estimates of losses in export earning for L.D.C.s but Professor Vernon suggested that there were two critical sets of figures here. The first were those for agricultural production; the second, those for American petrol quotas. Petrol quotas were calculated on market prices – but these were a basic part of a complicated oligopoly structure that kept oil prices up. Free market oil prices would be much lower now, despite shortages of petroleum, if it were not for these oligopoly arrangements. Something similar was true of cotton. The Mexican government would be upset if the United States ended controls over cotton. Since Mexican cotton competed with cotton exported from the United States at high prices, Mexico did very well. Professor Vernon thought it behoved any man of good will to reduce restrictions on trade. But it still behoved him to know whether history was with or against him.

On the usefulness of research and development in L.D.C.s, there was confusion in the paper between research and development carried out *in* underdeveloped countries and research and development intended *for the benefit* of these countries. The second could be undertaken anywhere in the world. For example, research on small oil refineries in developed countries had provided benefits for underdeveloped countries. Similarly, chemical plants for the U.S.A. might be designed in Bombay because it was cheaper. Research and development for underdeveloped countries taking place in these countries was no doubt best; however the paper should still have dealt with the two types separately.

Professor Bhagwati said that Professor Vernon had relied excessively on a casual reading of his paper. The history of reduced protectionism in the U.S.A. (and elsewhere) in the last two decades was familiar to everyone, but it did not mean that there was no danger of reversal now. This was what he had written about. Politics and ideology, as distinct from cold facts, were being introduced by Professor Vernon himself, in seeking to convince those present of the great benefits conferred by the U.S.A. on the world outside. His own paper had focussed on the changes in policies of both the L.D.C.s and the D.C.s where they conflicted with the requirements of rapid growth in the L.D.C.s.

Professor Okyar spoke about excessive protectionism in underdeveloped countries. He said that the paper brought out the problems of excessive import substitution during the last two decades in L.D.C.s. He agreed that the effect was to reduce their rates of growth so that one needed changes in policies. What were the underlying causes of these policies?

Professor Bhagwati dealt only with economic considerations. If, following him, we accepted the assumption that economic considerations had been the main influence behind the policies of the L.D.C.s, we should add to his correct remark about over-optimistic export predictions. The fact was that there had been under-estimation in the past of the future import needs of L.D.C.s by their governments and planning agencies. Professor Okyar questioned the assumption that decision-making in the L.D.C.s had relied predominantly upon economic considerations.

Professor Bhagwati had mentioned the tendency towards autarchy but did not elaborate. Professor Okyar thought we should not always assume rational economic behaviour in explaining such tendencies. We ought to look at non-economic factors like the desire of governments to be active, or to create employment, as was manifested in the setting up of factories. We ought also to look at the desire to create a nationally-integrated industrial structure based on heavy industry, or to introduce modern technology and complex production. These ideas were often far from rational economic calculation, but prevailed all the same among both politicians and economists in underdeveloped countries.

They were often accepted as indispensable features of industrialisation. All this probably played a bigger part in decision-making and in the current difficulties of L.D.C.s than the miscalculation of likely export proceeds. If we were interested in discovering what lay behind the policies of L.D.C.s, such non-economic elements should certainly be explicitly recognised, as well as the purely economic considerations mentioned by Professor Bhagwati.

Professor Srinivasan spoke about the problems of tied aid. There was confusion in what Professor Linder had said. If we supposed that aid was being given to three underdeveloped countries, but the three as a whole bought goods from developed countries and could shuffle the resources bought from aid, then untied aid meant a bigger real impact from the same transfer of resources.

On the psychological and political aspects of import substitution, Professor Srinivasan said one could argue that the economic effects were not so important. However, even if import substitution was necessary, other reasons were still worth looking at to see if it was correctly carried out. Even if there were a shift away from economic to political factors, there would still have to be an evaluation of the cost of import substitution in economic terms.

Professor Patinkin raised some points of presentation and emphasis in the paper, all derived from Israeli experience. He thought there was too much of an implication in the paper that imports were bad and exports good. One must emphasise the importance of imports. In Israel imports and G.N.P. had increased together for twenty years, implying unitary income-elasticity of demand for imports. The gap had been closed by a higher rate of growth of exports. This, too, raised imports because Israeli exports had a high import content. He did not say that this experience of unitary income elasticity of demand for imports was universal, but one *should* look carefully at the role of imports in development.

On what Professor Linder had said, Professor Patinkin wondered whether the Bhagwati position was that restrictive policies to help domestic industry were always wrong? Or was it that they *had* been correct but now ought to be dispensed with? Or were they useless? He thought the view of the paper was very much to argue for second-best solutions, but that was not clear, yet in many cases it would be very difficult to measure what was too much and what too little.

Professor Patinkin said he wanted to make a technical point on the effect of exchange rates. At the end of the paper, Professor Bhagwati pointed out (on page 268) that formal devaluation was often less important than one might imagine at first sight. This looked like a criticism. However, he would suggest that Professor Bhagwati should be thankful. Despite formally fixed exchange rates, there was a great deal of *de facto* flexibility which was all to the good. What we often had in practice was a series of informal devaluations, tidied up later by formal devaluation.

Professor Yenal wanted to endorse what had been said about harmful effects of import substitution. Two points were important for Turkey. One effect of import substitution was in diverting entrepreneurial talent towards the domestic market. For example, up to 1960 the best managerial brains in Turkey had been in the import business because that was the most lucrative. In 1960 the move towards import substitution came as the result of pressure on the government, mainly from economists. Business opposed it. However, when they saw that imports represented a serious problem they put up plans for large assembly plants within weeks. The government, however, had been determined to divide this up into several small plants – so that there was small-scale activity and monopoly profits.

It was true that this eliminated the domination of the automotive industry by one or two firms, but a shortage of foreign exchange and components meant high prices and high profits. The rents thus earned were attributable to import substitution and were very big. Where the currency had been over-valued for years this effectively meant that exports were taxed and imports subsidised. The best talent would then not move into exporting. If one tried to correct the situation by devaluation, this would not help enough. Exporters in Turkey were peasants. One therefore had to try and motivate export-groups. Professor Yenal wanted to repeat the question that Professor Linder had asked. What was the optimum degree of protection for the productive activities of the developing countries? Economists in recent years had contributed quite a lot to the discussion of which *methods* of protection were more desirable. But no clear answer seemed to emerge from the discussions to the problem of the optimal *degree* of protection. Restrictive measures resulting from the trade gap had blurred the issue. If one could not give an answer, one was forced to advocate free trade. However, we had not yet seen what were the correct criteria for an optimal trade policy in underdeveloped countries.

Professor Scott wanted to discuss Professor Bhagwati's reference to technical research and the economics of raw materials for underdeveloped countries. Professor Bhagwati asked an odd question: What was the optimal way to use research and development resources for the world's welfare? He should rather ask what was an appropriate policy for the L.D.C.s, given that so many imports of developed countries were raw material imports. We should look at the raw material users to see whether they were engaged in raw-material oriented or market-oriented research.

We got raw-material-saving when the final user had no property right or interest in raw materials. On the other hand, when the user was trying to maximise the value of his raw material deposits, research was oriented that way. Many raw material firms were concerned with the price and quality of their product rather than the source of the raw material. This was certainly not the bias implied in Professor Bhagwati's paper.

Professor Scott cited various examples. The oil industry had been once oriented to trade and distribution. Now it wished to stay in this business and this had led it into prospecting for oil and finding markets via research. Another good example was the contemporary paper industry in countries which produced the raw materials. It wanted to satisfy more of the world's needs from wood, using adaptations of traditional paper-making techniques. In other countries, there was research into devising substitutes for paper. So we should learn a different lesson from Professor Bhagwati, namely that the reallocation of research expenditure was less important than an increase in competitiveness. Where research and development was directed towards the ownership of raw materials, one often found that these were now owned by the L.D.C. itself. Then the L.D.C., as landlord, should be trying to maximise the value of the resources to the government. Research should also be carried out, not only into the final uses of the product but into prospecting, etc. Recently, there had been economic research into whether prospecting should be undertaken by governments. This was still a very new subject.

Professor Ohlin said that we liked to think that most underdeveloped countries were labour-surplus countries. He wondered whether there was some hidden reference to it in Professor Bhagwati's paper which he did not understand. At the end of the paper, Professor Bhagwati did not suggest that this should affect trade policy. But surely it *was* a problem for trade policy?

Professor Ghai replied to Professor Vernon. He agreed that there had been a good deal of trade liberalisation in the post-war period, but its main effect had been to expand trade among developed countries. The present structure of trade restrictions in rich countries discriminated against developing countries, whether one looked at tariffs or non-tariff barriers. It was extraordinary that adjustment problems faced by rich countries were emphasised only when it came to questions of liberalisation of imports from developing countries. There had been massive trade liberalisation among developed countries through the E.E.C., EFTA and the Kennedy Round, and adjustment problems were successfully overcome. Only when it came to trade liberalisation on products from developing countries were the adjustment problems exaggerated.

Professor Ranis commented on the day's discussion up to this point. He wondered how big a reduction in import substitution was contemplated. Where did we stop and what did we know about the relative attractiveness of different combinations of measures? He agreed that there was no good conceptual framework for an answer, but we did have rules of thumb. Tariffs were better than quotas; tariffs with bans were worse than tariffs alone. Uniform tariffs were better than discriminatory ones. Tariffs which reduced over time were good. Professor Ranis suggested that Professor Bhagwati had over-emphasised the difference between import substitution in Latin America and in Asia. The distinction between tariffs and quantitative restrictions was overdrawn. There were many quantitative restrictions in Latin America.

Professor Ranis pointed out that one cost of import substitution was the concentration of activity in local private firms. But why did Professor Bhagwati suggest that innovation was more frequent in big firms? Medium and small firms would probably innovate more than big ones.

On research and development, it seemed that Professor Bhagwati would argue for stopping research in synthetics, especially for the benefit of the L.D.C.s. Since Professor Bhagwati wanted the market mechanism to work in underdeveloped countries without the use of quantitative restrictions, he could not logically want to discriminate against particular pieces of research and development in developed countries. We were not clever enough to do this through government and tax policies.

Dr. Little did not think that what Professor Ghai had said was quite true. We ought to compare the oil and coal industries. There had been an enormous amount of redeployment of labour from the coal industries, especially of the U.K., Belgium, France and Germany; indeed so much that even if the already rapid rate of growth of manufactured exports from underdeveloped countries doubled, no industry would suffer on the scale of coal. He did not say that there would be no trouble in the future, but he did wonder why we did better in contracting some industries than others.

He wanted to make a positive suggestion. Why was there no confrontation procedure on trade, as distinct from aid, in the O.E.C.D.? The reasons seemed to be institutional. There was a Trade Division and the D.A.C., both in the O.E.C.D., but little or no co-operation. Perhaps the round table should write to the O.E.C.D. to ask them to institute a confrontation procedure on trade restrictions.

On the trade policies of underdeveloped countries, Dr. Little said he wanted to disagree with Professor Linder that efficient production (whatever the foreign exchange rate) was not the best one could hope for. Efficient production meant efficient trade. Certainly, this implied protection so far as the optimal-tariff argument went and it might not be the only reason for special favours to industry. But why protection? There were many other ways of encouraging industry. What we needed was industrial promotion policies and not protection, because protection inhibited exports. We ought also to dismantle a lot of protection in developed countries.

Professor Johnson referred to page 256 of Professor Bhagwati's paper. There Professor Bhagwati said that one could introduce an optimal tariff only after a foreign exchange gap had emerged. He wanted to make it clear that the optimal tariff argument always applied, though the emergence of a foreign exchange gap certainly allowed a country to introduce the optimal tariff with less objection. He argued that this paper was not the place to attack effective protection theory, especially as domestic resource cost had deficiencies of its own.

On research and development by foreign firms, Professor Bhagwati had fallen into the fallacy of ignoring costs and returns. Expenditure on research and development was investment; it was not obvious that investment in discovering techniques adjusted to the factors available in underdeveloped countries would be profitable. Possibly the local market would not be profitable enough, even in the long run, to justify such investment.

As for whether we could identify the objectives of research and development with the countries where this was *done*, R. & D. was often part of a company's integrated operation. For example, Professor Johnson mentioned that a unit in Pakistan did a great deal of research and development on products to be sold in Europe. The *process* of research and development mattered much more than its location.

Dr. Corden replied to a point made by Professor Linder, namely, how far the two-gap theory provided a case for protectionism. If one agreed with the two-gap theory (which he did not) one would hold the view that it was impossible to transform savings into export income. If a country wanted to keep imports within the bounds set by export income, the free trade solution would be to use the exchange rate, to devalue appropriately.

But why could one not transform savings into export earnings? First, the elasticity of supply of exports might be zero. Second, the elasticity of demand for exports might be unity or less. If the elasticity of supply of exports was zero, then there would be an income bonus to the export sector resulting from devaluation without any increase in exports resulting. There would then be an income distribution argument for preferring a tariff. If the elasticity of demand were unity or less, one had the optimal tariff argument in another guise. But the problem of what was the optimal pattern of protection remained. If the only argument for tariffs was the two-gap one, the optimal tariff was probably a uniform tariff, subject to qualifications.

Dr. Mahbub ul Haq went back to the effect of tied aid in limiting trade. On page 254 of his paper, Professor Bhagwati had said that underdeveloped countries were excluded from a market worth $7 billion because of the tying of aid. Perhaps there was another dimension to this question. The imports of underdeveloped countries came from tied sources at a fairly high cost, while their output was sold in competitive markets. For instance, tied aid from the U.S. in the form of industrial and agricultural raw materials often meant that Pakistan paid about 75 per cent more than international prices. Pakistan's exports were then at a disadvantage in the markets of the developed world since they had been produced with high-priced raw materials. Again, projects became over-capitalised and this compounded the problem.

The Bhagwati paper gave a very perceptive synthesis of the literature on trade policies for underdeveloped countries and for the developed world. But was the emphasis correct from the policy point of view? One could decide whether or not one believed Professor Vernon on the brave new gestures that the Western world would make in reducing protectionism – gestures which so far at least were conspicuous by their invisibility. From a policy point of view the burden of adjustment had to be borne by underdeveloped countries themselves. It was fruitless to continue to argue who was more at fault in the growing protectionism in international trade. It would be more realistic to explore what could be done by more enlightened trade policies of underdeveloped countries. This was especially true if Sir Arthur Lewis was right that rapid development in the L.D.C.s did not depend on a rapid expansion of trade with the developed world.

A lot could be done to adjust the trade policies of underdeveloped countries. He cited the experience of Pakistan where exports were stagnant in 1960 and manufacturing exports constituted hardly 3 per cent of total exports. Through a number of devices, particularly the export bonus scheme, Pakistan had been able to manage a rate of increase of 7 per cent per annum in exports during the 1960s; the share of manufacturing goods had risen by now to 50 per cent because of a 20 per cent annual increase. And this happened despite the fact that Pakistan's exchange rate policy was not the best possible, though it constituted a major improvement over that of the 1950s. Dr. Haq concluded by suggesting that more emphasis in the discussion should be placed on what could be done through an adjustment in the trade policies of underdeveloped countries rather than on arguing over who was to blame for what had happened in the past.

Mr. Streeten suggested that one might perhaps pay more attention to the common interests that ran across the national boundaries of underdeveloped and developed countries. This would lead to a policy of paying more attention to the cross-alignments of interests, to resist producers' lobbies. Consumers were harder to organise than producers, though Consumer Councils should be encouraged not only in the interest of rich consumers but also in those of low-cost, poor producers. One should enlist the help of independent retail chains. For example, the Atlantic and Pacific Stores in the U.S.A. might use pressure for imports of low-cost Brazilian processed coffee; or Marks and Spencer to push for cheap cotton textile imports. In this way Marks and Spencer might do more for the poor, not only of England but of the world, than Marx and Engels.

Dr. Baranson returned to the question of who lost and who gained from trade liberalisation. In the United States it was evident that the more-educated and higher-income groups obtained greater benefit from trade liberalisation than did the less-adaptable low income groups. This had been dramatised for him when he went to Taiwan. Economists representing the American Electrical Workers' Union prepared testimony indicating the large numbers of low-income wage earners who lost jobs when U.S.-based plants were moved to Taiwan, Singapore and other off-shore locations. An aggressive labour mobility policy to find new jobs for displaced workers was one answer, but the simple fact in the United States was that social policy was lagging behind trade liberalisation. The U.S. Trade Adjustment Act of 1962 had attempted to move in this direction, drawing on certain aspects of Swedish labour market policy. The U.S. Trade Act was allowed to expire in 1967, having exerted very limited influence.

To move to a more constructive point, he thought we needed more organised discussion on what we should do to help the orderly transportation of industries, when increasing labour costs meant they would have to be phased out in developed countries anyway. In many cases agreements could be made to phase out production in developed countries with increasing wages, and move it to underdeveloped countries where wage levels gave a country a comparative advantage. The emphasis on textiles (in view of the quotas levied against them) neglected other industrial opportunities. One large American vehicle manufacturer now in Germany was not likely to expand its production facilities there any further; but it might do so in Spain.

This led to the basic implication in the Bhagwati paper. Dr. Baranson recalled the musical 'Stop the World I Want to Get Off'. There was some of this attitude in Professor Bhagwati's paper, which argued that research and trade policies should be adjusted to the obvious and built-in difficulties of underdeveloped countries. Dr. Baranson was more in agreement with Professor Linder, who argued that the basic difficulties lay in the underdeveloped countries – in their inability to transform and adapt. Perhaps one should emphasise the need to do this now.

Dr. Nurul Islam introduced the paper by Professor Findlay into the discussion. The paper dealt with three main aspects of the inter-relation between trade and growth. These were: first, the relationship between the growth of exports and income; second, the foreign exchange gap of developing countries; and third, the Prebisch hypothesis on the adverse movement in the terms of trade of developing countries.

To start with the first aspect, he assumed there was no import component of domestic investment. If there were a perfectly elastic supply of international credit, an increase in the rate of growth of exports then reduced the rate of growth of income. With these assumptions an increase in the rate of growth of exports reduced the rate of growth of domestic capital stock. The higher the rate of growth of exports, the larger was the rate of accumulation of foreign exchange reserves; alternatively, the larger was the rate of growth of imports of consumer goods – since capital goods were not imported. The rate of growth of the capital stock was a function of the rate of growth of supply and domestic capital goods only. By the same reasoning, the higher the propensity to import, the lower the propensity to consume domestic output and the higher the rate of domestic saving and capital accumulation. With these unusual assumptions, the rate of growth of the capital stock, and hence the rate of growth of income, was inversely related to the rate of growth of exports and positively related to the propensity to import.

Once these assumptions were removed, the effect of a change in the rate of growth of exports would depend on a number of factors. Some of these were the following: first, sources of growth in exports – whether an increase in demand or a rise in productivity in the export sector; second, movements in the terms of trade – an increase in exports associated with the rise in the terms of trade could cause a rise in real income and savings and in investment; third, the relative rate of return on the investment abroad of additional foreign exchange earnings as against the return on domestic investment undertaken with the help of imported capital goods; fourth, changes in domestic savings and investment which accompanied changes in exports; fifth, increases in exports or changes in the flow of investment from abroad in response to the changes in demand for exports or changes in the flow of labour from abroad to exploit opportunities for increased production in the export sector. This had happened in the 19th century in Australia and North America.

The familiar theory of the foreign exchange gap, on the other hand, reversed the relationship between exports and economic growth because the assumptions behind the 'gap' theory were very different. The rate of growth of exports was positively related to the rate of growth of income. In the usual discussions of the foreign exchange gap, it was assumed that:

(a) domestic and imported goods were required in fixed proportions for investment;

(b) the quantum of imported consumer goods was held down to an irreducible minimum;

(c) foreign exchange earnings could not be expanded by increasing exports.

Under these conditions, increases in domestic savings did not lead to increases in investment. The volume of capital goods imported was limited by the supply of foreign exchange.

When exports could be expanded, even though with worsening terms of trade, investment could be increased through increased domestic savings, even if domestic and imported capital goods were used in fixed proportions. Investment increased at a declining rate in response to given increases in savings and exports. On the other hand, if there were an absolute limitation on export expansion, investment could be increased through savings, if domestic capital goods could be substituted for imported ones. Usually the output of domestic capital goods could be augmented, at an increasing cost in terms of domestic resources.

Professor Findlay showed in his paper that once the suitability of domestic and imported capital goods was admitted, as well as the possibility of expanding export earnings even though with worsening terms of trade, the appropriate allocation of domestic output or saving between exports and domestic investment followed the well-known principles of optimum allocation of resources, subject to constraints. Of course, the allocation of output or savings between exports and domestic investment determined the appropriate combination of domestic and imported capital of goods. The constraints in this case were: (a) declining terms of trade between exports and import capital goods; (b) increasing marginal rates of substitution in production between domestic conconsumer goods and domestic capital goods; and (c) a diminishing marginal rate of substitution between domestic and imported capital goods in investment. Professor Findlay provided us with a very elegant exposition, and a very neat technique. What was important in this context was to emphasise that, as empirical work in recent years had demonstrated, none of the restraints was independent of the economic policies pursued by both developing and developed countries.

It was true that inflexibilities and rigidities were more important in the short run than in the long run. Substantial price changes might be necessary to bring about adequate adjustments in demand or production structures. Such changes in relative prices might be significantly out of line with long-run equilibrium prices, so that special measures might be required to deal with disequilibrium between short-run demand and supply.

Experience had shown that import intensities of investment, as well as possibilities for export expansion, were critically influenced by several things. Among these were the exchange rate and the fiscal policies of developing countries. The role that trade policy played in both developed and developing countries in manipulating or aggravating the foreign exchange gap had been discussed in the paper by Professor Bhagwati. The pricing of imports at less than their scarcity price under a regime of direct control and import licensing encouraged an increased import intensity of investment. Similarly policies which restricted exports in the interest of domestic consumption, as well as over-valued currencies, adversely affected foreign exchange earnings.

In addition, with an over-valued currency and a licensing policy which provided import capital goods to domestic manufacturing industry at the official exchange rate, import substitution in the capital-goods sector was discouraged. The policy encouraged the adoption of capital-intensive techniques and projects. What was more disturbing, it led to the under-utilisation of the capital stock. In the process developing countries became increasingly dependent on imported raw materials to feed their domestic industries and import needs tended to increase. After a time any restriction on imports of raw material or of intermediate goods in favour of larger imports of capital goods, aggravated the problem of the under-utilisation of the existing stock of capital. Yet the move towards larger imports of capital goods was necessary if the rate of investment were to be increased. All these problems reduced the rate of growth of income. The foreign exchange gap theories, with their emphasis on the inflexibility of production and demand structures in developing countries, had paid too little attention to the role of domestic policies in generating inflexibility.

The 'foreign exchange gap' model, with its concentration on the import of capital goods for physical investment, had tended to neglect the role of investment in human capital. For example, it had overlooked education, training and research and development. The development of skill was an important input for economic growth, but one which had a much lower import component than investment in physical capital.

What was more important, in its attempt to provide a rationale of foreign aid in terms of its role in filling the exchange gap, the theory might also have had the unintended result of reducing the efforts of poor countries to correct domestic distortions in cost/price structures.

Ideally, the 'gap' theorists would argue that the cushion which foreign aid provided should be used by any sensible recipient country to undertake suitable reforms in the domestic economy; to meet the adverse effects of short-term dislocations due to big changes in domestic policy; and to insure against the risks and uncertainties of economic policy. They had, indeed, contended that investment policy in the L.D.C.s should be devoted toward trade improvement – to efficient import substitution and export expansion.

Dr. Nurul Islam said that Professor Findlay then took up the divergent roles of technical progress in developed and developing countries. It created foreign exchange bottlenecks for the primary-producing, developing countries. The important differences between developed and developing countries were facts of life. First, the elasticity of export demand was higher in developing than in developed countries, so that a rise in productivity in the export sector caused a smaller fall in export prices than in a poor country. Hence the terms of trade moved much more adversely in poor than in rich countries. Moreover, rising productivity, being associated with a smaller fall in export prices and incomes in the export sector, led to smaller falls in wages in rich than in poor countries. Second, differences in productivity between the export and import-competing sectors was less in rich than in poor countries. So, again, falling wages shifted the comparative advantage in favour if import-competing sectors more significantly than in a poor country. This helped to restrain the fall in the terms of trade in rich countries.

Professor Findlay suggested that a rise in productivity in the primary export sector, accompanied by a fall in income due to instability of demand, resulted in unemployment. This was not necessarily true. All depended on the flexibility of wages and the extent to which any fall in wages might encourage the substitution of labour for capital.

In the light of this discussion, and in the context of the development of poor countries, the crucial question was how the L.D.C.s could make optimum use of the opportunities which international trade presented for encouraging economic growth. How, and in what ways, could the poor countries use trade as an engine of growth? This led immediately to various issues of trade policy in both developed and developing countries, which Professor Bhagwati had considered. However, it also led to the whole range of domestic policies which impinged on the optimum allocation of resources between import substitution and exporting.

Two issues of trade policy, which concerned both developing and developed countries, had not been considered in the paper. They were: first, the prospects and problems of preferential access to the markets of rich countries; and second, the scope for the liberalisation of trade among the L.D.C.s themselves. Undoubtedly these subjects had been discussed at length in recent years. Professor Lewis had gone on to suggest that the developed countries were not as important for the L.D.C.s as they had thought. One would like to take a view on where the international community now stood on all these issues.

The second set of issues which deserved analysis was concerned with the appropriate domestic policies for L.D.C.s. Which policies would help to bring about greater flexibility and production and demand? And which would allow the optimal exploitation of trade opportunities for development?

This led us to a whole range of questions about the best techniques or instruments for import substitution. Domestic fiscal policy, including credit or interest rates, probably had important implications for import intensity or the capital intensity of production in developing countries.

Professor Chenery said that he had found Professor Findlay's re-statement of the two-gap model useful. It was good to have the same conclusions reached in different ways. However he was not happy with the argument on page 276. This showed the difficulty of economic development theorists and international trade theorists in agreeing on conclusions. The two-gap phenomenon was not a theoretical necessity but it was something commonly met with. It should therefore be analysed as a tendency in many countries. It was not simply the result of misjudged foreign exchange rate policies. It was a result of the dynamics of growth. What we needed was to introduce lags in adjustment.

First, there was the nature of comparative advantage. This was much affected by scales of production. There was little comparative advantage in machine tools, steel or chemicals. However there was also a whole range of products (both consumer and intermediate) with big economies of scale. Demand was also highly income-elastic. An increased rate of growth for goods where one had a comparative advantage, and whose output was growing at 4–6 per cent, led to an increased rate of growth for things where one had *no* comparative advantage of up to 10 per cent. So one had the two-gap theory.

Whether foreign exchange was actually short depended on how policy responded. Could one devise a market system to avoid the problem? Professor Chenery suggested that countries needed to vary their export products in advance of the need for them. We had seen that underdeveloped countries typically overstated the likely future demand for exports. If one thought there was a low elasticity of demand for traditional exports how did one add an additional range? The export of light manufactured goods and import substitution did not go the whole way against comparative advantage. It was a question of striking a balance. However he did not agree with what Professor Findlay had said. He also wondered why Professor Findlay had concentrated on import substitution in capital goods. Import substitution certainly did not only occur with domestic capital goods. There could be new kinds of machinery or buildings and structures. Professor Chenery suggested that it was therefore a question of a balance between import substitution and exports. Savings were not relevant to a country's ability to make capital goods. And capital goods were no different from other goods. So the main disagreement was over narrowing exchange possibilities too much. No one said that the two-gap system *must* emerge. But it would if there were no plans to meet the problem. For example, if education was regarded as domestic capital goods, one had to remember that there was a ten-year lead-time here. At the aggregate level one could not say very much. The linear programming model of Professor Bruno rarely gave the two-gap result.

This was probably because there was enough substitutability within the model to avoid it. But if the way in which such a model gave predominance to the value of foreign exchange showed the importance of external capital, then this was a measure of the problem.

Professor Horvat noted that Professor Findlay said that if at the margin a country had one ton of cement, it could use it either in building an apartment or for export. Or it might use the export earnings for doing something else. We should look at which was likely to give the biggest increase in G.N.P. Professor Horvat was not sure that this case had general validity. For example, if saving was limited, Professor Findlay now had just one ton of cement because this was the assumption he had made. However if he had two tons of cement he could still do both things. This was a typical problem in a centrally-planned economy.

Professor Horvat set out a model of a centrally-planned economy. He began with the Harrod-Domar identity:

$$g = \frac{s}{k}$$

Here, g was the growth rate, s savings ratio and k the capital output ratio. It was said that k was a technical element and s a policy element. This was not true. k partly depended on what one did; k was an increasing function of savings. At some point the marginal efficiency of investment became negative. So one had optimal savings, related to the maximum rate of growth. However in Yugoslavia there had been a period when the marginal efficiency of investment was negative. So one could say that output was a function of capital and of the absorptive capacity of the economy. One now had to maximise the absorptive capacity of the economy.

Professor Horvat explained that in his view this depended on labour, know-how and the social organisation of the economy. In the long run imports were a function of exports. If one wanted to maximise exports, one had to maximise the absorptive capacity of the economy. He wondered why one took imports as the final bottleneck? In principle one could use any variable. There were several reasons. In particular there was little that the international community could do about labour, know-how and the organisation of the social economy. That was the business of the country itself. All the international community could do was to help trade possibilities, which was why imports were crucial.

Professor Fei said that Professor Findlay based his views on the structrue of national income. Exports either enabled one to buy imports or provided either consumer goods or savings. Investment was financed by savings plus the difference between imports and exports. In other words: investment plus exports = savings plus imports.

Professor Fei wanted to comment on Professor Findlay's three models. The first was a resource model. Exports were a drain on the economy, while imports supported it: exports were 'bad' for growth. The weakness of this model was that exports were seen as an end in themselves rather than as a means of obtaining imports.

This led to the second model. The important point was that in this Professor Findlay sub-divided imports into capital and investment goods, while exports (which were exogenous) could be either consumer or investment goods. Consumption was related to income, so that foreign exchange not used for the import of consumer goods could be used for the import of capital goods. So exports became a blessing, because they led to the ability to buy capital goods, with domestic capacity the key element. What lay behind all this was Professor Findlay's views of the technological gap.

In the second model savings were no longer a limitation because any savings needed were automatically available. It was a reasonable assumption that this would be true. Dividing imports into capital and investment goods was very important because it touched on import substitution. It meant that one could substitute imported capital goods for imported consumer goods, which was a problem in the early stages of development. Professor Findlay did not go into this. However if the model were extended to link imported capital to domestic capital the results would be fruitful. At the same time the static formula linking imported capital to domestic capital was unsatisfactory. Later in development there would be a more dynamic process.

The key assumption here was also that of the planning school, namely, that exports were exogenous. Professor Fei agreed that this was a very important assumption if one wanted quick results for planning. However, perhaps it ignored the important problems of growth and development. A feature of transitional growth was that one got rapid changes in productive potential and that this was reflected in international trade. It was a reason why countries like Taiwan and Korea altered the composition of their exports as the transition progressed. Perhaps one could move away from the assumption of a constant rate of growth.

Professor Srinivasan said that Professor Findlay's conclusions on the relationship between the growth of exports and that of the whole system was misleading. The growth rate depended on $(s+m)b$, which did not depend on the rate of growth of exports at all. What *was* true was that the level of income or capital stock was lower if exports increased. One then had an *asymptotic* rate of growth of the whole system equal to $(s+m)b$.

Professor Bhagwati noted that there seemed to have been something of a confrontation between economists from the underdeveloped and developed countries in the discussion. However, he had wanted to emphasise that policies in *both* L.D.C.s *and* D.C.s required amendment and had tried to focus on the main reasons why these changes were necessary and why they might be difficult to implement.

On specific points Professor Linder had raised a question about the relevance of foreign exchange bottlenecks to trade policy. Professor Johnson had also argued that the foreign exchange bottleneck idea was erroneously understood by him. But this was not so. A foreign exchange bottleneck, as understood in the literature, described a situation where savings could not be translated into investments because of difficulties in transformation: e.g. saved corn could not be turned into imported tractors because of an inelastic export demand for corn. The concept therefore *necessarily* implied monopoly power in trade. This being so there must necessarily be an optimal tariff for a welfare maximum in this situation. As for Professor Linder's question about the relevance of the bottleneck to the problem of internal and external balance, he could see no problem there: there was no reason why external balance could not be obtained despite a foreign-exchange bottleneck. All that the bottleneck implied was a 'technological' transformation situation: it was fully consistent with 'internal' and 'external' balance in the Meade sense.

On tied aid he thought Professor Srinivasan had already explained the point well. Permitting other L.D.C.s to tender for aid contracts, even though there were restricted account arrangements, meant that the constraint of buying from expensive sources was weakened, even if only slightly. The recent extension of this practice by the United States to enable the Latin American aid recipients to buy from within Latin America was therefore a step in the right direction.

On research and development, he had been amused by the reaction of many economists from the D.C.s. Admittedly research was motivated by different objectives. Professor Scott had implied that some of it was even 'prestige' expenditure which was cut as soon as expenditures had to be cut; some research was aimed at opening up new markets, and some at improving existing products. But one could not deny that some, and possibly a major fraction of the R. & D. expenditure, did disrupt primary product markets. This was true no matter what motivated the research, a question which underlay the Nurkse-Cairncross debate. It was clear enough that the questions raised in his paper about the welfare effects of such research were both valid and important. Participants should have addressed themselves to these instead of reacting somewhat emotionally to them.

As for his proposal to have compensation arrangements worked into the international institutional system, so that those excluded from a market by the imposition of quotas and/or tariffs should be compensated, it had been suggested that this was unrealistic. But he was not sure that this scepticism was legitimate. Compensation arrangements were already being implemented for industries hurt by imports; they had a long way to go but were not ruled out. One merely needed to extend the same principles to injury to exporters from import-prohibitions. In fact this was a better route to aiding the L.D.C.s than recent proposals (by Professor Johnson, for instance) that the injuries imposed by the D.C.s on the L.D.C.s through their trade policies be used to arouse a 'guilt complex' which should then be deployed to get more aid. In any case, revolutionary-sounding proposals had a funny way of getting down to earth when their inherent justice and reasonableness were accepted with passage of time.

As for Professor Johnson's complaint that his paper had dwelt too long on the problems of effective rates of protection and too little on the domestic-resource-cost measure, the sole reason was that he had used effective-rate calculations extensively in his argument. This required their limitations to be put into proper perspective. He agreed that the domestic-resource-cost approach raised largely similar difficulties, but it also had definite advantages.

As for the optimal method of intervention in trade policy, Professor Bhagwati said that a theory of government was necessary before economists could make useful prescriptions. Experience seemed to show that selectivity degenerated into tariff-setting by pressure groups whereas the economist had a quite different kind of selectivity in mind, for example of the optimal tariff variety. Hence he preferred uniform tariffs, although admittedly these were theoretically not the best. Similarly he was for low tariffs.

Finally Professor Bhagwati wished to emphasise that the criticisms he levelled against L.D.C.s policies did not imply that these L.D.C.s were stupid. Mistakes were inevitable in policy-making. At the same time it was useful to remember what would have happened if all L.D.C.s had concentrated on export promotion, following the prescriptions now being given to them, instead of indulging in import substitution. The round table today would then have been advocating import substitution to the L.D.C.s and talking about the dangers of excessive export promotion!

Professor Findlay said he wanted to clarify the motivation of the early part of his paper. He certainly did not *believe* in the first model, where an increase in exports led to less growth. He thought there was something strange here. The beginning of all growth models was the Harrod-Domar equation. In discussions of trade growth theory one would expect to begin again from these equations. In fact an early paper by Professor Johnson had taken this line. Since then it had not been used. All he had done in his paper was to go back to the Harrod-Domar equation to get Professor Johnson's result. This result was obtained because the equation reminded us that exports competed with investment for resources. So in the 1950s, when the emphasis was on investment, the Harrod-Domar model had been used.

Then foreign exchange constraints came in and we had a situation like that in the second model. But competition between exports and domestic investment was lost, and one now had to emphasise that growth required increased exports. The second model was the Chenery model and it showed that one could reverse the process. If trade had to be balanced, then the rate of growth of exports gave the rate of growth of income. As Professor Fei said, in this model savings always adjusted. But more exports meant more resources being taken from domestic investment, so that exports were a curse, but also a blessing in part one. The contradiction was reconciled in the diagram, using simple marginal reasoning to show that there could be an optimal balance between exports and investment. Both models were rather extreme. His own leanings were towards the model implicit in the diagram on page 276.

To Professor Srinivasan, Professor Findlay said it was true that the dominant term in the Harrod-Domar equation was $(s+m)b$. This was the rate of growth to which the system tended. However the result was that a growth of exports led to a fall in the rate of growth of income. Asymptotically, the growth rate was not interdependent. But one was living at only one point of time.

To Professor Horvat, Professor Findlay said that if one had two tons of cement the curve shifted. Nothing else changed. The economy had done the maximum amount of belt-tightening. But in what form? There was still a problem of choice and the issue in the diagram was not the volume of investment but its choice.

To Professor Fei, Professor Findlay said that he had explained the first model already. It did bring out a useful point. As for the static nature of the diagram, he did not apologise. If one could make a useful point this way why not do so? He was making the simple point that growth depended on a *choice* between exports and investment. Any dynamic model would require institutional adjustments of this kind as a necessary condition.

On the problem of 'sinking into the sea' the effect would be to shift the curve inwards, so that the diagram could explain this phenomenon too. So growth *was* affected. Underdeveloped countries could make for themselves the capital goods that they obtained from developed countries, but at great cost. Finally there was the limitation of the model to capital goods. This made no difference of principle. If we extended it to imported consumer goods, this simply reduced the rigidity of the two-gap model.

12 Bridging the Technological Gaps between Rich and Poor Countries

Jack Baranson

STAFF ECONOMIST, WORLD BANK[1]

I. INTRODUCTORY

Implicit in the technological gap between rich and poor countries is something more than acquisition of technical knowledge and the training of technical manpower. Implanted capabilities to manufacture industrial products and intermediate goods entail sustained relationships over extended periods of time between technology donors and recipient firms. It should be noted that problems and issues associated with the transfer of technology among industrialised countries are of a different order than transfers between industrially-advanced and newly industrialised countries, stemming from the much wider disparities in respective levels of technical knowledge and industrial capabilities.[2] A further distinction also needs to be drawn between an ability to utilise acquired technology, with little or no alteration, and research and engineering capabilities to develop indigenous technology or to adjust acquired technology to local needs and conditions.

This paper focusses upon the problem and issues arising from enterprise-to-enterprise transfer of industrial technology. International relationships between Japanese automotive vehicle and parts manufacturers in Japan and their manufacturing affiliates in Taiwan are taken as a case in point. The factors which contribute to the technological gap between Taiwan and Japan are typical of other L.D.C. cases and include (a) differences in respective stages of industrial development and manpower resources, (b) the sets of economic policies in force in each country, and (c) market strategies of Japanese firms, which in turn are strongly influenced by economic

---

[1] The author is a staff economist of the World Bank. This paper is an outgrowth of a research project on enterprise-to-enterprise relationships between international firms and their manufacturing affiliates in developing countries, undertaken by the World Bank in co-operation with UNITAR (United Nations Institute for Training and Research) under the direction of Walter Chudson. Material presented on Taiwan and Japan is based in part upon visits to those countries in March–April 1970. Opinions expressed are the author's alone and therefore should not be taken as necessarily representing the views of UNITAR or of the World Bank.

[2] See recent Report of the Panel on International Transfer of Technology to the U.S. Department of Commerce Technical Advisory Board on *Factors Affecting the International Transfer of Technology Among Developed Countries* (U.S. Government Printing Office, 1970).

L

policies in both countries. The intricacy of the technology transferred, the absorptive capabilities of recipient firms and the transfer capabilities and motivation of donor firms, are determining elements in the cost feasibility of transfer.[1]

These considerations of the so-called 'technological gap' are part of the larger developmental questions related to factor endowments and long-term comparative advantage. In the short term, acquired technology is combined with available skills and other factor endowments; but over time factor productivities and technology itself can be upgraded through investments in education, in research and in institution building. Industrial activities in the comparative-advantage range is, in part, a question of which segments of production can be carried out with available and manageable technology – given available levels of skills and industrial organisation. In its electronics industry production for export is limited to value added based upon its comparative advantage in highly productive, low-wage labour, which is employed in plants scaled to international markets and combined with imported skill and technology – some of which is embodied in equipment and parts. Over time production activities can be shifted into activities of emerging comparative advantage based upon emerging factor productivities and the enlarged capabilities of enterprises to utilise technology and trade internationally. The question of whether these structural changes are best achieved through free market mechanisms or through purposeful price distortions (tariffs, exchange manipulations or public investments in research) I leave to the trade and development theorists.[2]

II. REDUCING TECHNOLOGICAL GAPS TO MANAGEABLE PROPORTIONS

Developing countries now produce a rather impressive array of industrial goods ranging from simple consumer items to sophisticated engineering

---

[1] A study of the transfer of jet aircraft manufacturing techniques from the U.S. to Japan shows that the ability to absorb technology depends upon the intricacy of the particular component and the manufacturing experience of the parts manufacturer. The degree of self-sufficiency reached was based upon a realistic appraisal of time and resources needed to bridge the gap for each of the hundreds of materials and parts that went into the jet aircraft and its engine. See George Hall and Robert Johnson, 'Transfer of U.S. Aerospace Technology to Japan', paper presented at *Conference on Technology and Competition in International Trade*, sponsored by Universities – National Bureau Committee for Economic Research (New York, 11–12 October 1968).

[2] For an analysis of the relevant theory, see Harry G. Johnson, *Comparative Cost and Commercial Policy Theory for a Developing World Economy*, Wicksell Lectures 1968 (Stockholm: Almqvist and Wicksell, 1968). On the general characteristics of Taiwan's post-1945 industrial development and the transition from import substitution to export manufacturing, see Ken C. Y. Lin, 'Industrial Development and Changes in the Structure of Foreign Trade: The Experience of the Republic of China in Taiwan, 1946–66', *International Monetary Fund Staff Papers*, Vol. XV, No. 2 (July 1968), pp. 290–321.

products, and from the processing of basic materials to the final stages of fabrication. Technological transfer and absorption has been both extensive and rapid in the past two decades among a dozen or more of the newly industrialising states. But this does not necessarily mean that the industrialisation has been efficient from an economic standpoint. Foreign exchange constraints and the need to expand industrial employment have moved the L.D.C.s (less developed countries) into an everwidening spectrum of industries producing at small scale for domestic markets of limited size. Such industrialisation has not only been costly by international standards, it often has moved the L.D.C.s into extensive areas of processing and fabrication that is beyond their technological capabilities.[1]

Protectionist policies have also introduced an inevitable lag in product designs and production techniques. For example, automotive vehicle models must be stabilised over much longer periods among L.D.C.s in order to amortise expensive tooling and dies for low-volume production. The techniques themselves are, from the outset, outmoded by international standards of high-volume production. Under the seller's market created by systems of protection, quality control and materials standards, which constitute a vital part of technological transfer, are difficult to establish and maintain. Furthermore high cost supplier industries tend to price manufactured goods out of world markets, where volume production might be possible. In regional markets, national protectionist interests have proven to be an insurmountable obstacle.[2]

In short, over-ambitious industrialisation programmes have *created* technological gaps, which are then difficult to bridge in terms of time and resources. In such cases the problem is primarily one of *narrowing* the gaps down to manageable proportions, before *bridging* the gaps between donors and recipients. Some of the gaps could be narrowed appreciably if L.D.C.s could take on technological tasks in manageable segments – that is to say, commensurate with their technical skills and the stage of development of their supplier industries. But this implies an international division of labour not only in finished products but in sub-assemblies and industrial materials. It also entails marketing and trading arrangements that are often difficult to attain in the world economy.

One basic dilemma confronting L.D.C.s is that whereas automated techniques are not suited to the limited size of their domestic markets and employment needs, the use of labour-intensive techniques encounters difficulties in attaining required precision in production and in training the necessary supervisory and operator's skills. There is also the problem of

[1] See author's *Manufacturing Problems in India: The Cummins Diesel Experience in India* (Syracuse University Press, 1967).
[2] See author's 'Integrated Automobiles for Latin America?', *Finance and Development*, Vol. 5, No. 4 (December 1968), pp. 25–29.

technical skills to convert technology to low-volume production requirements. The burden of technological development is thus shifted from
capital and foreign exchange scarcities to manpower and organisational
deficiencies. Thus, what may seem paradoxical to the uninitiated, the
more advanced industrial techniques associated with high volume production are often more readily transplanted to newly industrialised
economies than are the so-called labour-intensive or capital-saving techniques.[1]

Another basic dilemma concerns the L.D.C.s long-term technological
growth and development. Economists from developing countries have
used terms such as 'technological dependence' and 'technological imperialism' to describe relationships between developing and advanced
economies.[2] The dilemma is whether to invest in absorptive and adaptive
capabilities and sacrifice, if necessary, production efficiencies; or whether
to emphasise the acquisition of 'narrow-gap' technologies which maximise productive output in the short run and minimise absorption time and
effort – that is to say, the upgrading of technical and organisational skills.
A related set of issues concerns licensing, with a minimum of foreign
involvement, versus investment, which entails ownership and technical
control by foreign enterprise.[3]

III. TAIWAN'S AUTOMOTIVE INDUSTRY AND JAPAN'S ROLE IN ITS DEVELOPMENT

Taiwan's automotive industry has followed a path which is now familiar
in a dozen or more developing countries.[4] It is a small industry even by
L.D.C. standards (only 11,000 vehicles annually). Despite this low volume
there are now three plants with installed capacities for 50,000 vehicles,
which produce at least 8 basic models of light cars, in addition to several
local firms that also assemble about 3,000 trucks a year. (The recent
sanctioning of more plants followed a period of poor quality and high
costs by a single firm with a monopoly position.) Previously there had been
overdevelopment of the motorcycle industry, with 19 firms producing
115,000 units a year as compared to a total production of about 2,500,000

[1] See author's *The Relevance of Automated Techniques to Industrialisation in Developing Economies*, paper presented at Conference on Manpower Problems Associated
with Automation and Advanced Technology in Developing Countries, sponsored by
the International Labour Organisation, Geneva (1–3 July 1970).

[2] See, for example, Celso Furtado, *Development and Underdevelopment* (Berkeley:
University of California Press, 1964), pp. 60–62; and Victor L. Urquidi, 'Latin American
Development, Foreign Capital, and the Transmittal of Technology', *El Trimestre
Economico*, XXIX (January–March 1962), pp. 19–29.

[3] See author's 'Technology Transfer thru the International Firm', *American Economic
Review, Papers and Proceedings*, Vol. LX, No. 2 (May 1970), pp. 435–40.

[4] See author's *'Automotive Industries in Developing Economies'*, World Bank Staff
Occasional Paper No. 8 (Johns Hopkins Press, 1969).

in Japan. Diseconomies of small-scale production are exacerbated by high domestic-content requirements – 60 per cent in light motor vehicles and 70 per cent for motor-cycles. Supplying this local content are hundreds of small manufacturers of components and parts.

Minimum economies of scale by international standards are between 40,000–60,000 for assembly, 80,000–120,000 for manufacturing engines and transmissions and 160,000–240,000 for body stamping. Motor vehicle production volumes for a single series now run from 1,000–5,000 units annually in Taiwan. It is a considerable industrial achievement that production costs do not run higher than they do (the manufacturing costs of the 60 per cent value added domestically is between two to three times the cost of the c.i.f. equivalent).[1] This development has taken place under a regime of protection and progressive import substitution over the past ten years. Domestic content requirements, in effect, give absolute protection to local parts manufacturers.

Procurement of quality parts at reasonable costs has been a major problem in Taiwan. Small-scale production for the limited local market has been further fragmented through competition among many producers in the protected market, which has lead inevitably to a duplication of each other's product lines and production facilities – and further deterioration in the efficiency and quality of production. This duplication of production facilities has been especially evident among foundries and in die-making, with pitiful efforts to cast mouldings and make stamping dies at miniscule scale. Door frames produced under similar primitive conditions by small-scale, local suppliers have to be straightened out piece by piece by the vehicle manufacturer. Efforts to establish consolidated facilities for castings, forgings and die-making, have proven futile thus far. Among these small-scale suppliers there is widespread under-utilisation of equipment (for example, in many shops presses are used only a few days a month, and as much as a third of time is spent in changing dies).

The described fragmentation deeply influences the nature and quality of acquired technology and compounds the problem of transferring and implanting production systems. Typically, it requires up to a dozen foreign technicians over a period which may extend from several months to several years to transfer technical knowledge in manufacturing techniques, equipment utilisation, quality and production controls, and to develop the necessary supervisory and operator skills. The magnitude of the technological transfer problem is suggested by the reality that a single automotive engine manufactured in the United States depends upon as many as 200 plants to supply 60 per cent of the engine's content and as many as 15,000 separate machining and processing techniques to

---

[1] Because of the so-called 'deletion allowance', c.i.f. prices often *understate* actual international values. See *Automotive Industries*, p. 37.

complete the remaining 40 per cent value added by the engine manufacturer.[1]

Taiwan's vehicle and parts industry has been developed largely in technical co-operation with Japanese firms. The motor-car and motor-cycle industries are wholly-owned by Chinese, but there are about two dozen joint ventures with Japanese firms and a limited number of American and European firms engaged in manufacturing automotive parts. Until recently the local affiliate of Nissan held a monopoly in passenger-car manufacturer, but now three other firms – affiliated to Honda, Toyota and Toyo Kogyo – have entered or are entering the market as vehicle manufacturers. Parts produced in Taiwan were not only high cost but of poor quality, and it is only since the new entries into the market that the quality of production has shown signs of improvement. For example, a team of Japanese officials are meticulously supervising the installation of casting facilities for the new plant being built to manufacture Toyota cars.

In order to improve further the technical efficiency of the Taiwan vehicle and parts industry, it first will be necessary to (a) curb the further proliferation in models and makes, (b) reduce local content to a reasonable level of cost efficiency, and (c) develop specialised vehicle or parts production for world markets.[2] Japanese partners (like other international firms in the automotive field) are in a unique position commercially and geographically to help develop parts production for world markets.

Taiwan's highly successful export industry in electronics is indicative of the direction in which the auto parts industry might move. Electronic plants turn out components and sub-assemblies for radios, TV sets and other related equipment, including transistors and other sophisticated micro-electronic devices. Production for export is made possible by a judicious mix of foreign and domestic inputs. In the case of miniaturised devices, pinhead-size transistors are cut from silicon wafers using laser guns and microscopes for the fine welding. The 1,000 to 2,000 people employed locally in typical plants are supplemented by a dozen foreign technicians who are critical to the effective implantation of technology. Domestic materials and parts have been incorporated, in the Taiwan case only as local supplier capabilities have developed. It is true that these

---

[1] See author's *Manufacturing Problems*, p. 19.

[2] Several international firms have already concluded agreements with other developing countries which provide for export earnings from specialised manufacture of components and vehicle for world markets. For example, Massey-Ferguson concluded an agreement in Mexico two years ago, which provided for export of tractor components to help pay for the 30 per cent import requirement on production for the local market. Fiat concluded an agreement with Crvena Zastava in Yugoslavia to manufacture one of the smaller cars in Fiat's line for export, thereby moving into production volumes that could compete on the world market. See policy recommendations in author's *Automotive Industries*, pp. 66–80.

plants producing exclusively for export are wholly owned and controlled by foreign firms, but this pattern could change as indigenous capability to market internationally develops.

Several export ventures are now under way in the automotive field.[1] One Japanese firm now has a plant in Taiwan to manufacture its car radio antennas for their export market in Europe and North America, since production costs in their Taiwan plant are nearly 20 per cent below those in Japan. The savings are in labour costs, which account for nearly 25 per cent of total costs. Taiwan wages are one-third of Japan's, but productivity is near Japanese standards. This is because the scale of production is nearly the same in both plants, production techniques are virtually identical in both countries and labour productivity in Taiwan is comparable to Japan's.[2]

The Taiwan plant is also able to capitalise on low wages to produce its own copper tubing for the antenna rods.

There are many other opportunities for export expansion in automotive parts, provided the production series is of sufficient volume and the plants are well managed and integrated into world markets. There is a particular interest in products or product elements that are low-volume items in Japan, since these items tie up equipment in Japanese plants and require disproportionately higher amounts of labour. Japanese manufacturers have expressed interest in such items as distributor coils, starters and generators, lamps and horns, pistons and pumps, and shock absorbers and motor-cycle suspension systems. One Japanese motor-cycle manufacturer is considering the transfer of its lower volume series to Taiwan, leaving higher-volume production with more frequent design changes to Japanese plants. Foundry work and electrical components (with 40 per cent or more labour content) are two obvious areas for potential expansion in Taiwan. Other possibilities include items in relatively low-volume series or those that have a relatively high value-to-bulk ratio (to absorb freight and duty charges). Another step in the right direction is the formation of a new company in Taiwan by the Nissan Group, Taiwan Automotive Parts, which will manufacture both for the domestic and export markets. Production will include car locks and instruments, air and oil filters, and piston rings. These particular products were chosen with a view toward common tooling in a joint facility and in order to achieve volume production of common elements or sub-assemblies.

[1] There are about a dozen joint ventures in Taiwan with Japanese partners producing piston rings, engine metals, forging parts, engine bearings, engine belts, springs, brake liners, water pumps, horns, switches and wiring harnesses. Other ventures planned include rubber parts, meters, air filters, key locks, die casting parts, lamps, mirrors, engine values, radiators, drive shafts and clutches.

[2] An analysis of Mexican labour indicates attainable productivity levels if Mexican labour were used in U.S.-scale plants. See W. Paul Strassmann, *Technological Change and Economic Development* (Cornell University Press, 1968), pp. 71, 78 and 316–17.

Japanese firms are strongly influenced in their external relations with Taiwan by administrative guidelines issued by the Japanese Government. Recent policies seem to favour industrial expansion and technical developments in Taiwan as a competitive base for indirect exports to third markets – particularly to the United States and Europe, but not for production that will compete in the home market.[1] A leading wire harness manufacturer in Japan has been approved by MITI (Ministry of International Trade and Industry) to manufacture its products in Taiwan for export to Japan – but this was a rare case. Before permission was granted agreement had to be reached with the four other wire harness producers in Japan as to the type of products that would be permitted into the Japanese market, and provisions made for the absorption of displaced Japanese workers. It took two years to work out this agreement, and several other similar proposals have been turned down by MITI thus far.

But the fact is that the Japanese Government has recognised that in order to continue its economic growth Japan must export, and to export it must continue to improve its economic efficiency. For nearly two decades labour efficiency has continued to rise,[2] but for the first time this past year wages increased ahead of productivity gains. Measures adopted thus far by the Japanese Government consist mainly of incentives to invest in labour-saving equipment and encouragement of corporate mergers to improve production efficiencies. But a third possibility for maintaining competitive costs in the face of rising wages in Japan is to relocate industrial activities with high wage costs to low-wage countries such as Taiwan or Korea. The familiarity of Japanese business firms with the Taiwan and Korean markets make these countries doubly attractive as export sites. The dilemma has been to move Japanese labour into more productive activities without creating unemployment and idle capacity in Japan. It is for this reason that the Japanese Government has been reluctant to sanction plant expansions in Taiwan that would compete in the Japanese home market. Restructuring the international division of labour between Japan and Taiwan would contribute to the increased efficiencies of the Japanese automotive industry in a minor way, but it is of major importance to technical progress in Taiwan's economy.

Technical expansion into more efficient, high-volume production in the

---

[1] The car radio antenna plant cited earlier is a case in point. In many areas Japanese firms maintain a dual pricing system which keeps home prices well above export prices. For example, the ex-factory price on a colour TV set is $160 for the export market, compared with $530 in the home market. See 'Japan's TV Trade Told to Up Prices', *Journal of Commerce* (28 July 1970).

[2] See Kiyoshi Kojima, 'Japan's Trade Policy', *Economic Record*, Vol. 41, No. 93 (March 1965), pp. 54–77. Kojima notes that between 1953–60, when exports expanded by a factor of 324 (1953 = 100), relative labour costs declined to 89. That is to say, labour productivity increased by a factor of 182, as compared to 148 for money wages, *op. cit.*, p. 72.

comparative advantage range requires closer technical and marketing arrangements between firms in Taiwan and their Japanese partners. Certain Japanese firms, like many international firms throughout the world, are not willing to commit the scarce production and marketing personnel unless they are allowed equity participation, which is the only assurance of an adequate rate of return.[1] Export ventures in the electronics field in Taiwan have proven highly successful from a production viewpoint in a relatively short time mainly because sufficient personnel were assigned to assure high efficiencies in production and marketing. In the previously mentioned car radio antenna plant, sixteen Japanese engineers and technicians worked over a two-year period to assure the success of the operation. Such ventures also owe a major portion of their success to the judicious choice of product lines and the structuring of value added in Taiwan in combination with value added in Japan – embodied skill and technology from Japan used in combination with the low-wage, high-productivity labour in Taiwan.

Technical development in support of more efficient industries also requires a reversal of protectionist policies on the part of the industrialisation authorities in Taiwan. Businessmen in Taiwan, as in most developing countries, would prefer the quiet life of manufacturing in protected markets for themselves with limited entry for others. A reversal of the present trend toward proliferation of models and increased local content in vehicles produced for the local market is also needed, expanding instead into specialised production for world markets and limiting import substitution to the cost-efficient range.

IV. POLICIES AND MEASURES TO NARROW TECHNOLOGICAL GAPS

As indicated in the introduction, the first step toward bridging technological gaps is narrowing them down to 'bridgeable' sizes. This narrowing down may be achieved through

(1) adjustments in L.D.C. industrialisation policies,
(2) adjustments in the trade policies of industrially advanced countries,
(3) the development of indigenous research and engineering capabilities, and
(4) measures designed to solicit very specialised kinds of co-operation of foreign enterprise.

Policies and measures in each of these areas are outlined and summarised in this section.

[1] See reference in footnote 3, p. 302, *supra*. Government policy in Taiwan has been to welcome foreign equity proportional to export intentions.

L 2

(1) *L.D.C. Development Policies*

Indiscriminate import substitution creates ever-widening technological gaps in manpower and know-how. An industrialisation policy which is more selective in terms of scarcities in technical and managerial skills is the first step toward reducing technological gaps to manageable proportions. Understandably L.D.C. governments are concerned over foreign exchange flows and overall efficiencies in resource utilisation, but to the degree possible, decisions concerning the factor mix in production between foreign and domestic inputs, and in the product mix utself, should be left to the firm. This is so enterprises will have the maximum latitude to manufacture and procure materials and parts in areas where the technological gaps are 'bridgeable'. In this regard there is also a widespread tendency on the part of industrialisation authorities to create employment through small-scale enterprise and labour-intensive techniques. This places an excessive burden upon the technological transfer process where machine skills must then be replaced with human skills, and scarce technical and managerial resources are required to adapt acquired technology.[1]

(2) *Trade Policies of Industrially-Advanced Countries*

If L.D.C.s are to avoid the high-cost range of small-scale or technologically-difficult areas of production, they must be allowed to specialise in those products and intermediate industrial goods that are in their range of emerging industrial competence. Industrially-advanced countries should specialise in value added based upon high technology, high levels of technical and managerial skills, and heavy capital investment; and developing countries should take over an increasing share of industrial activities with high labour content in the middle-level skills.[2] Ideally production should be broken down to specialisations and complementaries based upon the respective capabilities of the trading partners – Taiwan's electronic industry provides a case in point. The modern world of communication and transport and the emergence of multinational marketing and manufacturing groups, has made such specialisation and interchange possible. But the further development of an internaiotnal division of labour along these lines is now hampered by discriminatory tariffs imposed by in-

[1] See reference in footnote 1, p. 302, *supra*.
[2] See Hal B. Lary, *Import of Manufactures from Less Developed Countries* (National Bureau of Economic Research, 1968). Lary ranks industrial products in world trade according to labour productivity – which is a composite including skill, technology and capital. I believe a further breakdown into segments of products would reveal that the comparative advantage of low-wage labour is *anywhere*, it can be used in combination with skills, technology and equipment or materials which embodied deficient factors. For guidelines to industrialisation in the comparative advantage range in the automotive industry, see author's *Automotive Industries*, pp. 70–76.

dustrially advanced countries which are progressively restrictive toward processed goods. The same applies to escalated freight rates. Indiscriminate and excessive import substitution can only be avoided if more economic paths to earn income and provide employment are opened up through world trade.[1]

(3) *Development of Indigenous Research and Engineering*

A distinction needs to be drawn between capabilities to convert acquired technology and absorptive capacity for unaltered technology. Involved in the later are measures to upgrade technical and managerial skills at the plant level. The former involves long-term programmes to develop research and engineering capabilities at the firm level and among cadres in economic planning and financial institutions engaged in industrial planning and related investment decisions. These engineering capabilities are needed both for marginal adjustments in technology and for long-range planning to utilise lower-range skills in larger numbers.[2]

Improving the quality and efficiency of the smaller-scale supplier industries is another basic task in bridging technological gaps. Smaller firms, as a rule, have very limited access to foreign technical assistance or opportunities for the 'sustained relationship' that is needed to implant technology. In the case of Taiwan's automotive parts industry a development corporation aimed at upgrading local supplier capabilities might prove a suitable means for channelling technical and financial resources from Japan and elsewhere. Vehicle manufacturers in Taiwan and their foreign affiliates would have a vested interest in improving parts supply, and they might provide equity for such institutions. A development corporation has been organised in Taiwan (Chunghwa Electronics Development Company) with precisely this purpose in mind. It should be possible to involve the technical and financial resources of vehicle manufacturers, since it serves the interests of these foreign corporations to develop supplier capabilities in markets where they themselves have a manufacturing role. Industrial and financial interests in Japan also probably would be receptive to such a proposal, which would reinforce the drive toward advancing productivity in the Japanese economy by helping to shift segments of Japanese industry with rising labour costs to areas with lower labour costs.

[1] These arguments are further developed in author's article to be published in *Finance and Development*, 'Clearing the Way for Exports'. On reorienting New Zealand's industrial economy to high levels of skills and know-how, see author's chapter in *The World Bank Report on the New Zealand Economy* (Wellington, N.Z.: Government Printer, 1968), pp. 34–35.

[2] For more detailed suggestions on the development of indigenous research and engineering capabilities, see author's 'Role of Science and Technology in Advancing Development of Newly Industrialised States', *Socio-Economic Planning Sciences*, Vol. 3, No. 4 (January–February 1970), pp. 351–83.

National programmes may be undertaken to broaden knowledge on trade in industrial technology between industrially-advanced and newly industrialising countries. Information on sources of technology, on prices charged and on qualitative differences among technology donors, could enhance the bargaining power of L.D.C. enterprises. It would be unreasonable to generate exhaustive details covering the vast spectrum of industrial alternatives, but it may prove feasible to develop some general guidelines and centralised services that can channel requests from local firms to knowledgeable sources of information.[1]

(4) *L.D.C. Policies Toward Foreign Enterprise*

The technological development of L.D.C.s is critically dependent upon foreign enterprise to provide *and implant* technical knowledge and managerial systems. The quality and operational effectiveness of implanted technologies in terms of high contributions to economic growth, depend upon the choice of partners and the arrangements negotiated. Competitive production particularly depends upon technical proficiency, which for a wide range of industries can only be acquired through a *sustained* relationship with an experienced industrial partner. This is necessary in order to absorb the myriad of processing specifications, material standards, tooling guidelines and control procedures that are associated with the manufacture and assembly of industrial products. Particularly advantageous are agreements which include (a) marginal adjustments in product designs and production techniques to accommodate factor availabilities, (b) the development of local supplier industries, and (c) help develop indigenous research and engineering personnel who can participate in worldwide marketing and production systems.[2]

As an example of the role international corporations can play in narrowing technological gaps, Volkswagen has put considerable efforts into its transfer techniques of production and related management systems.

---

[1] See, for example, recent work by Constantine V. Vaitsos, *Transfer of Industrial Technology to Developing Countries Through Private Enterprises*, paper prepared for Colombian National Planning Department (9 February 1970). For an analysis of the returns earned by foreign corporations on the technology package, see also C. V. Vaitsos, *Transfer of Resources and Preservation of Monopoly Rents*, paper prepared for Harvard University Development Advisory Service (28 April 1970).

[2] For an analysis of the adjustments made by an American diesel engine manufacturer in India, see reference to author's *Manufacturing Problems in India*, at pp. 63–66, 70–73. See also author's *Industrial Technologies for Developing Economies* (Praeger, 1969), pp. 45–53; James B. Quinn, 'Technology Transfer by Multinational Companies', *Harvard Business Review* (November–December 1969), pp. 147–61; and Hans Heymann, Jr. (Rand Corporation), *Promoting the 'D' in R & D: Dubious Models and Relevant Strategies*, paper presented at the Research and Development Planning Management Seminar organised by the Turkish Scientific and Technical Research Council (TUBITAK) and sponsored by the O.E.C.D. Technical Assistance Programme, Istanbul, Turkey (4–8 May 1970).

The firm has developed management and procedural guides covering every aspect of vehicle manufacture and assembly in overseas plants – from quality control to machine utilisation – with a view toward decreasing the need for management skills at the receiving end and reducing the number of VW personnel engaged in transferring production systems.[1]

L.D.C. governments must come to realise that foreign firms will not part with critical transfer resources (largely manpower and the technical knowledge embodied in them) to achieve the tasks outlined above, unless they earn an adequate return. Involved here are issues of licensing *v.* direct investment policies on the part of technology donors and the related issue of ownership and control in foreign ventures. L.D.C.s must develop a reasonable balance in their attitudes and policies toward foreign enterprise which takes into account, on the one hand, the price that must be paid in terms of resource costs and deference to foreign ownership and control.[2]

V. CONCLUDING REMARKS

In the final analysis, narrowing and bridging technological gaps is part of the general problem of advancing productivity in emerging areas of comparative advantage. A principal of comparative advantage for the L.D.C.s in early phases of industrialisation is low wage labour – provided it is employed to give the L.D.C. a comparative advantage in labour *costs*. The economic benefits derived from improvements in the technological transfer *modes* depend largely upon market orientations and production opportunities that permit the L.D.C. to operate in its area of 'emerging comparative advantage' – which in the long term means developing its own technical and managerial skills. But in the critical interim stages of development, opportunities for efficient production may be broadened through trade in intermediate goods and certain end-products in which the L.D.C.s factor supply of middle-range skills is combined with foreign technology and high skills through trade both in factors and end-products.

[1] See Werner P. Schmidt, *The International Transfer of Management Skills – Volkswagen's Needs, Experiences and Plans*, paper presented to AIESEC (Association Internationale des Etudiants en Sciences Economiques et Commerciales), Torino, Italy (19 November 1960).
[2] See reference in footnote 2, p. 302, *supra.* See also Detlev F. Vagts, 'The Multinational Enterprise: A Challenge for Transnational Law', *Harvard Law Review*, Vol. 83, No. 4 (February 1970), pp. 739–92.

13 Less Developed Country Innovation Analysis and the Technology Gap

John Fei and Gustav Ranis
YALE UNIVERSITY

I. INTRODUCTORY

Increases in material welfare, i.e. economic progress leading to increases in per capita consumption, can be achieved in the long run as the consequence of many factors, including capital accumulation, improvements in the quantity of human resources and technological change. However both economists with a theoretical and those with an empirical and historical bent [1] have increasingly come to the conclusion that, in the long run, technological change is the most crucial – as well as the most difficult to get hold of. On the one hand, the theoretical economists have reminded us of the inevitability of stagnation in per capita income if capital accumulation alone is at work [2]. On the other hand, those with an historical interest have identified modern growth, as the Western world has experienced it over the past 200 years, as an epoch characterised by the routinisation of innovations.

When we accept such a long-run historical perspective, the development of a 'typical' contemporary L.D.C. may be viewed as focussed on transitional growth, i.e. that period of some 30–50 years during which the country shakes off its economic heritage of pre-modern stagnation[1] and moves into an epoch of modern growth. Economic progress in general, and innovations in particular, must be viewed in the context of this transition.

At the present time our understanding of transition growth and of the role of innovation in it, are both admittedly still in a rather embryonic state. Consequently, any search for a better understanding of L.D.C. technological change, i.e. any attempt to theorise on this important subject in a viable fashion, must begin with some historical perspective and proceed to propose an analytical framework. It is the purpose of the present paper to attempt this twin task.

What is imperative about an historical perspective in which to imbed the analysis is that it provides a major focal point for deciding what factors out of the multitude of possible observations are essential and relevant – and which may be set aside as of secondary importance, at least as a

---

[1] In many a contemporary L.D.C. this heritage is that of a pre-independence open agrarian society operating typically as a colonial appendage to a mature industrial country.

first approximation. In section II, we shall try to cultivate this historical view by contrasting the role of innovation in the typical L.D.C. with the role of innovation in the industrially mature economy. Such a comparison then permits us to conclude that the major factors relevant to the innovational process in the L.D.C.s – our main concern – include (a) changes in the quality of domestic entrepreneurship, (b) changes in the factor endowment over time, and (c) the possibility of the international transfer of technology. These are the facets that will be explored as part of our analytical framework in sections III to VI.

This analytical framework of ours represents little more at this time than a preliminary attempt to let empirical insights, based mainly on the transitional growth experience of post-Meiji Japan, be integrated into a rather crude theoretical framework. To date, the innovational process has not yielded easily to analysis in any context, developed or underdeveloped – and it would be presumptuous for us to expect to change this situation in the context of this paper. While we think we have made some progress, especially in beginning to link the element of rational choice to the innovation inducement mechanism, the whole set of issues broached here is sufficiently complicated to threaten to involve us in a rather ambitious reformulation of development theory – something we have clearly not attempted. But even a first approximation must give due recognition to some of the following factors:

(i)   the relationship between rational entrepreneurial decision-making and the feasibility of technological borrowing abroad (section III);
(ii) the high cost of technological borrowing initially due to entrepreneurial immaturity – and the subsequent act of unconscious innovation as these entrepreneurs gradually learn by doing in the course of the transition process (section IV);
(iii) the attempt, later, by maturing entrepreneurs to consciously adopt biased innovations in response to changing factor endowments (section V).

Our overall analytical farmework, resulting from a synthesis of these elements in the context of a phase of transition theory, will then be subjected to some statistical verification (section VI).

II. INNOVATIONS IN HISTORICAL PERSPECTIVE

Since most of our knowledge about technological change is necessarily derived from our understanding of industrially advanced countries, it behoves us to make a preliminary assessment of the extent of transferability of that knowledge, i.e. to what extent the knowledge of innovations pertinent to 'mature industrial capitalism' is useful for the understanding of an underdeveloped country engaged in this transition. We propose to examine the transferability of innovation analysis from the point of view of (1) the socio-economic significance of innovations, (2) the sources of innovational ideas, and (3) the innovation-motivation mechanism proper. As we will discover, there exist significant differences between the rich and the poor countries in all three of these dimensions.

(1) *The Socio-Economic Significance of Innovation*

Economists are normally concerned with social as opposed to private objectives. In a wealthy industrial society three types of socio-economic problems may be said to have motivated economists' interest in innovations: (i) economic instability, (ii) distributional equity, and (iii) long-run stagnation. The relationship between innovations and instability stems from the fact that economic fluctuations are caused mainly by fluctuations of investment which, in turn, may be traced to the lack of dependability in the appearance of innovational ideas to be accommodated by capital accumulation [3]. The issue of 'distributional equity' stems from the natural focus of a wealthy society on issues of distributional conflicts (e.g. the distribution between labour and capital) which are affected by the factor bias of innovations. The distributional equity issue, moreover, has implication for long-run stagnation in that the natural tendency for the profit rate to decline in the long run as the consequence of capital deepening must be compensated for by innovations if secular stagnation is to be avoided, i.e. if the capital owning class is to be induced by a high enough profit rate to take the risk of investment and the exploration of new ideas.

The problems of instability and of distributional sensitivity are mainly problems of mature 20th-century capitalism in which innovational activities are assumed to have become institutionalised and routinised. This group of social problems is very different from that faced by a contemporary L.D.C. in the course of transition. Here the crucial socio-economic problem, one which lies at the heart of the transitional problem and tends to perpetuate L.D.C. poverty, is not the erratic up-and-down quality of innovational activities but rather their absolute low level. As a consequence, instead of 'instability' and 'distributional equity' the analysis of L.D.C. must be focussed on (i) the origins of innovational capacity, and (ii) the impact of innovations on relative factor utilisation.

One of the most important 'cultural' achievements during the transition phase is to acquire increased innovational capacity, and a major purpose of any analysis of innovational activity must be to study the process by which this ability is acquired. This, in turn, requires an understanding of the precise nature of entrepreneurial decision-making, given inherited human resources.[1] For it is by the very process of the formation and the

[1] Including such cultural factors as secularism, nationalism and a belief in the equality of access to scarce resources.

execution of entrepreneurial decisions that entrepreneurship is developed in a learning-by-doing context. In this respect the analysis should focus naturally on the identification of the particular entrepreneurial tasks which need to be performed in the transition process.

From the socio-economic point of view, the impact of innovations must be assessed in terms of their efficiency in utilising the resource endowment of the country. As a general rule we may visualise that, during the transition process, an L.D.C. moves from an almost exclusive reliance on land-based natural resources (e.g. in primary product exports) to the utilisation of its human resources (labour and entrepreneurship) and, still later, of its skill and capital resources. Thus the impact of an innovation in the 'early', i.e. land-based or labour surplus phase, must be gauged mainly in terms of its labour using (or capital saving) impact in meeting the basic requirements of efficiency. The common sense of the matter is that as long as there is a marked discrepancy between factor endowment and factor utilisation, given a particular state of the arts, innovations should be 'biased' in a labour-using direction, as a learning effort in the use of the country's relatively abundant resource (i.e. labour) and in conserving the relatively scarce resource (i.e. capital). For an L.D.C. in transition, the innovation effects could thus be statistically summarised in terms of changes in the overall capital-labour and capital-output ratios, at least for the industrial sector.

In summary, the two objectives of L.D.C. innovation analysis, augmenting innovational ability and improving the related efficiency of resources utilisation, are critical growth related objectives, i.e. objectives oriented toward increasing the output capacity of the economy. These objectives are quite different from the emphasis on instability and/or distribution in the industrially advanced countries where long-term growth can be taken more or less for granted.

(2) *The Sources of Innovational Ideas*

The defining property of 20th-century industrial capitalism is the institutionalisation of innovation activities. This process results from decades of cost-benefit analyses guiding the direction of R. & D. expenditures to explore the knowledge frontier, with the benefits reaped in terms of the actual industrial adoption of new ideas. Thus the sources of innovational ideas reside in the exploration of new knowledge. Moreover full analysis of the institutionalisation of the exploration process itself necessitates distinguishing between private (profit-seeking) and public (e.g. military-related) innovations [4].

The situation is again entirely different for an L.D.C. in transition. Here the source of technological ideas is not the simple consequence of the exploration of the knowledge frontier. Rather, the most important source of new technology is the transfer via the importation of ideas already proven to be industrially feasible in the mature countries. Cost-benefit analysis and the role of government in the innovation process are likely to be less important, except for search costs. Thus, for an L.D.C., the focal point of the analysis of innovations is more likely to be the absorption process proper, i.e. how foreign innovational ideas are transferred and possibly modified. Specifically, such analysis can be expected to be more concerned with the level of efficiency over time in the process of borrowing and simply transplanting knowledge – as well as with the efficiency of the domestic assimilation and innovation processes 'on top of' the imported technology.

In the total technology absorption process we may usefully distinguish between two facets, a private innovation process and a social innovation process. Like its counterpart in the industrially advanced countries, the private innovation process refers to the conscious calculations and actions of private profit seeking entrepreneurs, with respect to profits and losses, as related to, among other elements, factor bias in technology transfer. The social innovation process, on the other hand, refers to more unconscious acts of learning by doing, partly by entrepreneurs and partly by other economic agents, in the process of technological assimilation. As we shall argue, such 'unintentional' social innovations may be quite important, especially in the early phase of transition when the domestic entrepreneurship is, as yet, underdeveloped. This type of innovation is peculiar to an L.D.C. under transition, i.e. it represents a category of innovations not ordinarily emphasised in the mature industrialised society where the effects of most innovations tend to be 'internalised' or 'imputed'. It is likely to come earlier in the life of an L.D.C. since inefficiencies arising from pure transplantation are progressively eliminated as domestic entrepreneurs become more experienced.

(3) *Innovation-Motivation Analysis*

With respect to the analysis of the private or conscious motivation of innovation, the focal point in the industrially mature countries has been on the entrepreneurial calculation of the anticipated saving in factor cost [5]. A most important type of information relevant to this calculation is usually provided by the state of anticipation with respect to the supply of labour. This includes both (i) the anticipation of the real wage trend – generally upward in mature societies, and (ii) the anticipation of other (non-wage) difficulties in dealing with labour unions – generally upward too. For both these reasons, innovations in mature capitalist societies have had an inherent labour-saving bias, i.e. as exemplified by the marked trend towards 'automation'.

Once the L.D.C. entrepreneur is capable of making rational economic calculations, a similar innovation motivation analysis can be applied here. There are two points which need to be emphasised in this context. First, the full flowering of labour union development is a phenomenon still mainly reserved for the mature economy,[1] and hence the analysis of innovations can be simplified by the assumption of a trend towards perfect competition in the labour markets. Second, instead of anticipating continuing marked increases in the real wage, we may distinguish two stages of L.D.C. growth: a first stage characterised by an approximation to the 'unlimited supply of labour' condition, and hence the anticipation of fairly constant or only gently rising real wages; and a second stage characterised by anticipation of substantially increasing real wages. One of the major elements of contemporary growth theory enables us to accept this distinction as an operationally relevant one [6].

III. A PURE MODEL OF TECHNOLOGY TRANSFER

In the context of any 'pure' theory of technological transfer, at least three facets must be specified:

(1) the availability of technology from abroad as described by a technology shelf,
(2) the process of technological borrowing from that shelf based on rational entrepreneurial calculations, and
(3) the implications of such borrowing for 'growth', i.e. the tendency for capital deepening or shallowing, for employment and output generation, etc.

These three facets will be examined in turn. Moreover, it should be understood that the 'pure model' represents merely the skeleton of our analysis which will be modified and expanded in the subsequent sections.

(1) *Technology Shelf*

The important fact that, for an L.D.C., the primary source of technological ideas is from abroad may be described by the existence of a technology shelf, containing technologies of production which, either in the present or at some time in the historical past, have been demonstrated to be feasible in the industrially advanced countries, and from which an L.D.C. can borrow freely. The technology shelf is given by the curve SS' in Fig. 13.1(a) in which labour (capital) is measured on the horizontal (vertical) axis. A typical point A_i on this curve represents a pair (n_i, k_i) in which n_i is the labour co-efficient and k_i is the capital co-efficient. The point A_i may be referred to as a unit technology in that it describes the amount of labour inputs (n_i) and of capital inputs (k_i) required to produce one unit of output. The idea of a unit technology assumes factor complementarity and is shown diagrammatically by the fact that the point A_i is the 'corner point' of an L-shaped production contour (U_i) producing one unit of output.

[1] Less true for L.D.C.s which are at a later stage of transition, e.g. Latin America.

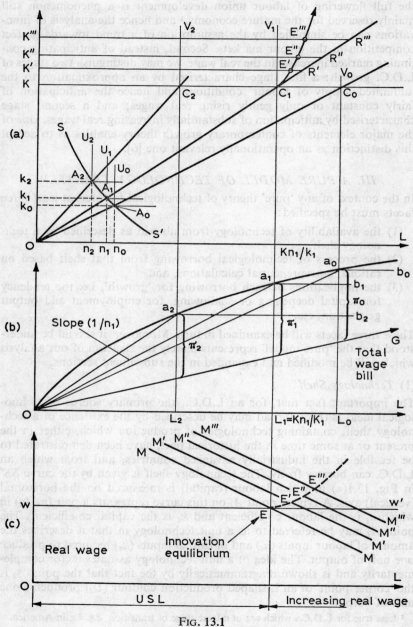

FIG. 13.1

Suppose the size of the capital stock for the whole industrial sector is K, as measured on the vertical axis. Then, when, for example, the unit technology A_1 is chosen from the shelf, it can be operated at a definite scale producing K/k_1 units of output and employing Kn_1/k_1 units of labour. In diagram (1a) the radial line through point A_1, i.e. the radial line with a slope (k_1/n_1) intersects the horizontal line through point 'K' at a point 'C_1'. This point 'C_1' is the 'corner point' of an L-shaped production contour indexed by V_1 – producing K/k_1 units of output and employing Kn_1/k_1 units of labour. Thus, associated with any technology choice (in this case A_1), the degree of capital intensity (i.e. capital per head, k_1/n_1) is determined. The size of the capital stock 'K' thus determines the amount of labour force which can be efficiently accommodated for each technological choice.

The complementary nature of capital and labour in the unit technology (e.g. A_1) can alternatively be shown by means of the TPP_L (total productivity of labour) curve oa_1b_1 in Fig. 13.1(b). This TPP_L-curve has a radial, i.e. homogeneously linear portion, Oa_1, before the size of the optimum labour force (KC_1 in Fig. 13.1a) is reached, and a horizontal portion, a_1b_1, beyond that point.[1] Thus, when the size of the capital stock K is given, by varying the unit technology A_0, A_1, A_2 ... on the shelf SS' in diagram 1a, we can determine a family of TPP_L curves (Oa_0b_0, Oa_1b_1, Oa_2b_2 ... in Fig. 13.1(b).

The technology shelf contains information on techniques demonstrated to have been feasible at some point in the historical past somewhere in an industrially advanced country. The fact that curve SS' (diagram 1a) is negatively sloped serves to emphasise the fact that, with respect to the more recent vintage of advanced country technology, i.e. as we move upward to the left along the shelf, A_0, A_1, A_2 ... three long run trends may be observed: increasing labour productivity (i.e. decreasing values of n_0, n_1, n_2 ...), continuous capital deepening (i.e. increasing slopes of radial lines OA_0, OA_1, OA_2 ...), and increasing capital-output ratios (i.e. increasing values of k_0, k_1, k_2.) The first two properties are among the well-known 'stylised' facts of economic growth in the history of the mature economics.[2]

---

[1] Given the capital stock, e.g. K and the unit technology e.g. A_1, the optimum labour force (kn_1/k_1) is an optimum in the sense that it represents the minimum amount of labour required to produce the maximum produceable output.

[2] E.g. Kaldor, 'A Model of Economic Growth', *E. J.* (December 1957) and Fellner, *Trends and Cycles in Economic Activity, op. cit.* The third condition, that of an increasing trend in the capital-output ratio, is less clear empirically and could easily be modified in our above analysis. For example, the technology shelf SS' is a horizontal line for a constant 'k'; an upward sloping curve would indicate a declining 'k'. Empirically the downward sloping shelf, as we have pictured it, seems the most realistic to us, but is not necessary for our argument.

(2) *Technological Borrowing and Rational Entrepreneurial Action*

Let us assume that, in addition to the technology shelf itself, we also know the value of the real wage, i.e. the height Ow of the horizontal supply curve of labour ww' in Fig. 13.1(c). From this we can construct a curve depicting the total wage bill, i.e. the radial line OG in Fig. 13.1(b), the slope of which is the real wage. If the technology chosen by the entrepreneur is A_1, for example, then profits π_1 are maximised at the point a_1 where the gap between the OG and the TPP_L-curve Oa_1b_1 is at a maximum. In other words, that amount of labour input which maximises profits is precisely the previously defined optimum labour force, i.e. that labour force which for the given capital stock, leaves neither labour nor capital disguisedly unemployed. This simple property follows directly from the competitive assumption, i.e. the fact that the real wage is constant and given for all firms.

When the size of the capital stock (K) for the representative, or average, firm is fixed, a rational entrepreneur will thus seek to adopt (i.e. borrow) that technology choice which maximises the rate of return to capital. In Fig. 13.1(b), alternative maximum profit levels π_0, π_1, π_2, represent the anticipated profit stream associated with each alternative technology choice – under the assumption of the expectation of near constancy of the real wage. A rational entrepreneur under these circumstances will adopt that technology which yields the maximum profit. In Fig. 13.1(b), the equilibrium technology choice turns out to be A_1, leading to the maximum profit π_1.

This equilibrium condition can be shown explicitly by treating the 'envelope curve' a_2, a_1, a_0 as an *ex ante* TPP_L curve.[1] For each amount of labour employed the curve shows the maximum output which can be obtained by a suitable technological choice. It so happens that the maximum output is obtained when the optimum technology, consistent with the given labour force, is chosen. The *ex ante* MPP_L-curve, i.e. the slope of the *ex ante* TPP_L curve, is the demand curve for labour as depicted by the negatively sloped MM curve in Fig. 13.1(c). Where this demand curve intersects the horizontal wage line ww', e.g. at a point E, the equilibrium position is determined.

The above skeleton of a theory of a rational entrepreneurial behaviour – under the admittedly restrictive condition that the capital stock is given to the firm at any point in time – shows that the technology choice can be deduced from a calculation of the rate of return to capital – which in turn can be traced to the combination of anticipated domestic real wage be-

---

[1] This is reminiscent of the putty-to-clay idea in the growth theory literature (see E. Phelps, 'Substitution, Fixed Proportion, Growth and Distribution', *International Economic Review* (1963). Our model, however, by permitting continuous full adjustment, is really more of the putty-to-putty type.

haviour and the technological information available from abroad. The result of such an entrepreneurial choice is not only the determination of the rate of return to capital (π_1) but also simultaneously of the degree of capital intensity (k_1/n_1) and of the total volume of labour which can be absorbed (wE).

(3) *Overall Implications for Growth*

The above framework for analysing technological choice also provides the groundwork for determining the impact on growth. In this simple model growth may be defined in terms of increased capital accumulation and increased employment opportunities. Both of these will be clearly affected by the anticipated long-run behaviour of wages. As pointed out earlier, wages may be assumed to be held roughly constant or increasing only modestly during the early labour surplus phase of transition, and to increase rapidly at the later phases when that labour surplus no longer overhangs the market.[1]

Thus far we have kept the capital stock constant at K. Now let the increase of that capital stock through time be represented by the points K, K', K''. . . on the vertical axis in Fig. 13.1(a). The larger capital stock will lead to 'higher' demand curves for labour MM, $M'M'$, $M''M''$. . . in Fig. 13.1(c), leading to increases in labour absorption. When the real wage is constant, the amount of labour force absorbed will always be proportional to the size of that capital stock. Starting from the initial point 'C_1' in Fig. 13.1(a) the expansion path would then be indicated by the locus of points R', R'', R'''. . . which fall on a radial line. Conversely, when the real wage is increasing (i.e. as represented by the dotted curve from the point E on), the expansion path will show a capital deepening tendency, as shown by the locus of points E', E'', E'''. . . . These conclusions follow readily from the assumption of constant returns to scale.[2]

In summary, we can thus see that the main implication of our view of L.D.C. innovation behaviour is that the behaviour of the real wage, as it makes itself felt through the choice of technology, determines the extent of capital intensity, i.e. a rapid increase in the real wage will induce rapid capital deepening. The pace at which employment opportunities are generated is thus controlled by capital accumulation, as modified, in an adverse direction, by the capital-deepening tendency resulting from wage

---

[1] Other, exogenous, pressures may combine with the termination of the unlimited supply of labour condition to differentiate this second phase from the first. As wages rise, moderately in phase 1 and rapidly in phase 2, the slope of the wage bill curve OG in Fig. 13.1(b) shifts up and the maximum profit point shifts to the left.

[2] As T. N. Srinivasan pointed out in the course of discussion of our paper at Bled, our analysis is more comparative static rather than fully dynamic since it does not accommodate the possible impact of entrepreneurial expectations concerning future wage increases on current technological choice.

increases. These simple relations must now be modified to accommodate other important dimensions of the technology transfer process.

IV. 'SOCIAL' INNOVATION ACTIVITIES

For a less developed country in transition, an important source of productivity gain may be traced to the elimination of inefficiency in the course of the above described process of technology transfer. As perfected and developed in the industrially advanced countries, such technologies assume factor efficiency and organisational efficiency which may be lacking in an L.D.C. The most important manifestation of factor efficiency is, of course, labour efficiency which can be traced to such factors as cultural heritage, accumulated experience, education, etc., the precise relationships as yet incompletely specified. In organisational efficiency we may include entrepreneurial capacity as well as organisational capacity traceable to economies of large-scale production. While we are not yet ready for finely specified answers, we may assume that both of these types of efficiency are related to learning by doing processes.

The aforementioned inefficiency is operationally described by an increment in the real cost (i.e. real capital cost and/or real labour cost) which an L.D.C. will have to incur, over and above that implied by the technology shelf, i.e. over and above the costs per unit of output prevailing historically in the advanced countries. In Fig. 13.2(a), the SS' curve represents the technology shelf containing unit technologies $A_0, A_1, A_2 \ldots$, and TT' represents the unit technologies after unit technologies A_i have been transplanted into the L.D.C. and converted into $B_0, B_1, B_2 \ldots$ at lower levels of efficiency. The incremental real costs due to inefficiency are indicated by the vectors (i.e. arrows) $A_0B_0, A_1B_1, A_2B_2 \ldots$ which have a 'direction' (i.e. slope) and a 'magnitude' (i.e. length). Notice that these arrows point to the North-East (i.e. they are positively sloped), indicating the fact that capital and/or labour co-efficients will be increased as a consequence of the existence of inefficiencies.

Generally speaking, an L.D.C. will incur a heavier real cost if it attempts to import technologies with a more recent vintage, i.e. further away from their own experience. This is shown by the increasing length of vectors $A_0B_0, A_1B_1, A_2B_2, \ldots$ as we move to the left. Our conjecture is that these arrows will also become steeper indicating the fact that as the L.D.C. attempts to import technologies of a more recent vintage, i.e. 'beyond their reach', the incremental real cost per unit of output is oriented increasingly toward capital rather than labour. This is due to the fact that the efficiency of modern capital intensive production depends more and more on organisational capacity as well as on the ability to maintain and repair the capital stock. On the other hand, when an L.D.C. attempts to import a technology of a considerably older vintage, e.g. a U.K. textile mill of

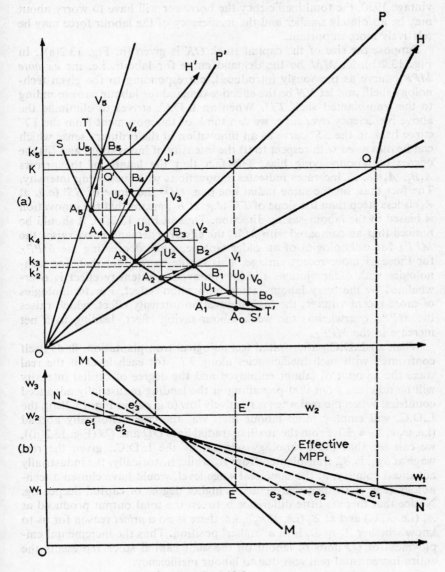

FIG. 13.2

vintage 1930, the total inefficiency the borrower will have to worry about may be absolutely smaller and the inefficiency of the labour force may be relatively more important.

Suppose the size of the capital stock OK is given (in Fig. 13.2(a)). In Fig. 13.2(b), let MM be the demand curve for labour, i.e. the *ex ante* MPP_L curve as previously introduced, corresponding to the given technology shelf, and let NN be the effective demand for labour corresponding to the transplanted shelf TT'. When an L.D.C. strives to eliminate the above inefficiency over time, we can think of the movement from the TT' curve back to the SS' curve as an innovation in the ordinary sense which can be measured with respect to (i) the intensity of innovation, and (ii) the degree of labour-saving bias. The fact that the length of the arrows A_1B_1, A_2B_2 . . . increases indicates innovations with increasing intensity. The fact that, on the same radial line (e.g. OQ) the slope of SS' (e.g. at A_2) is less steep than the slope of TT' (e.g. at B_2) means that the innovation is biased in the labour-saving direction. Thus in Fig. 13.2(b), it should be noticed that as compared with MM, the effective demand curve raises the MPP_L for technologies of an older vintage, while depressing the MPP_L for those of more recent vintage. This is due to the fact that, for technologies with older vintage, the low innovation intensity effect is overwhelmed by the 'very labour-saving innovation' effect. For technologies of more recent vintage, the high innovation intensity effect, which raises the MPP_L overwhelms the weak labour-saving effect, leading to a net increase in the MPP_L.

When an L.D.C., after initial technological transplantation, finds itself confronted with such inefficiencies along TT', for each level of the real wage the amount of labour employed and the degree of capital intensity will be different from that prevailing in the lending industrially advanced countries. When the real wage is relatively low (e.g. ow_1 in Fig. 13.2(b)), the L.D.C. will employ more labour than was the case historically abroad (i.e. $w_1 e_1 > w_1 E$). From the auxiliary radial lines OQ and QJ (Fig. 13.2(a)), we can see that the technology selected by the L.D.C., given the real wage at ow_1, is B_2, transplanted from A_2 while, historically, the industrially advanced country, at the same real wage level, would have chosen a technology (e.g. A_3) which represented a higher degree of capital deepening. Notice that there is little difference between the total output produced at A_3 (i.e. K/k_3) and at B_2 (i.e. K/k_2'), i.e. there is no *a priori* reason for us to know whether A_3 or B_2 is in a 'higher' position. Thus the incremental employment of QJ units of labour on the same capital stock represents the entire incremental real cost due to labour inefficiency.

Given a real wage at a somewhat higher level, we may note that the above situation is reversed. Here the depressing effect of MPP_L leads to the employment of less labour than was the case historically in the industrially advanced countries (i.e. $w_2 e_1' < w_2 E'$). In Fig. 13.2(a), at the given higher real wage level, the technology chosen by the L.D.C. is B_5 (transplanted from A_5) which represents a higher degree of capital intensity than that prevailing historically in the advanced countries (i.e. A_4). Because of this inefficiency the country now pays a double penalty in terms of output loss, i.e. the loss of output is $Q(1/k_4 - 1/k_5')$. In other words, the economy loses output on the given capital stock both because it chose a technology which is more capital using (i.e. by moving from A_4 to A_5) and because of the inefficiency in the utilisation of that technology (i.e. by moving from A_5 to B_5).[1]

For an L.D.C. which normally finds itself with such inefficiencies as part of its colonial heritage, their elimination over time clearly constitutes a major source of innovation, leading to gains in output capacity per unit of input. In Fig. 13.2(a) such 'innovations' may be represented by the gradual movement of the TT' curve through time towards the SS' position. In Fig. 13.2(b), similarly, the NN curve can be pictured as swivelling in a clockwise manner towards the MM position. It is then also easy to trace the impact of such a change. For a relatively low level of the real wage such 'innovations' lead to capital deepening, i.e. e_1, e_2, e_3 . . . E. Little effect on raising output is recorded, with the main impact the laying off of some redundant workers per unit of capital stock. For a relatively high level of the real wage, the impact of this type of 'innovation' leads to capital shallowing, i.e. e_1', e_2', e_3' . . . E' as more labour is employed per unit of capital. However, the major gain is now measured in terms of increased output brought about through a more effective use of the scarce capital stock.

The existence and elimination of these inefficiencies modifies the conclusions for the L.D.C.s growth path as analysed in the last section. For the low wage case (Ow_1) in Fig. 13.2(a), the expansion path as a result of only capital accumulation would, in the absence of elimination of inefficiences, have followed the radial line JP (as we noted earlier). The elimination of inefficiencies, on the other hand, leads to a growth path QH, marked by a capital-deepening tendency, which 'catches up' with the JP path over time. For the high wage case (Ow_2) the growth path $Q'H'$ now shows a capital-shallowing tendency approximating the radial path $J'P'$ over time.

[1] For lack of a better name, the above phenomenon may be referred to as a 'diseconomy' of premature modernisation. Such 'diseconomies' occur when the entrepreneurial and other infrastructure is still inadequate, requiring the use of relatively more capital and resulting in a lowering of the MPP_L. The inherent paradox can be seen in that the transplantation of a 'supermodern' factory, seemingly completely out of line with the prevailing relatively low level of real wages, may be viewed as necessary to raise the MPP_L to a high enough level to compensate for the inherent inefficiency. Differently put, in Fig. 13.2(b) we see that as the real wage level is raised to w_3, it will become uneconomic for *any* technology to be borrowed by the L.D.C. in the early stage, while some technology will still be economic in the lending country.

For an L.D.C. in transition, we can realistically visualise a situation in which the real wage increases only gradually as long as a labour surplus overhangs the market. In the absence of the 'inefficiency' element, we note an initial capital-deepening phenomenon, induced by this wage increase – as analysed in the previous section. When the argument of this section is added, however, we can see that while, in the early phase, the country will show a tendency toward capital deepening, this tendency may give way to some capital shallowing later – but only if the elimination of inefficiencies is sufficiently important to swamp the effects of moderate wage increases over time. Moreover, this capital-shallowing phase is likely to be accompanied by a substantial growth in income because of the huge output-raising effects associated with gains in the efficiency of using capital. This capital-shallowing phase is not likely, however, to go on for ever and will eventually give way to capital deepening when, first, this source of gain in efficiency is exhausted and, later, the accelerating real wage increase begins to dominate.

V. THE MOTIVATION FOR INNOVATIONAL BIAS

The unintentional or 'social' innovation of the last section is the result of learning by doing processes which are themselves a by-product of growth. This contrasts sharply with the more important intentional type of innovation which we will be concerned with in this section, i.e. as a consequence of a conscious entrepreneurial attempt to further reduce the real output costs (in terms of capital or labour inputs) in the process of technological assimilation. The core of this theory, as in the mature countries, must be a rational innovation analysis at the level of the individual entrepreneur. Since the amount of possible reductions in real costs, or innovational intensity, is, of course, constrained by the expansion of the entrepreneurial knowledge frontier, there is little that economists can say, on *a priori* grounds, about the magnitude of possible cost reductions. What the economist can hopefully speculate about on such *a priori* grounds is limited to the direction of the factor bias of innovations, which is what will be emphasised in this section.

In Fig. 13.3(a), let the point A (i.e. the point (n, k)) represent a pre-innovation unit technology. The real cost-reducing effect on an innovation is to shift this point towards the south-west (e.g. towards point D) which represents a reduction in the labour and/or capital co-efficient. In the same figure we have shown two special extreme cases: a move from A to A', which may be called a pure capital-saving innovation (i.e. yielding a reduction of the capital co-efficient only and leaving the labour co-efficient constant), and a move from A to A'', a pure labour-saving innovation. Useful *a priori* reasoning about the innovation-motivation

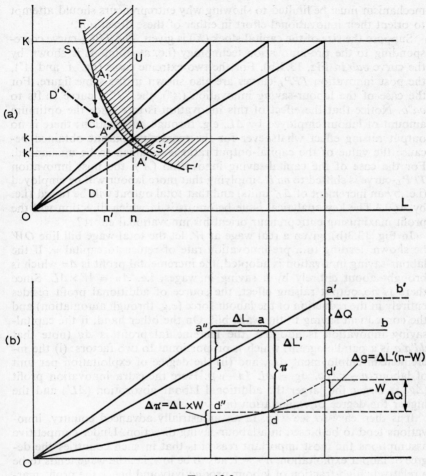

Fig. 13.3

mechanism must be limited to showing why entrepreneurs should attempt to orient their innovational effort in either of these directions.[1]

Suppose the size of the capital stock (K) is given. The TPP_L-curve corresponding to the pre-innovation technology (i.e. at point A) is shown by the curve oab in Fig. 13.3(b). For the two extreme cases (i.e. A' and A''), the post innovation TPP_L-curves are also shown in the same figure. For the case of the labour-saving innovation (A''), the TPP_L curve shifts to $oa''b$. Notice that the effect of this innovation is to reduce the optimum amount of labour employed by ΔL, e.g. through automation; there is no output raising effect whatsoever for the maximum output obtained because the value of the capital-output ratio is assumed to be unchanged. For the case of the capital-saving innovation (A'), the post innovation TPP_L-curve is shifted to $oa'b'$, implying that more labour will be employed (i.e. by an increment of Δ_L' units) and that total output will be raised (i.e. by ΔQ).[2] The key analytical issue before us is in which direction will the profit maximising entrepreneur orient his innovational effort?

In Fig. 13.3(b), given a real wage at W, let the total wage bill line OW be shown, leading to a pre-innovation rate of return to capital π. If the labour-saving innovation is adopted, the incremental profit is $\Delta\pi$ which is brought about entirely by a saving in wages, i.e. $\Delta\pi = W \times \Delta L$. Since there is no output raising effect, the source of additional profit resides entirely in the reduction of the labour force (e.g. through automation) and the consequent saving in the wage bill. On the other hand, if the capital-saving innovation is adopted, the incremental profit is Δg (note that $dd'a'a$ is a parallelogram) which is proportional to two factors: (i) the increment in employment $\Delta L'$, and (ii) the degree of exploitation per unit of labour $n - w$ (i.e. $\Delta g = \Delta L' (n - w)$). Here the extra innovation profit (Δg) is larger the larger the additional labour absorption ($\Delta L'$) and the higher the degree of exploitation ($n - w$).

It is then easy to see why, in an industrially advanced country, innovations tend to be biased in a labour-saving direction. Under competitive assumptions the most important reason is that in such countries the degree of labour exploitation, $n - w$, tends to be low, i.e. the wage tends to be a relatively high fraction of labour productivity and hence the profit margin tends to be low. Under these circumstances the saving associated with labour-saving innovations tend to be large and, at the same time, the extra profits due to capital-saving innovation tend to be small. This is clearly seen in the extreme case when the wage bill curve (OW) is steep enough to coincide with the TPP_L-curve oa, implying zero profits before innovation. In this case, the extra profit due to the labour-saving innovation is ja'' ($ja'' = \Delta L \times n$), while the extra profit due to a capital-saving innovation is zero.

---

[1] In the context of this paper the costs of R. & D. and of search are neglected.

[2] The radial portion of the TPP_L curve coincides with the pre-innovation curve because of the assumed constancy of the labour co-efficient.

This 'static' argument would be strengthened if the entrepreneur can be viewed as anticipating a rising trend in real wages. For the only way in which said entrepreneur can protect his profit margin (when threatened by wage hikes) is through adopting labour-saving innovations. Capital-saving innovations will not help when the profit margin is threatened.

We may cite two additional arguments based on market imperfections in the mature economy which tend to strengthen the above conclusion. First, labour-saving innovations result in lower levels of employment and hence in a lessening of the entrepreneurial dependence on labour – thus minimising labour control problems. Second, labour-saving innovations, to the extent that there is little or no output raising effect, lessen the entrepreneurial task in having to create new markets, which can be a serious problem in a wealthy economy constantly threatened by a deficiency of aggregate demand.

When we turn the argument around we can see why, in an L.D.C., the entrepreneurial effort should generally be oriented in the opposite or capital-saving direction. When the wage is relatively low and the profit margin (i.e. the degree of labour exploitation $n - w$) relatively high the entrepreneurial preference clearly lies in the capital-saving direction. For example, in the extreme case where the wage is zero (i.e. OW coincides with the horizontal axis), the gain in profits due to a labour-saving innovation approaches zero (i.e. $\Delta\pi = O$), while the gain in profit due to capital-saving innovation is equivalent to the gain in output (i.e. $\Delta g = \Delta Q$). On top of these competitive arguments we can again add a couple of non-competitive ones;

(1) entrepreneurs in L.D.C.s are likely to be more paternalistic or 'family oriented' and motivated by a desire to provide employment opportunities for relatives as long as there is no extra cost; and

(2) there is generally greater pressure for output expansion in economies characterised by poverty and Say's Law.

Returning now to Fig. 13.3(a), let us assume that, historically, the initial technology in the industrially advanced country was at point A. We may then let the shaded area represent the set of newly possible unit activities resulting from the R. & D. expenditures, bounded by the knowledge frontier FF'. The choice of the post-innovation technology is then shown to be at point A_1, as determined, on the one hand, by the new knowledge frontier and, on the other, by a desire for maximum labour saving as argued above. It is in this manner that the technology shelf SS' itself has been built up historically in the mature economy.

A contemporary L.D.C., on the other hand, faced with technology shelf SS', will mainly be concerned with engaging in capital-saving innovations in accordance with our earlier analysis. For example, if unit technology A_1 is borrowed, such innovations may bring the actual unit technology down to point C. Choices along curve CD', the post-assimilation locus of unit technology, thus represent all the points describing the net result of moving along the technology shelf SS' plus the capital-saving innovation. The actual final resting place will be determined by profit maximisation as described earlier.[1]

VI. SUMMARY AND STATISTICAL IMPLEMENTATION

As we pointed out in the introduction, any study of L.D.C. innovations must be related to phases in the transition to modern growth. This problem is, in turn, intrinsically related to the development of entrepreneurship and to the improvement in the efficiency of resource utilisation once entrepreneurial capacities improve.[2] In this connection we have made two special assumptions. On the one hand, we assume that the L.D.C. under consideration is of a labour surplus type. This means that it fits the general description of a country initially marked by a substantial overhang of unemployed labour leading to approximate constancy of the real wage – or only moderate increases in the wage – with rapid increases in the real wage to follow later in the transition process. On the other hand, we assume that the importation of technology from abroad represents the dominant source of innovational ideas. While both assumptions somewhat delimit the generalisation of our theory, we believe that our approach is addressed to an important type of contemporary L.D.C.

The major theoretical conclusions of our paper can be derived from a synthesis of the arguments presented earlier. The central notion of a transition period of thirty to fifty years for the typical contemporary L.D.C. is accepted. The various phases which make up that transition are a reflection of the more or less natural maturing process with respect to (i) the development of entrepreneurship, and (ii) changes in the basic endowment condition, i.e. from a labour-abundant to a labour-scarce situation.

In the first phase of the transition we envision that entrepreneurs are still very inexperienced, at least as far as industrial activities are concerned. Innovations at this time are mainly of the unintentional or unconscious variety exemplified by the elimination of inefficiencies inherent in the process of technology transfer. In this first place, since the real wage remains low, innovations, as we have seen, tend to be labour-saving in nature, with little output-raising impact. Thus we would expect to observe moderate rates of growth of output or capital stock – due to the relative inexperience of the entrepreneurs and the consequent inefficiency of the emerging industrial structure.

---

[1] See, however, footnote 2, p. 321, for a qualification of the argument of this section.

[2] In an open economy, the first phase is often highly correlated with a so-called import substitution regime, the second with liberalisation and a greater role for the market mechanism.

In the second phase of transition entrepreneurs have become more experienced. As a result the unintentional (or unconscious) type of innovation gradually gives way to the more conscious type. In this phase, in contrast to the first, there is a deceleration of the capital-deepening process or, when carried to its logical conclusion, the possibility of some capital shallowing. Two arguments may be cited in support of this conclusion. First, as long as the real wage remains low, the capital-deepening effect traceable to residual innovations of the unintentional variety is gradually swamped by the effects of the intentional type which is, as we have seen, mainly capital shallowing in nature.[1] The conclusion is that such capital shallowing or reduction in capital deepening should be what we expect of any rationally operating labour surplus economy in which relatively mature entrepreneurs, for the first time, learn to make use of the relatively abundant factor, i.e. labour. It is for this reason that we expect rapid growth, both in terms of a higher rate of capital accumulation and of a higher rate of per capita income, to accompany the capital-shallowing process.

In the third phase of transition the innovation effect may be traced entirely to the conscious type of innovation – as the unconscious variety is completely exhausted. Now the innovation bias gradually shifts from labour using to labour saving. This tendency toward capital deepening becomes pronounced when, with the elimination of the economy's surplus labour and the consequential sustained increase in the real wage, innovation takes on the character typical of an industrially advanced economy. Capital deepening will be accompanied by a slowing down of the growth rate, as the surplus labour (a hidden source of saving) runs out and the economy gradually closes its technology gap with the advanced countries. Once development becomes more skill- and capital-based, the economy relies more and more on her own internal entrepreneurial talents to fashion the initial innovational breakthroughs.

In Fig. 13.4 the historical time series for capital per head (K/L), the real wage (w) and the rate of growth of the capital/stock (n_K) for the industrial sector of Japan are shown. The fifty years of transition experience, between 1880 and 1930, can be seen by inspection to be divisible into three possible sub-phases marked off by the two vertical lines in 1905 and 1917. The year 1917 moreover appears to be a major turning point, marking off the labour surplus phase from the phase characterised by the exhaustion of the labour surplus in agriculture [6]. To us the operational significance of the turning point is that, in the labour surplus phase, there is strong population pressure keeping the real wage from rising very much and inducing labour-using innovations. This contrasts sharply with the rapid wage increase after 1917 which, according to our analysis, induces entrepreneurs to innovate in a labour-saving direction.

[1] When the real wage climbs to a relatively higher level, even the unintentional type of innovation will have capital-shallowing consequences.

M

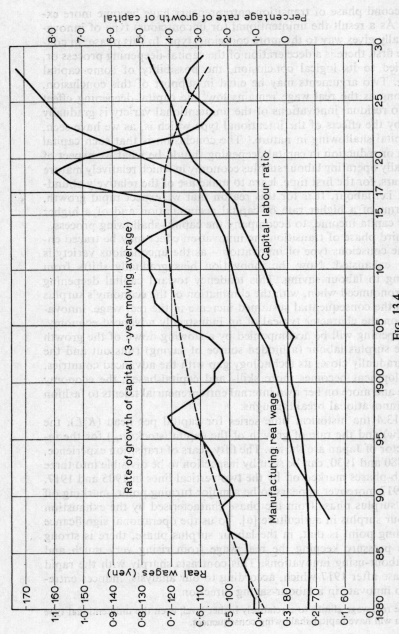

FIG. 13.4

Sources:

Manufacturing Real Wages are from Hakchung J. Choo, 'On the Empirical Relevancy of the Ranis-Fei Model of Economic Development: Comment', *American Economic Review*, to be published.

Capital stock estimates are from *Estimates of Long-Term Economic Statistics of Japan Since 1868*, Vol. 3, pp. 149–51, Total Net Capital Stock excluding Residences.

Based on these data, the average annual rate of increases of the real wage (w), capital per head (K/L) and capital stock (K) are presented in Table 13.1. The significance of the turning point in 1917 is seen by a comparison between rows (3) and (4). Moderate annual increases of real wage before 1917 (1·7 per cent) give way to much higher rates of increase (4·4 per cent) thereafter. Equally striking contrasts are shown for the rate of capital deepening (from 2·1 per cent to 4·0 per cent) and for the rate of growth of capital (from 2·9 per cent to 4·4 per cent) as between before and after the turning point.

TABLE 13.1

AVERAGE ANNUAL GROWTH RATES

Before 1917:	Real wage (w)[a]	Capital per head (K/L)	Capital (K)
(1) 1880–1905	1·8	1·2	2·3
(2) 1905–1917	1·6	4·0	4·4
(3) 1880–1917	1·7	2·1	2·9
After 1917:			
(4) 1917–1929	4·4	4·0	4·4

Note: [a] The real wage figures are based on a 5-year moving average beginning in 1880.

The year 1905 also appears to have some significance, by inspection of Fig. 13.4, possibly dividing the labour surplus phase into two sub-periods. For the period prior to 1905, there is a span of twenty-five years of near constancy of capital per head (1·2 per cent increase per year in Table 13.1), indicating a tendency towards 'capital shallowing growth'.[1] This is a significant phenomenon in the transition of a labour surplus economy. It signifies that entrepreneurs have, during this relatively long stretch of time, developed sufficient maturity and experience to be able to utilise the relatively abundant factor (i.e. the endowment of cheap labour) by innovating in a labour-using direction on top of the imported technology.

This rather remarkable entrepreneurial performance, of course, did not just happen but has to be viewed as resulting from the development of entrepreneurship in the earlier period. Our data begin in 1880, which is more than a decade after the Restoration in 1868. For the earlier period, in spite of the absence of reliable statistical data, there is ample qualitative evidence of the kind of inefficiencies, based on the immaturity of entrepreneurs just moving from agrarian and commercial pursuits into attempting to organise a 'modern' industrial sector, which characterised phase one on the analysis of our paper.[2]

[1] Earlier data led us to the conclusion of actual capital shallowing for this period (Fei and Ranis, ref. [5]). But the important point is that there is little capital deepening in spite of the modest increase in the real wage.

[2] This evidence includes the massive scale of early, rather frantic attempts to borrow technology, including whole factories, from abroad, once the economy had been

The period between 1905 and 1917 may be viewed as a transitional sub-phase between agricultural labour surplus and its ultimate exhaustion. During this subphase, the forces leading to the turning point begin to assert themselves. Entrepreneurs are, by now, fully matured. The fact that the real wage has climbed to a relatively higher level now induces them to begin to shift somewhat toward labour-saving innovations.[1] The result is that, after 1905, there begins a decided trend towards capital deepening growth, i.e. from 1·2 per cent before to 4·0 per cent thereafter (see Table 13.1).

The rapidity of growth of the economy as a whole during the fifty or so years of transition reflects three types of forces:

(i) an entrepreneurial maturing process,
(ii) the process of gradual exhaustion of the economy's surplus labour, and
(iii) the gradual narrowing of the technology gap (or the exhaustion of the advantage of the economy's 'latecomer status').

The first factor is the basic cause of the acceleration of the rate of expansion, especially in the early phase. The other two factors contribute to a deceleration effect on the rate of expansion. When we take the rate of capital accumulation as a proxy for the rate of growth of the whole economy, we can detect, in Fig. 13.4, a long-run inverse U-shaped curve (seen more clearly by the dotted curve fitted by free hand). This curve reaches a peak just before the turning point when the surplus labour is exhausted and when the economy's entrepreneurs have become fully matured.[2]

Any study of the transitional growth process through an investigation of macro-economic data must be accompanied by a reasonable theoretical framework. As noted earlier, the analysis of this paper constitutes only a preliminary attempt in this direction. If nothing else, we have demonstrated that what lies behind such macro data as capital-output and capital-labour ratios is an extremely complicated set of phenomena involving,

---

unceremoniously opened up after centuries of isolation. Secondly, the fact that many of the early factories were built by government on an experimental basis and sold to the private sector by around 1890 indicates the reduction of initial inefficiencies as the increased competence of private entrepreneurs could be harnessed. If we had the data our theory would predict finding capital deepening in the early post-Restoration years and an assist, by the unconscious type of innovation, to the capital shallowing tendency already noted above, thereafter.

[1] In addition to this conscious innovation argument is the capital shallowing effect traced to the exhaustion of the unconscious innovation possibilities accompanying the elimination of organisational inefficiency.

[2] From Table 13.1 we see that the rate of growth of capital increases from 2·3 per cent to 4·4 per cent annually (see rows 1 and 2). During the post-1917 period, the rate of growth of capital drastically decreases from its earlier peak as can be seen from Fig. 13.4, and could be observed statistically by calculating η_K for shorter time periods.

inter alia, the development of entrepreneurship and the coming into play of an entrepreneurial innovation inducement mechanism in assimilating imported technology, while making efficient use of a country's domestic resources. It is our hope that this approach can be further refined via a relaxation of some of our restrictive assumptions, and some of our behavioural patterns more fully specified as a consequence of more disaggregate empirical investigation.

REFERENCES

[1] R. M. Solow, 'Technical Change and the Aggregate Production Function', *RES* (August 1957); and S. Kuznets, *Modern Economic Growth* (New Haven: Yale University Press, 1966).
[2] R. M. Solow, 'A Contribution to the Theory of Economic Growth', *QJE* (February 1956); T. W. Swan, 'Economic Growth and Capital Accumulation', *Economic Record* (November 1956); and J. Fei, 'Per Capita Consumption and Growth', *QJE* (February 1965).
[3] Cf. J. A. Schumpeter, *The Theory of Economic Development* (Cambridge, Mass.: Harvard University Press, 1934); and Karl Marx, *Das Kapital* (London: George Allen & Unwin, Ltd., 1943).
[4] W. Fellner, 'Trends in the Activities Generating Technological Progress', *AER* (March 1970).
[5] W. Fellner, *Trends and Cycles in Economic Activity* (New York: Holt, Rinehart and Winston, 1956).
[6] J. Fei and G. Ranis, *Development of the Labor Surplus Economy: Theory and Policy* (Homewood, Ill.: Richard Irwin, Inc. 1964); and also J. Fei and G. Ranis, 'On the Empirical Relevancy of the Ranis-Fei Model of Economic Development: A Reply', to be published in the *AER*.

14 Science Policy in the Developing Countries: the Role of the Multinational Firm

Nicolas Jéquier

DIRECTORATE FOR SCIENTIFIC AFFAIRS, O.E.C.D.; PARIS

I. INTRODUCTION

One of the striking features of the evolution of the developing countries in the last ten years has been the substantial increase in their research and development (R. & D.) expenditures. Forecasts for the present decade show that this trend is accelerating: Latin American countries are planning to increase their R. & D. expenditures by 15 per cent per year, and several countries are preparing to devote 1 per cent of their gross national product to R. & D. by 1980.[1] Alongside with this one can observe a rapid build-up of specialised government bodies such as science ministries and science advisory councils. The assumption underlying these developments is that scientific research taken in the widest sense[2] can make an important contribution to economic growth, and therefore has an important role to play in any development strategy. Another factor which should not be overlooked is that research is a status symbol which no country, however underdeveloped, can afford not to have.

Numerous studies have shown, however, that the correlation between R. & D. expenditures and economic growth is at best inconclusive, and at worst negative. Nevertheless there does seem to be a good correlation between R. & D. expenditures and trade performance, especially if the analysis concentrates on well-defined industrial sectors. The low correlation with economic growth, best exemplified by the performance of the United States and the United Kingdom, might be construed as an indictment of R. & D. activities. However the real problem probably lies elsewhere: R. & D. expenditures, as far as they can be relied upon, only measure a country's inputs into original innovation. They give no indication as to the overall rate of technological change. The latter, which does indeed contribute very substantially to economic growth [1] consists not only of original innovation, but also of a very large amount of secondary innovation, which results from the importation of foreign licences and know-how, imitation and the normal effects of the learning curve. Were

[1] Cf. Pearson Report and UNESCO data.
[2] In this paper, science is taken in the German sense of *Wissenschaft*, and not in the traditional English sense. Science policy thus covers pure science as well as technology.

it possible to measure the way in which these total inputs are transformed by the scientific system into outputs, one might get a better idea of an eventual causal relationship between R. & D. and economic growth.

The initial hypothesis of this paper is that the scientific efforts of many developing countries, while they may in the long run make some contribution to economic growth and social development, are at present oriented in such a way that they cannot fulfil the purposes for which they were originally intended. It might therefore be necessary to envisage some fundamental revisions in the national science policies of developing countries. In a first stage, this paper will discuss some of the basic problems of science policy in the developing countries. In a second stage, it will discuss the role which could be played by the multinational corporations, and in particular their contribution towards the establishment of more responsive science policies in these countries. Multinational corporations, defined here in a very wide sense, account for at least half the total scientific and technological capability of the non-communist countries, and by virtue of this situation could become major partners in the scientific and technological policies of developing nations.

II. SHORTCOMINGS OF SCIENCE POLICY

Before considering what the new role of these firms might be, it is necessary to take a brief look at what has been traditionally called science policy, and in particular at some of its most conspicuous shortcomings:

  (a) The absence of any satisfactory yardsticks for measuring the successes and failures of science policy. In economic policy, export figures or growth data are a reasonably accurate way of measuring national performance; in science policy, R. & D. data tell nothing about performance, and governments operate more or less completely in the dark. At best one can surmise that there must be some sort of relationship between the amounts of money spent on research and the long-term returns it brings in. The uncertainty about performance is such that one can reasonably suspect that in many countries the scientific system operates satisfactorily not *because* of science policy, but *in spite* of it. In other terms, the distortions introduced in the system through national science policies (notably through massive programmes of military and prestige research) may well outweigh the benefits accruing to it as a result of increased government funding.

  (b) The imitative nature of science policy. In most countries, institutions, strategies and goals tend to follow the patterns set by a more 'advanced' country, and not the needs and capabilities of the country for which this policy is intended. Thus the larger European countries have a tendency to copy what has been done in the United States, and the developing countries to imitate the institutions and policies of the highly industrialised nations. This imitation effect is generally accompanied by an important time lag: European countries copy what the United States was doing five or ten years ago, and the developing nations copy what the more advanced countries were trying to do ten or fifteen years before.

(c) The practice of defining science policy primarily as a governmental policy. As a result, science policy as it is currently understood leaves out a substantial part of the scientific system, namely industrial research and the R. & D. activities of private institutions (foundations, non-profit companies, etc.). Furthermore, and partly as a result of this bias, science policy tends to concentrate upon the 'purer' end of the scientific spectrum, i.e. on fundamental research, and to neglect both the more mundane aspects of technological change, such as the role of imported innovation, and the highly complex issues, such as the influence of the social environment on creativity or a society's receptivity to change.

In the industrialised countries these shortcomings are serious, but they do not seem to have had any catastrophic effects, at least until now; in these countries the scientific system is sufficiently strong and adaptable to be able to weather the policies imposed upon it by government and, experience shows, has even been able to thrive on some of their basic flaws: thus military research has been for many American universities a golden opportunity for engaging in research programmes which otherwise would probably never have been undertaken.

In the developing countries the situation is generally far less satisfactory. First because the scientific system is inherently weak, both quantitatively and qualitatively. Government action tends to have a much wider impact than in the industrialised countries, and the balancing mechanisms of the scientific system are rather ineffective. This results not only from the state of underdevelopment of these countries, but also from the fact that government has a virtual monopoly in the allocation of research funds. Second, the imitation effect which pervades science policy is comparatively more damaging in the case of developing countries. This might be viewed as a result of history.

In Europe and in North America there was a well-established scientific system long before governments started to set up science policies. As a result, science policy tended to develop as a *superstructure* of the system. But in the developing countries, where there was generally no pre-existing scientific system, and few scientific traditions apart from old historical memories, science policy had another role to play: it was, or rather should have been, an *infrastructure*, i.e. a set of mechanisms and policies geared to the creation of a scientific tradition and a scientific system [2].

By imitating the highly industrialised countries, the developing nations have imported a superstructure-oriented type of science policy, when in fact what was required was an infrastructure-oriented policy. In many countries this situation has been very damaging, for the mechanisms which work reasonably well in a developed country often have the opposite effect when transposed into the very different environment of a developing nation.

The cause of this policy paradox is one of the most important questions which has to be faced by policy-makers in the developing countries. Why is it, for instance, that the increase in R. & D. expenditures has little if any effect on the quality and volume of research? In most developing countries these 'leakages' are very important, and the higher the level of government financing, the more rapidly they seem to increase. A similar phenomenon can be observed in the educational field: the increase in the number of university graduates, which in the industrialised countries is a precondition for the expansion of the scientific system, contributes in fact to undermining it in the developing countries. Increases in the output of university graduates seldom lead to better teaching or to more efficient research, and usually contribute to more social discontent and to substantially higher rates of emigration.

III. THE CONSTRAINTS OF THE SCIENTIFIC SYSTEM

A more responsive science policy cannot be envisaged if it does not take into account the constraints of the scientific system in the developing countries. A major policy reorientation might conceivably concentrate on some of the following points:

(a) The tendency for the 'scientific system' (the term system might seem too ambitious to describe the network of scientific activities in most developing nations) to form a ghetto in the society of the developing country. As a result contacts with other segments of society are very limited, and the political support which is needed by the scientific community in order to pursue its activities rests upon a very narrow base (usually a small group within the government bureaucracy or the party in power). Such a support may not be well accepted by society as a whole and it is far too dependent upon the whims of political fortune. The quality of research and the freedom necessary to the scientist suffer in consequence.

(b) The tendency for scientific and technological activities to remain aloof from the industrial and economic environment. A major

M 2

part of the research performed in developing countries is devoted to pure science, and what applied research there is cannot easily be transferred to industry or to agriculture. This aloofness is closely linked with the institutional set-up, and in particular with the weakness of industry and the inadequacy of the market mechanisms.

(c) The lack of communication between the scientific community of the developing country and the world scientific community. As a result research programmes in developing countries tend to duplicate what has been done elsewhere a few years previously. Because of this isolation these research activities are not subject to the constraints of intellectual competition on the world scientific market, and their quality is therefore often rather poor.

(d) The close link between research and higher education. In the developing countries, as in the highly industrialised countries, an important part of scientific activities (and virtually all fundamental research) is performed in the universities. This pattern, set in earlier decades by countries like Germany and the United States, may have been well adapted to the university of the past, but today it is showing clear signs of stress: it may be that the research function of the universities cannot be reconciled with the demands of mass education. In the developing countries the pressures put upon the universities by mass education are much stronger than elsewhere (the teacher-student ratio can measure this quite accurately) and there are serious doubts as to their ability to perform research, a task which after all did not come into the European universities until the late 19th century.[1]

(e) The mechanism of negative selection which operates on the scientific community of the developing countries. The high rate of emigration of local scientists and engineers means that the most enterprising and often the most creative people quit the country, leaving behind those who are unable to survive on the international scientific market and those who have a greater ability to compose with the local political and social structures.

(f) The tailoring of scientific activities of the developing countries to the fashions of the industrialised countries. This might be seen as a perversion of the system itself. However, it results essentially from the state of underdevelopment of these countries: in the absence of any 'market', or rather of any effective demand for the 'products' of the R. & D. effort, the only guideline which can be followed is the demand which can be found in the more advanced countries. Hence the emphasis on research projects which in many cases bear little or

---

[1] A classic case study of the conflict between mass education and research is A. B. Zahlan's article: 'Science in the Arab Middle East', *Minerva* (spring 1970).

no relationship with the real needs of the country. This tendency is further reinforced by the fact that, as in many Western countries, science policy is dominated by physicists; hence the emphasis on a group of scientific disciplines which are both costly and somewhat unrewarding [3].

IV. THE CAPABILITIES OF THE MULTINATIONAL FIRM

When looking at the role of the multinational corporation in the science policies of developing countries, two questions have to be raised. First, what type of policy is needed? And second, what are the particular assets of these firms which might play an important part in the elaboration and implementation of a science policy?

As noted earlier, science policies of the developing countries have tended to concentrate on the superstructural aspects to the detriment of the infrastructural aspects. Pushing the distinction a little further, one can outline three types of policies, or rather three stages:

(a) A primarily *infrastructural* policy.
(b) An *intermediary* science policy, whose main emphasis, together with the solution of infrastructural problems, is on the use of imported technology (through imports or imitation).
(c) A *superstructural* policy, which concentrates upon original innovation and a strong native R. & D. effort.

In practice the distinction between the three stages is seldom very clear, and government policies are generally a combination of the three, although the emphasis on each one may differ substantially from country to country. Each of these stages corresponds (or should correspond) to a certain level of development. The first applies primarily to the truly underdeveloped countries, the second to those which might be called semi-developed (like Mexico, Argentina, Brazil and, until recently, Japan) and the third to the highly industrialised nations. A policy of the third type does not preclude certain aspects of a policy of the second type: the best illustrations of this are probably Germany and the Soviet Union which, alongside with their own original innovative ability, have made considerable use of imported innovation.

In the case of the developing countries, the role of the multinational corporation has to be defined primarily in terms of an infrastructural policy and secondarily in terms of an intermediary policy. This might seem to run contrary to most policy suggestions in this matter, but it appears more adequate in view of the fundamental shortcomings of science policy in most developing countries.

One of the classical proposals of a superstructure-oriented policy is that multinational corporations expand their research activities in developing countries.[1] Experience shows that, while this may be beneficial in some specific instances (one might cite here cases of firms like Syntex in Mexico or Ciba in India), it cannot be a substitute for an infrastructural policy, and is at any rate quite insufficient to serve as a basis for a far-reaching science policy: in the Western world there are no more than 100 companies (and in fact probably far less) which are in a position to have several foreign research centres. Given an average of five foreign centres, at least three of which are almost necessarily located in a highly industrialised country (for purely scientific and technological reasons), the more than 100 developing countries of the world might be able to share some 200 important foreign laboratories, i.e. an average of two per country. Clearly this can only be a complement, and not the basis of a wide-ranging scientific strategy.

The idea that multinational corporations might foster research activities which are geared primarily to the needs of the developing countries in which they operate appears at first sight a more satisfactory proposal. However it can probably only work in a country which already represents a large market (i.e. a relatively big gross national product); furthermore it seems to run contrary to the logical evolution of many multinational corporations, whose strategies tend to be integrated on a world-wide basis and no longer, as was often the case before, to be defined in terms of a series of national markets.

An attempt to link multinational corporations to a superstructural type of science policy may well be self-defeating. First, because it does not correspond to the organisation and goals of the firm; second, because what developing countries generally need is an infrastructure-oriented science policy. In the framework of the latter one can see that multinational firms have a certain number of assets which, given the necessary policy adjustments, could make useful contributions to the scientific and technological development of many poor nations. Let us list some of these assets:

(a) The ability to transfer technology rapidly and efficiently. In fact there are reasons to believe that the internal transfer mechanisms of these firms are the most effective ones yet devised; at any rate, transfers from parent company to foreign subsidiaries are more efficient than transfers to unaffiliated foreign firms, and considerably more efficient than the transfers which take place through government channels. This capability has been developed in response both to market necessities and to the constraints of technology. A rapid transfer can be a decisive factor in the competition with other firms, both local and foreign; if production is organised

[1] This proposal has been raised among others by R. Demonts: 'La recherche dans la firme plurinationale', *Economie appliquée*, Tome XX, No. 4 (1967).

on an international basis, with one subsidiary providing parts or subsystems to others located in neighbouring countries, interface tolerances have to be very strict, and the technological level of each subsidiary must be at least equivalent to that of the parent firm and of the subsidiaries located in the industrialised countries.[1] In other terms the subsidiaries in the developing countries tend to be in close contact with the state of the art (i.e. the most advanced technology of that particular industry).

(b) The ability of the multinational corporation to select first-rate people to man its foreign operations. And on a more general level, its ability to train its personnel, both at the professional level and at the managerial level [4]. In the highly industrialised countries the large companies, which are usually multinational corporations, have succeeded to some extent in overcoming the deficiencies of the local education system. Thus in the computer industry, virtually all the programmers and systems analysts have, until quite recently, been trained by private companies and not by the governmental educational system. The same phenomenon can be observed in the managerial field: in Europe, where high level management schools are rare, American subsidiaries have to a large extent overcome this deficiency by developing their own internal management schools.

(c) The tendency of the large multinational corporation to serve as a breeding ground, or spin-off basis, for new companies. This depends of course on a large number of factors: the involuntary parent firm's managerial ability, its technological capability, its financial situation, its sector of operation (science-based industries are more spin-off prone than the more traditional industries). This ability to spin-off new companies also depends on certain environmental factors: anti-trust legislation, cartel agreements, labour mobility, sub-contracting practices, the possibility of enforcing technological embargoes upon former employees and, in a wider sense, the social conditions of the country in which such developments take place.

(d) Finally, and this is perhaps the most important factor, even though it may not be the most obvious one, there is what one may call the multinational firm's 'systems capability', i.e. its ability to deal with complex problems on an integrated basis (software and hardware). To some extent this might be viewed primarily as an extension of its managerial ability and its experience in dealing with projects which interact closely with the social environment (one illustration here would be construction, with its impact on urban development).

---

[1] This factor comes out quite clearly in the case of the computer industry. See *Gaps in Technology: Electronic Computers* (O.E.C.D., Paris, 1969).

There are as yet few pure 'systems firms', but many large corporations already have a significant capability in this field. Typical cases would be certain large American conglomerates (Litton Industries, TRW, Ling Temco Vought) and the large Japanese trading companies (Mitsui & Co., Marubeni Iida, C. Itoh). At present most of the systems firms are relatively less multinational than the traditional industrial corporations, but there are indications that many of them are planning to expand their operations on a world-wide basis.

V. THE ROLE OF POLICY

If things are left to run their own way, there are no reasons to believe that the subsidiaries of multinational corporations in the developing countries will ever come to play a significant role in the science policy-making process of these countries. The normal market mechanisms, as in so many other issues relating to these countries, tend to operate to the detriment of the latter, and not to their benefit. The problem, therefore, is to replace this failing market mechanism by something else, and this might be one of the main objectives of government policy in the scientific and technological field.

The assumption here is that something can be done, and should be done. Policy might be viewed as a means of creating the future, and the absence of policy as an acceptance of the *status quo*, and in particular of the failings of the market mechanisms. The problem is not simply to anticipate the trends which multinational corporations will follow in the scientific or technological field, but rather to foster new trends which are more in accordance with the long-term needs and possibilities of the developing countries. Such a policy reorientation has to take into account the constraints discussed above but it might also make use of certain capabilities of the multinational firm. This might be done in the form of direct agreements between the government of a developing country and the central management of the multinational firm. The idea of such agreements is relatively new, but experience shows that it can work. A model which might be followed in this respect is the agreement concluded by Chrysler Corp. with the British Ministry of Technology; when Chrysler took over the ailing Rootes Company it accepted certain conditions set by the British authorities (export policy, employment practices) and subsequent developments show that this agreement was reasonably successful. In fact there are reasons to believe that, apart from its purely technical aspects, it also helped to take the steam out of the political problems raised by such a takeover.

If such agreements were to be generalised in the developing countries, one can conceive that the latter would have to set up within their science policy machinery a new body whose aim would be to deal specifically with foreign subsidiaries. Such a body might conceivably be set up jointly with the Ministry of Industry and the Ministry of Education. Taking into account the capabilities of the multinational firms, such agreements could in a first stage cover some of the following issues:

(a) Provisions for facilitating the spin-off of new firms from the subsidiaries of multinational corporations. This might include joint-financing of the companies thus formed, long-term sub-contracting agreements and the prohibition of technological embargoes. For the moment, the number of such spin-offs in developing countries has been relatively small, but given a few incentives and a clear policy, it might be increased substantially.[1]

(b) A better utilisation of the subsidiary's contacts with the state of the art in its country of origin. This might take the form of a more effective information system, either through personal contacts (visits of scientists and technologists from the parent firm to the subsidiary and to partners of the latter in the developing country – be they universities, private research institutions or industrial firms) or through a more formalised information network (transfer of scientific papers and preprints to local scientists; use of the subsidiary's computerised information system by local people). Such a policy might be set up with the financial help of the developing country's science policy bodies. Compared to specific scientific projects, the expenditures would be minimal and the return on such investments probably very high. Such measures might be integrated in a broader policy aimed at fostering much wider contacts with the world scientific community.

(c) A reversal of the brain-drain through the employment of émigré scientists by the foreign subsidiaries. These subsidiaries offer the advantage of a more congenial environment than local firms, both in terms of salaries and intellectual rewards. Such a policy might include provisos, like that of letting these returnees devote a certain amount of their time to teaching or to consulting with government bodies. Many multinational firms have already on their own accord and for their own interest sought to engage émigré scientists from the country in which some of their main subsidiaries are located (Pfizer Corporation for instance has brought back several Taiwanese and Portuguese scientists from the United States). The aim here is not to create a new movement *ex nihilo*, but rather to

[1] American firms in South-East Asia have recently begun to spin-off a few new companies. See J. Morton, 'Licensee Relations – Japanese Style' (Bell Telephone Laboratories, Murray Hill, 1967, mimeo) and M. Evers, 'World Electronics to 1980' (Stanford Research Institute, Menlo Park, 1969).

encourage in a more systematic way the one which has already begun to take place.

(d) Closer ties between the foreign subsidiaries and the educational system of the developing country. In the management field the experiences of Nestlé and ALCAN in Switzerland (with management schools like IMEDE and the Centre d'Études Industrielles) offer a good example of what could also be done in some developing countries. This effort need not necessarily be limited to the management field: it could extend to the training of technicians and to refresher courses for middle level scientists. In most developing countries the subsidiaries of multinational corporations already have such programmes, but they tend to be reserved to employees of the company. Governments might therefore consider a widening of the functions of these training programmes, and in effect sub-contract part of their educational responsibilities to these subsidiaries.

(e) Application of the systems capability of certain large multinational firms to some of the most pressing issues of the developing countries. From a political point of view, this is probably the most sensitive field of all, and it is unlikely that these companies would be given a monopoly in this field. These systems problems would have to be tackled on a joint-venture basis. Typical cases in which such a capability might be used would be for instance the development of a mass education system (through TV and communications satellites); such a project could bring together a consortium of foreign subsidiaries (electronics firms, communications companies, publishing houses, etc.) and local firms. Another field which could be tackled on an integrated basis might be urban development: the explosive growth of cities in the developing countries is probably a far more complex issue than agricultural development [5]. Such a joint-venture approach would also help the developing countries to create the systems capability which many of them lack so conspicuously.

These suggestions are only a modest beginning. The purpose is simply to foster the idea that multinational corporations could play a very substantial and, if correctly channelled, a very positive role in the science policies of developing countries. However the fundamental issue, both in developing nations and in the highly industrialised countries, is whether science policy can continue to develop as a set of self-sufficient mechanisms: should it not be part of a much broader *societal policy*, which still has to be defined?

REFERENCES

[1] Cf. E. Dennison, *Why Growth Rates Differ* (Brookings Institution, Washington, D.C., 1967).
[2] Cf. C. Cooper: 'Science and Underdeveloped Countries', in *Problems of Science Policy* (O.E.C.D., Paris, 1968).
[3] Cf. J. Leite Lopes: 'La Science dans le Tiers-Monde', *Le Monde* (13 April 1967).
[4] See: *Pilot Survey on Technical Assistance Extended by Private Enterprise* (O.E.C.D., Paris, 1967) and A. Maddison, *Foreign Skills and Technical Assistance* (O.E.C.D., Paris, 1967).
[5] B. Ward, 'The Poor World's Cities' (*The Economist*, 6 December 1969).

Discussion of Papers by
Jack Baranson, Gustav Ranis and John Fei, and
Nicolas Jéquier

Professor Tuncer began by introducing the paper by Dr. Baranson. He said there were several ways of transferring technology from industrialised countries to the L.D.C.s. In his paper, Dr. Baranson focussed attention on the way technology was transferred through the multinational firm. His proposition was that before we thought of completely closing the gap we should first concentrate our efforts on reducing the existing technological gap to manageable proportions.

In the early pages of the paper the author asserted that in recent years there had been an extensive transference of technology to a relatively large number of newly industrialised countries. However, from an economic point of view, this kind of industrialisation had not been efficient in the past. Under pressure from the necessity to create industrial employment for a rapidly increasing labour force, and under foreign exchange restrictions, industries were established on a small scale to meet demand in local markets. The same protectionist policies also adversely affected product design and production techniques. All these developments, according to Dr. Baranson, led to serious technological gaps.

To illustrate these points, Dr. Baranson took the case of Taiwan's automotive industry, developed in technical co-operation with Japanese firms. It was a small industry producing 11,000 vehicles annually, in three plants, with eight basic models. The number of cars produced was far below the minimum for economies of scale by international standards and was the result of a protectionist regime. The fragmentation of the market was even more obvious when one considered spare parts. Later, Dr. Baranson suggested that this industry should move in the direction of Taiwan's electronics industry which was producing for export and was very successful. The firms operating in this field were wholly owned and operated by foreign firms.

According to Dr. Baranson, Taiwan could develop the production of specialised vehicles and parts for the world market in the automotive field as well. Wages were about one-third of Japan's. Japanese firms were now anxious to carry out this industrial activity in low-wage countries like Taiwan, to maintain their competitive position in the export field.

After giving these examples from Taiwan Dr. Baranson repeated that, to bridge the technological gap, it must first be narrowed to a 'bridgeable' size. This should be done by taking action on more than one front. First, and most important, the L.D.C.s should change their industrialisation policies. Indiscriminate import-substitution policies had caused the widening of the gap in the past. Second, industrially advanced countries should change their trade policies. They should concentrate on those fields where high technology and heavy capital investment were required, and leave industrial activity with a high labour content, which required middle-level skills, to less developed countries. Third, measures should be taken in the L.D.C.s towards the development of indigenous research and engineering. Fourth, the policies followed by the L.D.C.s should also change. A sustained relationship with an experienced industrial partner was essential for the implantation of technical knowledge and managerial systems suitable to the needs of the host country. Agreements should provide marginal adjustments in product designs and production techniques, the development of local supply industries and assistance to indigenous research and development.

A closer examination of the Baranson paper showed that it relied heavily on the old, static comparative-advantage theory and he advocated that the developing countries should specialise in activities with high labour content and middle-level skills. Professor Tuncer did not think the arguments were convincing enough on how this would contribute to the growth of the L.D.C.s in the long run. He further observed that, interesting as the examples from Taiwan might be, they had limited application to some other countries. In many parts of the underdeveloped world, social security legislation and labour unions pushed wage rates up in the non-agricultural sectors. Indeed they pushed them up to where there was little comparative advantage left in labour-intensive industries.

With his considerable experience in the economics of the Far-Eastern countries, Dr. Baranson gave vivid examples of how successful some Japanese firms had been in taking the opportunities created by low labour costs in countries like Taiwan. These examples showed clearly how it helped Japan to replace high-cost labour at home with cheap and abundant labour elsewhere, in order to maintain export competitiveness. Nevertheless it was not equally clear in the paper how this practice would narrow the technological gap and eventually help to close it. Dr. Baranson might wish to elaborate on this point during the discussion.

We should also not overlook the fact that technological change was more difficult in L.D.C.s than in industrialised countries, because major changes in the former were often opposed by strong traditional forces. For technological change to have a continuing impact on economic growth, these socio-economic barriers had to be removed and technological change had to become self-sustaining in the long run. This point also came out strongly in the Baranson paper, where the author suggested, '. . . but over time, factor productivities and technology itself can be upgraded through investment in education, in resources and in institution building'. Professor Tuncer thought it would have helped greatly if the author had shown more clearly the necessary link between overseas investment and the prerequisites of technological change.

It was also important to note that there were various means of transferring technology to the L.D.C.s. One of these was transfer through the multinational firm. It was undeniable that modern technological knowledge was concentrated in manufacturing firms in industrialised countries and that foreign investment had been an important carrier of this technology. Nevertheless there were certain problems inherent in this type of transfer that were not mentioned in the paper, but needed to be resolved if this kind of transfer were to be profitable to L.D.C.s. One problem was that, in a world of fixed exchange rates, these investments could create adverse effects on the balance of payments of the receiving country. Even if one thought in terms of flexible exchange rates, the fact still remained that there was a possibility of loss to the economy, possibly from adverse effects on the terms of trade.

Another potential conflict arose from the fact that the multinational firm sought to optimise its own profits. It would be wishful thinking to imagine that these benefits always coincided with the benefits of the host country. A further threat to harmonious co-operation stemmed from the fact that, sooner or later, the government of the host country found that large foreign firms became influential, and sometimes even a threat to their own sovereignty.

There were other possible areas of conflict of interest. Professor Lewis put this very convincingly in terms of the impact of foreign firms on domestic savings. Mr. Streeten had turned our attention to the possible shift in consumption functions. All these factors made other changes rather attractive as a source of the transfer of technology, including licensing, management contracts and the hire of the services of consulting firms.

Professor Tuncer thought that, in the final analysis, most of these questions ought to be resolved before the multinational firm was instrumental in bridging the technological gap. Private overseas investment was an important instrument for transferring technology to the L.D.C.s and would continue to be so in the years to come. He agreed with Dr. Baranson over his suggestions about policy changes, and would go further. Indeed he would say that the main responsibility lay with policy-makers in the less developed countries. Government there could and should pursue more consistent policies and the project-evaluation techniques suggested by Mr. Little could be a step in the right direction.

Professor Tsuru wanted to begin his comments on the paper by Professor Ranis and Fei by looking at their Figure 13.1. The conceptual framework was made up of three postulates and a set of definitions. The three postulates were these: first, there was a labour-surplus economy – the wage rate was at first constant and then rose; second, entrepreneurs were at first immature and then improved; third, there was borrowing of foreign technology. The technological situation was represented by the production function – a technology shelf. This was represented by S-S' in Fig. 13.1(a).

There was then the set of definitions about types of innovation. The authors distinguished social innovation from intentional innovation. Social innovation meant eliminating inefficiencies due to a pre-modern heritage. Thus in Fig. 13.2(a) the T-T' curve was to the North East of the S-S' curve. Both capital and labour costs were higher. The movement from T-T' to S-S' showed the degree of inefficiency overcome by social innovation. This had to be distinguished from intentional innovation where the entrepreneur acted rationally, accepting or rejecting a technology according to his judgement.

This was the conceptual framework. The theory worked mainly in terms of factor proportions. If the capital-labour ratio increased, there was capital deepening; if the capital-labour ratio fell, there was capital shallowing.

The theory distinguished three phases of development. First, there was a labour-surplus economy with entrepreneurial immaturity. Social innovation was predominant, and innovations tended to be labour-saving. In Fig. 13.2(a) this was shown in the lower range of the diagram at A_1 or A_2 where the vector of As was nearly horizontal. Development was more labour-saving at this stage. At A_5, the vector of As become almost vertical with capital-saving, now more important. So development was labour-saving in the early stages but output did not increase very much. Output was given by dividing K by k; by dividing K by the capital-output ratio.

In the second phase, entrepreneurs began to use the country's factor endowments. Social innovation gradually gave way to conscious innovation. Entrepreneurs began to use cheap labour. Development was now dependent on labour-using innovations. Capital intensity fell so that there was capital-shallowing, and output rose faster. What happened was more complex in this phase, and the paper gave three complicated reasons for this capital-shallowing.

In the third phase, the labour surplus had gone and entrepreneurs had matured. Now conscious innovation dominated there. There was a shift towards labour-saving innovations, so that one had capital-deepening again, and a fall in the growth rate. The essential conclusion of the whole theory was that factor proportions changed during growth.

Professor Tsuru said he wanted to make some theoretical comments. First, what was the unit of capital? Was it in value terms or in physical terms? What did the paper mean when it said that the capital stock was given or increasing? The result was that the increase in the capital/output ratio during development seemed to depend on a rather odd concept of capital.

Second, when we spoke of technical transformation we ought rather to speak of an increment of the capital stock (ΔK rather than K). For an innovation usually involved a small fraction.

Third, a crucial element in the theory was the relation of the S-S' and T-T' curves in Fig. 13.2(a). From inspection we could not know the properties of the diagram. However, they divided into two – direction and length. Direction was given by the arrows in the figure; length was shown by the degree of capital or labour saving in innovations. One therefore had a much longer distance from A_5 to B_5 than from A_1 to B_1. The greater technical content of development required more intense innovation. It was also more capital-saving.

It was important to emphasise that the shape of the T-T_1 curve in relation to the S-S_1 curve was an *assumption*. There might be good empirical grounds for it but intuitively it was not convincing. Yet the assumption was crucial to the later discussion – for example, the way MM and NN crossed in Fig. 13.2(b). For a less developed society, social innovation meant a movement from e_1 to E, with a falling labour content. A high labour content (with less capital) was shown in the move from e_1' to e_3'.

He should perhaps mention the intersection of the W-W curve with the marginal productivity curve in Fig. 13.2(b). Either E or e_1 was determined first; one went to J or Q. This determined what technology was used. Once the capital stock was given, the intersection of the wage line with the marginal productivity curve determined the choice of technique.

Professor Tsuru pointed out that, incidentally, the assumption that there was 'the same real wage level' during a historical period in developed countries and in the present period in underdeveloped countries had little meaning. It was most likely that the real wage rate in developed countries had been higher than that in less developed countries when the former adopted the technology which was now being adopted by the latter. In other words, the real wage rate in this sense was not the determinant of the choice of technique. This problem related to the question of what was the unit of capital.

In the remarks on the optimal labour force on page 320, Professor Tsuru wondered how the authors knew that there was no disguised unemployment of labour when that optimum existed.

On profit, Professor Tsuru said that the authors used profit and the rate of profit interchangeably, because they started with a given capital stock where the two were unambiguous. However, if one changed the capital stock through gross investment, or if one included working capital, he thought it would be wiser to distinguish the amount of profit from the rate of profit. In Fig. 13.1(b), A_1 was chosen from the three possibilities of A_0, A_1 and A_2, because the total amount of profit was maximised. However, A_2 gave a high profit too and, if one included working capital, it was possible that A_2 gave more profit than A_1. So, he was not entirely happy with the conceptual framework in the paper.

As for the remarks on Japan, he hesitated to say anything because theorists did a great deal of injustice to history in any case. He did not have enough data to be sure of his facts, but felt that the trend of real wages from which the paper apparently inferred that Japan had a labour surplus, in fact reflected a shift in the structure of the labour force – a shift from female to male labour and the emergence of the so-called 'dual structure'. If the authors had looked at the same type of labour and the same kind of firm, he doubted whether they would have found this shift. Furthermore, the emergence of factory labour was part of a historical process involving complex factors. The dearth of modern factory labour must have been considerable. How else could one explain the dependence of Japanese industrialisation on the use of prison labour, female labour and labour from the agricultural sector? The size of the agricultural labour force in Japan, in terms of families, was very constant from 1870 to 1940. Labour which moved from agriculture into the cities obviously came from a net addition to the agricultural population. The low wage level should be explained more in terms of the character of exploitation in Japanese agriculture.

On entrepreneurial maturity, Professor Tsuru thought those institutional factors more important which created a social condition where entrepreneurs could carry on rational economic calculations based on their own expectations. For example, there was increased monetary stability after the Bank of Japan was set up in 1885, and there was the development of social overhead capital. This process was not completed until 1900. There was also stability of foreign-exchange rates under the Gold Standard after 1897. Orderly and predictable government policies were then possible. Until the end of the Russo-Japanese war in 1905 entrepreneurs had found it hard to plan, and tariff autonomy came only in 1905. One very important aspect of Japanese growth was that it was linked to Japanese trade. A modern wage-labour market, responding to changes in the supply and demand for labour, came only after 1905.

In Fig. 13.4, Professor Tsuru looked at the rate of growth of capital stock in Japan. This increased after 1895, fell and rose again after 1905. It went up again after 1917. All these changes were connected with war and with reparations from China. Russia and elsewhere. The three curves in the diagram were too aggregated for the purpose of proving the Ranis/Fei thesis.

Professor Lundberg said that the paper by M. Jéquier was very different from some other papers, not least in its ease of reading. However, ease of reading or lucidity of writing had nothing to do with the complexity of the problems tackled.

He would take up the main theme and concentrate on certain questions. Our problem was that this was a topic where facts were minimal – something which economists often enjoyed. However, the seriousness of the problems was clear from the way in which M. Jéquier dealt with them. M. Jéquier took up the role of multinational corporations in helping to bring a change in science policy and research activities in underdeveloped countries. He argued that a number of weaknesses were apparent in underdeveloped countries on these fronts, and that these could be much improved by the use of multinational corporations. Indeed he gave the impression that he thought that this was the only efficient way to get a revision of science policy. He suggested that the use of multinational corporations would help underdeveloped countries to get away from the lack of contact between scientific policy and industry. He also noted the lack of communication between developed and underdeveloped countries on science policy and technical development, and thought that using the multinational corporation could help underdeveloped countries to develop research programmes better geared to their needs.

Professor Lundberg thought that it was very hard to define science policy. M. Jéquier took the term in a very broad sense, considering not only university science but the research and development of corporations too. He had a good deal to say about the need for the development of infrastructure in the form of a transfer mechanism to underdeveloped countries but gave a warning about building a superstructure of science policy with too little attention to what underdeveloped countries really needed.

M. Jéquier was sceptical. He noted how hard it was to link research and development to real economic growth. However, Professor Lundberg missed one thing in the paper. Looking at the research and development expenditure of industry in developed countries, one found that it concentrated on a limited field. In the U.K. a third went on the aircraft industry, which accounted for only 2 per cent of industrial output. Two-thirds of British and American research and development was on aircraft, electrical equipment and chemicals. These were not the first industries which would be setting up subsidiaries in underdeveloped countries.

M. Jéquier gave a very vivid picture of the failures of science policy in all countries. One distortion was the imitative nature of technical development and science policy in underdeveloped countries. M. Jéquier thought that these imitations probably had little to do with the real needs of the countries. However, Professor Lundberg suggested that what was useful for underdeveloped countries might, in fact, be just imitation. He thought that M. Jéquier had not looked sufficiently at the alternative of using the multinational corporations. M. Jéquier might have compared the cost of licensing in various forms, looking at the experiences of small European countries which had developed it in recent years. Buying and selling technical know-how represented a big element in their balance of payments. Such transfer of technical knowledge could be linked to the country's development of its own science policy.

Professor Lundberg mentioned that M. Jéquier had said that the shakiness of science policy had no catastrophic effect in developed countries because they had strong and adaptable structures. But were not these structures adaptable rather than strong? Professor Lundberg referred to the fact that much R. & D. expenditure in developed countries went into defence. This certainly could have catastrophic effects.

M. Jéquier said that some benefits of multinational corporations could be strengthened by government policy. They were a response to market needs and led to the training of first-rate local men and the spin-off through subcontracting. M. Jéquier added – and this was most important – that multinational corporations had people with systems-capacity which could be used in underdeveloped countries. He gave examples of how mass education with television might be important. This was politically dangerous – so that joint ventures were needed.

The market mechanism was not reliable on questions that had to do with research and development and science. What could governments do? How could governments make multinational corporations do what M. Jéquier had in mind? And could this happen on a large enough scale? M. Jéquier thought one might induce multinational corporations to help some countries' science policies, for example, by subcontracting part of the education system to them. The problem was that one needed to have governments strong enough to deal with the multinational corporation, while offering it enough incentives to bring in the desired benefits. Multinational corporations sought markets and profits. Very few underdeveloped countries offered good markets in fields where research was being done. Governments could certainly insist on the sort of drastic condition that Dr. Haq had mentioned in Pakistan. Then they would keep multinational corporations out. If governments wanted to impose conditions, they would have to consider the elasticity of supply of multinational corporations with respect to those conditions.

M. Jéquier thought that tariffs could help to stimulate the transfer of technology. However, Professor Lundberg thought we had agreed in the Round Table that it would be both dangerous and costly to do this, not least because of the profit which foreign firms would earn from import substitution policies. It would be better to pay lump sums to the multinational corporations and, if possible, thereby use international aid. Tariff barriers were much more costly.

M. Jéquier had a good sense of proportion; he did not expect wonders. He hoped for a modest beginning but more success later. What Professor Lundberg missed was an analysis of the limitations, costs and dangers of this special method of helping science policy and introducing research and development in underdeveloped countries. Professor Lundberg would have liked more reference to experience. The cost of multinational corporations to underdeveloped countries could be high. It could lead to an instability of decision-taking because the decision centres of the multinational corporations themselves were very far away. There was always an element of creative destruction inhibiting local production. And there were serious political issues too. There were reasons to fear multinational corporations, and these fears were far from being least in science policy. How many underdeveloped countries could rely on this type of policy? What were the alternatives?

Professor Lundberg had felt sometimes at Round Table discussions that when we dealt with underdeveloped countries, we did not remember that it was not only the stage of development that mattered, but the size of the country too. This must affect the possibility of taking advantage from introducing the activities of multinational corporations. There was the alternative of making contracts with teams of managers and engineers to start production, research and education. Could feasible policies of contracts often be safer alternatives? This surely was a problem that had been dealt with by Dr. Rosenstein-Rodan years ago.

In all circumstances the transfer of scientific policy and research and development through the multinational corporation *could* be an effective way to transfer knowledge. The great issue was how, and with what success, governments could deal with them. Dealing with multinational corporations in order to get results along the lines suggested by M. Jéquier was certainly a great art.

Professor Ghai said that these papers, and indeed much of the discussion in the literature on technology, focussed attention on only one aspect of the technological problems of underdeveloped countries, namely the transfer of already available technology from developed countries to L.D.C.s. This was unfortunate because it distracted attention from what he saw as the more important problem – the development of new technology and new products more appropriate to the economic and social circumstances of the L.D.C.s. It was now widely accepted that, apart from industries like petro-chemicals where there might be no real choice of technique, in most cases, particularly in agriculture, technology in advanced countries was inappropriate for developing countries. There might also be a few other industries where the latest technology was dominant in the sense that it used less of both capital and labour per unit of output.

The technology developed in the advanced countries fifty or sixty years ago might also be inappropriate to present-day L.D.C.s. There were, first, all the well-known problems associated with the revival of a defunct technology. The capital equipment was no longer produced, nor were spare parts; nor were engineers and technicians familiar with them. Second, of course, 1970 was different from 1870; the quality and design of products had changed, as had people's tastes. New materials had been discovered which were not known a hundred years ago. For all these reasons it might be found that, in many cases, the technological 'shelf' developed in the rich countries, whether over the past decade or the past century, was inappropriate for present-day L.D.C.s.

So the developing countries faced the great challenge of devising new technology including, wherever feasible, the adaptation of existing technology developed in rich countries. This technology would not only be appropriate to factor endowments in the narrow economic sense, but would also be in tune with the social environment. And the new technology was needed not just to produce, by different techniques, products already known. The new technology was needed to produce modified products, for example, a means of family transport halfway between a car and a bicycle, or a car minus all the frills required by consumers in rich societies. Or it might be the development of new agricultural machinery somewhere between the traditional man-and-oxen and modern tractors and bulldozers. Or it might be the development of a technology capable of constructing modern houses at vastly lower cost.

The question was how could the task of developing new technology in the sense just described be best organised? An essential condition was large-scale research, often carried out over long periods. The characteristics of such research, as was well known, were: (a) that it was expensive; (b) that it required high-quality and scarce professional talent; and (c) that it was risky, with uncertain results.

Because of these characteristics, it seemed that neither the multinational corporation nor local entrepreneurs in L.D.C.s were capable of carrying out research leading to the development of new kinds of technology and product. For the former, operations in L.D.C.s were a marginal part of their activities; investment in research was risky and they might not be able to appropriate enough of the gains. Since such R. & D. was beyond the resources of most domestic corporations in underdeveloped countries, we were forced back to governments. While a few underdeveloped countries might feel able to commit large resources to research of this kind, most were either too small or too unwilling to take the risks involved. A novel way of organising such research might be through international research institutions located in developing countries, but carrying out intensive research on technological problems relevant to a large number of developing countries and financed by foreign aid. A prototype of such an organisation already existed in the International Rice Research Institute in the Philippines and the Wheat Research Institute in Mexico. The spectacular results achieved by research in these institutions demonstrated the enormous potential pay-off from concentrated, organised research into these problems. The International Institute for Tropical Agriculture recently established in Nigeria was another example. Perhaps the most interesting innovation in this field was the creation of the Canadian International Development Research Center, through which 5 per cent of all Canadian assistance would be channelled. It was charged with the aim of promoting research on problems of developing countries. It seemed that technological break-throughs, relevant to L.D.C.s, would come from research organised in this kind of way.

Professor Rasmussen said that Professors Fei and Ranis assumed the capital stock given but a range of choice of techniques. He thought the idea that there was not much choice was more fruitful and wondered whether they had given thought to allowing this. On M. Jéquier's paper, he was unhappy that it was so narrow. It really considered science policy only in relation to multinational corporations. Perhaps the Programme Committee had narrowed the choice, but he would have liked a more general view of science policy in underdeveloped countries and its possible contribution to reducing the gap. One heading might be: 'Science Policy as a Vehicle for the Transfer of Technology from Abroad'. He thought that one should look not only at underdeveloped but also at the smaller developed countries in this respect.

Professor Vernon commented on the paper by Dr. Baranson. This had a series of implicit and explicit generalisations about static and dynamic comparative advantage, and he wondered whether Dr. Baranson was right in his assumptions. He thought the evidence showed that the Heckscher-Ohlin proposition was right and that the Leontief paradox was something of a red herring. Perhaps there was confusion because of the mis-specification of where it was that the developed countries had advantages.

Professor Vernon wondered whether it was not also true that comparative advantage changed satisfactorily over time, in the way that we would expect. Few comparative advantages were frozen; they changed, as we would expect them to do. Underdeveloped countries, for example, shifted in general from primary products to some manufacturing. All this was reassuring and satisfactory.

At the level of the firm, one found a similar pattern. Once the degree of oligopoly for a product fell, the multinational corporation gave up market share and left production to local enterprises. It went from import substitution to simple exporting, and then to more complex exporting. Professor Tuncer was right that this was not the only way to get technology. One study had reconstructed the sources of technology for 375 petro-chemical plants, covering all plants producing certain petro-chemicals outside the Communist world. Many of these plants were not owned by multinational corporations, but these had been established after it had become easy to get the technology by licensing. So there were trade-offs. Waiting made local ownership easier, but many countries did not want to wait. A price had to be paid for using other than the quickest and easiest channel for the transmission of technology. But if a country was prepared to pay the cost, why should it not be allowed to do so?

Professor Correa thought we should define the characteristics of the technology to be transferred. Professors Ranis and Fei had referred to Solow's evaluation of the contribution of increased productivity to economic growth. Not all the technological change measured by Solow could be transferred. For example, his own estimates showed that an important increase in productivity in L.D.C.s was due to improved nutrition and health.[1] This was not a transfer of technology via the profit-maximising firms. So a change which was appropriate for one level of development might not be appropriate at another.

The technical shelf did not exist, even for marginal increments of productivity. What was available to underdeveloped countries depended on the best practice in developed countries. Perhaps markets in L.D.C.s were too small to influence the techniques embodied in new capital goods. Even if there was a technological shelf, underdeveloped countries might not choose well from it because their entrepreneurs lacked the ability to choose by rational cost-benefit analyses, but listened to foreign salesmen instead. The paper made the obvious point that in the early industrialisation of Japan there were mistakes of direction in the short period. But the evidence suggested that this period lasted longer in the underdeveloped countries than the paper implied.

Professor Khachaturov said that on pages 337 and 338 of M. Jéquier's paper he wrote of the low efficiency of the research and development in underdeveloped countries. What suggestions had M. Jéquier on how to maximise the effectiveness of expenditure on research and development for economic growth?

Professor Chenery spoke about the level of aggregation in the Ranis–Fei paper. Their studies were about national economies so that the technological shelf represented a weighted average for all sectors. This was not a very useful concept, not least because it included agriculture and services. Once one had aggregated all kinds of argument could be used to show how one was wrong in given cases.

Working sectorally was more useful and would show how one could improve the model. If one were looking at production functions industry by industry, there was a lot of earlier work. For example, such research had found technological substitution and borrowing from the technical shelf different in the U.S. from Japan in different sectors. In steel and petrol Japanese productivity was equal to American; in textiles it was only about 50 per cent.

Another study of Japan and Peru gave similar results. The more capital-intensive activity used more modern technology. He doubted whether there was

[1] Correa, H., 'Sources of Economic Growth in Latin America', *The Southern Economic Journal*, Vol. XXXII, No. 1 (July 1970), pp. 17, 31.

a difference in the figures because the more capital-intensive activity showed less difference between countries. The same was true for different size of firm and economies of scale. Once one used sectoral analysis, great variety appeared. One needed other factors as well as labour productivity. Highly capital-intensive industries showed high efficiency because they used a lot of capital and the rate of labour productivity was not very significant. There was some benefit from co-operating factors. For example, a steel mill *must* have a good manager; too much was at stake. Management was less important in a textile mill. If one distinguished traded and non-traded goods, Japan was closer to the U.S. in traded goods. So sectoral differences were more than just a matter of wage rates and productivity.

Professor Srinivasan said he wanted to question two of the Ranis–Fei conclusions. First, they concluded that entrepreneurs in developed countries devoted their researches to labour-saving innovations, since they anticipated a steady growth in wage rates and a steady increase in the difficulties of dealing with trade unions. It seemed to him that any innovation, regardless of its bias, reduced unit costs, and an entrepreneur would choose that innovation which would reduce unit costs by the largest amount assuming that the cost of 'innovating' was the same for each innovation. Such an innovation need not be labour-saving, in the context of rising wages. He had illustrated this below.

Assume that there were only two factors, labour and capital. Their initial

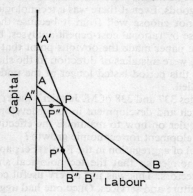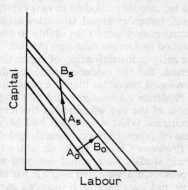

FIG. 1

relative price was indicated by the slope of AB. Let the initial factor combination per unit of output be indicated by the point P on AB. Further assume that there was an increase in the wage rate relatively to the price of capital, so that the relative price line was $A'B'$. We could now consider two alternative innovations, represented by the factor combinations P' and P'', for producing a unit of output. P' represented a capital-saving innovation, since it reduced the capital/output ratio without changing the labour coefficient. Similarly, P'' represented a labour-saving innovation. The line $A''B''$ was drawn through P', parallel to the line $A'B'$.

It was obvious from the diagram that the labour-saving innovation, represented by P'', resulted in higher unit costs at the price represented by the slops $A'B'$, than the capital-saving innovation P'. A cost-minimising entrepreneur would opt for P' rather than P'', despite the fact that he was reacting to an increase in the wage rate. This illustration ignored the cost of innovation. Once we recognised this cost, it was clear that an entrepreneur allocating his research resources would be concerned with efforts to find that innovation which would maximise his return from such resources, regardless of its factor bias.

Professor Srinivasan said that his second point related to the Fei–Ranis diagram (Fig. 13.2(a)). They argued that an L.D.C. would bear heavier real costs if it attempted to import technologies of more recent vintage. This was shown, in Fig. 13.2(a), by the increasing length of the vectors A_0B_0, A_1B_1, A_2B_2, etc., as one moved to the left. He doubted if this was correct. He had tried to construct a diagram similar to their Fig. 13.2(a) in his own Figure 2. In order to keep it fairly simple, he had drawn only A_0B_0 and A_5B_5. He had also drawn the price lines on which these points lay. The diagram was so constructed that the inefficiency associated with B_0 as compared with A_0 was the same as that one got when comparing B_5 and A_5. In other words, the increase in unit cost at B_0 as compared with A_0 was the same as the increase in unit cost at B_5 as compared with A_5. Thus despite the vector A_5B_5 being longer than A_0B_0, the inefficiency associated with B_5 did not involve as heavy a real cost as the inefficiency associated with B_0.

In conclusion, he would like to find out from the authors whether they were saying much more than that efficiency was better than inefficiency; and that it was better to devise or borrow technology relative to one's own factor endowments.

Professor Patinkin wanted to raise a point on what Professor Tsuru had said. Professor Tsuru had argued that what had happened in Japan had not been the use of surplus labour but a shift from male to female labour. Was this not largely a semantic point? Surely what had happened was that Japan had used up all labour of one type. In some sense one was simply saying that the whole of a particular kind of surplus labour was used up.

He would like to ask all the authors of the papers why they made the implicit assumption that the market mechanism did not lead developed countries to develop technology which was relevant to the L.D.C.s. He genuinely wanted to know. Why did not international corporations do it? Did they not see market possibilities? Perhaps they had done so, but he did not know about it. Certainly tractors had become smaller. Basically, he remained puzzled.

To Dr. Ghai, Professor Patinkin said that his example of a vehicle between a car and a bicycle was a bad one. One could see in underdeveloped countries that both cycles and cars served rather different functions from those they served in developed countries. They were modified to suit local needs and local industries did indeed improvise and make use of vehicles between cars and bicycles.

Professor Robinson said he wanted to ask a naïve question on the whole range of problems. If a country had a labour surplus, was not only one question important – how to minimise the amount of capital per unit of output? The capital/labour ratio was almost irrelevant. What the country needed to do was obtain results with minimal amount of capital. Much of the discussion at the Round Table had suggested that more labour could be equally efficient with less capital. But did we ask engineers if this made engineering sense? Often, he suspected, it did not. He wanted to give some examples. In automated car factories almost all basic machining of the cylinder block was carried out by automatic transfer machinery. This was part of the labour saving operation, it was true, but it also saved capital. Automatic transfer worked more quickly and more accurately so that one got more efficient work from the rest of the capital. Similarly, the electronic control of the machine had the same effect of making the machine work faster and more efficiently and was in this sense capital-saving. In one sense, this was what Professor Vernon had said when he had remarked that the machine set the tempo. There were many cases, he believed, in which minimising the amount of capital almost inevitably saved labour.

To Professor Robinson this meant that we must study both capital- and labour-intensive products and activities. It was important to concentrate on the choice of product rather than of technique. One should concentrate on activities with low capital-intensity. A difficulty here arose because most of the capital-intensive technology went into the infrastructure needed for later development. But that did not mean there was no problem of choice of technique. What should a country do, for example, if it was asking how to increase investment in electricity? If it decided it needed energy for industrialisation, it still had the choice between thermal, hydro and nuclear electricity plants. This was an ordinary choice of technology, but perhaps economists spent too much time finding economic solutions to problems where the economic solution would not work in engineering practice.

Professor Horvat made a comment on what Professor Tsuru had said. On changes in capital/output ratio over time, the Ranis–Fei assumptions were rather like the threshold theory of Professor Bičenič. Empirical tests had shown that the world did not quite comply with these assumptions. So Professor Horvat had himself collected all the data on capital-output ratios. He had found a tendency for the capital-output ratio to rise in 1914 and to fall ever since. This applied even to countries as diverse as Yugoslavia, South Africa and the U.S.A. It applied not only overall but to the components: to manufacturing, agriculture and mining. The reasoning might be correct, but overwhelmed by technological progress at both high and low levels of development.

To Professor Robinson, Professor Horvat said he had asked the same question of engineers in the Yugoslav Federal Planning Bureau. The answer was that there was nothing one could do with the basic technology. What was efficient in the

U.S.A. was also efficient in Yugoslavia, India, etc. But one could alter the ancillary equipment.

Dr. Baranson replied to the discussion. Professor Tuncer had agreed that countries like Taiwan and Korea might well benefit from relations with Japan, but had asked: what about L.D.C.s? Taiwan was a rather special case. Wages were only one-third of those in Japan, which was not representative of the higher labour costs encountered in other underdeveloped countries. For example, in Puerto Rico after ten years, wage advantages had withered away. How could these plants survive without the advantage of low wage costs? Dr. Baranson argued that the lesson to be drawn from the Puerto Rican case was that an underdeveloped country might only have low wages for a limited time period – say fifteen years – during which it had to capitalise on its comparative advantage. Places like Singapore and Hong Kong had found activities where they could specialise even as wages began rising. They would have to move on to new activities and raise productivity in the process.

Dr. Baranson then turned to investment in education and research. In the short term, multinational corporations could help to establish production capabilities in areas of static comparative advantage. But, even more important for the L.D.C. in the long run, it could help a country to develop a more appropriate technology and to select products in which to specialise according to its productive capability. This would give a developing country a share of production of advanced products for world markets.

On private foreign investment, Dr. Baranson thought that one had to look at the overall contribution to long-term industrial growth and development. For example, Taiwan was involved in negotiations with a Japanese multinational corporation which enabled it to make a specialised product for Japanese and world markets. There was not just the question of profit flows to the multinational corporations; the country also had to ask what were its long-term goals in moving from import substitution to more efficient production for world markets, and build these goals into basic agreements.

On the question whether current or new technology should be transferred, he had a divided view. At one point he had emphasised adapted technology for L.D.C.s but, the more he saw of the world, the more he saw the force of Professor Robinson's points. The technology already on the shelf consisted of all the things that engineers could presently make. Major efforts should go into making appropriate selections and finding more effective transfer modes.

On static comparative advantage, he had tried to emphasise that a country needed to pick up those segments of production where it had available skill and, taking state-of-the-art technology, get into production. Over time the country could move into more sophisticated and advantageous activities. The dynamic effects of learning how to do these things got the country to the plateau of take-off. His paper had said that a country should always be asking: what are the necessary steps to reach the take-off point?

The critical factor was scale. For motor vehicle and parts manufacture, for example, it was pathetic to see engineers breaking down processes in L.D.C. plants because they could not use automatic transfer machines. They inevitably ended up with a higher capital-output ratio for the lower scales.

Professor Ranis said that, as Professor Tsuru had emphasised, they had tried to deal with three main elements: most innovation came from abroad, most entrepreneurs were immature and drastic changes were needed in the factor endowments of developing countries. They had looked at the interaction between these three at the aggregate level, and also at the figure at entrepreneurial level. However they had not looked at the problem at Professor Chenery's sectoral level. He agreed with Professor Chenery that to move to the sectoral level would be useful.

On social innovation, Professor Tsuru had argued that things other than entrepreneurial maturity were important. Professor Ranis agreed that, at an early stage of development, the preconditions and the creation of overhead capital were important. At the aggregate level most of the emphasis for Japan was on entrepreneurial inducement in the second phase, when private innovations were being made. Japan had concentrated on a conscious attempt to bias innovation, plus the import of technology.

Professor Ranis said that Professor Ghai obviously thought that they did not emphasise indigenous innovations sufficiently. It was not just a question of importing 1890-machines. A country had to take a piece of the production process from abroad and make new modern innovation 'on top' of it.

Professor Ranis then discussed Professor Tsuru's theoretical points. The definition of a unit of capital was an old controversy which he wanted to leave to one side here. However he had not argued that the capital-output ratio had to rise during development. It might be constant or declining, and the curve in Figure 13.1, page 318 had simply been drawn in that way. On the issue of the capital stock versus the increase in the capital stock, and whether entrepreneurs already had to choose, theirs was an *ex ante* shelf. It assumed that the choice was made by entrepreneurs in terms of the wage rate and a particular technology and decisions were not expected to change every year. Professor Tsuru's interpretation of the S-S' curve was not the same as theirs, though this was not crucial to the paper. Most of their empirical work had been done on innovation and did not depend on the S-S' curve.

As one moved to the micro-level, one could look at why entrepreneurs did not move to labour-saving processes when there was an increase in the wage rate. This was a profitable area for work, as he agreed with Professor Chenery.

To Professor Robinson, Professor Ranis said that they had been doing interview work in Korea and Taiwan and had found a lot of difference in processes between firms, even when engineers said there was none. When one asked engineers why things were different in a particular plant, one was told that they were the same. In fact one found differences in numbers of shifts, speed of work, the ratio of repair to operative workers, and so on. They had been looking, like Professor Robinson, at how far the amount of capital per labour unit was falling.

Professor Ranis suggested that one reason why there seemed to be a marked inadequacy in the transfer of technology was that markets in underdeveloped countries were very small, and that so far there had been little demand for intermediate technology. He agreed that intermediate technologies could be more appropriate in L.D.C.s. However, once the market was there, he saw no reason why profit-maximising firms should not respond to it.

Professor Fei said that there were many problems in the paper because of the limitations of the aggregate model. However, the aggregate model did allow technical change to be integrated into a growth model with capital accumulation, population growth, etc.

The big question was what were the appropriate production conditions to assume, in order to analyse technical change. Some spoke of technical change embodied in the labour force; Professor Tsuru obviously thought of 'vintage-capital'. In the choice of appropriate production conditions, one had to remember: First, that production conditions had to be conducive to a rational theory of innovation and motivation. How did entrepreneurs choose? Little evidence had emerged. Second, data needed to be statistically identifiable. They had therefore chosen the Leontieff factor-complementarity type of function, allowing them to look at motivation and test this statistically. Similarly, on the remarks of Professor Srinivasan, one should note that in Professor Srinivasan's diagram a higher wage rate led to a more labour-saving method.

Professor Tsuru had asked whether economists should study economic history. There were always historical events like war, and all time series were affected by them. Perhaps the economic historians would allow us to isolate from these historical influences the problems we wanted so study.

M. Jéquier said that various speakers had suggested that his concentration on the role of multinational corporations in science policy was narrow. Professor Rasmussen had given him the excuse that the programme committee had narrowed his topic. It would have been easy to take this way out, but he ought to accept the responsibility of narrowing the paper himself. The main reason for concentrating on multinational corporations was that they accounted for approximately half the research and development effort in the western world. In most developing countries the national scientific system was very weak, and science policies often ineffective. The problem was therefore to investigate the ways in which multinational corporations might contribute to strengthening the scientific and technological infrastructure of the developing countries.

This was obviously a very delicate political issue, and the multinational corporation was not the only instrument whereby this infrastructure could be reinforced. Large firms could, however, contribute to improving the climate for science and technology in a developing country and could, among other things, create a demand for the products of the local scientific system.

Unfortunately little was known about the links between the scientific system and the social environment. It did appear that it was far more difficult to create a favourable environment for research and development than it was to destroy a pre-existing favourable environment. The story of Germany in the 1930s, and of many developing countries which in recent years had undergone political upheavals, was probably the best illustration of this.

M. Jéquier agreed with Professor Lundberg that a lot of the research and development effort of multinational corporations went to military and prestige projects which were not directly relevant to the problems of the developing nations. However, these firms had a managerial capability and an experience of complex systems which could be, and already had been, applied to non-military problems. Professor Lundberg had rightly emphasised the profit orientation of the multinational corporation. But one should not ignore the large firm's concern for much wider social issues. We now needed to focus this for the benefit of L.D.C.s. He agreed with Professor Lundberg that his treatment of the tariff

N

problem had been cursory and would just like to say that one did not necessarily
have to choose between a tariff and an outright grant. One could have the intermediate solution of a temporary tariff.

Professor Khatchaturov had raised one of the very complex issues of science
policy: what was the relationship between research and development and economic growth? Most of the data we had were rather inconclusive, and there was
no way of establishing a meaningful correlation between R. & D. and economic
growth. Part of the problem stemmed from the fact that R. & D. data measured
only a country's original innovation, while economic growth was a much broader
phenomenon, relying often more on imported innovation than on local, original
innovation. In other terms, what one should attempt to measure was the total
process of scientific and technological change rather than simply the relatively
small part of it concerned with original innovation. One of the problems of the
developing countries was that too little attention was paid to the fact that
science policy and technological policy could perhaps more profitably concentrate on imported innovation (or secondary innovation) rather than on
original (or primary) innovation. It was probably no coincidence that in most
developing countries science policy had developed quite independently from,
and without any interactions with, technical assistance programmes.

Professor Patinkin had asked why market forces did not work. One possible
explanation for this was that the scientific system was highly international,
while science policies were essentially national. The market forces might well be
operating correctly at the international level, but for many countries this could
be highly detrimental, and was certainly politically unacceptable. In terms of the
international system, it would probably be more efficient to concentrate all R. &
D. activities in the most highly industrialised countries, but this process of
polarisation, which would result from the free working of international market
forces, would probably contribute to widening the gap between the rich and the
poor nations. The problem therefore appeared to be how to create new market
forces, either national or transnational, to counteract the negative effects of un-
restrained competition between unequal nations.

15 The Brain Drain and the Development Process[1]

Richard Jolly and Dudley Seers

INSTITUTE OF DEVELOPMENT STUDIES AT THE UNIVERSITY OF SUSSEX,
BRIGHTON

I. INTRODUCTORY

In spite of the publication of many factual and analytical studies of the
brain drain in recent years, very little systematic attention has been paid
to its links with the process of development, or perhaps rather with distortions in the process of development. In the past decade there have been
two conspicuous distortions in many poor countries. One has been the
growth of unemployment; the other, the persistence of (or even increase
in) the concentration of income. These are linked with each other in
mutual causation. They are also each aspects of growing imbalances in
the world economy.

The purpose of this paper is to widen the somewhat sterile controversy
about who gains and who loses from the migration of the professionally
qualified, by attempting to sketch out the approach to a systematic integration of the analysis of the brain drain with the analysis of the whole
development process, placing the discussion within the framework of the
widening gap between rich countries and poor.

The paper is in five parts: a brief summary of 'brain drain' literature with
a critique of the neo-classical treatment of unemployment and the brain
drain; a summary of the failures in the development process in the 'developing' countries; a critical evaluation of the brain drain in the light of
this analysis; a section on the 'reverse' flow towards poor countries; and a
note on research needs.

II. THE BRAIN DRAIN LITERATURE

The economic literature on the brain drain in recent years has been dominated by analysis of a general model of the economic losses and gains
from the international migration of educated manpower, assuming free
markets in long-run equilibrium.

These analytical arguments have generally taken little account of the

---

[1] The version of this paper presented at Bled has subsequently been revised to take
account of comments made there and by other colleagues. We are particularly grateful
for helpful comments from Michael Lipton.

structure of the qualified manpower involved in the brain drain. The welfare analysis of gains and losses has been constructed on supposedly general characteristics of educated manpower, with little reference to the particular characteristics of the doctors, engineers and scientists, who are the professionals mainly concerned. The underlying model has been of a private, profit-maximising, full employment and output to changing stocks of skilled manpower, with other factors held constant. The model has assumed that each individual's output is readily identifiable and satisfactorily measured in terms of economic returns.

In practice, however, the brain drain has comprised a high proportion of doctors, scientists and engineers; these persons are in occupations in which output is not all easy to identify (for instance, scientists). Nor is it satisfactorily measured by economic returns (for instance, doctors) even on the assumption that the existing distribution of income is satisfactory, which is hard to sustain whether we are discussing distribution within most countries or between countries. Moreover, a high proportion of those in these professional categories are] employed either within public administration or education (where the rules of profit-maximisation hardly apply) or on work heavily dependent on government contracts (where the links with 'consumer demand' are tenuous, to say the least).

Economists working within this framework have tended to discount the long-run effects of the brain drain on the grounds that, when there are free markets, the allocation of factors will soon adjust to their marginal returns. Voluntary migration, almost by definition, is presumed to increase the welfare of the migrant himself (misinformation and imperfect decision-making are usually ignored). The only question, therefore, is whether the brain drain reduced the welfare of those left behind. Their possible losses from the brain drain are discussed under five headings:

   (i) Short-term dislocations, which cause a temporary reduction of output until there is time for the allocation of factors to adjust to the reduced quantity of skilled manpower.

  (ii) Non-marginal changes.

 (iii) External economies or dis-economies, in which social marginal product of individuals is not adequately represented by their earnings.

 (iv) Changes in the supply of other factors, due to the brain drain.

  (v) Effects on government finances, in cases where the loss of taxation revenue from the emigration of professional manpower is different from the reduction in the claims made on social and other services provided by government by the families of the professional manpower involved.

Although the analysis we give later emphasises rather different factors, it may be useful at this stage to indicate briefly why we would expect several or all of the five factors to be important causes of welfare loss for the inhabitants of 'developing' countries with sizeable emigration of skilled manpower.

  (i) In many such countries the dislocations due to the loss of skills, far from being temporary, may last five or ten years. This is certainly true in some African countries where the numbers in the pipeline of higher education are still small and expatriate skills are an inadequate economic substitute for local skills;[1] the loss of local skilled manpower may therefore take five or ten years to replace.

 (ii) In many 'developing' countries the brain drain makes more than a marginal reduction in the stock of skilled persons. While the loss may appear marginal from aggregate figures, it is not really so when one classifies emigrants from particular professions by age or professional standing.

(iii) We have already expressed our dissatisfaction with the assumption that earnings satisfactorily measure the marginal products of the sort of manpower involved in the brain drain. Given our value premises it is difficult to accept the presumption that a doctor makes a bigger contribution to human welfare in the United States or England simply because he earns more there than he does in India. The average ratio of doctors to population in India is scarcely one-tenth of the ratio in the United States or England and far worse in the rural areas. *Prima facie* this seems to us an argument that the contribution to human welfare of a doctor in India is greater than in England or the United States. Similar arguments could be developed for other categories of professional manpower involved in international migration.

 (iv) Nor is it safe to assume that the supply of other factors is unaffected by the brain drain. The flow of foreign investment to developed countries is highly influenced by the availability of a skilled and professional labour force, the quality of educational and medical facilities available to expatriate workers, etc., and therefore by the brain drain.

  (v) Recent evidence suggests that the effects of skilled migration in reducing taxation may well outweigh the reductions in claims on the

[1] Because, for instance, expatriate manpower generally lacks local experience and stays too short a period to acquire it, is often politically acceptable only when employed in certain occupations or particular sectors. Such characteristics matter little if expatriates form only a small minority of skilled manpower – the benefits they bring may well then outweigh these disadvantages. But when their numbers are large, these characteristics can be important.

social services. In Britain, professionals seem to pay tax in excess of government-provided services received.[1] In less developed countries, where professional earnings are much higher in relation to per capita income and the level of welfare services provided by the government is much lower, there is *a priori* a higher probability that the departure of skilled migrants will reduce revenue more than they reduce claims on government expenditure, provided that personal income tax is a significant source of revenue.

Ultimately, as has often been emphasised in the literature, the importance of these possible causes of damage to welfare can only be decided after empirical research. Our point here is that the presumption – sometimes almost taken for granted in the economic literature – that these potential losses from the brain drain are likely to be *exceptional* rather than typical is by no means likely in the context of 'developing' countries. The exceptions are more likely to turn out to be the general case.[2]

[1] See M. Blaug, 'Economic Aspects of Vouchers for Education' in *Education: a Framework for Choice* (Institute of Economic Affairs, London, 1967).

[2] This may be the point at which to add a post-conference footnote to make clear a frequent and somewhat value-loaded characterisation of the two sides of the debate which has crept into the literature, largely unchallenged. Those who have argued that the brain drain tends to increase the welfare of the migrants without reducing the welfare of those left behind have appropriated to themselves the title of 'internationalists' (although the early articles of this position primarily stressed *individual welfare*, e.g. H. G. Grubel and A. D. Scott, 'The International Flow of Human Capital', *American Economic Review Proceedings*, May 1966, pp. 268–74). Those who argued that the brain drain was likely to represent a real loss were dubbed 'nationalists' on the grounds that their argument was 'most nearly always valid when we consider the "country" to be a nation state whose national objective is to maximise its military and economic power' (Grubel and Scott, *op. cit.*). In fact, the arguments of the so-called nationalists have frequently been in terms of the same *value premises* as the internationalists, the difference being that the former have believed that the brain drain was likely to have involved some loss in welfare to the *individuals* remaining behind while the latter believe that this is unlikely.

The 'internationalists' have helped to clarify some of the issues in the debate, but they have laid themselves open to the counter-charge that they are really the 'nationalists' because their arguments in fact tend to justify a manpower flow that benefits the rich countries of the world and ignore the need to correct the international income distribution. At the Bled conference Professor Johnson strongly objected to the implication that the 'internationalists' were apologists for the rich countries. We certainly did not wish to suggest implications about the personal motivations of any participants in the brain drain debate. But in our view, it is important for the advance of economic, as of other social services to question whether the social and economic context in which theories or viewpoints are formed is itself introducing systematic biases into that analysis. Our personal view is that much of the economic analysis of the brain drain has been inadequate through neglecting questions of income distribution, both between and within countries.

It is interesting to note some other changes in the 'internationalist' position which have taken place as the debate proceeded. Professor H. G. Johnson's article was care-

But, in our judgement, the real weakness in this approach is different – its failure to grapple with the long-run structural imbalances which are among the causes of unemployment as opposed to short-term departures from competitive equilibrium. The framework of analysis is essentially static when it needs to be dynamic; it ignores crucial linkages which are essential to the explanation of growing unemployment and inequality.

III. THE FAILURE OF DEVELOPMENT AND ITS INTER-NATIONAL SETTING

In recent years two big defects have been widely visible in the development process – unemployment and inequality. Indeed such clues as we have suggested that both these problems are growing more acute.[1]

Unemployment is one of the main roots of inequality, both directly (because, in a society with only limited social security systems, most of the

---

ful to restrict his argument to the developed countries, but Grubel and Scott (*op. cit.*) suggested that the effects of the brain drain on those remaining behind were generally likely to be favourable. More recently they have specified more general conditions under which there would apparently be losses from the emigration of graduate manpower from low income countries (H.G. Grubel and A. D. Scott, *The Theory of Migration and Human Capital*, unpublished mimeo). Blaug *et al.* loosen this argument even more, arguing *not* that those remaining behind will be unaffected, but only that their loss is likely to be *less* than the welfare gain of those who have left. This position Blaug characterises as 'individualistic' although it rests on the narrower value premises than concern with the 'collective welfare of individuals' used by Grubel and Scott. Moreover, by his comparisons of the losses of some people with the gains to others Blaug admits the need to introduce the very interpersonal comparisons which we feel are at the heart of the problem neo-classical analysis seeks to avoid. (M. Blaug, P. E. G. Layard, M. Woodhall, *The Causes of Graduate Unemployment in India*, L.S.E. Studies in Education (Penguin Press, 1969), Ch. 6).

Underlying our own approach, we would characterise our basic value premises as 'redistributive', an over-riding priority for the development of the poorer countries and, in particular, of the poorest sections of their populations. Much of our argument in fact rests on much weaker premises than these, and could be defended in terms of *not reducing* the welfare of any persons, rich or poor in rich or poor countries. But, if pressed, we would go further than this, by giving particular weight to measures which raise the welfare of poorer persons in the poorer countries even at the cost of some reduction of welfare among persons in the richer (and in the poorer too!).

[1] Data on these points are scarce and not very reliable. An unpublished paper by Dr. Jaffe read to the latest I.A.R.I.W. conference lead us to a tentative conclusion that concentration by size is increasing in Latin America. David Turnham (in '*The Employment Problem in Less Developed Countries*', O.E.C.D., June 1970, p. 105) comes to the conclusion that 'we have been unable to find in recent literature grounds for optimism'. The same source shows available data on overt unemployment; this does not reveal marked trends for recent years in the countries concerned, but in at least one of the cases quoted (Trinidad) longer series would certainly reveal rising unemployment, and it is difficult to believe that the present heavy urban unemployment has always been with us. There is in addition evidence of growing disguised unemployment in service sectors. See also '*1967 Report on the World Social Situation*' (U.N., 1969).

unemployed live at the margin of subsistence) and indirectly (because the existence of unemployment often prevents the poorer workers forcing up wages or peasants leaving smallholdings). But conversely inequality promotes unemployment, because of the tendency of the rich and of town dwellers to spend their income on luxuries which are imported or which incorporate a high import content, thus pre-empting the use of foreign exchange for capital equipment and thereby reducing the potential long-run growth of output and employment. Unemployment and inequality have, between them, meant the persistence of poverty and of related evils such as ill-health and illiteracy; these social evils also are in turn contributory causes of unemployment and inequality.

Such interactions are examined at length in a country study of Colombia, in which we were both recently involved, and on which we shall draw for illustration.[1] In this study we identified three major institutional weaknesses in Colombia: an extremely unequal system of land holding, which meant artificial shortages of arable land for the mass of the rural population; an education system that was very deficient, especially in rural areas (as were other rural services); labour legislation and institutions which created a small, high-wage aristocracy of labour.[2] (The major obstacles to agricultural progress are not everywhere the same, but shortages in rural social services and the existence of a labour elite are universal.)

Within this institutional framework, we identified four major dynamic factors primarily responsible for the failure of development (in the sense of chronic unemployment and inequality)[3]:

(i) The rapid growth of the working population, accelerating over recent decades;

(ii) The slow increase in foreign exchange earnings, limiting the growth of output;

---

[1] *Towards Full Employment: A programme for Colombia prepared by an international mission organised by the I.L.O.* (I.L.O., Geneva, 1970). See also Dudley Seers, 'Income Distribution and Employment – a note on some issues raised by the Colombia Report', *Bulletin of the Institute of Development Studies*, Vol. 2, No. 4.

[2] One important consequence of Colombia's labour legislation is the tendency to employ existing employees overtime, rather than to take on additional workers. This is encouraged by a number of features in the legislation, particularly prohibitions against dismissals and several statutory payments required by government in respect of each worker, regardless of his hours of work or pay. The result is that nearly 60 per cent of the employed urban labour force work 48 hours a week or more, of whom about a third work 60 hours or more. The full-time equivalent of this overtime work is about 12 per cent of the urban labour force, of the same order of magnitude as the percentage seeking work in 1969.

[3] Another cause, to which we only referred in passing in the Colombia report, was the spreading use of advertising (especially on TV) to create demand for generally capital-intensive manufactures as well as imported products, foreign travel, etc.

(iii) Rising real wages in the modern sectors, absolutely and relative to rural incomes;[1]
(iv) The increasing use of capital-intensive techniques.

These dynamic factors within Colombia reflect, and are directly related to, the existence of a division in the world economy between rich countries and poor. We would not want to suggest that they are all beyond the reach of policy, but they are in fact, to some degree, exogenous, from the viewpoint of any single economy.

Population growth has been accelerated by the advances in medical technology, in large part pioneered by the developed countries.[2]

The demand for agricultural products has proved rather inelastic with respect to world income increases, and this elasticity may actually be falling as the world distribution of income becomes more unequal. In the past two decades the terms of trade have also moved against most exporters of primary products. These tendencies have been aggravated by restrictionist import policies on the part or industrial countries (notably the adoption of quotas on textile imports). It is true that they are mitigated to some extent by an increasing flow of aid, but this flow has now levelled off – in any case the value of aid is greatly reduced by tying practices.

The rise in modern-sector wages, in spite of open unemployment, has many origins yet to be properly analysed. But one of the important causes has been the growing power of government and unions in wage settlements. In the case of 'developing' countries, this has been to some extent imitative of practices in those which are richer; indeed the trade union organisation is also largely an institutional transfer. The wage rise has also been influenced by growing knowledge about living standards in more developed countries, and in some cases it had been initiated by high wages paid by foreign companies (e.g. in petroleum economies). In Africa the high proportion of expatriates in skilled jobs is in part responsible for extending expatriate standards to local skilled personnel. Any brief explanation is bound to be over-simplified, but it seems difficult to explain the *worldwide tendency* towards higher real wages in modern

---

[1] In the last five years the rise in real wages has been slower than it was earlier, making it a less important factor in Colombia than in many other 'developing' countries. Nevertheless relative to the cost of capital, which is increasingly made cheaper by tax concessions to investment, the cost of labour has probably continued to rise. But we do not wish to suggest that these factors alone were the only ones responsible for unemployment in Colombia, though they seem to be both important and common to many developing countries.

[2] Other factors are of course also important, particularly improved transportation within developing countries and between them and the rest of the world, both of which reduce the risk of local famines leading to widespread death from starvation.

N 2

sectors without reference to the growing gap between developed countries and the remainder.[1]

The spread of capital-intensive technologies from the rich countries to those where factor proportions are very different has been a theme of much economic literature. One recent estimate suggests that 98 per cent of all expenditure on research and development takes place within the industrialised countries of North America, Western Europe and the Communist bloc.[2] Sometimes research in the industrial countries produces technologies which can displace those which are more labour-intensive on grounds of absolute efficiency. Even when this is so, however, monopoly power (often based on technology) enables firms to insist that their technology, capital equipment and often intermediate goods are used by countries overseas if they want to start certain lines of production. Moreover governments and private entrepreneurs in many of these countries are often ignorant of alternatives,[3] and there are many cultural and political channels for transmission of capital-intensive technologies, including aid.[4]

The interaction of these four factors has helped to produce a distorted growth process, marked by slow progress and lack of structural transformation in major sectors of the economy, notably agriculture and artisan industry. The turning of the terms of trade against primary producers in world markets is reflected by a similar trend inside each country, reinforced by the heavy protection given to large-scale industry to encourage import substitution (which also enables industry to pay relatively high wages). Nearly all private investment takes place in the towns. (Foreign managers, in particular, prefer the capital or another large city since these provide amenities similar to those to which they are accustomed, as well as international airports.) The economic and social gap between the towns and the countryside therefore widens, with the towns imitating in many

[1] For data and some hypothesis explaining the 'extraordinary similarity between the experiences of the advanced and the less advanced economies' in respect of money wages, prices and real wages, see H. A. Turner and D. A. S. Jackson, 'On the Determination of the General Wage Level – A World Analysis', *Economic Journal* (Dec. 1970).

[2] *World plan of Action for the Application of Science and Technology to Development: Introductory Statement by the Sussex Group* (mimeo report of a conference at the Institute of Development Studies, sponsored by the United Nations, 1969), p. 12.

[3] We gained a good deal from discussions with Constantine Vaitsos, an adviser to the Colombian Government, on the role of technology as a reinforcement of monopolistic market structure in Colombia.

[4] It could also be argued that the institutional factors reflect international forces as well. The weaknesses of the educational and health systems in the Third World are often due to attempts to copy the systems (in particular the universities) of industrial countries. In many countries, especially those where foreign capital is an important influence, the political power of the governments of industrial countries operates to discourage far-reaching land reform (especially if it would affect foreign-owned plantations).

respects the life of the industrial countries. Yet the swelling flood of migrants to the cities is not fully absorbed into employment, and social contrasts emerge within the urban community almost as stark as those between town and country.

Our analysis in Colombia made it clear that increasing the aggregate rate of economic growth was not a sufficient solution to the problems of inequality and unemployment. Many methods of raising the growth rate involve the 'Verdoorn effect', according to which productivity growth rises along with the aggregate growth rate. Although if it were possible to accelerate the growth of output sufficiently, it would seem possible to expand productive employment as fast as the growing supply of labour, there are two severe difficulties with this approach. First, the required rate of growth of output will probably not be feasible, in terms of either foreign exchange earnings or organisational capacity. Our calculations suggested that even an 8 per cent growth rate would only be sufficient to reduce unemployment in Colombia if the rise in output per man-years were slowed down. Secondly, even if a total growth rate were sufficient to reduce unemployment, it would not necessarily solve the basic problem of inequality. The reduction of unemployment would certainly make some difference to income distribution, but it could well leave unchanged the pattern of land tenure and fail to prevent a widening gap between rural and urban incomes.

IV. REPERCUSSIONS OF THE BRAIN DRAIN

Increasing unemployment and inequality are linked to the brain drain in two ways: each is to some extent a cause of the other and both are in part symptoms of deeper, more general causes – in particular, (i) the failure to achieve balanced growth and development within the country, and (ii) increasing inequality in the world economy.

Of the various ways in which the brain drain is a part cause of unemployment and inequality, five seem of greatest importance: its biased influence on (a) wage structure and wage trends, (b) educational and social services, (c) rural-urban migration, (d) the development and application of local technology, and (e) the general rate of economic growth. Of the reverse influence of unemployment and inequality on the brain drain, unemployment is important at the higher levels of education and skills, because it reduces the attractiveness to skilled persons of remaining in the country instead of leaving it. But more generally, the cause of the brain drain is inequality, the widening gap between countries leading in turn to the associated gaps opening up within countries – rural-urban, skilled-unskilled, educated-uneducated, expatriate-local. The differentials created in the domestic economy are not only out of line with the structure needed to provide incentives for development, but often lead to activities (as the brain drain itself) perversely opposite to the needs of accelerated development.

(a) Links with Wages Structure and Trends

Through the brain drain, actual or potential, the widening gap between rich and poor countries has opened up a major new channel of distortions within the domestic economy away from the priorities of development. In those occupations where there is an international market, the attraction of foreign professional salaries (and research facilities etc.) has greatly increased since the war. This is due in large part to the growing dispersion of per capita incomes.[1] The earnings of doctors, scientists and engineers in *developed* countries thus play an increasing part in the determination of salaries of the same occupational groups in the 'developing' countries. The market price of scarce professional skills there is forced up and this in turn raises the payment for other skills which are not internationally marketable (because of conventional rigidities in government and university salary scales). This aggravation of inequality – which can take place even if there is no actual brain drain – has been analysed by one of us elsewhere.[2]

(b) Links with Education and Social Services

The actual emigration of professional manpower directly affects inequality through some of the other institutional and dynamic influences mentioned earlier. The effect on land tenure is not very great, except in as far as emigration of agronomists, surveyors, etc. impedes land reform. Obviously, however, outflows of professional skills play a big part in the inadequacies of the educational system; if the overseas stock of graduates could be added to the domestic stock, there would be far fewer shortages of qualified teachers, especially in mathematics and the natural sciences at university and secondary levels, thus easing the shortage of professional personnel. The upward pressure on salaries also sets a ceiling on the quantum of social services which governments can afford.

(c) Links with Internal Migration

Some of the links between the brain drain and rural-urban contrasts have already been covered, because urban wages are affected by the brain drain. In addition, rural areas suffer particularly from the shortages of doctors and teachers, for which emigration overseas is in part responsible.

[1] The relative reduction in the cost of international travel and standardisation of higher education (under the influence of the textbooks and research of the developed countries) have also encouraged the brain drain.

[2] 'The International Transmission of Inequality', unpublished paper prepared for the Haile Selassie Prize trust conference, Addis Ababa, 1965. See also 'Graduate Migration as an obstacle to Equality' in *Unfashionable Economics, Essays in Honour of Lord Balogh* (Weidenfeld & Nicolson, London, 1970).

The gaps in the city's manpower structure, e.g. in medicine, created by international emigration,[1] opens opportunities for the ambitious country-dweller with professional qualifications, just as the emigration of doctors from Britain to the United States creates openings for Indian doctors in Britain.[2] Moreover, professional expectations and standards are often dominated by rich-country practices; these can only partially be realised in the cities but they lie quite beyond the reach of the doctor, teacher or other professional person practising in the rural areas.

This internal brain drain has not only characteristics but also effects analogous to those of the international brain drain. Rural professional salaries are pulled up to levels out of proportion to other local incomes and to what local authorities can pay. Moreover, such research as is done is often on the problems of the city dwellers (or if rural, on those of the big commercial farmer).[3]

Like the international brain drain, the internal one has been gathering momentum, also partly because of the widening socio-economic gaps. Each type of brain drain is in fact self-reinforcing; by making the losing area (countryside or 'developing' country) less attractive to live in (and perhaps by contributing to political unrest), the migration of other brains is encouraged.[4]

(d) Links with Technology

In science and engineering, actual and potential emigration means simply that fewer people are capable and willing to work on the development of appropriate technologies for the country concerned. (It does not necessarily follow from this that, if such persons did not migrate, they would necessarily be engaged in such work or that they would necessarily make a positive contribution – other issues will also be involved.) In assessing the effect of this aspect of the brain drain, the crucial test is whether scientists who emigrate would make a greater contribution to their own country's development by going abroad. Of course, in some cases, because of the wrong type of education, or too slow a pace of development, there is no place at home for some types of scientists and engineers. But much bigger

[1] In the case of Colombia, emigrating physicians and surgeons accounted for from 17 per cent of the annual output in the years 1960–61 to 1965–66 (Gustavo Gonzalez, 'Migration of Latin American Manpower', *International Labour Review*, December 1968).

[2] 'International Medical Migration: Britain and Ireland', 1969, unpublished thesis by Oscar Gish.

[3] There are two big differences, however. The internal brain drain covers a far bigger range of professions – including, for example, lawyers, administrators and politicians who have little possibility of international migration. It is also of course accompanied by unskilled labour, against which controls on international immigration now discriminate.

[4] The internal drain is affected by the accelerating international movement, precisely because of the links between them.

questions are raised. It is sometimes claimed that emigrants of this type indirectly help their own country's technical progress because the results of their work add to the world store of knowledge on which all can draw. But, as we have seen, technology is by no means neutral. Not only are the technologies in the rich countries usually more capital-intensive; they are often designed for types of production of little relevance, perhaps of positive harm, to the developing countries. Over 40 per cent of research and development expenditure in the 'developed' countries is spent in the fields of defence and space research.[1] (Moreover it is in part demand for research on this work which has initiated some of the more important brain drain flows). It is not obvious that the spillover effects from such research are much to the advantage of the 'developing' countries; indeed one consequence is to increase the disparity of military strength in the world, which has further implications for international economic relationships.[2] Moreover much of the research for non-military ends, e.g. on the development of synthetic materials, is directly contrary to the interests of those relying on exports of primary products.

(e) Links with Rate and Structure of Growth

Finally, in our concern with the process of growth, we must not lose sight entirely of its rate, especially since here the effects of the brain drain are clear. Its implications for the educational system have been discussed above; there, however, the context was the implications for equality. When scarcity of professional skills is a constraint on a sector's growth, however, anything which increases that scarcity reduces the sector's contribution to providing jobs – this is a straightforward case of complementarity. It may be particularly serious for manufacturing where the expansion depends, sooner or later, on hacking out a route into new export markets.[3]

We sometimes forget that the emergence of a viable national strategy for development also depends on leadership, especially in politics and administration. This itself depends in some degree on the proportion of educated people in the population (whatever the definition of 'educated'), but also on the *content* of their education. The usefulness of the educational system for this purpose is often impaired by the tendency for syllabuses and (at higher levels) research topics to be influenced by the desire of the teachers and students to maintain links with the international market for professional skills – so that students can take further degrees and jobs overseas.[4]

[1] See the Sussex Group Report (*op. cit.*) Table 2, based on O.E.C.D. data.
[2] Some 'developing' countries, for example, are subject to military attack.
[3] Similarly the loss of doctors affects the country's whole productive capacity, since this is to some extent a function of its health.
[4] On this and other aspects developed above see V. M. Dankekar in *The Brain Drain*, edited by Walter Adams (of Michigan State, not L.S.E.), New York, 1968.

V. THE 'REVERSE' FLOW OF BRAINS

It is sometime argued that the effects of the brain drain are exaggerated because the *net* flows are much smaller than the *gross* flows. If the analytical approach of this paper is accepted, the reverse flows of professional manpower towards the 'developing' countries have distinct effects, which may reinforce rather than offset the original brain drain influences. The reverse flows are of two main types – nationals of the country returning after higher education or work overseas, and foreigners on technical assistance.

Both types can help to relieve skill shortages, and thus ease upward pressures on salaries and restraints on the growth of output and employment. On the other hand they may both, especially experts on technical assistance, encourage (by emulation) the raising of local salaries, and this influence could well predominate. Moreover both help to reinforce preferences for foreign consumption patterns, with a high import content.

Both types may also bring with them inappropriate techniques (e.g. capital-intensive medicine, highly mechanical construction techniques, foreign administrative systems or industrial-country economics), and this is perhaps more likely than not, even for the returning national. They may also bring inappropriate ideologies: failure to understand the process of development may make the work of the arrival from overseas unproductive or worse, in any central field of policy (e.g. finance, trade, education or industry).

Key questions are the place and type of work. The analysis above suggests a very positive role for appropriately trained professional personnel prepared to work in rural areas – something which seems to be more common among short-service technical assistance personnel (especially volunteers) than returning nationals, who would consider this a step further down, in a sense, than working in their own capital.

One clear priority would be for medical personnel capable of (and willing to accept) work in the family planning field, provided that the political and social climate permits this type of work to be productive. Another would be for agricultural specialists, on the assumption that the land tenure system is such as that advice would be heeded – better still if the technical assistance facilitates land reform.

VI. RESEARCH NEEDS

This new set of relationships carries implications not only for policy conclusions about the brain drain but also for further research. As regards the agenda for research, the crucial need is to identify, analyse and quantify more precisely this wider set of relationships between the brain drain and development. As a start these should include the relationships between the international brain drain and:

(a) real salaries and wages;
(b) education (and other social services);
(c) incentives and motivation to work in the rural areas;
(d) the transfer of technology;
(e) the rate and structure of economic growth.

A vigorous attempt should be made to specify, test and quantify these relationships on similar lines as other macro-relationships in socio-economic systems. Data are increasingly available – or in principle could be collected – on many of the variables involved. In other cases it will be more difficult. But much we believe is possible, and even where the capacity to quantify of current techniques of the social sciences is limited, we should not be lead to ignore totally relationships which appear, *a priori*, to be important.

We should in addition mention our conviction that adequate explanations of the relationships specified will only emerge from multi-disciplinary research.

VII. CONCLUSIONS

The economics profession showed, on the whole, a rather discreditable slowness in reacting to the chronic unemployment of the inter-war years. Let us hope that on this occasion we are not again left clutching the wrong model. Once more massive and worldwide unemployment has appeared – and of a far more menacing kind, because endogenous to the process of development. (We are, of course, not speaking of the minority of countries which are industrialised.) It is moreover accompanied now by chronic and severe inequalities within countries and in the world as a whole. This is the framework for any major subject, especially an international one such as the brain drain. Any analysis has to take account of this context – and any policy prescription starts from the moral need to change it.

APPENDIX

Postscript on the Economic Model Assumed

One of the important questions raised at the Bled Conference about our paper was the nature of the economic model implicit within our analysis. We accept the need to specify this more precisely, though point out that our primary concern was to analyse some of the partial functional relationships linking the brain drain to key variables (particularly the quantity and quality of skilled manpower resources, differentiated by occupation and level of education) and to the initiated framework and key parameters (particularly those related to the limits specified in section IV of the paper). The nature of the model would need to be varied according to the particular characteristics of the economy being analysed, but essentially we would wish to construct a dynamic model of labour force supply and demand, with demand for labour linked to sectoral and aggregative output and productivity and output related to a fairly conventional sectoral growth model, differentiating at least sectors – modern and traditional manufacturing, modern and traditional agriculture, and series. A model on these lines for Colombia is given in the appendix to the I.L.O. Report, *Towards Full Employment, op. cit.*

16 Labour Mobility and the Brain Drain

Harry G. Johnson
THE LONDON SCHOOL OF ECONOMICS AND POLITICAL SCIENCE
AND THE UNIVERSITY OF CHICAGO

I. CONCERN ABOUT THE BRAIN DRAIN

The movement of labour, and especially of educated labour, from poorer to richer countries has excited considerable public concern in many countries during the past decade, under the popular description of 'brain drain'. Two types of such concern may be noted: concern in lower-income advanced countries such as Canada and the United Kingdom about the flow of native talent to the United States, and concern in various developing countries and in the United States about the flow of educated talent from the former to the latter, conceived in the United States as the problem of student non-return. The latter concern is the one relevant to this Conference, though it may be worth noting that the flows that occasioned the former concern appear to have been, at least in magnitude, a temporary phenomenon associated with university expansion, a build-up of scientific research endeavour and an expansion of demand for medical services in the United States, funds for the first two of which at least have been recently sharply cut back. Indeed some sections of public opinion in Canada are now concerned about the reverse 'problem' of an inflow of foreign (and especially American) academics attracted by the recent rapid expansion of the Canadian University system, while Britain has been besieged by inquiries for suitable employment from British scientists and engineers who have lost their jobs in the United States. This reversal should serve as a reminder both that flows of labour migration are a response to market forces, and that demand-supply situations can change fairly rapidly, and should not be incautiously identified as permanent structural economic features.

Our concern is with 'the gap between the rich and the poor nations'. I do not like that definition of the problem, for reasons to be explained later. But if the concept of the 'gap' is taken literally, it means the difference between average living standards, somehow defined and measured, between the rich and the poor nations. Such a definition – unless the measurements are considerably more sophisticated (and probably also more questionable) than those standard in the field – rules out a great deal of the discussion that has gone on about the economic effects of brain drain, which discussion has typically appealed to externalities and excesses of social over private benefits not measured in market prices. The argument frequently advanced, for example, that the services of a doctor in a poor country are worth far more than his salary there – indeed, it is sometimes suggested worth more than the salary he would obtain by emigrating to a rich country – has the logical corollary that the gap is seriously over-stated by the standard measurements, which do not revalue services in the light of such extra-economic considerations (and would have difficulty establishing a scientifically acceptable basis for so doing). A literal concern with the gap, also, could lead to strange results, because it is quite possible for the migration of an educated person to raise the average income in the poor country he leaves and lower it in the rich country he joins, thus narrowing the gap.[1] Yet if such were the case, it is doubtful that any of those concerned about the gap would be prepared to recommend accelerated migration as a gap-closing policy.

My objection to the gap as the focus of analysis is not merely that the use of statistical averages can produce unnecessary paradoxes or nonsense results, but that it assumes the nation as the unit of analysis rather than the people that are born and live in a world divided into national states, and hence biases thinking towards a nationalist rather than a cosmopolitan view of the nature of the problem and of solutions to it, and towards a neglect of the welfare of the individuals who better themselves by moving. No one seriously disputes the economic benefits, in the form of both improved allocative efficiency and competitive pressures for increasing productivity, that result from the mobility of labour within the nation; in fact nations typically seek to increase labour mobility by public policy. But the same type of movement of labour in search of better opportunities, but between rather than within nations, is widely regarded as a serious problem, damaging to the economic development of the poor nations.

If one takes a cosmopolitan point of view, there can be no doubt that efficiency, growth and the relief of world poverty would be very effectively promoted by unlimited freedom of migration. The only possible economic objection, which is a real one but exists already, is that the propensity of populations in important parts of the world to grow in response to expanding economic opportunities, rather than translate those opportunities into rising living standards, might become generalised and swamp the world in general poverty. That important consideration apart, the prevalence of poverty among the nations, and the need for transfers of capital and knowledge to help remedy it, can be attributed to an important extent to the barriers to immigration imposed by the advanced countries,

---

[1] This result will occur if the wage of an educated man, in both countries, exceeds the average wage by less than per capita income from capital and other property. For migration of the educated necessarily to widen the gap, the differential earned by educated people over the average wage must be greater than per capita non-wage income in both countries.

coupled with tariff and other barriers to trade that restrict 'indirect immigration' from poor to rich countries via the export of goods and services.

The problem in hand is that, for a mixture of cultural and nationalistic reasons, immigration barriers are not non-discriminatorily restrictive – in that case the advanced countries would receive their quotas of the poor from the poor nations, and so contribute directly to the relief of world poverty – but instead discriminate selectively against the poor and unskilled and in favour of the well-off and the educated and skilled, the latter being our concern.[1] The problem is whether the migration of scientific and professional personnel from poor to rich countries promoted by selective immigration laws is damaging or helpful to the economic development of the poor countries, the common presumption being that it must be damaging.

II. THE BENEFITS FROM MIGRATION[2]

I have dealt with this issue extensively in previous papers, as have a number of others, and will merely summarise some of the main points that have emerged from the preceding discussion that are relevant to the present Conference. In particular, I shall eschew a 'cosmopolitan' analysis of the net effect of the migration of talented people from poor to rich nations, which requires appeal either to the compensation principle or to some kind of international welfare function, and concentrate on the effects such emigration may have on the welfare and economic growth of the poor countries.

To begin with it is necessary to establish some sense of proportion and perspective on the problem. It is only too easy for economists discussing it to conjure up visions of a country being completely depopulated of its educated talent overnight, and to envisage consequential economic disasters that they would not for a moment entertain as realistic possibilities for an impersonal commodity market, or even for a national labour market. As a broad generalisation, the 'brain drain' phenomenon tends to be either a long-standing structural feature of a country's educational system, reflecting a relative over-supply of certain kinds of talent

---

[1] A question that has received very little attention, perhaps much less than it deserves, is the implications for the development of the poor countries of the hospitality of the rich countries towards the rich citizens of the poor countries, as tourists and permanent or part-time residents. This permits the latter to enjoy the benefits of modern civilisation while relieving them of pressures to create such civilisation for their poorer homebound fellow-citizens.

[2] Harry G. Johnson, 'The Economics of Brain Drain', *Sixth Annual Seminar on Canadian-American Relations*, 1964, pp. 37–50; also *Minerva*, Vol. III, No. 3 (spring 1965), pp. 299–311; 'Some Economic Aspects of Brain Drain', *Pakistan Development Review*, Vol. VII, No. 3 (autumn 1967), pp. 379–411 and Walter Adams (ed.) *The Brain Drain* (New York: Macmillan, 1968).

in relation to the country's economy – and a characteristic way by which people born in poor countries seek to better their lot – or else a marginal matter to which countries can and do adjust by making marginal substitutions among human and non-human resources.[1] In either case, brain drain is likely to be characteristic of countries that have a reasonably well-developed education system and hence some economic sophistication and flexibility. Further, it is necessary to remember that some important cases of substantial brain drain have been occasioned by political upheavals, and that to view such cases as constituting an economic problem is to impose a political judgement that the citizen should be the slave of the state; that much of what appears as brain drain at any particular time may be a statistical reflection of the acquisition of on-the-job training subsequent to formal education, or of career patterns that involve the international mobility of the trained person; and that apparently drained brains may merely be parked abroad at foreign expense pending the development of opportunities for them to be used at home, either intermittently or permanently (this point is discussed below).

As a starting point for analysis of the economic consequences of migration of educated people from poor to rich countries for the poor countries, we may note some cases in which such migration may be of positive benefit to the poor countries.

First comes the case of the potentially great scientist capable of making basic contributions to scientific knowledge. Since such contributions cannot be appropriated commercially, and once made are available to the whole world of learning, it is of no national consequence where they are made (apart from considerations of national prestige, which can be enjoyed equally by country of residence and country of birth). On the other hand, such contributions increasingly seem to require both a large scale of research community and extreme specialisation of individual researchers, supported by massive public funds for the researchers, their supporting staff and their research equipment. They are therefore most efficiently located in the large rich countries, which can better afford the luxury of long-range possibly-very-low-pay-off investments in the general advance of knowledge of the character of an internationally public good.

A related case is that of the highly-trained and experienced professional specialist. The development of such specialists (certain kinds of doctors,

---

[1] There has been an unfortunate tendency in development economics for writers to base their analyses on the assumption of fixed coefficients in production and consequently on a single factor as limitational to output, to the exclusion of the traditional concern of economics with choice and substitution possibilities. Formerly the limitational factor was taken to be capital, more recently it has been taken to be formally-educated professional people. There is much less justification for the assumption in the latter than in the former case, since people are more capable of teaching themselves than of creating capital equipment, and until the very recent development of elaborate university systems most them had to do so.

economists, statisticians, demographers, anthropologists, and so forth) involves a heavy investment both of resources and of the personal time of the specialist. Poor countries generally cannot either afford the development of such specialisms, or utilise them profitably on a full-time basis once they have been developed, and often find it economically more advantageous to hire them temporarily from the outside to advise on or solve particular problems. In such cases the emigration of some of its potentially competent specialist citizens may benefit a poor country by adding to the pool of specialists and hence reducing the cost of specialist advice. This encourages the development of specialisms in subjects of special concern to the country – in which such citizens tend to be motivated to specialise – and makes available to it, when required, specialist citizens of its own at a cost lowered by loyalty below what it might otherwise be.

A third, and obvious, possibility of gain lies in the remittances of emigrants to relatives at home – which may well exceed any conceivable loss to the home country from emigration – and the repatriation of capital assets accumulated abroad by returning residents. This possibility is associated with the fact that for a variety of reasons a number of poor countries consistently produce more educated people in certain categories than their educational and economic systems can absorb. In the past the reason has frequently been a religious or cultural emphasis on the value of scholarship for its own sake; more recently, in the poor countries, the reason has been a democratic insistence on the extension of educational opportunities, based on a set of rewards for education inherited from colonial times of necessity to import a limited amount of foreign-educated talent at internationally competitive prices, and implemented in disregard of the laws of demand and supply as they determine relative wages. For such situations, emigration of educated people provides a political safety-valve against disgruntlement with the results of over-optimistic educational planning, both by removing some of the more ambitious and impatient from the scene and, in so doing, by moderating the frustration of the rest by slowing or preventing the rate of decline of the rewards for educational investment.

Finally, emigration of a proportion of the educated may make a dynamic contribution to the process of social and economic change that constitutes economic development, by 'stirring things up' through imposing new economic and social pressures on the domestic society and economy. This may occur in two major ways: (i) through the influence of letters, visits back and forth between relatives and the eventual return of emigrants in raising questions about whether traditional ways of doing things are really as reasonable and inevitable as tradition has taught, and (ii) through the economic pressure of foreign demand for educated people in making governments and businesses aware that such people are more valuable and potentially more useful than traditionally they have been considered to be.

III. LOSSES TO THE POOR COUNTRIES

So much for the potential benefits to the poor countries of the emigration of educated people; I now turn to the possibilities of economic losses. As the earlier literature on the subject has made clear, there is an initial distinction to be drawn between a 'nationalist' conception of economic loss, which takes total G.N.P. as an index of welfare, and an 'individualist' or 'economic welfare' definition of loss, which is concerned with potential losses from the emigration of educated people to those remaining behind, the emigrants being assumed to enjoy a private benefit from their emigration.

The obvious economic tools to employ here are the tools of comparative statics, and the concept of divergence of private from social cost or benefit. Analysis along these lines has produced four major cases of potential loss.[1]

The first arises when the education of the individual is financed by the public, in the expectation that once educated he will repay society either through taxes on the earnings he obtains by virtue of his education, or through working for a socially-determined wage lower than the social value of his services, or both. If he emigrates on completion of his education, society loses the return on its investment. Whether this is a real loss, however, depends on whether that investment was understood to be an inter-generational gift or an inter-generational loan; in the former case there is no repayment obligation on the educated person, but on the contrary his choice to use it to emigrate is an optimising decision that presumably has the blessing of the donors of the gift. In other words, while governments may rue the exodus of educated people as involving a loss of tax revenue or cheap public servants, the parents of the people involved may delight in their children's economic success.

The second arises, or may arise, through the change in factor proportions that will occur as a result of the emigration of skilled people. Such changes in factor proportions may be approached on several different assumptions. First, the economy may be treated as a closed economy producing an aggregate commodity for consumption, using raw labour and capital invested in both material and human capital form. In this case it can be established that those remaining behind must lose, unless the emigrating human packages of labour and capital possess and

---

[1] Since Professor A. D. Scott, in a review of the proceedings volume of a 1967 Conference on the brain drain (Walter Adams (ed.), *The Brain Drain* (New York: Macmillan, 1968), reviewed in the *Journal of Political Economy*, Vol. 77, No. 3 (May–June 1969), pp. 440–43) to be discussed in more detail below, has complained that 'the full resources of positive international trade theory have not been consulted', I should point out that the theoretical appendices to my Lausanne Conference paper, while not reproduced in the Conference volume, were published that year in the *Pakistan Development Review;* see the reference in footnote 2, p. 382.

leave behind them enough material capital to raise the overall ratio of capital to labour in the economy. A second assumption is that the emigrating educated produce a non-traded good (e.g. medical services); in that case the price of the good in question will rise and the remaining population suffer a loss of consumers' surplus. In both cases it can be shown that the loss per capita to the remaining residents will be very small indeed, for reasonable magnitudes of the extent of the brain drain and the elasticities of substitution and structural parameters involved.

A third approach employs the Heckscher-Ohlin model of trade, and assumes that educated people are employed in the production of tradeable goods. If the country is small enough for its terms of trade to be given to it, emigration leads to no change in factor prices, being accommodated by a change in the pattern of production, so long as emigration leaves the economy within the limits of incomplete specialisation (i.e. with an overall capital-labour ratio between the optimal ratios in the two industries at the factor prices implicit in the given terms of trade). If the terms of trade are a function of the volume of trade and the effects of educated emigration on the foreign offer curve are neglected, the country will gain on its terms of trade if import substitutes are capital-intensive and emigration raises the overall ratio of capital to labour and vice versa, and lose on its terms of trade if exports are capital-intensive and emigration raises the overall ratio of capital to labour and vice versa. Unfortunately, this analysis provides no presumption about the probable effects of educated emigration on the terms of trade of poor countries, because import-substitutes may be assumed to be both human-capital and material-capital intensive relative to exports, and the two initial effects of educated emigration – reducing human capital per head and raising material capital per head – work in opposite directions.

The analysis of the previous paragraph ignores the influence on welfare effects of the presence of domestic tariffs on imported goods. Where such tariffs exist, as they almost invariably do, and where the terms of trade can be taken as constant, as they may be assumed to be as a first approximation for most poor countries, economic changes that shift production out of import-substitutes towards exports are welfare-increasing and changes producing converse shifts are welfare-reducing. But, again, there is no obviously plausible basis for predicting the probable direction of shift consequent on educated emigration.

Such a basis could be provided by modifying the assumption implicit in the preceding analysis that in the long run capital is allocated between investments in human and in material capital so as to equalise the rates of return, and instead treating unskilled labour, educated labour and material capital as complementary but substitutable factors of production. On that assumption, which I would regard as a short-run assumption (though it might be justified for the longer run by the willingness of governments to subsidise education to a level yielding a substantially lower rate of return than material investment), and on the additional assumption that import-substitutes are human-capital-intensive, educated emigration would tend to reduce a country's production of import-substitutes, thereby tending to worsen its terms of trade but also reduce the economic losses it imposes on itself through protection of import-substitution industries. The net effect would depend on the relation of its existing tariffs to the optimum tariff rate; and there is a certain presumption that existing protection in the poor countries is above the optimum tariff rate, so that there would be a net gain in economic welfare from educated migration.

The third possibility of economic loss arises through the loss of scale economies through the reduction in total resources of the economy consequent on educated emigration. Such possibilities appear to be of negligible importance, though one might be able to construct a case for potentially significant loss if one accepted as true the Kaldor hypothesis that the growth of productivity is determined by the rate of growth of manufacturing, and coupled it with the hypothesis that the level of manufacturing production is correlated with the supply of educated talent.

The fourth possibility of economic loss is associated with the possibility that educated residents create externalities (inherently, and apart from the fiscal externalities first discussed) which are not captured by themselves in the form of cash earnings. Such externalities can be interpreted to include dynamic contributions to economic growth through the communication of knowledge and the invention or transplantation of new ways of doing things. The contention that this source of potential loss is important raises several questions. One is whether on balance such externalities are positive: an education typically confers on its recipient both knowledge and a vested interest in maintaining society as it is so as to reap the monopoly rewards of acquired knowledge, and there is no reason to think that the presence of educated people in society is typically and reliably a force for progressive change rather than for conservation of whatever exists. Educated people have an economic interest in high rents and a quiet life rather than in incurring the risks of inciting genuine (and not merely conventionally defined) change, and most of the paraphernalia of both academic and professional life are designed with this interest in view. Another question is whether, where such externalities are important, they do not enter into the utility functions of the educated people concerned and hence become internalised and a deterrent to emigration in search of a higher cash income, but less social recognition and personal self-respect. History abounds with cases of people who have thrown up promising career prospects in order to devote themselves to promoting the welfare of some small lower-income group – frequently with disappointing or problematical results. Probably the key question, to which empirical research has not yet provided an answer, is whether educated people do in fact provide an externality of some sort in the form of a stimulus to the growth of the economy for which they do not receive compensation. Here the evidence of history and social anthropology, for what it is worth, tends to suggest that a potent source of economic growth is the presence or immigration of minority groups debarred from participation in the political process and equipped with certain specific attitudes towards the general population that enable them to concentrate their energies on raising productive efficiency and lowering costs for the goods they produce – not very comforting evidence for those who simultaneously deplore the emigration of natives and the immigration of foreigners.[1]

IV. SOME CRITICISMS OF THIS APPROACH

The foregoing approach to the question of possible economic losses from educated emigration has been challenged by Professor A. D. Scott, in a review referred to earlier, and directed at the 'cosmopolitan' approach to net world gain from such migration elaborated elsewhere by the present author.[2] Professor Scott's attack is directed at the assumption that, in the case of non-traded goods provided by educated people, losses should be measured in terms of the domestic values of goods forgone. He asserts instead that 'To me it is obvious that the "social contribution" of such goods and services (in absence of flows of goods and unskilled people) should not be based on their low local demand prices' (p. 442).

I have an initial quarrel with the model Professor Scott sets up to develop this conclusion, a model which involves no flows whatever of goods and capital other than that of the capital embodied in educated emigrants. I find it impossible, realistically, to conceive of a country with no participation whatsoever in international commercial relations, but still capable of producing educated emigrants with a marginal product higher enough abroad than at home to make emigration worth while. On the contrary, I would expect than no country could produce eligible emigrants unless its involvement in international economic relations were great enough for its educational system to produce people useful enough to the outside world to be able to gain by emigrating, and that the existence of emigration flows would be a symptom either of a comparative advantage in pro-

---

[1] It is one of the puzzles of social psychology in the development literature that both the emigration of educated natives and the domestic employment of educated foreigners are viewed as undesirable. Most of the economic arguments for retaining educated natives in the country apply equally well to the obtention and retention of educated foreigners. The former arguments therefore appear to rest implicitly on discrimination between natives and foreigners based on nationalistic emotion rather than economic logic.

[2] See footnotes 2 on p. 382 and 1 on p. 385.

ducing such people or of a disequilibrium of some kind between the resources devoted to producing such people and the capacity of the domestic economy to absorb their talents.

That remark, however, concerns the question of the realism of a proposed theoretical model. The more fundamental question concerns Professor Scott's argument that because the low valuation placed on certain kinds of services in poor countries is low as a result of their general poverty, the social value of the services is understated and that therefore the emigration of those who provide these services, in search of higher incomes elsewhere, may entail a social loss at the world level. This argument seems to me to represent an elementary confusion of analysis that was evident at the Lausanne Conference on the Brain Drain, the absence of a report of which Professor Scott laments in his review of the Conference volume. As suggested earlier, if we are to be concerned with the measurement of losses as people perceive them (or should perceive them), then we must take market prices as we find them; if a high utility value of services according to some definition is overbalanced by a high marginal utility of money, the result is a low money valuation of the services, and that has to be accepted for purposes of measurement of losses in terms of money. Only if we are concerned with constructing a hedonical index of welfare levels should we attempt to take account of differences in prices between countries occasioned by the differential effects of differing wealth or relative wages. If we do so – and this implicitly involves interpersonal comparisons of utility for citizens of different countries, on the assumption that everyone should be considered equal – we will wind up with two propositions. The first is that incomes are far less unequal internationally than standard calculations show, because in poor countries consumers of non-traded goods produced by educated people are subsidised by the low wages earned by the providers of those goods. The second is that international migration of the providers of those goods is not necessarily beneficial for the world, because the consumers lose a substantial subsidy when the producers emigrate in order to gain their economic rents.

This, however, is price-less economics. The important consideration is not the transfer from producers to consumers implicit in low prices associated with low producers' incomes, but the loss of efficiency from keeping labour (and consumption of its services) in locations where the price is low compared with what is available and will be paid elsewhere. Scott's argument implicitly asserts, without saying so, that people in poor countries should be supplied with services *as if* they had the same capacity to pay for them as as people in rich countries.[1] The fallacy of this argument

[1] This is a quite different proposition from one that may seem very similar, namely that it may be considered desirable, as a social policy, that the state hire veterinarians at competitive wages to poor farmers to improve their methods for maintaining the health of their livestock, as a means of improving their incomes.

stems from the introduction of the extraneous and non-economic assertion that all people ought to be treated as equal regardless of their contributions to the productive process, an assumption whose irrelevance and unscientific character is masked by Christian and other motives for placing faith in the assumed equality of man as a fact of economics. No economist would support the proposition that a veterinarian should be obliged to devote his attention to preserving the health of the cattle on a poor farmer's ranch, in return for whatever pittance he can get, because if the poor farmer were only a better farmer he could afford to pay as much for the service as a rich farmer, and that it is therefore socially damaging for the veterinarian to earn more money by looking after the cattle of rich farmers if he has the opportunity to do so. True, the poor farmer would lose as a result; but his losses are not to be reckoned by what a rich farmer might have lost in the absence of veterinary service.

I conclude that Professor Scott has let his humanitarian sentiments in favour of poor countries carry him away into bad economics. I expect many others will be equally carried away by the assumption of human economic equality as a value judgement – an assumption not applied to pieces of land or of material capital, and whose implications in terms of social policy in those connections they would be the first to reject.

To say this is not to deny the right of Professor Scott or of anyone else to make the value judgement concerned – most economists share it, defenceless as it is on theoretical grounds – but to insist that money measurements of losses are money measurements under existing circumstances, and should not be inflated by tender social consciences in order to provide apparently 'objective' evidence for the proposition that the market is failing to perform its task of resource allocation properly and needs to be interfered with for the social good. It may well be – and is in fact the case – that many economists believe that educated people from poor countries should be forced by policy (their own country's or that of the advanced countries) to make their careers in their countries of origin at a substantial alternative-opportunity-cost loss to themselves in order to subsidise the welfare of their fellow-citizens. Such a policy can perhaps be justified, as a very much second-best policy, if the education these people command is paid for by their own or an advanced-country government as a social investment in the promotion of economic development – though in that case the compulsion should be confined to the subgroup of students so invested in. But to insist on such compulsion as a policy of income-redistribution between rich and poor nations is to endorse what is primarily a tax on the educated citizens of poor countries for the benefit of their poorer fellow-citizens, and only marginally a transfer from the citizens of rich countries to the citizens of poor countries (mediated through marginal changes in the price of educated services in the two types of countries). To dress up such a conscience-saving but virtually costless (to advanced countries) type of income redistribution as a correction of market failure, the alleged market failure being created by an ethically-based revaluation of market prices, is to conceal what is really being recommended in a cloud of spurious scientific objectivity.

Discussion of the Papers by
Richard Jolly and Dudley Seers, and Harry G. Johnson

Professor Correa introduced the paper by Mr. Jolly and Professor Seers. The authors stated that they attempted to sketch out a systematic integration of the. analysis of the brain drain with the analysis of the whole development process. He interpreted this to mean that they would study one of the following three models:

First, there was the model explaining how the structural and dynamic characteristics of developed and underdeveloped countries determined the existence of the brain drain.

Second, there was a model explaining the influence of the brain drain on the situational and dynamic characteristics of developed and underdeveloped countries.

Third, there was a model which amalgamated the two.

Unfortunately, Jolly and Seers did not carry out the task they had set for themselves. None of the three possible models was presented in the paper. They seemed to prefer the first type of model, and presented some of the building blocks needed for it. For instance, they characterised L.D.C.s as having unemployment and inequality. They were seen to have unequal distribution of land, deficient educational systems and labour legislation that had created a small high-wage aristocracy of labour. They also indicated that four dynamic factors were primarily responsible for the failure of development. These were:

(a) the rapid growth of the working population;
(b) the slow increase in foreign exchange earnings;
(c) rising real wages in the modern sector, both absolutely and relatively to rural incomes; and
(d) the increased use of capital-intensive techniques.

However, in this characterisation of the L.D.C.s, the author did not interrelate the elements they considered important. They therefore failed to produce a model of growth. On this basis they could not proceed to explain how the characteristics of L.D.C.s influenced the brain drain. At no point had Professor Correa been able to find the objective of every scientific investigation. In the present case there was no qualitative or quantitative index of the brain drain as a function of qualitative or quantitative indices for the characteristics of developed and developing countries.

The second model he had mentioned earlier was the one explaining the influence of the brain drain by the characteristics of developed and underdeveloped countries. Most of the work done up to now fell into this classification, as could be seen by the paper presented by Professor Johnson. It could also be seen in the introduction to the paper by Mr. Jolly and Professor Seers, though the latter authors dismissed this approach as sterile. Nevertheless, most of their paper was a discussion of some specific points in the second approach. In their first section, they argued that the brain drain was an important cause of welfare losses for the inhabitants of the L.D.C. In the third section, they pointed to the effects of the brain drain on the income structure and the urban-rural contracts within an economy. Finally, they argued that the reverse flow of brains from developed to underdeveloped countries, in the form of returning immigrants or advisers, might also be disadvantageous.

In this presentation the authors brought out some new ideas that should be elaborated, ideas which might make it necessary to revise the analysis of the brain drain. For example, the suggested influence of the brain drain on income distribution might make it necessary to revise some of the assumptions and conclusions of the models used by Professors Johnson and Scott. Unfortunately the authors failed to present their ideas in a systematic way.

Despite these criticisms, Professor Correa agreed with the basic goal of the paper and hoped that the authors would reach it. This paper was a courageous first study which he hoped would be followed by many others.

Professor Scott then introduced the paper by Professor Johnson. He said that the brain drain was a surprisingly new topic for economists. The educational level of migrants was a subject *not* to be found in many inter-war or early post-war conferences or symposia on population. Nor was it found in the literature of factor movements. It bloomed in the 1960s, in the U.K., as a term for popular concern about the departure of important scientists for the U.S.A.

To his knowledge, the notion was first analysed in economics by Brinley Thomas, who dealt with world-wide flows from the poorer to the richer countries, and by Professor Johnson, who dealt with Canadian outflows to the U.S.A. Since then many research and governmental agencies, and various branches of economics, industrial relations and manpower studies, as well as sociologists, had carried out surveys, and had attempted quantitative measures of stocks, flows and migratory behaviour.

However, in economics itself, theoretical or *a priori* analyses of the welfare consequence of the brain drain had predominated at the expense of growth processes, prediction or even of precise policy proposals. At various times, indeed, a number of people in the present Round Table had contributed to the literature. He thought not only of Professors Johnson and Seers, but also of Professors Patinkin, Bhagwati, Boulding, Ohlin and probably several others.

The Johnson paper took the form of a survey of a cost-benefit analysis of the emigration of skilled people emigrating from a developing country. In effect it consisted of an abbreviated check list of possible sources of benefit or cost, along with a commentary on the importance or the sign of these.

As with most cost-benefit analyses, and with much of welfare theory as applied to international trade, the categories were all concerned with comparative statics rather than dynamics, linkages, perceptions or lags in the development process. These *processes*, or dynamic categories, were the province of the other paper by Mr. Jolly and Professor Seers.

One difficulty with both papers, as with much of the extensive literature on the brain drain, was that the alternative state, or proposed policy change, was not really specified. Thus we did not really learn much about what was the welfare loss or gain from modifying or expanding migration. However, we were presumably considering some all-or-nothing change. The brain drain might be just as necessary a cost of building a professional and scientific corps as occasional physical damage, failure and unexpected obsolescence might be a necessary cost of having a large stock of physical capital. Certainly it was not clear that a benefit-cost, with-and-without study of the brain drain dealt with any real-world, operational, problem.

Within these comparative-static limits, Professor Johnson's paper was short, clear and easy to summarise. It was divided into four parts. In the first, from pages 380–3, Professor Johnson dealt with the size of the brain drain and the importance of its correct measurement. It was essential to emphasise that this was not a massive flow. A migration of the order of 50,000 people per annum might be wrong by two orders of magnitude, but certainly not by ten. It was important that we should have a true idea of the size of the problem, whether the migration concerned was one-way or not.

On pages 383–4, Professor Johnson noted five benefits to underdeveloped countries from emigration. These were as follows:

> First, the output of a pure scientist was most valuable if he worked under the best possible conditions. He would then be of most value to every country, including his own country of origin. The benefit of his research might well go back to the underdeveloped country, because it was a public good.

> Second, Professor Johnson extended the analysis to the case of some specialists, such as economists and consultants, suggesting that economists worked much better in their own countries.

> Third, there were remittances – which were the subject of an important part of the literature.

> Fourth, Professor Johnson suggested that the brain drain was a safety valve for 'inappropriate' and 'excessive' manpower and educational systems in countries of origin.

> Fifth, he argued that the brain drain might have a catalytic effect back in the L.D.C.

So, there were five categories of benefits. Two of these were short-run, and the others were likely to be met with only in comparative-static cases.

On pages 385–8, Professor Johnson considered losses. However he again argued that it was important to be sure of the 'point of view'. There were four kinds of 'point of view':

(a) cosmopolitan or global;
(b) total size of a country's G.D.P.;
(c) total G.D.P. per head;
(d) G.D.P. per head of those remaining in the country.

Professor Johnson's discussion was almost entirely from the fourth point of view. Professor Scott suggested that at least some economists thought that the two most important points of view were those of the total size and scale of the G.D.P.

Because Professor Johnson's analysis was one of comparative statics, he distinguished three time periods. He also distinguished three analytical models of human and/or physical capital. First, there were instantaneous situations where the stock of capital was fixed in form. In the short run, even human capital was malleable. In the long run, the rate of saving and capital-replacement varied. Professor Johnson was not always explicit about which period he was considering, but mostly he was concerned with the short run when human capital was malleable.

Professor Johnson now moved on to five categories of loss:

(1) the unwanted or unexpected loss of future fiscal or family combinations. This must be undesired *and* unexpected.
(2) a change in factor proportions beyond those previously existing and beyond the range of easy substitution of products. A variant of this second case was where there was a loss of consumers' surplus for non-traded services. Both these losses were seen as 'small'.
(3) terms-of-trade losses. Professor Johnson followed up the possibility of mass immigration actually changing the supply of import-competing goods, and thus having an adverse effect on the terms of trade but a favourable efficiency effect.
(4) the scale effect, which was dismissed. It was significant only if there was a change in the scale of the whole economy. There was the minor point that, in science, the loss of one man might then be important in breaking up a team.
(5) externalities, namely, distinctions between professional people in terms of their work and personal characteristics. For example, a public health doctor always helped the country in which he worked; some did more than this. This was important in terms of the short run versus the very short run. In the very short run, all externalities were a loss; in the short run, when professionals could be replaced, only those externalities associated with particular individuals could not be made up.

On a static basis, and on balance, Professor Johnson felt that the benefits of the brain drain exceeded the costs – apart from any effect it had on altering the ratio of labour to capital among those remaining in the losing country.

There were, however, some additional matters to be considered if one were looking at the gap. There was an important literature on the size of the brain drain, especially by Bowman, Myers and the O.E.C.D. Second, Professor Johnson ignored measures of human capital, a slightly different subject from welfare economics. At the Lausanne conference it had been suggested that some countries should go in for the export of brains as an activity. A measure of human capital might suggest a basis for measuring losses and gains. Professor Johnson might have referred to the distribution of local incomes from a different structure of manpower in the losing country. He mentioned a paper by West at the University of Canterbury, which had been published in the *Southern Economic Journal*.

At the end of his paper, Professor Johnson went to global welfare and referred to the reviews of the Adams book on the brain drain. The basic question was: did unrestricted emigration lead to the maximisation of global welfare? Professor Johnson would say yes, either because each individual could go to wherever his pay was the highest, or because unrestricted migration led to the location of production or services where they were most efficient and cheap.

This was a first-best solution. Professor Scott's own point of view was that although international income maximisation did bring about a first-best solution, migration was defective in bringing about rapidly the best location of the production of a particular kind of output; non-traded goods and services.

For years, or generations, the adjustment process would bring, for example,

O

doctors into high-income locations, although that would *not* improve the quality of their services much or at all. Here 'ideal location' was entirely the result of the distribution of patients' incomes, not of the technical advantages of the grouping of people. Consequently restraint on the migration of producers of non-traded goods would (a) at least produce a good second-best *distribution* of real income; and (b) might not reduce the global output of *other* goods from the first-best, or Pareto, location of production.

Professor Scott said that his final remarks were these. First, he was unrepentant about everything he had said about the brain drain in the past. Second, Professor Johnson had discussed only the static effects of the brain drain. What we needed was a policy proposal, and this must take some account of growth and adjustment in developing countries.

Professor Johnson said that Professor Scott and he had discussed the paper before the Round Table meeting and decided to cast it in its present form, because Professor Scott's review of the Lausanne volume was important and needed discussion. He would therefore like to make it clear that this paper had been an invitation to a duel that was accepted, and not an unpremeditated attack on a defenceless individual.

Dr. Corden noted that many of the members of the Conference were representatives of the brain drain. He was not sure whether this made the Round Table more or less competent to discuss the paper.

He would like to relate what he had to say to the theory of welfare economics. There were certain requirements for a Pareto optimum, but the outcome depended on the pattern of tastes and the distribution of income. He would grant that free labour movement led to a Pareto optimum. With the present, far from ideal, income distribution, there was a different distribution of brains from that which would exist if income distribution were optimal. On this point, he thought Professor Johnson was correct.

However, the first-best policy had two elements. First, one had to get the Pareto optimum; second, one had to get the right income distribution. Given that one did not have the desired international distribution of incomes, was it right to use migration as a second-best policy? The Scott/Johnson debate was peripheral to this.

Professor Bhagwati commented on the paper by Jolly and Seers. He agreed with the problems identified by them as stemming from the brain drain from L.D.C.s, especially the problem of income distribution in the L.D.C.s.

As for the question of the impact on the L.D.C.s, however, the analysis had to be pushed further. Admittedly more doctors were critical to a country such as India. But if they were not allowed to migrate, would they really go to the villages where their social marginal product was very high or would they stick around in the urban areas where they were too many doctors anyway? Even in China force had to be deployed repeatedly, as during the Cultural Revolution, to get the necessary transfer of talent to the countryside.

A still further qualification arose from the fact that many discussions of brain drain assumed that the brain was 'static'. Either it stayed at home or it 'drained out'. But it was clear enough that the brain could drain away pretty rapidly just sitting around at home! Thus, for example, a hierarchical or a bureaucracy-ridden society in the L.D.C.s could well stultify the academic environment and impair creativity and efficiency. Occasional migration could well be fruitful in making such a society more responsive to the need to use its brains more efficiently by treating them better.

Mr. Streeten wondered what followed from this discussion for salary policies in underdeveloped countries. Should one raise or lower salaries? One had to distinguish the effect on new entrants and established members of any profession. If one lowered salaries, one would deter new entrants and absorb some unemployed, but one might also cause members of the profession to emigrate. If one increased salaries, one might keep more at home but also increase the flow of new entrants and discourage employment. So, whatever salary policy was followed, there was a dilemma.

Mr. Streeten noted that Professor Johnson allowed an exception to his cosmopolitan view, where he said that free labour movement might lead to population growth and swamp the world in poverty. He did not say in so many words that a possible solution was to admit only professionals to the country and bar the unskilled. But if he followed his argument through, this was the result. Surely, to a cosmopolitan, there would be a benefit if the increased mobility of unskilled labour led to a fall in mortality rates. Even an increase in fertility rates had some positive welfare aspects. How could a true cosmopolitan reach this conclusion? If one had to limit free immigration, why not let in a limited number of skilled *and* unskilled people, in fixed proportions? The Johnson argument could be used to justify the present deplorable immigration policies of the U.K.

Professor Findlay commented on the paper by Professor Johnson. On page 381, Professor Johnson pointed out the logical possibility that a reduction in the numbers leaving an underdeveloped country could increase average income. A footnote said that this would happen 'if the wage of an educated man, in both countries, exceeds the average wage by less than per capita income from capital and other property'. A rough calculation suggested that if an educated person was a university graduate, the excess of his income over average per capita income was so big that this was most unlikely to happen. It would certainly not happen in Asia.

Dr. Mahbub ul Haq distinguished two types of brain drain. The first was a brain drain within the country, while the second was to countries outside. As he had said earlier, there were large foreign firms operating in countries like India and Pakistan. These firms were obliged by legislation to hire some local staff and to pay equal wages, which in many cases were completely out of proportion to domestic wages. Thus there was a considerable flow of very highly educated people to these firms even when those concerned were required to do small administrative jobs and were kept on the payrolls of foreign firms mostly for influence – peddling with the government. This kind of brain drain was probably worse than a brain drain abroad as there were adverse repercussions all round, especially the demonstration effect on luxury consumption and the misallocation of scarce resources. The policy options in this case were under the control of the relevant governments, so that the problem could be more easily tackled. He suggested that some analysis should be devoted to this type of brain drain, to bring out its quantitative magnitude and its implications for policy-makers in underdeveloped countries.

The second kind of brain drain was emigration. One could not analyse this problem adequately unless one stopped treating brains as homogeneous. He would like to make a distinction between high- and low-quality brains. The latter could become a major source of remittances if immigration laws abroad permitted labourers from underdeveloped countries to work there. For example, many labourers who left Pakistan worked in restaurants abroad and their remittances now gave Pakistan its second biggest source of export earnings. He also made a distinction between temporary and permanent emigration. Many who left underdeveloped countries temporarily were in Professor Johnson's words 'parked abroad'. They generally acquired a good deal of expertise and experience and returned to their countries when economic and political conditions were favourable.

The brain drain of really skilled people like doctors was, however, different since there were critical shortages of these skills in the countries concerned, which had also made a fairly sizeable investment in them. The solution lay in the relative price policy of underdeveloped countries. If they insisted on paying their doctors much less than they paid their general administrators, as was the case in Pakistan, they should not be surprised if they lost 500 out of 700 doctors trained each year, as Pakistan was losing annually to the outside world. The acquisition of higher skills greatly increased the international mobility of skilled people in underdeveloped countries so that their salary structure had to be judged not in relation to per capita income in the countries concerned but in relation to what would have to be paid for such skills in a competitive international market or to an outside expert. This might be the real alternative in many such cases.

Professor Patinkin said that Professor Johnson and he had already disagreed about the brain drain in Lausanne.[1] To some extent their differences depended on their different personal experiences.

He would like to register a point on the use of the word 'cosmopolitan'. To take the 'world approach' said little unless one specified the kind of world one wanted. If one wanted a world with a variety of cultural and economic centres, then one would get a different answer from Professor Johnson. So it was important to have a world social-welfare function to begin with.

To some extent the terms of reference of the Round Table postulated a world of nation states. Professor Johnson had accepted these terms of reference, though perhaps reluctantly. Professor Patinkin just wanted to say that the nation state was not a chance classification. Modern economic development was concomitant with (and probably helped by) the emergence of nation states. So perhaps the nation state was a relevant unit for an analysis of the process of economic development. What should be emphasised here was that development was dynamic – almost as good an 'O.K.' word as cosmopolitan.

There were two points in dynamic development. First, why accept that the

---

[1] Professor Patinkin referred here, for a fuller discussion of his points, to his contribution to *The Brain Drain* (ed. Walter Adams, New York, 1968), pp. 92–108. He noted that the title originally given to his paper was 'Some Reflections on the Brain Drain', and not (as it now appeared under the title imposed upon it by the editor) 'A "Nationalist" Model'. This unauthorised change in title created a misrepresentation of his main point: namely, that the views expressed reflected a certain 'world viewpoint' about the role of national cultures and states.

market would not develop new machinery and techniques for underdeveloped countries? This question had still not been answered, although he had raised it in the earlier discussion of the transfer of technology. His own feeling was that the main element was that those in developed countries were not sensitive to the technical problems of underdeveloped countries. Relevant technological development could be encouraged by living in underdeveloped countries. This was not a necessary or sufficient condition, but it still increased the probability of success. Second, the social milieu was important. If a scientist was given credit for solving problems, he was encouraged to go on. In the U.K. no one would be a hero if he found how to use orange peel in the chemical industry. But in Israel the situation would be quite different.

Another question was that of entrepreneurial ability. We had discussed the transfer of technical knowledge. Those entrepreneurs who were able to borrow it must be reasonably well educated and hence the loss of such people to the 'brain drain' could create serious external diseconomies. He wondered what were the experiences of the multinational corporations. Had the presence of locally trained personnel helped them to integrate into the local economy? Dr. Haq now talked of the internal brain drain, but this reflected internal policies.

He wanted to take up Professor Johnson on the 'great scientist who *should* go abroad'. He would like to point out some facts not usually discussed in this cost-benefit analysis. First, what did a great scientist give in addition to his own work? We all knew how a university worked, and if the university lost him it would lose several things. It would lose an ability to spot good people; probably a research team; high standards of judgement and academic work.

He found it significant that in the discussion of this question the possibility that the scientist could bring research funds to his own university because of his ability was not mentioned. Because of lower professional salaries, the marginal productivity of a research dollar in an underdeveloped country was often greater than in a developed one. The policy implications of this were that – from a world viewpoint – the free international flow of research funds should be encouraged.

He was not saying that one should impede the flow of people. In all world communities one would have a flow of manpower. If there was no flow of people from and to a country, it was not part of the world scientific community. He thought it was important how one looked at the issue. Did one look with equanimity or with concern? We needed policies, consistent with freedom, to mitigate the dangers that a brain drain could bring to underdeveloped countries.

Professor Johnson said it was probably unfortunate that, at Lausanne, he had accepted the cosmopolitan-national distinction from Adams. He agreed with Professor Patinkin that universities depended on a few talented men, but those with this role did not usually go abroad. Those who attracted foreign research funds also stayed. British experience was that a man did not break up a research team until after years of frustration. Indeed many brains often did not drain when they should, but put up with frustrations for too long. Professor Patinkin had set up a straw man.

Professor Ranis said that the answer to Professor Patinkin's question about why developed countries did not develop technology for underdeveloped countries might take us in a dangerous direction. Professor Patinkin had not gone far enough. The question was why this happened. The answer was that demand for such research and development was not exercised in developed countries because of scientific and technical policies.

If Professor Patinkin argued that one should keep people at work in the underdeveloped countries, he would not deny the pay-off but perhaps question whether a lot of R. & D. expenditure would be a waste of resources. These countries did not use sufficiently appropriate techniques as the basis for their research. Formal education was much more expensive than learning by doing.

Professor Patinkin did not want to dwell on the 'great scientist' problem. All he had been saying was that his other points had not been mentioned in the papers. And it was wrong to say that research funds were always obtained by good researchers. Those interested in the international approach should take as their first problem the fact that U.S. government and foundations discriminate in the granting of research funds between scholars in the U.S. and in other countries. The same scholar was much more likely to obtain a research grant if he moved to the U.S. than if he stayed in his home country. This had clear implications for the brain drain.

Dr. Pfaff thought that Professor Patinkin had made an important point in suggesting that, if one used a social welfare function to evaluate the effect of the 'brain drain', one had to ask as to what was the relevant unit of observation. The very concept of the *type* of social welfare function employed depended on assumptions about the nature of the economic system. If one assumed that separate, atomic individuals, characterised in economic terms by independent utility functions, were the basic unit of analysis, this did not provide strong economic logic for taking the national rather than the cosmopolitan view. On the other hand, if one did *not* view the individual as an atomic entity different conclusions would follow. Individuals could no longer be viewed as 'brains freely floating on the surface of the globe'. When focussing on interdependence, community and social structure, the nation-state would appear as a more relevant unit, simply because community patterns of interdependence were more pronounced at the national than at the cosmopolitan level.

The relevant unit of observation thus depended on the patterns of interdependence prevailing in the real world. A social welfare function, when viewed as an aggregate reflection of the interdependence patterns prevailing at the micro-level, necessarily had to be related to the very patterns of interdependence that gave rise to its existence.

Professor Patinkin was also right in asking what were the functions and limitations of the market in evaluating the brain drain. In particular, why did the market mechanism not lend itself to the measurement of the effects of the brain drain. There were several reasons. First, markets expressed individual rather than social choice. Second, market choices were guided by the planning horizons of individual actors and these were generally shorter than those of the government or society. In fact, if one were to postulate functions and time-attributes of implicit goals to various levels of society, the market could be viewed as operating in the very short run; the overall economic system in the short run; the political system in the intermediate run; the social system in the long run; and the cultural system in the very long run. If this view were accepted, there was little surprise in the conclusion that market signals expressed through prices did not express the complete *social* welfare implications of the brain drain.

Dr. Pfaff defended Professor Scott for taking the equity norm into consideration. Even if the international mobility of labour were to be economically efficient, it might not be considered equitable by those less developed countries whose high-talent manpower had emigrated to industrialised countries. Accordingly, in their view, their *social* welfare must necessarily have been diminished. One could view the problem of assessing the welfare implications of the brain drain as an optimisation problem under conditions of conflicting goals. Market-efficiency-goals could be measured on one axis; equity goals on another; growth goals on the third, and so on. The first axis would measure a purely economic utility while the other axes would include social goals. Such a system of goals could be postulated for an n-dimensional Euclidean space of norms measurable, at least in principle, through a set of economic and social indicators. In order to evaluate a particular plane in this space we would require a social welfare function which expressed the relevant unit's (say the nation's) social function as a weighted function of the various goals. A tangency point between such a welfare function and a complex socio-economic utility possibility function would indicate the optimum point which might serve as basis for evaluation.

There was little doubt that an evaluation of this type, which added not only equity but other goals, would differ from the evaluation suggested by neo-classical welfare economics. This based its judgement solely on criteria of market efficiency.

Professor Seers explained that he had recently been in Latin America and had discussed the ideas in the paper by Richard Jolly and himself, which drew on their recent work in Colombia. There was therefore a strong Latin-American, especially Colombian, influence on the framework of analysis. Perhaps it needed to be modified for use elsewhere.

To summarise, the best approach was to ask what was happening to the view of development in Latin America. He wanted to stress that the old, simplistic models of the 1950s and 1960s were being discarded. At that time the dominant model had been partly based on the Prebisch analysis which put heavy emphasis on the need to use tariff protection to develop the growth of modern (especially industrial) sectors. One should rely on private foreign investment and foreign aid to make up for savings deficiencies. This was expected to lead to growth elsewhere, but the expectation had not been fulfilled.

Any assessment needed qualification for particular regions. The statistics were also poor. However, it was fairly clear that growth remained concentrated in the modern sector, with industrial output sometimes rising by as much as 10 per cent per annum. Yet there was little spreading of its benefits, and technology in the industrial sector was becoming increasingly modern. Salaries, even wages, reflected overseas standards, while consumption patterns were heavily influenced by overseas tastes.

All this had been accompanied by growing unemployment. Taking urban employment, sample surveys had shown that this was often now more than 10 per cent. In Colombia, growth had been accompanied by a rise in 'disguised' unemployment – for example, work in family businesses or withdrawal from the labour force. So total unemployment was bigger than the official figures suggested. Again, income distribution was becoming more concentrated. There seemed to have been no increase in real wages in rural areas from the early 1930s to the 1960s. This was certainly not true for urban areas. Fragmentary data showed that even in fast-growing economies unemployment and inequality in income was increasing, as it was in Jamaica, Trinidad and Venezuela.

All this had led to a reappraisal of the philosophy of development. The 'spread' mechanism had not worked and cumulative tendencies were operating. The most useful way of looking at 'the gap' was to treat it as a 'gap' between those countries where there were mechanisms for spreading growth from the fastest-growing sectors and the remainder. On this basis, Argentina was less underdeveloped than Venezuela (which had a higher income). It was not easy for Argentinian economists to make the required change of view. He was not saying that there had been no government policy mistakes, but governments themselves were partially endogenous to the process, because political power was concentrated in the advanced, urban sectors.

How could this be linked to the 'brain drain'? He and Richard Jolly had only given some bricks for constructing models in their paper. They thought it would help to get away from purely quantitative cost and benefit measures to focus attention on the links between the 'brain drain' and the uncritical importation of various types of technology. It would also help to concentrate attention on its relation to salaries; if salaries increased in a country losing professional skills this might ease the brain drain, but it would worsen the income distribution. We should also look critically at the appropriateness of copying Western educational systems.

Professor Lewis pointed out that neither paper said much about policy. We ought to distinguish countries with a labour surplus that they wanted to export, from other countries. For example, Barbados needed to export about 50 per cent of its population and therefore felt that it had a duty to educate them before they went. This helped, because it made it easier for them to get good jobs when they left, and also because it increased the remittances that they were able to send back. We should not take it for granted that all persons now in underdeveloped countries should stay there.

In the other cases, the question was how far the rate of growth in the underdeveloped country was affected by the brain drain. The answer was not much. The rate of growth of G.N.P. had increased, from 3 per cent to 5 per cent to 6 per cent or even 8 per cent in some cases. Shortage of skill had not been a major constraint. We had net inflows of talent now rather than net outflows. Indeed one had to remember that it was very easy for underdeveloped countries to over-produce skill. The problem of the underdeveloped countries as a whole was that there were too many university graduates though, again, different countries were in different positions. Much of this was because of bad educational policies. There were too many graduates in the non-natural sciences. The fundamental remedy was better science training in schools.

The main need was to treat professional people well. The brain drain was not a question of salary but of frustration. In the West Indies most of those who were potential candidates for the brain drain worked for governments. The degree of brain drain depended on how well the governments treated them. The West Indies needed more trained peopele, and in this case it was important to pay them properly. Why should one not pay professionals according to the value of their skills? We gave enormous incentives to foreigners to bring in capital; why should we not give equal incentives to our own valuable human resources.

Professor Lewis also wondered why the few we had who did want to become professionals through hard work should be discriminated against. As youngsters they were sneered at by their contemporaries for being 'swots'. When they graduated, were they to be specially taxed in the interest of those same pleasure-loving contemporaries? However, he did think that they should be made to pay for their education. 'Free' education for the middle class was regressive. We ought to make those who wanted higher education pay for it themselves through loans.

Professor Hicks wanted to agree with Sir Arthur Lewis and reply to Dr. Corden. It seemed that part of the disagreement between Professors Scott and Johnson reflected a fundamental point in welfare economics, on which the whole of the session's discussion depended.

Dr. Corden suggested that the Pareto-optimum theory implied that it was all a matter of getting to a frontier with a lot of different positions on it, each with a different distribution of income. This was correct up to a point, but the essential thing was that the theory was concerned with an analysis where the initial position was one with people and resources as they were now. The income distribution arising from this was part of the organisation. One was varying this, and trying to classify the results. So one had to remember that it was hard to find lump-sum income redistributions that did not affect other general conditions of the optimum.

A system that satisfied the Pareto test was not independent of income distribution, but put severe constraints on it. If the income distributions that emerged were not satisfactory, then one had to go to a second-best alternative. Professor Johnson was going for a first-best solution, and so was implying things about income distribution. Professor Scott and others were doing something different.

Professor Eastman thought that the challenging tone of Professor Seers' paper had obscured its policy recommendations. It referred to unsatisfactory kinds of education. Professor Eastman believed that the problem of education was analogous to that of designing capital goods appropriate to relative factor prices in developing countries. The emigration of doctors because of low salaries in their countries of origin, and similar problems, indicated the necessity of designing less capital-intensive education. The supply price would be lower and the service more appropriate to demand conditions. Any policy aiming at reducing the income of the intra-marginal, rent-receiving practitioner in the interests of social welfare had certain dangers. The intra-marginal man was a sitting duck, but defended by his protective colouring, and attacks on his rent often fell on others who were mobile and left the country. In any event, taxing intra-marginal individuals to finance the services they supplied raised the question of who was included in the social group for which welfare should be maximised.

Professor Kuznets argued that the two papers illustrated a basic disagreement on the theory of economic growth. The fascinating but rambling character of the discussion in the Round Table was also a result of this. One view, implicit in the Johnson paper, denied the basic importance of *national* brain power. The

Jolly–Seers paper was based on the theory that the availability of some brain-endowed factors in a country, who were nationals of that country, was a pre-condition of the full employment of other resources and of retaining political viability. If this were true the theory could be extended to the whole educational and scientific system of the country. He was sorry that the Round Table had not given more attention to science policy than that which the discussion of multi-national corporations allowed. Such a discussion might have led the Conference to distinguish the *types* of brain-endowed factors that were needed *within* the country for economic growth.

This would also have led to a reformulation of the theory of capital invest-ment; and to a classification of types of capital investment in brain-endowed factors that might yield a better measure of the brain drain – internal or ex-ternal – or the drains of different types of brain would have assumed different meanings. We could then also have more useful discussions of the pricing of factors and its effect on the brain drain.

Professor Seers might have provided us with some bricks, but their shape depended upon the theory for which they were needed. The papers and dis-cussion dealt with an interlocking process, closely related to transfer of tech-nology and factor complementarities in the process of growth.

Professor Vernon pointed out that the Jolly-Seers paper was based on a per-ception of what happened to the income and welfare of different groups in a country. On Latin America, Professor Seers explained that there was room for different views drawn from the same data. He would suggest alternative con-clusions along these lines. On unemployment; there was certainly a high rate of unemployment in Latin America. This was a serious social problem, but what did it mean in welfare terms? It was part of the development process by which dis-guised unemployment on the land had converted into open unemployment in the cities. In the process, as various sociological studies indicated, slum dwellers that had migrated from rural areas in Latin America usually saw themselves as better off.

Turning to income distribution, he would agree at once that there was an 'upper-income lump', as more entrepreneurs came in. Professor Seers had quoted interesting statistics on income distribution, but it was not clear whether income distribution was becoming more or less skewed. If one went back to census data and created indexes of social welfare based on literacy, health, housing, etc., by region, it was clear by the 1960s that there were growing similarities between regions. For example, this happened in Venezuela and Mexico. He thought that the 1970 data would show even more similarities.

Professor Seers had cited the Navarrete study which took a sample of wage earners – giving all profit to the top decile. This was an absurdly arbitrary esti-mate and it produced a skewed distribution that would raise anyone's eyebrows.

Professor Ghai wanted to add a new distinction. Brains also drained to inter-national institutions in developed countries. He wondered what percentage of them went there. He thought that it represented an increasing percentage, par-ticularly of economists, and the effect was probably quite different according to what they went to do.

Brains from underdeveloped countries going to international agencies could probably do good for the L.D.C.s. They would work on development problems and perhaps make more contribution there than in their own countries. International agencies were becoming more and more powerful and needed representatives from underdeveloped countries. Again, it was through international agencies that experts from one L.D.C. could serve in another.

Professor Horvat had been provoked by Professor Johnson because there were ideological elements in the paper. Professor Johnson took a cosmopolitan view; but we did not know what kind of cosmos.

On page 381 of his paper, Professor Johnson said that, 'a literal concern with the gap . . . could lead to strange results, because it was quite possible for the migration of an educated person to raise the average income in the poor country he leaves and lower it in the rich country he joins, thus narrowing the gap'.

This was possible, but irrelevant, so that its insignificant probability did not matter. The effect could be the other way. The problem of most international agencies was that they did not help by sending experts. For example, a man from the U.K. had been sent to Ethiopia to help with industrialisation. His report to the U.N. agency argued that what was necessary was technological education. The Ethiopians were unused to technology and did not even care about it, so one had to interest them, and this would be easier if one started young. One needed toys to encourage this, and the expert therefore recommended the establishment of toy factories.

Also on page 381 Professor Johnson said, 'My objection to the gap as a focus for analysis is not merely that the use of statistical averages can produce unnecessary paradoxes or nonsense results, but it assumes the nation as a unit of analysis rather the people that are born and live in a world divided into nation states, and hence biases thinking towards a nationalist rather than a cosmopolitan view of the problem and of solutions to it, and towards a neglect of the welfare of the individuals who better themselves by moving'.

Let us suppose that we had a man with a wife and two children. The man decided to leave his family in order to increase his individual economic welfare. While we knew that there was nothing 'cosmopolitan' about such a decision, and could agree that it was a bad one, we did not learn this from neo-classical economics. We should remember that the historical development of solidarity had gone from solidarity within the family, to that of the village, the nation and now that of the whole of humanity. But we should not forget this developmental process. We had the highest and lowest amounts of solidarity at the ends of the scale. So, while it was not right to try to maximise the welfare of the government, we should certainly try to maximise the welfare of the community.

Dr. Little said that Sir John Hicks had suggested that it was hard to find policies to allow a shift along a Pareto welfare function. He would just add that it was quite impossible. He would also say that economists still had a very static view both of how to shift wealth and of inequality. In theory one needed to define these for all eternity. It was not clear how far one knew what one was doing for equality, if one said, for example, that one should reduce salaries and allow a brain drain to take place. This was particularly so if one took a long-run view of equality. In the end everything was a matter of common sense and elasticities. One could sometimes pay people salaries below their marginal social product and yet lose very few of them. This worked if elasticity was low; but it was rather silly if it were high.

Professor Johnson replied to the discussion, Professor Scott was right that the quantitative brain drain was a small problem, though some small countries might have non-marginal brain drains. Perhaps attention to the brain drain had therefore been overdone. We must remember that demand *and* supply factors were at work. What was deplorable from the one point of view was desirable from the other.

Professor Johnson said there had recently been much emotion over the brain drain in developed countries, mainly from those who knew little of under-developed countries but used very vivid imagery. The issue was of disproportions in the education systems and absorptive capacity of countries. He agreed that remittances were often ignored in discussions in developed countries, yet they were often very important to underdeveloped countries, not least because of the difference in levels of income between L.D.C.s and developed countries. The brain drain could help to remedy policy deficiencies. This was a question of pricing policies for educated people, and the way governments under-priced scarce resources to encourage their use. So, the pricing system discriminated against very expensive talent. A fruitful part of the discussion would concentrate on the micro-economics of the subject.

Dr. Haq mentioned the internal brain drain to foreign firms, and perhaps more attention should be given to the economics of this matter. If a country forced foreign firms to hire indigenous managers, it created the problem for itself. If one were trying to transplant technology, perhaps the foreign firm should bring in a complete labour force. It should leave the nationals of the country to do things which were better for growth. We usually tried to achieve the opposite. There had been no work done on these internal brain drains, but work in Canada suggested that they might be desirable. However it was certainly impossible to have a policy to make foreign firms hire only incompetent nationals.

The problem of welfare measurement was at the heart of the discussion. The standard procedure in welfare economics was to use, on the one hand, the Pareto-optimum concept and on the other, both current prices and the current income distribution. If one thought current prices inappropriate, then one should aim at a different income distribution rather than inflate costs to reflect assumed social welfare. It was a long step from objecting to an unfair world income distribution to preventing the emigration of skilled labour, which was probably a fourth best solution. Moreover given what Professor Bhagwati had said, perhaps emigration did not always represent a loss. For example, if one looked at Canada and the U.S.A. one found economists like Galbraith going from Canada to America. After some time many less able Canadian economists employed in the U.S.A. could not have got jobs at home, and found them in small American colleges.

Everything came down in the end to a matter of taste. If one thought it important to have highly educated people in underdeveloped rather than developed countries, then one could take steps to achieve this. But it was not clear why one should. Surely the proper policy was to pay the right price rather than coerce individuals; if one paid them to stay, it was not necessary to coerce them.

Professor Seers also replied to the discussion. He agreed that income distribution lay at the nub of the problem. To Professor Vernon he said that the problem was not simply the regional distribution of income. He had concentrated on the rural–urban balance which was not the same thing, but there was also the question whether inequality was growing in the distribution of income (and social services, infrastructure, etc.) between towns on the one hand and villages on the other, and between large and small towns. In addition, there seemed to be growing disparities within urban areas. Regional figures alone could not by themselves prove a tendency for income differences to become less severe.

However, income distribution had other implications, both for the consumption pattern and for the level of employment. High salaries in the modern sector could impede the adaptation of the consumption structure to match the production structure, an adaptation which must be made if high levels of employment were to be reached. Furthermore, those who were paid high salaries tended to be almost as cut off from the population as foreigners were, which limited the usefulness of their advice on policy issues.

What about policy implications? These had been ignored in the paper, partly because he and Richard Jolly had dealt with them elsewhere. However, there were more important reasons. First, policy recommendations were specific to countries. Second, one had to specify objectives and indeed find the frame of reference for the welfare function. One could then abandon the rate of growth as the central target; he thought one must, and could, tackle specific problems.

We ought to look at the 'brain' drain as part of the development process. One way to reduce it was by making education more appropriate. The balance of argument on the need for restricting migration would differ with, for example, one's moral view of the government. Moreover, it could well be against a country's interests to do so. For example, Cuba had decided that it would be best to allow an outflow of professional people rather than face the political consequences of keeping them. This was understandable, though perhaps the Cuban view would have been different if the country had had fewer skilled people.

For developed countries the major requirement was that they should look after their own professional needs. This was not happening at present. For example, in the case of medicine in the United Kingdom, there would be shortages of doctors up to 1980, given current plans.

He had not suggested that the transfer of technology was unimportant; contact should not be cut off from research and teaching in developed countries. One simply wanted a more selective use of research (and teaching) material from countries with entirely different structures and problems.

Professor Scott wanted to thank those economists who had distinguished the ideal distribution of goods from the ideal location of their production. He had been happy with the discussion until Professor Johnson had spoken of the distribution of goods and services with respect to the location of scientists. He wanted to draw attention to the fact that he himself had talked of *non-traded* services, like medicine. With free migration, everyone went where he was best off. He had two problems in convincing people that a case could be made for preventing free migration of doctors, when much of world population was immobile.

First, one had to make the unprovable, subjective assertion that the loss, for example, to doctors, was less than the gains to their patients. Second, one had to make the conceptually-verifiable prediction that more equal income distributions would have little or no effect on the output of traded products. If these points were accepted, one had a second-best solution.

Professor Johnson said that in believing that emigration was a good thing, he was trying to improve income distribution. Migration laws were contrary to improving income distribution. They prevented people emigrating and were often accompanied by barriers to removing such differences by trade. For some, migration could improve income per head, but only, perhaps, if it harmed those left behind.

Part 3

The Outlook

17 Objectives and Prognostications

W. Arthur Lewis

PRINCETON UNIVERSITY

I. OBJECTIVES

Assignment to such a title as this affords an author little scope for systematic investigation; it seems rather to invite rambling reflections, appropriate to a closing session. I shall take it in this sense, though lacking the advantage of reading the preceding papers.

I have never been much impressed by 'the revolution of rising expectations', or 'the demonstration effect', or 'the importance of closing the gap', so these remarks will concentrate on the prospects of the less developed countries, without reference to what may happen simultaneously to the living standards of the more developed.

The central objective is taken to be to raise the level of living of the masses of the people in L.D.C.s as rapidly as is feasible, with all the problems hidden in the word 'feasible'. One will thus begin by studying those constraints which make it desirable to keep the growth rate lower than is technically possible; the second half of the paper will reflect on what is technically possible.

(1) Present v. Future Consumption

Economists' formulae for deriving the optimal growth rate of consumption assume (subject to discounting the future) that a man at time n equals a man at time zero; that my son and I are the same person. The assumption is of course false. I may wish to save most of my income to make my children rich; or, expecting that the continuous increase in productivity will inevitably make them richer than I, I may feel that it is they who should mortgage their future for my present rather than I my present for their future. Economics has no basis for calculating an optimal rate of savings, or of economic growth.

Three factors counsel restraint. One is current poverty, especially in some overpopulated rural areas and some metropolitan slums. Some part of current output should be devoted to relieving these miseries now, rather than (via saving) in the future. A second restraining factor is the political dislocation created by rapid social change, which makes some absolutely poorer and others relatively poorer for reasons which they may neither understand nor accept. A wider spreading of the benefits of growth is to be desired, even at the expense of reducing the rate of growth.

The third factor emphasises that a high rate of growth of *commodities* is not all that important in the public's sense of well being. If asked what they most need from the economic system, those at the bottom of the ladder seem almost everywhere to concentrate on a few simple needs: (a) continuous employment, (b) a somewhat higher income[1], (c) more or better schooling for the children, (d) better medical services, (e) pure water at hand, and (f) cheap transport.[2] This list does involve greater output of some commodities, whether for direct use by their producers, or indirectly to supply the men who produce the services; but an economic plan which gave more emphasis to the wants listed here would devote relatively less resources to commodity production. It would have less saving, more taxes and a relatively slower rate of growth, as national income statisticians measure growth.[3]

These arguments do not run against increasing the ratio of savings, which is still too low in most L.D.C.s. They run against setting too high a target for the marginal ratio of savings. A ratio of 0·2 would be comfortable, whereas 0·4 would be excessive, except in an economy which was already growing very rapidly. One must raise the average savings ratio, but gradually.

Some economists have argued for very high savings in order to promote rapid industrialisation and so solve the unemployment problem. But unemployment can be eliminated without industrialisation (via public works, higher agricultural output, expansion of public services, housing programmes, national wage policies, restrictions on capital intensity, etc.). The level of employment is indeed tied to the availability of wage goods, which requires some capital; but the availability of wage goods is only rather loosely tied to the expansion of modern factory industry, which anyway eats up so much capital and employs so little labour. The need to cope with unemployment is one of the reasons why it may be desirable to keep taxes high and investment in industry low.

(2) *Economic Independence v. Neo-Colonialism*

One would like to have the most of both – consumption and investment. This is possible if one uses foreign funds and personnel. Leaving aside foreign aid and public borrowing, a word is in order here about foreign private investment.

[1] I have read, but cannot trace the reference, that when people are asked how much more income they would need to make them really comfortable, the modal demand is only for about 20 per cent more.

[2] Surprisingly, better housing is low on the list of L.D.C. felt needs; if one gets more housing space, one is likely to take in more tenants or relatives. Housing space is, like whisky, an acquired taste.

[3] In valuing goods and services at cost, they pass over the fact that those which are in short supply (e.g. hospital service in L.D.C.s) are valued by the poor at more than cost.

One reason for the unexpectedly high growth rate of manufacturing in L.D.C.s since the war has been substantial private foreign investment. In the thirties and forties African and Asian political leaders were very hostile towards foreign investment. This attitude relaxed notably in the fifties and sixties, but there are signs that the atmosphere is again changing.

Relaxation was associated with mutual adjustment. Governments passed a series of new laws – licensing investment, regulating inflows and outflows of funds, controlling immigration so as to enforce hiring of local personnel, and so on. Investors in their turn learned to accept controls and tried to accommodate to new political leadership.

Nevertheless hostility is reviving, especially among the young generation coming out of schools and universities, and demanding to pass beyond the political independence won by their fathers to what they call economic independence. The new term 'neo-colonialism' has many meanings; in one it describes a society which has political independence, but whose economy is controlled by foreign shareholders. They argue that it is better for the economy to grow slowly than to succumb to neo-colonialism.

Economic independence also has many meanings, in some of which it is unattainable – all modern economies are interdependent through international trade. But in the limited sense of absence of foreign ownership, any L.D.C. could become independent if it were willing to save more or to grow less rapidly. There are a few cases where foreign firms have a monopoly of advanced technology which they will share only if allowed to invest. But for the most part L.D.C.s can buy technology and management, and can grow with independence at the rate determined by their own willingness to save.

Whether the fears of neo-colonialism are justified on economic or political grounds has no doubt been investigated in earlier papers, so the exercise is not needed here. Even if there were no grounds – and there are some – nationalist feeling is still a factor that cannot be ignored. It will probably significantly restrain the level of private foreign investment in the 1970s; and since those who advocate such restraints are not noticeably forward in promoting domestic savings, the net result will probably be a lower rate of economic growth than would otherwise be possible.

(3) *Growth v. Equality*

During the period when a traditional economy is transformed into a modern economy, a few people inevitably benefit more than the general mass. This is so even when the engine of growth is in small farm agriculture (e.g. cocoa), for usually the profitable crop flourishes only in some regions of the country and not in others. It is still more the case when the transformation occurs through the establishment of a new sector (e.g. factories, mines) which grows by attracting labour from the rest, since the smallness of that sector will ensure it labour with an almost infinite elasticity of supply; and most of the benefits of the new technology will accrue to profit and 'rent' receivers in the new sector. In a modern economy income seems to grow at the same rate at all levels (i.e. distribution remains unchanged), but in the transforming economy most of the poor stay poor while the rich get richer.

Several aspects of this attract particular attention. One is that the transforming economy spawns a middle class (professional, administrative and managerial) whose earnings tend to be rather high in relation to per capita income, when compared with the similar relationship in advanced economies. Where this middle class also holds the potential power, it accumulates privileges for itself (e.g. taxes the farmers to give its own children free university education) without effective political opposition. But where politics is dominated by groups suspicious of 'the establishment' (e.g. Tanzania) the tensions between the government and the middle class can easily erupt into constraints on the rate of economic expansion. Indeed a significant part of the so-called brain drain results from the unwillingness of traditional societies to adjust to men with modern education – not merely in the sense of paying salaries, but rather in the sense of giving them the freedom to exercise their talents which they could expect to find in more modern environments.

The problem is compounded when the society is divided into tribes or races or religious groups, one of which is more successful economically than the rest (e.g. Ibos in Northern Nigeria, Indians in Kenya, Chinese in Malaysia). Left exclusively to market forces, such situations tend to get worse rather than better. The superiority of the advanced group resides in its culture, which gives greater emphasis to the factors that ensure economic success (e.g. education, saving, attention to detail, responsibility and reliability in fulfilling contracts or meeting obligations). For the same reason members of such a group prefer to hire or do business with each other. The disadvantaged groups do not therefore get the opportunity to learn and resent their exclusion from superior opportunities for employment and business. The situation can be righted only by deliberate action to break the monopoly (reserving special educational, financial or business opportunities for the disadvantaged) but it is hard to do this without in the interim restraining growth.

It used to be argued that economic growth required the emergence of large personal fortunes to yield the savings for new investment, but the socialist countries have demonstrated that this is not so. If the state is well managed, it can raise all the required savings through budget surpluses and the profits of public enterprises. There is in many L.D.C.s a yearning to develop through socialist institutions and bypass the robber baron stage. One of the chief obstacles between the L.D.C.s and development on socialist lines is the fact that they are not well managed. Inept administration is not the major problem since, if the governments could save the capital, they could contract with foreign firms to manage the government enterprises until a domestic cadre was formed. The obstacle is rather inability to save; government current expenditure tends to outrun revenue and public enterprises make losses instead of profits. In these circumstances the drift towards socialism in L.D.C.s will restrain economic growth until they learn the principles of sound socialist finance.

(4) Conclusion

Availability of foreign aid – grants and cheap loans – makes all these problems easier, but they persist at any reasonably likely level of aid. They explain why politicians do not see the development process quite as economists see it, and do not always give it top priority. They know the disadvantages of development, and will sometimes deliberately stand in its way. The growth rates of L.D.C.s show a wide range over the past fifteen years. A substantial part of this is explained by the differing degrees of priority accorded to development by different governments.

It follows that the rate of economic growth would be faster if governments were more ruthless. However, ruthlessness does not identify with ideology; the Ivory Coast grows rapidly, with indifference to the charge of neo-colonialism; but despite their ideologies, Burma, Mali and Guinea have lagged. Neither does ruthlessness identify with administrative competence, lack of which constrains the effectiveness of most L.D.C. governments, whatever their ideologies may be; to this we shall return.

II. POSSIBILITIES

In this part of the paper I consider what is technically possible given adequate savings (or foreign aid) and top priority for development.

On this subject the climate of opinion has changed drastically over the past decade. When 5 per cent growth was chosen as the target for the first development decade, it was chosen as an almost unmeetable challenge. It was then assumed that such a high growth rate (higher than the now developed countries had ever achieved before 1950) would not be possible in L.D.C.s without major changes in attitudes, social institutions and land ownership. That this rate has been achieved still comes as a surprise to economists when they first hear of it. Now Professor Tinbergen has informed us that a 6 per cent growth rate is a feasible target for the second development decade, and most of the dissent comes from younger members of our profession who wish to accelerate the pace. What are the technical constraints?

(1) Population

Growth of population is a constraint on the growth of output per head. Traditionally economists have worried about food supplies, but we are not at the moment in that mood; on the contrary some of our number are asking whether the 'green revolution' is not about to bankrupt the farmers of the L.D.C.s (especially in Asia). It looks as if the next decade should be free from worries about food; beyond that we cannot guess.

There is a new worry about exhaustible raw materials, especially fuels and metals. We are warned that it will not be possible for all countries in the world to consume that at the same per capita rate as the U.S.A., and this is seen as a constraint on growth. If we take refuge in scientific progress, which is bound to produce some substitute materials (not to speak of nuclear fission) we are accused of burying our heads in the clouds. Suffice it to say that if a shortage of materials is going to constrain growth, this is still some years ahead.

When we worry about population today we worry not about natural resources but about the drain on savings. It is very expensive to provide houses, schools, hospitals, water supplies and factory space and equipment for a population which doubles every twenty-five years – even if one is merely keeping up with numbers. A lower population growth makes possible more capital per head.

Progress is being made in population control. The problem is not in popular attitudes; the proportion of L.D.C. women who wish to plan their families is already much larger than the resources available to help them. One of the problems is that the technologies we now use are either expensive (like pills) or not entirely reliable (like I.U.D.s). Birth rates are coming down, but rather slowly, except in countries which have legalised abortion. Population growth will continue to be a major constraint on per capita growth for at least the rest of this century.

(2) *Agriculture*

Balance of payments pressure has moved agriculture from low to top priority. The need to earn foreign exchange has promoted concern for agricultural exports, while the need to save foreign exchange on food imports for swiftly rising populations has given equal urgency to domestic food production. Still more recently the relevance of agriculture to unemployment has begun to stand out. Rising urban unemployment seems likely to be the most intractable problem of the 1970s. It is due in part to excessive development of the towns relatively to the countryside, with the higher wages and greater amenities of the towns attracting more young people than the towns can absorb even in casual employment. It is easy to demonstrate that the towns cannot grow fast enough even to absorb the annual increase in the population,[1] let alone also to reduce the

[1] If non-agricultural occupations are 30 per cent of the labour force, and grow by 5 per cent a year, they can take in 1·5 per cent of the labour force in any year. So if the rate of natural increase is 3 per cent, half the natural increase must be added to the agricultural population.

absolute numbers in agriculture. Hence agricultural prosperity is an essential part of any programme for reducing the growth of urban un-employment.

Thanks to the 'green revolution', the current prospect is good. Our pessimism about L.D.C. small farmers has proved unfounded; we do not have to chivvy them into vast communes, or to control by edict what they may plant and when, or to abandon them in favour of opening up new lands with highly capital-intensive techniques. The solutions to their problems lie more in biology than in capital or organisation, though these last two will also help.

The green revolution, however, is a phenomenon of the wet tropics, or areas which can be irrigated. Vast millions, however, live in the dry tropics, especially in parts of India and in Africa. The comparative advantage of such areas does not lie in agriculture. West Africa's response to this problem, during the first seventy years of this century, was a vast migration from north to south, from the dry savannahs to the wetter coastlands; but the enforcement of national boundaries is now reducing this migration.

The immediate prospect is then that agriculture is not likely to be a constraint on growth in the wet L.D.C.s; on the contrary such countries may need at least a 6 per cent growth of domestic product to keep their agriculture prosperous. But agriculture will continue to lag in the drier L.D.C.s, and their growth rates will continue to be below the average.

(3) *Industry*

Contrary to expectation, industrial production now grows more swiftly in L.D.C.s than it does in developed countries. Problems of management and of productivity are solvable, especially if use is made of foreign managerial skills. Developed countries, from traditionally sneering at the industrial incompetence of L.D.C.s, are now hastily erecting barriers to keep out L.D.C. manufactures.

In many L.D.C.s, industry has been growing by more than 10 per cent per annum. Since the growth rate of domestic use of manufactures does not exceed 7 or 8 per cent, output can maintain a rate of 10 per cent only if it is eating into imports or spilling over into exports. Import sub-stitution kept industry buoyant during the 1960s, but in much of Asia and Latin America the limits of import substitution have already been reached in light consumer goods. To continue at a 10 per cent rate for industry one must do one of three things: (1) raise the growth rate of G.D.P. as a whole to 8 per cent – this would require an impossibly high growth rate for agriculture; (2) move over into import substitution of capital goods; or (3) export manufactures (with a growth rate for exports exceeding 10 per cent).

Only two L.D.C.s have made substantial inroads into producing capital goods – India and Brazil. In most L.D.C.s the market is too small, but one can think of another dozen or so which ought to be further advanced than they are, and which are likely to become substantial producers of capital goods both for themselves and for their neighbours.[1] The rest will retain their high growth rates of industrial production only if they move over into exporting light manufactures.

In fact, manufactures have been the fastest growing export of L.D.C.s over the past decade, even when metals are excluded. About a dozen countries have participated, showing that it is quite possible to beat the developed countries at their own game. The list would be larger if so many Latin American countries were not continuously pricing themselves out of the market with high rates of continuous inflation. And the volume would be larger still if the developed countries were willing to play the game, and refrained from discriminating against the exports of manufactures from L.D.C.s.

(4) *Trade*

This brings us to trade, a crucial constraint on growth. One reason why L.D.C.s grew so rapidly in the 1960s was the fact that the prosperity of the developed countries caused world trade to grow faster than at any time in the preceding century.

Even so, there were weaknesses. The demand for the 'traditional' agricultural exports from L.D.C.s now grows relatively slowly – by 3 per cent per annum or less. These can no longer support the import requirements of L.D.C.s. If L.D.C. income grows by 6 per cent, L.D.C. imports will grow at about the same rate[2] and L.D.C. exports must grow at about the same rate.[3]

It follows that if L.D.C. growth is not to be constrained by the balance of payments, L.D.C.s must

    (a) sell more non-traditional exports to developed countries;
    (b) become individually more self-sufficient; or
    (c) sell more to each other.

As to the first, L.D.C. exports of fuels, minerals, metals and manufactures to developed countries have been mounting swiftly. Unfortunately the concentration of manufactures on textiles and clothing makes difficulties in those markets, which invite restrictions. The situation calls both

---

[1] For figures relevant to this paragraph and the next see my Wicksell Lectures, *Aspects of Tropical Trade, 1883–1965* (Stockholm, 1969).

[2] Imports grew faster than income over the past two decades because investment was accelerating, and investment has a higher import content than consumption. Imports cannot grow faster than income permanently.

[3] This assumes that net foreign aid and investment grow as fast as imports; exports must grow even faster if the net transfer grows only as fast as the G.D.P. of developed countries.

for greater understanding in the developed countries and also for a wider range of exports of manufactures from the L.D.C.s.

As to the second, L.D.C.s now import from the developed countries over $4 billion of food in a good year and over $7 billion of light manufactures. There is clearly room for more import substitution both in agriculture and in industry. The larger L.D.C.s could also make more of their own capital goods.

Thirdly, L.D.C.s must trade more with each other. If the income of the developed countries grows by 4 per cent per annum, they are not likely to be wanting to increase their imports from L.D.C.s by 6 per cent per annum, especially if this includes manufactures growing by 12 per cent per annum. So if the imports and exports of L.D.C.s are to grow by 6 per cent per annum they must buy and sell more from and to each other. The green revolution should make it possible to eliminate altogether the current food import from the developed countries, and there are also immense possibilities for exchanging exports of manufactures.

Trade is the main potential obstacle in the way of achieving the 6 per cent target of the second development decade. This almost certainly must be a decade in which L.D.C.s trade much more with each other. But this development requires new patterns – new tariff structures, new institutions for financing inter-L.D.C. trade, new selling organisations, etc. (ground doubtless covered in earlier papers). Progress in creating these patterns has been slow, and one cannot confidently predict that it will henceforth be adequate. The growth of Latin America is especially tied to greater exploitation of the opportunities presented by foreign trade; a prerequisite for this is greater stability of the prices of exportable manufactures.

(5) *Commitment*

The rate of economic growth depends to some extent on the degree of government commitment – on willingness to raise taxes, willingness to create infrastructure, treatment of entrepreneurs, incentives offered, amount of administrative delay, control of inflation, and so on.

Commitment to development has generally been low, if measured by actions rather than by words. The first half of this paper gave one reason for this: awareness of the disadvantages of growth, which led to caution. But beyond this the commitment of L.D.C. governments is constrained by their low average quality. Some Ministers are deeply interested in the affairs of their departments, which they labour to promote, but a high proportion are more interested in other matters.

The quality of economic administration has been much improved by the creation of planning agencies, usually staffed by enthusiastic and well-educated young men and women. They have experimented a lot with planning, going through a phase of vast statistical documentation, and another phase of over-licensing of private activity, but we have all learnt a great deal about these matters during the past two decades, and a moderate consensus is coming to be the mode.

One cannot write with equal confidence about the political situation. There is a crisis of legitimacy in nearly every L.D.C., whether in Asia, Africa or Latin America. These countries are so divided by tribe, religion, language, race or class that it is hard to establish a government which the majority of the politically active will regard as having the right to rule. So they are subject to a succession of political takeovers which create uncertainty, even in the cases where the administration of economic affairs is not actually changed. This has to be listed as one of the constraints on growth.

III. CONCLUSIONS

I see no reason to doubt that 6 per cent is a feasible growth target for the 1970s, at any rate for the wetter tropics. It is on the margin of what is possible without excessive acceleration of savings ratios; with reasonable priority for public services and for relieving current poverty; without too much dependence on private foreign investment; and without too uneven a distribution of income, if adequate reliance is placed on public saving. It corresponds reasonably to the potential growth rates of industry and of agriculture, and is menaced only by need for considerable changes in the pattern of trade if the balance of payments is not to be a major constraint.

A growth rate of 6 per cent reduces to about 3·5 per cent per head. This is without historical precedent. Continued for only sixty years it would bring income per head in the average L.D.C. (say Ghana or Ceylon) to about the present level in Great Britain (assuming the current real difference to be about 8 : 1). To those with a sense of history this would seem to be a remarkable achievement, but a sense of history is not widespread and is also a conservative bias.

I cannot answer the question whether a higher rate of growth would be possible if the developed countries gave aid more generously than the 1 per cent of G.D.P. which this 6 per cent growth rate assumes. I doubt that it would be possible in the 1970s; although if 6 per cent were achieved in the seventies, 7 per cent might become feasible in the eighties, with the kind co-operation of further biological change in agriculture.

What will happen to the gap between the rich and the poor countries? This could not be answered without a paper of equal length on the prospects of the rich countries. I do not know the answer and, to end where I began, since I think what matters is the absolute progress of the L.D.C.s and not the size of the gap, I do not care.

Discussion of the Paper by Arthur Lewis

Mr. Streeten said that this was a brief, stimulating and lucid paper. Professor Lewis held that the objective of underdeveloped countries should be to raise the level of living of the masses of the people as rapidly as was feasible. The paper discussed what was feasible. Professor Lewis saw two constraints; (1) a constraint on growth, identified with constraints on the savings ratio (or the growth of that ratio), and (2) technical constraints – assuming that the savings ratio was adequate. Under the first point, Professor Lewis said that there were three problems. First, there was the choice between present and future consumption; second, the choice between independence and neo-colonialism; and third, between growth and equality.

Under the first choice, between present and future consumption, Professor Lewis dealt with three subheadings: (1) one might try to relieve current poverty; (2) one might want to avoid the political dislocation of rapid growth by compensating those harmed by it; and (3) there might be a statistical illusion. Many components of output were not adequately measured by current measures of growth and deserved greater weights.

Under the issue of independence and colonialism, there was the problem that growth might be faster if private foreign investment were brought in; yet it was often resisted.

Under the issue of growth versus equality, there was the fact that while, in principle, one could combine growth and equality (through public savings and well-managed state enterprises), many underdeveloped countries had not succeeded. To get equality one had to sacrifice growth, and Mr. Streeten noted that maybe one did not always get all that much equality.

On technical constraints, Professor Lewis included under this heading: population, agriculture, industry, trade and the government's commitment to development. Talking of population growth, he said that this presented a problem not so much because of scarcity of land, food or resources, as because of its drain on savings. Mr. Streeten argued that it was not *high*, but *accelerated* population growth that reduced savings rates on some reasonable savings hypothesis (e.g. life-time savings). Mr. Streeten concluded that Professor Lewis's views could be summarised by saying that a country would have the best chance if it was wet, had legalised abortion, exported light manufactures and enjoyed a ruthless government.

There was then the question of whether the gap mattered. Professor Lewis thought it was irrelevant. Mr. Streeten felt he ought to mention that Professor Lewis's position in the Conference, that it would not matter if the developed countries 'sank under the sea', had not been qualified as it had been elsewhere. In a U.N. booklet he did so in two ways. First, he assumed that the developed countries would not sink until the year A.D. 2000. Second, he made it clear that this was not a recommendation. Even if the sinking were to occur, there were thirty years to go – which most of us would regard as quite a long time. And he submitted that there was a cost (though not an infinite cost), even in the year A.D. 2000. One wondered whether Professor Lewis thought that the gap would not matter after thirty years, because interdependence was unimportant or because benefits and losses, though possibly substantial, cancelled out. If they did cancel out, though, one could accelerate development by operating through policies, increasing the benefits and reducing the losses, unless one felt extremely pessimistic about changing policies.

In the discussion of what was feasible, Professor Lewis concentrated on economic, social and political restraints on the rate of increase in the savings ratio. Its rigid linkage to the growth rate implied, of course, a fixed capital/output ratio. However, Mr. Streeten wondered why one should emphasise the savings ratio rather than use a generalised approach to capital formation, as Professor Johnson had suggested. In this approach, any expenditure or indeed any activity that raised the stream of production over what it would otherwise have been, was regarded as capital investment. In many countries one could make an important contribution to growth, not just by a *squeeze* of consumption, but also by a *twist* of consumption. One could improve the quality of the labour force by health measures, education or nutrition.

In addition, one could accelerate development by many activities, like acquisition of know-how, of administrative and other skills, institutional reforms, like land reforms, or just doing things in a different way, like sowing seeds in a row instead of broadcasting them. These things might require *some* savings, but success was only tenuously related to squeezing consumption. All he was saying was, in a sense, that one could not tacitly assume that capital/output ratios would be constant.

In the discussion of increases in the savings ratio, Professor Lewis was mainly concerned with weighting – inter-temporal and inter-personal. His discussion of the need to relieve poverty (apart from higher weighting for lower incomes) boiled down to a positive rate of time discount. But it should be remembered that present relief might be at the expense of future relief.

The discussion at the end of page 411 and the top of page 412 seemed to imply that qualifications (a) to (f), and the footnote, gave reasons why the government should accept a slower rate of growth. The fact that people wanted just 20 per cent more income could be used as an argument for slower growth and a 'somewhat higher income'. More plausibly it could justify accelerated growth, because when incomes increased by 20 per cent, people would want another 20 per cent increase, and so on.

Mr. Streeten said there need not be a conflict between 'continuous employment' and growth. Professor Lewis ignored the danger of increasing employment now at the expense not only of growth but of future employment, which depended upon output.

It could, of course, quite easily be true that the community (or the politicians) had a different rate of time discount for employment and for consumption growth. But it was quite plausible to argue that the time discount rate for employment growth was *lower* than for consumption growth (because an unemployed man in a future, richer society was just as bad as in the present, poor society). So, an employment-maximising strategy might have to go for a *faster* rather than a slower rate of output growth.

Mr. Streeten went on to discuss the diagrams below (taken from a paper by Frances Stewart and himself). He had used semi-logarithmic scales, with an

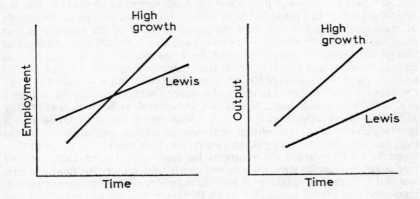

ordinary scale for the horizontal axis showing time. In the left-hand diagram employment was measured up the vertical axis; output was measured up the vertical axis in the right-hand diagram. The curve marked 'Lewis' showed Professor Lewis's strategy; the high growth curve showed what might happen with high growth. With high growth one had less employment for a while. At some point, in the not so distant future however, it overtook the Lewis curve and for ever after employment was higher. While he agreed with Professor Lewis that income accruing to the poorest people should be given a greater weight, he thought that it was too simple to advocate lowering growth rates (or, as Professor Lewis argued, savings ratios) below what they might be, in order to raise current employment.

On private foreign investment, Professor Lewis said that hostility to it would slow down growth. Professor Johnson had said that 'nationalism' was a consumer good to which growth was sacrificed, rather than an investment good. If one regarded it as an investment good – a spur to greater effort, greater saving or structural reforms – growth might be accelerated.

On population, recent evidence in India was more pessimistic. Perhaps people were less keen to accept birth control than we had thought and a lack of will rather than of facilities was the constraint. Whereas, in the case of nationalism, the developmental task was to transform a consumer good into an investment good, in tackling the population problem the task was the opposite. It was to transform children from a producer good into a consumer good.

In his discussion of international trade, Professor Lewis thought this was 'a crucial constraint on growth' and that 'trade is the main political obstacle in the way of achieving the 6 per cent target'. To one who had not read Professor Lewis's Wicksell Lectures it might seem odd that he emphasised trade and de-emphasised the importance of the developed countries. He advocated more trade between less developed countries and warned them not to try to compete on the home ground of the industrial countries.

Mr. Streeten thought Professor Lewis would regard it as irrelevant to say that well over two-thirds of poor countries' trade was still with the rich; that the rate of growth of this trade had been two or three times as high as the growth of trade among themselves; that the terms of trade of the underdeveloped countries were largely determined by what happened in developed countries; and that protectionism of underdeveloped countries against one another was at least as fierce as, and probably fiercer than (because unmitigated by a bad conscience), the protectionism of the rich against the poor. But it was not clear why the question must be posed in terms of solidarity between developing countries as a block. Why should South Korea look to Indonesia rather than Japan? Why Mexico to Brazil rather than the U.S.A.? Why should countries not be guided by comparative advantage plus propaganda to abolish protectionism by the rich, and sell wherever they got the best returns? He would also ask why Professor Lewis disregarded the prospects for trade with the centrally planned economies, potentially dynamic markets which were hungry for food and raw material imports and might well become suppliers of low-cost, standardised, mass-produced capital goods (for which Professor Patinkin had asked and had found the market economies wanting). Or of consumer goods – perhaps a £10 refrigerator?

Mr. Streeten was still left with some doubts about the thesis that the developed countries did not matter. For trade and for the supply of capital and of ideas, the rich countries did seem to matter. Admittedly, they mattered for good and ill. The problem was to eradicate the ill.

Professor Srinivasan said that Professor Lewis first focussed attention on the constraints that 'make it desirable to keep the growth rate lower than technically possible'. This way of posing the problem suggested two interpretations. First, one might argue that the rate of growth of income or consumption was one of the many variables that affected welfare, and one might give up a little on the rate of growth to gain something elsewhere. Second, one could argue that the rate of growth was indeed the index of welfare that one wanted to maximise. However, there were several constraints, a subset of which included specification of tolerable levels of unemployment, or inequalities of income distribution, etc. Though there were these two ways of looking at the problem, they were equivalent theoretically. In practice the second approach might be more relevant, since it was easier to set a target on levels of employment, etc. than to specify the social welfare function.

It was not clear why the fact that the poorer group in L.D.C.s had to concentrate on a few simple needs necessarily implied less saving, and so a relatively slower growth rate. This seemed to confuse the pattern of allocation of investment with the level of savings. One could easily think of mobilising larger savings from their income and investing such savings in providing the goods and services mentioned by Professor Lewis. One could thus raise levels of living faster, with a more rapid rate of growth than was otherwise possible, and with a lower rate of savings. In other words, though the question of the level of savings, and of its allocation, were interdependent, the level was more influenced by time preference and the allocation by preferences for particular consumer goods.

It was not necessarily true that to cope with unemployment it might be desirable to keep investment in industry small. Here again, the choice of capital intensity of investment seemed to be mixed up with its sectoral allocation. It was not hard to imagine two alternative strategies for development. (For the moment he was ignoring foreign trade.) The first chose a pattern of investment which emphasised the production of capital goods and intermediate goods at the cost of light consumer goods in the near future. So, both output and employment rose faster in the far future. Of course, even with this strategy, in any particular sector one would choose the capital intensity that would generate maximum employment.

The second way emphasised employment in the near future, presumably by investing in the production of light consumer goods. The choice between the two strategies would, of course, depend on other things, such as social time preference.

Professor Srinivasan was not quite sure what exactly Professor Lewis meant when he said that we could have most consumption and investment if we used foreign funds and personnel. Perhaps he meant that, given the magnitude of investment, one could have more consumption if a greater proportion of that investment was financed by a foreign capital inflow. Similarly, given the level of consumption, we could have a bigger investment the bigger the foreign capital inflow. It seemed to him that most of those who argued against narrowing the foreign capital inflow were questioning this very hypothesis. They suggested that domestic savings, particularly government savings, were not independent of the foreign capital inflow. They went on to suggest, and there was some evidence to support them, that foreign capital inflow acted more as a substitute for domestic savings than as a supplement. In an extreme version of this thesis the size of investment was determined by other considerations, and the bigger the capital inflow the laxer the government became in its tax and expenditure policies. If this were true, one need not accuse foreign investors of being neo-colonialists to be against them.

Professor Lewis had stressed the short-run conflict between growth and the egalitarian distribution of the gains from growth. He was absolutely right in drawing attention to the fact that in L.D.C.s the so-called middle class (professional, administrative and managerial) held potential power and accumulated privileges for itself without effective political opposition. If he could be permitted to quote a few instances from India, the government had fixed the price of domestically-produced automobiles at a level below that which would clear the market. It had instituted a queue for its allocation in which government servants, members of parliament, doctors, etc. got priority. What was more, the government had yielded to pressure to invest in yet another automobile plant, this time to produce a 'small car' to cater for the demands of the middle class.

Professor Lewis suggested that, in principle, even if the income distribution were egalitarian, this fact need not reduce aggregate savings if public savings could be substituted for private savings. Public savings arose from the surpluses of public enterprises and the revenue surpluses of governments. However there were some constraints: public enterprises were badly managed, grossly overstaffed and operated at less than capacity. So these were deficits rather than surpluses. The incompetence and lack of care of some L.D.C. governments in introducing vigorous tax efforts were well known and documented. He thought that Professor Lewis was not quite right in saying that the bad management of public enterprise was again due to its inability to raise savings. He argued that, if one had the resources, one could always have foreign managers to run the enterprises. There was a tendency, at least in India, to appoint administrators from the Civil Service as managers of public enterprises. These administrators, besides having no particular managerial skills, tended to run the enterprises more or less as government departments and would stoutly resist any outside managers being brought in. Moreover, if foreign managers could be hired without domestic opposition, the surplus they generated through managerial skill should at least cover their own cost! So the question of savings would not arise. Good managers would earn enough at least to pay for themselves.

Professor Lewis was again right in suggesting that politicians did not see the development process in the same way as economists saw it. Nor did they always give it top priority. In so far as the distribution of political power was the base on which politicians depended, it was positively correlated with income and wealth, particularly in the form of land, in agricultural countries. There was therefore no hope of getting around the problem without a thorough institutional reform.

Professor Lewis rightly pointed out that the so-called 'green revolution' was as yet confined to a small area. He might add that in India the green revolution had had significant effects only on the wheat crop. Rice, which amounts to nearly 40 per cent of indigenous food output, had barely been affected. This was to say nothing of pulses, cash crops like cotton, oil, seeds, etc. Even in the case of wheat, though the effect on the growth of output had been accelerated, there was some evidence to suggest that the impact on unemployment and on the wages of agricultural labour had not been very significant. Disparities between small peasants and bigger landlords had increased. If the social tensions generated by this process went further, the 'green revolution' and indeed any development along the present lines, would be ended.

Professor Lewis pointed out that once the phase of rapid growth in industry made possible by import substitution was over, the old L.D.C.s would not be able to sustain a 10 per cent growth rate in industry unless one of two things happened. Either the overall rate of growth of income would have to be very high, or the country would have to gear the rate of growth of industry to manufactured exports. Since high rates of growth of income would generate impossibly high rates of growth in agricultural production, L.D.C.s would have to look to trade for sustaining industrial growth. He entirely agreed with Professor Lewis that L.D.C.s had to trade more with each other.

Professor Bhagwati had already drawn our attention to the fact that aid-tying arrangements for the developing countries inhibited the growth of such trade. In so far as some L.D.C.s would be selling capital goods to others, it would require the development of appropriate institutions for the supply of credit, etc.

He did want to take issue with Professor Lewis on one aspect of this intra-L.D.C. trade. Professor Lewis argued that the green revolution should make it possible to eliminate the food imports into developing ones. This was true. But it also meant that some developing countries, like Thailand and Burma, which had been exporters of food grains, were likely to be affected if the L.D.C.s (as well as Japan) became self-sufficient in foods. He supposed the way out of this situation would probably be both to shift the cropping pattern in these countries to fodder crops and to alter the pattern of food consumption towards more consumption of meat and dairy products.

Professor Lewis had emphasised the need for a commitment to development on the part of L.D.C. governments. He wondered if such committed governments were at all likely to come into power, given the present distribution of political and economic power in these countries.

To conclude, Professor Srinivasan accepted and re-emphasised Professor Lewis's conclusion that what mattered was the absolute rate of progress of the underdeveloped countries. The size and the dynamics of the gap between underdeveloped and developed countries was irrelevant.

Professor Lewis wanted to elaborate the connection between the gap and trade. Professor Kuznets had asked a question which had not been answered: Was it desirable to bridge the gap? This would worsen the terms of trade of underdeveloped countries. If the rate of growth in underdeveloped countries was 10 per cent, and that in developed countries was 12 per cent, then the terms of trade of underdeveloped countries would improve; but there would be trouble for L.D.C.s if the rate of growth in developed countries were only 6 per cent. If one accepted the interdependence thesis, one must want a rapid rate of growth in developed countries and even a widening gap. But he did not believe that the growth of L.D.C.s need depend on their trade with developed countries; they did not need the gap.

On the choice between the rate of growth and other objectives, he assumed that the government was the marginal saver. To increase the savings ratio therefore meant raising taxes. But what was the best use for these taxes? To Professor Islam he might say that we now needed schools and medicine more urgently than factories. Or, to Mr. Streeten he might say that we wanted, not factories, but big rural public works programmes. One might prefer investment creating much employment to investment that would increase G.N.P. rather faster.

Professor Kuznets said that Professor Lewis gave a picture of the success of L.D.C.s in the past decade. He should examine this picture further. Professor Kuznets found it hard to accept the proposition that the major underdeveloped countries showed 5 per cent per annum growth rates in G.D.P. over the past decade to decade and a half, which given the increase in population, presumably meant that G.D.P. per head was going up by about $2\frac{1}{2}$ per cent per year. This was not true of India, Indonesia, Pakistan or China – the four giants of the less developed world; nor could it be true of many politically and war-disturbed countries in North and Sabsaharan Africa. If one took *properly* weighted aggregate growth rates per capita (weighted by constant population, not by changing shares in a product), he thought that these would not be more than $1\frac{1}{2}$ per cent per annum.

Professor Kuznets also thought that in many populous less developed countries, inequality in income had widened. This appeared to have been true of the inequality in sectoral product per worker as between agriculture and other sectors in the production system. So perhaps the lower 50 per cent of the population gained little in real income, even though it had gained from factors like a falling death rate and other relatively costless changes.

Third, there was a question of future growth. According to Professor Lewis a 6 per cent growth rate would bring Ceylon to parity with the U.K. in sixty

P

years, but perhaps Professor Lewis was over-optimistic. He had been reminded
by the paper just how much difficulty there was in handling figures like these. A
difference between a 6 per cent and 4 per cent growth rate in total product meant
a disparity between about $3\frac{1}{2}$ and $1\frac{1}{2}$ growth rates in per capita product (if
population continued to grow at $2\frac{1}{2}$ per cent). The cumulation of the latter growth
rates might mean no convergence to the U.K. at all, even though it would mean
a substantial absolute rise over sixty years. Professor Lewis should use growth-
rate statistics with the caution that the explosive power of their cumulation over
long periods required. We should not say that figures were no good, and then
use them incautiously.

Would the relative gap widen? Professor Kuznets quoted West German
projections for the years 1970–85, which suggested that per capita product would
double over these fifteen years. If such projections were valid for other developed
countries, these, or even lower growth rates, would not warrant an expectation
that the relative gap would narrow. This perhaps was unimportant if incomes
and standards of living in the less developed countries would improve materially
and rapidly. And it was true that such improvement did occur in the recent
past, at least as indicated by falling mortality rates. But there was much dissatisfaction and turmoil, perhaps because people in L.D.C.s felt the absence of
'fruits of progress' at all comparable to what was desirable and feasible, or to
those attained elsewhere.

Dr. Mahub ul Haq spoke about the role of economists in narrowing the gap.
He felt that he should say something on this in the final session since the economists had been engaged, directly or indirectly, in a crusade to reduce the gap.

He felt that economists from the underdeveloped and developed worlds had
really been playing a game throughout the 1950s and the 1960s. The rules were
often simple and civilised. The economists from the underdeveloped countries
would blame all the troubles and problems of these countries on the policies of
the developed world. If the exports of underdeveloped countries had not expanded this was blamed on the restrictive trade policies of the developed world,
irrespective of the fact that some of the underdeveloped countries did not even
meet their fixed quotas, as Pakistan did not in the case of textiles. If the technology used in underdeveloped countries was inappropriate to the conditions of
these countries, the fault was that of the developed world for not developing a
suitable technology to transfer to these countries. Yet this ignored the fact that
many underdeveloped countries themselves did very little to encourage the
adoption of appropriate technology. For instance, Pakistan had been spending
more on research in nuclear energy than on research in jute, which was its major
natural resources. On the other hand, economists from the developed countries
kept arguing how wrong the development or planning policies of the underdeveloped countries had been. Or they explained how useless it was to come to
any definite conclusions regarding the terms of trade between primary producing and industrialised countries; or how even the limited foreign assistance
that was available was being spent inefficiently by underdeveloped countries.
They paid much less attention to influencing policies in the developed world.

This game was interesting in certain respects but did not do much credit to
economists and was certainly of little help to the policy-makers. Probably the
time had come when economists must return to the fields where they had com-

parative advantage. Economists from underdeveloped countries should turn their attention inwards and try to explore the means through which underdeveloped countries could improve their policy performance. Economists from developed countries should urge more enlightened policies in their own countries, where they might have some influence. This was essentially, he thought, the message of Professor Lewis when he suggested that developing countries should turn inwards and look after their own affairs. He concluded that while economists had urged the need for a rational division of labour in all other fields, and and for everyone else, they were rather reluctant to accept one in their own profession.

Professor Horvat commented on some points in the paper. First, on page 411, Professor Lewis said, 'economics has no basis for calculating the optimal rate of savings, or of economic growth'. This implied, Lewis argued, that his son and he were the same person. So there was no answer. The solution was to assume that he, today and in twenty years time, was one and the same person, and that his utility discount rate was less than 30 per cent or 40 per cent per annum. These were reasonable, testable hypotheses, so that one could calculate an optimal rate of savings.

On page 412, Professor Lewis said, 'a ratio of 0·2 would be comfortable, whereas 0·4 would be excessive, except in an economy which was already growing very rapidly'. This choice was abstract. One could choose only 0·2, because 0·4 was in the range of the negative marginal efficiency of investment. The marginal rate of savings of 0·2 meant a ratio of investment to income going up by about 1½ percentage points per annum. This was all that one could do. So that what was comfortable was also the maximum possible.

On page 414, Professor Lewis said, 'in a modern economy income seems to grow at the same rate at all levels (i.e. distribution remains unchanged), but in the transforming economy most of the poor stay poor while the rich get richer'. Professor Horvat recalled there were countries where this was not true, and perhaps Yugoslavia served as a paradigm. Yugoslavia had reduced the incomes of the rich, even of those who were not very rich, including those participating in the conference, and increased the incomes of the poor.

On page 416, Professor Lewis continued, 'Population growth will continue to be a major constraint on per capita growth for at least the rest of the century'. This implied a slow rate of G.N.P. If the rate of growth of G.N.P. could be increased to 10 per cent, it would not be important if population increased by 1½ per cent, 2 per cent or 3 per cent. One got arithmetically the same result if one reduced population growth or increased the rate of growth of G.N.P. But the strategy – and for this conference – the difference mattered very much. One ought to put the emphasis on G.N.P. rather than on population.

Professor Findlay said Professor Lewis was right that in the short run the gap-narrowing and interdependence theses were independent. If income in underdeveloped countries was positively correlated with income in developed countries, then to increase income in L.D.C.s one wanted to have income in developed countries as high as possible. Since, logically, it was impossible to have a narrowing gap if there was interdependence, Professor Lewis gave up interdependence. He would himself give up the idea of immediately narrowing the gap.

Even if incomes in underdeveloped countries fell in the short run, one could still narrow the gap in the long run. He was not alone, he thought, in believing that interdependence was a fact. Since the conference was on how to narrow the gap, and most of us agreed that we wanted maximum income per head in underdeveloped countries, should we not give up the idea of closing the gap in the short run?

Dr. Baranson said that what Dr. Haq had said about the role of economists suggested that there was a certain *Zeitgeist* in institutions and government policies. Sometimes economists had to bide their time for a receptive atmosphere for their suggestions. Up to two years ago economists were not widely used for industrial analysis at the World Bank, but now the climate had improved considerably. On what Professor Lewis said on page 417, he thought that the distinction had to be made between cancer and growth. A 10 per cent rate of growth of industrial output, brought about by industrialisation under protection, might simply mean that goods were being produced at progressively increased costs. If one allowed for this, perhaps one had to reduce the apparent rate of growth by half.

In the long run, the question of investment in research and development and of finding appropriate technologies must be emphasised. But much of the derived usefulness of such activities would depend upon market mechanisms to properly gauge expenditures on product and process adaptation or innovation.

Professor Chenery thought that if the aim was to maximise the growth of underdeveloped countries, one should not look at averages but at growth of the lower income group. This implied something about employment. If one said one wanted to maximise employment, one was saying something about the consumption of the rich in poor countries. He would rather accept the widening of the gap. Professor Lewis suggested that one might alter the composition of consumption. To him, this seemed a short-run measure which might work for five years but not for two or twenty. One was stuck with a high rate of growth if one wanted high employment.

Wanting developed countries to grow rapidly emphasised that trade was particularly important. So was aid. Aid was being given increasingly by Japan, Germany, etc. There was much less aid from countries like the U.K. and the U.S.A. with problems of growth and the balance of payments. Military expenditure aside, he thought one could get a good aid/growth function for developed countries. Up to 25 per cent of investment in underdeveloped countries (5 per cent of G.N.P.) could be generated by widening the gap to increase the rate of growth. Studies showed that if aid reduced savings, this was not important. What mattered was whether aid increased investment – and the evidence was that it did.

Should we get away from industrialisation? The answer was no. We looked too much at the employment it created and not sufficiently at the transfer of technology. We had to get this from the transfer of industrialisation. One ought not to look at employment per dollar for industrialisation, but income per dollar.

Professor Correa wanted to ask Professor Lewis how far his observations on the relationship between population and income growth were definitive. The current rate of growth of population could not continue very long, or the universe would be occupied by human tissue. The reason for reducing population growth was not that it was an obstacle to the rate of growth of income per head. While population growth did have a reducing effect on income per head, it could have a positive effect – due to bigger markets. Perhaps this was bigger than the negative effect. Blind population control might simply be disadvantageous.

If a country were used to a high rate of population growth, it would have trouble if this rate were reduced. For example, in underdeveloped countries parents saw children as an insurance for their old age. One would disrupt this arrangement if one stopped population growth suddenly.

Professor Ghai said that the discussion of the gap, here and elsewhere, had generated much pessimism. Economists since the days of Ricardo had been given to projections of various trends to doom and damnation. It was thus not without justification that economics had been labelled as a science of despair. So that the conference could end on a note of optimism, he would like to argue that the relative gap between the poor and the rich nations, and thus over time the absolute gap, must decline.

If was, of course, not possible to go into the details of the argument. In summary, his views were these. First, he thought it would be surprising if, in the eighties and nineties, a growth rate of 7 per cent to 10 per cent was not considered normal for most developing countries. In the past twenty years the developing countries had achieved growth rates which only thirty years ago would have seemed unattainable. At the same time, a dozen or so countries had achieved growth rates of 7 per cent to 10 per cent in the sixties. There were strong reasons to believe that marked acceleration of economic growth would occur in other developing countries too. Systematic efforts, both at national and international level, to intensify development in poor countries were relatively recent. They went back no more than two decades, and for many countries for less than a decade. During this time a great deal had been learned which should help rapid development. Massive investment in almost all L.D.C.s had been made in social and economic overheads, and all this should begin to yield results. There was also an enormous backlog of technology already developed to draw from.

With the continuing shrinkage of the world, transfers of innovation from one part of the world to another should be greatly speeded up. Above all, it was only very recently that systematic, organised research directed at the problems of the L.D.C.s had been undertaken on any significant scale. If more resources were put into it, as appeared likely, it would be surprising if there were not a steady stream of innovations of the sort that had triggered off the green revolution. It was for these reasons that he thought that his estimate of rates of growth of 6 per cent to 8 per cent by the eighties, and 8 per cent to 10 per cent by the nineties might, if anything, be underestimates.

The prospect of such high and accelerating growth rates for L.D.C.s were, however, heavily dependent on two sets of circumstances. First, the maintenance of political stability; second, continuing rapid growth in rich countries and of international trade.

Professor Vernon wanted to suggest a point of collective interest. Professor Lewis had called attention to a question: did private foreign investment close the gap via increased domestic savings or not? Economists made a number of assumptions about this *ex cathedra*. Yet this was a researchable issue. First, had it increased domestic savings? Second, could it do so? Or, should one do more to ensure that it did?

The issues were complex. Some foreign investment affected savings by its depressant effect on local industry. However, foreign investment went beyond this. Only one dollar of each four or five dollars in foreign-owned businesses came from capital crossing the exchanges. Did foreign investment, then, increase the rate of personal savings? There had been speculation, including speculation in Yugoslavia, that there would be more savings if there were more joint ventures with foreign capital. Did foreign investment increase business savings? The investment in foreign-owned businesses was often higher than in domestic firms. Could the existence of foreign investment increase government savings? Governments were quick to exempt foreign firms from taxation. But perhaps foreign firms were more tax-inelastic in their investment decisions than had been thought. He said that all these were researchable issues and he hoped that much more empirical work would be done on them soon.

Professor Robinson said that if we were generalising at this stage in the discussions, he wanted to say that seldom in the Round Table had any reference been made to questions of scale. Once one began to work on practical issues, one was all the time up against these questions. To see what would happen in twenty years one must look at scale. Few underdeveloped countries would be able to sustain many modern industries even by 1990. This had implications for the pattern of development. There would have to be more development in the form of collaboration between groups of underdeveloped countries. Collaborative development, and its political pre-conditions, were something that needed more thought.

Professor Patinkin argued that there was another dimension to what Professor Vernon had been saying. Once one looked at the effect of foreign investment on domestic saving, one had to broaden the definition of savings. Not all foreign aid or foreign investment went to consumption, and here he was not just thinking of education but of the development of human capital generally. For example, we had already seen that the brain-drain took skilled people away from L.D.C.s. The effects of the brain-drain were a function of the gap. Perhaps some investment programmes could be used to keep in L.D.C.s some human capital that would otherwise leave. He did not know how, but thought it was important to try.

Dr. Nurul Islam said that some people in the conference had been arguing that it was unimportant whether the gap closed. Professor Lewis said that to import from underdeveloped countries, developed countries must grow. But, even now, there would be more imports from underdeveloped countries if there were no protection in advanced countries. Increasing trade between L.D.C.s did not rule out increased trade with developed countries. The experience of increased trade among underdeveloped countries in the last ten years had led to no conclusive evidence. The ideal was world trade liberalisation with more preferences given to underdeveloped countries. This would be more efficient than liberalisation of trade between L.D.C.s, but with the degree of protection in developed countries.

Mr. Streeten wanted to clarify what he had said about the choice between maximum employment and maximum output. He was assuming that extra output was linked to extra employment, partly through extra capital goods that provided jobs and partly through extra consumption goods on which wages were spent. If one sacrificed output (correctly measured), one sacrificed future employment. The inter-temporal choice remained.

Second, it was not clear from the discussion why the widening gap should help the underdeveloped countries, or improve the transfer of resources to them. If there were a high rate of growth in developed countries because of population growth, this had implications for their demand for primary products. The results would be different if the same total growth rate took the form of rising incomes per head. Apart from the different pattern of demand for primary products, there were a host of other considerations, such as the effects on the supply of capital and skills. A widening gap might, in the one case, improve the developing countries' terms of trade, but deprive them of skilled manpower and capital. In the second case, it might present them with more manpower and skills, but worse terms of trade. The net advantages were not clear.

Professor Lewis said that Mr. Streeten and Professor Correa had introduced the relationship between population growth and capital formation. His paper must have been misunderstood. Mr. Streeten had distinguished between an increasing rate of growth of population and a high and steady level of population. He was not concerned with this. His assumption was simply that one had a given amount of savings. So, more people meant less savings left to raise income per head, after providing accommodation and education for extra people.

Professor Lewis said he could not allay Professor Kuznet's worries. All he could say was that United Nations and the O.E.C.D. gave sectoral figures for growth rates. These showed growth rates for manufacturing of 7–8 per cent, agriculture 3 per cent and services 5–6 per cent. Overall, this came out at a round figure of 5 per cent. He could not vouch for the figures, and could not expect to persuade Professor Kuznets on this subject. As for whether what mattered was savings or raising the inducement to invest, he did not see these as alternatives. He would say that one should worry about both.

Professor Lewis said he had assumed that the government raised funds to assist employment. He had noted with approval that in Professor Seers's report on Colombia the growth rate had not been mentioned – only welfare. He would say this too. In increasing employment, governments would increase welfare. Admittedly, this was a short-run strategy, but unemployment now had the highest priority. One could turn later to restoring priority to growth.

One point that did worry him was that the Round Table was called to discuss how to narrow the gap. Now it seemed as if everyone was here on false pretences, since closing the gap was being rejected. He had said that his thinking was not dominated by the gap, but that was all. He did not like the gap; he wanted to close it. But his primary aim was to increase the level of welfare in underdeveloped countries, not to close the gap.

A major interest had been in the conditions for regional trade, where he agreed with Professor Robinson. Underdeveloped countries simply *had* to combine in larger groupings to expoit the economies of scale.

Professor Nurul Islam had said that the rate of growth of developed countries was satisfactory, if only they would import more. But one had to make a distinction between their level of imports and their rate of growth. The removal of protectionism, etc., could only operate in the short run. He would like to ask

Professor Islam how developed countries could go on increasing the rate of growth of imports more than their rate of growth of G.N.P. If developed countries were growing at 5 per cent, but underdeveloped countries were growing at 10 per cent, the trade of the L.D.C.s would have to grow up by 10 per cent. One could not increase the imports of developed countries indefinitely at 10 per cent, without growth at a similar rate.

Index

Entries in the Index in **bold type** under the names of participants in the conference indicate their papers or discussions of their papers. Entries in *italic* indicate contributions by participants to the discussions.